AF848761

Logic in Asia: Studia Logica Library

Series Editors

Fenrong Liu, Tsinghua University and University of Amsterdam, Beijing, China

Hiroakira Ono, Japan Advanced Institute of Science and Technology (JAIST), Ishikawa, Japan

Kamal Lodaya, Bengaluru, India

Editorial Board

Natasha Alechina, University of Nottingham, Nottingham, UK

Toshiyasu Arai, University of Tokyo, Tokyo, Japan

Sergei Artemov, City University of New York, New York, NY, USA

Mattias Baaz, Technical university of Vienna, Austria, Vietnam

Lev Beklemishev, Institute of Russian Academy of Science, Russia

Mihir Chakraborty, Jadavpur University, Kolkata, India

Phan Minh Dung, Asian Institute of Technology, Thailand

Amitabha Gupta, Indian Institute of Technology Bombay, Mumbai, India

Christoph Harbsmeier, University of Oslo, Oslo, Norway

Shier Ju, Sun Yat-sen University, Guangzhou, China

Makoto Kanazawa, National Institute of Informatics, Tokyo, Japan

Fangzhen Lin, Hong Kong University of Science and Technology, Hong Kong

Jacek Malinowski, Polish Academy of Sciences, Warsaw, Poland

Ram Ramanujam, Institute of Mathematical Sciences, Chennai, India

Jeremy Seligman, University of Auckland, Auckland, New Zealand

Kaile Su, Peking University and Griffith University, Peking, China

Johan van Benthem, University of Amsterdam and Stanford University, The Netherlands

Hans van Ditmarsch, Laboratoire Lorrain de Recherche en Informatique et ses Applications, France

Dag Westerstahl, Stockholm University, Stockholm, Sweden

Yue Yang, Singapore National University, Singapore

Syraya Chin-Mu Yang, National Taiwan University, Taipei, China

Logic in Asia: Studia Logica Library

This book series promotes the advance of scientific research within the field of logic in Asian countries. It strengthens the collaboration between researchers based in Asia with researchers across the international scientific community and offers a platform for presenting the results of their collaborations. One of the most prominent features of contemporary logic is its interdisciplinary character, combining mathematics, philosophy, modern computer science, and even the cognitive and social sciences. The aim of this book series is to provide a forum for current logic research, reflecting this trend in the field's development.

The series accepts books on any topic concerning logic in the broadest sense, i.e., books on contemporary formal logic, its applications and its relations to other disciplines. It accepts monographs and thematically coherent volumes addressing important developments in logic and presenting significant contributions to logical research. In addition, research works on the history of logical ideas, especially on the traditions in China and India, are welcome contributions.

The scope of the book series includes but is not limited to the following:

- Monographs written by researchers in Asian countries.
- Proceedings of conferences held in Asia, or edited by Asian researchers.
- Anthologies edited by researchers in Asia.
- Research works by scholars from other regions of the world, which fit the goal of "Logic in Asia".

The series discourages the submission of manuscripts that contain reprints of previously published material and/or manuscripts that are less than 165 pages/ 90,000 words in length.

Please also visit our webpage: http://tsinghualogic.net/logic-in-asia/background/

Relation with Studia Logica Library

This series is part of the Studia Logica Library, and is also connected to the journal Studia Logica. This connection does not imply any dependence on the Editorial Office of Studia Logica in terms of editorial operations, though the series maintains cooperative ties to the journal.

This book series is also a sister series to Trends in Logic and Outstanding Contributions to Logic.

For inquiries and to submit proposals, authors can contact the editors-in-chief Fenrong Liu at fenrong@tsinghua.edu.cn or Hiroakira Ono at ono@jaist.ac.jp.

More information about this series at http://www.springer.com/series/13080

Toshiyasu Arai

Ordinal Analysis with an Introduction to Proof Theory

Springer

Toshiyasu Arai
University of Tokyo
Tokyo, Japan

ISSN 2364-4613 ISSN 2364-4621 (electronic)
Logic in Asia: Studia Logica Library
ISBN 978-981-15-6458-1 ISBN 978-981-15-6459-8 (eBook)
https://doi.org/10.1007/978-981-15-6459-8

© The Editor(s) (if applicable) and The Author(s), under exclusive license to Springer Nature Singapore Pte Ltd. 2020
This work is subject to copyright. All rights are solely and exclusively licensed by the Publisher, whether the whole or part of the material is concerned, specifically the rights of translation, reprinting, reuse of illustrations, recitation, broadcasting, reproduction on microfilms or in any other physical way, and transmission or information storage and retrieval, electronic adaptation, computer software, or by similar or dissimilar methodology now known or hereafter developed.
The use of general descriptive names, registered names, trademarks, service marks, etc. in this publication does not imply, even in the absence of a specific statement, that such names are exempt from the relevant protective laws and regulations and therefore free for general use.
The publisher, the authors and the editors are safe to assume that the advice and information in this book are believed to be true and accurate at the date of publication. Neither the publisher nor the authors or the editors give a warranty, expressed or implied, with respect to the material contained herein or for any errors or omissions that may have been made. The publisher remains neutral with regard to jurisdictional claims in published maps and institutional affiliations.

This Springer imprint is published by the registered company Springer Nature Singapore Pte Ltd.
The registered company address is: 152 Beach Road, #21-01/04 Gateway East, Singapore 189721, Singapore

Preface

Ordinal analysis is a field in proof theory, in which ordinals play a central role. Let us expound how theories relate to ordinals.

Let T be a computable theory comprising a small portion of arithmetic, where by a computable theory we mean the set of axioms in the theory is computable under a suitable encoding of syntax. We are supposing that the theory T is Π^1_1-sound. Namely, for every Π^1_1-sentence A on natural numbers, or in an equivalent form, if T proves the sentence A, then A is supposed to be true in the standard model $\mathbb{N}$.

On the other side, we see easily that the cut-free fragment of the ω-logic with the following ω-rule is Π^1_1-complete.

$$\frac{\cdots \Gamma, A(n) \quad \cdots (n \in \mathbb{N})}{\Gamma, \forall x A(x)}$$

Furthermore for every true Π^1_1-sentence A, there exists a computable and cut-free derivation d_A of A in ω-logic. This means that there exists a computable, and *well-founded* tree $tree(A) \subset^{<\omega} \omega$ for which there exists a computable decoration, i.e., a function on $tree(A)$ such that $tree(A)$ with the decoration is a cut-free ω-derivation of A (the decoration assigns a sequent, an inference rule, etc. to each node in $tree(A)$).

Therefore, when T is Π^1_1-sound, there must exist an ordinal $\alpha_A < \omega_1^{CK}$ for each T-provable Π^1_1-sentence A such that the ordinal α_A gives an upper bound for the depth of the well-founded tree $tree(A)$. Then there would exist an ordinal $|T| < \omega_1^{CK}$ which is the supremum of the ordinals α_A for T-provable Π^1_1-sentences A.

In ordinal analysis, we describe the ordinal $|T|$ for a given theory T without assuming that T is Π^1_1-sound. In many cases, the description of the ordinal $|T|$ is done as follows. Some operations on ordinals are defined in such a way that $|T| > 0$ is the least ordinal which is closed under the operations. For example, when T is the first-order arithmetic PA, two operations on ordinals are typically considered: the ordinal ω and the exponential function $\alpha \mapsto 2^{\alpha}$. The first epsilon number ε_0 is the least ordinal closed under these two.

Which operations on ordinals are associated with theories? This depends not only on theories, but also on the methods how the theories are expressed and analyzed. The main approaches in ordinal analysis are cut-elimination in sequent calculi (Gentzen, Schütte) and epsilon substitution method (Hilbert, Ackermann). In this monograph, we focus on the first, which has been the dominant one in ordinal analysis.

The associated operations on ordinals correspond to or express a structural complexity of procedures in cut-elimination. We transform derivations to eliminate cut inferences in sequent calculi, and the operations are closely related to the transformations.

$$\frac{\Gamma, \neg C \quad C, \Gamma}{\Gamma}\,(cut)$$

These operations warrant the executability of the procedures. Specifically let us assume that the associated operations on ordinals are well defined, by which we mean that an operation yields a well ordering from well orderings. Then we see that a cut-elimination procedure with these operations gives us a cut-free derivation. Once a cut-free derivation with a subformula property is gained, we can conclude that the end formula is true by transfinite induction on depths of the cut-free derivations, where the depth is bounded by the least ordinal closed under the associated operations.

Thus, we comprehend what structure is involved in derivations of the theory T through the associated operations on ordinals as long as we are concerned with cut-elimination. Moreover, the Π^1_1-soundness of T follows from the well-definedness of the operations. In this way, we obtain a deep understanding of T in terms of the ordinal analysis of T.

The ordinal $|T|$ is called *proof-theoretic ordinal* of the theory T, and it can be alternatively defined by the supremum of the order types of computable, strict partial orders such that T proves its well-foundedness. Although the definition of the ordinal $|T|$ concerns only with provable Π^1_1-sentences, it turns out in almost all cases that $|T|$ characterizes some proof-theoretic limitations of T. For example, let f be a computable total function. We see that T proves the fact that f is a total function iff f is defined by a transfinite recursion on ordinals up to an ordinal $< |T|$. Note that the fact is written in a Π^0_2-sentence. By the equivalence we could yield an independent Π^0_2-statement.

Let us mention the contents of the monograph.

In Chap. 1, some prerequisites are explained such as one-sided sequent calculi, recursion-theoretic prerequisites, and the definition of the proof-theoretic ordinal. Our base theory, the elementary (recursive) arithmetic EA, is introduced, and the Kripke-Platek set theory KP is also defined. These materials are scattered in text-books on logic.

Though this monograph concerns mainly with ordinal analysis through cut-elimination in sequent calculi, Chaps. 2 and 3 are intended to be an introduction to proof theory. The reason for such an introduction is due to the fact that the ordinal analysis is based on proof-theoretic analyses of finite derivations. There are two topics in Chap. 2. First, the completeness of cut-free fragments is proved through a canonical proof-search method or refutation method. The sequent calculus for the *classical* first-order logic is best seen as a refutation procedure. Inference rules are regarded as searching step of a counter-model of the endsequent when we turn inferences upside down. Besides the classical first-order logic, the same method is employed to applied logic calculi, predicative second-order logic, and the ω-logic. Since the calculi with the cut inference are sound, this yields the cut-elimination theorem (Hauptsatz). It is convenient for us to have cut-free derivations for a further analysis. Second, some consequences of the cut-elimination are presented. Herbrand's theorems for formulas in prenex normal form are proved through the midsequent theorem. Moreover, witnesses for existential quantifiers are extracted from cut-free derivations. An example of the witnessing theorem is the Parikh's theorem stating that if a Σ_1-formula is provable in a bounded theory, then there exists a term bounding the unbounded existential quantifier in the Σ_1-formula. The theorem is applied to bounded arithmetic and employed to characterize proof-theoretically the class of rudimentary functions in set theory. The second example of the witnessing theorem is on primitive recursion. In theories with induction schema for existential formulas, only a primitive recursive function is proved to be total. The Parsons-Mints-Takeuti theorem is the prominent example: provably computable functions in a fragment $I\Sigma_1$ of arithmetic are primitive recursive functions. The proof of the theorem is based on a witnessing argument due to S. Buss and is modified to obtain a proof-theoretic proof of a theorem due to H. Friedman, which states that the second-order arithmetic WKL_0 for the weak König's lemma is Π^0_2-conservative over $I\Sigma_1$. A proof-theoretic proof of the fact was first obtained by W. Sieg. Our proof deviates from Sieg's in replacing the weak König's lemma by an equivalent reduction property. Furthermore, the witnessing argument is employed to show a theorem due to M. Rathjen, which states that only the primitive recursive set functions in the sense of Jensen-Karp are provably total Σ_1-functions in a restricted Kripke-Platek set theory with Σ_1-induction schema.

The proof of the cut-elimination theorem via a canonical proof search provides us no quantitative information. In Chap. 3, cut-elimination procedures are presented, by which we obtain a bound of the depth of the resulting cut-free derivations. The bound is given by an iteration of exponential functions of the depth of the given derivation. Logics dealt in the chapter are classical logic, intuitionistic logic, and fixed point logics in which a predicate constant I_φ together with inference rules is added for positive formula φ. The inference rules are for the axiom $\forall \mathbf{x}[\varphi(I_\varphi, \mathbf{x}) \leftrightarrow I_\varphi(\mathbf{x})]$ stating that I_φ is a fixed point of φ. When the underlying logic is intuitionistic, φ is a strictly positive formula. For the cut-elimination in the classical fixed point logic, an asymmetric interpretation is employed to replace the fixed point I_φ by stages I^n_φ of inductive definitions. The replacement is done according to contexts. As contrasted with the classical logic, the cut inferences from derivations in the intuitionistic fixed logic are eliminated quickly through a parallel elimination procedure.

Chapter 4 is of central importance in ordinal analysis. The target theories in the chapter are theories with induction schemata, i.e., complete induction schema, transfinite induction schema, and foundation schema in set theory. Let PA $+\mathrm{TI}(<\Lambda)$ denote an extension of the first-order arithmetic PA with transfinite induction schema for a standard and computable well-order $<$ of type Λ. Assuming that the ordinal Λ is an epsilon number, the proof-theoretic ordinal of the theory PA $+\mathrm{TI}(<\Lambda)$ is shown to be equal to the ordinal Λ. First the fact is proved by eliminating cut inferences from derivations of transfinite induction $\mathrm{TI}(\prec)$ for a computable strict partial order $\prec$ in ω-logic. We see that the ordinal Λ is an upper bound of the depths of the resulting cut-free derivations. On the other side, each cut-free derivation of $\mathrm{TI}(\prec)$ is seen to express the well-foundedness of $\prec$ directly. This means that the depth of the cut-free derivation is nearly equal to the order type of $\prec$. Moreover, it is easy to embed finitary proofs in the theory PA $+\mathrm{TI}(<\Lambda)$ into infinitary derivations with cut inferences with depth $<\Lambda$. Thus, we get an upper bound Λ of the proof-theoretic ordinal of PA $+\mathrm{TI}(<\Lambda)$, which is at the same time the least upper bound. By analyzing cut-free infinitary derivations, we show over a weak arithmetic that each Π^0_3-theorem in PA $+\mathrm{TI}(<\Lambda)$ follows from a weakly descending chain principle up to an ordinal $<\Lambda$.

To obtain a finer analysis, i.e., not just the proof-theoretic ordinal, but a characterization of consequences in lower complexity such as $\Pi^0_i (i = 1, 2)$, it is convenient for us to analyze finitary proofs directly following Gentzen's consistency proof. We show over a weak arithmetic that each Π^0_2-theorem follows from a descending chain principle, and each Π^0_1-theorem follows from an inference rule for a transfinite induction, each of which is up to an ordinal $<\Lambda$. For example, the class of provably computable functions in PA $+\mathrm{TI}(<\Lambda)$ is shown to be equal to the class $\mathscr{R}^{<\Lambda}$ of computable functions defined by transfinite recursion up to an ordinal $<\Lambda$.

The importance of these results lies in the fact that when a stronger theory T is analyzed proof-theoretically, the analysis shows in many cases that T is proof-theoretically reducible to a PA $+\mathrm{TI}(<\Lambda)$. Specifically T is shown to be Π^1_1-conservative over PA $+\mathrm{TI}(<\Lambda)$.

Next we examine closely the class $\mathscr{R}^{<\varepsilon_0}$ of provably computable functions in PA. First the descending chain principle up to ε_0 is shown to be equivalent to apparently weaker principle stating that there is no primitive recursive, slowly descending chain of ordinals $<\varepsilon_0$. The equivalence is based on a representation of natural numbers using Grzegorczyk functions $\{F_n\}_n$, which dominates each primitive recursive function. This yields Π^0_2-independence statements from PA: terminations of Goodstein sequences and Grzegorczyk sequences. Second we introduce fundamental sequences of ordinals $<\varepsilon_0$ and Hardy functions $H_\alpha\,(\alpha<\varepsilon_0)$, a classic approach to the class $\mathscr{R}^{<\varepsilon_0}$. We show a theorem stating that each provably computable function in PA is dominated by an H_α. Although the theorem is seen from a fact that each function in $\mathscr{R}^{<\varepsilon_0}$ is dominated by an H_α, we prove directly the theorem through a finer derivability relation $k \vdash^\alpha_c \Gamma$ to control numerical witnesses occurring in derivations. Though the approach with fundamental sequences is elegant and intuitively appealing, it would be complicated when we need to handle larger ordinals. For the obstacle, we introduce thirdly a syntactic approach called the norm-bounding recursion.

Finally, we show that the intuitionistic fixed point theory $\mathrm{Fi}X^i(T)$ over theories $T = \mathsf{PA}, \mathsf{KP}$ is a conservative extension of T. To illustrate an idea of a proof, let us consider the intuitionistic fixed point theory $\mathrm{Fi}X^i(\mathsf{HA})$ over the intuitionistic arithmetic HA. Note that this yields the fact that $\mathrm{Fi}X^i(\mathsf{PA})$ is a conservative extension of PA.

Given a finitary proof of an arithmetic formula A in $\mathrm{Fi}X^i(\mathsf{HA})$, let us embed it to an infinitary derivation, and cut inferences are eliminated quickly as in Chap. 3. This results in an almost cut-free derivations in depth $<\varepsilon_0$. By a partial truth definition we can conclude that the end formula A is true. By formalizing the proof in HA, we obtain $\mathsf{HA} \vdash A$. Although the above-sketched proof does work, it is cumbersome in formalizing the proof through infinitary derivations. Instead of this we give a finitary analysis of the proofs in the intuitionistic fixed point theories, since a formalization of the finitary analysis is a trivial matter.

Furthermore, the conservation theorem is utilized in showing that a theory T is Π^1_1-conservative over, e.g., a theory $\mathsf{PA} + \mathrm{TI}(<\Lambda)$, where Λ is the proof-theoretic ordinal of T as follows. T is analyzed proof-theoretically through infinitary derivations and cut-elimination. We need to handle a derivability relation $\vdash^\alpha_c \Gamma$ here. Suppose that the relation is definable as a fixed point. Then a proof of cut-elimination is carried out in an intuitionistic fixed point theory $\mathrm{Fi}X^i(\mathsf{PA} + \mathrm{TI}(<\Lambda))$. Since $\mathrm{Fi}X^i(\mathsf{PA} + \mathrm{TI}(<\Lambda))$ is conservative over $\mathsf{PA} + \mathrm{TI}(<\Lambda)$, we conclude that T is Π^1_1-conservative over $\mathsf{PA} + \mathrm{TI}(<\Lambda)$. Therefore, it is desirable to have a finitary analysis of intuitionistic fixed point theories.

In Chap. 5, we discuss straightforward extensions of results in Chap. 4, which are obtained by iterating cut-elimination procedures for first-order arithmetic. In iterating procedures, the (binary) Veblen hierarchy $\{\varphi_\alpha\}_{\alpha<\omega_1}$ appears, where each φ_α is a normal, i.e., strictly increasing and continuous function on ω_1 defined as follows. $\varphi_0(\beta) = \omega^\beta$, and for $\alpha > 0$, φ_α enumerates the common fixed points of functions $\varphi_\gamma(\gamma<\alpha)$. We establish equivalences between second-order arithmetics $\mathsf{ATR}_0 = \mathsf{FP}_0 = \mathrm{WOP}(\lambda X.\varphi X0)_0$ and the proof-theoretic ordinal of these is equal to the first strongly critical number also known as the Feferman-Schütte ordinal Γ_0, where ATR_0 is a second-order arithmetic whose main axiom is the arithmetical transfinite recursion admitting a jump hierarchy of sets along a well ordering. FP_0 is another second-order arithmetic whose main axiom states that a fixed point of a positive formula exists as a set. The main axiom of the second-order arithmetic $\mathrm{WOP}(\lambda X.\varphi_X(0))_0$ is the well-ordering principle for the normal function $\alpha \mapsto \varphi_\alpha(0)$, which states that if X is a well ordering, then a linear ordering $\varphi_X(0)$ is well founded. It is easy to see that FP_0 comprises ATR_0, and ATR_0 proves the well-ordering principle $\mathrm{WOP}(\lambda X.\varphi X0)_0$. We show by a proof-search method in Chap. 2, the fact that the well-ordering principle $\mathrm{WOP}(\lambda X.\varphi X0)_0$ implies FP_0. For the proof-theoretic ordinal of these second-order arithmetic, FP_0 is reduced to a theory $(\Pi^{0-}_1 - \mathrm{CA})_{<\Gamma_0}$ of the jump hierarchy via asymmetric interpretations as for fixed point logic in Chap. 3, and proving a cut-elimination theorem for $(\Pi^{0-}_1 - \mathrm{CA})_{<\Gamma_0}$ is a straightforward extension of the proof in Chap. 3. Finally, we extend proof-theoretic analyses for predicative theories to a metapredicative theory $\mathsf{ATR}_0{}^+$, whose main axiom states that there exists an arbitrarily large countable coded ω-model of ATR_0. A theory is said to be *metapredicative* if its proof-theoretic ordinal is larger than the limit Γ_0 of predicativity (over $\mathbb{N}$), but we can analyze it through a straightforward extension of analyses for predicative theories.

In Chap. 6, we analyze impredicative theories proof-theoretically. To extract computational (or countable) contents, we employ a technique, *collapsings*, by which uncountable infinitary derivations and uncountable ordinals are collapsed down to countable ones. This is done through Mostowski collapsings of Skolem hulls as in the Condensation lemma, which is a key to prove the fact that the GCH (generalized continuum hypothesis) holds in the constructible universe L. We introduce for each computable well order of type ν, theories ID_ν for iterated positive elementary inductive definitions over natural numbers, and set theories KP_ν for iterated admissibility. The intended model of KP_ν is the constructible set L_{Ω_ν}, where $0<\alpha \mapsto \Omega_\alpha$ denotes the continuous closure of the function $0<\alpha \mapsto \tau_\alpha$ for the α-th admissible ordinal τ_α. Next an iterated Skolem hull $\mathcal{H}_\alpha(X)$ of sets X of ordinals and a collapsing function $(\sigma, \alpha) \mapsto \psi_\sigma(\alpha)$ are introduced simultaneously, where σ is a recursively regular ordinal. It turns out that $\mathcal{H}_{\varepsilon_{\Omega_\nu+1}}(\{0\})$ is isomorphic to a computable set of ordinal terms, thereby yielding a notation system of ordinals. The theory ID_ν is shown to prove the well-foundedness of the notation system up to each ordinal term. We consider the simplest case to illustrate the ideas in cut-elimination procedures for impredicative theories. Namely, a theory $\mathsf{ID}_1{}^{\mathbb{O}}$, which is ID_1 with ordinals, is analyzed through the operator controlled derivations, and ID_1 through the Ω-rule. Then an ordinal analysis of the set theory KP_ν is given. Finally, we give two applications of the method of the operator controlled derivations. The first one is a relativized ordinal analysis. An operator to control derivations is a relativized Skolem hull $\mathcal{H}^\theta_\alpha$ relative to a function f_θ on ordinals. In the second, a set theory $\mathsf{KP}\Pi_{N+1}$ for Π_{N+1}-reflections is proof-theoretically reduced to a set theory of iterations of Π_N-recursively Mahlo operations. A transitive and well-founded model of $\mathsf{KP}\omega$ controls derivations in the second.

In the end of each chapter except Chap. 1, we include a list of problems, Exercises. Some of them provides additional topics and applications of techniques developed in the texts. Answers of the selected problems are found in Appendix 7.

In the final section, Notes, of each chapter, sources and credits are collected, and suggestions for further reading are given. We don't intend by no means to give a complete list of references since it is practically impossible.

For other topics not handled here, readers are suggested to read monographs by Takeuti, Schütte, Girard, Pohlers, and articles in the handbook.

I'd like to thank to Prof. Hiroakira Ono for encouraging me to write this monograph, and to the anonymous reviewers and Dr. Kentaro Sato for helpful comments.

Tokyo, Japan
October 2019

Toshiyasu Arai

References

Girard, J.-Y.: Proof Theory and Logical complexity, vol. 1. Bibliopolis, Napoli (1987)

Handbook of Proof Theory. S. R. Buss (ed.) Elsevier (1998)

Pohlers, W.: The First step Into Impredicativity. Universitext. Springer-Verlag, Berlin (2009)

Schütte, K.: Proof Theory. Translated from the Revised German. In: Crossley J. N. (ed.) Grundlehren der Mathematischen Wissenschaften, Band 225. Springer-Verlag, Berlin-New York (1977)

Takeuti, G.: Proof Theory, 2nd edn, North-Holland, Amsterdam (1987) reprinted from Dover Publications (2013)

Contents

Chapter 1
Introduction

In this chapter some prerequisites are explained such as one-sided sequent calculi, recursion-theoretic prerequisites, and the definition of the proof-theoretic ordinal. Our base theory, the elementary (recursive) arithmetic EA, is introduced, and the Kripke–Platek set theory KP is also defined. These materials are scattered in textbooks on logic.

1.1 Languages

In this book, languages considered are restricted to be *countable* unless otherwise stated. Let $\mathcal{L}$ be a countable language for predicate logic *without equality*, which consists of function symbols and relation symbols. Each symbol receives a non-negative integer called the arity of the symbol. 0-ary function symbols are *individual constants* denoted c. *Terms* in $\mathcal{L}$ or $\mathcal{L}$-terms are generated from countable lists of *free variables* denoted $a_0, a_1, \ldots$ or a, b by applying function symbols. *Closed terms* are terms in which no (free) variable occurs.

When we analyze *classical* logic or theories in classical logic proof-theoretically, we assume that each formula is in *negation normal form*. By a formula in negation normal form we mean a formula in which the implication $\rightarrow$ does not occur, and the negation $\neg$ is applied only to atomic formulas. Then the set of relation (predicate) symbols contains the *complement* $\overline{R}$ for each relation symbol R in the set. Thus the set of relation symbols $\mathcal{R} = \{R_i, \overline{R}_i : i \in I\}$($I$: a non-empty countable set), where R and $\overline{R}$ is the *complement* each other. Set $\overline{(\overline{R})} := R$. By a *literal* we mean an atomic formula, i.e., one of formulas $R(t_1, \ldots, t_n)$, $\overline{R}(t_1, \ldots, t_n)$ for terms $t_1, \ldots, t_n$ and n-ary relation symbols $R, \overline{R}$.

Formulas in negation normal form are generated from literals by means of *logical connectives*, boolean (or propositional) connectives $\vee, \wedge$, and quantifiers $\exists, \forall$ with *bound variables* denoted $x_0, x_1, \ldots$ or x, y. Let us specify quantifications. When A

© The Editor(s) (if applicable) and The Author(s), under exclusive license to Springer Nature Singapore Pte Ltd. 2020

T. Arai, *Ordinal Analysis with an Introduction to Proof Theory*, Logic in Asia: Studia Logica Library, https://doi.org/10.1007/978-981-15-6459-8_1

is a formula and x a bound variable not occurring in A, $\exists x\, A[x/a]$ and $\forall x\, A[x/a]$ are formulas, where $A[x/a]$ denotes the result of replacing every occurrence of a free variable a in A by x. We denote $A(x)$ instead of $A[x/a]$ when no confusion likely occurs.

The *negation* $\neg A$ of a formula A is defined recursively by de Morgan's law and the elimination of double negations:

1. $\neg L :\equiv \bar{L}$ for a literal L.
2. $\neg(A \vee B) :\equiv \neg A \wedge \neg B$ and $\neg(A \wedge B) :\equiv \neg A \vee \neg B$.
3. $\neg \exists x A(x) :\equiv \forall x \neg A(x)$ and $\neg \forall x A(x) :\equiv \exists x \neg A(x)$.

Closed formulas (or sentences) are formulas in which no free variable occurs. Formulas are denoted $A, B, C, \ldots$ $Var(e)$ denotes the set of free variables occurring in terms and formulas e.

A formula is said to be *positive* with respect to a predicate R, or R-*positive* if $\overline{R}$ does not occur in it. Alternatively we say that the predicate R occurs only positively in the formula. Similarly a formula is said to be R-*negative* if R does not occur in it.

When we consider intuitionistic logics and theories in intuitionistic logic, the implication $\to$ is a primitive logical connective, and $\perp$ is an atomic formula denoting the absurdity. Set $\neg A :\equiv (A \to \perp)$.

1.2 Sequent Calculi

We adopt *one-sided sequent calculi*, when we analyze *classical* logic or theories in classical logic proof-theoretically. Structural rules (weakening or thinning, contraction and exchange) are not included in one-sided sequent calculi since these are admissible rules or implicit in inference rules. A finite set $\{A_0, \ldots, A_{n-1}\}$ $(n \geq 0)$ of formulas is said to be a *sequent* or a *cedent*. Its intended meaning is the disjunction $\bigvee_{i<n} A_i$. Hence the empty sequent denotes the absurdity. Sequents are denoted $\Gamma, \Delta, \ldots$. Let Γ and Δ be sequents, and A a formula. Γ, Δ denotes the union $\Gamma \cup \Delta$ and $\Gamma, A := \Gamma \cup \{A\}$.

Now we define one-sided sequent calculus $\boldsymbol{G}_1$ for classical first-order predicate logic.

Axiom

$$\Gamma, \bar{L}, L$$

for any sequent Γ and a *literal* L.

Inference rules Rules for the propositional connectives $\vee, \wedge$:

$$\frac{\Gamma, A_0 \vee A_1, A_i}{\Gamma, A_0 \vee A_1}\ (\vee)_i\ (i = 0, 1) \qquad \frac{\Gamma, A_0 \wedge A_1, A_0 \quad \Gamma, A_0 \wedge A_1, A_1}{\Gamma, A_0 \wedge A_1}\ (\wedge)$$

$(\lor)$ denotes one of $(\lor)_i$. Note that

$$\frac{\Gamma, A_0 \lor A_1, A_0, A_1}{\Gamma, A_0 \lor A_1} \; (\lor)_{01}$$

is an admissible rule by applying $(\lor)$ twice, and vice versa with a weakening, cf. Lemma 1.3 below.

Rules for the quantifiers $\exists, \forall$:

$$\frac{\Gamma, \exists x A(x), A(t)}{\Gamma, \exists x A(x)} \; (\exists) \qquad \frac{\Gamma, \forall x A(x), A(a)}{\Gamma, \forall x A(x)} \; (\forall)$$

where, in $(\forall)$, the free variable a does not occur in the *lower sequent* $\Gamma, \forall x A(x)$, and is said to be the *eigenvariable* of the inference rule $(\forall)$.

In each inference rule the displayed formula in the lower sequent is the *main formula* (or the principal formula) of the inference rule. In the above figures $A_0 \lor A_1$, $A_0 \land A_1$, $\exists x A(x)$ and $\forall x A(x)$ are main formulas. Note that each main formula is assumed to be in the *upper sequent* of the inference rule. Other displayed formulas in upper sequents are the *minor formulas* (or the auxiliary formulas) of the inference rules. A_i is the minor formulas in $(\lor)$ and $(\land)$. $A(t)$ is the minor formula of the $(\exists)$, while $A(a)$ is the minor formula of the $(\forall)$.

The *cut* rule, which is not an inference rule in $\boldsymbol{G}_1$, is:

$$\frac{\Gamma, \neg C \quad C, \Delta}{\Gamma, \Delta} \; (cut)$$

where C is the *cut formula* of the (cut).

Let $\boldsymbol{G}$ be one of the two calculi $\boldsymbol{G}_1(+(cut))$ with or without (cut) rule. A *proof* or a *derivation* in $\boldsymbol{G}$ is a finite binary tree with sequents as labels which is correct with respect to **Axiom** and **Inference rules** in $\boldsymbol{G}$. The *endsequent* Γ of a proof is the sequent which is a label of the root of the proof tree. In this case the proof is said to be a proof of the endsequent Γ, and Γ is provable in $\boldsymbol{G}$, denoted $\boldsymbol{G} \vdash \Gamma$. A proof in $\boldsymbol{G}_1 + (cut)$ is *cut-free* if it is a proof in $\boldsymbol{G}_1$, i.e., a proof without (cut) rules.

Proposition 1.1 (Soundness) *Any provable sequent in* $\boldsymbol{G}_1 + (cut)$ *is valid. This means that if* $\boldsymbol{G}_1 + (cut) \vdash \Gamma$*, then the universal closure of the formula* $\bigvee \Gamma$ *is true in any structure.*

Definition 1.1 *The degree* $\mathrm{dg}(A)$ *of a formula* A.

1. $\mathrm{dg}(L) = 0$ for a literal L.
2. $\mathrm{dg}(A_0 \lor A_1) = \mathrm{dg}(A_0 \land A_1) = \max\{\mathrm{dg}(A_i) : i = 0, 1\} + 1$.
3. $\mathrm{dg}(\exists x A(x)) = \mathrm{dg}(\forall x A(x)) = \mathrm{dg}(A(a)) + 1$.

Note that $\mathrm{dg}(\neg A) = \mathrm{dg}(A)$.

Lemma 1.1 $\vdash \Gamma, \neg A, A$ *for each sequent* Γ *and formula* A.

Proof By induction on the degree $dg(A)$ of formulas A.

When A is a literal L, $\Gamma, \overline{L}, L$ is an axiom.

Let $A \equiv (B_0 \vee B_1)$. By IH(=Induction Hypothesis) we have $\Gamma_A, \neg B_i, B_i$ for $\Gamma_A = \Gamma \cup \{\neg B_0 \wedge \neg B_1, B_0 \vee B_1\}$ and $i = 0, 1$. Then the left figure below shows that $\vdash \Gamma, \neg B_0 \wedge \neg B_1, B_0 \vee B_1$.

Next let $A \equiv (\exists x B(x))$. By IH we have $\Gamma_A, \neg B(a), B(a)$ for $\Gamma_A = \Gamma \cup \{\forall x \neg B(x), \exists x B(x)\}$ and a free variable a not occurring in Γ_A. Then the right figure shows that $\vdash \Gamma, \forall x \neg B(x), \exists x B(x)$.

$$\dfrac{\dfrac{\Gamma_A, \neg B_0, B_0}{\Gamma_A, \neg B_0}\,(\vee)_0 \quad \dfrac{\Gamma_A, \neg B_1, B_1}{\Gamma_A, \neg B_1}\,(\vee)_1}{\Gamma_A}\,(\wedge) \qquad \dfrac{\dfrac{\Gamma_A, \neg B(a), B(a)}{\Gamma_A, \neg B(a)}\,(\exists)}{\Gamma_A}\,(\forall)$$

□

Definition 1.2 The set $Sbfml(A)$ of *subformulas* of a formula A (in Gentzen's sense) is defined as follows:

1. $Sbfml(L) = \{L\}$ for literals L.
2. $Sbfml(A) = \{A\} \cup \bigcup\{Sbfml(A_i) : i = 0, 1\}$ if $A \in \{A_0 \vee A_1, A_0 \wedge A_1\}$.
3. $Sbfml(A) = \{A\} \cup \bigcup\{Sbfml(B(t)) : t \text{ is a term}\}$ if $A \in \{\exists x B(x), \forall x B(x)\}$.

Clearly $B \in Sbfml(A) \Rightarrow dg(B) \leq dg(A)$.

Lemma 1.2 (Subformula property of cut-free proofs) *Any formula occurring in a cut-free proof (in* $\boldsymbol{G}_1$*) is a subformula of a formula occurring in the endsequent.*

Proof In an inference rule $(\vee)_{01}, (\wedge), (\exists), (\forall)$ of $\boldsymbol{G}_1$, each formula in the upper sequent is a subformula of a formula in the lower sequent. □

Lemma 1.3 (Weakening Lemma)

$$\vdash \Gamma \;\Rightarrow \vdash \Gamma, \Delta.$$

Proof This is seen by induction on $\vdash \Gamma$.

Let P be a proof of Γ in $\boldsymbol{G}$, and $P * \Delta$ a tree obtained from P by appending Δ to each sequent in P. Then P, Δ is a desired proof provided that one renames eigenvariables to new ones not occurring in Δ if necessary. □

We assume that the language contains an individual constant in the next definition.

Definition 1.3 *A proof* P *enjoys the pure variable condition* if a free variable can occur in an uppersequent of an inference but not in the lowersequent only in the case when the variable is the eigenvariable of the inference, i.e., the eigenvariable of a $(\forall)$ for the logic calculus $\boldsymbol{G}_1 + (cut)$.

If a free variable other than eigenvariables occurs in an uppersequent of an inference but not in the lowersequent, then one can substitute an individual constant for the variable. Note that free variables of such a proof are eigenvariables and free variables of its endsequent.

1.3 Arithmetic

1.3.1 Subrecursive Functions and Weak Arithmetic

Definition 1.4 1. $f^{(x)}$ denotes the xth iterate of a unary function f on $\mathbb{N}$, defined by $f^{(0)}(y) = y$ and $f^{(x+1)}(y) = f(f^{(x)}(y))$.
2. The *nth Grzegorczyk function* F_n denotes the function on integers defined recursively on n as follows. $F_0(x) = x + 1$ and $F_{n+1}(x) = F_n^{(x)}(x)$.

Definition 1.5 1. $\mathcal{B} = \{\text{zero}, S, x \dot{-} y, \max\} \cup \{I_i^k : 1 \leq i \leq k, k > 0\}$ denotes a class of initial functions. The 0-ary function zero $= 0$, the successor function $S(x) = x + 1$, the modified subtraction $x \dot{-} y = \max\{x - y, 0\}$, the maximum $\max(x, y)$ and projections $I_i^k(x_1, \ldots, x_k) = x_i$.
2. f is defined from $h, g_1, \ldots, g_m$ by **Composition** if $f(\mathbf{x}) = h(g_1(\mathbf{x}), \ldots, g_m(\mathbf{x}))$ for $\mathbf{x} = x_1, \ldots, x_k$.
3. f is defined from g, h by **Primitive Recursion** if $f(\mathbf{x}, 0) = g(\mathbf{x})$ and $f(\mathbf{x}, y + 1) = h(\mathbf{x}, y, f(\mathbf{x}, y))$.
4. f is defined from g by **Summation** if $f(\mathbf{x}, y) = \sum_{i<y} g(\mathbf{x}, i)$, where by definition $\sum_{i<0} g(\mathbf{x}, i) := 0$.
5. f is defined from g by **Product** if $f(\mathbf{x}, y) = \prod_{i<y} g(\mathbf{x}, i)$, where $\prod_{i<0} g(\mathbf{x}, i) := 1$.
6. The *elementary closure* of a class $\mathcal{F}$ of functions on $\mathbb{N}$ is the smallest class $\mathcal{G}$ such that $\mathcal{B} \cup \mathcal{F} \subset \mathcal{G}$, and $\mathcal{G}$ is closed under **Composition**, **Summation** and **Product**.
7. Let $3 \leq n \leq \omega$. The nth class $\mathcal{E}^n$ in the Grzegorczyk hierarchy is defined to be the elementary closure of the functions $\{F_m : 2 < m < n\}$.
   $\mathcal{E}^3$ is the class of *elementary recursive functions*.
8. PRIM denotes the class of all primitive recursive functions, which is the smallest class $\mathcal{G}$ such that $\{\text{zero}, S\} \cup \{I_i^k : 1 \leq i \leq k, k > 0\} \subset \mathcal{G}$, and $\mathcal{G}$ is closed under **Composition** and **Primitive Recursion**.
9. For a class $\mathcal{G}$ of functions, $\mathcal{G}_*$ denotes the class of relations whose characteristic functions are in $\mathcal{G}$.

Proposition 1.2 *Let $\mathcal{E}(\mathcal{F})$ be the elementary closure of a class $\mathcal{F}$ of functions.*

1. *The equality relation $x = y$ is in $\mathcal{E}(\mathcal{F})_*$, and $\mathcal{E}(\mathcal{F})_*$ is closed under boolean operations and bounded quantifications: If R is in $\mathcal{E}(\mathcal{F})_*$, then so is $\exists z < y\, R(z, \mathbf{x})$.*

2. *$\mathcal{E}(\mathcal{F})$ is closed under bounded minimizations: If R is in $\mathcal{E}(\mathcal{F})_*$, then $f(y, \mathbf{x}) = \min\{z : (z < y \land R(\mathbf{x}), z) \lor z = y\}$ is in $\mathcal{E}(\mathcal{F})$.*
3. *For each $f(\mathbf{x}) \in \mathcal{E}(\mathcal{F})$, its graph $R = \{(\mathbf{x}, y) : f(\mathbf{x}) = y\}$ is in $\mathcal{E}(\mathcal{F})_*$. Conversely if the graph of $f(\mathbf{x})$ is in $\mathcal{E}(\mathcal{F})_*$ and $f(\mathbf{x}) \leq j(\mathbf{x})$ for a $j(\mathbf{x}) \in \mathcal{E}(\mathcal{F})$, then $f(\mathbf{x})$ is in $\mathcal{E}(\mathcal{F})$.*
4. *Each of the following functions is elementary: the function $n \mapsto p_n$ with the nth prime p_n, $(x_0, \ldots, x_{n-1}) \mapsto \langle x_0, \ldots, x_{n-1}\rangle := \prod_{i<n} p_i^{1+x_i}$, $exp(x, i) = \max\{y \leq x : p_i^y | x\}$ with $y|x :\Leftrightarrow \exists z \leq x(yz = x)$, $(x)_i = exp(x, i) \dot{-} 1$, $lh(x) = \min\{i \leq x : exp(x, i) = 0\}$.*
5. *$\mathcal{E}(\mathcal{F})$ is closed under* **Limited Recursion***: Let f be a function defined from $g, h \in \mathcal{E}(\mathcal{F})$ by* **Primitive Recursion***. If $f(\mathbf{x}, y) \leq j(\mathbf{x}, y)$ for a $j(\mathbf{x}, y) \in \mathcal{E}(\mathcal{F})$, then $f(\mathbf{x}, y) \in \mathcal{E}(\mathcal{F})$.*

Proof It is easy to see Propositions 1.2.1–4. The modified subtraction $\dot{-}$ and max handle the equality, the boolean operations, and **Summation** the bounded quantifications and bounded minimizations. Proposition 1.2.3 follows from Proposition 1.2.2 since $f(\mathbf{x}) = F(j(\mathbf{x}) + 1, \mathbf{x})$ for $F(y, \mathbf{x}) = \min\{z : (z < y \land R(\mathbf{x}, z) \lor z = y\}$. By **Product** we see that the exponential function x^y is elementary.

For the closure under **Limited Recursion**, let $f(\mathbf{x}, 0) = g(\mathbf{x})$ and $f(\mathbf{x}, y + 1) = h(\mathbf{x}, y, f(\mathbf{x}, y))$ with $f(\mathbf{x}, y) \leq j(\mathbf{x}, y)$. Then $f(\mathbf{x}, y) = z$ iff there exists a sequence $w = \langle w_0, \ldots, w_y\rangle$ such that $w_0 = g(\mathbf{x})$, $w_{i+1} = h(\mathbf{x}, i, w_i)$ $(i < y)$, $w_y = z$, and each $w_i \leq J(\mathbf{x}, y) = \max\{i \leq y : j(\mathbf{x}, i)\}$, where $w \leq p_{y+1}^{K(\mathbf{x},y)}$ with $K(\mathbf{x}, y) = (1 + J(\mathbf{x}, y))(y + 1)$. We see $f(\mathbf{x}, y) \in \mathcal{E}(\mathcal{F})$ from Proposition 1.2.3. □

Proposition 1.3 *1. $F_n(x) > x$ for $x > 0$.*
2. *$F_n^{(y)}(x) \geq x$.*
3. *$(x, y) \mapsto F_n^{(y)}(x)$ is strictly increasing both in $x > 0$ and y.*
4. *$F_{n+1}(x) > F_n(x)$ for $x \geq 2$.*

Proof Propositions 1.3.1, 1.3.2 and 1.3.3 are proved simultaneously by induction on n. The case $n = 0$ is easily seen.

Let $x > 0$. Then $F_{n+1}(x) = F_n(F_n^{(x-1)}(x)) \geq F_n(x) > x$ by IH. Proposition 1.3.4 is proved by $F_{n+1}(x) = F_n^{(x-1)}(F_n(x)) > F_n(x) > 0$. From this we see $F_{n+1}^{(y)}(x) \geq x$ by induction on y. Again by IH we obtain $F_{n+1}(x + 1) = F_n(F_n^{(x)}(x + 1)) > F_n(F_n^{(x)}(x)) \geq F_n^{(x)}(x) = F_{n+1}(x)$. From this we see $F_{n+1}^{(y)}(x + 1) > F_{n+1}^{(y)}(x)$ by induction on y. $F_{n+1}^{(y+1)}(x) > F_{n+1}^{(y)}(x)$ is seen from Proposition 1.3.1. □

Lemma 1.4 *For each primitive recursive function $f(\mathbf{x})$, there exists an n for which $f(\mathbf{x}) \leq F_n(\max\{\mathbf{x}, 2\})$ holds for any $\mathbf{x} = x_1, \ldots, x_k$.*

Proof We show the lemma by induction on the definitions of primitive recursive functions f. For the initial functions $f(\mathbf{x}) \equiv 0$, $f(\mathbf{x}) = x_i$, $f(\mathbf{x}) = x_i + 1$, $f(\mathbf{x}) \leq F_0(\max\{\mathbf{x}, 2\})$ holds.

Let $f(\mathbf{x}) = h(g_1(\mathbf{x}), \ldots, g_m(\mathbf{x}))$ by **Composition**. By IH with Proposition 1.3.4 we have an n such that $g_i(\mathbf{x}) \leq F_n(\max\{\mathbf{x}, 2\})$ for any $\mathbf{x}$ and any $i \leq m$. Moreover $h(y_1, \ldots, y_m) \leq F_n(\max\{y_1, \ldots, y_m, 2\})$ for any y_i. Then Propositions 1.3.3 and

1.3.1 yield $f(\mathbf{x}) \leq F_n(\max\{g_1(\mathbf{x}), \ldots, g_m(\mathbf{x}), 2\}) \leq F_n(F_n(\max\{\mathbf{x}, 2\})) \leq F_{n+1}(\max\{\mathbf{x}, 2\})$.

Finally let $f(\mathbf{x}, 0) = g(\mathbf{x})$ and $f(\mathbf{x}, y+1) = h(\mathbf{x}, y, f(\mathbf{x}, y))$ by **Primitive Recursion**. By IH with Proposition 1.3.4 we have an n such that $g(\mathbf{x}) \leq F_n(\max\{\mathbf{x}, 2\})$ and $h(\mathbf{x}, y, z) \leq F_n(\max\{\mathbf{x}, y, z, 2\})$ for any $\mathbf{x}$ and any y, z. By induction on y we show that $f(\mathbf{x}, y) \leq F_n^{(y+1)}(\max\{\mathbf{x}, y, 2\})$. From this we see that for $z = \max\{\mathbf{x}, y, 2\} \geq 2$, $f(\mathbf{x}, y) \leq F_n^{(y+1)}(z) \leq F_n^{(z+1)}(z+1) = F_{n+1}(z+1) \leq F_{n+1}^{(2)}(z) \leq F_{n+2}(z)$.

When $y = 0$, $f(\mathbf{x}, 0) = g(\mathbf{x}) \leq F_n(\max\{\mathbf{x}, 2\}) = F_n^{(1)}(\max\{\mathbf{x}, 2\})$. For $y > 0$, $f(\mathbf{x}, y) = h(\mathbf{x}, y-1, f(\mathbf{x}, y-1)) \leq F_n(\max\{\mathbf{x}, y-1, f(\mathbf{x}, y-1), 2\}) \leq F_n(\max\{\mathbf{x}, y-1, F_n^{(y)}(\max\{\mathbf{x}, y-1, 2\}), 2\}) \leq F_n^{(y+1)}(\max\{\mathbf{x}, y, 2\})$ by Propositions 1.3.3 and 1.3.1. □

Corollary 1.1 $\mathscr{E}^\omega = \mathsf{PRIM}$.

Proof $\mathscr{E}^\omega \subset \mathsf{PRIM}$ is obvious. To see $\mathsf{PRIM} \subset \mathscr{E}^\omega$ inductively, let f be a function defined from $g, h \in \mathscr{E}^{n+1}$ by **Primitive Recursion**. By Lemma 1.4 we can assume that $f(\mathbf{x}) \leq F_n(\max\{\mathbf{x}, 2\})$. Proposition 1.2.5 yields $f \in \mathscr{E}^{n+1}$. □

Definition 1.6 The *elementary (recursive) arithmetic* EA for $\mathscr{E}^3$ is a fragment of the first-order arithmetic in the language $\mathscr{L}(\mathsf{EA}) = \{=, \leq, 0, S, +, \cdot, exp\}$, where $exp(x) = 2^x$ is the function symbol for the exponential. EA^4 is another fragment in an expanded language $\mathscr{L}(\mathsf{EA}^4) = \mathscr{L}(\mathsf{EA}) \cup \{tower\}$, where $tower(x) = 2_x = exp^{(x)}(1)$ is the function symbol for the tower of exponentials.

$\mathscr{L}(\mathsf{PRA}) = \{=, \leq\} \cup \{\mathsf{f} : f \in \mathsf{PRIM}\}$ denotes a language for PRA, *primitive recursive arithmetic* having function symbols f for each primitive recursive function $f \in \mathsf{PRIM}$.

The *defining axioms* of function symbols are: $x + 0 = x$, $x + S(y) = S(x + y)$, $x \cdot 0 = 0$, $x \cdot S(y) = x \cdot y + x$, $exp(0) = 1 := S(0)$, $exp(S(x)) = exp(x) \cdot 2$, $(2 := S(1))$, $tower(0) = 1$, $tower(S(x)) = exp(tower(x))$. If f is defined from $h, g_1, \ldots, g_m$ by **Composition**, then $\mathsf{f}(\mathbf{x}) = \mathsf{h}(\mathsf{g}_1(\mathbf{x}), \ldots, \mathsf{g}_m(\mathbf{x}))$ is its defining axiom. If f is defined from g, h by **Primitive Recursion**, then $\mathsf{f}(\mathbf{x}, 0) = \mathsf{g}(\mathbf{x})$ and $\mathsf{f}(\mathbf{x}, S(y)) = \mathsf{h}(\mathbf{x}, y, \mathsf{f}(\mathbf{x}, y))$ are its defining axioms.

The *axioms for the discrete order* $\leq$ are $0 \leq x$, $x \leq S(y) \leftrightarrow x \leq y \vee x = S(y)$, $x \leq x$, $x \leq y \leq z \to x \leq z$, $x \leq y \vee y \leq x$, $x \leq y \leq x \to x = y$.

In the following $\mathscr{L}$ is a language with a binary relation symbol $\leq$.

1. A formula in $\mathscr{L}$ is said to be *bounded* if every quantifier occurring in it is bounded by a term in $\mathscr{L}$, $\exists x \leq t$, $\forall x \leq t$, where $\exists x \leq t\, A(x) :\equiv (\exists x (x \leq t \wedge A(x)))$ and similarly for bounded universal quantifier.
2. $\Delta_0(\mathscr{L}) = \Sigma_0(\mathscr{L}) = \Pi_0(\mathscr{L})$ denotes the class of *bounded formulas* in the language $\mathscr{L}$.
3. $\Sigma_n(\mathscr{L})$ denotes the class of Σ_n*-formulas* in $\mathscr{L}$, each of which is of the form $\exists x_1 \forall x_2 \cdots Q x_n\, B$ with $B \in \Delta_0(\mathscr{L})$ and $Q = \forall$ when n is even, and $Q = \exists$ else.
4. Let $\{=, \leq, 0, S\} \subset \mathscr{L} \subset \mathscr{L}(\mathsf{PRA})$. $\mathrm{I}\Sigma_n(\mathscr{L})$ denotes a fragment of first-order arithmetic in the language $\mathscr{L}$. Its axioms are the *Peano axioms* $\forall x(S(x) \neq 0)$,

$\forall x, y(S(x) = S(y) \to x = y)$, the defining axioms for function symbols f for $\mathsf{f} \in \mathcal{L}$, the equality axioms, the axioms for the discrete order $\leq$, and the complete induction schema for $\Sigma_n(\mathcal{L})$-formulas A:

$$A(0) \land \forall x(A(x) \to A(S(x))) \to \forall x\, A(x).$$

The *Peano arithmetic* or the *first-order arithmetic* in the language $\mathcal{L}$ is defined to be $\mathsf{PA}(\mathcal{L}) := \mathrm{I}\Sigma_\omega(\mathcal{L}) := \bigcup_{n<\omega} \mathrm{I}\Sigma_n(\mathcal{L})$. Also *elementary arithmetic* $\mathsf{EA} := \mathsf{EA}^3 := \mathrm{I}\Sigma_0(\mathcal{L}(\mathsf{EA}))$, and $\mathsf{EA}^4 := \mathrm{I}\Sigma_0(\mathcal{L}(\mathsf{EA}^4))$.
The *primitive recursive arithmetic* $\mathsf{PRA} := \mathsf{EA}^\omega := \mathrm{I}\Sigma_0(\mathcal{L}(\mathsf{PRA}))$.

Note that for $\mathcal{E}^3 \subset \mathcal{G}$, each bounded formula is equivalent to an equation modulo defining axioms for function symbols.

Due to the following Proposition 1.4, $I\Sigma_n$ denotes ambiguously a theory $I\Sigma_n(\mathcal{L})$ for $n > 0$ and classes $\{\mathsf{f} : f \in \mathcal{E}^3\} \subset \mathcal{L}$.

Proposition 1.4 *Let $0 < n \leq \omega$. Then for any languages $\mathcal{L}, \mathcal{L}'$ such that $\{\mathsf{f} : f \in \mathcal{E}^3\} \subset \mathcal{L} \cap \mathcal{L}'$ and $\mathcal{L} \cup \mathcal{L}' \subset \mathcal{L}(\mathsf{PRA})$, $I\Sigma_n(\mathcal{L}) = I\Sigma_n(\mathcal{L}')$ holds.*

Proof This is seen from the fact that each primitive recursive function is $\Sigma_1(\mathcal{L})$-definable in $I\Sigma_1(\mathcal{L})$ for $\mathcal{L} = \{\mathsf{f} : f \in \mathcal{E}^3\}$. □

Proposition 1.5 *1. The partial truth definition for $\Sigma_0(\mathcal{L}(\mathsf{EA}))$-formulas is definable by a $\Sigma_0(\mathcal{L}(\mathsf{EA}^4))$-formula provably in the arithmetic EA^4.*
2. For each *$n > 0$ a partial truth definition for $\Sigma_n(\mathcal{L}(\mathsf{EA}))$-formulas is definable by a $\Sigma_n(\mathcal{L}(\mathsf{EA}))$-formula Tr_n provably in the arithmetic EA.*

Proof Note that EA is strong enough to encode finite sequences of natural numbers, cf. Proposition 1.2.4. Then an arithmetization of syntax and a partial truth definition are carried out in EA, cf. [6]. Proposition 1.5.1 is seen from the fact that each $\mathcal{E}^3$-function $f(x_1, \ldots, x_n)$ is bounded by a function $2_c(\max\{x_1, \ldots, x_n\})$ for a c, and there is an $\mathcal{E}^4$-function sending Gödel numbers $\lceil t \rceil$ of closed terms t in the language $\mathcal{L}(\mathsf{EA})$ to their values $t^{\mathbb{N}}$ in the standard model $\mathbb{N}$. □

1.3.2 Incompleteness

As said above, the language is assumed to be countable. We assume tacitly a suitable encoding of the syntax, such as terms, formulas, sequents. $\lceil A \rceil$ is then the code (Gödel number) of formulas A. Furthermore we are concerned only with formal (first-order or second-order) theories T, which are *elementary recursive*. This means that the set of coeds of axioms in T is elementary recursive.

Proposition 1.6 (Craig's trick) *Any r.e.(=recursively enumerable=computably enumerable) theory is axiomatizable by an elementary recursive set of sentences.*

Proof Let Th be an r.e. theory. We can assume that $Th \neq \emptyset$. Let e be a number such that $\forall x(x \in Th \leftrightarrow \exists y\, T(e, x, y))$ for the Kleene's T-predicate. Pick an $a \in Th$. Then for inverses $(n)_i$ $(i = 0, 1)$ of a bijective pairing function, let $f(n) = \begin{cases} (n)_0 \text{ if } T(e, (n)_0, (n)_1) \\ a \quad \text{otherwise} \end{cases}$. Since each of T and $(n)_i$ is elementary recursive, so is f. Moreover it is clear that $rng(f) = Th$. Now let $Th' = \{A^{(n+1)} : \ulcorner A \urcorner = f(n), n \in \mathbb{N}\}$, where for formulas A, $A^{(1)} \equiv A$ and $A^{(n+1)} \equiv (A \wedge A^{(n)})$. Then Th' axiomatizes the theory Th, and we see easily that Th' is elementary recursive. □

Let $\mathrm{Pr}_T(y) :\equiv \exists x \mathrm{Prf}_T(x, y)$ be a standard Σ_1-provability predicate for an elementary recursive theory $T \supset \mathsf{EA}$, where $\mathrm{Prf}_T(x, y)$ is an elementary recursive relation codifying 'x is a code of a proof of a formula y in T'. Assume that $\mathrm{Pr}_T(y)$ enjoys the Löb's derivability conditions, **D1**: $T \vdash A \Rightarrow \mathsf{EA} \vdash \mathrm{Pr}_T(\ulcorner A \urcorner)$ for formulas A, **D2**: $\mathsf{EA} \vdash \mathrm{Pr}_T(\ulcorner A \to B \urcorner) \to \mathrm{Pr}_T(\ulcorner A \urcorner) \to \mathrm{Pr}_T(\ulcorner B \urcorner)$ for formulas A, B, and **D3**: $\mathsf{EA} \vdash \mathrm{Pr}_T(\ulcorner A \urcorner) \to \mathrm{Pr}_T(\ulcorner \mathrm{Pr}_T(\ulcorner A \urcorner) \urcorner)$ for formulas A.

Let Φ be a class of sentences. $\mathrm{Rfn}_\Phi(T)$ denotes the *local reflection schema* for T with respect to sentences in Φ:

$$\mathrm{Rfn}_\Phi(T) = \{\mathrm{Pr}_T(\ulcorner A \urcorner) \to A : A \in \Phi\}.$$

$\mathrm{RFN}_{\Sigma_n}(T)$ denotes the *uniform reflection schema* for T with respect to Σ_n-sentences:

$$\mathrm{RFN}_{\Sigma_n}(T) = \forall \ulcorner A \urcorner \in Snt_n[\mathrm{Pr}_T(\ulcorner A \urcorner) \to Tr_n(\ulcorner A \urcorner)]$$

where Snt_n denotes the set of codes (Gödel numbers) of Σ_n-sentences, and Tr_n a Σ_n-formula defining a partial truth definition for Σ_n-sentences. The uniform reflection schema $\mathrm{RFN}_{\Pi_n}(T)$ for Π_n-sentences is defined similarly.

$\mathrm{RFN}_{\Sigma_n}(T)$ is said to be the *n-consistency* statement of T when $n = 1, 2$. It is easy to see that $\mathrm{RFN}_{\Pi_{n+1}}(T)$ is equivalent (over EA) to $\mathrm{RFN}_{\Sigma_n}(T)$ for each $n < \omega$, and $\mathrm{RFN}_{\Pi_1}(T)$ is equivalent to the consistency statement $\mathrm{CON}(T) :\Leftrightarrow \neg\mathrm{Pr}_T(\ulcorner \bot \urcorner)$, where $\bot$ is a false sentence $\bot$, e.g., $0 = 1$.

Gödel's second incompleteness theorem states that $T \nvdash \mathrm{CON}(T)$ unless T is inconsistent. Moreover $\mathrm{Rfn}_{\Sigma_1}(T)$ is stronger than the consistency $\mathrm{CON}(T)$, i.e., $T + \mathrm{Rfn}_{\Sigma_1}(T) \vdash \mathrm{CON}(T)$, but $T + \mathrm{CON}(T) \nvdash \mathrm{Rfn}_{\Sigma_1}(T)$ unless $T + \mathrm{CON}(T)$ is inconsistent. Moreover $T + \mathrm{Rfn}_{\Sigma_1}(T) \vdash \mathrm{CON}(T + \mathrm{CON}(T))$ is seen from the fact that $\mathrm{CON}(T)$ is a Π_1-sentence. In general the following holds.

Theorem 1.1 (Kreisel–Lévy Essential unboundedness theorem) *Let $T \supset \mathsf{EA}$ be one of fragments in Definition 1.6, and $n \geq 0$.*

1. *For any Σ_{n+1}-sentence C, $T + C \vdash \mathrm{Rfn}_{\Pi_{n+1}}(T) \Rightarrow T \vdash \neg C$.*
2. *For any Π_{n+1}-sentence C, $T + C \vdash \mathrm{Rfn}_{\Sigma_{n+1}}(T) \Rightarrow T \vdash \neg C$.*

Proof First consider the case $n = 0$ in Theorem 1.1.2. Suppose $T + C \vdash \mathrm{Rfn}_{\Sigma_1}(T)$ for a Π_1-sentence C. An instance $\mathrm{Pr}_T(\ulcorner \neg C \urcorner) \to \neg C$ of $\mathrm{Rfn}_{\Sigma_1}(T)$ yields $T + C \vdash \neg\mathrm{Pr}_T(\ulcorner \neg C \urcorner)$, i.e., $T + C \vdash \mathrm{CON}(T + C)$. Hence $T + C$ is inconsistent.

Next we show Theorem 1.1.1. Theorem 1.1.2 for $n > 0$ is seen similarly. Assume $T + C \vdash \mathrm{Rfn}_{\Pi_{n+1}}(T)$ for a Σ_{n+1}-sentence C. We show $T \vdash \neg C$.

Let A denote a Π_{n+1}-sentence such that

$$\mathsf{EA} \vdash A \leftrightarrow [C \to \neg \mathrm{Pr}_T(\ulcorner C \to A \urcorner)] \tag{1.1}$$

Since $T + C \vdash \mathrm{Rfn}_{\Pi_{n+1}}(T)$, we obtain $T + C \vdash \mathrm{Pr}_T(\ulcorner C \to A\urcorner) \to C \to A$. Hence $T + C \vdash \neg A \to \neg \mathrm{Pr}_T(\ulcorner C \to A\urcorner)$. Thus (1.1) yields $T + C \vdash \neg A \to A$. Therefore $T + C \vdash A$ and $T \vdash C \to A$. By the derivability condition **(D1)** we have $T + C \vdash \mathrm{Pr}_T(\ulcorner C \to A\urcorner)$. By (1.1) we conclude $T + C \vdash \neg A$, and $T \vdash \neg C$. □

1.3.3 Jumps and Trees

Let $T^{\mathcal{X}}(e, x, y)$ be Kleene's T-predicate with an oracle $\mathcal{X}$, which means that y is the code of a halting computation of a program P with its code $e = \ulcorner P \urcorner$ under the input x and the oracle $\mathcal{X} \subset \mathbb{N}$. For the result extracting function U, $\{e\}^{\mathcal{X}}(x) \simeq z :\Leftrightarrow \exists y[T^{\mathcal{X}}(e, x, y) \land U(y) = z]$. $\{e\}^{\mathcal{X}}(x)\downarrow :\Leftrightarrow \exists y[\{e\}^{\mathcal{X}}(x) \simeq y]$. A set A of natural numbers is computable (recursive) in $\mathcal{X}$ if there exists an e such that $A = \{x \in \mathbb{N} : \{e\}^{\mathcal{X}}(x) \simeq 0\}$ and $\forall x(\{e\}^{\mathcal{X}}(x)\downarrow)$. Then the *jump* of the set $\mathcal{X}$, denoted by $\mathcal{X}'$ is the set $\{x \in \mathbb{N} : \{x\}^{\mathcal{X}}(x)\downarrow\}$. The *jump operation* $\mathcal{X} \mapsto \mathcal{X}'$ can be iterated. Define $\mathcal{X}^{(n)}$ recursively by $\mathcal{X}^{(0)} = \mathcal{X}$ and $\mathcal{X}^{(n+1)} = (\mathcal{X}^{(n)})'$. It is well known that a set A of natural numbers is *arithmetical in* $\mathcal{X}$, i.e., $A = \{x \in \mathbb{N} : \mathbb{N} \models B[\mathcal{X}, x]\}$ for a first-order formula B in the language $\mathcal{L}(\mathsf{EA}) \cup \{X\}$ iff there exists an $n < \omega$ such that A is computable in the jump $\mathcal{X}^{(n)}$.

RCA_0 and WKL_0 are two of the big five of the subsystems of second order arithmetic. The axioms of RCA_0 are purely universal ones which define $0, S, +, \cdot, \leq$, the complete induction schema for Σ^0_1-formulas, and Δ^0_1-Comprehension Axiom Δ^0_1-CA: $\forall n(A(n) \leftrightarrow \neg B(n)) \to \exists X \forall n(X(n) \leftrightarrow A(n))$ $(A, B \in \Sigma^0_1)$. In these axioms, by a Σ^0_1-formula we mean a formula $\exists x\, R(x, \mathbf{a}, \mathbf{X})$ with a bounded formula, i.e., Δ^0_1-formula R possibly having first-order parameters $\mathbf{a}$, and second-order ones $\mathbf{X}$.

WKL_0 is obtained from RCA_0 by adding the *weak König's lemma*, i.e., König's lemma for binary trees.

Definition 1.7 1. For strings $\sigma, \tau \in {}^{<\omega}\omega$, $lh(\sigma)$ denotes the length of σ, and $\sigma(n)$ the n-component of σ for $n < lh(\sigma)$. $\tau \subset_e \sigma$ iff τ is an initial segment of σ. $\tau \subsetneq_e \sigma$ iff τ is a proper initial segment of σ. $\sigma * (i)$ is the concatenated string such that $lh(\sigma * (i)) = lh(\sigma) + 1$ and $(\sigma * (i))(lh(\sigma)) = i$.

2. $T \subset {}^{<\omega}\omega$ is a *tree* on ω iff $T \neq \emptyset$ and $\forall \sigma \in T \forall \tau \subset_e \sigma(\tau \in T)$.
   In general a tree is a partial order $(A, \leq_A)$ such that A has a largest element (*root*), and $\{b \in A : a \leq_A b\}$ is linearly ordered by $\leq_A$ for each $a \in A$.
3. A tree $(A, \leq_A)$ is *well-founded* if there is no infinite path $f : \omega \to A$ through A, i.e., $\neg \exists f \in {}^{\omega}A \forall n < \omega(f(n+1) <_A f(n))$. When $T \subset {}^{<\omega}\omega$, by an infinite

path through T we mean an infinite series $f : \omega \to T$ such that $\forall n < \omega(f(n) \subsetneq_e f(n+1))$.

4. For well-founded trees $(A, \leq_A)$ and $a \in A$, let $|a|_A := \sup\{|b|_A + 1 : b <_A a\}$, and $|A| := |r|_A$ for the root r of A.
5. The *Kleene–Brouwer ordering* $<_{KB}$ on a tree $T \subset {}^{<\omega}\omega$ is defined by $\sigma <_{KB} \tau$ iff either $\tau \subsetneq_e \sigma$ or there exists an $n < \min\{lh(\sigma), lh(\tau)\}$ such that $\sigma(n) < \tau(n)$ and $\forall i < n(\sigma(i) = \tau(i))$.
6. A tree $T \subset {}^{<\omega}\omega$ is *finitely branching* if the set $\{i \in \mathbb{N} : \sigma * (i) \in T\}$ is finite for any σ.
7. A tree T is *binary* if $T \subset {}^{<\omega}2$.

The *König's (infinity) lemma* states that for any infinite, and finitely branching tree T there exists an infinite path through T, while the *weak König's lemma* states that for any infinite binary tree T there exists an infinite path through T. Note that an infinite path through a binary tree T can be replaced by an infinite series $f : \omega \to 2$ of 0 and 1 such that $\forall n(\bar{f}(n) \in T)$, where $\bar{f}(n) = (f(0), \ldots, f(n \dot{-} 1))$.

For trees T and S on ω, let $T \otimes S$ denote the set of sequences $\tau \otimes \sigma := ((t_1, s_1), \ldots, (t_n, s_n))$ of pairs (t_i, s_i) such that $\tau = (t_1, \ldots, t_n) \in T, \sigma = (s_1, \ldots, s_n) \in S$ with $n \geq 0$. It is clear that $T \otimes S$ is a tree.

Proposition 1.7 *Assume that T is not well-founded, while S is well-founded. Then $T \otimes S$ is well-founded, and $|T \otimes S| \geq |S|$.*

Proof We see easily that $T \otimes S$ is well-founded from the well-foundedness of S.

Let $\{t_i\}_i$ be an infinite path through T, and $\tau_n = (t_1, \ldots, t_n)$. By induction on $\sigma = (s_1, \ldots, s_n) \in S$ we show

$$|\tau_n \otimes \sigma|_{T \otimes S} \geq |\sigma|_S$$

Let $\sigma * (s) \in S$. By IH we obtain $|\tau_{n+1} \otimes (\sigma * (s))|_{T \otimes S} \geq |\sigma * (s)|_S$. Hence $|\tau_n \otimes \sigma|_{T \otimes S} \geq \sup\{|\tau_{n+1} \otimes (\sigma * (s))|_{T \otimes S} + 1 : \sigma * (s) \in S\} \geq \sup\{|\sigma * (s)|_S + 1 : \sigma * (s) \in S\} = |\sigma|_S$. □

Proposition 1.8 *Over* RCA_0, *the weak König's lemma is equivalent to the following* Π_1-Reduction axiom, Π_1–RD[1]*:*

$$\neg\exists n(A(n) \land B(n)) \to \exists X \forall n[(A(n) \to X(n)) \land (X(n) \to \neg B(n))]\ (A, B \in \Sigma_1) \tag{1.2}$$

Proof First we show Π_1-RD from the weak König's lemma. For $i = 0, 1$, let $A_i(n) \equiv \exists m B_i(n, m)$ be Σ_1-formulas with Δ_0-matrices B_i. Suppose $\neg\exists n(A_0(n) \land A_1(n))$. Let T be the set of binary strings $\sigma \in {}^{<\omega}2$ such that

$$\bigwedge_{i<2} \forall m, n < lh(\sigma)(B_i(n, m) \to \sigma(n) = 1 - i).$$

[1]Although the axiom is called the Σ_1-Separation axiom in the literature, let us call it the 'Π_1-Reduction axiom' to avoid a possible confusion of it and the axiom of Σ_1-separation in set theory.

T exists as a set by Δ_0-Comprehension Axiom. We see readily that T is an infinite binary tree. By the weak König's lemma pick an infinite path f through T, and let $X = \{n : f(n) = 1\}$. Then we see that $\forall n[(A_0(n) \to X(n)) \land (X(n) \to \neg A_1(n))]$.

Second we show the weak König's lemma from Π_1-RD. Let T be an infinite binary tree. Let

$$B(n, \sigma) :\Leftrightarrow \exists \tau < 2^{n+1}[lh(\tau) = n \land \tau \in T \land \sigma \subset \tau]$$
$$A_i(\sigma) :\Leftrightarrow \exists n(B(n, \sigma * (i)) \land \neg B(n, \sigma * (1 - i)))$$

We see readily that $\neg\exists\sigma(A_0(\sigma) \land A_1(\sigma))$. By Π_1-RD pick a set X such that $\forall\sigma[(A_0(\sigma) \to X(\sigma)) \land (X(\sigma) \to \neg A_1(\sigma))]$. Define a sequence $\{\sigma_k\}_k \subset {}^{<\omega}2$ by starting with the empty string σ_0, and

$$\sigma_{k+1} = \begin{cases} \sigma_k * (0) \text{ if } X(\sigma_k) \\ \sigma_k * (1) \text{ otherwise} \end{cases}$$

Clearly $lh(\sigma_k) = k$. We show that $\forall n \forall k \leq n\, B(n, \sigma_k)$ by induction on $k \leq n$. $B(n, \sigma_0)$ is seen from the assumption that T is infinite. Assume that $B(n, \sigma_k)$ for $k < n$. We have $B(n, \sigma_k * (0)) \lor B(n, \sigma_k * (1))$. If $\neg B(n, \sigma_k * (i))$ for an $i < 2$, then we obtain $A_{1-i}(\sigma_k)$, and $(\neg)^{1-i} X(\sigma_k)$, where $(\neg)^1 C = \neg C$ and $(\neg)^0 C = C$. This means that $\sigma_{k+1} = \sigma_k * (1 - i)$. Moreover $B(n, \sigma_k * (1 - i))$. Hence $B(n, \sigma_{k+1})$. Otherwise, i.e., if $\bigwedge_{i<2} B(n, \sigma_k * (i))$, then $B(n, \sigma_{k+1})$ for $\sigma_{k+1} \in \{\sigma_k * (i) : i < 2\}$. Thus we have shown $\forall n \forall k \leq n\, B(n, \sigma_k)$. In particular we obtain $\forall n\, B(n, \sigma_n)$, i.e., $\forall n(\sigma_n \in T)$. Then $f(n) = i \Leftrightarrow \sigma_{n+1}(n) = i$ is an infinite path through T. □

ACA_0 is obtained from RCA_0 by adding the *arithmetic comprehension axiom* $\forall Z \exists X \forall y[y \in X \leftrightarrow A(y, Z)]$ for first-order formulas A.

Proposition 1.9 ACA_0 *proves the König's lemma.*

Proof Let T be an infinite, and finitely branching tree. Define $T^\infty \subset T$ by $\sigma \in T^\infty$ iff the set $\{\tau \in T | \sigma \subset_e \tau\}$ is infinite. By the arithmetic comprehension axiom, T^∞ exists as a set. For each $\sigma \in T^\infty$, there exists an i such that $\sigma * (i) \in T^\infty$ since T is finitely branching. Moreover the empty sequence $\emptyset$ is in T^∞ since T is infinite. By recursion define an infinite path (the leftmost branch) $\{\sigma_n\}_n$ through T^∞ by $\sigma_0 = \emptyset$, and $\sigma_{n+1} = \sigma_n * (i)$, where i is the least number such that $\sigma_n * (i) \in T^\infty$. □

It is easy to see that the Kleene–Brouwer order $<_{KB}$ on T is a linear ordering.

Proposition 1.10 ACA_0 *proves the following equivalence:*
a tree T is well-founded iff the Kleene–Brouwer order $<_{KB}$ on T is a well ordering.

Proof If there is an infinite path $\{\sigma_n\}_n$ through T, then $\sigma_n \subsetneq_e \sigma_{n+1}$, and $\sigma_{n+1} <_{KB} \sigma_n$ for any n.

Conversely assume that the tree T is well-founded, and let $\{\sigma_n\}_n$ be an infinite descending chain in T with respect to $<_{KB}$. Let $S = \{\sigma \in T | \exists n(\sigma \subset_e \sigma_n)\}$. S is a set by the arithmetic comprehension axiom, and an infinite subtree of T.

We claim that S is finitely branching. Then S, a fortiori T, would have an infinite path by Proposition 1.9. Let $\sigma \in S$ be such that $\sigma * (i) \in S$ for an i. Let i_0 be the least number such that $\sigma * (i_0) \in S$. Pick an n such that $\sigma * (i_0) \subset_e \sigma_n$. Then we see that the set $X = \{j > i_0 | \sigma * (j) \in S\}$ has at most n elements as follows. For each $j \in X$ let n_j be the least number m such that $\sigma * (j) \subset_e \sigma_m$. Then for $i, j \in X$, if $i < j$, then $\sigma_n <_{KB} \sigma_{n_i} <_{KB} \sigma_{n_j}$, and $n_j < n_i < n$. □

1.3.4 Π^1_1-Completeness of *W*

Theorem 1.2 (Π^1_1-normal form) *Let* $\forall f (\in^{<\omega} \omega) A(f, n)$ *be a* Π^1_1*-formula. Then there exists an elementary recursive predicate* $S_A(n, s)$ *such that the following is provable in* ACA$_0$*: for any* $n \in \omega$ *and any* $s, t \in {}^{<\omega}\omega$

1. $\forall f A(f, n) \leftrightarrow \forall f \exists x\, S_A(n, \bar{f}(x))$ *with* $\bar{f}(x) = \langle f(0), \dots, f(x \dot{-} 1)\rangle$, *and*
2. $s \subset_e t \,\&\, S_A(n, s) \to S_A(n, t)$.

$\forall f \exists x\, S_A(n, \bar{f}(x))$ *is said to be a* Π^1_1-normal form *of the* Π^1_1*-formula* $\forall f A(f, n)$.

Proof Pick an elementary recursive relation R such that ACA$_0 \vdash \forall f A(f, n) \leftrightarrow \forall f \exists x R(n, f, x)$ as follows. We can assume that the arithmetical A is in prenex normal form. Then using the following equivalences, which are provable in ACA$_0$, we get a desired R with a pairing function $\langle x, y\rangle$.

$$\begin{aligned} &\forall f \forall x B(f, x) \leftrightarrow \forall g B(g_0, g_1(0)) \text{ for } g_i(x) = g(\langle i, x\rangle) \\ &\exists x \forall y B(x, y) \leftrightarrow \forall g \exists x B(x, g(x)) \end{aligned} \tag{1.3}$$

In showing the implication $\forall g \exists x B(x, g(x)) \to \exists x \forall y B(x, y)$, let $g(x) = y \leftrightarrow y \simeq \mu y.\neg B(x, y)$. The (graph of the) function g exists by the arithmetic comprehension axiom.

The idea to get an S_A is as follows. Since R is computable, $\exists x R(n, f, x)$ means that for the inputs n, f there exists a halting computation x for a program e_A. Hence for the Kleene's T-predicate, which is elementary recursive,

$$\begin{aligned} \forall f A(f, n) &\leftrightarrow \forall f \exists x R(n, f, x) \\ &\leftrightarrow \forall f \exists x T(e_A; n, \bar{f}(x); x) \end{aligned}$$

Now let

$$S_A(n, s) :\Leftrightarrow \exists x \le lh(s) T(e_A; n, s; x).$$

This is a desired one since $T(e_A; n, s; x)$ means that s includes a sufficient information of an input function f for computation.

Formally given an elementary recursive relation $R(n, f, x)$ with a function variable f, let $\exists w\, R_1(n, f, x, w) \leftrightarrow R(n, f, x)$ be an f-normal form of R. This means that the variable f occurs in R_1 only in the form $f(y) = z$ for some variables y, z. Such a normal form is obtained from R by logical equivalences. Therefore we can assume that $R(n, f, x)$ is in f-normal form.

Second for a fresh variable s let $S_A(n, s)$ be obtained from $R(n, f, x)$ as follows. Replace each atomic formula $f(y) = z$ [$f(y) \neq z$] by $(s)_y = s \land y < lh(s)$ [by $(s)_y \neq z \land y < lh(s)$], resp. Then let $S_A(n, s) :\Leftrightarrow \exists x < lh(s)\, S_0(n, s, x)$ for the result S_0 of the replacements. Then we obtain

$$\exists x\, R(n, f, x) \leftrightarrow \exists s \left(s = \bar{f}(lh(s)) \land S_A(n, s)\right) \tag{1.4}$$

and S_A is a desired one. □

Remark 1.1 Let $F(x, y)$ be a formula in the language of the second-order arithmetic, SOA. The full complete induction schema Π^2_0-IND yields $\forall x \exists ! y\, F(x, y) \to \forall x \exists s(s = \bar{F}(x))$, and hence in (1.4) we can substitute the formula F for the variable f:

$$\Pi^2_0\text{-IND} \vdash \forall x \exists ! y\, F(x, y) \to [\exists x\, R(n, F, x) \leftrightarrow \exists s \left(s = \bar{F}(lh(s)) \land S_A(n, s)\right)]$$

since the equivalence (1.4) is seen logically.

Definition 1.8 W denotes the set of codes of computable well-founded trees.

$$e \in W :\Leftrightarrow Set(e) := \{s \in {}^{<\omega}\omega : \{e\}(s) \simeq 0\} \text{ is a well-founded tree.} \tag{1.5}$$

To sum up, we have proved the following theorem.

Theorem 1.3 *W is Π^1_1-complete. Namely for any Π^1_1-formula $\forall f\, A(f, n)$, there exists an elementary recursive function w_A such that*

$$\forall n [\forall f\, A(f, n) \leftrightarrow w_A(n) \in W].$$

Proof $w_A(n)$ is a code of the tree $\{s \in {}^{<\omega}\omega : \neg S_A(n, s)\}$ in the proof of Theorem 1.2. □

1.3.5 Inductive Definitions

Let $\mathscr{A}[X, n]$ denote an X-positive elementary, i.e., first-order formula in the language of arithmetic. Then $\mathscr{A}$ defines a *monotonic operator* $\mathscr{A} : \mathscr{P}(\mathbb{N}) \to \mathscr{P}(\mathbb{N})$, where $\mathscr{A}(\mathscr{X}) := \{n \in \mathbb{N} : \mathbb{N} \models \mathscr{A}[\mathscr{X}, n]\}$ such that $\mathscr{X} \subset \mathscr{Y} \Rightarrow \mathscr{A}(\mathscr{X}) \subset \mathscr{A}(\mathscr{Y})$.

By transfinite recursion on ordinals define stages $I^\alpha_{\mathscr{A}} \subset \mathbb{N}$ by

$$I^\alpha_{\mathscr{A}} := \mathscr{A}(I^{<\alpha}_{\mathscr{A}}) \text{ where } I^{<\alpha}_{\mathscr{A}} := \bigcup_{\beta<\alpha} I^\beta_{\mathscr{A}}, \text{ and } I_{\mathscr{A}} := \bigcup_\alpha I^\alpha_{\mathscr{A}}.$$

We call $I_{\mathscr{A}}$ the *set inductively defined by* $\mathscr{A}$.

Lemma 1.5 *1.* $\beta < \alpha \Rightarrow I^{\beta}_{\mathscr{A}} \subset I^{\alpha}_{\mathscr{A}}$.
2. *There exists an ordinal* $\lambda < \omega_1$ *such that* $I_{\mathscr{A}} = I^{\lambda}_{\mathscr{A}} = I^{<\lambda}_{\mathscr{A}}$. *Call the least such* λ *the* closure ordinal *of* $\mathscr{A}$, $\lambda = |\mathscr{A}|$.
3. $I_{\mathscr{A}}$ *is the smallest fixed point of* $\mathscr{A}$, *i.e.,* $\mathscr{A}(I_{\mathscr{A}}) = I_{\mathscr{A}}$ *and*

$$I_{\mathscr{A}} = \bigcap\{\mathscr{X} \subset \mathbb{N} : \mathscr{A}(\mathscr{X}) = \mathscr{X}\} = \bigcap\{\mathscr{X} \subset \mathbb{N} : \mathscr{A}(\mathscr{X}) \subset \mathscr{X}\}. \quad (1.6)$$

Definition 1.9 A set $\mathscr{X} \subset \mathbb{N}$ is said to be *inductive* if it is a *section* of a set inductively defined by a positive elementary operator $\mathscr{A}$. This means that $\mathscr{X} = \{n \in \mathbb{N} : \langle m, n\rangle \in I_{\mathscr{A}}\}$ for an $m \in \mathbb{N}$. $\mathscr{X}$ is said to be *coinductive* if it is a complement of an inductive set. $\mathscr{X}$ is said to be *hyperelementary* if it is both inductive and coinductive.

Corollary 1.2 *The set* $I_{\mathscr{A}}$ *inductively defined by a positive elementary operator* $\mathscr{A}$ *is* Π^1_1. *Any inductive set is* Π^1_1.

Let T be an arithmetical tree, and $T_s := \{t : s * t \in T\}$. Define

$$\mathscr{T}[X, s] :\Leftrightarrow T_s = \emptyset(\leftrightarrow s \notin T) \lor \forall m[s * \langle m\rangle \in X].$$

Then we see easily that for any $s \in {}^{<\omega}\omega$

$$s \in I_{\mathscr{T}} \Leftrightarrow T_s \text{ is well-founded.} \quad (1.7)$$

In particular

$$\langle\rangle \in I_{\mathscr{T}} \Leftrightarrow T \text{ is well-founded.}$$

Theorem 1.4 *Any* Π^1_1 *subset of* ω *is inductive.*

Proof For a given Π^1_1 set $\{n \in \omega : \forall f A(f, n)\}$ pick a recursive predicate $S_A(n, s)$ given in Theorem 1.2: $\forall f A(f, n)$ iff the tree $T^n = \{s : \neg S_A(n, s)\}$ is well-founded iff $\forall f \exists x\, S_A(n, \bar{f}(x))$.

Now define an operator by

$$\mathscr{T}[X, \langle n, s\rangle] :\Leftrightarrow T^n_s = \emptyset(\leftrightarrow S_A(n, s)) \lor \forall m[\langle n, s * \langle m\rangle\rangle \in X].$$

Then by (1.7) we have

$$\langle n, s\rangle \in I_{\mathscr{T}} \Leftrightarrow T^n_s \text{ is well-founded } \Leftrightarrow \forall f \exists x\, S_A(n, s * \bar{f}(x)).$$

In particular

$$\langle n, \langle\rangle\rangle \in I_{\mathscr{T}} \Leftrightarrow T^n_{\langle\rangle} = T^n \text{ is well-founded } \Leftrightarrow \forall f \exists x\, S_A(n, \bar{f}(x)) \Leftrightarrow \forall f A(f, n).$$

Therefore $\{n \in \omega : \forall f A(f, n)\}$ is a section of the set $I_{\mathscr{T}}$ inductively defined by the positive elementary $\mathscr{T}$. □

1.4 Proof-Theoretic Ordinals

In this section we consider theories in a language $\mathcal{L} \supset \mathcal{L}(\mathsf{EA}) \cup \{U\}$ with a unary relation symbol U. Let $\prec$ be an arithmetically definable relation on ω. This means that $n \prec m$ is a formula $A(n, m)$ in the language of first-order formula without the relation variable U whose free variables are among n, m. Although the relation $\prec$ is supposed to be well-founded, but we don't assume it. A *strict partial order* $\prec$ is an irreflexive, $\forall x(x \not\prec x)$ and transitive relation, $\forall x, y, z(x \prec y \prec z \to x \prec z)$. An ordinal α is said to be *recursive* iff there exists a recursive (computable) well ordering on ω of type α. ω_1^{CK} (*Church–Kleene* ω_1) denotes the least non-recursive ordinal.

Definition 1.10 1. $Prg[\prec, U] :\Leftrightarrow \forall x[\forall y \prec x(y \in U) \to x \in U]$ (U is *progressive* with respect to $\prec$).
2. $\mathrm{TI}[\prec, A] :\Leftrightarrow Prg[\prec, A] \to \forall x\, A(x)$ for formulas $A(x)$, and $\mathrm{TI}[\prec, U] \Leftrightarrow Prg[\prec, U] \to \forall x\, U(x)$ (transfinite induction on $\prec$).
3. Let $\prec$ be a computable strict partial order on ω. If $\prec$ is well-founded, then let $|n|_\prec := \sup\{|m|_\prec + 1 : m \prec n\}$, and $|\prec| := \sup\{|n|_\prec + 1 : n \in \omega\}$ (the order type of $\prec$). Otherwise let $|\prec| := \omega_1^{CK}$.

Definition 1.11 For a theory T comprising elementary recursive arithmetic EA the *proof-theoretic ordinal* $|T| \leq \omega_1^{CK}$ of T is defined by

$$|T| := \sup\{|\prec| : T \vdash \mathrm{TI}[\prec, U] \text{ for some recursive strict partial order } \prec\}. \quad (1.8)$$

Now, most brutally speaking, the aim of the ordinal analysis is to compute and/or describe the proof-theoretic ordinals of natural theories, thereby measuring the proof-theoretic strengths of theories with respect to Π^1_1-consequences.

Let us give some comments and remarks on Definition 1.11.

A formula in the language of second-order arithmetic (SOA) is said to be Π^1_1 if it is of the form $\forall X(\subset \omega)A(X)$ or $\forall f(\in {}^\omega\omega)A(f)$ for a first-order (Π^1_0) formula A. The dual form $\exists X(\subset \omega)A(X)$ or $\exists f(\in {}^\omega\omega)A(f)$ is a Σ^1_1-formula.

When T is a first-order theory in the following Theorem 1.5, by a 'Π^1_1-sentence' we mean a first-order formula $A(U)$ possibly with the relation symbol U. Such a formula is true in $\mathbb{N}$ iff $\langle \mathbb{N}, \mathcal{P}(\mathbb{N})\rangle \models \forall U\, A(U)$.

Theorem 1.5 *For recursive theories* $T \supset \mathsf{ACA}_0$, $|T| < \omega_1^{CK}$ *iff* T *is* Π^1_1-sound, *namely any provable* Π^1_1*-sentences in* T *is true (in the standard model).*

Proof First let us assume that T is Π^1_1-sound. For each $p \in \omega$ let $<_p$ denote a recursive relation defined as follows:

1. The case when p is a Gödel number of a proof in T whose endformula is $\mathrm{TI}[\prec, U]$ for a recursive relation $\prec$.: Then put $<_p := \prec$.
2. Otherwise: Then let $<_p$ denotes an empty ordering, i.e., $dom(<_p) = \emptyset$.

Glue these ordering together to get a recursive relation $<^T$:

$$\langle n, p\rangle <^T \langle m, q\rangle :\Leftrightarrow [p = q \,\&\, n <_p m] \vee p < q$$

for a bijective pairing function $\langle n, p\rangle$. Then $<^T$ is a recursive and well-founded relation by the assumptions, and $|T| \leq \sup\{|<_p| : p \in \omega\} \leq |<^T| < \omega_1^{CK}$ as desired.

Conversely suppose that T is not Π^1_1-sound. Let A be a false Π^1_1-sentence for which $T \vdash A$. Let $\forall f \exists x\, S_A(n, \bar{f}(x))$ be a Π^1_1-normal form of A such that $T \vdash \forall f\, A(f, n) \leftrightarrow \forall f \exists x\, S_A(n, \bar{f}(x))$ for $T \supset \mathsf{ACA}_0$. Then the elementary recursive tree $T_A = \{\sigma \in {}^{<\omega}\omega : \neg S_A(n, \sigma)\}$ is not well-founded. Now let $\alpha < \omega^{CK}$, and S be a recursive well-founded tree such that $\alpha \leq |S|$. Since T proves that the tree T_A is well-founded, we see that T proves that the recursive tree $T_A \otimes S$ is well-founded. On the other side Proposition 1.7 yields $|T_A \otimes S| \geq |S| \geq \alpha$. Hence $|T| \geq \alpha$ for any $\alpha < \omega_1^{CK}$. This means $|T| = \omega_1^{CK}$ even for well orders. □

Theorem 1.6 *Let T be a recursive, Π^1_1-sound SOA comprising* ACA_0.

1. *The proof-theoretic ordinal remains the same even for Σ^1_1-ordering.*

$$|T| = \sup\{| \prec | : T \vdash \mathrm{TI}[\prec, U] \text{ for some } \Sigma^1_1\text{−strict partial order } \prec\}.$$

2. *Adding true Σ^1_1-sentences does not raise the proof-theoretic ordinal: Let $Tr_{\Sigma^1_1}$ denote the set of true Σ^1_1-sentences. Then*[2]

$$|T| = |T + Tr_{\Sigma^1_1}|.$$

Proof Theorem 1.6.1. Let $\prec$ be a Σ^1_1-strict partial order for which $T \vdash \mathrm{TI}[\prec, U]$. Let $Emb(y)$ denote the formula, cf. (1.5) in Definition 1.8, $Set(y) \neq \emptyset \wedge \exists f \forall s, t \in {}^{<\omega}\omega[t \in Set(y) \wedge s \subsetneq_e t \rightarrow s \in Set(y) \wedge f(t) \prec f(s)]$, i.e., $Set(y)$ is a tree, and there exists an embedding f from the tree $Set(y)$ to the order $\prec$. Then by $T \vdash \mathrm{TI}[\prec, U]$ we obtain $T \vdash \forall y(Emb(y) \rightarrow y \in W)$.

Let $Emb^{nf}(y)$ be a Σ^1_1-normal form such that $T \vdash \forall y(Emb^{nf}(y) \rightarrow Emb(y))$ and $\mathbb{N} \models \forall y(Emb^{nf}(y) \leftrightarrow Emb(y))$. By Theorem 1.3, i.e., Π^1_1-completeness of W, pick a number n such that $T \vdash Emb^{nf}(\bar{n}) \leftrightarrow \bar{n} \notin W$ for the nth numeral $\bar{n}$.

Then $T \vdash \neg Emb^{nf}(\bar{n})$ and $T \vdash \bar{n} \in W$. Since T is assumed to be Π^1_1-sound, we obtain $\neg Emb^{nf}(\bar{n})$, $\neg Emb(\bar{n})$ and $\bar{n} \in W$. Therefore $| \prec | < | <_n | \leq |T|$, where $<_n$ denotes the recursive strict partial order defined by $t <_n s :\Leftrightarrow (s, t \in Set(n) \wedge s \subsetneq_e t)$.

Theorem 1.6.2. Assume $T \vdash A \rightarrow \mathrm{TI}[\prec, U]$ for a recursive strict partial order $\prec$ and a true Σ^1_1-sentence A.

Define a Σ^1_1-order $\prec_A$ by $n \prec_A m :\Leftrightarrow (n \prec m \wedge A)$. Then we obtain $T \vdash \mathrm{TI}\,[\prec_A, U]$. By Theorem 1.6.1, the order type of $\prec$ which is equal to the order type of $\prec_A$, is less than or equal to $|T|$. □

Note that $T \vdash \mathrm{TI}[\prec, U]$ means that the transfinite induction along the order $\prec$ is *uniformly* provable in T. If the proofs of $\mathrm{TI}[\prec, A]$ may depend on formulas A, we

---

[2]The theory $T + Tr_{\Sigma^1_1}$ is not recursive.

see that the order types of $\prec$ reaches ω_1^{CK} in Theorem 1.8 below. Let $\mathrm{TI}[\prec, \Pi_0^{1-}] = \{\mathrm{TI}[\prec, A] : A \in \Pi_0^{1-}\}$ denote the transfinite induction schema along a relation $\prec$ applied to arithmetic formulas $A \in \Pi_0^{1-}$ without set (second-order) parameters.

Theorem 1.7 *There exists a* PA*-provably linear elementary recursive order* $\prec$*, which is not well-founded, but* PA *proves transfinite induction schema along* $\prec$*, applied to arithmetic formulas* $\mathrm{TI}[\prec, \Pi_0^{1-}]$.

Proof We construct an elementary recursive tree such that any infinite path through the tree defines the arithmetic truth. Hence the tree has an infinite path, i.e., non well-founded, but the tree has no arithmetic infinite path by the undefinability of the arithmetic truth by means of any arithmetic formulas.

Let us formulate the first-order arithmetic in the language with function constants for addition and multiplication. Then we see that there exists an elementary recursive predicate Q such that the characteristic function f for arithmetic truth of sentences $A \in \Pi_0^{1-}$ such that $f(\ulcorner A \urcorner) = 0 \leftrightarrow A$, enjoys the Π_2^0-formula $\forall x \exists y\, Q(x, y, f)$, and conversely if $\forall x \exists y\, Q(x, y, f)$ holds, then f is the characteristic function. This is seen as follows. We can assume that each formula is in negation normal form. For literals, $f(\ulcorner t = s \urcorner) = 0 \leftrightarrow t^{\mathbb{N}} = s^{\mathbb{N}}$ and $f(\ulcorner t \neq s \urcorner) = 0 \leftrightarrow t^{\mathbb{N}} \neq s^{\mathbb{N}}$ for closed terms t, s and their values $t^{\mathbb{N}}$ in the standard model, and $f(\ulcorner \exists x\, A(x) \urcorner) = 0 \leftrightarrow \exists y\, f(\ulcorner A(\dot{y}) \urcorner) = 0$, where $\dot{y}$ denotes the Gödel number of the yth numeral. Similarly for universal quantifiers. A conjunction of these conditions for f is a boolean combination of Σ_1^0-formulas, and hence logically equivalent to a Π_2^0-formula Q.

As in the proof of Theorem 1.2, let us associate an elementary recursive tree $\mathcal{T} = \{t \in {}^{<\omega}\omega : \neg S(t)\}$ such that the tree $\mathcal{T}$ is well-founded, i.e, $\forall f \exists x\ S(\bar{f}(x))$ iff $\forall f \neg \forall x \exists y\, Q(x, y, f)$. Let us consider the Kleene–Brouwer order $\prec$ on the tree $\mathcal{T}$. The order $\prec$ is a linear order provably in EA, not well-founded since there is a truth definition of arithmetic formulas, but there is no arithmetically definable infinite descending chain in $\mathcal{T}$. Therefore $\mathrm{TI}[\prec, \Pi_0^{1-}]$ holds otherwise there would exist an arithmetically definable infinite descending chain in the tree $\mathcal{T}$. □

Theorem 1.8 *For theories* $Th \supset \mathsf{ACA}_0$,
$\sup\{|\prec| : Th \vdash \mathrm{TI}[\prec, \Pi_0^{1-}]$ *for some recursive well order* $\prec\} = \omega_1^{CK}$.

Proof Let $\prec$ be a recursive and non well-founded linear order given in Theorem 1.7 such that PA proves transfinite induction schema $\mathrm{TI}[\prec, \Pi_0^{1-}]$. Let T be the tree consisting of the descending chain $(t_1, \ldots, t_n)$ $(n \geq 0)$, $t_n \prec \cdots \prec t_1$, and $<_{KB}^T$ the Kleene–Brouwer order on T. Then for $Th \supset \mathsf{ACA}_0$, we see $Th \vdash \mathrm{TI}[<_{KB}^T, \Pi_0^{1-}]$ from the proof of Proposition 1.10. Let $\alpha < \omega_1^{CK}$, and $S \subset {}^{<\omega}\omega$ be a recursive well-founded tree such that $|S| \geq \alpha$. By Proposition 1.7 we obtain $|T \otimes S| \geq |S| \geq \alpha$.

Let $<_{KB}$ be a lexicographic order on $T \otimes S$ defined as follows. $\tau_1 \otimes \sigma_1 <_{KB} \tau_2 \otimes \sigma_2$ iff either $\tau_1 <_{KB}^T \tau_2$ or $\tau_1 = \tau_2 \,\&\, \exists n < lh(\sigma_1) \forall i < n(\sigma_1(i) = \sigma_2(i) \wedge \sigma_1(n) < \sigma_2(n))$. Then $\tau_2 \subsetneq_e \tau_1 \,\&\, \sigma_2 \subsetneq_e \sigma_1 \Rightarrow \tau_1 \otimes \sigma_1 <_{KB} \tau_2 \otimes \sigma_2$, and $Th \vdash \mathrm{TI}[<_{KB}, \Pi_0^{1-}]$ for the recursive well order $<_{KB}$ of type $|<_{KB}| \geq |T \otimes S| \geq |S| \geq \alpha$. □

In the definition (1.8) of the proof-theoretic ordinal of T, $\alpha \leq |T|$ iff there exists *some* recursive strict partial order $\prec$ of type α for which T proves $\mathrm{TI}[\prec, U]$. If we requires that T should prove $\mathrm{TI}[\prec, U]$ for *arbitrary* such order $\prec$ of type α, then the supremum of ordinals α becomes much smaller, independent from theories T. Next consider the least ordinal α such that the consistency of T follows from a transfinite induction along an order $\prec$ of type α. Again such ordinals collapse to small ordinals. Therefore theories are not ranked in order of these ordinals unless we restrict our attentions to a single specific well order. As far as the notion of 'natural well orders' remains vague, we cannot obey the restriction.

Theorem 1.9 *Let* $T \supset \mathsf{EA}$ *be a* consistent *and elementary recursive theory, cf. Craig's trick, Proposition 1.6. Let* $\mathrm{CON}(T)$ *denote the consistency statement of the theory* T.

1. *The supremum of recursive ordinals* α *for which* T *proves* $\mathrm{TI}[\prec, U]$ *for* arbitrary *recursive well-founded strict partial order* $\prec$ *of type* α *is equal to* 0*: There exists an elementary recursive well-founded strict partial order* $\prec$ *of type* 1 *such that* $\mathsf{EA} \vdash \mathrm{TI}[\prec, A] \to \mathrm{CON}(T)$ *for some elementary recursive predicate* A.
2. *The infimum of recursive ordinals* α *for which there exists a recursive well order* $\prec$ *of type* α *such that* $\mathsf{EA} \vdash \mathrm{TI}[\prec, A] \to \mathrm{CON}(T)$ *for some elementary recursive predicate* A *is less than or equal to* ω*: There exists an elementary recursive well order* $\prec$ *of type* ω *such that* $\mathsf{EA} \vdash \mathrm{TI}[\prec, A] \to \mathrm{CON}(T)$ *for some elementary recursive predicate* A.

Proof Theorem 1.9.1. Let Prov denote an elementary recursive (canonical!) proof predicate for T: $\mathrm{Prov}(x, y)$ means x is (the Gödel number of) a proof of a formula y in T. Let $\mathrm{CON}(T, n) :\Leftrightarrow \forall x \leq n \neg \mathrm{Prov}(x, \ulcorner 0 = 1 \urcorner)$ denoting a partial consistency of T up to n. Now let $n \prec m$ us define as follows. If $\mathrm{CON}(T, \ell)$ for $\ell = \min\{n, m\}$, then $n \prec m$ does not hold. Otherwise let $n \prec m :\Leftrightarrow n > m$. Argue in $T \supset \mathsf{EA}$.

1. The case $\mathrm{CON}(T)$: Then $\{(n, m) : n \prec m\} = \emptyset$, and hence $|\prec| = 1$ since T is assumed to be consistent.
2. The case $\neg\mathrm{CON}(T)$: Let $n_0 := \min\{x : \mathrm{Prov}(x, \ulcorner 0 = 1 \urcorner)\}$. Then

   a. $\min\{n, m\} < n_0 \to n \not\prec m$, and
   b. $\min\{n, m\} \geq n_0 \to [n \prec m \leftrightarrow n > m]$.

Also let $A(n) :\Leftrightarrow \mathrm{CON}(T, n)$. Then we see $\neg\mathrm{CON}(T) \to [Prg[\prec, A] \land \exists n \neg A(n)]$. Hence by Gödel's second incompleteness theorem we obtain $T \nvdash Prg[\prec, A] \to \forall n A(n)$. Here is a proof of $\neg\mathrm{CON}(T) \to Prg[\prec, A]$. Assume $\neg\mathrm{CON}(T)$ and let n_0 denote the number defined as above. Then $A(n) \leftrightarrow n < n_0$. For $m > n \geq n_0$ we have $\neg A(n) \land \neg A(m) \land m \prec n$.

Theorem 1.9.2 is seen similarly for Theorem 1.9.1. Modify the definition of $\prec$ as follows. $n \prec m :\Leftrightarrow n < m$ if $\mathrm{CON}(T, \ell)$ for $\ell = \min\{n, m\}$. □

Remark 1.2 In the definition (1.8) of the proof-theoretic ordinal of theories T, the relations concerned are restricted to computable and strict partial orders, i.e., irreflexive and *transitive* relations. If we drop the transitivity in the definition, the ordinal

$$|T|' := \sup\{|\prec| : T \vdash \mathrm{TI}[\prec, U] \text{ for some recursive irreflexive relation } \prec\}$$

grows by one exponential. For example, $|I\Sigma_n| = 2_n(\omega^2)$ for the fragment $I\Sigma_n$ of PA, while $|I\Sigma_n|' = 2_{n+1}(\omega^2)$ for each $n \geq 0$, cf. Exercises 4.4 and 4.5 in Chap. 4.

Definition 1.12 The *natural sum* $\alpha\#\beta$ and the *natural product* $\alpha \times \beta$ of ordinals α and β are defined as follows. $0\#\alpha = \alpha\#0 = \alpha$ and $0 \times \alpha = \alpha \times 0 = 0$.

Let $\beta = \omega^{\beta_0} + \cdots + \omega^{\beta_n}$ with $\beta_0 \geq \cdots \geq \beta_n$, and $i = \min(\{i \leq n : \alpha > \beta_i\} \cup \{n+1\})$. Then $\omega^\alpha\#\beta = \beta\#\omega^\alpha = \omega^{\gamma_0} + \cdots + \omega^{\gamma_{n+1}}$ where $\gamma_i = \alpha, \gamma_j = \beta_j$ for $j < i$ and $\gamma_j = \beta_{j-1}$ for $j > i$. Also $\omega^\alpha \times \beta = \beta \times \omega^\alpha = \omega^{\alpha\#\beta_0} + \cdots + \omega^{\alpha\#\beta_n}$.

$\alpha\#\beta = \beta\#\alpha = \big((\alpha\#\omega^{\beta_0})\#\cdots\big)\#\omega^{\beta_n}$ and $\alpha \times \beta = \beta \times \alpha = (\alpha \times \omega^{\beta_0})\#\cdots\#(\alpha \times \omega^{\beta_n})$.

1.5 Kripke–Platek Set Theory

In this section Kripke–Platek set theory KP, a fragment of Zermelo–Fraenkel set theory ZF, is introduced, and some rudimentary facts on it are shown. These results are needed only in Chap. 6. Let $\mathcal{L}_{set} = \{\in, =\}$ be the set-theoretic language. In this section we deal only with set-theoretic models $\langle X; \in\restriction(X \times X)\rangle$, and the model is identified with the sets X.

Definition 1.13 ($\Delta_0, \Sigma_1, \Pi_2, \Sigma$)

1. A set-theoretic formula is said to be a Δ_0-*formula* if every quantifier occurring in it is *bounded* by a set. *Bounded quantifiers* is of the form $\forall x \in u, \exists x \in u$.
2. A formula of the form $\exists x\, A$ with a Δ_0-matrix A is a Σ_1-*formula*.
   Its dual $\forall x\, A$ is a Π_1-*formula*.
3. The set of Σ-formulas [Π-formulas] is the smallest class including Δ_0-formulas, closed under positive operations $\wedge, \vee$, bounded quantifications $\forall x \in u, \exists x \in u$, and existential (unbounded) quantification $\exists x$ [universal (unbounded) quantification $\forall x$], resp.
   For example $\forall x \in u \exists y\, A$ ($A \in \Delta_0$) is a Σ-formula but not a Σ_1-formula.
4. A formula of the form $\forall x\, A$ with a Σ_1-matrix A is a Π_2-*formula*.

We see easily that Δ_0-formulas are *absolute* in the sense that for any transitive sets $X \subset Y$ (X is transitive iff $\forall y \in X \forall x \in y (x \in X)$), $X \models A[\vec{x}] \Leftrightarrow Y \models A[\vec{x}]$ for any Δ_0-formula A and $\vec{x} = x_1, \ldots, x_n$ with $x_i \in X$.

Definition 1.14 Axioms of KP are **Extensionality** $\forall a, b[\forall x \in a(x \in b) \wedge \forall x \in b(x \in a) \to a = b]$, **Null set**(the empty set $\emptyset$ exists), **Pair** $\forall x, y \exists a(x \in a \wedge y \in a)$, **Union** $\forall a \exists b \forall x \in a \forall y \in x(y \in b)$, and the following three schemata.

Δ_0-**Separation** For any set a and any Δ_0-*formula* A, the set $b = \{x \in a : A(x)\}$ exists. Namely $\exists b \forall x[x \in b \leftrightarrow x \in a \land A(x)]$.
Δ_0-**Collection** $\forall x \in a \exists y\, A(x, y) \to \exists b \forall x \in a \exists y \in b\, A(x, y)$ for Δ_0-*formulas* A.
Foundation or $\in$-**Induction** $\forall x[\forall y \in x F(y) \to F(x)] \to \forall x F(x)$
for *arbitrary formula* F.

For classes Φ of formulas, fragments KP_Φ is obtained from KP by restricting **Foundation** schema to formulas $F \in \Phi$. Another fragment $\mathsf{KP}^- = \mathsf{KP}_\emptyset$ is obtained from KP by dropping **Foundation** schema.

1.5.1 Σ-Reflection and Its Consequences

We see that the fragment KP_{Σ_1} is strong enough in the sense that some elementary constructions such as recursions can be carried in KP_{Σ_1}. Here is a list of examples of Δ_0-*predicates*:

$x \subset y$, $a = \langle x, y\rangle (= \{\{x\}, \{x, y\}\})$, $Tran(a)(\leftrightarrow a$ is transitive),

$ON(x)(x$ is an ordinal)$\leftrightarrow Tran(x) \land \forall y \in x\, Tran(y)$, $Lim(x)(\leftrightarrow x$ is a limit ordinal)$\leftrightarrow ON(x) \land x \neq 0 \land \forall y \in x \exists z \in x(z = y \cup \{y\})$,

$x \in \omega(\leftrightarrow x$ is a natural number)$\leftrightarrow ON(x) \land \forall y \in x \cup \{x\} \neg Lim(y)$,

f is a function, $y = f(x)$, $a = \mathrm{dom}(f)(=$ the domain of $f)$, $a = \mathrm{rng}(f)(=$ the range of $f)$.

Proposition 1.11 $\mathsf{KP}^- \vdash \forall a, b \exists! c[c = a \times b]$.

Proof From $\forall x \in a \forall y \in b \exists z[z = \langle x, y\rangle]$ and Δ_0-**Collection**, we see $\forall x \in a \exists w \forall y \in b \exists z \in w[z = \langle x, y\rangle]$. Once again by Δ_0-**Collection** pick a set d so that $\forall x \in a \exists w \in d \forall y \in b \exists z \in w[z = \langle x, y\rangle]$.

Now for $c_1 = \bigcup d$ we obtain $\forall x \in a \forall y \in b[\langle x, y\rangle \in c_1]$. Δ_0-**Separation** yields $\{z \in c_1 : \exists x \in a \exists y \in b[z = \langle x, y\rangle]\} = a \times b$. □

For a formula B and a variable a not occurring in B, $B^{(a)}$ denotes the result of restricting every unbounded quantifier in B to a.

Lemma 1.6 (Σ-Persistency) *For any Σ-formula B the following are logically valid:*

1. $B^{(u)} \land u \subset v \to B^{(v)}$.
2. $B^{(u)} \to B$.

Proof By induction on the length of the Σ-formulas B. □

Theorem 1.10 (Σ-Reflection) *For any Σ-formula B*

$$\mathsf{KP}^- \vdash B \leftrightarrow \exists a B^{(a)}.$$

Proof By induction on the length of the Σ-formulas B.
Case 1 $B \equiv C_1 \wedge C_1$: By IH we have $C_i \leftrightarrow \exists a_i\, C_i^{(a_i)}$ $(i = 0, 1)$. Assume B, and pick sets a_0, a_1 such that $C_0^{(a_0)} \wedge C_1^{(a_1)}$. Then for $a = a_0 \cup a_1$ we have $C_0^{(a)} \wedge C_1^{(a)}$ by **Σ-Persistency** 1.6. The converse direction is easy.
Case 2 $B \equiv \forall x \in u\, C(x)$: IH yields $C(x) \leftrightarrow \exists y\, C^{(y)}(x)$. Assume B, i.e., $\forall x \in u \exists y\, C^{(y)}(x)$. Pick a set b by **Δ_0-Collection** so that $\forall x \in u \exists y \in b\, C^{(y)}(x)$. Let $a = \cup b$. Then $\forall x \in u\, C^{(a)}(x) \equiv B^{(a)}$ as desired.
Case 3 $B \equiv \exists u\, C(u)$: IH yields $C(u) \leftrightarrow \exists b\, C^{(b)}(u)$. Assume B, and let u denote a set such that $C(u)$. Pick a b so that $C^{(b)}(u)$, and let $a = b \cup \{u\}$. Then $u \in a \,\&\, b \subset a$. Hence $\exists u \in a\, C^{(a)}(u) \equiv B^{(a)}$ by **Σ-Persistency** 1.6. □

Corollary 1.3 (Σ-Collection) *For any Σ-formula B*

$$\mathsf{KP}^- \vdash \forall x \in a \exists y\, B(x, y) \to \exists b[\forall x \in a \exists y \in b\, B(x, y) \wedge \forall y \in b \exists x \in a\, B(x, y)].$$

Proof By **Σ-Reflection** 1.10, $\mathsf{KP}^- \vdash \forall x \in a \exists y\, B(x, y) \to \exists c \forall x \in a \exists y \in c\, B^{(c)}(x, y)$. $b = \{y \in c : \exists x \in a\, B^{(c)}(x, y)\}$ is a desired one. □

Corollary 1.4 (Σ-Reduction *and* Δ-Separation) *For any $A \in \Pi$ and $B \in \Sigma$*

$$\mathsf{KP}^- \vdash \{x \in c : A(x)\} \subset \{x \in c : B(x)\} \to \exists a[\{x \in c : A(x)\} \subset a \subset \{x \in c : B(x)\}].$$

In particular

$$\mathsf{KP}^- \vdash \{x \in c : A(x)\} = \{x \in c : B(x)\} \to \exists a[a = \{x \in c : A(x)\}].$$

Proof Assume $\forall x \in c[A(x) \to B(x)]$. By **$\Sigma$-Reflection** 1.10, pick a b so that $\forall x \in c[A^{(b)}(x) \to B^{(b)}(x)]$. Then $a = \{x \in c : B^{(b)}(x)\}$ is a desired one. □

Corollary 1.5 (Σ-Replacement) *For $B \in \Sigma$*

$$\mathsf{KP}^- \vdash \forall x \in a \exists! y\, B(x, y) \to \exists f[\mathrm{dom}(f) = a \wedge \forall x \in a\, B(x, f(x))].$$

Proof Assume $\forall x \in a \exists! y\, B(x, y)$. By **$\Sigma$-Collection** 1.3 pick a b so that $\forall x \in a \exists! y \in b\, B(x, y)$. Let, by **$\Delta$-Separation** 1.4, $f = \{\langle x, y \rangle \in a \times b : B(x, y)\} = \{\langle x, y \rangle \in a \times b : \neg \exists z (B(x, z) \wedge z \neq y)\}$. □

Definition 1.15 (Σ-function and Δ-predicate) Let T be a set theory. Assume that $B \in \Sigma$ such that $T \vdash \forall \bar{x} \exists! y\, B(\bar{x}, y)$. Then the function F defined by

$$F(\bar{x}) = y :\Leftrightarrow B(\bar{x}, y)$$

is said to be a *Σ-function* in T.

A predicate $P(\bar{x})$ is a *Δ-predicate* in T if there are Σ-formula $A(\bar{x})$ and Π-formula $B(\bar{x})$ such that $T \vdash \forall \bar{x}(A(\bar{x}) \leftrightarrow B(\bar{x}))$ and the formula A defines the predicate P in the whole universe V.

Lemma 1.7 *The transitive closure* $\mathrm{TC}(x)$ *is a* Σ*-function in* KP_{Σ_1}.

Proof Let $P(x, a)$ denote $x \subset a \land Tran(a) \land \forall z \in a \exists n \exists f[n \in \omega \land \mathrm{dom}(f) = n + 1 \land z = f(0) \land f(n) \in x \land \forall m < n\{f(m) \in f(m+1)\}]$. Then $P \in \Sigma$ and $\mathrm{TC}(x) = a \leftrightarrow P(x, a)$. We show $\forall x \exists! a\, P(x, a)$ by $\in$-induction on x. The uniqueness of a is obvious. Assume $\forall y \in x \exists! a_y\, P(y, a_y)$. By **$\Sigma$-Replacement** 1.5 pick an f so that $\forall y \in x\, P(y, f(y))$. Then $a = x \cup \bigcup_{y \in x} f(y)$ is a desired one. □

Theorem 1.11 (Σ-Recursion) *For* Σ*-function* $G(\bar{x}, y, a)$ *in* $T \supset \mathsf{KP}_{\Sigma_1}$ *the function defined by*

$$F(\bar{x}, y) := G(\bar{x}, y, \{\langle z, F(\bar{x}, z)\rangle : z \in \mathrm{TC}(y)\}) \tag{1.9}$$

is again a Σ*-function in* T.

Proof Let $P(\bar{x}, y, a)$ denote

$$\exists f[\mathrm{dom}(f) = \mathrm{TC}(y) \land \forall z \in \mathrm{TC}(y)\{f(z) = G(\bar{x}, z, f \restriction \mathrm{TC}(z))\} \land a = G(\bar{x}, y, f)]].$$

Then $P \in \Sigma$ and $F(\bar{x}, y) = a \leftrightarrow P(\bar{x}, y, a)$. It is easy to see that $\forall y \exists! a\, P(\bar{x}, y, a)$ by induction on y. □

A variant of (1.9)

$$F(\bar{x}, y) := G(\bar{x}, y, \{\langle z, F(\bar{x}, z)\rangle : z \in y\}) \tag{1.10}$$

is seen to be a Σ-function for Σ-functions G by letting $G'(\bar{x}, y, f) = G(\bar{x}, y, f \restriction y)$.

Corollary 1.6 (Δ-Recursion) *Let* $P(\bar{x}, y, a)$ *be a* Δ*-predicate in* $T \supset \mathsf{KP}_{\Sigma_1}$. *Then the predicate defined by*

$$R(\bar{x}, y) :\Leftrightarrow P(\bar{x}, y, \{z \in \mathrm{TC}(y) : R(\bar{x}, z)\})$$

is also a Δ*-predicate in* T.

Proof Let G, F denote the characteristic functions of P, R, resp. Then $F \in \Sigma$ and $R(\bar{x}, y) \leftrightarrow F(\bar{x}, y) = 1 \leftrightarrow F(\bar{x}, y) \neq 0$. Hence $R \in \Delta$. □

The followings are Σ-operations in KP_{Σ_1} defined by recursion:

rank	$rk(x) = \sup\{rk(y) + 1 : y \in x\}$
ordinal addition	$\alpha + \beta = \alpha \cup \sup\{(\alpha + \gamma) + 1 : \gamma < \beta\}$
ordinal multiplication	$\alpha\beta = \sup\{\alpha\gamma + \alpha : \gamma < \beta\}$
Mostowski collapsing	$C_a(x) = \{C_a(y) : y \in x \cap a\}$

A small portion of **Foundation** (or $\in$-**Induction**) schema seems to be indispensable in the following theorem.

Theorem 1.12 (Second Recursion Theorem) *For each Σ-formula $R(X, x, y)$ in which a predicate symbol X occurs only positively, there exists a Σ-formula $F(x, y)$ such that*

$$\mathsf{KP}_{\Sigma_1} \vdash F(x, y) \leftrightarrow R(\{x' : F(x', y)\}, x, y).$$

Proof Let $M_a := \langle a; \in\restriction (a \times a)\rangle$, the set-theoretic structure with the universe a. Obviously the map $a \mapsto M_a$ is Σ. Also let $\ulcorner B \urcorner$ denote the code (Gödel number) of a formula B. Then the satisfaction relation $M_a \models \ulcorner B \urcorner [s]$ (read: M_a satisfies the sentence $B[s]$ for the assignment s of sets in a to (free) variables in B.) is seen to be a Δ-relation of $a, \ulcorner B \urcorner, s$.

Let, for each $n < \omega$,

$$\begin{aligned} &\mathrm{Sat}^n_\Sigma(y, x_1, \ldots, x_n) :\Leftrightarrow y = \ulcorner B(v_1, \ldots, v_n) \urcorner \text{ for a formula } B \wedge \\ &\exists a[a \text{ is transitive } \wedge x_1, \ldots, x_n \in a \wedge M_a \models \ulcorner B(x_1, \ldots, x_n) \urcorner]. \end{aligned}$$

Then Sat^n_Σ is a Σ-predicate for each n.

We see, for each Σ-formula $B(v_1, \ldots, v_n)$

$$B(x_1, \ldots, x_n) \leftrightarrow \mathrm{Sat}^n_\Sigma(\ulcorner B \urcorner, x_1, \ldots, x_n).$$

Now let $S(z, x, y) :\Leftrightarrow R(\{x' : \mathrm{Sat}^3_\Sigma(z, z, x', y)\}, x, y)$, and $F(x, y) :\Leftrightarrow S(\ulcorner S \urcorner, x, y)$. Then S as well as F is Σ and

$$\begin{aligned} F(x, y) &\leftrightarrow S(\ulcorner S \urcorner, x, y) \leftrightarrow R(\{x' : \mathrm{Sat}^3_\Sigma(\ulcorner S \urcorner, \ulcorner S \urcorner, x', y)\}, x, y) \\ &\leftrightarrow R(\{x' : S(\ulcorner S \urcorner, x', y)\}, x, y) \leftrightarrow R(\{x' : F(x', y)\}, x, y). \end{aligned}$$

□

Definition 1.16 A set a is *extensional* iff

$$\forall b_1 \in a \forall b_2 \in a[a \cap b_1 = a \cap b_2 \rightarrow b_1 = b_2].$$

In other words a is extensional iff $\langle a; \in\restriction (a \times a)\rangle \models$ **Extensionality**. Any transitive set is extensional.

For the Mostowski's collapsing function C we have the following lemma.

Lemma 1.8 *The following are provable in* KP_{Σ_1}.

1. *If a is transitive and $a \subset b$, then $\forall x \in a[C_b(x) = x]$.*
2. *For any b $\mathrm{clpse}(b) := C_b(b) = \{C_b(x) : x \in b\}$ is transitive.*
3. *If a is extensional, then the restriction c_a of C_a to a is an isomorphism of $\langle a; \in\restriction (a \times a)\rangle$ onto $\langle \mathrm{clpse}(a); \in\restriction (\mathrm{clpse}(a) \times \mathrm{clpse}(a))\rangle$.*

Proof Lemma 1.8.1 by $\in$-induction. Assume $x \in a$. Since a is transitive, $x \subset a \subset b$. Hence by IH $C_b(x) = \{C_b(y) : y \in x \cap b\} = \{C_b(y) : y \in x\} = \{y : y \in x\} = x$.

Lemma 1.8.2. Let $z \in y \in C_b(b)$. Then $y = C_b(x) = \{C_b(u) : u \in x \cap b\}$ for some $x \in b$. Hence $z = C_b(u)$ for some $u \in b$. Thus $z \in C_b(b)$.

Lemma 1.8.3. We need to show that c_a is one-one, and $c_a(x) \in c_a(y) \to x \in y$. We show simultaneously $c_a(x) = c_a(y) \to x = y$ and $c_a(x) \in c_a(y) \to x \in y$ for any $x, y \in a$ by $\in$-induction (by induction on the natural sum $rk(x)\#rk(y)$). Suppose $x_0, y_0 \in a$.

First assume $c_a(x_0) = c_a(y_0)$. Suppose $x_0 \neq y_0$. Then, since a is extensional, there exists a $z \in a$ such that $z \in (x_0 \cup y_0) - (x_0 \cap y_0)$. Thus $c_a(z) \in c_a(x_0) = c_a(y_0)$. On the other side IH yields $z \in x_0 \cap y_0$. A contradiction.

Second assume $c_a(x_0) \in c_a(y_0)$. Then $c_a(x_0) = c_a(z)$ for some $z \in y_0 \cap a$. IH yields $x_0 = z \in y_0$. □

1.5.2 Constructible Hierarchy and Admissible Sets

Let $\mathcal{F}_i$ $(1 \leq i \leq N)$ be a finite list of Σ-operations which generate the constructible hierarchy $\{L_\alpha : \alpha \in ON\}$.

1. $L_0 := \emptyset$.
2. $L_{\alpha+1} := \mathcal{D}(L_\alpha \cup \{L_\alpha\}) := L_\alpha \cup \{L_\alpha\} \cup \{\mathcal{F}_i(\bar{x}) : \bar{x} \subset L_\alpha \cup \{L_\alpha\}, 1 \leq i \leq N\}$.
3. $L_\lambda := \bigcup_{\alpha<\lambda} L_\alpha$ for limits λ.
4. $L := \bigcup_{\alpha \in ON} L_\alpha$.

Note that $\alpha \mapsto L_\alpha$ is a Σ-operation in $T \supset \mathsf{KP}_{\Sigma_1}$ by Theorem 1.11.

We assume that these operations enjoy the followings demonstrably in KP_{Σ_1}, cf. [1] for such a list $\{\mathcal{F}_i\}_{1 \leq i \leq N}$ of operations.

1. $\mathcal{F}_i(x, y) = \{x, y\}$ and $\mathcal{F}_j(x, y) = \cup x$ for some i and j.
2. For each Δ_0-formula $B(y, \bar{x})$, there exists a term $\mathcal{F}$ built from $\mathcal{F}_i$ $(1 \leq i \leq N)$ so that $\mathcal{F}(a, \bar{x}) = \{y \in a : B(y, \bar{x})\}$.
3. From $\mathcal{F}_i$ $(1 \leq i \leq N)$ and a bijective pairing function on ON we can define a Σ-surjection $F : ON \to L$ such that $F"\alpha = \{F(\gamma) : \gamma < \alpha\} = L_\alpha$ holds for each multiplicative principal number $\alpha = \omega^{\omega^\beta}$.
4. Each L_α is transitive.
5. $\alpha < \beta \Rightarrow L_\alpha \subset L_\beta$.
6. $L_\alpha \in L_{\alpha+1}$.
7. $o(L_{\omega\alpha}) := L_{\omega\alpha} \cap ON = \omega\alpha$ for any ordinal $\alpha \in ON$.

Note that $L_{\omega\alpha} \models \mathsf{KP} - (\Delta_0-\textbf{Collection})$ for $\alpha > 0$, and $\omega \in L_{\omega\alpha}$ if $\alpha > 1$.

Definition 1.17 1. A transitive set A is *admissible* if $(A; \in) \models \mathsf{KP}$.
2. An ordinal α is *admissible* if L_α is admissible.
3. A relation R on an admissible set A is *A-recursive* [*A-recursively enumerable*, *A-r.e.*] (*A-finite*) if R is Δ_1 $[\Sigma_1]$ $(R \in A)$, resp.
4. A function on an admissible set A is *A-recursive* if its graph is A-r.e.

5. $\mathsf{KP}\omega$ [$\mathsf{KP}\omega_{\Sigma_1}$] denotes KP [KP_{Σ_1}] *plus* Axiom of **Infinity** $\exists x \neq \emptyset \forall y \in x[y \cup \{y\} \in x]$, resp.
6. An ordinal α is *recursively regular* iff $L_\alpha \models \mathsf{KP}\omega$.

Observe that an ordinal α is recursively regular iff α is a multiplicative principal number$> \omega$, and for any L_α-recursive function $f : \beta \to \alpha$ with a $\beta < \alpha$, $\sup\{f(\gamma) : \gamma < \beta\} < \alpha$ holds.

Proposition 1.12 *Let $\Gamma[X, n]$ be an arithmetical formula in which the predicate X occurs only positively. The least fixed point $I_\Gamma = \bigcup_\alpha I_\Gamma^\alpha$ of a positive elementary (arithmetical) Γ is Σ-definable in $\mathsf{KP}\omega_{\Sigma_1}$, i.e., the stages $n \in I_\Gamma^\alpha$ $(\alpha < \lambda)$ is a Δ-predicate in $\mathsf{KP}\omega_{\Sigma_1}$.*

Proof Since ω exists as a set in $\mathsf{KP}\omega_{\Sigma_1}$, the predicate $P(n, x) :\equiv (\Gamma[x, n] \wedge n \in \omega \wedge x \subset \omega)$ is a Δ_0-predicate with bounded quantifiers $\exists m \in \omega, \forall m \in \omega$. By **$\Delta$-Recursion** 1.6, the stages $n \in I_\Gamma^\alpha$ is a Δ-predicate in $\mathsf{KP}\omega_{\Sigma_1}$. □

Theorem 1.13 (Π_2-Reflection on L) *For any Σ-predicate A*

$$\mathsf{KP}\omega_{\Sigma_1} \vdash \forall x \in L \exists y \in L\, A(x, y) \to \exists z \in L \forall x \in z \exists y \in z\, A(x, y).$$

In particular for recursively regular ordinals Ω,

$$\forall \alpha < \Omega \exists \beta < \Omega\, A(\alpha, \beta) \to \exists \gamma < \Omega \forall \alpha < \gamma \exists \beta < \gamma\, A(\alpha, \beta).$$

Proof Assume $\forall x \in L \exists y \in L\, A(x, y)$. Then $\forall \alpha \forall x \in L_\alpha \exists \beta \exists y \in L_\beta A(x, y)$. Define an increasing series $\{\alpha_n\}_{n \in \omega}$ of ordinals by starting with an arbitrary $\alpha_0 > 0$ and $\alpha_{n+1} = \min\{\beta > \alpha_n : \forall x \in L_{\alpha_n} \exists y \in L_\beta A(x, y)\}$. Then the series $\{\alpha_n\}$ is a Σ-function. Let $\lambda = \sup\{\alpha_n : n \in \omega\}$. Then $\forall x \in z \exists y \in z A(x, y)$ for $z = L_\lambda \in L$. □

1.6 Notes

Sequent calculi were introduced in Gentzen's dissertation [3]. One-sided calculus for the classical logic is sometimes called Tait calculus for the contribution in [13]. However a variant of it was already appeared in Schütte [11]. More comprehensive accounts on proof theory are found in [14] by Troelstra and Schwichtenberg.

Grzegorczyk functions $\{F_n\}_n$ and Lemma 1.4 are in [5]. Kreisel–Lévy Essential unboundedness theorem 1.1 is proved in [10]. Proposition 1.8 is Lemma IV.4.4 in Simpson's monograph [12], which is the main source for the second-order arithmetic, SOA. Theorem 1.5 with Proposition 1.7 is took from Girard [4].

Theorem 1.6 is due to Kreisel [8], which seems to be inspired from Spector's boundedness theorem. Theorem 1.7 is took from Kreisel [7], and Theorem 1.8 from Beckmann [2]. Theorem 1.9 is found in [9], but it has already given in a course note given by Kreisel dated 1968.

For more on Kripke–Platek set theory sketched in Sect. 1.5, see the book [1] by Barwise.

References

1. Barwise, J.: Admissible Sets and Structures. Springer, Berlin (1975)
2. Beckmann, A.: A non-well-founded primitive recursive tree provably well-founded for co-r.e. sets. Arch. Math. Log. **41**, 251–257 (2002)
3. Gentzen, G.: Untersuchungen über das logische Schließen. Math. Z. **39**, I, 176–210: II, 405–431 (1934/35)
4. Girard, J.-Y.: Proof Theory and Logical Complexity, vol. 1. Bibliopolis, Napoli (1987)
5. Grzegorczyk, A.: Some Classes of Recursive Functions. Rozprawy Mate, No. IV. Warsaw (1953)
6. Hájek, P., Pudlák, P.: Metamathematics of First-order Arithmetic. Perspectives in Mathematical Logic. Springer, Berlin (1993)
7. Kreisel, G.: A variant to Hilbert's theory of foundations of arithmetic. Br. J. Philos. Sci. **4**, 107–127 (1953)
8. Kreisel, G.: The status of the first ε-number in first order arithmetic. J. Symb. Log. **25**, 390 (abstract) (1960)
9. Kreisel, G.: Wie die Beweistheoire zu ihren Ordinalzahlen kam und kommt. Jahresbereicht Dtsch. Math.-Ver. **78**, 177–223 (1977)
10. Kreisel, G., Lévy, A.: Reflection principles and their use for establishing the complexity of axiomatic systems. Z. Math. Log. Grundlagen Math. **14**, 97–142 (1968)
11. Schütte, K.: Schlussweisen-Kalküle der Prädikatenlogik. Math. Ann. **122**, 47–65 (1950)
12. Simpson, S.G.: Subsystems of Second Order Arithmetic. Perspectives in Logic, 2nd edn. Cambridge UP, Cambridge (2009)
13. Tait, W. W.: Normal derivability in classical logic. In: Barwise. J. (ed.) Syntax and Semantics of Infinitary Languages. Lecture Notes in Mathematics, vol. 72, pp. 204–236 (1968)
14. Troelstra, A. S., Schwichtenberg, H.: Basic Proof Theory, 2nd edn. Cambridge Tracts in Theoretical Computer Science, vol. 43. Cambridge UP, Cambridge (2000)

Chapter 2
Calculi for Classical Logic

The sequent calculus $\boldsymbol{G}_1$ for the *classical* first-order logic in Sect. 1.2 is best seen as a refutation procedure. Inference rules are regarded as searching step of a counter-model of the endsequent when we turn inferences upside down. In Sect. 2.1 we follow the idea to prove the completeness of the cut-free fragment $\boldsymbol{G}_1$ by a canonical proof search. This together with Soundness 1.1 yields the cut-elimination theorem (Hauptsatz, normal form theorem). Furthermore the same method is employed to applied calculi, predicative second order logic and the ω-logic.

In Sect. 2.2 we show some consequences of cut-elimination theorem for the first-order calculus $\boldsymbol{G}_1$ such as the midsequent theorem, Herbrand's theorem and Π_2-analyses, by which a witness of a purely existential formula is extracted from cut-free proofs of the formula.

2.1 Completeness of Cut-Free Fragments

2.1.1 Canonical Proof Search

We show the following theorem for completeness of the cut-free fragment $\boldsymbol{G}_1$.

Theorem 2.1 (Completeness of the cut-free fragment) *If* $\bigvee \Lambda$ *is valid, then* $\boldsymbol{G}_1 \vdash \Lambda$.

From this together with Proposition 1.1 (Soundness) we see that the cut-elimination theorem holds.

Corollary 2.1 (Cut-elimination)

$$\boldsymbol{G}_1 + (cut) \vdash \Lambda \Rightarrow \boldsymbol{G}_1 \vdash \Lambda .$$

© The Editor(s) (if applicable) and The Author(s), under exclusive license to Springer Nature Singapore Pte Ltd. 2020

T. Arai, *Ordinal Analysis with an Introduction to Proof Theory*, Logic in Asia: Studia Logica Library, https://doi.org/10.1007/978-981-15-6459-8_2

Assume that $G_1 \nvdash \Lambda$. By a canonical proof search, we find a 'model' M which refutes Λ.

Let us describe the search method. Let $\{t_n : n \in \omega\}$ denote an enumeration of all terms, and $\{a_n : n \in \omega\}$ an enumeration of free variables.

Starting with the given sequent Λ at the bottom node, we construct a binary tree $\mathcal{T} \subset {}^{<\omega}2$ recursively. Each node $\sigma \in \mathcal{T}$ has three data as labels: two sequents $Seq_i(\sigma)$ $(i = 0, 1)$, a linear ordering $ON(\sigma)$ on $Seq_0(\sigma)$ and a finite set $Term(\sigma; \exists x B(x))$ of terms for each existential formula $\exists x B(x)$. $Seq_0(\sigma)$ consists solely in non-literal formulas. Set $Seq(\sigma) := Seq_0(\sigma) \cup Seq_1(\sigma)$, which is denoted also by $Seq_0(\sigma); Seq_1(\sigma)$. Let $Term(\sigma)$ denote the function which maps $\exists x B(x)$ to $Term(\sigma; \exists x B(x))$.

At the stage σ, $Seq_0(\sigma)$ denotes the set of unanalyzed formulas, while $Seq_1(\sigma)$ the set of analyzed formulas. The terms t in the set $Term(\sigma; \exists x B(x))$ has been already substituted for x in $B(x)$.

For a sequent Γ, let $\Gamma = NL(\Gamma) \cup L(\Gamma)$ with the set $L(\Gamma)$ of literals in Γ and $NL(\Gamma) = \Gamma \setminus L(\Gamma)$.

For the bottom node $\emptyset$, set $Seq_0(\emptyset) = NL(\Lambda)$, $Seq_1(\emptyset) = L(\Lambda)$, $Term(\emptyset; \exists x B(x)) = \emptyset$. Fix an ordering $ON(\emptyset)$ on $NL(\Lambda)$ arbitrarily.

Suppose that the tree $\mathcal{T}$ has been constructed up to a node σ. Let $\Gamma_i = Seq_i(\sigma)$. If $Seq(\sigma)$ is an axiom in G_1 (**Leaf condition**), then σ is a leaf in $\mathcal{T}$. If $Seq(\sigma)$ is not an axiom and $\Gamma_0 = \emptyset$, then $\sigma * (0) \in \mathcal{T}$, $Term(\sigma * (0)) = Term(\sigma)$ and $Seq_i(\sigma * (0)) = Seq_i(\sigma)$ for $i = 0, 1$. We say that (Rep) (repetition) is applied.

$$\frac{\emptyset; \Gamma_1}{\emptyset; \Gamma_1}\ (Rep)$$

Otherwise pick the first non-literal formula $B \in \Gamma_0$ in the ordering $ON(\sigma)$. The next level is defined according to the outermost connective of B:

($\vee$) $B \equiv A_0 \vee A_1$: Then $\sigma * (0) \in \mathcal{T}$, $Term(\sigma * (0)) = Term(\sigma)$. Let $\Delta_i = Seq_i(\sigma * (0))$. Then $\Delta_0 = (\Gamma_0 \cup NL(A_0, A_1)) \setminus \{A_0 \vee A_1\}$ and $\Delta_1 = \Gamma_1 \cup L(A_0, A_1) \cup \{A_0 \vee A_1\}$. $ON(\sigma * (0))$ on Δ_0 is the ordering induced by $ON(\sigma)$ with the elements in $NL(A_0, A_1)$ as last ones.

($\wedge$) $B \equiv A_0 \wedge A_1$: Then $\sigma * (n) \in \mathcal{T}$ $(n = 0, 1)$, $Term(\sigma * (n)) = Term(\sigma)$. Let $\Delta_{ni} = Seq_i(\sigma * (n))$. Then $\Delta_{n0} = (\Gamma_0 \cup NL(A_n)) \setminus \{A_0 \wedge A_1\}$ and $\Delta_{n1} = \Gamma_1 \cup L(A_n) \cup \{A_0 \wedge A_1\}$. $ON(\sigma * (n))$ on Δ_{n0} is the ordering induced by $ON(\sigma)$ with the element in $NL(A_n)$ as last one.

Let us depict the cases $L(A_0, A_1) = \emptyset$. In the following figures, sequents in $Seq(\sigma)$ are arranged in such a way that formulas in $Seq_0(\sigma)$ first according to the ordering $ON(\sigma)$ (larger formula is to the right of smaller formula) and formulas in $Seq_1(\sigma)$ next:

$$\frac{\Psi, A_0, A_1; \Gamma_1, A_0 \vee A_1}{A_0 \vee A_1, \Psi; \Gamma_1} \quad \frac{\Psi, A_0; \Gamma_1, A_0 \wedge A_1 \quad \Psi, A_1; \Gamma_1, A_0 \wedge A_1}{A_0 \wedge A_1, \Psi; \Gamma_1}$$

($\exists$) $B \equiv \exists x A(x)$: Then $\sigma * (0) \in \mathcal{T}$. Let t be the first term in the enumeration $\{t_n\}$ not in $Term(\sigma; B)$. $Term(\sigma * (0); B) = Term(\sigma; B) \cup \{t\}$, and $Term(\sigma * (0); C) = Term(\sigma; C)$ for $C \not\equiv B$. Let $\Delta_i = Seq_i(\sigma * (0))$. Then $\Delta_0 = \Gamma_0 \cup NL(A(t))$ and $\Delta_1 = \Gamma_1 \cup L(A(t))$. Let $\exists x A(x), \Psi = \Gamma_0$ in the ordering $ON(\sigma)$. Then $\Delta_0 = \Psi, NL(A(t)), \exists x A(x)$ in the ordering $ON(\sigma * (0))$.

($\forall$) $B \equiv \forall x A(x)$: Then $\sigma * (0) \in \mathcal{T}$, $Term(\sigma * (0)) = Term(\sigma)$. Let $\Delta_i = Seq_i(\sigma * (0))$, and a be the first variable in the enumeration $\{a_n\}$ not occurring in $\Gamma_0 \cup \Gamma_1$. Then $\Delta_0 = (\Gamma_0 \cup NL(A(a))) \setminus \{\forall x A(x)\}$ and $\Delta_1 = \Gamma_1 \cup L(A(a)) \cup \{\forall x A(x)\}$. $ON(\sigma * (0))$ on Δ_0 is the ordering induced by $ON(\sigma)$ with the element in $NL(A(a))$ as last one.
Let us depict the cases $L(A(t)) = L(A(a)) = \emptyset$:

$$\frac{\Psi, A(t), \exists x A(x); \Gamma_1}{\exists x A(x), \Psi; \Gamma_1} \quad \frac{\Psi, A(a); \Gamma_1, \forall x A(x)}{\forall x A(x), \Psi; \Gamma_1}$$

This ends the description of the tree $\mathcal{T}$. We see easily the following properties on $\mathcal{T}$:

$$\mathcal{T} \text{ is computable.} \tag{2.1}$$

$$\sigma \subset \tau \in \mathcal{T} \Rightarrow Seq(\sigma) \subset Seq(\tau) \tag{2.2}$$

$$\frac{\{Seq(\sigma * (i)) : \sigma * (i) \in \mathcal{T}\}}{Seq(\sigma)} \text{ is an admissible rule in } \mathbf{G}_1 \tag{2.3}$$

Claim 2.1 *There exists an infinite path $\mathcal{P}$ through $\mathcal{T}$ if $\mathbf{G}_1 \nvdash \Lambda$.*

Proof By $\mathbf{G}_1 \nvdash \Lambda$ the tree is infinite. Thus there is an infinite path through $\mathcal{T}$ by weak König's lemma in Definition 1.7. □

Pick an infinite path $\mathcal{P}$ through $\mathcal{T}$. Let

$$Seq^+(\mathcal{P}) := \bigcup \{Seq(\sigma) : \sigma \in \mathcal{P}\}$$

Then

$$A_0 \vee A_1 \in Seq^+(\mathcal{P}) \Rightarrow \{A_0, A_1\} \subset Seq^+(\mathcal{P}) \tag{2.4}$$

$$A_0 \wedge A_1 \in Seq^+(\mathcal{P}) \Rightarrow \{A_0, A_1\} \cap Seq^+(\mathcal{P}) \neq \emptyset \tag{2.5}$$

$$\exists x A(x) \in Seq^+(\mathcal{P}) \Rightarrow \{A(t_n) : n \in \omega\} \subset Seq^+(\mathcal{P}) \tag{2.6}$$

$$\forall x A(x) \in Seq^{+}(\mathscr{P}) \Rightarrow \{A(a_n) : n \in \omega\} \cap Seq^{+}(\mathscr{P}) \neq \emptyset \tag{2.7}$$

No $Seq(\sigma)$ $(\sigma \in \mathscr{T})$ is an axiom. In other words

$$\{\bar{L}, L\} \not\subset Seq^{+}(\mathscr{P}) \text{ for any literal } L \tag{2.8}$$

Let

$$Seq^{-}(\mathscr{P}) := \{\neg A : A \in Seq^{+}(\mathscr{P})\} \text{ and } Seq(\mathscr{P}) := Seq^{+}(\mathscr{P}) \cup Seq^{-}(\mathscr{P})$$

Now we define a truth valuation $M(A) \in \{\bot, \top\}$ for $A \in Seq(\mathscr{P})$ as follows:

$$M(A) := \begin{cases} \bot \text{ if } A \in Seq^{+}(\mathscr{P}) \\ \top \text{ otherwise} \end{cases} \tag{2.9}$$

Observe that M is computable in $\mathscr{P}$.

Claim 2.2 *1. $M(A) \neq M(\neg A)$ for $A \in Seq(\mathscr{P})$.*
2. M enjoys the Tarski's conditions, e.g., $M(\exists x B(x)) = \top$ iff there exists a term t such that $M(B(t)) = \top$.

Proof These are proved simultaneously by induction on $\mathrm{dg}(A)$ for $A \in Seq(\mathscr{P})$. By the definition we have $M(A) = \top \Rightarrow M(\neg A) = \bot$. Thus it suffices to refute $M(A) = M(\neg A) = \bot$ for Claim 2.2.1.

First for a literal $L \equiv A$ we have $\{\bar{L}, L\} \not\subset Seq^{+}(\mathscr{P})$ by (2.8). Hence $M(L) \neq M(\bar{L})$ and $M(L) = \bot \Leftrightarrow M(\bar{L}) = \top$.

Next consider the case $A \equiv A_0 \vee A_1$. If $M(A) = M(\neg A) = \bot$, then we would have $M(A_i) = M(\neg A_i) = \bot$ for an $i = 0, 1$ by (2.4) and (2.5). This contradicts IH(=Induction Hypothesis). From this and (2.4), (2.5) we see $M(A) = \bot[\top] \Leftrightarrow M(A_0) = M(A_1) = \bot\,[M(A_0) = \top \text{ or } M(A_1) = \top]$, resp.

Finally consider the case $A \equiv \exists x B(x)$. If $M(A) = M(\neg A) = \bot$, then we would have $M(B(t)) = \bot$ for a term t by (2.6) and (2.7). This contradicts IH. From this and (2.6), (2.7), we see $M(A) = \bot \Leftrightarrow M(B(t)) = \bot$ for any t, and $M(A) = \top \Leftrightarrow M(B(t)) = \top$ for some t.

This completes a proof of Claim. □

Now the proof of Theorem 2.1 is completed as follows. By the definition we have $M(A) = \bot$ for any $A \in \Lambda = Seq(\emptyset) \subset Seq^{+}(\mathscr{P})$. On the other we see from Claim 2.2 that M determines a model with the universe $\{t_n : n \in \omega\}$.

Remark 2.1 We could define alternatively the counter model M for Λ by setting $M \models L :\Leftrightarrow L \notin Seq^{+}(\mathscr{P})$ for literals L, and expand the satisfaction relation $M \models A$ by recursion on $\mathrm{dg}(A)$. However, then, the relation $M \models A$ is not computable in $\mathscr{P}$ since we need ω-times jump operators.

2.1.2 Applied Calculi

In this subsection we consider applied logic calculi obtained from $G_1 + (cut)$ by adding some axioms and inference rules. Although (cut) inferences are not eliminable completely from such a proof, they are eliminable partially.

Let T be a *theory*, i.e., a set of closed formulas. The easiest way for any formula A in T to be provable is to add new axioms Γ, A. This is equivalent to add a new inference rule

$$\frac{\neg A, \Gamma}{\Gamma}\ (A)$$

When A is a formula $\forall \mathbf{y}[\bigwedge_i \forall \mathbf{x}_i \bigvee \Phi_i(\mathbf{x}_i; \mathbf{y}) \to \bigvee \Phi(\mathbf{y})]$, assuming A is equivalent to add the inference rule

$$\frac{\{\Phi_i(\mathbf{a}_i; \mathbf{t}), \Gamma\}_i}{\Phi(\mathbf{t}), \Gamma}$$

where $\mathbf{t}$ is a list of terms, and $\mathbf{a}_i$ are eigenvariables not occurring in the lower sequent $\Phi(\mathbf{t}) \cup \Gamma$. Or alternatively

$$\frac{\{\Phi_i(\mathbf{a}_i; \mathbf{t}), \Gamma\}_i \quad \{\neg B, \Gamma\}_{B \in \Phi(\mathbf{t})}}{\Gamma}$$

We denote ambiguously one of applied logic calculi for T by $G_1 + T$ or $G_1 + T + (cut)$ with the (cut)-rule.

Examples

1. Equality axioms $\forall x(x = x), \forall x, y, z(x = y \land z = y \to x = z)$,
$\forall x_1, \ldots, x_n, y_1, \ldots, y_n(\bigwedge_i (x_i = y_i) \to f(x_1, \ldots, x_n) = f(y_1, \ldots, y_n))$, and
$\forall x_1, \ldots, x_n, y_1, \ldots, y_n(\bigwedge_i (x_i = y_i) \to R(x_1, \ldots, x_n) \to R(y_1, \ldots, y_n)$ are codified by the following inference rules.

$$\frac{t \neq t, \Gamma}{\Gamma} \qquad \frac{\Gamma, t_1 = t_2 \quad \Gamma, t_3 = t_2 \quad t_1 \neq t_3, \Gamma}{\Gamma}$$

$$\frac{\Gamma, t_1 = s_1 \quad \cdots \quad \Gamma, t_n = s_n \quad f(t_1, \ldots, t_n) \neq f(s_1, \ldots, s_n), \Gamma}{\Gamma}$$

$$\frac{\Gamma, t_1 = s_1 \quad \cdots \quad \Gamma, t_n = s_n \quad \Gamma, R(t_1, \ldots, t_n) \quad \overline{R}(s_1, \ldots, s_n), \Gamma}{\Gamma}$$

2. Complete induction schema
$\forall \mathbf{y} \forall x[A(0, \mathbf{y}) \land \forall z(A(z, \mathbf{y}) \to A(Sz, \mathbf{y})) \to A(x; \mathbf{y})]$ is codified by the inference rule with the eigenvariable a.

$$\frac{\Gamma, A(0, \mathbf{t}) \quad \neg A(a, \mathbf{t}), \Gamma, A(Sa, \mathbf{t}) \quad \neg A(s, \mathbf{t}), \Gamma}{\Gamma}$$

3. Transfinite induction schema $\forall \mathbf{y} \forall x[\forall z(\forall w < z A(w, \mathbf{t}) \to A(z, \mathbf{t})) \to A(x, \mathbf{y})]$ is codified by the inference rule with the eigenvariable a.

$$\frac{\Gamma, \neg\forall w < a A(w, \mathbf{t}), A(a, \mathbf{t}) \quad \neg A(s, \mathbf{t}), \Gamma}{\Gamma}$$

where $\forall w < a A(w, \mathbf{t})$ is an abbreviation for $\forall w(w < a \to A(w, \mathbf{t}))$.

Theorem 2.2 *Let T be a countable list of closed formulas. Then the cut-elimination holds for applied logic calculus $\mathbf{G}_1 + T$: $\mathbf{G}_1 + T + (cut) \vdash \Lambda \Rightarrow \mathbf{G}_1 + T \vdash \Lambda$.*

Proof Assume $\mathbf{G}_1 + T \nvdash \Lambda$. Define a proof search procedure as in Sect. 2.1.1, but here we analyze each $A_n \in T$ at stage $2n$. Let A_n be the formula $\forall \mathbf{y}[\bigwedge_{i<k} \forall \mathbf{x}_i \bigvee \Phi_i (\mathbf{x}_i; \mathbf{y}) \to \bigvee \Phi(\mathbf{y})]$. Let $\langle n, m\rangle$ be a surjective pairing function on $\mathbb{N}$, e.g., $\langle n, m\rangle = \dfrac{(n+m+1)(n+m)}{2} + n$. When the length $lh(\sigma) = 2\langle n, m\rangle$, let $\sigma * (i) \in \mathcal{T}$ and $Term(\sigma * (i); B) = Term(\sigma; B)$ for $i < k + \ell$, where ℓ is the cardinality of the finite set $\Phi(\mathbf{y})$. For each $k > 0$, enumerate the set of sequences $\mathbf{t} = (t_1, \ldots, t_k)$ of terms t_i in length k. The tree is extended by adding nodes with mth entry $\mathbf{t}_m$ in the enumeration $\mathbf{t}_0, \mathbf{t}_1, \ldots$.

$$\frac{\{Seq_0(\sigma), \Phi_i(\mathbf{a}_i; \mathbf{t}_m); Seq_1(\sigma)\}_{i<k} \quad \{Seq_0(\sigma), NL(\neg B); Seq_1(\sigma), L(\neg B)\}_{B \in \Phi(\mathbf{t}_m)}}{Seq_0(\sigma); Seq_1(\sigma)}$$

The assumption yields that the tree is infinite, and the existence of an infinite path $\mathcal{P}$ through $\mathcal{T}$. From the path $\mathcal{P}$, define a truth valuation M, in which $M(A_n) = \top$ for any $A_n \in T$. □

2.1.3 Predicative Second Order Logic

Let $\mathcal{L}_1$ be a first order language. Π_0^{1-} denotes the set of formulas in $\mathcal{L}_1$. A second order language $\mathcal{L}_2$ is obtained from $\mathcal{L}_1$ by adding n-ary predicate variables (or second-order variables)[1] $\{X_i^n : i \in \omega\}$ for each $n \geq 0$. Hence $X_i^n(t_1, \ldots, t_n)$ and its complement $\overline{X_i^n}(t_1, \ldots, t_n)$ are literals in $\mathcal{L}_2$ besides literals in $\mathcal{L}_1$. The set of *first-order formulas* denoted Π_0^1 is then obtained from literals by applying first-order logical connectives $\vee, \wedge, \exists x, \forall x$ (first-order quantifications). While the set of formulas in $\mathcal{L}_2$ is obtained by applying the *second-order quantifiers* $\exists X$ and $\forall X$. Thus a formula is first-order iff no second-order quantifier occurs in it. The negation $\neg A$

[1] For simplicity free and bound second-order variables are discriminated only in the context, not formally.

of second-order formulas A is defined recursively by $\neg\exists X F(X) \equiv \forall X \neg F(X)$ and $\neg\forall X F(X) \equiv \exists X \neg F(X)$.

Definition 2.1 1. An *n-ary abstract* is a formal expression of the form $\{\mathbf{x}\}F(\mathbf{x})$ for a formula F and a list $\mathbf{x} = (x_1, \ldots, x_n)$ of first-order variables.
2. An abstract $\{\mathbf{x}\}F(\mathbf{x})$ is said to be first-order denoted $\{\mathbf{x}\}F(\mathbf{x}) \in \Pi^1_0$ if $F \in \Pi^1_0$.
3. Let $A(X^n)$ be a formula with an n-ary predicate variable X^n and $\{\mathbf{x}\}F(\mathbf{x})$ an n-ary abstract. Then $A(\{\mathbf{x}\}F(\mathbf{x}))$ denotes the result of replacing any literals $X^n(\mathbf{t})$ ($\mathbf{t} = (t_1, \ldots, t_n)$) by $F(\mathbf{t})$ and $\overline{X^n}(\mathbf{t})$ by $\neg F(\mathbf{t})$ where we rename bound variables if necessary.

For example for $A(X) \equiv \forall x \forall y[x = y \to (X(x) \leftrightarrow X(y))]$ and $V = \{x\}F(x)$, $A(V)$ denotes $\forall x \forall y[x = y \to (F(x) \leftrightarrow F(y))]$.

Now we define a predicative second order logic $\boldsymbol{G}_2$.

Axiom

$$\Gamma, \overline{L}, L$$

for any sequent Γ and a literal L.

Inference rules Inference rules $(\vee)$, $(\wedge)$, $(\exists)$, $(\forall)$ for first-order connectives are the same as in $\boldsymbol{G}_1$, cf. Sect. 1.2.

Inference rules for the second-order quantifiers:

$$\frac{\Gamma, \exists X A(X), A(V)}{\Gamma, \exists X A(X)}\ (\exists^2_{1st})$$

where V is a *first-order abstract*, $V \in \Pi^1_0$.

$$\frac{\Gamma, \forall X A(X), A(Y)}{\Gamma, \forall X A(X)}\ (\forall^2)$$

where, in $(\forall^2)$, the variable Y does not occur freely in the lowersequent, and is said to be the *eigenvariable*.

Corollary 2.2 *Any first-order sequent provable in* $\boldsymbol{G}_2 + (cut)$ *is provable in* $\boldsymbol{G}_1$.

Proof This follows from the completeness of $\boldsymbol{G}_1$ and the soundness of $\boldsymbol{G}_2 + (cut)$ for models $(\mathcal{M}, Df(\mathcal{M}))$, where $Df(\mathcal{M})$ denotes the set of (first-order) definable relations on the $\mathcal{L}_1$-structures $\mathcal{M}$. □

Definition 2.2 The 2-degree $\mathrm{dg}_2(A)$ of a formula A.

1. $\mathrm{dg}_2(A) = 0$ if $A \in \Pi^1_0$.
2. $\mathrm{dg}_2(A_0 \vee A_1) = \mathrm{dg}_2(A_0 \wedge A_1) = \max\{\mathrm{dg}_2(A_i) : i = 0, 1\} + 1$ if $\{A_i : i = 0, 1\} \not\subset \Pi^1_0$.
3. $\mathrm{dg}_2(\exists x A(x)) = \mathrm{dg}_2(\forall x A(x)) = \mathrm{dg}_2(A(x)) + 1$ if $A \notin \Pi^1_0$.
4. $\mathrm{dg}_2(\exists X A(X)) = \mathrm{dg}_2(\forall X A(X)) = \mathrm{dg}_2(A(X)) + 1$

Note that $\text{dg}_2(A(V)) = \text{dg}_2(A(X))$ for first-order abstracts V.

Theorem 2.3 *The cut-elimination holds for predicative second-order logic calculus* $\mathbf{G}_2$*:* $\mathbf{G}_2 + (cut) \vdash \Lambda \Rightarrow \mathbf{G}_2 \vdash \Lambda$.

Proof Assume $\mathbf{G}_2 \nvdash \Lambda$. Define a proof search procedure as in Sect. 2.1.1, but here we analyze also second-order quantifications. Let $\{Y^k_n : n \in \omega\}$ be an enumeration of all k-ary predicate variables, and $\{V^k_n : n \in \omega\}$ an enumeration of all k-ary first-order abstracts. $Term(\sigma; \exists X F(X))$ is a finite set of first-order abstracts substituted for X before the stage σ. Let B be the first formula in $\Gamma_0 = Seq_0(\sigma)$ in the ordering $ON(\sigma)$.

Let us consider the case $B \equiv \exists X^k\, F(X)$ first. Then $\sigma * (0) \in \mathcal{T}$. Let V be the first k-ary abstract in the enumeration $\{V^k_n\}_n$ not in $Term(\sigma; B)$. $Term(\sigma * (0); B) = Term(\sigma; B) \cup \{V\}$, and $Term(\sigma * (0); C) = Term(\sigma; C)$ for any $C \not\equiv B$. Let $\Delta_i = Seq_i(\sigma * (0))$. Then $\Delta_0 = \Gamma_0 \cup NL(F(V))$ and $\Delta_1 = \Gamma_1 \cup L(F(V))$. Let $\exists X F(X), \Psi = \Gamma_0$ in the ordering $ON(\sigma)$. Then $\Delta_0 = \Psi, NL(F(V)), \exists X F(X)$ in the ordering $ON(\sigma * (0))$.

Next let $B \equiv \forall X^k F(X)$. Then $\sigma * (0) \in \mathcal{T}$, $Term(\sigma * (0)) = Term(\sigma)$. Let $\Delta_i = Seq_i(\sigma * (0))$, and Y be the first variable in the enumeration $\{Y^k_n\}$ not occurring freely in $\Gamma_0 \cup \Gamma_1$. Then $\Delta_0 = (\Gamma_0 \cup NL(F(Y))) \setminus \{\forall X F(X)\}$ and $\Delta_1 = \Gamma_1 \cup L(F(Y)) \cup \{\forall X F(X)\}$. $ON(\sigma * (0))$ on Δ_0 is the ordering induced by $ON(\sigma)$ with the element in $NL(F(Y))$ as last one.

Let us depict the cases $L(F(V)) = L(F(Y)) = \emptyset$:

$$\frac{\Psi, F(V), \exists X F(X); \Gamma_1}{\exists X F(X), \Psi; \Gamma_1} \quad \frac{\Psi, F(Y); \Gamma_1, \forall X F(X)}{\forall F(X), \Psi; \Gamma_1}$$

The assumption yields that the binary tree is infinite, and the existence of an infinite path $\mathcal{P}$ through $\mathcal{T}$. For $Seq^+(\mathcal{P}) = \bigcup\{Seq(\sigma) : \sigma \in \mathcal{P}\}$ we see that

$$\exists X^k F(X) \in Seq^+(\mathcal{P}) \Rightarrow \{F(V^k_n) : n \in \omega\} \subset Seq^+(\mathcal{P}) \tag{2.10}$$

$$\forall X^k F(X) \in Seq^+(\mathcal{P}) \Rightarrow \{F(Y^k_n) : n \in \omega\} \cap Seq^+(\mathcal{P}) \neq \emptyset \tag{2.11}$$

From the path $\mathcal{P}$, define a truth valuation $M(A) \in \{\bot, \top\}$ on $Seq(\mathcal{P}) = Seq^+(\mathcal{P}) \cup \{\neg A : A \in Seq^+(\mathcal{P})\}$ as before. Then Claim 2.2 is seen by induction on $\omega \cdot \text{dg}_2(A) + \text{dg}(A)$. Specifically $M(\exists X^k F(X)) = \bot$ iff $M(F(V)) = \bot$ for any k-ary abstract V, and $M(\exists X^k F(X)) = \top$ iff $M(F(V)) = \top$ for some k-ary abstract V. □

2.1.4 Predicative Extensions

Let T be a first-order theory over a language $\mathcal{L}_1$. (We can) Assume that the set of axioms in T consists of the instances $F_i(V)$ of *axiom schemata* $F_i(X^{n_i}) \in$

Π^1_0 (with an n_i-ary predicate variable X) for first order abstracts $V \in \Pi^{1-}_0$. Namely $\mathrm{T} = \{F_i(V) : V \in \Pi^{1-}_0, i \in I\}$.

Then its *predicative extension* T_2 is formulated in the predicative second order logic $\boldsymbol{G}_2 + (cut)$ by $\mathrm{T}_2 := \{\forall X F_i(X) : i \in I\}$.

For example in the predicative extension of the first-order arithmetic PA, the axiom schemata for equality is replaced by the single second order sentence $\forall X \forall x \forall y[x = y \to (X(x) \leftrightarrow X(y))]$, and the induction schema by $\forall X[X(0) \land \forall y(X(y) \to X(Sy)) \to \forall x X(x)]$. Following H. Friedman, PA_2 is denoted ACA_0 (=Arithmetical Comprehension Axiom with restricted induction).

Another example is the Bernays–Gödel set theory $\mathsf{BG} = \mathsf{ZF}_2$, in which Collection axiom schema $\forall x \in a \exists y A(x, y) \to \exists b \forall x \in a \exists y \in b A(x, y)$ $(A \in \Pi^{1-}_0)$ is replaced by $\forall Y^2 \forall a[\forall x \in a \exists y Y(x, y) \to \exists b \forall x \in a \exists y \in b Y(x, y)]$ and Separation axiom schema $\exists b[b = \{x \in a : A(x)\}]$ $(A \in \Pi^{1-}_0)$ follows from $\forall X \forall a \exists b[b = a \cap X]$ and $(\exists^2)$.

In this subsection we show the

Theorem 2.4 T_2 *is a conservative extension of* T. *Namely for any* $A \in \Pi^{1-}_0$

$$\mathrm{T}_2 \vdash A \Rightarrow \mathrm{T} \vdash A.$$

Proof Let $\Gamma_0 \subset \Pi^{1-}_0$ such that $\mathrm{T}_2 \vdash \Gamma_0$. Then there are finitely many axioms $\Theta_0 := \{\forall X F_i(X) : i \leq n\} \subset \mathrm{T}_2$ such that $\boldsymbol{G}_2 + (cut) \vdash \neg\Theta_0, \Gamma_0$. By Cut-elimination theorem 2.3 for the second order logic $\boldsymbol{G}_2$ pick a proof P of $\neg\Theta, \Gamma_0$ in $\boldsymbol{G}_2 + (cut)$ whose cut formulas are first-order. Now we show, by induction on the depth of P, that $\mathrm{T} \vdash \Gamma_0$ with $\Gamma_0 \subset \Pi^{1-}_0$. Observe that since $\neg\Theta_0, \Gamma_0 \subset \Sigma^1_1 \cup \Pi^{1-}_0$ there is no second-order inference $(\forall^2)$ in P, i.e., there is no second-order eigenvariables. Hence we can assume that no second-order free variable occurs in P for otherwise substitute any first order formulas for second order free variables. Therefore any sequent occurring in P is of the form $\neg\Theta_0, \Gamma$ with $\Gamma \subset \Pi^{1-}_0$.

If $\neg\Theta_0, \Gamma$ is an **Axiom** $\Delta, \bar{L}, L$ with a literal L, then so is Γ. Suppose that $\neg\Theta_0, \Gamma$ is a lowersequent of an inference $(\exists^2)$:

$$\frac{\neg F_i(V), \neg\Theta_0, \Gamma}{\neg\Theta_0, \Gamma}\ (\exists^2)$$

where $\forall X F_i(X) \in \Theta_0 \subset \mathrm{T}_2$ and $\neg F_i(V) \in \Pi^{1-}_0$. IH yields $\mathrm{T} \vdash \neg F_i(V), \Gamma$. On the other hand we have $\mathrm{T} \vdash F_i(V)$. Hence $\mathrm{T} \vdash \Gamma$. □

Model-theoretically Theorem 2.4 is seen easily: Suppose $\mathrm{T} \nvdash A$ for a first order sentence $A \in \Pi^{1-}_0$. By Gödel's completeness theorem pick a model $M \models \mathrm{T} \cup \{\neg A\}$. Expand the model M for the second-order language $\mathcal{L}_2$ by taking the set $Def(M)$ of first-order definable predicates as the second-order universe. Call the expansion M^2: $\mathcal{X} \in Def(M)$ iff there exists a formula A in $\mathcal{L}_1(M)$ such that $\mathcal{X} = \{a \in |M| : M \models A[a]\}$, and $M^2 \models \exists X F(X)$ iff $M^2 \models F[\mathcal{X}]$ for some $\mathcal{X} \in Def(M)$.

Then it is clear that $M^2 \models F(V) \to \exists X F(X)$ and $M^2 \models \mathrm{T}_2$. Hence $M^2 \models \mathrm{T}_2 \cup \{\neg A\}$, and $\mathrm{T}_2 \nvdash A$.

2.1.5 ω-Logic

Let us specify the language $\mathcal{L}_\omega$ for the ω-logic. Its predicate symbols are $\{=, \neq\} \cup \{X_i, \bar{X}_i : i < \omega\}$ for unary relation symbols (set variables) X_i.

For each function symbol $f \in \mathcal{L}_\omega$, we assume that its *interpretation* $\bar{f}$ is assigned, where $\bar{f}$ is a k-ary number-theoretic function, $\bar{f} : \mathbb{N}^k \to \mathbb{N}$, for k-ary function symbol f. In particular we assume that $\mathcal{L}_\omega$ contains an individual constant 0 and a unary function symbol S, the *successor* function, and their interpretations are given by $\bar{0} := 0$ and $\bar{S}(n) = n + 1$. $S \cdots S0$ is a *numeral*, denoted $\bar{n}$ and identified with the natural number n when S occurs n-times in it.

Terms in $\mathcal{L}_\omega$ are defined as usual once the set of function symbols is fixed. For a closed term t, $t^{\mathbb{N}} \in \mathbb{N}$ denotes its *value* under the interpretation of function symbols. t is identified with its value $t^{\mathbb{N}}$. $n \in X$ denotes $X(n)$, and $n \notin X$ denotes $\bar{X}(n)$. Formulas in $\mathcal{L}_\omega$ are restricted to *closed formulas* (formulas without first-order free variables) in the language $\mathcal{L}_\omega$. Therefore a literal in $\mathcal{L}_\omega$ is either an equation $n = m$ or $n \in X$, or their complements.

This means that we are concerned with an ω-model $\mathcal{M} = (\mathbb{N}; \bar{f}, \ldots, X_i^{\mathcal{M}})$, where $X_i^{\mathcal{M}} \subset \mathbb{N}$. Since interpretations $\bar{f}$ of function symbols are fixed, an ω-model is determined by assigning interpretations $X_i^{\mathcal{M}} \subset \mathbb{N}$ for unary relation symbols X_i. A closed formula A is said to be valid in ω-models if $\mathcal{M} \models A$ for any ω-models $\mathcal{M}$.

Axiom for the infinitary calculus $\boldsymbol{G}_\omega$ for ω-logic.

$$\Gamma, \bar{L}, L$$

for any sequent Γ and a literal L,[2] and

$$\Gamma, t_0 = t_1 \text{ (with } t_0^{\mathbb{N}} = t_1^{\mathbb{N}}) \text{ and } \Gamma, s_0 \neq s_1 \text{ (with } s_0^{\mathbb{N}} \neq s_1^{\mathbb{N}}).$$

Inference rules for the ω-logic are $(\vee)$, $(\wedge)$, $(\exists)$ and the following infinitary rule $(\forall\omega)$ (, which is called the *ω-rule*):

$$\frac{\{\Gamma, \forall x A(x), A(n) : n \in \omega\}}{\Gamma, \forall x A(x)}\ (\forall\omega)$$

Proposition 2.1 (Soundness) *Any provable sequent in $\boldsymbol{G}_\omega$ + (cut) is valid in ω-models.*

Subformula property of cut-free proofs, Lemma 1.2, holds for $\boldsymbol{G}_\omega$: Any formula occurring in a cut-free proof in $\boldsymbol{G}_\omega$ is a subformula of a formula occurring in the endsequent.

---

[2] In $\boldsymbol{G}_\omega$ **Axiom** $\Gamma, \bar{L}, L$ can be restricted to the case when L is a formula $t \in X$, since for a *closed* literal $t_0 = t_1$ one of $t_0 \neq t_1$ and $t_0 = t_1$ is true..

$\boldsymbol{G}_\omega \vdash \Gamma$ designates that there exists a (well-founded) derivation of Γ in $\boldsymbol{G}_\omega$. $\boldsymbol{G}_\omega + (cut) \vdash \Gamma$ is defined similarly with cut inferences.

Theorem 2.5 (Completeness of ω-logic) *If* $\bigvee \Lambda$ *is valid in* ω*-models, then* $\boldsymbol{G}_\omega \vdash \Lambda$.

From this together with Proposition 2.1 (Soundness) we see the following.

Corollary 2.3 (Cut-elimination for ω-logic)

$$\boldsymbol{G}_\omega + (cut) \vdash \Lambda \Rightarrow \boldsymbol{G}_\omega \vdash \Lambda.$$

To prove Theorem 2.5, assume that $\boldsymbol{G}_\omega \nvdash \Lambda$. We construct a counter model M of Λ by proof search method, where M is a function which interpretes predicate symbols X as $M(X) \subset \mathbb{N}$. In the proof let $\vdash \Gamma :\Leftrightarrow \boldsymbol{G}_\omega \vdash \Gamma$. Modify the construction of the refutation tree $\mathcal{T} \subset {}^{<\omega}\omega$ in Sect. 2.1.1 as follows.

Suppose that the tree $\mathcal{T}$ has been constructed up to a node σ. Let $\Gamma_i = Seq_i(\sigma)$. **Leaf condition** is literally the same as before: If $Seq(\sigma)$ is an axiom in $\boldsymbol{G}_\omega$, then σ is a leaf in $\mathcal{T}$. If $\Gamma_0 = \emptyset$, then repeat. Otherwise pick the first non-literal formula $B \in \Gamma_0$ in the ordering $ON(\sigma)$.

($\exists$) $B \equiv \exists x A(x)$: Instead of an enumeration of all terms $\{t_n : n \in \omega\}$, let $t_n \equiv n$.

($\forall\omega$) $B \equiv \forall x A(x)$: Then $\sigma * (n) \in \mathcal{T}$ $(n \in \omega)$, $Term(\sigma * (n)) = Term(\sigma)$. Let $\Delta_{ni} = Seq_i(\sigma * (n))$. Then $\Delta_{n0} = (\Gamma_0 \cup NL(A(n))) \setminus \{\forall x A(x)\}$ and $\Delta_{n1} = \Gamma_1 \cup L(A(n)) \cup \{\forall x A(x)\}$. $ON(\sigma * (n))$ on Δ_{n0} is the ordering induced by $ON(\sigma)$ with the element in $NL(A(n))$ as last one.

Let us depict the case $L(A(n)) = \emptyset$ for any (some) n:

$$\frac{\{\Psi, A(n); \Gamma_1, \forall x A(x) : n \in \omega\}}{\forall x A(x), \Psi; \Gamma_1}$$

Then (2.1), (2.2), (2.3) holds. In particular $\mathcal{T}$ is computable in the interpretation $\bar{f}$. Since we are assuming $\boldsymbol{G}_\omega \nvdash \Lambda$, the tree $\mathcal{T}$ is not well-founded, i.e., there exists an infinite path $\mathcal{P}$ through $\mathcal{T}$. Pick an infinite path $\mathcal{P}$ through $\mathcal{T}$. For $Seq^+(\mathcal{P}) = \bigcup\{Seq(\sigma) : \sigma \in \mathcal{P}\}$ we have (2.4), (2.5), (2.6) and

$$\forall x A(x) \in Seq^+(\mathcal{P}) \Rightarrow \{A(n) : n \in \omega\} \cap Seq^+(\mathcal{P}) \neq \emptyset \tag{2.12}$$

and for $n \neq m$,

$$\{\bar{L}, L\} \not\subset Seq^+(\mathcal{P})\,\&\,(n = n) \notin Seq^+(\mathcal{P})\,\&\,(n \neq m) \notin Seq^+(\mathcal{P}) \tag{2.13}$$

Then define as in (2.9) truth valuation $M(A) \in \{\bot, \top\}$ for $A \in Seq(\mathcal{P}) = Seq^+(\mathcal{P}) \cup Seq^-(\mathcal{P})$ with $Seq^-(\mathcal{P}) = \{\neg A : A \in Seq^+(\mathcal{P})\}$.

Claim 2.2 stating that $M(A) \neq M(\neg A)$ for $A \in Seq(\mathcal{P})$, and M enjoys the Tarski's conditions, is seen as before. Specifically M determines an ω-model with the universe $\mathbb{N}$ by (2.13), and $M(\forall x A(x)) = \top$ iff $M(A(n)) = \top$ for any $n \in \omega$. Each X is interpreted as the set $\{n \in \mathbb{N} : X(n) \notin Seq^+(\mathcal{P})\}$. This shows Theorem 2.5.

From the construction of the search tree (2.2), we see the following.

Corollary 2.4 *If $\bigvee \Lambda$ is valid in ω-models, then there exists a computable-in-interpretation derivation of Λ in $\boldsymbol{G}_\omega$.*

2.2 Consequences of Cut-Elimination

In this section we show some consequences of cut-elimination theorem.

Remark 2.2 These consequences follow from the cut-elimination theorems finitistically. Although the cut-elimination theorems (except one for ω-logic and Mints' normal form theorem 2.16 in Exercise 2.4) are proved in the previous Sect. 2.1 by invoking the weak König's lemma, the cut-elimination theorems are proved in the $\mathcal{E}^4$-arithmetic $\mathcal{E}^4\mathsf{A}$ in the next Chap. 3. Hence all of the consequences in this section are proved in $\mathcal{E}^4\mathsf{A}$. This remark is important for the Π_2-conservativity result of WKL_0 over PRA.

Subformula property of cut-free proofs, Lemma 1.2 yields the non-finite axiomatizability of PA.

Proposition 2.2 *The first-order arithmetic* PA *is not finitely axiomatizable unless* PA *is inconsistent: there is no closed formula A such that $\mathsf{PA} \vdash B \Leftrightarrow A \vdash B$ for any B.*

Proof First PA is a *reflexive theory*. Namely PA proves the consistency of any finite fragment of it. Let PA_0 be a finite fragment of PA. Then $\mathsf{PA} \vdash \mathrm{CON}(\mathsf{PA}_0)$ by Corollary 2.1 (cut-eliminability in $\boldsymbol{G}_1$) and the partial truth definition. Now assume that there exists a closed formula A such that $\mathsf{PA} \vdash B \Leftrightarrow A \vdash B$ for any B. Pick a finite fragment PA_0 of PA such that $\mathsf{PA}_0 \vdash A$ and $\mathsf{EA} \subset \mathsf{PA}_0$. Then $\mathsf{PA} \vdash \mathrm{CON}(\mathsf{PA}_0)$, and hence $\mathsf{PA}_0 \vdash \mathrm{CON}(\mathsf{PA}_0)$. This contradicts with the second incompleteness theorem unless PA is inconsistent. □

2.2.1 *Midsequent Theorem*

Let T be a set of purely universal closed formulas. Each $A \in T$ is of the form $\forall \mathbf{x}\, B(\mathbf{x})$ for quantifier-free B. T may contain equality axioms. Let $\boldsymbol{G}_1 + T$ denote a formalization in a sequent calculus of the theory T. $\boldsymbol{G}_1 + T$ is obtained from $\boldsymbol{G}_1$ by adding some inference rules (T) to state that $\forall \mathbf{x}\, B(\mathbf{x}) \in T$ holds as in Sect. 2.1.2. It may be formulated by one of the inferences:

$$\frac{\neg B(\mathbf{t}), \Gamma}{\Gamma}\ (T) \quad \text{or} \quad \frac{\Gamma_0, B_0(\mathbf{t}) \quad \cdots \quad \Gamma_n, B_n(\mathbf{t})}{\Gamma_0, \ldots, \Gamma_n}\ (T)$$

where $\bigwedge_i B_i(\mathbf{x}) \leftrightarrow \neg B(\mathbf{x})$ is a tautology.

Definition 2.3 An occurrence of a sequent in a proof is said to be a *midsequent* in the proof, if any inference rule occurring above the sequent is either a propositional one $(\vee)_{01}$, $(\wedge)$ or one of inference rules (T), and any inference rule occurring below it is one of $(\exists)$, $(\forall)$.

A formula in prenex normal form is a *prenex formula* $Q_1x_1 \cdots Q_nx_n\, B$, where $Q_i \in \{\exists, \forall\}$ and B is a *quantifier-free* formula in which there occurs no quantifiers $\exists, \forall$.

Although the existence of a cut-free proof of prenex formulas with a midsequent is seen through proof search, cf. Exercise 2.3 in this chapter, it is seen from the cut-elimination theorem with proof transformations as follows.

Theorem 2.6 *Let* $\boldsymbol{G}_1 + T$ *be a sequent calculus for a purely universal theory* T *as described above, and* Γ *a sequent consisting solely of prenex formulas.*

If $\boldsymbol{G}_1 + T + (cut) \vdash \Gamma$*, then there exists a (cut-free)* $\boldsymbol{G}_1 + T$*-proof of* Γ *with a midsequent.*

Proof For the proof let's assume that each inference does not share contexts (side formulas). This means that the inference rule $(\wedge)$ is formulated as

$$\frac{\Gamma_0, A_0 \wedge A_1, A_0 \quad \Gamma_1, A_0 \wedge A_1, A_1}{\Gamma_0, \Gamma_1, A_0 \wedge A_1}\ (\wedge)$$

Assume $\boldsymbol{G}_1 + T + (cut) \vdash \Gamma$ with a set Γ of prenex formulas. By cut-elimination we can assume that we have a $\boldsymbol{G}_1 + T$-proof P of Γ. For each inference $I \in \{(\exists), (\forall)\}$ in P let $n(I)$ be the number of occurrences of propositional inferences $(\vee)$, $(\wedge)$ and inference rules (T) below I. Let $n(P)$ be the sum of the numbers $n(I)$ for occurrences I of $(\exists)$, $(\forall)$ in P. If $n(P) = 0$, then there is a midsequent in P. Specifically the upper sequent of the uppermost inference $(\exists)$, $(\forall)$ is a midsequent when such a rule exists in P. Otherwise the endsequent is a midsequent.

Assume $n(P) > 0$. Let us transform P to another P' with the same endsequent such that $n(P') < n(P)$. Pick one of the lowest inference $I \in \{(\exists), (\forall)\}$ in P such that $n(I) > 0$. Since I is a lowest such one, the lower sequent of I is an upper sequent of an inference J, which is either a propositional one or an inference (T). Suppose that I is an inference $(\forall)$ with the main formula $\forall x\, A(x)$. The formula $\forall x\, A(x)$ is not a minor formula of J since every minor formula of inferences (T) is quantifier-free, and every formula in the end sequent is in prenex normal form. We can interchange inferences I and J. To get P', transform

$$\frac{\Gamma_0, C_0 \wedge C_1, C_0 \quad \dfrac{\Gamma_1, C_0 \wedge C_1, C_1, \forall x\, A(x), A(a)}{\Gamma_1, C_0 \wedge C_1, C_1, \forall x\, A(x)}\ (\forall)}{\Gamma_0, \Gamma_1, \forall x\, A(x), C_0 \wedge C_1}\ (\wedge)$$

to

$$\frac{\dfrac{\Gamma_0, C_0 \wedge C_1, C_0 \quad \Gamma_1, C_0 \wedge C_1, C_1, \forall x\, A(x), A(a)}{\Gamma_0, \Gamma_1, \forall x\, A(x), A(a), C_0 \wedge C_1}\ (\wedge)}{\Gamma_0, \Gamma_1, \forall x\, A(x), C_0 \wedge C_1}\ (\forall)$$

Obviously $n(P') < n(P)$. Other cases are similar. □

2.2.2 Interpolation Theorem

Let $\top$ be a 0-ary relation symbol not in the language $\mathcal{L}$, and its complement $\bot :\equiv \overline{\top}$. $\mathbf{G}_1 + (\top)$ is a sequent calculus in the expanded language with $\top$, which is obtained from $\mathbf{G}_1$ by adding an axiom

$$(\top)\ \Gamma, \top$$

Recall that each relation symbol R in a language is accompanied by its complement $\overline{R}$ in the following Definition 2.4.

Definition 2.4 A relation symbol $R \notin \{\top, \bot\}$ occurs *positively* [*negatively*] in a formula A, denoted $R \in Rel^+(A)$ [denoted $R \in Rel^-(A)$] if R [$\overline{R}$] occurs in A, resp.

For a relation symbol $R \notin \{\top, \bot\}$, A is an *R-positive* formula [*R-negative* formula] if $R \notin Rel^-(A)$ [$R \notin Rel^+(A)$], resp.

Obviously $Rel^{\pm}(\neg A) = Rel^{\mp}(A)$.

Theorem 2.7 (Lyndon's Interpolation theorem) *Assume* $\mathbf{G}_1 + (cut) \vdash A \to B$. *Then we can find an interpolant* C *of* A, B *such that*

1. $\mathbf{G}_1 + (\top) \vdash A \to C$ *and* $\mathbf{G} + (\top) \vdash C \to B$.
2. $Rel^{\pm}(C) \subset Rel^{\pm}(A) \cap Rel^{\pm}(B)$, *resp.*

Assume $\mathbf{G}_1 + (cut) \vdash A \to B$. Then by Corollary 2.1 $\mathbf{G}_1 \vdash \neg A, B$. We show the theorem by the method of splitting sequents due to S. Maehara. For sequents Γ, $Rel^{\pm}(\Gamma) = \bigcup\{Rel^{\pm}(A) : A \in \Gamma\}$, resp. It suffices to show the

Lemma 2.1 *Assume* $\mathbf{G}_1 \vdash \Gamma, \Delta$. *Then we can find an interpolant* C *such that*

1. $\mathbf{G}_1 + (\top) \vdash \Gamma, C$ *and* $\mathbf{G}_1 + (\top) \vdash \neg C, \Delta$.
2. $Rel^{\pm}(C) \subset Rel^{\mp}(\Gamma) \cap Rel^{\pm}(\Delta)$, *resp.*

Proof By induction on the depths of cut-free proof P of Γ, Δ.

First consider the case $\Lambda, \overline{L}, L = \Gamma, \Delta$ is an axiom. If $\overline{L} \in \Gamma$ and $L \in \Delta$, then let $C \equiv L$. Otherwise we can assume, e.g., $\{L, \overline{L}\} \subset \Delta$. Then let $C \equiv \top$.

Next consider the case when the last inference in P is a $(\wedge)$.

$$P = \dfrac{\begin{array}{cc} P_0 & P_1 \\ \Gamma, \Delta, A_0 & \Gamma, \Delta, A_1 \end{array}}{\Gamma, \Delta}\ (\wedge)$$

where $A_0 \wedge A_1 \in \Gamma \cup \Delta$.

First suppose $A_0 \wedge A_1 \in \Delta$. Split the endsequent of P_i in Γ and $\Delta \cup \{A_i\}$. IH yields an interpolant C_i such that $\boldsymbol{G}_1 + (\top) \vdash \Gamma, C_i, \boldsymbol{G}_1 + (\top) \vdash \neg C_i, \Delta, A_i$, and $Rel^{\pm}(C_i) \subset Rel^{\mp}(\Gamma) \cap Rel^{\pm}(\Delta \cup \{A_i\})$. Then let $C \equiv C_0 \wedge C_1$.

Next suppose $A_0 \wedge A_1 \in \Gamma$. Split the endsequent of P_i in $\Gamma \cup \{A_i\}$ and Δ. IH yields an interpolant C_i for this splitting. Then let $C \equiv C_0 \vee C_1$.

Third consider the case when the last inference in P is a $(\forall)$.

$$P = \cfrac{\begin{matrix} P_0 \\ \Gamma, \Delta, A(a) \end{matrix}}{\Gamma, \Delta}\ (\forall)$$

where $\forall x A(x) \in \Gamma \cup \Delta$ and the eigenvariable a does not occur in Γ, Δ.

First suppose $\forall x A(x) \in \Delta$. Split the endsequent of P_0 in Γ and $\Delta \cup \{A(a)\}$. IH yields an interpolant $C_0(a)$ such that $\boldsymbol{G}_1 + (\top) \vdash \Gamma, C_0(a), \boldsymbol{G}_1 + (\top) \vdash \neg C_0(a), \Delta, A(a)$, and $Rel^{\pm}(C_0(a)) \subset Rel^{\mp}(\Gamma) \cap Rel^{\pm}(\Delta \cup \{A(a)\})$. Then let $C \equiv \forall x C_0(x)$. By Weakening lemma 1.3 we get

$$\cfrac{\begin{matrix} \vdots \\ \Gamma, \forall x C_0(x), C_0(a) \end{matrix}}{\Gamma, \forall x C_0(x)}\ (\forall) \quad \text{and} \quad \cfrac{\cfrac{\begin{matrix} \vdots \\ \neg C_0(a), \neg \forall x C_0(x), \Delta, A(a) \end{matrix}}{\neg \forall x C_0(x), \Delta, A(a)}\ (\exists)}{\neg \forall x C_0(x), \Delta}\ (\forall)$$

Next suppose $\forall x A(x) \in \Gamma$. Split the endsequent of P_0 in $\Gamma \cup \{A(a)\}$ and Δ. IH yields an interpolant $C_0(a)$ such that $\boldsymbol{G}_1 + (\top) \vdash \Gamma, A(a), C_0(a), \boldsymbol{G}_1 + (\top) \vdash \neg C_0(a), \Delta$, and $Rel^{\pm}(C_0(a)) \subset Rel^{\mp}(\Gamma \cup \{A(a)\}) \cap Rel^{\pm}(\Delta)$. Then let $C \equiv \exists x C_0(x)$.

The cases when the last inference in P is either a $(\vee)_{01}$ or an $(\exists)$ is similar. □

2.2.3 *Herbrand's Theorems*

Herbrand's theorem is known in several forms. Let us mention the simplest two of them.

In this subsection we assume that the language $\mathcal{L}$ contains an individual constant. For simplicity let us quit to make a distinction between free and bound variables.

Definition 2.5 Let A be a formula.

1. The *Herbrand universe* of A is the set of all terms over $Cnst(A)$, $Var(A)$ and $Fnc(A)$, where $Cnst(A)$ denotes the set of individual constants occurring in A, $Var(A)$ the set of variables occurring freely in A, and $Fnc(A)$ the set of function symbols occurring in A. If $Cnst(A) \cup Var(A) = \emptyset$, then let $Cnst(A) = \{c\}$ for an individual constant c. $\mathcal{L}_{H(A)}$ denotes the language of the Herbrand universe consisting of $Cnst(A) \cup Var(A) \cup Fnc(A)$ and the relation symbols occurring in A.

2. Let A be a *purely existential formula*, $A \equiv \exists \mathbf{x} B(\mathbf{x}; \mathbf{a})$ with a quantifier-free matrix B. For a list $\{\mathbf{t}^i : i \leq r\}$ of lists $\mathbf{t}^i$ of terms, $\bigvee\{B(\mathbf{t}^i; \mathbf{a}) : i \leq r\}$ is said to be an *instance* of A. When each term in the list $\mathbf{t}^i$ $(i \leq r)$ is in the Herbrand universe of A, then the instance is said to be an *H-instance*.

Theorem 2.8 (Herbrand's theorem for purely existential formulas) *For purely existential formulas $A \equiv \exists \mathbf{x} B(\mathbf{x}; \mathbf{a})$, $G_1 \vdash A$ iff there is an H-instance of A, which is a propositional tautology.*

Proof Supposing $G_1 \vdash A$, pick a cut-free proof P of A. Each formula occurring in P is purely existential. Let us remove all of formulas with existential quantifiers and inferences $(\exists)$ in P.

$$\frac{\Gamma, \exists x_j \cdots \exists x_n B(\ldots, t_{j-1}, x_j, \ldots, x_n; \mathbf{a})}{\Gamma, \exists x_{j-1} \exists x_j \cdots \exists x_n B(\ldots, x_{j-1}, x_j, \ldots, x_n; \mathbf{a})} \ (\exists)$$

We obtain a propositional proof of an instance $\{B(\mathbf{t}^i; \mathbf{a}) : i \leq r\}$. If the instance is not an H-instance, then there occurs a term in the instance, which is not in the Herbrand universe. Substitute a term in the Herbrand universe for such a term, and we get an H-instance of A, which is a tautology. □

Next consider formulas in prenex normal form.

Definition 2.6 Let A be a prenex formula.

1. For each universal quantifier $\forall x_l$ in $A \equiv (\cdots \exists x_1^l \cdots \exists x_{n_l}^l \forall x_l \cdots)$, let $\exists x_1^l, \ldots, \exists x_{n_l}^l$ be the list of prefix existential quantifiers occurring to the left of the quantifier $\forall x_l$. Pick a new n_l-ary function symbol f_l not occurring in A, erase the universal quantifier $\forall x_l$ and substitute $f_l(x_1^l, \ldots, x_{n_l}^l)$ for the variable x_l in the matrix of A. It results in a purely existential formula A^H, the *Herbrand normal form* A^H of A. The new function symbols f_l are *Herbrand functions*.
2. Let $A \equiv Q_1 z_1 \cdots Q_{E+U} z_{E+U}\, B(\mathbf{y}; \mathbf{x}; \mathbf{a})$ with the matrix B, where $Q_k \in \{\exists, \forall\}$, $\{z_1, \ldots, z_{E+U}\} = \mathbf{y} \cup \mathbf{x}$, $\mathbf{y} = y_1, \ldots, y_E$ are existentially quantified variables, $\mathbf{x} = x_1, \ldots, x_U$ universally quantified, $\mathbf{a}$ parameters, and $Q_k = \exists$ iff $z_k = y_j$ for a j.
   Let $\{\mathbf{x}^i : i \leq r\}$ $(\mathbf{x}^i = x_1^i, \ldots, x_U^i)$ be a list of lists of distinct variables. Next let $\{\mathbf{t}^i : i \leq r\}$ $(\mathbf{t}^i = t_1^i, \ldots, t_E^i)$ be a list of lists of terms in the Herbrand universes. Let $u_k^i \equiv x_m^i$ if $z_k = x_m$, and $u_k^i \equiv t_m^i$ if $z_k = y_m$. Assume that there exists a linear order $<$ on the set $\{u_k^i : i \leq r, k \leq E+U\} = \{x_m^i : i \leq r, m \leq U\} \cup \{t_k^i : i \leq r, k \leq E\}$ such that $u_k^i < u_{k+1}^i$, and

$$Var(t_k^i) \subset \mathbf{a} \cup \{x_m^j : x_m^j < t_k^i\} \tag{2.14}$$

   where $Var(t)$ denotes the set of variables occurring in terms t.
   Then the quantifier-free formula $A^+ \equiv \bigvee\{B(\mathbf{t}^i; \mathbf{x}^i; \mathbf{a}) : i \leq r\}$ in the language $\mathcal{L}_{H(A)}$ is said to be an *H-instance* of A.

For instance the Herbrand normal form A^H of an $\exists\forall$-formula $A \equiv \exists y \forall x B(y; x; a)$, its instance A^{H+} and an H-instance A^+ constructed from terms $t^i = t^i(x^1, \ldots, x^{i-1}; a)$ with the order $t^0 < x^0 < t^1 < x^1 < \cdots$ are:

$$
\begin{aligned}
A &\equiv \exists y \forall x B(y; x; a)\\
A^H &\equiv \exists y B(y; f(y); a)\\
A^{H+} &\equiv \bigvee_i \{B(s^i; f(s^i); a)\} \ (f \text{ may occur in } s^i)\\
A^+ &\equiv \bigvee \{B(t^i(x_1, \ldots, x_{i-1}; a); x^i; a) : i \leq r\}\\
&\equiv B(t^0(; a); x^0; a) \lor B(t^1(x^0; a); x^1; a) \lor \cdots \lor B(t^r(x^0, \ldots, x^{r-1}; a); x^r; a)
\end{aligned}
$$

Theorem 2.9 (Herbrand's theorem for prenex formulas) *For prenex formulas A, the following conditions are mutually equivalent:*

1. $G_1 \vdash A$.
2. $G_1 \vdash A^H$.
3. *An H-instance A^{H+} of the Herbrand normal form A^H is a tautology.*
4. *An H-instance A^+ of A is a tautology.*

Proof $1 \Rightarrow 2$. $G_1 \vdash A \to A^H$.
$2 \Leftrightarrow 3$ is seen from Theorem 2.8.
$4 \Rightarrow 1$. For simplicity let $A \equiv \exists y_1 \forall x_1 \exists y_2 \forall x_2 B(y_1, y_2; x_1, x_2; a)$ and an H-instance A^+ is a tautology. From a propositional proof of the H-instance, deduce A by inferences $(\forall)$, $(\exists)$ according to the linear order $<$ enjoying (2.14), the larger first. For instance when the order is given by

$$t_1^0(;\ ; a) < x_1^0 < t_2^0(; x_1^0; a) < x_2^0 < t_1^1(x_1^0, x_2^0;\ ; a) < x_1^1 < t_2^1(x_1^0, x_2^0; x_1^1; a) < x_2^1$$

let

$$
\begin{array}{cl}
\vdots & \\
B(t_1^0(;\ ; a), t_2^0(; x_1^0; a); x_1^0, x_2^0; a), B(t_1^1(x_1^0, x_2^0;\ ; a), t_2^1(x_1^0, x_2^0; x_1^1; a); x_1^1, x_2^1; a)(\equiv A^+) & \\
\hline
B(t_1^0(;\ ; a), t_2^0(; x_1^0; a); x_1^0, x_2^0; a), \forall x_2^1 B(t_1^1(x_1^0, x_2^0;\ ; a), t_2^1(x_1^0, x_2^0; x_1^1; a); x_1^1, x_2^1; a) & (\forall)\\
\hline
B(t_1^0(;\ ; a), t_2^0(; x_1^0; a); x_1^0, x_2^0; a), \exists y_2 \forall x_2^1 B(t_1^1(x_1^0, x_2^0;\ ; a), y_2; x_1^1, x_2^1; a) & (\exists)\\
\hline
B(t_1^0(;\ ; a), t_2^0(; x_1^0; a); x_1^0, x_2^0; a), \forall x_1^1 \exists y_2 \forall x_2^1 B(t_1^1(x_1^0, x_2^0;\ ; a), y_2; x_1^1, x_2^1; a) & (\forall)\\
\hline
B(t_1^0(;\ ; a), t_2^0(; x_1^0; a); x_1^0, x_2^0; a), A & (\exists)\\
\hline
\forall x_2^0 B(t_1^0(;\ ; a), t_2^0(; x_1^0; a); x_1^0, x_2^0; a), A & (\forall)\\
\hline
\exists y_2 \forall x_2^0 B(t_1^0(;\ ; a), y_2; x_1^0, x_2^0; a), A & (\exists)\\
\hline
\forall x_1^0 \exists y_2 \forall x_2^0 B(t_1^0(;\ ; a), y_2; x_1^0, x_2^0; a), A & (\forall)\\
\hline
A & (\exists)
\end{array}
$$

$3 \Rightarrow 4$. For simplicity suppressing parameters and let $A \equiv \exists y_1 \forall x_1 \exists y_2 \forall x_2 B(y_1, y_2; x_1, x_2)$. Assume that the following H-instance of A^H is a tautology.

$$A^{H+} \equiv \bigvee_{i \leq r} \{B(t_1^i, t_2^i; f_1(t_1^i), f_2(t_1^i, t_2^i))\}$$

We are going to replace the terms $f_1(t_1^i)$, $f_2(t_1^i, t_2^i)$ by fresh variables, thereby we obtain an H-instance A^+ of A. Note that A^+ is a tautology.

In what follows assume that any term of the form $f_1(t)$, $f_2(t, s)$ occurring in A^{H+} is one of terms $f_1(t_1^i)$, $f_2(t_1^i, t_2^i)$. Such a term may occur in t_1^i, t_2^i. Substitute an arbitrary term in the Herbrand universe for such a term.

Let $Tm = \{f_1(t_1^i), f_2(t_1^i, t_2^i) : i \leq r\} = \{s_1 < s_2 < \cdots < s_{r_0}\}$ be the set of all terms with function symbols f_1, f_2 occurring in A^{H+}, and arrange these terms in a linear order in such a way that $f_1(t_1^i) < f_2(t_1^i, t_2^i)$, and s is not a subterm of t if $t < s$, where $r_0 \leq 2(r + 1)$ is the cardinality of the set Tm of terms. Pick fresh and distinct variables $x_1, \ldots, x_{r_0}$.

First consider the last term s_{r_0}. We can assume that $s_{r_0} \equiv f_2(t_1^r, t_2^r)$. Replace s_{r_0} by the variable $x_{r_0} (\equiv x_2^r)$ in A^{H+}. The replacement dose not affect terms in $\{s_k : 1 \leq k < r_0\}$, and the variable x_{r_0} does not occur in these terms. Next replace $s_{r_0 - 1}$ by the variable x_{r_0-1}, and s_k by x_k. This results in a tautology in the language $\mathscr{L}_{H(A)}$

$$A^+ \equiv \bigvee_{i \leq r} \{B(t_1^{i+}, t_2^{i+}; x_1^i, x_2^i\}$$

where $f_1(t_1^i)$ is replaced by x_1^i, and $f_2(t_1^i, t_2^i)$ by x_2^i, with some $\{x_1^i, x_2^i\} \subset \{x_1, \ldots, x_{r_0}\}$.

We need to define a linear order on $\{t_1^{i+}, t_2^{i+}, x_1^i, x_2^i : i \leq r\}$ so that the condition (2.14) is fulfilled. First let $x_k < x_j$ iff $s_k < s_j$ iff $k < j$.

If $f_1(t_1^i) \equiv s_k$, then define t_1^{i+} to be the predecessor of x_k in the order, and if $f_2(t_1^i, t_2^i) \equiv s_k$, then t_2^{i+} to be the predecessor of x_k. We see $t_1^{i+} < x_1^i < t_2^{i+} < x_2^i$ from $f_1(t_1^i) < f_2(t_1^i, t_2^i)$.

Assume that x_k occurs in t_j^{i+}, and let $x_m \equiv x_j^i$ be the successor of t_j^{i+}. t_j^i is a subterm of s_m. We claim that $m > k$. Suppose $m < k$. Then s_k is not a subterm of s_m, and hence the substituting x_k for s_k does not change s_m, a fortiori not change t_j^{i+}. Therefore $m \geq k$. Furthermore $m \neq k$ since t_j^i is a subterm of s_m. Thus we have shown $m > k$.

Since t_j^{i+} is the predecessor of x_m, we obtain $x_k < t_j^{i+} < x_m$. This means that the condition (2.14) is enjoyed by the order $<$ on $\{t_1^{i+}, t_2^{i+}, x_1^i, x_2^i : i \leq r\}$, and A^+ is an H-instance of A.

$1 \Rightarrow 4$ is seen from Midsequent theorem 2.6 with $T = \emptyset$. Let $\{B(\mathbf{t}^i; \mathbf{x}^i; \mathbf{a}) : i \leq r\}$ be the midsequent of a proof of A, where $B(\mathbf{y}; \mathbf{x}; \mathbf{a})$ is the matrix of A in which $\mathbf{y} = y_1, \ldots, y_E$ are existentially quantified variables, $\mathbf{x} = x_1, \ldots, x_U$ universally quantified, and $\mathbf{a}$ parameters. Also $\{\mathbf{x}^i : i \leq r\}$ ($\mathbf{x}^i = x_1^i, \ldots, x_U^i$) and $\{\mathbf{t}^i : i \leq r\}$ ($\mathbf{t}^i = t_1^i, \ldots, t_E^i$). Then a linear order $<$ on $\bigcup\{\mathbf{x}^i : i \leq r\} \cup \bigcup\{\mathbf{t}^i : i \leq r\}$ enjoying the condition (2.14) is read off from the order of inferences $(\forall)$, $(\exists)$ in the proof. Specifically let $x_m^j < t_k^i$ iff the inference rule $(\exists)$ with the witnessing term t_k^i occurs above (or precedes) the inference rule $(\forall)$ with its eigenvariable x_m^j in the proof. □

2.2.4 Epsilon Theorems

In this subsection we apply Herbrand theorem 2.9 to yield some epsilon theorems.

Theorem 2.10 (Skolem's theorem) *Assume that* $\boldsymbol{G}_1 \vdash \forall\mathbf{x}A(\mathbf{x}, f(\mathbf{x})) \to B$ *for a function symbol* f *not occurring in formulas* $A(\mathbf{x}, y), B$. *Then* $\boldsymbol{G}_1 \vdash \forall\mathbf{x}\exists y A(\mathbf{x}, y) \to B$.

Proof Let $C(\mathbf{x}, y)$ be a prenex normal form of the formula $\neg A(\mathbf{x}, y) \vee B$. Then we have $\boldsymbol{G}_1 \vdash \exists\mathbf{x}C(\mathbf{x}, f(\mathbf{x}))$, and $\boldsymbol{G}_1 \vdash (\exists\mathbf{x}C(\mathbf{x}, f(\mathbf{x})))^H$ for an Herbrand normal form $(\exists\mathbf{x}C(\mathbf{x}, f(\mathbf{x})))^H$ of $\exists\mathbf{x}C(\mathbf{x}, f(\mathbf{x}))$. Since $(\exists\mathbf{x}C(\mathbf{x}, f(\mathbf{x})))^H$ is also an Herbrand normal form of $\exists\mathbf{x}\forall y C(\mathbf{x}, y)$, we obtain $\boldsymbol{G}_1 \vdash \exists\mathbf{x}\forall y C(\mathbf{x}, y)$ by Theorem 2.9. Hence $\boldsymbol{G}_1 \vdash \forall\mathbf{x}\exists y A(\mathbf{x}, y) \to B$. □

Let us introduce *epsilon calculus*. For a language $\mathcal{L}_1$, let $\mathcal{L}_{1\varepsilon} = \mathcal{L}_1 \cup \{\varepsilon\}$. The symbol ε is the *epsilon operator*, which yields a term $\varepsilon x.A$ from a formula A. Thus the set of terms and the set of formulas are simultaneously generated in the language $\mathcal{L}_{1\varepsilon}$ for ε-calculi.

- If $A(a)$ is a formula, then $\varepsilon x.A(x)$ is a term (ε-*term*), where the occurrences of the variable x is bound by the epsilon operator εx.

An ε-term $\varepsilon x.A(x)$ is intended to denote an object e such that $A(e)$ holds when such an object exists. Otherwise $\varepsilon x.A(x)$ denotes an arbitrary object. This is codified in the *epsilon axiom.*

$$A(t) \to A(\varepsilon x.A(x)) \tag{2.15}$$

where A is a formula and t a term in the language $\mathcal{L}_{1\varepsilon}$.

$\boldsymbol{G}_{1\varepsilon}$ denotes a sequent calculus for ε-calculus, which is obtained from $\boldsymbol{G}_1$ in a language $\mathcal{L}_{1\varepsilon}$ by adding the following sequents as the sequent form of the ε-axioms (2.15).

$$\Gamma, \neg A(t), A(\varepsilon x.A(x))$$

Remark 2.3 In the presence of the ε-axiom (2.15), quantifiers are definable by

$$\exists x\, A(x) :\equiv A(\varepsilon x.A(x))\ ;\ \forall x\, A(x) :\equiv A(\varepsilon x.\neg A(x))$$

In the calculus $\boldsymbol{G}_{1\varepsilon}$ we are keeping quantifiers formally to state the following second epsilon theorem.

Theorem 2.11 (the second epsilon theorem) *Assume* $\boldsymbol{G}_{1\varepsilon} + (cut) \vdash \Gamma$, *and* Γ *is* ε-*free. Then* $\boldsymbol{G}_1 \vdash \Gamma$.

Proof By an ε-free sequent we mean a sequent in which the symbol ε does not occur. The second epsilon theorem 2.11 follows from Skolem's theorem 2.10 as follows.

Let us write $A(y; \mathbf{t})$ for a formula $A(y)$, where $\mathbf{t} = t_1, \ldots, t_n$ denotes the list of all terms occurring maximally in A, i.e., each occurrence of t_i is not a proper subterm in A. The epsilon operator can be regarded to denote a Skolem function $f_A : \mathbf{a} \mapsto \varepsilon y.A(y; \mathbf{a})$. Then the ε-axiom (2.15) turns to $A(s; \mathbf{t}) \to A(f_A(\mathbf{t}); \mathbf{t})$, which follows from

$$\forall \mathbf{x}[\exists y\, A(y; \mathbf{x}) \to A(f_A(\mathbf{x}); \mathbf{x})]$$

Assume $\boldsymbol{G}_{1\varepsilon} + (cut) \vdash \Gamma$. Γ follows logically from a finite number of ε-axioms, $A_1(s_1) \to A_1(\varepsilon x_1.A_1(x_1)), \ldots, A_n(s_n) \to A_n(\varepsilon x_n.A_n(x_n))$. Introduce new function symbols f_i, and replace each ε-term (including semi-terms, i.e., a bound variable may occur in $\mathbf{s}$) $\varepsilon x_i.A_i(x_i; \mathbf{s})$ by $f_i(\mathbf{s})$ successively. The ε-axiom $A_i(s_i; \mathbf{t}_i) \to A_i(\varepsilon x_i.A_i(x_i; \mathbf{t}_i); \mathbf{t}_i)$ turns to $A_i(s'_i; \mathbf{t}'_i) \to A_i(f_i(\mathbf{t}'_i); \mathbf{t}'_i)$. Replace remaining ε-terms by an individual constant. Thus we obtain an ε-free $\boldsymbol{G}_1$-proof of the sequent $\neg E_1, \ldots, \neg E_n, \Gamma$ for $E_i \equiv \forall \mathbf{x}[\exists x_i\, A_i(x_i; \mathbf{x}) \to A_i(f_i(\mathbf{x}); \mathbf{x})]$. We can assume that if $i > j$, then an ε-term $\varepsilon x_j.A_j(x_j; \mathbf{s})$ does not occur in the scope $A_i(x_i; \mathbf{x})$ of the ε-operator εx_i in such a way that the variable x_i occurs in $\varepsilon x_j.A_j(x_j; \mathbf{s})$, i.e., x_i occurs in the list $\mathbf{s}$ of terms. Then the function symbol f_j does not occur in E_i for $i > j$.

From $\boldsymbol{G}_1 \vdash \neg E_1, \neg E_2, \ldots, \neg E_n, \Gamma$ we obtain by Skolem's theorem 2.10 $\boldsymbol{G}_1 \vdash \neg\forall \mathbf{x}\exists y[\exists x_1\, A_1(x_1; \mathbf{x}) \to A_1(y; \mathbf{x})], \neg E_2, \ldots, \neg E_n, \Gamma$. On the other side $\forall \mathbf{x}\exists y[\exists x_1\, A_1(x_1; \mathbf{x}) \to A_1(y; \mathbf{x})]$ is logically (classically) valid, i.e., $\boldsymbol{G}_1 \vdash \forall \mathbf{x}\exists y[\exists x_1\, A_1(x_1; \mathbf{x}) \to A_1(y; \mathbf{x})]$. Therefore $\boldsymbol{G}_1 \vdash \neg E_2, \ldots, \neg E_n, \Gamma$. Repeat this elimination procedure until we obtain $\boldsymbol{G}_1 \vdash \Gamma$. □

2.2.5 *Parikh's Theorem*

Let $\mathcal{L}$ be a first-order language with an individual constant and a distinguished binary relation symbol $\prec$. A quantifier is *bounded* (with respect to $\prec$) if it is one of the forms $\exists x \prec t\, A(x) :\equiv \exists x(x \prec t \land A(x))$ or $\forall x \prec t\, A(x) :\equiv \forall x(x \prec t \to A(x))$ for a term t in which the variable x does not occur. A formula is said to be *bounded* (with respect to $\prec$) iff every quantifier occurring in it is bounded. $\Delta_0^{\prec}(\mathcal{L})$ or simply $\Delta_0^{\prec}$ denotes the set of bounded $\mathcal{L}$-formulas with respect to $\prec$. An $\mathcal{L}$-theory T, i.e., a set of closed formulas in $\mathcal{L}$, is a *bounded theory* if each axiom in T is a universal closure of a bounded formula. Note that each equality axiom is a universal closure of a bounded formula, and any Π_1*-theory* is a bounded theory, where each axiom in a Π_1-theory is a Π_1-formula $\forall \mathbf{x} B(\mathbf{a}, \mathbf{x})$ with a bounded formula B.

Let $FVar(t)$ denote the set of free variables occurring in terms t, $FVar(A)$ the set of free variables occurring in formulas A and $FVar(\Gamma) = \bigcup\{FVar(A) : A \in \Gamma\}$.

Theorem 2.12 (Parikh) *Let T be a bounded theory in a language with an individual constant and a distinguished binary relation symbol $\prec$. Suppose that the following three conditions are met.*

1. *For each terms s and t, there exists a term r such that* $FVar(r) \subset FVar(s) \cup FVar(t)$*, and* $T \vdash \forall x \prec s(x \prec r) \land \forall x \prec t(x \prec r)$.
2. *For each terms s and t, there exists a term r such that* $FVar(r) \subset FVar(s) \cup FVar(t)$*, and* $T \vdash s \prec r \land \forall x \prec t(x \prec r)$.
3. *For each terms s and t(b), there exists a term r such that* $FVar(r) \subset FVar(s) \cup (FVar(t(b)) \setminus \{b\})$*, and* $T \vdash \forall x \prec s \forall y \prec t(x)(y \prec r)$.

Let $A(\mathbf{a}, \mathbf{b})$ *be a bounded formula, and assume that* $T \vdash \forall \mathbf{x} \exists \mathbf{y}\, A(\mathbf{x}, \mathbf{y})$. *Then there exists a term* $t(\mathbf{a})$ *such that* $T \vdash \forall \mathbf{x} \exists \mathbf{y} \prec t(\mathbf{x})\, A(\mathbf{x}, \mathbf{y})$*, where* $\exists (y_1, \ldots, y_n) \prec t :\Leftrightarrow \exists y_1 \prec t \cdots \exists y_n \prec t$.

Here are two typical examples.

1. $\mathcal{L}$ is a language for arithmetic with an individual constant 0 (zero) and the less than relation $<$. Then the first condition says that $\max\{s, t\} \leq r$, the second $\max\{s + 1, t\} \leq r$, and the third $\max\{t(b) : b < s\} \leq r$ provided that T proves the transitivity of $<$ and $x < x + 1$.
2. $\mathcal{L}$ is a language for set theory with an individual constant $\emptyset$ and the membership relation $\in$. Then the first condition says that $s \cup t \subset r$, the second $\{s\} \cup t \subset r$, and the third $\bigcup\{t(b) : b \in s\} \subset r$.

Proof Let us show Theorem 2.12. Assume $T \vdash \exists \mathbf{y}\, A(\mathbf{a}, \mathbf{y})$. Then there is a list of axioms $\forall \mathbf{z} B_i$ $(B_i \in \Delta_0^{\prec})$ in T such that $G_1^{\prec} \vdash \Gamma_0, \exists \mathbf{y}\, A(\mathbf{a}, \mathbf{y})$ for $\Gamma_0 = \{\exists \mathbf{z} \neg B_i\}_i$, where $G_1^{\prec}$ denotes a sequent calculus obtained from G_1 by adding two inference rules for bounded quantifiers:

$$\frac{\Gamma, s \prec t \quad \Gamma, A(s)}{\Gamma}\ (b\exists) \qquad \frac{\Delta, a \not\prec t, \neg A(a)}{\Delta}\ (b\forall)$$

where $(\exists x \prec t\, A(x)) \in \Gamma$ in $(b\exists)$, and $(\forall x \prec t \neg A(x)) \in \Delta$ with the eigenvariable a in $(b\forall)$. Obviously $G_1^{\prec}$ admits a cut-elimination, and we can assume that each cut-free proof enjoys the pure variable condition in Definition 1.3.

Each formula in the cut-free proof of $\Gamma_0, \exists \mathbf{y}\, A(\mathbf{a}, \mathbf{y})$ is either bounded or a $\Sigma_1^{\prec}$-formula. Let us show by induction on the depth of cut-free proofs that there exists a term t such that $FVar(t) \subset FVar(\Gamma_0 \cup \Delta)$ and $T \vdash \Gamma_0, \Delta^t$, where Γ_0, Δ is a sequent in the cut-free proof, and $\Delta^t = \{B^t : B \in \Delta\}$ and B^t is obtained from B by restricting every unbounded existential quantifier $\exists y$ in B to $\exists y \prec t$. Then for $\Delta = \{\exists \mathbf{y}\, A(\mathbf{a}, \mathbf{y})\}$ we obtain $T \vdash \Gamma_0, \exists \mathbf{y} \prec t\, A(\mathbf{a}, \mathbf{y})$ for a term t.

Inference rules are $(\lor)$, $(\land)$, $(b\exists)$, $(b\forall)$, $(\exists)$. We consider $(\land)$, $(b\forall)$, $(\exists)$.

First suppose that the last inference rule is an $(\land)$.

$$\frac{\Gamma_0, \Delta, B_0 \quad \Gamma_0, \Delta, B_1}{\Gamma_0, \Delta}\ (\land)$$

where $B_0 \land B_1$ is in $\Gamma_0 \cup \Delta$.

By IH we have terms t_i $(i = 0, 1)$ such that $FVar(t_i) \subset FVar(\Gamma_0 \cup \Delta)$ and $\Gamma_0, \Delta^{t_i}, B_i$ is provable in T. By the first condition in the theorem pick a term t such that $\forall x(x \prec t_0 \lor x \prec t_1 \to x \prec t)$. Then Γ_0, Δ^t, B_i, and hence Γ_0, Δ^t in T.

Next suppose that the last inference rule is an $(\exists)$.

$$\frac{\Gamma_0, \Delta, \exists \mathbf{y}^i A(\mathbf{a}, \mathbf{s}_i, s, \mathbf{y}^i)}{\Gamma_0, \Delta} \ (\exists)$$

where $\exists y_i, \mathbf{y}^i A(\mathbf{a}, \mathbf{s}_i, y_i, \mathbf{y}^i)$ is in Δ, $\mathbf{s}_i = s_1, \ldots, s_{i-1}$ a list of terms, $\mathbf{y}^i = y_{i+1}, \ldots, y_n$ for $\mathbf{y} = y_1, \ldots, y_n$.

By IH we have a term t such that $FVar(s) \cup FVar(t) \subset FVar(\Gamma_0 \cup \Delta)$ and $\Gamma_0, \Delta^t, \exists \mathbf{y}^i \prec t A(\mathbf{a}, \mathbf{s}_i, s, \mathbf{y}^i)$ is provable in T. By the second condition in the theorem pick a term r such that $s \prec r$ and $\forall y \prec t(y \prec r)$. Then $T \vdash \Gamma_0, \Delta^r$.

Finally suppose that the last inference rule is a $(b\forall)$.

$$\frac{\Gamma_0, \Delta, b \not\prec s \quad \Gamma_0, \Delta, B(b)}{\Gamma_0, \Delta} \ (b\forall)$$

where $\forall x \prec s\, B(x) \in \Gamma_0 \cup \Delta$.

By IH we have a term $t(b)$ such that $FVar(t) \subset FVar(\Gamma_0 \cup \Delta) \cup \{b\}$ and $\Gamma_0, \Delta^{t(b)}, B(b)$ is provable in T. By the third condition pick a term r such that $\forall x \prec s \forall y \prec t(x)(y \prec r)$. Then we obtain $\Gamma_0, \Delta^r, b \not\prec s, B(b)$, and hence Γ_0, Δ^r.

□

In the following Corollary 2.5.1, $\mathcal{L}_0$ denotes a language for arithmetic such that $\{0, S, <\} \subset \mathcal{L}_0$, where $S(x)$ is the successor function $S(x) = x + 1$. Assume that there exists a term $t_{\max}(a, b)$ such that $a, b \le t_{\max}(a, b)$, and for each term $t(\mathbf{a}, b)$, there is a term s such that $s(\mathbf{a}, c) \ge \max\{t(\mathbf{a}, b) : b < c\}$. Let $I\Delta_0(\mathcal{L}_0)$ denote a bounded arithmetic in $\mathcal{L}_0$, i.e., each axiom in $I\Delta_0(\mathcal{L}_0)$ is a universal closure of a bounded formula in $\mathcal{L}_0$. Assume that $I\Delta_0(\mathcal{L}_0)$ proves the above facts, e.g., $\forall x(x < S(x))$, the fact that $<$ is a linear ordering, $b < c \to t(\mathbf{a}, b) \le s(\mathbf{a}, c)$. $I\Delta_0(\mathcal{L}_0)$ may comprise the complete induction schema for $\Delta_0(\mathcal{L}_0)$-formulas: $A(0) \land \forall y < a(A(y) \to A(S(y))) \to A(a)$ for $A \in \Delta_0(\mathcal{L}_0)$,

Here are two examples: $\mathcal{L}_0 = \{0, S, <, +\}, \{0, S, <, +, \cdot\}$.

In Corollary 2.5.2, $\mathcal{L}_1$ denotes a language for set theory such that the set $\mathcal{F}_1$ of function symbols in $\mathcal{L}_1$ is rudimentary closed, i.e., the projections $\pi^n_i(a_1, \ldots, a_n) = a_i$, the pair $\{a, b\}$, the difference $a - b$ are in $\mathcal{F}_1$, and $\mathcal{F}_1$ is closed under composition and rudimentary union $f(\mathbf{x}, z) = \bigcup\{g(\mathbf{x}, y) : y \in z\}$. Also assume that the individual constant $\emptyset$ is in $\mathcal{L}_1$. Then for each term t, there is a term s such that $s(\mathbf{a}, c) = \bigcup\{t(\mathbf{a}, b) : b \in c\}$.

Let $\mathsf{RUD}(\mathcal{L}_1)$ denote a bounded set theory in $\mathcal{L}_1$. The axiom $a \subset b \land b \subset a \to a = b$ of extensionality is assumed to be in $\mathsf{RUD}(\mathcal{L}_1)$. Also assume that $\mathsf{RUD}(\mathcal{L}_1)$ comprises the defining axioms for function symbols, e.g., $a \in \bigcup\{g(\mathbf{x}, y) : y \in z\} \leftrightarrow \exists y \in z(a \in g(\mathbf{x}, y))$.

$\mathcal{L}_1$ may contain a function symbol $\mathscr{P}(a)$ of the power set of a. The axiom for it is a Π_1-formula, $\forall x \in \mathscr{P}(a)(x \subset a) \land \forall x(x \subset a \to x \in \mathscr{P}(a))$. Or $\mathcal{L}_1$ may contain an individual constant ω with the axiom $\emptyset \in \omega \land \forall x \in \omega(x \cup \{x\} \in \omega)$ and $\forall y[\emptyset \in y \land \forall x \in y(x \cup \{x\} \in y) \to \omega \subset y]$. Or $\mathcal{L}_1$ may contain a function symbol $\mathrm{TC}(a)$ of the transitive closure of a together with the axiom: $Tran(\mathrm{TC}(a)) \land a \subset \mathrm{TC}(a) \land \forall x(Tran(x) \land a \subset x \to \mathrm{TC}(a) \subset x)$ for $Tran(a) :\Leftrightarrow \forall x \in a \forall y \in x(y \in a)$. When $\mathrm{TC}(a)$ is in the language, the transfinite induction schema for $\Delta_0(\mathcal{L}_1)$-formulas A is in $\mathsf{RUD}(\mathcal{L}_1)$: $\forall x \in \mathrm{TC}(a \cup \{a\})(\forall y \in x\, A(y) \to A(x)) \to A(a)$.

Note that in these examples, there is a Π_1-formula $A(\mathbf{x}, y)$ defining the graph of the function $f(\mathbf{x}) = y$ such that $\bigwedge_{i=0,1} A(\mathbf{x}, y_i) \to y_0 = y_1$ follows solely from the axiom of extensionality.

Corollary 2.5 *1. If $I\Delta_0(\mathcal{L}_0) \vdash \forall \mathbf{x} \exists y A(\mathbf{x}, y)$ with a $\Sigma_1(\mathcal{L}_0)$-formula A. Then there is a term t such that $I\Delta_0(\mathcal{L}_0) \vdash \forall \mathbf{x} \exists y < t(\mathbf{x}) A(\mathbf{x}, y)$.*

2. If $\mathsf{RUD}(\mathcal{L}_1) \vdash \forall \mathbf{x} \exists y A(\mathbf{x}, y)$ with a $\Sigma_1(\mathcal{L}_1)$-formula A. Then there is a term t such that $\mathsf{RUD}(\mathcal{L}_1) \vdash \forall \mathbf{x} \exists y \in t(\mathbf{x}) A(\mathbf{x}, y)$.

2.2.6 *Primitive Recursion*

Let T be either an arithmetic or a set theory. When T is an arithmetic, D denotes the set of natural numbers $\mathbb{N}$, and Σ_n, Π_n the class of formulas in a language of arithmetic, which define sets in the arithmetical hierarchy in $D = \mathbb{N}$. When T is a set theory, D denotes a well-founded universe such that $(D, \in) \models T$, and Σ_n, Π_n the class of formulas in the Lévy hierarchy.

A formula $A(x_1, \ldots, x_k, y)$ *defines a total function* in a theory T if

$$T \vdash \forall x_1, \ldots, x_k \exists ! y\, A(x_1, \ldots, x_k, y) \tag{2.16}$$

A total function $f : D^k \to D$ is said to be a *provably total Σ_n-function* in T, or *provably Σ_n-definable* in T if there exists a Σ_n-formula $A(x_1, \ldots, x_k, y)$ which defines a total function in T, and

$$\forall a_1, \ldots, a_k, b \in D[f(a_1, \ldots, a_k) = b \Leftrightarrow D \models A(\bar{a}_1, \ldots, \bar{a}_k, \bar{b})] \tag{2.17}$$

where $\bar{a}$ denotes the name of $a \in D$.

In this case we say that the Σ_n-formula A defines the function f in T, or the formula A Σ_n-defines f in T. A provably total Σ_1-function in T is said to be *provably computable* (or provably recursive) in T.

Let us denote the class of provably total Σ_n-functions in a theory T by $Fnc_{\Sigma_n}(T)$.

Proposition 2.3 *The class $Fnc_{\Sigma_n}(T)$ is closed under composition for $n > 0$.*

Proof For simplicity let us consider unary functions. Let $h(x) = g(f(x))$ for $f, g \in Fnc_{\Sigma_n}(T)$. Pick Σ_n-formulas A, B which define the functions f, g in T. Then the Σ_n-formula $C(x, z) :\Leftrightarrow \exists y[A(x, y) \wedge B(y, z)]$ defines the function h in T. □

Next we show that no new function becomes provably Σ_n-definable in the presence of true Σ_{n+1}-assumptions for arithmetics $T \supset I\Sigma_{n-1}$. Tr_{Σ_n} denotes the set of true Σ_n-sentences on $\mathbb{N}$.

Let $B\Pi_n$ denote the collection schema for Π_n-formulas, where $B\Pi_{-1}$ denotes a true sentence $0 = 0$. $L\Pi_n$ denotes the least number principle for Π_n-formulas. It is known that $I\Sigma_n = I\Pi_n = L\Pi_n \supset B\Sigma_{n+1} = B\Pi_n$, cf. [10], p. 63.

Proposition 2.4 *Let $T \supset I\Sigma_{n-1}$ an arithmetic for an $n > 0$. Then $Fnc_{\Sigma_n}(T + \mathrm{Tr}_{\Sigma_{n+1}}) = Fnc_{\Sigma_n}(T)$: If a function is provably Σ_n-definable in $T + \mathrm{Tr}_{\Sigma_{n+1}}$, then so is in T.*

Proof Let f be provably Σ_n-definable in $T + \mathrm{Tr}_{\Sigma_{n+1}}$, and $A \equiv \exists z\, A_0(x_1, \ldots, x_k, y, z)$ a Σ_n-formula for which (2.17) and (2.16) holds with the theory $T + \mathrm{Tr}_{\Sigma_{n+1}}$.

Let $\exists z \forall w \neg B(z, w)$ be a true Σ_{n+1}-sentence such that T proves $\exists z \forall w \neg B(z, w) \to \forall x_1, \ldots, x_k \exists y\, A(x_1, \ldots, x_k, y)$. Pick a number p so that $\forall w \neg B(\bar{p}, w)$ is true. Then $T \vdash \forall w \neg B(\bar{p}, w) \to \forall x_1, \ldots, x_k \exists y\, A(x_1, \ldots, x_k, y)$, and for a projection $(y)_i$ such that $(\langle y_0, y_1 \rangle)_i = y_i$ for a paring function $\langle y_0, y_1 \rangle$ we obtain $T \vdash \forall x_1, \ldots, x_k \exists y[B(\bar{p}, y) \vee A_0(x_1, \ldots, x_k, (y)_0, (y)_1)]$. Obviously these functions $(y)_i$ and $\langle y_0, y_1 \rangle$ are in $Fnc_{\Sigma_1}(T)$.

For the formula $C(y) \equiv [B(\bar{p}, y) \vee A_0(x_1, \ldots, x_k, (y)_0, (y)_1)]$, let $y = \mu y.C(y) :\Leftrightarrow (C(y) \wedge \forall z < y \neg C(z))$, which is equivalent to a Σ_n-formula over $T \supset B\Pi_{n-2}$ for the Π_{n-1}-formulas B, A_0. Since we are assuming that $L\Pi_{n-1} \subset T$, we obtain $T \vdash \forall x_1, \ldots, x_k \exists! y[y = \mu y.C(y)]$.

Thus the Σ_n-formula $y = \mu y.C(y)$ defines a function g in T such that $f(x_1, \ldots, x_k) = (g(x_1, \ldots, x_k))_0$ since $\mathbb{N} \models \forall w \neg B(\bar{p}, w)$. We see that $f \in Fnc_{\Sigma_n}(T)$ from Proposition 2.3. □

Proposition 2.5 *Let $T \supset I\Sigma_{n-1}$ an arithmetic for an $n > 0$. Then each function in $Fnc_{\Sigma_n}(T)$ is elementary in a function in $Fnc_{Bool(\Pi_{n-1})}(T)$, where $Bool(\Pi_{n-1})$ denotes the set of Boolean combinations of Π_{n-1}-formulas.*

Proof Let f be provably Σ_n-definable in T, and $A \equiv \exists z\, A_0(x_1, \ldots, x_k, y, z)$ a Σ_n-formula for which (2.17) and (2.16) holds with the theory T. For the Π_{n-1}-formula $C(y) \equiv [A_0(x_1, \ldots, x_k, (y)_0, (y)_1)]$, $y = \mu y.C(y) :\Leftrightarrow (C(y) \wedge \forall z < y \neg C(z))$ is equivalent to a Boolean combination of Π_{n-1}-formulas over $T \supset B\Pi_{n-2}$, for which $T \vdash \forall x_1, \ldots, x_k \exists! y[y = \mu y.C(y)]$. $y = \mu y.C(y)$ defines a function g in T such that $f(x_1, \ldots, x_k) = (g(x_1, \ldots, x_k))_0$, which is elementary in g. □

Theorem 2.13 *Let $A^+ \equiv \forall u \exists v\, A(u, v)$ be a true Π_2-sentence in a language of arithmetic, and g the computable function defined by $g(u) = \mu v.A(u, v)$. Then $Fnc_{\Sigma_1}(\mathsf{EA} + A^+) \subset \mathcal{E}^3(g)$. Conversely if $\mathsf{EA} + A^+ \vdash A(u, v) \wedge A(u + 1, w) \to v \leq w$, then $\mathcal{E}^3(g) \subset Fnc_{\Sigma_1}(\mathsf{EA} + A^+)$.*

Proof Let $\mathcal{L}_0$ denote the language obtained from the language $\{=, <, 0, 1, +, \cdot, 2^x\}$ of EA by adding function symbols h for each function $h \in \mathcal{E}^3(g)$ elementary in g, and $I\Delta_0(\mathcal{L}_0)$ a definitional extension of $\mathsf{EA} + A^+$ in the language $\mathcal{L}_0$ with defining axioms for function symbols h. Each axiom in $I\Delta_0(\mathcal{L}_0)$ is a Π_1-sentence in $\mathcal{L}_0$. Specifically the axiom for the function g is $\forall u[A(u, \mathsf{g}(u)) \land \forall v < \mathsf{g}(u) \neg A(u, v)]$. Then each term in the language denotes a function in $\mathcal{E}^3(g)$, and the conditions in Theorem 2.12 are enjoyed. For example, $s(\mathbf{a}, c) = \max\{t(\mathbf{a}, b) : b < c\}$ denotes a function in $\mathcal{E}^3(g)$. Suppose $f \in Fnc_{\Sigma_1}(\mathsf{EA} + A^+)$, and let $B \equiv (\exists z\, B_0)$ be a Σ_1-formula which defines f in $\mathsf{EA} + A^+$. Then $\mathsf{EA} + A^+ \vdash \forall x \exists! y\, B$, and hence $I\Delta_0(\mathcal{L}_0) \vdash \forall x \exists y\, B$. By Corollary 2.5.1 pick a term $t(x)$ such that $I\Delta_0(\mathcal{L}_0) \vdash \forall x \exists y < t(x) \exists z < t(x)\, B_0$. Therefore $f(x) = \mu y < t(x)[\exists z < t(x)\, B_0]$ is in $\mathcal{E}^3(g)$.

Conversely assume that g is weakly monotonic provably in $\mathsf{EA} + A^+$. First observe that for each function $f(\mathbf{x})$ in $\mathcal{E}^3(g)$, there exists a weakly monotonic term $t_f(x)$ in $\{2^x, \mathsf{g}\}$ such that $f(\mathbf{x}) \leq t_f(\max \mathbf{x})$, where $t_f(x) \leq t_f(y)$ if $x \leq y$. Then by induction on the construction of $f \in \mathcal{E}^3(g)$, show that there exist a bounded formula $A_f(\mathbf{x}, y, s)$ in the language $\{=, <, 0, 1, +, \cdot, 2^x\}$ and a weakly monotonic term $s_f(x)$ in $\{2^x, \mathsf{g}\}$ such that $\mathsf{EA} + A^+ \vdash s = \bar{g}(s_f(\mathbf{x})) \to \exists! y\, A_f(\mathbf{x}, y, s)$, where $s = \bar{g}(a)$ designates that s is a sequence of length a such that for any $u < a$, $A(u, (s)_u)$. Moreover $f(\mathbf{x}) = y$ iff $\mathbb{N} \models \exists s[A_f(\mathbf{x}, y, s) \land s = \bar{g}(s_f(\mathbf{x}))]$. On the other hand we have $\mathsf{EA} + A^+ \vdash \forall a \exists s(s = \bar{g}(a))$ since such an s is a finite function from $\{0, \ldots, a \dot{-} 1\}$ to $\{0, \ldots, g(a \dot{-} 1)\}$. Hence $f \in Fnc_{\Sigma_1}(\mathsf{EA} + A^+)$. □

Let $I\Sigma_1(PR)$ denote a fragment of first-order arithmetic with function symbols for primitive recursive functions. The complete induction schema is restricted to $\Sigma_1(PR)$-formulas: $B(0) \land \forall x < a(B(x) \to B(S(x)) \to B(a)$ for $\Sigma_1(PR)$-formula $B(x)$.

Proposition 2.6 $I\Sigma_1(PR) \vdash \Sigma_1(PR)\text{-Col} = B\Sigma_1(PR)$.

Proof We show that $I\Sigma_1(PR)$ proves $\forall x < a \exists y\, B(x, y) \to \exists z \forall x < a \exists y < z\, B(x, y)$ for $\Delta_0(PR)$-formulas B. Assuming $\forall x < a \exists y\, B(x, y)$, we show $C(b) :\equiv (b \leq a \to \exists z \forall x < b \exists y < z\, B(x, y))$ by induction on b. $C(0)$ is clear, and supposing $C(b)$, let $b + 1 \leq a$. Pick a z such that $\forall x < b \exists y < z\, B(x, y)$ by $C(b)$. On the other side let y be such that $B(b, y)$ by the assumption. Then for $w = \max\{z, y + 1\}$ we obtain $\forall x < b + 1 \exists u < w\, B(x, u)$. We have shown that $\forall x < a \exists y\, B(x, y) \to [C(0) \land \forall b(C(b) \to C(b + 1))]$. Hence $\forall x < a \exists y\, B(x, y) \to \exists z \forall x < a \exists y < z\, B(x, y)$ by $\Sigma_1(PR)$-induction in $\Sigma_1(PR)$.

When B is a $\Sigma_1(PR)$-formula $\exists u\, C$, consider the $\Delta_0(PR)$-formula $B_0(x, v) :\Leftrightarrow \exists y, u < v\, C$. Note that we have $\exists y\, B(x, y) \to \exists v\, B_0(x, v)$ and $\exists v < w\, B_0(x, v) \to \exists y < w\, B(x, y)$. □

In the following theorem let $A^+ \equiv \forall u \exists v\, A(u, v)$ be a true Π_2-sentence in a language of arithmetic, and g the computable function defined by $g(u) = \mu v.A(u, v)$. $I\Delta_0(PR(g)) + \forall u\, A(u, \mathsf{g}(u))$ denotes an arithmetic in the language with function symbols f for (the definitions of) primitive-recursive-in g functions f. The complete induction schema is restricted to bounded formulas in the language, and the axiom $\forall u\, A(u, \mathsf{g}(u))$ is augmented for a function symbol g for the function g.

Theorem 2.14 (Parsons–Mints–Takeuti) *If* $I\Sigma_1(PR) + A^+ \vdash \forall \mathbf{x} \exists y\, C(\mathbf{x}, y)$ *with* $C \in \Sigma_1(PR)$*, then* $I\Delta_0(PR(g)) + \forall u\, A(u, \mathsf{g}(u)) \vdash \forall \mathbf{x}\, C(\mathbf{x}, f(\mathbf{x}))$ *for a function* f *primitive recursive in* g.

Proof It suffices to show the existence of a primitive-recursive-in g function f such that $I\Delta_0(PR(g)) + \forall u\, A(u, \mathsf{g}(u)) \vdash \forall \mathbf{x}\, C(\mathbf{x}, f(\mathbf{x}))$ assuming $I\Sigma_1(PR(g)) \vdash \forall u\, A(u, \mathsf{g}(u)) \to \forall \mathbf{x} \exists y\, C(\mathbf{x}, y)$ with $C \in \Delta_0$.

Assume that $\mathbf{G}^< + (\Sigma_1(PR(g))\text{-Ind}) \vdash \Gamma_0, \exists u \neg A(u, \mathsf{g}(u)), \exists y\, C(\mathbf{a}, y)$, where Γ_0 is a finite set of negations of bounded axioms other than $(\Sigma_1(PR(g))\text{-Ind})$, and $\mathbf{G}^< + (\Sigma_1(PR(g))\text{-Ind})$ is obtained from $\mathbf{G}^<$ by adding the following inference rule for the $\Sigma_1(PR(g))$-induction schema:

$$\frac{\Gamma, \exists y\, B(0, y) \quad \Gamma, b \not< t, \neg B(b, y), \exists z\, B(b+1, z) \quad \neg B(t, a), \Gamma}{\Gamma}\ (\Sigma_1(PR(g))\text{-Ind})$$

for terms t, eigenvariables b, y, a and $B \in \Delta_0(PR(g))$.

$\mathbf{G}^< + (\Sigma_1(PR(g))\text{-Ind})$ admits a cut-elimination. Each sequent in the cut-free proof of $\Gamma_0, \exists u \neg A(u, \mathsf{g}(u)), \exists y\, C(\mathbf{a}, y)$ is of the form Γ_0, Δ with $\Delta \subset \Delta_0(PR(g)) \cup \Sigma_1(PR(g))$.

As in the proof of Theorem 2.12, show by induction on the depth of cut-free proofs that there exists a term t such that $FVar(t) \subset FVar(\Gamma_0 \cup \Delta)$ and $I\Delta_0(PR(g)) \vdash \Gamma_0, \Delta^t$. In particular we obtain $I\Delta_0(PR(g)) \vdash \exists u < t(\mathbf{a}) \neg A(u, \mathsf{g}(u)), \exists y < t(\mathbf{a})\, C(\mathbf{a}, y)$. Hence $I\Delta_0(PR(g)) + \forall u\, A(u, \mathsf{g}(u)) \vdash C(\mathbf{a}, f(\mathbf{a}))$ for $f(\mathbf{a}) = \min\{y < t(\mathbf{a}) : C(\mathbf{a}, y)\}$.

Consider the case when the last inference rule is a $(\Sigma_1(PR(g))\text{-Ind})$.

$$\frac{\Gamma_0, \Delta, \exists y\, B(0, y) \quad \Gamma_0, \Delta, b \not< s, \neg B(b, y), \exists z\, B(b+1, z) \quad \neg B(s, a), \Gamma_0, \Delta}{\Gamma_0, \Delta}\ (\Sigma_1(PR(g))\text{-Ind})$$

By IH we have a term t_0 such that $FVar(t_0) \subset \mathbf{a} := FVar(\Gamma_0 \cup \Delta)$ and $I\Delta_0(PR(g)) \vdash \Gamma_0, \Delta^{t_0}, \exists y < t_0\, B(0, y)$, and a term $t_1(b, y)$ such that $FVar(t_1) \subset FVar(\Gamma_0 \cup \Delta) \cup \{b, y\}$ and $I\Delta_0(PR(g)) \vdash \Gamma_0, \Delta^{t_1(b,y)}, b \not< s, \neg B(b, y), \exists z < t_1\, B(b+1, z)$. Also there is a term t_2 such that $FVar(t_2) \subset FVar(\Gamma_0 \cup \Delta) \cup \{a\}$ and $I\Delta_0(PR(g)) \vdash \neg B(s, a), \Gamma_0, \Delta^{t_2(a)}$.

Let $f(\mathbf{a}, b)$ be the function defined by $f(\mathbf{a}, 0) = t_0(\mathbf{a})$, $f(\mathbf{a}, b+1) = \max(\{t_1(\mathbf{a}, b, y) : y < f(\mathbf{a}, b)\} \cup \{f(\mathbf{a}, b)\})$. By induction on b we see that $I\Delta_0(PR(g)) \vdash \Gamma_0, \Delta^{f(\mathbf{a},b)}, \exists y < f(\mathbf{a}, b)\, B(b, y)$. Hence $I\Delta_0(PR(g)) \vdash \Gamma_0, \Delta^{f(\mathbf{a},s)}, \exists y < f(\mathbf{a}, s)\, B(s, y)$. On the other hand we have $I\Delta_0(PR(g)) \vdash \forall y < f(\mathbf{a}, s) \neg B(s, a), \Gamma_0, \Delta^{k(\mathbf{a})}$ for $k(\mathbf{a}) = \max\{t_2(a) : a < f(\mathbf{a}, s)\}$. Therefore a (cut) yields $I\Delta_0(PR(g)) \vdash \Gamma_0, \Delta^{h(\mathbf{a})}$ for $h(\mathbf{a}) = \max\{f(\mathbf{a}, s), k(\mathbf{a})\}$. □

Corollary 2.6 WKL_0 *is* Π_2*-conservative over* $I\Sigma_1$.

Proof (Cf. Sect. 1.3 for WKL_0.) First let us formulate a sequent calculus $\mathbf{G}(\mathsf{WKL}_0)$ for the subsystem WKL_0 using Proposition 1.8 and the fact that Π_1-RD yields Δ_1-Comprehension Axiom. $\mathbf{G}(\mathsf{WKL}_0)$ is obtained from the calculus $\mathbf{G}^< + (\Sigma_1(PR)\text{-Ind})$ in the proof of Theorem 2.14 by adding the following inference rule for Π_1-Reduction axiom: for bounded formulas A_0, B_0 possibly with first-order and second-order parameters

$$\frac{\Gamma, \neg A_0(m,n) \lor \neg B_0(k,n) \quad \exists m,n,k[(A_0(m,n) \land \overline{X}(n)) \lor (X(n) \land B_0(k,n))], \Gamma}{\Gamma} \; (\Pi_1\text{-RD})$$

where m, n, k, X are eigenvariables. The inference rule says the Π_1-Reduction axiom in (1.2) for Σ_1-formulas $A(n) :\equiv \exists m\, A_0(m,n)$ and $B(n) :\equiv \exists k\, B_0(k,n)$.

Suppose that $\mathsf{WKL}_0 \vdash \exists y\, C(a,y)$ for a Δ_0-formula C. There exists a cut-free $G(\mathsf{WKL}_0)$-proof of $\Gamma_0, \exists y\, C(a,y)$ for negations Γ_0 of Π_1-axioms. Each sequent in the cut-free proof is of the form Γ_0, Δ with $\Delta \subset \Delta_0(PR) \cup \Sigma_1(PR)$. Let us show that there exists a term t such that $FVar(t) \subset FVar(\Gamma_0 \cup \Delta)$ and $I\Delta_0(PR) \vdash \Gamma_0, \Delta^t$ by induction on the number of nested applications of the inference rules (Π_1-RD). From the proof of Theorem 2.14 we see the existence of such a term t when the inference rule (Π_1-Red) does not occur in the cut-free proof. Consider the inference.

$$\frac{\Gamma_0, \Delta, \neg A_0(m,n) \lor \neg B_0(k,n) \quad \exists m,n,k[(A_0(m,n) \land \overline{X}(n)) \lor (X(n) \land B_0(k,n))], \Gamma_0, \Delta}{\Gamma_0, \Delta} \; (\Pi_1\text{-RD})$$

By IH we have a term t_0 such that $I\Delta_0(PR) \vdash \exists m,n,k < t_0[(A_0(m,n) \land \overline{X}(n)) \lor (X(n) \land B_0(k,n))], \Gamma_0, \Delta^{t_0}$. In the $I\Delta_0(PR)$-proof, substitute the bounded formula $\exists m < t_0\, A_0(m,n)$, i.e., the abstract $\{n\}(\exists m < t_0\, A_0(m,n))$ for $X(n)$. This results in a $I\Delta_0(PR)$-proof of $\exists n,k < t_0[(\exists m < t_0\, A_0(m,n) \land \neg\exists m < t_0\, A_0(m,n)) \lor (\exists m < t_0\, A_0(m,n) \land B_0(k,n))], \Gamma_0, \Delta^{t_0}$. Hence we obtain $I\Delta_0(PR) \vdash \exists m,n,k < t_0 [A_0(m,n) \land B_0(k,n)], \Gamma_0, \Delta^{t_0}$. On the other side IH yields a term $t_1(m,n,k)$ such that $I\Delta_0(PR) \vdash \Gamma_0, \Delta^{t_1(m,n,k)}, \neg A_0(m,n) \lor \neg B_0(k,n)$. For the term $t = \max(\{t_1(m,n,k) : m,n,k < t_0\} \cup \{t_0\})$ we obtain $I\Delta_0(PR) \vdash \Gamma_0, \Delta^t, \neg\exists m,n,k < t_0[A_0(m,n) \land B_0(k,n)]$. A (cut) yields $I\Delta_0(PR) \vdash \Gamma_0, \Delta^t$. □

2.2.7 *Primitive Recursion on Sets*

The set of primitive-recursive-in-$\mathcal{G}$ functions is generated from functions in a collection $\mathcal{G}$ of functions on sets, projections, null $\emptyset$, conditional $C(a,b,c,d) = a$ if $c \in d$, b else, and $M(a,b) = a \cup \{b\}$, and operating composition and set recursion:

$$f(x, \mathbf{y}) = h(x, \mathbf{y}, \{f(z, \mathbf{y}) : z \in x\}).$$

Assume that the collection $\mathcal{G}$ is *extensionally Π_1-definable*. This means that for each $g \in \mathcal{G}$, a Π_1-formula θ_{g} is assigned so that for any $\mathbf{a} = (a_0, \ldots, a_{m-1})$ and any b,

$$[g(\mathbf{a}) = b \Leftrightarrow V \models \theta_{\mathrm{g}}(\mathbf{a}, b)] \text{ and } [Ext \vdash \bigwedge_{i=0,1} \theta_{\mathrm{g}}(\mathbf{x}, y_i) \to y_0 = y_1] \quad (2.18)$$

where Ext denotes the axiom of extensionality. For example the power set $\mathcal{P}(a)$, ω and the transitive closure $\mathrm{TC}(a)$ are extensionally Π_1-definable, cf. Sect. 2.2.5.

Introduce a function symbol g denoting the function $g \in \mathcal{G}$, and $\Delta_0(\mathcal{G})$ denotes the set of bounded formulas in the language $\mathcal{L}(\mathcal{G}) = \{\in\} \cup \{\mathsf{g} : g \in \mathcal{G}\}$, cf. Sect. 1.5. Let $\mathsf{KP}_{\Sigma_1}(\mathcal{G})$ denote the set theory KP_{Σ_1} in the language $\mathcal{L}(\mathcal{G})$. Its axioms are extensionality, pair, union, $\Delta_0(\mathcal{G})$-Separation schema, $\Delta_0(\mathcal{G})$-Collection schema and equality axioms for function symbols g, $\forall \mathbf{x} \forall \mathbf{y}[\mathbf{x} = \mathbf{y} \to \mathsf{g}(\mathbf{x}) = \mathsf{g}(\mathbf{y})]$ and $\forall \mathbf{x}\, \theta_{\mathsf{g}}(\mathbf{x}, \mathsf{g}(\mathbf{x}))$ where θ_{g} is a Π_1-formula assigned to the function g with (2.18).

A set-theoretic function F is said to be *$\Sigma_1(\mathcal{G})$-definable in* $\mathsf{KP}_{\Sigma_1}(\mathcal{G})$ if there exists a $\Sigma_1(\mathcal{G})$-formula A such that $\mathsf{KP}_{\Sigma_1}(\mathcal{G}) \vdash \forall \mathbf{x} \exists! y\, A(\mathbf{x}, y)$, and $F(\mathbf{x}) = y$ iff $V \models A(\mathbf{x}, y)$ for any $\mathbf{x}$, y.

Let $\mathsf{KP}_{\Sigma_1}(\mathcal{G})^{PR}$ denote a definitional extension of $\mathsf{KP}_{\Sigma_1}(\mathcal{G})$ with function symbols f for primitive-recursive-in $\mathcal{G}$ functions f.

Theorem 2.15 *Suppose that* $\mathsf{KP}_{\Sigma_1}(\mathcal{G}) \vdash \forall \mathbf{x} \exists! y\, A(\mathbf{x}, y)$ *for a* $\Sigma_1(\mathcal{G})$*-formula* A. *Then there exists a primitive-recursive-in* $\mathcal{G}$ g *such that* $\mathsf{KP}_{\Sigma_1}(\mathcal{G})^{PR} \vdash A(\mathbf{a}, \mathsf{g}(\mathbf{a}))$.

In particular a set-theoretic function is $\Sigma_1(\mathcal{G})$*-definable in* $\mathsf{KP}_{\Sigma_1}(\mathcal{G})$ *iff it is primitive recursive in* $\mathcal{G}$.

Proof It is easy to see that each primitive-recursive-in-$\mathcal{G}$ function is $\Sigma_1(\mathcal{G})$-definable in $\mathsf{KP}_{\Sigma_1}(\mathcal{G})$. Note that the transitive closure $b = \mathrm{TC}(a)$ of sets a is Σ_1-definable in KP.

For example let $f(x, \mathbf{y}) = h(x, \mathbf{y}, \{f(z, \mathbf{y}) : z \in x\})$ be defined from h by primitive recursion, and φ_h be a $\Sigma_1(\mathcal{G})$-formula for h. We have $\forall z, \mathbf{y}, e \exists! b\, \varphi_h(z, \mathbf{y}, e, b)$ and $h(z, \mathbf{y}, e) = b \Leftrightarrow \varphi_h(z, \mathbf{y}, e, b)$.

Let

$$\begin{aligned} \varphi(x, \mathbf{y}, b; c) :\Leftrightarrow\ & (c \text{ is a function on } \mathrm{TC}(x \cup \{x\})) \land \\ & \forall z \in \mathrm{TC}(x \cup \{x\})\, \varphi_h(z, \mathbf{y}, c''z, c'z) \land (c'x = b) \end{aligned} \tag{2.19}$$

where $c''x = \{c'z : z \in x\}$. Then $f(x, \mathbf{y}) = b$ iff $\exists c\, \varphi(x, \mathbf{y}, b; c)$.

Modulo $\Delta_0(\mathcal{G})$-Collection, $\varphi(x, \mathbf{y}, b; c)$ is equivalent to a $\Sigma_1(\mathcal{G})$-formula $\exists d[d = \mathrm{TC}(x \cup \{x\}) \land \exists e \forall z \in d(\varphi_h(z, \mathbf{y}, \mathbf{a}, c''z, c'z))^{(e)}]$, where unbounded existential quantifiers in φ_h are restricted to e.

We show $\forall \mathbf{y}, x \exists!(b, c)\, \varphi(x, \mathbf{y}, b; c)$. There is nothing to prove for the uniqueness of b. Let $\theta(x, c) :\equiv \varphi(x, \mathbf{y}, c'x; c)$. By ($\Delta_0(\mathcal{G})$-**Collection**), $c''z$ exists as a set for any c and any z. The uniqueness of c, i.e., $\theta(x, c) \land \theta(x, d) \to c = d$ follows from $\Delta_0(\mathcal{G})$-induction.

Suppose $\forall z \in x \exists c\, \theta(z, c)$. We show $\exists c\, \theta(x, c)$ assuming $x \in d_0 = \mathrm{TC}(x_0 \cup \{x_0\})$. Then by $\Sigma_1(\mathcal{G})$-induction we obtain $\forall x \in d_0 \exists c\, \theta(x, c)$. Hence $\exists c\, \theta(x_0, c)$.

By $\Delta_0(\mathcal{G})$-collection pick a d so that $\forall z \in x \exists c \in d(\theta(z, c))^{(d)}$. Let $e = \{c \in d : \exists z \in x(\theta(z, c))^{(d)}\}$ by $\Delta_0(\mathcal{G})$-separation, and $c_0 = \cup e$. Then c_0 is seen to be a function on $\mathrm{TC}(x)$. For $c_1, c_2 \in e$ and $z \in d_1 \cap d_2$ with $d_i = \mathrm{dom}(c_i)$ $(i = 1, 2)$, if $c_1''z = c_2''z$, then $\varphi_h(z, \mathbf{y}, c_i''z, c_i'z)$ for $i = 1, 2$. Hence $c_1'z = c_2'z$. Δ_0-induction with $d_1 \cup d_2 \subset d_0$ yields $c_1 \restriction (d_1 \cap d_2) = c_2 \restriction (d_1 \cap d_2)$. Hence c_0 is a function.

Let b be such that $\varphi_h(x, \mathbf{y}, c_0''x, b)$, and let $c_x = c_0 \cup \{\langle x, b\rangle\}$. Then $\theta(x, c_x)$ as desired.

Conversely let F be $\Sigma_1(\mathcal{G})$-definable in $\mathsf{KP}_{\Sigma_1}(\mathcal{G})$, and A a $\Sigma_1(\mathcal{G})$-formula such that $\mathsf{KP}_{\Sigma_1}(\mathcal{G}) \vdash \forall \mathbf{x}\exists! y\, A(\mathbf{x}, y)$ and $A(\mathbf{x}, y)$ defines the graph of $F(\mathbf{x}) = y$.

Let T be a definitional extension of $\mathsf{KP}_{\Sigma_1}(\mathcal{G})$. T is obtained from $\mathsf{KP}_{\Sigma_1}(\mathcal{G})$ by adding a finite number of function symbols f for Gödel's fundamental operations f together with a defining axiom $\mathsf{f}(\mathbf{x}) = y \leftrightarrow B_{\mathsf{f}}(\mathbf{x}, y)$ with a $B \in \Delta_0(\mathcal{G})$. The axioms for pair, union and $\Delta_0(\mathcal{G})$-Separation are dispensable. Specifically for each $\Delta_0(\mathcal{G})$-formula $B(x; \mathbf{y})$ there exists a term $t_B(a; \mathbf{y})$ such that $t_B(a; \mathbf{y}) = \{x \in a : B(x; \mathbf{y})\}$ is provable from these defining axioms. Cf. [3].

Let us formulate the definitional extension in a sequent calculus $G(\Sigma_1(\mathcal{G}))$. It is obtained from $G^{\in}$ in Sect. 2.2.5 by adding the following inference rules.

1. For $g(\mathbf{x}) \in \mathcal{G}$, let $\theta_{\mathsf{g}}(\mathbf{x}, a) \equiv (\forall c\, \psi_{\mathsf{g}}(\mathbf{x}, a, c))$ be a Π_1-formula assigned to g as in (2.18). Then
$$\frac{\exists c \neg \psi_{\mathsf{g}}(\mathbf{t}, \mathsf{g}(\mathbf{t}), c), \Gamma}{\Gamma}\ (\mathsf{g})$$

2. $$\frac{\Gamma, x \notin t, \exists a\, B(x, a) \quad \exists x \in t \forall a \in c\, B(x, a), \Gamma}{\Gamma}\ (\Delta_0(\mathcal{G})\text{-Col})$$
where B is a $\Delta_0(\mathcal{G})$-formula, and x and c are the *eigenvariables*.

3. $$\frac{\exists x \in y \forall a \in c \neg B(x, a), \exists a\, B(y, a), \Gamma \quad \neg B(t, a), \Gamma}{\Gamma}\ (\Sigma_1(\mathcal{G})\text{-Ind})$$
where B is a $\Delta_0(\mathcal{G})$-formula, and c, y, a are the *eigenvariables*.
Note that $\exists c \forall x \in y \exists a \in c\, B(x, a)$ is equivalent to $\forall x \in y \exists a\, B(x, a)$ in the presence of $(\Delta_0(\mathcal{G})\text{-Col})$.

Suppose that $\mathsf{KP}_{\Sigma_1}(\mathcal{G}) \vdash \forall \mathbf{x}\exists! y\, A(\mathbf{x}, y)$. Let Eq denote the set of equality axioms $\forall a[a = a]$, $\forall a, b, c[a = b \to a = c \to b = c]$, $\forall a, b, c[a = b \to b \in c \to a \in c]$, and equality axioms for function symbols in $\mathcal{L}(\mathcal{G})$. Also let $Ext = \{\forall a, b[\forall c \in a(c \in b) \wedge \forall c \in b(c \in a) \to a = b]\}$ for the extensionality. There exists a cut-free proof of $\neg Eq, \neg Ext, \exists y\, A(\mathbf{a}, y)$ in the sequent calculus $G(\Sigma_1(\mathcal{G}))$. Each sequent in the cut-free proof of $\neg Eq, \neg Ext, \exists y\, A(\mathbf{a}, y)$ is of the form Γ, Δ with $\Gamma \cup \Delta \subset \Delta_0(\mathcal{G}) \cup \Sigma_1(\mathcal{G})$. We show by induction on the depth of cut-free proofs that there exists a primitive-recursive in $\mathcal{G}$ function $f(\mathbf{a})$ such that $\mathbf{a} = FVar(\Gamma \cup \Delta)$ and $\mathsf{KP}_{\Sigma_1}(\mathcal{G})^{PR} \vdash \Gamma, \Delta^{f(\mathbf{a})}$. In particular we have $\mathsf{KP}_{\Sigma_1}(\mathcal{G})^{PR} \vdash \exists y \in f(\mathbf{a})\, A(\mathbf{a}, y)$. On the other hand we have $\mathsf{KP}_{\Sigma_1}(\mathcal{G}) \vdash \exists! y\, A(\mathbf{a}, y)$. Hence $\mathsf{KP}_{\Sigma_1}(\mathcal{G})^{PR} \vdash A(\mathbf{a}, g(\mathbf{a}))$ for $g(\mathbf{a}) = \bigcup f(\mathbf{a})$.

Consider the case when the last inference rule is a $(\Sigma_1(\mathcal{G})\text{-Ind})$.

$$\frac{\exists x \in y \forall a \in c \neg B(x, a), \exists a\, B(y, a), \Gamma, \Delta \quad \neg B(t, a), \Gamma, \Delta}{\Gamma, \Delta}\ (\Sigma_1(\mathcal{G})\text{-Ind})$$

By IH we have a primitive-recursive-in $\mathcal{G}$ function $h(y, c, \mathbf{a}) = h(y, c)$ (for simplicity suppress the parameters $\mathbf{a}$) such that $\exists x \in y \forall a \in c \neg B(x, a), \exists a \in h(y, c) B(y, a), \Gamma, \Delta^{h(y,c)}$, i.e., $\forall y, c[\forall x \in y \exists a \in c\, B(x, a) \to \exists a \in h(y, c)\, B(y, a) \vee \bigvee \Delta^{h(y,c)}] \vee \bigvee \Gamma$. Let $g(y) = \bigcup\{f(x) : x \in y\}$ and $f(y) = h(y, g(y)) \cup g(y)$. f is primitive-recursive-in $\mathcal{G}$. By induction on y we show that $\exists a \in f(y)\, B(y, a) \vee \bigvee \Delta^{f(y)} \vee \bigvee \Gamma$. Assume $\forall x \in y[\exists a \in f(x)\, B(x, a) \vee \bigvee \Delta^{f(x)}]$ and $\neg \bigvee \Delta^{f(y)} \wedge \neg \bigvee \Gamma$. Then $\forall x \in y \exists a \in g(y)\, B(x, a)$. We obtain $\exists a \in h(y, g(y))\, B(y, a) \vee \bigvee \Delta^{h(y,g(y))}$, and hence $\exists a \in f(y)\, B(y, a) \vee \bigvee \Delta^{f(y)}$. Therefore $\exists a \in f(t)\, B(t, a), \Delta^{f(t)}, \Gamma$.

On the other hand we have a primitive-recursive-in $\mathcal{G}$ function $k(a) = k(a, \mathbf{a})$ such that $\neg B(t, a), \Gamma, \Delta^{k(a)}$. Let $p(\mathbf{a}) = f(t) \cup \bigcup\{k(a, \mathbf{a}) : a \in f(t)\}$. Then we obtain $\exists a \in f(t)\, B(t, a), \Delta^{p(\mathbf{a})}, \Gamma$ and $\forall a \in f(t) \neg B(t, a), \Gamma, \Delta^{p(\mathbf{a})}$. A (cut) yields $\Gamma, \Delta^{p(\mathbf{a})}$. □

Exercises

2.1 Let $\boldsymbol{G}_0$ be the propositional fragment of $\boldsymbol{G}_1$. Inference rules in $\boldsymbol{G}_0$ are $(\vee)$ and $(\wedge)$. A set T of propositional formulas is satisfiable iff there is a truth valuation under which every formula in T is true. T is finitely satisfiable iff any finite subset of T is satisfiable. A formula is a logical consequence of T iff the formula is true under any truth valuation validating all formulas in T. Show the followings for sets T of propositional formulas.

1. (Completeness) Show the completeness of $\boldsymbol{G}_0$ by a proof search: If $\bigvee \Lambda$ is a logical consequence of T, then $\boldsymbol{G}_0 + T \vdash \Lambda$.
2. (Cut-elimination) $\boldsymbol{G}_0 + T + (cut) \vdash \Lambda \Rightarrow \boldsymbol{G}_0 + T \vdash \Lambda$.
3. (Compactness) Any finitely satisfiable set T of formulas is satisfiable.

2.2 Show $\boldsymbol{G}_2 \vdash \exists Y^n \forall \mathbf{x}[Y(\mathbf{x}) \leftrightarrow F(\mathbf{x})]$ for any first-order $F \in \Pi^1_0$. (Π^1_0-, or Elementary Comprehension Axiom).

Observe that $(\exists^2_{1st})$ is an admissible rule with Π^1_0-Comprehension Axiom, (cut) and a weak inference rule

$$\frac{\Gamma, \exists X A(X), A(Y)}{\Gamma, \exists X A(X)}$$

2.3 Show the Midsequent Theorem 2.6 by proof search.

2.4 Show that the following Mints normal form theorem 2.16 by proof search.

We assume that the language contains an individual constant. An inference in $\boldsymbol{G}_1$ is said to be *reducible* iff the minor formula in one of its uppersequents can be refuted in the predicate logic. For example, in the figures in Sect. 1.2 $(\wedge)$ is reducible if $\boldsymbol{G}_1 \vdash \neg A_i$ for an $i = 0, 1$, while $(\vee)_i$ is reducible if $\boldsymbol{G}_1 \vdash \neg A_i$. If an inference is reducible, then it can be eliminated by using a (cut). A cut-free proof P enjoying the pure variable condition, cf. Definition 1.3 is said to be in *Mints normal form* if there is no reducible inference in P.

Theorem 2.16 (Mints normal form theorem) *Every sequent provable in first order logic* $G_1 + (cut)$ *has a proof in Mints normal form.*

2.5 Show that Mints normal form theorem 2.16 implies the 2-consistency of PA (over $\mathrm{I}\Sigma_1$).

2.6 Conversely show that Mints normal form theorem 2.16 is implied from the 2-consistency of PA (over $\mathrm{I}\Sigma_1$).

2.7 (Beth's Implicit definability theorem)
Let $Rel(A) = Rel^+(A) \cup Rel^-(A)$, the set of relation symbols occurring in formulas A, cf. Definition 2.4. Let $\mathbf{x} = x_1, \ldots, x_n$ be a list of distinct bound variables, and R, Q n-ary relation symbol such that $Q \notin Rel(\varphi(R))$ and $R \notin Rel(\varphi(Q))$ for a formula φ. Assuming $G_1 \vdash \varphi(R) \land \varphi(Q) \to \forall \mathbf{x}[R(\mathbf{x}) \leftrightarrow Q(\mathbf{x})]$, show that there is a formula C such that $R \notin Rel(C)$ and $G_1 \vdash \varphi(R) \to \forall \mathbf{x}[R(\mathbf{x}) \leftrightarrow C(\mathbf{x})]$.

2.8 Let $\mathbf{x} = x_1, \ldots, x_n$ be a list of distinct bound variables, and R an n-ary relation symbol. Show that the following two condition on formulas $\varphi(R, \mathbf{x})$ is equivalent.

1. φ is logically monotonic with respect to R: For an n-ary relation symbol $Q \notin Rel(\varphi(R, \mathbf{x}))$, $G_1 \vdash \forall \mathbf{x}[Q(\mathbf{x}) \to R(\mathbf{x})] \to \forall \mathbf{x}[\varphi(Q, \mathbf{x}) \to \varphi(R, \mathbf{x})]$.
2. φ is logically equivalent to an R-positive formula: there is a formula $\theta(R, \mathbf{x})$ such that $R \notin Rel^-(\theta)$ and $G_1 \vdash \forall \mathbf{x}[\varphi(R, \mathbf{x}) \leftrightarrow \theta(R, \mathbf{x})]$.

2.9 Assume that $I\Sigma_0(\mathscr{E}^3) \vdash \forall c[A^+(c) \leftrightarrow \neg A^-(c)]$ for Σ^0_2-formulas A^+, A^- with $A^+(c) \equiv \exists z \forall u B(z, u, c)$ and $\neg A^-(c) \equiv \forall x \exists y A(x, y, c)$ for some quantifier-free formulas A, B.

1. Show that there exist a list of variables $\{a_i, b_i : i \leq r\}$ and a list of terms $\{t_i, s_i : i \leq r\}$ such that
$$\bigvee \{A(t_i, a_i, c) \to B(s_i, b_i, c) : i \leq r\} \tag{2.20}$$
is provable in $I\Sigma_0(\mathscr{E}^3)$, and variables occurring in t_i, s_i are among a_j, b_j for $j < i$ besides the parameter c.
2. For simplicity consider the case when $r = 1$. The following is provable in $I\Sigma_0(\mathscr{E}^3)$:
$$\neg A(t_0, a_0, c) \lor B(s_0, b_0, c) \lor \neg A(t_1(a_0, b_0), a_1, c) \lor B(s_1(a_0, b_0), b_1, c) \tag{2.21}$$
Let f denote the elementary recursive predicate such that $f(c, w) = 0$ if either $\{t_0 \leq w \land \exists y \leq w A(t_0, y, c)\} \land \{s_0 \leq w \land \forall u \leq w B(s_0, u, c)\}$ or $\exists a_0, b_0 \leq w$ $\{A(t_0, a_0, c) \land \neg B(s_0, b_0, c) \land \exists a_1 {\leq} w A(t_1(a_0, b_0), a_1, c) \land \forall b_1 {\leq} w B(s_1(a_0, b_0), b_1, c)\}$, and $f(c, w) = 1$ otherwise.
For the number $K := 1 + 2r + 2 (= 5 \text{ if } r = 1)$, let $h : \omega \times \omega \to K$ denote the elementary recursive function defined by $h(c, 0) = K - 1$, and

$$h(c, w+1) := \begin{cases} h(c, w) & \text{if } f(c, w+1) = f(c, w) \\ h(c, w) \dot{-} 1 & \text{if } f(c, w+1) \neq f(c, w) \end{cases}$$

Show that $I\Sigma_0(\mathscr{E}^3)$ proves the following facts.

a. (weakly descending) $K > h(c, w) \geq h(c, w+1)$.
b. (lowering) $f(c, w) \neq f(c, w+1) \to h(c, w) > h(c, w+1)$.
c. (reduction) $\lim_{w\to\infty} f(c, w) = 0 \to \exists z \forall u B(z, u, c)$, $\lim_{w\to\infty} f(c, w) = 1 \to \exists x \forall y \neg A(x, y, c)$, and $\exists z \forall u B(z, u, c) \to \forall x \exists y A(x, y, c)$.

3. Show that provably Δ^0_2-sets in $I\Sigma_0(\mathscr{E}^3)$ are boolean combinations of Σ^0_1-sets. Specifically let A^+, A^- be Σ^0_2-formulas, and assume that $I\Sigma_0(\mathscr{E}^3) \vdash \forall x[A^+(x) \leftrightarrow \neg A^-(x)]$. Then there is a boolean combination C of Σ^0_1-formulas such that $I\Sigma_0(\mathscr{E}^3) \vdash \forall x[A^+(x) \leftrightarrow C(x)]$.

2.10 Consider a first-order language $\mathscr{L}(\{X_i\}_i)$ with predicate variables X_i $(i < \omega)$. For simplicity let us assume that these variables X_i are unary. X denotes an X_i. Let $\forall$-Reduction be the following inference rule for purely universal formulas A, B possibly with first-order and second-order parameters

$$\frac{\Gamma, \forall x(A(x) \vee B(x)) \quad \exists y \exists x(\neg A_0(y, x) \wedge X(x)) \vee \exists z(\overline{X}(z) \wedge \neg B(z)), \Gamma}{\Gamma} \;(\forall\text{-Red})$$

where $A(x) \equiv (\forall y\, A_0(y, x))$ with quantifier-free A_0, and the variable X does not occur in A, B, Γ.

The inference rule says in a second-order logic that if $\forall x(A(x) \vee B(x))$, then $\exists X[\forall x(X(x) \to A(x)) \wedge \forall z(\overline{X}(z) \to B(z))]$.

Let T denote a set of formulas in a first-order language $\mathscr{L}(\{X_i\}_i)$ with predicate variables such that each formula in T has no first-order free variable possibly with predicate variables, and T is closed under substituting quantifier-free formulas C for predicate variables X_i. The latter means that if $A(X) \in T$, then $T \vdash A(C)$, where $A(C)$ is obtained from $A(X)$ by replacing each literal $X(t)$ $[\bar{X}(t)]$ by $C(t)$ $[\neg C(t)]$, resp.

Show that the inference rule $\forall$-Reduction is an admissible rule in T. Namely if $T \vdash \Gamma, \forall x(A(x) \vee B(x))$ and $T \vdash \exists y \exists x(\neg A_0(y, x) \wedge X(x)) \vee \exists z(\overline{X}(z) \wedge \neg B(z)), \Gamma$ for purely universal formulas $A(x) \equiv (\forall y\, A_0(y, x))$ and B, and X does not occur in A, B, Γ, then $T \vdash \Gamma$.

2.11 Let S and T be theories such that $\mathsf{EA} \subset S \subset T$. Assume that S is universally axiomatized, i.e., axioms in S are purely universal formulas $\forall x_1, \dots, x_n A$ with quantifier-free matrices A, and T is a recursively enumerable theory. Let $\mathrm{Con}(T) :\Leftrightarrow \forall x\, \neg \mathrm{Prov}_T(x, \ulcorner \bot \urcorner)$ denote a consistency statement for T, where $\mathrm{Prov}_T(x, y)$ is a standard T-proof predicate such that $Pr_T(y) :\Leftrightarrow \exists x\, \mathrm{Prov}_T(x, y)$ enjoys the three derivability conditions provably in S. Then $\mathrm{Con}^{(n)}(T)$ denotes the iterated consistency of T for $n < \omega$: $\mathrm{Con}^{(0)}(T) :\Leftrightarrow \forall x(0 = 0)$, and $\mathrm{Con}^{(n+1)}(T) :\Leftrightarrow \mathrm{Con}(T + \mathrm{Con}^{(n)}(T))$.

Show that $S + \mathrm{RFN}_{\Sigma_1^0}(T)$ is Π_1^0-conservative over $S + \{\mathrm{Con}^{(m)}(T)) : m < \omega\}$.

2.12 Let T be a bounded theory in a language with an individual constant and a distinguished binary relation symbol $\prec$. Suppose that T enjoys the three conditions in Theorem 2.12.

Let $\Sigma_1^{\prec}$-Col or $B\Sigma_1^{\prec}$ denotes the collection schema

$$\forall x \prec a \exists y\, B(x, y) \to \exists z \forall x \prec a \exists y \prec z\, B(x, y)$$

for $\Sigma_1^{\prec}$-formula $B(x, y) \equiv \exists w\, C(x, y, w)$ with $C \in \Delta_0^{\prec}$.

Show that $T + (\Sigma_1^{\prec}\text{-Col})$ is $\Pi_2^{\prec}$-conservative over T: if $T + (\Sigma_1^{\prec}\text{-Col}) \vdash \forall x \exists y\, C$ with $C \in \Sigma_1^{\prec}$, then $T \vdash \forall x \exists y \prec t\, C$ for a term t.

2.13 $I\Delta_0(\mathcal{L}_0)$ denotes a bounded arithmetic, and $\mathsf{RUD}(\mathcal{L}_1)$ a bounded set theory as in Corollary 2.5. $B\Sigma_1(\mathcal{L}_0)$ denotes a collection schema: $\forall x < a \exists y\, A(x, y) \to \exists z \forall x < a \exists y < z\, A(x, y)$ for $\Sigma_1(\mathcal{L}_0)$-formulas A, and $\Sigma_1(\mathcal{L}_1)$-Col denote a collection schema: $\forall x \in a \exists y\, B(x, y) \to \exists z \forall x \in a \exists y \in z\, B(x, y)$ for $\Sigma_1(\mathcal{L}_1)$-formulas B. Show the following.

1. If $I\Delta_0(\mathcal{L}_0) + (B\Sigma_1(\mathcal{L}_0)) \vdash \forall \mathbf{x} \exists y A(\mathbf{x}, y)$ with a $\Sigma_1(\mathcal{L}_0)$-formula A. Then there is a term t such that $I\Delta_0(\mathcal{L}_0) \vdash \forall \mathbf{x} \exists y < t(\mathbf{x}) A(\mathbf{x}, y)$.
2. If $\mathsf{RUD}(\mathcal{L}_1) + (\Sigma_1(\mathcal{L}_1)\text{-Col}) \vdash \forall \mathbf{x} \exists y A(\mathbf{x}, y)$ with a $\Sigma_1(\mathcal{L}_1)$-formula A. Then there is a term t such that $\mathsf{RUD}(\mathcal{L}_1) \vdash \forall \mathbf{x} \exists y \in t(\mathbf{x}) A(\mathbf{x}, y)$.

For example, the arithmetic $B\Sigma_1$ is Π_2-conservative over $I\Delta_0$. Let KP^- be obtained from the Kripke–Platek set theory KP by deleting the foundation schema. In Exercise 2.13.2 we see that each Σ_1-*definable* set-theoretic function in the theory KP^- is rudimentary.

2.14 Show the following theorem.

Theorem 2.17 (Parsons–Mints) *The Π_2^0-induction rule is an admissible rule in $I\Delta_0(PR)$: $I\Delta_0(PR) \vdash B(0) \land \forall z(B(z) \to B(z + 1)) \Rightarrow I\Delta_0(PR) \vdash \forall z\, B(z)$ for any Π_2^0-formula B.*

2.15 Show over $I\Sigma_1$ that Π_2^0-induction rule proves the totality of the Ackermann function $A(x, y)$ defined by $A(0, y) = y + 1$, $A(x + 1, 0) = A(x, 1)$ and $A(x + 1, y + 1) = A(x, A(x + 1, y))$.

2.16 Let T be a bounded theory in a language with an individual constant and a distinguished binary relation symbol $\prec$. Suppose that T enjoys the three conditions in Theorem 2.12. Let $A(\mathbf{b}, \mathbf{c})$ be a bounded formula with $FV(\exists \mathbf{y} \forall \mathbf{z}\, A(\mathbf{y}, \mathbf{z})) \subset \mathbf{a}$, and assume that $T \vdash \exists \mathbf{y} \forall \mathbf{z}\, A(\mathbf{y}, \mathbf{z})$.

Show that there are terms $t_i(\mathbf{c}_0, \ldots, \mathbf{c}_{i-1})$ such that $FV(t_i(\mathbf{c}_0, \ldots, \mathbf{c}_{i-1})) \subset \mathbf{a} \cup \mathbf{c}_0 \cup \cdots \cup \mathbf{c}_{i-1}$, and T proves
$\exists \mathbf{y}_0 \prec t_0 \forall \mathbf{z}_0 \left[A(\mathbf{y}_0, \mathbf{z}_0) \lor \exists \mathbf{y}_1 \prec t_1(\mathbf{z}_0) \forall \mathbf{z}_1\, (A(\mathbf{y}_1, \mathbf{z}_1) \lor \cdots \lor \exists \mathbf{y}_k \prec t_k \forall \mathbf{z}_k A(\mathbf{y}_k, \mathbf{z}_k))\right]$.

2.17 Let $A^+ \equiv \forall u \exists v\, A(u, v)$ be a true Π^0_2-sentence in a language of arithmetic, and g the computable function defined by $g(u) = \mu v.A(u, v)$. Show that a number-theoretic function is provably computable in $I\Sigma_1 + A^+$ iff it is primitive recursive in g: $Fnc_{\Sigma_1}(I\Sigma_1 + A^+) = PR(g) = \mathcal{E}^{\omega}(g)$.

2.18 Let $T \supset I\Sigma_n$ be an arithmetic for an $n > 0$. Show that $Fnc_{\Sigma_n}(T)$ is closed under primitive recursion.

2.3 Notes

2.3.1 Section 2.1

The canonical proof search goes back to Beth [5], Hintikka [12], Schütte [26] and Kanger [14]. For more on the search method see Kreisel, Mints and Simpson [15].

2.3.2 Section 2.2

Midsequent theorem 2.6 is found in [9]. Theorem 2.7 is due to Lyndon [16], and the method of splitting sequents in the proof of Lemma 2.1 is due to Maehara [18, 29].

For more on Herbrand's theorem in a general form, see Buss [7].

The second epsilon theorem 2.11 goes back to Hilbert and Bernays [11]. Our proof of the theorem is similar to Maehara's in [17].

Corollary 2.5.1 is proved in Parikh [22]. Our proofs of Theorems 2.12 and 2.15 are based on Buss' witnessing argument in his dissertation [6]. Corollary 2.5.2 together with Exercise 2.13.2 seems to be new.

Parsons–Mints–Takeuti Theorem 2.14 is proved in [19, 23, 29].

Corollary 2.6 is due to H. Friedman [28]. A proof-theoretic proof of it is found by Sieg [27], and the proof is directly formalizable in $I\Sigma_1$ (or even in $I\Sigma_0(\mathcal{E}^4)$). Our proof via Π_1-RD is took from a course note (Japanese) given in Research Institute of Mathematical Science, Kyoto, 1991.

Theorem 2.15 is due to Rathjen [25], and the class of primitive recursive set functions is introduced in Jensen and Karp [13].

2.3.3 Exercises

Mints normal form theorem 2.16 in Exercise 2.4 is found in Mints [21], and a proof of it by proof search is in [2]. Exercises 2.5 and 2.6 are also took from [2]. Beth's Implicit definability theorem in Exercise 2.7 is proved in [4]. Exercise 2.8 is due to Feferman [8].

Exercise 2.9 is took from [1]. Parsons–Mints theorem 2.17 in Exercise 2.14 is proved in [20, 24].

References

1. Arai, T.: Provably Δ_2^0 and weakly descending chains. In: Arai, T. Feng, Q., Kim, B., Wu, G., Yang, Y. (eds.) Proceedings of the 11th Asian Logic Conference, pp. 1–21. World Scientific (2011)
2. Arai, T., Mints, G.: Extended normal form theorems for logical proofs from axioms. Theor. Comput. Sci. **232**, 121–132 (2000)
3. Barwise, J.: Admissible Sets and Structures. Springer, Berlin (1975)
4. Beth, E.W.: On Padoa's method in the theory of definition. Indag. Math. **15**, 330–339 (1953)
5. Beth, E.W.: Semantic entailment and formal derivability. Mededelingen der Koninklijke Nederlandse Akademie van Wetenschappen (Amsterdam), Afdeling Letterkunde, Nieuwe Reeks 18, pp. 309–342 (1955)
6. Buss, S.R.: Bounded Arithmetic. Bibliopolis, Napolis (1986)
7. Buss, S.R.: Introduction to Proof Theory. In: Buss, S.R. (ed.) Handbook of Proof Theory, pp. 1–78. Elsevier, Amsterdam (1998)
8. Feferman, S.: Formal theories for transfinite iteration of generalized inductive definitions and some subsystems of analysis. In: Kino, A., Myhill, J., Vesley, R.E. (eds.) Intuitionism and Proof Theory, Proceedings of the Summer Conference at Buffalo, N. Y., 1968, pp. 303–325. North-Holland, Amsterdam (1970)
9. Gentzen, G.: Untersuchungen über das logische Schließen. Math. Z. **39**, I, 176–210: II, 405–431 (1934/35)
10. Hájek, P., Pudlák, P.: Metamathematics of first-order arithmetic. Perspectives in Mathematical Logic. Springer, Berlin (1993)
11. Hilbert, D., Bernays, P.: Grundlagen der Mathematik II, Die Grundlehren der mathematischen Wissenschaften, Bd. 50. Springer, Berlin (1939)
12. Hintikka, K.J.J.: Form and content in quantification theory. Two papers on symbolic logic. Acta Philos. Fenn. **8**, 7–55 (1955)
13. Jensen, R., Karp, C.: Primitive recursive set functions. In: Scott, D. (ed.) Axiomatic Set Theory. Proceedings of Symposia in Pure Mathematics, vol. 13, Part I, pp. 143–176. American Mathematical Society, Providence, RI (1971)
14. Kanger, S.: Provability in logic. Acta Universitatis Stockholmiensis (Stockholm Studies in Philosophy), vol. 1. Almqvist and Wiksell, Stockholm (1957)
15. Kreisel, G., Mints, G.E., Simpson, S.G., The use of abstract language in elementary mathematics: some pedagogic examples. In: Parikh, R. (ed.) Logic Colloquium. Lecture Notes in Mathematics, vol. 453, pp. 38–131. Springer, Berlin (1975)
16. Lyndon, R.C.: An interpolation theorem the predicate logic. Pac. J. Math. **9**, 129–142 (1959)
17. Maehara, S.: The predicate calculus with ε-symbol. J. Math. Soc. Jpn. **7**, 323–344 (1955)
18. Maehara, S.: On the interpolation theorem of Craig (Japanese). Sugaku **12**, 235–237 (1960)
19. Mints, G. E.: Quantifier-free and one-quantifier systems. Zap. Nauchnykh Semin. POMI **20**, 115–133 (1971). Translation in J. Sov. Math. 1, 71–84 (1973)
20. Mints, G. E., What can be done with PRA? Zap. Nauchnykh Semin. POMI **60**, 93–102 (1976). Translation in J. Sov. Math. 14, 1487–1492 (1980)
21. Mints, G.E.: A normal form for logical derivations implying one for arithmetic derivations. Ann. Pure Appl. Log. **62**, 65–79 (1993)
22. Parikh, R.: Existence and feasibility in arithmetic. J. Symb. Log. **36**, 494–508 (1971)
23. Parsons, C.: Ordinal recursion in partial systems of number theory (abstract). Not. AMS **13**, 857–858 (1966)

24. Parsons, C.: On a number-theoretic choice schema and its relation to induction. In: Kino, A., Myhill, J., Vesley, R.E. (eds.) Intuitionism and Proof Theory, Proceedings of the Summer Conference at Buffalo, N. Y., 1968, pp. 459–473. North-Holland, Amsterdam (1970)
25. Rathjen, M.: A proof-theoretic characterization of the primitive recursive set functions. J. Symb. Log. **57**, 954–969 (1992)
26. Schütte, K.: Ein System des verknüpfenden Schlißens. Arch. Math. Log. Grundlagenforschung **2**, 34–67 (1956)
27. Sieg, W.: Fragments of arithmetic. Ann. Pure Appl. Log. **28**, 33–71 (1985)
28. Simpson, S.G.: Subsystems of second order arithmetic. Perspectives in Logic, 2nd edn. Cambridge UP, Cambridge (2009)
29. Takeuti, G.: Proof Theory, 2nd edn. North-Holland, Amsterdam (1987). Reprinted from Dover Publications (2013)

Chapter 3
Cut-Elimination with Depths

In this chapter we first introduce a standard cut-elimination procedure for the first-order logic and the ω-logic, by which we see that the tree-height of the resulting cut-free proofs is bounded by a tower of exponential functions. Such a control of the tree-heights in cut-elimination is one of the most important results in ordinal analysis. A partial cut-elimination with a control holds as well for applied calculi. The partial result is sometimes helpful for us to analyze mathematical theories.

Next we consider a fixed point logic FiX. FiX is obtained from the first-order logic by introducing predicate symbols I_φ for each R-positive formula $\varphi(R, x)$ together with the axiom $I_\varphi(x) \leftrightarrow \varphi(I_\varphi, x)$. Although it is easy to see that FiX is a conservative extension of the first-order logic, a proof of this fact by the completeness theorem does not yield a sharp upper bound for speed-up of FiX over the first-order logic. We give a cut-elimination procedure for FiX, by which we see that the tree-height of the resulting cut-free proofs is bounded by a superexponential function. For a cut-elimination procedure of FiX we employ an *asymmetric interpretation* due to J.-Y. Girard, which is a powerful tool to analyze provable implications of existential formulas.

Third a cut-elimination procedure for the intuitionistic logic $\boldsymbol{G}_1^i$ is given, where (cut) inferences are eliminated in parallel. Here a complexity $\mathrm{dg}^i(A)$ of formulas A is defined so that $\mathrm{dg}^i(A) = 0$ if A is monotonic, i.e., if the implication $\to$ (and the negation $\neg$) does not occur in A. It is shown that monotonic (cut) inferences yield only an elementary speed-up over the cut-free fragment. The result is applied to an intuitionistic fixed point logic FiX^i.

Finally an elimination theorem of epsilon terms is proved.

© The Editor(s) (if applicable) and The Author(s), under exclusive license to Springer Nature Singapore Pte Ltd. 2020

T. Arai, *Ordinal Analysis with an Introduction to Proof Theory*, Logic in Asia: Studia Logica Library, https://doi.org/10.1007/978-981-15-6459-8_3

3.1 Classical Logic

Let $\boldsymbol{G}$ denote one of the calculi $\boldsymbol{G}_i + T + (cut)$ $(i = 1, \omega)$, where T is a set of closed formulas, and each $A \in T$ is codified in $\boldsymbol{G}_i + T$ as an inference rule with *no major formula*, cf. Sect. 2.1.2.

Definition 3.1 $\boldsymbol{G} \vdash^{\alpha}_{c} \Gamma$ iff there exists a proof of Γ in $\boldsymbol{G}$ such that its tree-height is at most α and degree of any cut formula in it is less than c.

Specifically $\boldsymbol{G} \vdash^{\alpha}_{c} \Gamma$ is defined inductively as follows:

1. $\boldsymbol{G} \vdash^{\alpha}_{c} \Gamma$ holds for any α and c if Γ is an axiom in $\boldsymbol{G}$.
2. Let $\dfrac{\{\Gamma_i : i \in I\}}{\Gamma}$ be an inference rule in $\boldsymbol{G}$ other than cut rule. Then $\forall i \in I[\boldsymbol{G} \vdash^{\beta}_{c} \Gamma_i \,\&\, \beta < \alpha] \Rightarrow \boldsymbol{G} \vdash^{\alpha}_{c} \Gamma$.
3. For the cut rule if $\boldsymbol{G} \vdash^{\beta}_{c} \Gamma, \neg C$ and $\boldsymbol{G} \vdash^{\beta}_{c} C, \Delta$ with $\beta < \alpha$ and $\mathrm{dg}(C) < c$, then $\boldsymbol{G} \vdash^{\alpha}_{c} \Gamma, \Delta$.

When no confusion likely occurs, we write $\vdash^{\alpha}_{c} \Gamma$ for $\boldsymbol{G} \vdash^{\alpha}_{c} \Gamma$.

Lemma 3.1 (Weakening lemma with depths) *Assume $\beta \leq \alpha$ and $d \leq c$. Then*

$$\vdash^{\beta}_{d} \Gamma \Rightarrow \vdash^{\alpha}_{c} \Gamma, \Delta.$$

Proof This is seen by induction on β. □

Lemma 3.2 (Inversion lemma)

1. $\boldsymbol{G} \vdash^{\alpha}_{c} \Gamma, A_0 \wedge A_1 \Rightarrow \boldsymbol{G} \vdash^{\alpha}_{c} \Gamma, A_i$ *for* $i = 0, 1$.
2. $\boldsymbol{G}_1 + T + (cut) \vdash^{\alpha}_{c} \Gamma, \forall x A(x) \Rightarrow \boldsymbol{G}_1 + T + (cut) \vdash^{\alpha}_{c} \Gamma, A(t)$ *for any term* t.
3. $\boldsymbol{G}_\omega + T + (cut) \vdash^{\alpha}_{c} \Gamma, \forall x A(x) \Rightarrow \boldsymbol{G}_\omega + T + (cut) \vdash^{\alpha}_{c} \Gamma, A(\bar{n})$ *for any numeral* $\bar{n}$.

Proof We show Lemma 3.2.2 by induction on α.

If $\Gamma, \forall x A(x)$ is an axiom, then so is $\Gamma, A(t)$ since $\forall x A(x)$ is not a major formula of an axiom in $\boldsymbol{G}_1$.

Assume $\Gamma, \forall x A(x)$ is the lowersequent of an inference. If a formula other than $\forall x A(x)$ is the major formula of the inference, then IH(=Induction Hypothesis) yields the assertion. For example

$$\dfrac{\vdash^{\beta}_{c} \Lambda, \forall x A(x), \forall y B(y), B(z)}{\vdash^{\alpha}_{c} \Lambda, \forall x A(x), \forall y B(y)} \ (\forall)$$

for a $\beta < \alpha$, turns into another $(\forall)$

$$\dfrac{\vdash^{\beta}_{c} \Lambda, A(t), \forall y B(y), B(u)}{\vdash^{\alpha}_{c} \Lambda, A(t), \forall y B(y)} \ (\forall)$$

provided that we rename the eigenvariable z if necessary.

Suppose the major formula of the inference is the formula $\forall x A(x)$.

$$\frac{\vdash^{\beta}_{c} \Gamma, \forall x A(x), A(y)}{\vdash^{\alpha}_{c} \Gamma, \forall x A(x)} \ (\forall)$$

for a $\beta < \alpha$. By IH we have $\vdash^{\beta}_{c} \Gamma, A(t), A(y)$. We can assume that y does not occur in t. Then substitute t for y in the whole proof of $\Gamma, A(t), A(y)$ to get $\vdash^{\beta}_{c} \Gamma, A(t), A(t)$. $\beta < \alpha$ yields the assertion. □

Lemma 3.3 (Eliminating false arithmetic literals) *Let L be a false arithmetic literal $\bar{n} = \bar{m}$ $(n \neq m)$, $\bar{n} \neq \bar{n}$ in the language of $\mathbf{G}_\omega$. Then $\mathbf{G}_\omega + T + (cut) \vdash^{\alpha}_{c} \Gamma, L \Rightarrow \mathbf{G}_\omega + T + (cut) \vdash^{\alpha}_{c} \Gamma$.*

Proof By induction on α.

Consider the case when Γ, L is an axiom. If Γ is an axiom,[1] then there is nothing to prove. Otherwise L is a major formula of the axiom. Namely $\Gamma, L = \Lambda, \bar{L}, L$. Since L is false, its complement $\bar{L}$ is a true literal. Hence $\Gamma = \Lambda, \bar{L}$ is another axiom. □

Definition 3.2 A formula is said to be a $\forall$-formula, if it is either a literal or a conjunction $A_0 \wedge A_1$ or a universal formula $\forall x B(x)$.

Lemma 3.4 *Let C be an $\forall$-formula with* $\mathrm{dg}(C) \leq c$. *Then*

$$\mathbf{G} \vdash^{\alpha}_{c} \Gamma, C \;\&\; \mathbf{G} \vdash^{\beta}_{c} \neg C, \Delta \Rightarrow \mathbf{G} \vdash^{\alpha+\beta}_{c} \Gamma, \Delta.$$

Proof By induction on β. By Weakening Lemma 3.1 and $\alpha \leq \alpha + \beta$, we can assume that $C \notin \Delta$ for otherwise $\Gamma \cup \{C\} \subset \Gamma \cup \Delta$.

First consider the case when $\neg C, \Delta$ is an axiom. We can assume that Δ is not an axiom. Since $\neg(\neg C) = C \notin \Delta$, $\neg C$ is a true arithmetic literal and $\mathbf{G} = \mathbf{G}_\omega + T + (cut)$. Use Lemma 3.3 to eliminate the false arithmetic literal C to get $\mathbf{G} \vdash^{\alpha}_{c} \Gamma$. Weakening Lemma 3.1 yields the assertion.

Assume $\neg C, \Delta$ is the lowersequent of an inference. If the major formula of the inference is not the formula $\neg C$, then IH yields the assertion. For example[2]

$$\cfrac{\vdash^{\alpha}_{c} \Gamma, C \qquad \cfrac{\vdash^{\gamma}_{c} \neg C, \Phi, \neg D \quad \vdash^{\gamma}_{c} D, \neg C, \Psi}{\vdash^{\beta}_{c} \neg C, \Phi, \Psi (= \neg C, \Delta)} \ (cut)}{\Gamma, \Delta}$$

for a $\gamma < \beta$ and $\mathrm{dg}(D) < c$. Since $\beta \mapsto \alpha + \beta$ is strictly increasing, IH yields

[1] **Axioms** $\Gamma, \bar{L}, L$ in $\mathbf{G}_\omega$ could be restricted to $L \equiv (t \in X)$, cf. footnote 2. Therefore if Γ, L is an axiom for a false closed literal L, then so is Γ.

[2] Wlog we can assume $\neg C$ occurs in both uppersequents. Otherwise augment $\neg C$ by Weakening Lemma 3.1.

$$\frac{\vdash_c^{\alpha+\gamma} \Gamma, \Phi, \neg D \quad \vdash_c^{\alpha+\gamma} D, \Gamma, \Psi}{\vdash_c^{\alpha+\beta} \Gamma, \Phi, \Psi (= \Gamma, \Delta)} \ (cut)$$

Suppose the major formula of the inference is the formula $\neg C$. There are two cases to consider $C \equiv A_0 \wedge A_1$ and $C \equiv \forall x A(x)$. Consider first the case $C \equiv A_0 \wedge A_1$.

$$\frac{\vdash_c^\alpha \Gamma, A_0 \wedge A_1 \qquad \dfrac{\vdash_c^\gamma \neg A_0 \vee \neg A_1, \Delta, \neg A_i}{\vdash_c^\beta \neg A_0 \vee \neg A_1, \Delta} \ (\vee)_i}{\Gamma, \Delta}$$

for a $\gamma < \beta$. By IH we have $\vdash_c^{\alpha+\gamma} \Gamma, \Delta, \neg A_i$. On the other hand we have $\vdash_c^\alpha \Gamma, A_i$ by Inversion Lemma 3.2, and hence $\vdash_c^{\alpha+\gamma} \Gamma, A_i$ by Weakening Lemma 3.1. Thus $\mathrm{dg}(A_i) < \mathrm{dg}(A_0 \wedge A_1) \leq c$ yields

$$\frac{\vdash_c^{\alpha+\gamma} \Gamma, \Delta, \neg A_i \quad \vdash_c^{\alpha+\gamma} \Gamma, A_i}{\vdash_c^{\alpha+\beta} \Gamma, \Delta} \ (cut)$$

Next let $C \equiv \forall x A(x)$.

$$\frac{\vdash_c^\alpha \Gamma, \forall x A(x) \qquad \dfrac{\vdash_c^\gamma \exists x \neg A(x), \Delta, \neg A(t)}{\vdash_c^\beta \exists x \neg A(x), \Delta} \ (\exists)}{\Gamma, \Delta}$$

for a $\gamma < \beta$. By IH we have $\vdash_c^{\alpha+\gamma} \Gamma, \Delta, \neg A(t)$. On the other hand we have $\vdash_c^\alpha \Gamma, A(t)$ by Inversion Lemma 3.2, and hence $\vdash_c^{\alpha+\gamma} \Gamma, A(t)$ by Weakening Lemma 3.1. Thus $\mathrm{dg}(A(t)) < \mathrm{dg}(\forall x A(x)) \leq c$ yields

$$\frac{\vdash_c^{\alpha+\gamma} \Gamma, \Delta, \neg A(t) \quad \vdash_c^{\alpha+\gamma} \Gamma, A(t)}{\vdash_c^{\alpha+\beta} \Gamma, \Delta} \ (cut)$$

We are done. □

Lemma 3.5 $G \vdash_{c+1}^\alpha \Gamma \Rightarrow G \vdash_c^{2^\alpha} \Gamma$.

Proof By induction on α.

Since $\alpha \mapsto 2^\alpha$ is strictly increasing, it suffices to consider the case when Γ is the lowersequent of a (cut):

$$\frac{\vdash_{c+1}^\beta \Lambda, C \quad \vdash_{c+1}^\beta \neg C, \Delta}{\vdash_{c+1}^\alpha \Lambda, \Delta (= \Gamma)}$$

for a $\forall$-cut formula C with $\mathrm{dg}(C) < c + 1$ and a $\beta < \alpha$. By IH, Lemma 3.4 and $2^\beta + 2^\beta \leq 2^\alpha$, we obtain

$$\frac{\vdash_c^{2^\beta} \Lambda, C \quad \vdash_c^{2^\beta} \neg C, \Delta}{\vdash_c^{2^\alpha} \Lambda, \Delta (= \Gamma)}$$

□

For ordinals α, β with $\beta \geq 2$ and $c < \omega$, let $\beta_0(\alpha) := \alpha$ and $\beta_{c+1}(\alpha) := \beta^{\beta_c(\alpha)}$. Now Lemma 3.5 yields the

Theorem 3.1 (Cut-elimination theorem) $\boldsymbol{G} \vdash^{\alpha}_{c} \Gamma \Rightarrow \boldsymbol{G} \vdash^{2_c(\alpha)}_{0} \Gamma$ *for* $c < \omega$.

Remark 3.1 Let $\boldsymbol{G}$ be one of the calculi $\boldsymbol{G}_i + T + (cut)$ $(i = 1, \omega)$, where each $A \in T$ is codified in an applied calculus $\boldsymbol{G}_i + T$ as an inference rule possibly with *major formulas*. For example in the inference rules for complete induction schema

$$\frac{\Gamma, A(0, \mathbf{t}) \quad \neg A(a, \mathbf{t}), \Gamma, A(Sa, \mathbf{t}) \quad \neg A(s, \mathbf{t}), \Gamma}{\Gamma} \qquad \frac{\neg A(a, \mathbf{t}), \Gamma, A(Sa, \mathbf{t})}{\neg A(0, \mathbf{t}), \Gamma, A(s, \mathbf{t})}$$

the left one has no major formula, but the right one has two.

Still, a *partial cut elimination theorem* holds for such calculus $\boldsymbol{G}$: If Γ is provable in $\boldsymbol{G}$, then there exists a proof P of Γ in $\boldsymbol{G}$ such that each formula occurring in the proof P is either a subformula of a formula in Γ, or a subformula of a major formula of an inference rule for an axiom in T. This is seen as follows. Given a proof P_0 in $\boldsymbol{G}$, replace inference rules for axioms in T with major formulas by equivalent inference rules without major formulas. Then eliminate (cut) inferences from the resulting proof, and replace inference rules for axioms in T without major formulas by inference rules with major formulas together with (cut) inferences. Each cut formula arising from the last replacement is a major formula of an inference rule for an axiom in T.

3.1.1 Elimination Procedure for Classical Calculus

Let us explain the proof of Theorem 3.1, i.e., the algorithm eliminating cuts from a given proof P in $\boldsymbol{G}_1 + (cut)$. Consider the cut inferences of the maximal degree, i.e., whose cut formulas have the maximal degree c. Pick an uppermost such one. Apply Lemma 3.4 to get a proof of the lowersequent of lesser degrees $< c$. Iterate this process $n_c(P)$-times until a proof P_1 of a lesser degree is obtained (cf. Lemma 3.5), where $n_c(P)$ denote the number of cut inferences of degree c in the given proof P. Note that $n_{c-1}(P_1)$ may be much bigger than $n_{c-1}(P)$. Next eliminate cuts of degree $c - 1$, and so on.

An algorithm behind the proof of Lemma 3.4 is described as follows. Lift the proof of Γ, C up to the inferences in the proof of $\neg C, \Delta$ whose major formula is $\neg C$. Then apply Inversion Lemma 3.2 to get the complement of the minor formulas, and cut it out of lesser degrees. If C is a literal, then lift the proof of Γ, C up to the axioms in the proof of $\neg C, \Delta$.

The reason why the Inversion Lemma 3.2 holds is that there are only two ways to introduce a $\forall$-formula $A_0 \wedge A_1$ $[\forall x A(x)]$ in a proof. One is to apply an inference rule $(\wedge)$ $[(\forall)]$ with its main formula, resp. The other is to introduce the formula in an axiom other than major formulas, i.e., as a weakening formula in an axiom. Furthermore each axiom or each inference rule needs to be closed under substituting terms for variables.

Let us consider a variant $\boldsymbol{G}_1'$ of the sequent calculus $\boldsymbol{G}_1$, in which there is another way to introduce a formula in a proof. In $\boldsymbol{G}_1'$

$$\Gamma, \neg A, A$$

is an axiom for any formula A.

We need to modify a cut-elimination procedure for $\boldsymbol{G}_1' + T$. First Weakening Lemma 3.1 holds for the variant $\boldsymbol{G}_1' + T$. Obviously Inversion Lemma 3.2 does not hold. For example $\boldsymbol{G}_1' \vdash_0^0 \neg\forall x A(x), \forall x A(x)$, but $\boldsymbol{G}_1' \nvdash_0^0 \neg\forall x A(x), A(t)$. Still we can substitute a term for a free variable in a proof, since each axiom or each inference rule in $\boldsymbol{G}_1'$ is closed under substituting terms for variables. To avoid a clash of variables, rename eigenvariables.

Lemma 3.6 *If* $\boldsymbol{G}_1' + T + (cut) \vdash_c^\alpha \Gamma(a)$, *then* $\boldsymbol{G}_1' + T + (cut) \vdash_c^\alpha \Gamma(t)$ *for any term* t.

Lemma 3.7 *Let* C *be a formula with* $\mathrm{dg}(C) \leq c$. *Then*

$$\boldsymbol{G}_1' + T \vdash_c^\alpha \Gamma, C \;\&\; \boldsymbol{G}_1' + T \vdash_c^\beta \neg C, \Delta \Rightarrow \boldsymbol{G}_1' + T \vdash_c^{\alpha\#\beta} \Gamma, \Delta.$$

Proof By induction on the natural sum $\alpha\#\beta$,[3] cf. Definition 1.12. This means that we treat two given proofs symmetrically. In the proof let us write $\vdash_c^\alpha \Gamma$ for $\boldsymbol{G}_1' + T \vdash_c^\alpha \Gamma$.

By Weakening Lemma 3.1 and $\alpha, \beta \leq \alpha\#\beta$, we can assume that $C \notin \Delta$ and $\neg C \notin \Gamma$. Hence if $\neg C, \Delta$ $[\Gamma, C]$ is an axiom, then so is Δ $[\Gamma]$, resp.

In what follows assume that both Γ, C and $\neg C, \Delta$ are the lowersequents of inference rules. If the major formula of the inference concluding $\neg C, \Delta$ is not the formula $\neg C$, then IH yields the assertion. The same for the case when the major formula of the inference concluding Γ, C is not the formula C. Here we need the fact that $(\alpha, \beta) \mapsto \alpha\#\beta$ is strictly increasing in both arguments.

Suppose the major formulas of the last inferences are C and $\neg C$. Let us consider the case $C \equiv \forall x A(x)$.

$$\dfrac{\dfrac{\vdash_c^\delta \Gamma, \forall x A(x), A(a)}{\vdash_c^\alpha \Gamma, \forall x A(x)}\,(\forall) \qquad \dfrac{\vdash_c^\gamma \exists x \neg A(x), \Delta, \neg A(t)}{\vdash_c^\beta \exists x \neg A(x), \Delta}\,(\exists)}{\Gamma, \Delta}$$

for $\delta < \alpha$ and $\gamma < \beta$. By IH we have $\vdash_c^{\alpha\#\gamma} \Gamma, \Delta, \neg A(t)$. On the other hand we have $\vdash_c^\delta \Gamma, \forall x A(x), A(t)$ by Lemma 3.6. Hence we obtain $\vdash_c^{\delta\#\beta} \Gamma, \Delta, A(t)$ by IH. From $\mathrm{dg}(A(t)) < \mathrm{dg}(\forall x A(x)) \leq c$ and $\alpha\#\gamma, \delta\#\beta < \alpha\#\beta$ we see

[3]For the finitary calculus $\boldsymbol{G}_1'$, $\alpha < \omega$ suffices, but for an infinitary calculus such as $\boldsymbol{G}_\omega'$, we need the natural sum of ordinals.

$$\frac{\vdash_c^{\alpha\#\gamma} \Gamma, \Delta, \neg A(t) \quad \vdash_c^{\delta\#\beta} \Gamma, \Delta, A(t)}{\vdash_c^{\alpha\#\beta} \Gamma, \Delta} \ (cut)$$

The whole process is depicted as follows.

$$\dfrac{\dfrac{\Gamma, \forall x A(x), A(a)}{\Gamma, \forall x A(x)} \quad \dfrac{\exists x \neg A(x), \Delta, \neg A(t)}{\exists x \neg A(x), \Delta}}{\Gamma, \Delta} \rightsquigarrow \dfrac{\dfrac{\Gamma, \forall x A(x) \quad \exists x \neg A(x), \Delta, \neg A(t)}{\Gamma, \Delta, \neg A(t)} \quad \dfrac{\Gamma, \forall x A(x), A(t) \quad \exists x \neg A(x), \Delta}{\Gamma, \Delta, A(t)}}{\Gamma, \Delta}$$

The (cut) rule in the left is replaced by the so called 'cross cuts' in the right. □

Lemma 3.5 and Theorem 3.1 follow from Lemma 3.7 and $2^\beta \# 2^\beta \leq 2^\alpha$.

Lemma 3.8 $G_1' + T + (cut) \vdash_{c+1}^{\alpha} \Gamma \Rightarrow G_1' + T + (cut) \vdash_c^{2^\alpha} \Gamma$.

Theorem 3.2 (Cut-elimination theorem for G_1') $G_1' + T + (cut) \vdash_c^{\alpha} \Gamma \Rightarrow G_1' + T \vdash_0^{2_c(\alpha)} \Gamma$ *for* $c < \omega$.

3.1.2 Predicative Second Order Logic

In this subsection we discuss a cut-eliminating procedure for the predicative second-order calculus G_2', in which

$$\Gamma, \neg A, A$$

is an axiom for any sequent Γ and a *first-order formula* A.

Let us define the 1-degree $\mathrm{dg}_1(A)$ by letting $\mathrm{dg}_1(\exists X A) = 0$ for $A \in \Pi_0^1$, cf. Definitions 1.1 and 2.2,. Namely $\mathrm{dg}_1(\neg A) = \mathrm{dg}_1(A)$, $\mathrm{dg}_1(A) = \mathrm{dg}(A)$ when $\mathrm{dg}_2(A) = 0$, $\mathrm{dg}_1(\exists X A) = 0$ for $A \in \Pi_0^1$. For $\mathrm{dg}_2(A) \neq 0 \neq \mathrm{dg}_2(B)$, $\mathrm{dg}_1(A) = \max\{\mathrm{dg}_1(A_0), \mathrm{dg}_1(A_1)\}$ when $A \equiv (A_0 \vee A_1)$, $\mathrm{dg}_1(A) = \mathrm{dg}_1(B)$ when $A \equiv \exists x B$, and $\mathrm{dg}_1(A) = \mathrm{dg}_1(B)$ when $A \equiv \exists X B$. For an abstract $\{\mathbf{x}\}F(\mathbf{x})$, let $\mathrm{dg}_1(\{\mathbf{x}\}F(\mathbf{x})) := \mathrm{dg}_1(F(\mathbf{x}))$. Then it is easy to see by induction on $\mathrm{dg}_1(A)$ that for first-order abstracts V

$$\mathrm{dg}_1(A(V)) \leq \mathrm{dg}_1(A) + \mathrm{dg}_1(V) \tag{3.1}$$

$G_2' + T + (cut) \vdash_{c,d}^{\alpha} \Gamma$ holds if there is a proof of Γ in $G_2' + T + (cut)$ such that its depth is at most α, and the 2-degrees $\mathrm{dg}_2(C)$ of its cut formulas C are less than c, its 1-degrees $\mathrm{dg}_1(C)$ are less than d, in $\dfrac{\Gamma, \exists X F(X), F(V)}{\Gamma, \exists X F(X)} \ (\exists_{1\mathrm{st}}^2)$, the 1-degrees of the witnessing abstract V are at most d, and the 1-degrees of the formula F are less than d.

Definition 3.3 Let $G = G_2' + T + (cut)$. $G \vdash_{c,d}^{\alpha} \Gamma$ is defined inductively as follows:

1. $G \vdash_{c,d}^{\alpha} \Gamma$ holds for any α and c, d if Γ is an axiom in G.

2. Let $\dfrac{\{\Gamma_i : i \in I\}}{\Gamma}$ be an inference rule in $\boldsymbol{G}$ other than cut rule and $(\exists^2_{1st})$. Then $\forall i \in I[\boldsymbol{G} \vdash^{\beta}_{c,d} \Gamma_i \,\&\, \beta < \alpha] \Rightarrow \boldsymbol{G} \vdash^{\alpha}_{c,d} \Gamma$.
3. For the cut rule if $\boldsymbol{G} \vdash^{\beta}_{c,d} \Gamma, \neg C$ and $\boldsymbol{G} \vdash^{\beta}_{c,d} C, \Delta$ with $\beta < \alpha$ and $\mathrm{dg}_2(C) < c$ and $\mathrm{dg}_1(C) < d$, then $\boldsymbol{G} \vdash^{\alpha}_{c,d} \Gamma, \Delta$.
4. Let $\boldsymbol{G} \vdash^{\beta}_{c,d} \Gamma, \exists X F(X), F(V)$ with $\beta < \alpha$. Assume $\mathrm{dg}_1(V) \le d$ and $\mathrm{dg}_1(F) < d$. Then $\boldsymbol{G} \vdash^{\alpha}_{c,d} \Gamma, \exists X F(X)$.

Lemma 3.9 (Inversion Lemma for $\boldsymbol{G}_2'$)

1. *Let* $\mathrm{dg}_2(A_0 \wedge A_1) > 0$. *Then* $\boldsymbol{G}_2' + T + (cut) \vdash^{\alpha}_{c,d} \Gamma, A_0 \wedge A_1 \Rightarrow \boldsymbol{G}_2' + T + (cut) \vdash^{\alpha}_{c,d} \Gamma, A_i$ *for* $i = 0, 1$.
2. *Let* $\mathrm{dg}_2(\forall x A(x)) > 0$. *Then* $\boldsymbol{G}_2' + T + (cut) \vdash^{\alpha}_{c,d} \Gamma, \forall x A(x) \Rightarrow \boldsymbol{G}_2' + T + (cut) \vdash^{\alpha}_{c,d} \Gamma, A(t)$ *for any term* t.
3. *Assume* $\boldsymbol{G}_2' + T + (cut) \vdash^{\alpha}_{c,d} \Gamma, \forall X A(X)$ *and let* V *be a first-order abstract with* $\mathrm{dg}_1(V) = \mathrm{dg}(V) = v$. *Then* $\boldsymbol{G}_2' + T + (cut) \vdash^{\alpha}_{c,d+v} \Gamma, A(V)$.

Proof For Lemma 3.9.3 use (3.1) and $\mathrm{dg}_2(B(V)) = \mathrm{dg}_2(B(X))$. □

Lemma 3.10 *Let* C *be a* $\forall$*-formula with* $0 < \mathrm{dg}_2(C) \le c$ *and* $\mathrm{dg}_1(C) < d$. *Then*

$$\boldsymbol{G}_2' + T + (cut) \vdash^{\alpha}_{c,d} \Gamma, C \,\&\, \boldsymbol{G}_2' + T + (cut) \vdash^{\beta}_{c,d} \neg C, \Delta \Rightarrow \boldsymbol{G}_2' + T + (cut) \vdash^{\alpha+\beta}_{c,d\cdot 2} \Gamma, \Delta.$$

Proof By induction on β as in Lemma 3.4. Write $\vdash^{\alpha}_{c,d} \Gamma$ for $\boldsymbol{G}_2' + T + (cut) \vdash^{\alpha}_{c,d} \Gamma$ in this proof.

Assume $\neg C, \Delta$ is the lowersequent of an inference and the major formula of the inference is the formula $\neg C$. There are three cases to consider $C \equiv A_0 \wedge A_1$, $C \equiv \forall x A(x)$ and $C \equiv \forall X A(X)$. Consider the last case.

$$\dfrac{\vdash^{\alpha}_{c,d} \Gamma, \forall X A(X) \qquad \dfrac{\vdash^{\gamma}_{c,d} \exists X \neg A(X), \Delta, \neg A(V)}{\vdash^{\beta}_{c,d} \exists X \neg A(X), \Delta}\,(\exists^2_{1st})}{\Gamma, \Delta}$$

for a $\gamma < \beta$ and a $V \in \Pi^1_0$ with $\mathrm{dg}_1(V) \le d$ and $\mathrm{dg}_1(A) < d$. By IH we have $\vdash^{\alpha+\gamma}_{c,d\cdot 2} \Gamma, \Delta, \neg A(V)$. On the other hand we have $\vdash^{\alpha}_{c,d\cdot 2} \Gamma, A(V)$ by Inversion Lemma 3.9.3. From $\mathrm{dg}_2(A(V)) < \mathrm{dg}_2(\forall X A(X)) \le c$ and $\mathrm{dg}_1(A(V)) < d \cdot 2$, we see

$$\dfrac{\vdash^{\alpha+\gamma}_{c,d\cdot 2} \Gamma, \Delta, \neg A(V) \quad \vdash^{\alpha}_{c,d\cdot 2} \Gamma, A(V)}{\vdash^{\alpha+\beta}_{c,d\cdot 2} \Gamma, \Delta}\,(cut)$$

□

Lemma 3.11 $\boldsymbol{G}_2' + T + (cut) \vdash^{\alpha}_{1+c+1,d} \Gamma \Rightarrow \boldsymbol{G}_2' + T + (cut) \vdash^{2^\alpha}_{1+c,d\cdot 2^\alpha} \Gamma$.

Proof By induction on α using Lemma 3.10. □

Let $d(0,\alpha) = d$ and $d(c+1,\alpha) = d(c,\alpha) \cdot 2_{c+1}(\alpha)$. The following Theorem 3.3 is seen by induction on c using Lemma 3.11.

Theorem 3.3 $\boldsymbol{G}_2' + T + (cut) \vdash^{\alpha}_{1+c,d} \Gamma \Rightarrow \boldsymbol{G}_2' + T + (cut) \vdash^{2_c(\alpha)}_{1,d(c,\alpha)} \Gamma$ *for* $c < \omega$.

As in Lemma 3.7 we see the

Lemma 3.12 *Let* C *be a first-order formula with* $\mathrm{dg}(C) \leq d$. *Then*

$$\boldsymbol{G}_2' + T \vdash^{\alpha}_{1,d} \Gamma, C \;\&\; \boldsymbol{G}_2' + T \vdash^{\beta}_{1,d} \neg C, \Delta \Rightarrow \boldsymbol{G}_2' + T \vdash^{\alpha\#\beta}_{1,d} \Gamma, \Delta.$$

Finally we obtain a complete cut-elimination for $\boldsymbol{G}_2'$.

Theorem 3.4 $\boldsymbol{G}_2' + T + (cut) \vdash^{\alpha}_{1+c,d} \Gamma \Rightarrow \boldsymbol{G}_2' + T \vdash^{2_{c+d(c,\alpha)}(\alpha)}_{0,d(c,\alpha)} \Gamma$ *for* $c, d < \omega$.

3.1.3 Propositional Logics

In this subsection we consider a cut-elimination procedure in finitary and infinitary propositional logics.

First let us introduce a finitary propositional logic. Formulas are generated from atoms $p, q, \ldots$ and their complements $\bar{p}, \bar{q}, \ldots$ by means of variadic propositional connectives $\bigvee, \bigwedge$: if $A_0, \ldots, A_{n-1}$ are formulas with $n \geq 0$, then $\bigvee_{i<n} A_i$ and $\bigwedge_{i<n} A_i$ are formulas. These propositional formulas are intended to denote bounded arithmetic formulas.

The degree of formulas is redefined to count the number of disjuncts and conjuncts so that the following holds.

$$m < n \Rightarrow \max\{\mathrm{dg}_0(A_m), \mathrm{dg}_0(\bigvee_{i<m} A_i)\} < \mathrm{dg}_0(\bigvee_{i<n} A_i) \tag{3.2}$$

$\mathrm{dg}_0(L) = 0$ for literals L, and $\mathrm{dg}_0(\bigvee_{i<n} A_i) = \mathrm{dg}_0(\bigwedge_{i<n} A_i) = \max\{\mathrm{dg}_0(A_i) : i < n\} + n$.

In a sequent calculus $\boldsymbol{G}_0$, axioms are $\Gamma, \bar{p}, p$ for atoms p, and inference rules $(\vee)$, $(\wedge)$ for binary connectives are changed as follows.

$$\frac{\Gamma, \bigvee_{i<n} A_i, A_0, \ldots, A_{n \dot{-} 1}}{\Gamma, \bigvee_{i<n} A_i} \,(\bigvee) \qquad \frac{\Gamma, \bigwedge_{i<n} A_i, A_0 \quad \cdots \quad \Gamma, \bigwedge_{i<n} A_i, A_{n \dot{-} 1}}{\Gamma, \bigwedge_{i<n} A_i} \,(\bigwedge)$$

$\boldsymbol{G}_0 \vdash^a_c \Gamma$ then designates that there exists a $\boldsymbol{G}_0 + (cut)$-proof of Γ whose depth is at most a, and $\mathrm{dg}_0(A) < c$ for any cut formula A occurring in the proof. Let us write $\vdash^a_c \Gamma$ for $\boldsymbol{G}_0 \vdash^a_c \Gamma$.

The following inversion lemma for $\boldsymbol{G}_0$ is easily seen.

Lemma 3.13 *1.* $\vdash^a_c \Gamma, \bigvee_{i<0} A_i \Rightarrow \vdash^a_c \Gamma$.
2. $\vdash^a_c \Gamma, \bigvee_{i<n+1} A_i \Rightarrow \vdash^a_c \Gamma, A_n, \bigvee_{i<n} A_i$.
3. If $\vdash^a_c \Gamma, \bigwedge_{i<n+1} A_i$*, then* $\vdash^a_c \Gamma, A_n$ *and* $\vdash^a_c \Gamma, \bigwedge_{i<n} A_i$.

Lemma 3.14 *If* $\vdash^a_{1+c} \Gamma, \neg C$ *and* $\vdash^a_{1+c} C, \Delta$ *with* $\mathrm{dg}_0(C) \leq 1 + c$*, then* $\vdash^{a+2}_{1+c} \Gamma, \Delta$.

Proof This is seen from Lemma 3.13 and (3.2). □

Theorem 3.5 *1.* $\vdash^a_{1+c+1} \Gamma \Rightarrow \vdash^{2a}_{1+c} \Gamma$.
2. $\vdash^a_{1+c} \Gamma \Rightarrow \vdash^{2^c a}_1 \Gamma$.
3. $\vdash^a_c \Gamma \Rightarrow \vdash^{2^{2^{c \dot{-} 1} a}}_0 \Gamma$.

Proof Theorem 3.5.1. By induction on a using Lemma 3.14.
Theorem 3.5.2. This follows from Theorem 3.5.1.
Theorem 3.5.3. This follows from Theorem 3.5.2 and the fact that $\vdash^a_0 \Gamma, \overline{L}$ & $\vdash^b_0 L, \Delta \Rightarrow \vdash^{a+b}_0 \Gamma, \Delta$ for literals L. □

Next let us introduce an infinitary propositional logic. Formulas are generated from atoms $p, q, \ldots$ and their complements $\bar{p}, \bar{q}, \ldots$ by means of infinitary propositional connectives $\bigvee, \bigwedge$: if $A_0, A_1, \ldots$ are formulas, then $\bigvee_{i<\omega} A_i$ and $\bigwedge_{i<\omega} A_i$ are formulas. These infinitary formulas are intended to denote first-order arithmetic formulas.

The degree of formulas is defined as follows. $\mathrm{dg}_{0\omega}(L) = 0$ for literals L, and $\mathrm{dg}_{0\omega}(\bigvee_{i<\omega} A_i) = \mathrm{dg}_{0\omega}(\bigwedge_{i<\omega} A_i) = \sup\{\mathrm{dg}_{0\omega}(A_i) + 1 : i < \omega\}$.

In a sequent calculus $\boldsymbol{G}_{0\omega}$, axioms are $\Gamma, \bar{p}, p$ for atoms p, and the following inference rules for infinitary disjunctions and conjunctions.

$$\frac{\Gamma, \bigvee_{i<\omega} A_i, A_n}{\Gamma, \bigvee_{i<\omega} A_i} (\bigvee) (n < \omega) \qquad \frac{\cdots \quad \Gamma, \bigwedge_{i<\omega} A_i, A_n \quad \cdots (n < \omega)}{\Gamma, \bigwedge_{i<\omega} A_i} (\bigwedge)$$

$\boldsymbol{G}_{0\omega} \vdash^a_c \Gamma$ then designates that there exists a $\boldsymbol{G}_{0\omega} + (cut)$-proof of Γ whose depth is at most a, and $\mathrm{dg}_{0\omega}(A) < c$ for any cut formula A occurring in the proof. Let us write $\vdash^a_c \Gamma$ for $\boldsymbol{G}_{0\omega} \vdash^a_c \Gamma$.

Lemma 3.15 *Let C be either a literal or a disjunctive formula. If* $\vdash^a_c \Gamma, \neg C$ *and* $\vdash^b_c C, \Delta$ *with* $\mathrm{dg}_{0\omega}(C) \leq c$*, then* $\vdash^{a+b}_c \Gamma, \Delta$.

Proof We see the lemma as usual by induction on b. □

Theorem 3.6 *1.* $\vdash^a_{c+1} \Gamma \Rightarrow \vdash^{2^a}_c \Gamma$.
2. *For* $c < \omega$, $\vdash^a_c \Gamma \Rightarrow \vdash^{2_c(a)}_0 \Gamma$.

Proof Theorem 3.6.1. By induction on a using Lemma 3.15.
Theorem 3.6.2. This is seen from Theorem 3.6.1 by induction on $c < \omega$. □

3.2 Fixed Point Logic

Definition 3.4 Let us define a logic calculus FiX for fixed points over a first-order language $\mathcal{L}_1$. Let $\varphi(R, \mathbf{x})$ be a (first-order) formula in which an n-ary relation symbol R occurs only positively, and whose free variables are among the list $\mathbf{x} \equiv x_1, \ldots, x_n$ of variables. For each such formula introduce an n-ary predicate constant I_φ, and thus extend the language $\mathcal{L}_1$ to $\mathcal{L}(FP) = \mathcal{L}_1 \cup \{I_\varphi, \overline{I}_\varphi : \varphi \text{ is a positive formula in} \mathcal{L}_1\}$. Let $\neg I_\varphi(\mathbf{t}) :\equiv \overline{I}_\varphi(\mathbf{t})$.

Then a logic calculus FiX is obtained from the first-order logic calculus $\boldsymbol{G}_1$ by adding the following inference rules for the fixed points:

$$\frac{\Gamma, I_\varphi(\mathbf{t}), \varphi(I_\varphi, \mathbf{t})}{\Gamma, I_\varphi(\mathbf{t})}\ (I_\varphi) \qquad \frac{\Gamma, \neg I_\varphi(\mathbf{t}), \neg\varphi(I_\varphi, \mathbf{t})}{\Gamma, \neg I_\varphi(\mathbf{t})}\ (\neg I_\varphi)$$

Note that $\Gamma, \neg I_\varphi(\mathbf{t}), I_\varphi(\mathbf{t})$ is an axiom in $\boldsymbol{G}_1$ in the language $\mathcal{L}(FP)$.

$$\forall \mathbf{x}[\varphi(I_\varphi, \mathbf{x}) \leftrightarrow I_\varphi(\mathbf{x})]$$

is equivalent to these two inference rules over $\boldsymbol{G}_1$.

In what follows let φ be an arbitrary but fixed positive formula, and let us restrict the calculus FiX for this single φ and I_φ.

Let FiX $\vdash^a_c \Gamma$ designate that there exists an FiX-proof P of Γ such that the depth of the proof tree P is at most a, and the degree of cut formulas in P is less than c, where $\text{dg}(I_\varphi(\mathbf{t})) = 0$. In this section we show that the calculus FiX admits a cut-elimination.

Theorem 3.7 FiX $\vdash^a_c \Gamma \Rightarrow$ FiX $\vdash^{E(c,a)}_0 \Gamma$ *for an* $E \in \mathcal{E}^4$.

Since a cut-free FiX-proof of an I_φ-free sequent Γ is a $\boldsymbol{G}_1$-proof, we obtain FiX $\vdash^a_c \Gamma \Rightarrow \boldsymbol{G}_1 \vdash^{E(c,a)}_0 \Gamma$. It is easy to see through the completeness theorem that FiX is a conservative extension of the first-order logic. The point here is that FiX has at most a superexponential speed-up over the first-order logic.

Our proof of Theorem 3.7 is based on an asymmetric interpretation. Introduce predicates $I^n_\varphi, \neg I^n_\varphi$ $(n \in \omega)$. Intuitively $I^0_\varphi(\mathbf{a}) \Leftrightarrow \bot$ and $I^{n+1}_\varphi(\mathbf{a}) \Leftrightarrow \varphi(I^n_\varphi, \mathbf{a})$. For these there are two axioms and two inference rules:

$$\Gamma, \neg I^0_\varphi(\mathbf{t}) \qquad\qquad \Gamma, \neg I^n_\varphi(\mathbf{t}), I^m_\varphi(\mathbf{t})\ (0 < n \leq m)$$

$$\frac{\Gamma, \varphi(I^m_\varphi, \mathbf{t}), I^{m'}_\varphi(\mathbf{t})}{\Gamma, I^{m'}_\varphi(\mathbf{t})}\ (m+1 \leq m') \qquad \frac{\Gamma, \neg\varphi(I^n_\varphi, \mathbf{t}), \neg I^n_\varphi(\mathbf{t})}{\Gamma, \neg I^n_\varphi(\mathbf{t})}$$

Call the resulting calculus FiX$^{<\omega}$ in a language $\mathcal{L}_1 \cup \{I^n_\varphi, \overline{I}^n_\varphi : I_\varphi \in \mathcal{L}(FP), n < \omega\}$.

In a cut inference, numbers assigned to both cut formulas have to coincide:

$$\frac{\Gamma, I^m_\varphi(\mathbf{t}) \quad \neg I^m_\varphi(\mathbf{t}), \Delta}{\Gamma, \Delta}$$

We show first that cut inferences are eliminable from proofs in the calculus $\text{FiX}^{<\omega}$. Let $\text{dg}_I(C)$ denote the I-degree of a formula C in the language $\text{FiX}^{<\omega}$ defined recursively by $\text{dg}_I(I^0_\varphi(\mathbf{t})) = \text{dg}_I(\neg I^0_\varphi(\mathbf{t})) = 0$ and $\text{dg}_I(I^{n+1}_\varphi(\mathbf{t})) = \text{dg}_I(\neg I^{n+1}_\varphi(\mathbf{t})) = \text{dg}_I(\varphi(I^n_\varphi, \mathbf{t})) + 1$. Other cases are defined as usual, e.g., $\text{dg}_I(QxA(x)) = \text{dg}_I(A(x)) + 1$ for $Q \in \{\exists, \forall\}$.

Let $\vdash^a_c \Gamma$ designates that there exists an $\text{FiX}^{<\omega}$-proof P of Γ such that the depth of the proof tree P is at most a, and $\text{dg}_I(C) < c$ for any cut formula C in P.

Proposition 3.1 *1. Let $\vdash^a_c \Gamma$, and $n' \leq n \leq m \leq m'$. Let Γ' denote a result of replacing some $\neg I^n_\varphi$ by $\neg I^{n'}_\varphi$ and some I^m_φ by $I^{m'}_\varphi$ in Γ. Then $\vdash^a_c \Gamma'$.*
2. Let $\vdash^a_c \Gamma, I^0_\varphi(\mathbf{t})$. Then $\vdash^a_c \Gamma$.

Proof These are seen readily by induction on a. □

As in Lemma 3.7 we see by induction on the sum $a + b$ that

$$\vdash^a_c \Gamma, \neg C \ \& \vdash^b_c C, \Delta \Rightarrow \vdash^{a+b}_c \Gamma, \Delta \tag{3.3}$$

First consider the case when C, Δ is an axiom for non-axiom sequent Δ. If $C \equiv I^m_\varphi(\mathbf{t})$ and $\neg I^n_\varphi(\mathbf{t}) \in \Delta$ with $n \leq m$, then by Proposition 3.1.1 we obtain $\vdash^a_c \Gamma, \neg I^n_\varphi(\mathbf{t})$ from $\vdash^a_c \Gamma, \neg I^m_\varphi(\mathbf{t})$. If $C \equiv \neg I^n_\varphi(\mathbf{t})$ and $I^m_\varphi(\mathbf{t}) \in \Delta$ with $n \leq m$, then by Proposition 3.1.1 we obtain $\vdash^a_c \Gamma, I^m_\varphi(\mathbf{t})$ from $\vdash^a_c \Gamma, I^n_\varphi(\mathbf{t})$. If $C \equiv \neg I^0_\varphi(\mathbf{t})$. Then we obtain $\vdash^a_c \Gamma$ from $\vdash^a_c \Gamma, I^0_\varphi(\mathbf{t})$ and Proposition 3.1.2. In each case we obtain $\vdash^a_c \Gamma, \Delta$ by weakening. The case when $\Gamma, \neg C$ is an axiom is similar.

Suppose the major formulas of the last inferences are C and $\neg C$. Let us consider the case $C \equiv I^{m'}_\varphi(\mathbf{t})$.

For $a_0 < a$, $b_0 < b$, $m_0 < m$ and $\text{dg}_I(\varphi(I^{m_0}_\varphi, \mathbf{t})) < \text{dg}_I(I^m_\varphi(\mathbf{t})) \leq c$, convert

$$\dfrac{\dfrac{\vdash^{a_0}_c \Gamma, \neg I^m_\varphi(\mathbf{t}), \neg\varphi(I^m_\varphi, \mathbf{t})}{\vdash^a_c \Gamma, \neg I^m_\varphi(\mathbf{t})} \quad \dfrac{\vdash^{b_0}_c I^m_\varphi(\mathbf{t}), \Delta, \varphi(I^{m_0}_\varphi, \mathbf{t})}{\vdash^b_c I^m_\varphi(\mathbf{t}), \Delta}}{\Gamma, \Delta}$$

to

$$\dfrac{\dfrac{\overset{\vdots\ \text{Proposition 3.1.1}}{\vdash^{a_0}_c \Gamma, \neg I^m_\varphi(\mathbf{t}), \neg\varphi(I^{m_0}_\varphi, \mathbf{t})} \quad \vdash^b_c I^m_\varphi(\mathbf{t}), \Delta}{\vdash^{a_0+b}_c \Gamma, \Delta, \neg\varphi(I^{m_0}_\varphi, \mathbf{t})} \quad \dfrac{\vdash^a_c \Gamma, \neg I^m_\varphi(\mathbf{t}) \quad \vdash^{b_0}_c I^m_\varphi(\mathbf{t}), \Delta, \varphi(I^{m_0}_\varphi, \mathbf{t})}{\vdash^{a+b_0}_c \varphi(I^{m_0}_\varphi, \mathbf{t}), \Gamma, \Delta}}{\vdash^{a+b}_c \Gamma, \Delta}$$

From (3.3) we see that the cut-elimination holds for $\text{FiX}^{<\omega}$:

Lemma 3.16 $\vdash^a_c \Gamma \Rightarrow \vdash^{2_c(a)}_0 \Gamma$ *for* $c < \omega$.

An FiX-proof is said to be *almost normal* if any cut formula in it is a fixed point formula $I_\varphi(\mathbf{t})$.

Let us assign a pair of positive integers (n, m) $(0 < n \leq m)$ to occurrences of sequents in almost normal proofs. When a pair (n, m) is assigned to a sequent Γ, then replace any negative occurrences of I_φ(i.e., positive occurrences of $\neg I_\varphi$) in Γ by $\neg I^n_\varphi$, and any positive occurrences of I_φ by I^m_φ. Denote the result of the replacing by $\Gamma^{(n,m)}$.

Define depths of an FiX-proof by counting the number of nesting of cut inferences and inferences (I_φ) only.

Proposition 3.2 *Let P be an almost normal proof of Γ with depth$\leq k$. For each $n > 0$ we can find an* $\text{FiX}^{<\omega}$*-proof of $\Gamma^{(n,n+2^k)}$ in the same tree-height.*

Proof By induction on the size of almost normal proofs P of Γ, we show that, for any n, $\Gamma^{(n,n+2^k)}$ is $\text{FiX}^{<\omega}$-provable, where the depth of P is at most k.

The axiom

$$\Gamma, \neg I_\varphi(\mathbf{t}), I_\varphi(\mathbf{t})$$

is converted to the axiom in $\text{FiX}^{<\omega}$:

$$\Gamma^{(n,n+2^0)}, \neg I^n_\varphi(\mathbf{t}), I^{n+2^0}_\varphi(\mathbf{t}).$$

For the inference rule

$$\frac{\Gamma, \varphi(I_\varphi, \mathbf{t}), I_\varphi(\mathbf{t})}{\Gamma, I_\varphi(\mathbf{t})}\ (I_\varphi)$$

assume that we have a proof of $\Gamma^{(n,m)}, \varphi(I^m_\varphi, \mathbf{t}), I^m_\varphi(\mathbf{t})$ for $m = n + 2^{k-1}$. By Proposition 3.1 the proof is converted to a proof of $\Gamma^{(n,m')}, \varphi(I^m_\varphi, \mathbf{t}), I^{m'}_\varphi(\mathbf{t})$ for $m' = n + 2^k > m$. We obtain

$$\frac{\Gamma^{(n,m')}, \varphi(I^m_\varphi, \mathbf{t}), I^{m'}_\varphi(\mathbf{t})}{\Gamma^{(n,m')}, I^{m'}_\varphi(\mathbf{t})}$$

Consider the cut inference

$$\frac{\Gamma, I_\varphi(\mathbf{t}) \quad \neg I_\varphi(\mathbf{t}), \Delta}{\Gamma, \Delta}\ (cut)$$

By IH we have proofs of $\Gamma^{(n,n+2^{k-1})}, I^{n+2^{k-1}}_\varphi(\mathbf{t})$ and of $\neg I^{n+2^{k-1}}_\varphi(\mathbf{t}), \Gamma^{(n+2^{k-1},n+2^k)}$. A cut inference yields a proof of $\Gamma^{(n,n+2^{k-1})}, \Gamma^{(n+2^{k-1},n+2^k)}$, and Proposition 3.1 yields a proof of $\Gamma^{(n,n+2^k)}$.

The inference rule

$$\frac{\Gamma, \neg\varphi(I_\varphi, \mathbf{t}), \neg I_\varphi(\mathbf{t})}{\Gamma, \neg I_\varphi(\mathbf{t})}\ (\neg I_\varphi)$$

is converted to

$$\frac{\Gamma^{(n,m)}, \neg\varphi(I^n_\varphi, \mathbf{t}), \neg I^n_\varphi(\mathbf{t})}{\Gamma^{(n,m)}, \neg I^n_\varphi(\mathbf{t})}$$

Other inference rules are converted as for $(\neg I_\varphi)$. This shows Proposition 3.2. □

Proof Let us show Theorem 3.7. Let FiX $\vdash^a_{1+c} \Gamma$. First eliminate cut inferences partially to get an almost normal proof of Γ, i.e., FiX $\vdash^{2_c(a)}_1 \Gamma$. Then by Proposition 3.2 we obtain $\text{FiX}^{<\omega} \vdash^{2_c(a)}_d \Gamma^{(1,k)}$ for $k = 1 + 2_{c+1}(a)$ and $d = \text{dg}_I(I^k_\varphi(\mathbf{t})) + 1$. Then $\text{FiX}^{<\omega} \vdash^{2_{c+d}(k)}_0 \Gamma^{(1,k)}$ by Lemma 3.16. From the cut-free proof, erase all the super indices, i.e., replace I^n_φ by I_φ. The result is a cut-free FiX-proof of Γ. □

3.3 Intuitionistic Logic

In this section we briefly touch upon sequent calculus for intuitionistic logic. Logical connectives are $\to$ for implication, $\bot$ for the absurdity and $\top$ for the true proposition besides $\vee, \wedge, \exists, \forall$. Let $\neg A :\equiv (A \to \bot)$. Formulas are generated from $\bot, \top$ and atomic formulas $P(t_1, \dots, t_n)$ for n-ary relation symbol P and terms $t_1, \dots, t_n$ by $\to, \vee, \wedge, \exists, \forall$.

An *intuitionistic sequent* is a pair (Γ, A) of cedents (finite sets of formulas) Γ and formulas A, denoted $\Gamma \Rightarrow A$. Γ is the *antecedent* and A the *succedent* (formula) of the sequent $\Gamma \Rightarrow A$. Axioms and inference rules in the sequent calculus $\boldsymbol{G}^i_1$ for the intutionistic (first-order predicate) logic are the followings.

[**Axioms**] For atomic formulas A and arbitrary C, the followings are axioms or *initial sequents*:

$$\Gamma, A \Rightarrow A\,; \qquad \Gamma, \bot \Rightarrow C\,; \qquad \Gamma \Rightarrow \top$$

[**Inference rules**] are $(L\vee)$, $(R\vee)$, $(L\wedge)$, $(R\wedge)$, $(L\to)$, $(R\to)$, $(L\exists)$, $(R\exists)$, $(L\forall)$, and $(R\forall)$.

$$\frac{\Gamma, A_0 \vee A_1, A_0 \Rightarrow C \quad \Gamma, A_0 \vee A_1, A_1 \Rightarrow C}{\Gamma, A_0 \vee A_1 \Rightarrow C}\,(L\vee)\,; \quad \frac{\Gamma \Rightarrow A_i}{\Gamma \Rightarrow A_0 \vee A_1}\,(R\vee)\,(i = 0, 1)$$

$$\frac{\Gamma, A_0 \wedge A_1, A_i \Rightarrow C}{\Gamma, A_0 \wedge A_1 \Rightarrow C}\,(L\wedge)\,(i = 0, 1)\,; \quad \frac{\Gamma \Rightarrow A_0 \quad \Gamma \Rightarrow A_1}{\Gamma \Rightarrow A_0 \wedge A_1}\,(R\wedge)$$

$$\frac{\Gamma, A \to B \Rightarrow A \quad \Gamma, A \to B, B \Rightarrow C}{\Gamma, A \to B \Rightarrow C}\,(L\to)\,; \quad \frac{\Gamma, A \Rightarrow B}{\Gamma \Rightarrow A \to B}\,(R\to)$$

$$\frac{\Gamma, \exists x B(x), B(a) \Rightarrow C}{\Gamma, \exists x B(x) \Rightarrow C} (L\exists) ; \frac{\Gamma \Rightarrow B(t)}{\Gamma \Rightarrow \exists x B(x)} (R\exists)$$

$$\frac{\Gamma, \forall x B(x), B(t) \Rightarrow C}{\Gamma, \forall x B(x) \Rightarrow C} (L\forall) ; \frac{\Gamma \Rightarrow B(a)}{\Gamma \Rightarrow \forall x B(x)} (R\forall)$$

In $(L\exists)$ and $(R\forall)$, a is the eigenvariable not occurring in the lower sequent.

Remark 3.2 The major formulas in upper sequents could be absent except the inference rules $(L \rightarrow)$ and $(L\forall)$, cf. [17]. In other words, contractions in the antecedents are hidden in these rules.

$$\frac{\Gamma, A \rightarrow B \Rightarrow A \quad \Gamma, B \Rightarrow C}{\Gamma, A \rightarrow B \Rightarrow C} (L \rightarrow) ; \frac{\Gamma, \forall x B(x), B(t) \Rightarrow C}{\Gamma, \forall x B(x) \Rightarrow C} (L\forall)$$

The following is the cut inference with the cut formula A.

$$\frac{\Gamma \Rightarrow A \quad \Gamma, A \Rightarrow C}{\Gamma \Rightarrow C} (cut)$$

Although we can eliminate cut inferences from $\boldsymbol{G}^i_1$-proofs as before, an alternative measure of formula complexity is met for the calculus $\boldsymbol{G}^i_1$.

Definition 3.5 The *intuitionistic degree* $\mathrm{dg}^i(A)$ of formulas A is defined recursively.

1. $\mathrm{dg}^i(A) = 0$ for atomic formulas A including $\bot, \top$.
2. $\mathrm{dg}^i(A_0 \lor A_1) = \mathrm{dg}^i(A_0 \land A_1) = \max\{\mathrm{dg}^i(A_0), \mathrm{dg}^i(A_1)\}$.
3. $\mathrm{dg}^i(\exists x A(x)) = \mathrm{dg}^i(\forall x A(x)) = \mathrm{dg}^i(A(x))$.
4. $\mathrm{dg}^i(A \rightarrow B) = \max\{\mathrm{dg}^i(A) + 1, \mathrm{dg}^i(B)\}$.

Let $\vdash^\alpha_c \Gamma \Rightarrow C$ mean that there exists a proof of $\Gamma \Rightarrow C$ in $\boldsymbol{G}^i_1 + (cut)$ such that its depth is at most α, and the intuitionistic degree of all its cut formulas is less than c.

The following lemmas are seen as usual.

Lemma 3.17 (Weakening) *If* $\vdash^\alpha_c \Gamma \Rightarrow A$, $d \geq c$ *and* $\beta \geq \alpha$, *then* $\vdash^\beta_d \Delta, \Gamma \Rightarrow A$.

Lemma 3.18 (Inversion) *Assume* $\vdash^\alpha_c \Gamma \Rightarrow A$.

1. If $A \equiv \bot$, *then* $\vdash^\alpha_c \Gamma \Rightarrow C$ *for any* C.
2. $\vdash^\alpha_c (\Gamma \setminus \{\top\}) \Rightarrow A$.

The elimination procedure is performed in parallel. Let

$$f(\alpha_1, \ldots, \alpha_k; \beta) = (1 + \alpha_1 + \cdots + \alpha_k) \cdot 3_2(\beta)$$

with $3_2(\beta) = 3^{3^\beta}$.

Lemma 3.19 *Suppose* $\vdash^{\alpha_i}_{c} \Gamma \Rightarrow A_i$ *and* $\vdash^{\beta}_{c+1} \Delta, A_k, \dots, A_1 \Rightarrow C$ *with* $\mathrm{dg}^i(A_i) \leq c$ *for* $i = 1, \dots, k$ $(k \geq 0)$. *Then*

$$\vdash^{f(\alpha_1,\dots,\alpha_k;\beta)}_{c} \Delta, \Gamma \Rightarrow C \tag{3.4}$$

Proof We prove Lemma 3.19 by main induction on β with subsidiary induction on $\alpha_1 + \cdots + \alpha_k + k$.

Case 1. The case when one of $\Gamma \Rightarrow A_i$, and $\Delta, A_k, \dots, A_1 \Rightarrow C$ is an initial sequent.

First consider the case when $\Delta, A_k, \dots, A_1 \Rightarrow C$ is an initial sequent.

If $\Delta, A_k, \dots, A_1 \Rightarrow C$ is an initial sequent such that one of the cases $C \equiv \top$, $\bot \in \Delta$ or $C \in \Delta$ occurs, then $\Delta \Rightarrow C$, and hence $\Delta, \Gamma \Rightarrow C$ is an initial sequent.

If $\Delta, A_k, \dots, A_1 \Rightarrow C$ is an initial sequent with the major formula $A_i \equiv C$, then $\vdash^{f(\alpha_1,\dots,\alpha_k;\beta)}_{c} \Delta, \Gamma \Rightarrow A_i (\equiv C)$ follows by weakening from the premise $\vdash^{\alpha_i}_{c} \Gamma \Rightarrow A_i$ and $f(\alpha_1, \dots, \alpha_k; \beta) \geq \alpha_i$.

If $A_i \equiv \bot$, then Inversion Lemma 3.18.1 with a weakening yields $\vdash^{\alpha_i}_{c} \Delta, \Gamma \Rightarrow C$.

Next assume $\Gamma \Rightarrow A_i$ is an initial sequent for an i. This implies $k > 0$. For simplicity assume $i = 1$.

If $A_1 \in \Gamma$, then by SIH(=Subsidiary Induction Hypothesis) we obtain $\vdash^{f(\alpha_2,\dots,\alpha_k;\beta)}_{c}$ $\Delta, A_1, \Gamma \Rightarrow C$ with $A_1 \in \Gamma$ and $f(\alpha_2, \dots, \alpha_k; \beta) \leq f(\alpha_1, \alpha_2, \dots, \alpha_k; \beta)$.

If $\bot \in \Gamma$, then $\Delta, \Gamma \Rightarrow C$ is an initial sequent.

If $A_1 \equiv \top$, then Inversion Lemma 3.18.2 yields $\vdash^{\beta}_{c+1} \Delta, A_k, \dots, A_2 \Rightarrow C$, and by SIH $\vdash^{f(\alpha_2,\dots,\alpha_k;\beta)}_{c} \Delta, \Gamma \Rightarrow C$.

In what follows assume that none of $\Gamma \Rightarrow A_i$, and $\Delta, A_k, \dots, A_1 \Rightarrow C$ is an initial sequent.

Case 2. Consider the case when $\Delta, A_k, \dots, A_1 \Rightarrow C$ is a lowersequent of a cut. For a $\gamma < \beta$

$$\dfrac{\vdash^{\alpha_i}_{c} \Gamma \Rightarrow A_i \qquad \dfrac{\vdash^{\gamma}_{c+1} \Delta, A_k, \dots, A_1 \Rightarrow A_0 \quad \vdash^{\gamma}_{c+1} \Delta, A_k, \dots, A_1, A_0 \Rightarrow C}{\vdash^{\beta}_{c+1} \Delta, A_k, \dots, A_1 \Rightarrow C}\,(cut)}{\Delta, \Gamma \Rightarrow C}$$

with $\mathrm{dg}^i(A_0) \leq c$.

MIH(=Main Induction Hypothesis) yields $\vdash^{f(\alpha_1,\dots,\alpha_k;\gamma)}_{c} \Delta, \Gamma \Rightarrow A_0$, and once again by MIH, and by $3_2(\gamma) \cdot 3_2(\gamma) + 3_2(\gamma) < 3_2(\gamma + 1)$

$$\begin{aligned} f(f(\alpha_1, \dots, \alpha_k; \gamma), \alpha_1, \dots, \alpha_k; \gamma) &= (\alpha \cdot 3_2(\gamma) + \alpha)\, 3_2(\gamma) = \alpha(3_2(\gamma) \cdot 3_2(\gamma) + 3_2(\gamma)) \\ &\leq \alpha \cdot 3_2(\beta) = f(\alpha_1, \dots, \alpha_k; \beta) \end{aligned}$$

with $\alpha = \alpha_1 + \cdots + \alpha_k + 1$, we conclude $\vdash^{f(\alpha_1,\dots,\alpha_k;\beta)}_{c} \Delta, \Gamma \Rightarrow C$.

We will depict a 'derivation' to illustrate the arguments.

$$\dfrac{\vdash_c^{\alpha_i} \Gamma \Rightarrow A_i \quad \dfrac{\vdash_c^{\alpha_i} \Gamma \Rightarrow A_i \quad \vdash_{c+1}^{\gamma} \Delta, A_k, \dots, A_1 \Rightarrow A_0}{\vdash_c^{f(\alpha_1,\dots,\alpha_k;\gamma)} \Delta, \Gamma \Rightarrow A_0} \text{MIH} \quad \vdash_{c+1}^{\gamma} \Delta, A_k, \dots, A_1, A_0 \Rightarrow C}{\vdash_c^{f(\alpha_1,\dots,\alpha_k;\beta)} \Delta, \Gamma \Rightarrow C} \text{MIH}$$

In what follows assume that $\Delta, A_k, \dots, A_1 \Rightarrow C$ is the lower sequent of an inference rule J other than a cut.

Case 3. If the major formula of J is not in $A_k, \dots, A_1$, then lift up the left upper part: for a $\gamma < \beta$

$$\dfrac{\vdash_c^{\alpha_i} \Gamma \Rightarrow A_i \quad \dfrac{\cdots \quad \vdash_{c+1}^{\gamma} \Delta_i, A_k, \dots, A_1 \Rightarrow C_i \quad \cdots}{\vdash_{c+1}^{\beta} \Delta, A_k, \dots, A_1 \Rightarrow C} (J)}{\Delta, \Gamma \Rightarrow C}$$

$$\dfrac{\cdots \quad \dfrac{\vdash_c^{\alpha_i} \Gamma \Rightarrow A_i \quad \vdash_{c+1}^{\gamma} \Delta_i, A_k, \dots, A_1 \Rightarrow C_i}{\vdash_c^{f(\alpha_1,\dots,\alpha_k;\gamma)} \Delta_i, \Gamma \Rightarrow C_i} \text{MIH} \quad \cdots}{\vdash_c^{f(\alpha_1,\dots,\alpha_k;\beta)} \Delta, \Gamma \Rightarrow C} (J)$$

Note that $f(\alpha_1, \dots, \alpha_k; \gamma) < f(\alpha_1, \dots, \alpha_k; \beta)$ since $\alpha_1 + \cdots + \alpha_k + 1 > 0$.

Case 4. Finally suppose that the major formula of J is a cut formula $A_i \in \{A_k, \dots, A_1\}$ with $\mathrm{dg}^i(A_i) \leq c$. For simplicity suppose $i = 1$, and let J' denote the last rule in $\vdash_c^{\alpha_1} \Gamma \Rightarrow A_1$.
Case 4.1. J' is either a left rule or a cut.
Case 4.1.1. The case when J' is an $(L\exists)$ with the main formula $\exists y D(y)$.

$$\dfrac{\vdash_c^{\alpha_0} \Gamma, D(a) \Rightarrow A_1}{\vdash_c^{\alpha_1} \Gamma \Rightarrow A_1} (L\exists)$$

Then $\alpha_0 < \alpha_1$, and hence $\alpha_0 + \alpha_2 + \cdots + \alpha_k < \alpha_1 + \alpha_2 + \cdots + \alpha_k$. Thus SIH yields $\vdash_c^{f(\alpha_0,\alpha_2,\dots,\alpha_k;\beta)} \Delta, \Gamma, D(a) \Rightarrow C$.

$$\dfrac{\dfrac{\vdash_c^{\alpha_i} \Gamma \Rightarrow A_i \ (i \neq 1) \quad \vdash_c^{\alpha_0} \Gamma, D(a) \Rightarrow A_1 \quad \vdash_{c+1}^{\beta} \Delta, A_k, \dots, A_2, A_1 \Rightarrow C}{\vdash_c^{f(\alpha_0,\alpha_2,\dots,\alpha_k;\beta)} \Delta, \Gamma, D(a) \Rightarrow C} \text{SIH}}{\vdash_c^{f(\alpha_1,\alpha_2,\dots,\alpha_k;\beta)} \Delta, \Gamma \Rightarrow C} (L\exists)$$

Case 4.1.2. The case when J' is an $(L \to)$ with the major formula $D \to E$.

$$\dfrac{\vdash_c^{\alpha_0} \Gamma \Rightarrow D \quad \vdash_c^{\alpha_0} \Gamma, E \Rightarrow A_1}{\vdash_c^{\alpha_1} \Gamma \Rightarrow A_1} (L \to)$$

Then

$$\dfrac{\vdash^{\alpha_0}_c \Gamma \Rightarrow D \quad \dfrac{\vdash^{\alpha_i}_c \Gamma \Rightarrow A_i \ (i \neq 1) \quad \vdash^{\alpha_0}_c \Gamma, E \Rightarrow A_1 \quad \vdash^{\beta}_{c+1} \Delta, A_k, \ldots, A_2, A_1 \Rightarrow C}{\vdash^{f(\alpha_0,\alpha_2,\ldots,\alpha_k;\beta)}_c \Delta, \Gamma, E \Rightarrow C}\,\text{SIH}}{\vdash^{f(\alpha_1,\alpha_2,\ldots,\alpha_k;\beta)}_c \Delta, \Gamma \Rightarrow C}\,(L\rightarrow)$$

Case 4.1.3. The case when J' is a cut with cut formula D.

$$\dfrac{\vdash^{\alpha_0}_c \Gamma \Rightarrow D \quad \vdash^{\alpha_0}_c \Gamma, D \Rightarrow A_1}{\vdash^{\alpha_1}_c \Gamma \Rightarrow A_1}\,(\text{cut})$$

$$\dfrac{\vdash^{\alpha_0}_c \Gamma \Rightarrow D \quad \dfrac{\vdash^{\alpha_i}_c \Gamma \Rightarrow A_i \ (i \neq 1) \quad \vdash^{\alpha_0}_c \Gamma, D \Rightarrow A_1 \quad \vdash^{\beta}_{c+1} \Delta, A_k, \ldots, A_2, A_1 \Rightarrow C}{\vdash^{f(\alpha_0,\alpha_2,\ldots,\alpha_k;\beta)}_c \Delta, \Gamma, D \Rightarrow C}\,\text{SIH}}{\vdash^{f(\alpha_1,\alpha_2,\ldots,\alpha_k;\beta)}_c \Delta, \Gamma \Rightarrow C}\,(\text{cut})$$

Other cases are seen similarly.

Case 4.2. J' is a right rule.

Case 4.2.1. The case when $A_1 \equiv \exists x B(x)$. We have for an $\alpha_0 < \alpha_1$ and a $\gamma < \beta$

$$\dfrac{\vdash^{\alpha_0}_c \Gamma \Rightarrow B(t)}{\vdash^{\alpha_1}_c \Gamma \Rightarrow \exists x B(x)}\,(R\exists) \quad \text{and} \quad \dfrac{\vdash^{\gamma}_{c+1} \Delta, A_k, \ldots, A_1, B(a) \Rightarrow C}{\vdash^{\beta}_{c+1} \Delta, A_k, \ldots, A_1 \Rightarrow C}\,(L\exists)$$

Then for $\text{dg}^i(B(t)) \leq \text{dg}^i(A_1) \leq c$

$$\dfrac{\vdash^{\alpha_i}_c \Gamma \Rightarrow A_i \quad \vdash^{\alpha_0}_c \Gamma \Rightarrow B(t) \quad \vdash^{\gamma}_{c+1} \Delta, A_k, \ldots, A_1, B(t) \Rightarrow C}{\vdash^{f(\alpha_0,\alpha_1,\alpha_2,\ldots,\alpha_k;\gamma)}_c \Delta, \Gamma \Rightarrow C}\,\text{MIH}$$

and we obtain $(\alpha_0 + \alpha)3_2(\gamma) \leq \alpha \cdot 2 \cdot 3_2(\gamma) < \alpha \cdot 3_2(\beta)$ with $\alpha = \alpha_1 + \cdots + \alpha_k + 1 \geq \alpha_0$. Namely

$$f(\alpha_0, \alpha_1, \ldots, \alpha_k; \gamma) < f(\alpha_1, \ldots, \alpha_k; \beta) \tag{3.5}$$

Case 4.2.2 The case when $A_1 \equiv (B \rightarrow A_0)$ with $\text{dg}^i(B) + 1, \text{dg}^i(A_0) \leq \text{dg}^i(A_1) \leq c$. We have for an $\alpha_0 < \alpha_1$ and a $\gamma < \beta$

$$\dfrac{\vdash^{\alpha_0}_c \Gamma, B \Rightarrow A_0}{\vdash^{\alpha_1}_c \Gamma \Rightarrow A_1}\,(R\rightarrow) \quad \text{and} \quad \dfrac{\vdash^{\gamma}_{c+1} \Delta, A_k, \ldots, A_1 \Rightarrow B \quad \vdash^{\gamma}_{c+1} \Delta, A_k, \ldots, A_1, A_0 \Rightarrow C}{\vdash^{\beta}_{c+1} \Delta, A_k, \ldots, A_1 \Rightarrow C}\,(L\rightarrow)$$

Then by (3.5) and MIH for two upper 'inferences' we obtain

$$\dfrac{\dfrac{\vdash^{\alpha_i}_c \Gamma \Rightarrow A_i \quad \vdash^{\gamma}_{c+1} \Delta, A_k, \ldots, A_1 \Rightarrow B}{\vdash^{f(\alpha_1,\ldots,\alpha_k;\gamma)}_c \Delta, \Gamma \Rightarrow B} \quad \dfrac{\vdash^{\alpha_i}_c \Gamma \Rightarrow A_i \quad \vdash^{\alpha_0}_c \Gamma, B \Rightarrow A_0 \quad \vdash^{\gamma}_{c+1} \Delta, A_k, \ldots, A_1, A_0 \Rightarrow C}{\vdash^{f(\alpha_0,\alpha_1,\ldots,\alpha_k;\gamma)}_c \Delta, \Gamma, B \Rightarrow C}}{\vdash^{f(\alpha_1,\ldots,\alpha_k;\beta)}_c \Delta, \Gamma \Rightarrow C}\,(\text{cut})$$

Case 4.2.3. The case when $A_1 \equiv \forall x B(x)$. We have for an $\alpha_0 < \alpha_1$ and a $\gamma < \beta$

$$\frac{\vdash_c^{\alpha_0} \Gamma \Rightarrow B(a)}{\vdash_c^{\alpha_1} \Gamma \Rightarrow A_1} (R\forall) \text{ and } \frac{\vdash_{c+1}^{\gamma} \Delta, A_k, \ldots, A_1, B(t) \Rightarrow C}{\vdash_{c+1}^{\beta} \Delta, A_k, \ldots, A_1 \Rightarrow C} (L\forall)$$

For $\mathrm{dg}^i(B(t)) \leq \mathrm{dg}^i(A_1) \leq c$ we obtain by (3.5)

$$\frac{\vdash_c^{\alpha_i} \Gamma \Rightarrow A_i \quad \vdash_c^{\alpha_0} \Gamma \Rightarrow B(t) \quad \vdash_{c+1}^{\gamma} \Delta, A_k, \ldots, A_1, B(t) \Rightarrow C}{\vdash_c^{f(\alpha_1,\ldots,\alpha_k;\beta)} \Gamma, \Delta \Rightarrow C} \text{MIH}$$

Other cases $A_1 \equiv B_0 \vee B_1, B_0 \wedge B_1$ are seen similarly. This shows Lemma 3.19. □

The case $k = 0$ in Lemma 3.19 means that if $\vdash_{c+1}^{\beta} \Delta \Rightarrow C$, then $\vdash_c^{3_2(\beta)} \Delta \Rightarrow C$. Hence we obtain

Theorem 3.8 (Cut-elimination in the intuitionistic calculus $\boldsymbol{G}_1^i$) *If* $\boldsymbol{G}_1^i \vdash_c^{\beta} \Delta \Rightarrow C$, *then* $\boldsymbol{G}_1^i \vdash_0^{3_{2c}(\beta)} \Delta \Rightarrow C$.

In particular

$$\text{if } \boldsymbol{G}_1^i \vdash_1^{\beta} \Delta \Rightarrow C, \text{ then } \boldsymbol{G}_1^i \vdash_0^{3_2(\beta)} \Delta \Rightarrow C$$

Note that $\mathrm{dg}^i(A) = 0$ iff A is a *monotonic formula* iff the implication $\rightarrow$ (and the negation $\neg$) does not occur in A. This means that monotone cuts (cut inferences with monotonic formulas) are quickly eliminable from the intuitionistic sequent calculus $\boldsymbol{G}_1^i$, i.e., the depth of the resulting cut-free proof is bounded by an elementary recursive function of the depth of the given proof.

3.3.1 Elimination Procedure for Intuitionistic Calculus

Let us try to explain the cut elimination procedure in the proof of Lemma 3.19.

$$P = \frac{\begin{array}{c}\vdots\, P_k \\ \Gamma \Rightarrow A_k\end{array} \quad \cdots \quad \begin{array}{c}\vdots\, P_1 \\ \Gamma \Rightarrow A_1\end{array} \quad \begin{array}{c}\vdots\, Q \\ \Delta, A_k, \ldots, A_1 \Rightarrow C\end{array}}{\Delta, \Gamma \Rightarrow C}$$

First lift up the left subproofs $P_k, \ldots, P_1$ up to an inference rule with a major formula A_i, cf. **Case 2** and **Case 3**. When the last rule in the subproof Q is a (cut), subproofs $P_k, \ldots, P_1$ are duplicated, and the list $A_k, \ldots, A_1$ is prolonged by the cut formula A_0, cf. **Case 2**. At the same time the subproof Q_0 of the right upper sequent becomes a subproof of a proof of $\Delta, \Gamma \Rightarrow A_0$ in the prolonged list.

$$Q = \dfrac{\overset{\vdots\ Q_0}{\Delta, A_k, \ldots, A_1 \Rightarrow A_0} \quad \overset{\vdots\ Q_1}{\Delta, A_k, \ldots, A_1, A_0 \Rightarrow C}}{\Delta, A_k, \ldots, A_1 \Rightarrow C}$$

Assume that the last rule in Q is an inference rule with a major formula A_i. We can assume that $i = 1$. Second, then, lift up the subproof Q in P_1 until we encounter a right rule, cf. **Case 4.1**.

Finally assume that the last rule in P_1 is a right rule, cf. **Case 4.2**. Then the list $A_k, \ldots, A_1$ is prolonged by the minor formula in the antecedent, and the subproof P_1 is duplicated due to a hidden contraction of major formulas in the upper sequent. Furthermore when A_1 is an implicational formula $B \to A_0$, the minor formula B in the antecedent remains after the above rewritings. We need to introduce a (cut) with the cut formula B, cf. **Case 4.2.2**. Thus the intuitionisitc degree is defined by $\text{dg}^i(B \to A_0) = \max\{\text{dg}^i(B) + 1, \text{dg}^i(A_0)\}$.

After the whole procedure is performed, cut inferences with lesser intuitionistic degrees remain, and all of the cut inferences are eliminated by iterating the procedures c-times for the maximal intuitionistic degree c of the cut formula in the given proof. In a whole of a procedure subproofs $P_k, \ldots, P_1$ are duplicated at most the number of inference rules in Q. This means that in the resulting proof, subproofs P_i has a doubly exponential copies in the depth of the subproof Q. On the other side, the number of duplications of the subproof Q is independent from subproofs P_i.

Here the elimination procedure deviates from one for classical logic. In the procedure for classical logic, the left and right upper parts are treated symmetrically as in the cross cuts in the proof of Lemma 3.7.

3.3.2 Intutionistic Fixed Point Logic

In this subsection an intuitionistic fixed point logic calculus FiX^i is introduced, and a cut-elimination theorem for it is shown. We see from it that FiX^i is conservative over $\boldsymbol{G}_1^i$.

Let $\mathcal{L}_1$ be a first-order language, and I a fresh predicate symbol not in $\mathcal{L}_1$, and let $\mathcal{L}_1(I)$ denote $\mathcal{L}_1 \cup \{I\}$. For simplicity let us assume that I is a unary predicate. Let $\text{dg}^i(I(t)) = 0$. A class $SP_{\mathcal{L}_1}$ of $\mathcal{L}_1(I)$-formulas is defined recursively such that $A \in SP_{\mathcal{L}_1}$ iff I occurs only *strictly positive* in A.

Definition 3.6 Define recursively a class of formulas $SP_{\mathcal{L}_1}$ in $\mathcal{L}_1(I)$ as follows. $\mathcal{L}_1$ denotes the set of $\mathcal{L}_1$-formulas.

1. Each atomic formula in $\mathcal{L}_1$ belongs to $SP_{\mathcal{L}_1}$.
2. Each atomic formula $I(t)$ belongs to the class $SP_{\mathcal{L}_1}$.
3. If $R, S \in SP_{\mathcal{L}_1}$, then $R \vee S$, $R \wedge S$, $\exists x R$, $\forall x R \in SP_{\mathcal{L}_1}$.
4. If $L \in \mathcal{L}_1$ and $R \in SP_{\mathcal{L}_1}$, then $L \to R \in SP_{\mathcal{L}_1}$.

Let $\Phi(I, x) \in SP_{\mathscr{L}_1}$ in which only a fixed variable x occurs freely. Then FiX^i is obtained from $\boldsymbol{G}_1^i$ by adding the following inference rules, which state that $\forall x[I(x) \leftrightarrow \Phi(I, x)]$.

$$\frac{\Gamma, I(t), \Phi(I, t) \Rightarrow C}{\Gamma, I(t) \Rightarrow C}\ (LI)\ ; \quad \frac{\Gamma \Rightarrow \Phi(I, t)}{\Gamma \Rightarrow I(t)}\ (RI)$$

Definition 3.7 The *SP-degree* $\mathrm{dg}^{SP}(A)$ of formulas A is defined by

$$\mathrm{dg}^{SP}(A) := \begin{cases} 0 \text{ if } A \in \mathscr{L}_1 \\ 1 \text{ if } A \in (SP_{\mathscr{L}_1} \setminus \mathscr{L}_1) \\ 2 \text{ otherwise} \end{cases}$$

Now $\vdash_c^\alpha \Gamma \Rightarrow C$ designates that there exists an FiX^i-proof of $\Gamma \Rightarrow C$ such that its depth is at most α, and the SP-degree of cut formulas in P is less than c. Let $f(\alpha_1, \ldots, \alpha_k; \beta) = (\alpha_1 \# \cdots \# \alpha_k \# 1) \times 3_2(\beta)$.

Lemma 3.20 *Suppose* $\vdash_1^{\boldsymbol{\alpha}} \Gamma \Rightarrow \mathbf{A}$ *and* $\vdash_2^\beta \Delta, \mathbf{A} \Rightarrow C$ *with* $\mathrm{dg}^{SP}(A_i) \leq 1$ *for* $i = 1, \ldots, k$. *Then* $\vdash_1^{f(\alpha_1, \ldots, \alpha_k; \beta)} \Delta, \Gamma \Rightarrow C$.

Proof As in Lemmas 3.19, 3.20 is proved by main induction on β with subsidiary induction on $\alpha_1 \# \cdots \# \alpha_k \# k$. There are two new cases in **Case 4.2** of the proof of Lemma 3.19. Namely we are considering the case when both of the proofs of $\Delta, A_k, \ldots, A_1 \Rightarrow C$ and of $\Gamma \Rightarrow A_1$ end with inference rules with its main formula A_1.

First the case when $A_1 \equiv (B \to A_0)$ with $B \in \mathscr{L}_1$ and $A_0 \in SP_{\mathscr{L}_1}$. We have for an $\alpha_0 < \alpha_1$ and a $\gamma < \beta$

$$\frac{\vdash_1^{\alpha_0} \Gamma, B \Rightarrow A_0}{\vdash_1^{\alpha_1} \Gamma \Rightarrow A_1}\ (R\to) \quad \text{and} \quad \frac{\vdash_2^\gamma \Delta, A_k, \ldots, A_1 \Rightarrow B \quad \vdash_2^\gamma \Delta, A_k, \ldots, A_1, A_0 \Rightarrow C}{\vdash_2^\beta \Delta, A_k, \ldots, A_1 \Rightarrow C}\ (L\to)$$

Then by (3.5) and MIH twice we obtain

$$\cfrac{\cfrac{\vdash_c^{\alpha_i} \Gamma \Rightarrow A_i \quad \vdash_2^\gamma \Delta, A_k, \ldots, A_1 \Rightarrow B}{\vdash_1^{f(\alpha_1, \ldots, \alpha_k; \gamma)} \Delta, \Gamma \Rightarrow B} \quad \cfrac{\vdash_1^{\alpha_i} \Gamma \Rightarrow A_i \quad \vdash_1^{\alpha_0} \Gamma, B \Rightarrow A_0 \quad \vdash_2^\gamma \Delta, A_k, \ldots, A_1, A_0 \Rightarrow C}{\vdash_1^{f(\alpha_0, \alpha_1, \ldots, \alpha_k; \gamma)} \Delta, \Gamma, B \Rightarrow C}}{\vdash_1^{f(\alpha_1, \ldots, \alpha_k; \beta)} \Delta, \Gamma \Rightarrow C}\ (\text{cut})$$

Next the case when $A_1 \equiv I(t)$. We have for an $\alpha_0 < \alpha_1$ and a $\gamma < \beta$

$$\frac{\vdash_1^{\alpha_0} \Gamma \Rightarrow \Phi(I, t)}{\vdash_1^{\alpha_1} \Gamma \Rightarrow A_1}\ (RI) \quad \text{and} \quad \frac{\vdash_2^\gamma \Delta, A_k, \ldots, A_1, \Phi(I, t) \Rightarrow C}{\vdash_2^\beta \Delta, A_k, \ldots, A_1 \Rightarrow C}\ (LI)$$

Then by (3.5) for strictly positive $\Phi(I, t)$

$$\frac{\vdash_1^{\alpha_i} \Gamma \Rightarrow A_i \quad \vdash_1^{\alpha_0} \Gamma \Rightarrow \Phi(I,t) \quad \vdash_2^{\gamma} \Delta, A_k, \ldots, A_1, \Phi(I,t) \Rightarrow C}{\vdash_1^{f(\alpha_1,\ldots,\alpha_k;\beta)} \Gamma, \Delta \Rightarrow C} \text{MIH}$$

□

$\mathrm{FiX}^i \vdash_c^a \Delta \Rightarrow C$ designates that there exists an FiX^i-proof P of $\Delta \Rightarrow C$ such that the depth of P is at most a, and every cut formula A in P has the intuitionistic degree $\mathrm{dg}^i(A) < c$.

Theorem 3.9 *If* $\mathrm{FiX}^i \vdash_c^a \Delta \Rightarrow C$, *then* $\mathrm{FiX}^i \vdash_0^{E^i(c,a)} \Delta \Rightarrow C$ *for an* $E^i \in \mathcal{E}^4$.

Proof Let $\mathrm{FiX}^i \vdash_{1+c}^{\beta} \Delta \Rightarrow C$. First by Theorem 3.8 we have $\mathrm{FiX}^i \vdash_1^{3_{2c}(\beta)} \Delta \Rightarrow C$, i.e., eliminate cuts partially, leaving cuts with cut formulas $I(t)$. This means that $\vdash_2^{3_{2c}(\beta)} \Delta \Rightarrow C$ with SP-degree. Lemma 3.20 yields $\vdash_1^{3_{2+2c}(\beta)} \Delta \Rightarrow C$, i.e., there is a proof P of $\Delta \Rightarrow C$ in FiX^i all of whose cut formulas B are in $\mathcal{L}_1$. From the proof of Lemma 3.20 we see that B is a negative subformula of Φ. Hence we have $\mathrm{FiX}^i \vdash_k^{3_{2+2c}(\beta)} \Delta \Rightarrow C$, where $k = \mathrm{dg}^i(\Phi) > \mathrm{dg}^i(B)$ for cut formulas $B \in \mathcal{L}_1$ in the witnessing proof. Therefore we conclude by Theorem 3.8 that $\mathrm{FiX}^i \vdash_0^{3_{2(1+k+c)}(\beta)} \Delta \Rightarrow C$.

Corollary 3.1 *If* $\mathrm{FiX}^i \vdash \Delta \Rightarrow C$ *and no relation symbol for fixed points occurs in* $\Delta \cup \{C\}$, *then* $\boldsymbol{G}_1^i \vdash \Delta \Rightarrow C$.

3.4 Epsilon Calculi

In Sect. 2.2.4 an epsilon calculus $\boldsymbol{G}_{1\varepsilon}$ is defined in a language $\mathcal{L}_{1\varepsilon} = \mathcal{L}_1 \cup \{\varepsilon\}$ with quantifiers $\exists, \forall$. In this section let us introduce another epsilon calculus $\boldsymbol{G}_\varepsilon$ in a language $\mathcal{L}_\varepsilon$, which is obtained from a first-order language $\mathcal{L}_1$ by deleting quantifiers and adding the epsilon operator ε. Quantifiers are defined through epsilon terms with epsilon axioms (2.15), cf. Remark 2.3. Terms and (quantifier-free) formulas in $\mathcal{L}_\varepsilon$ are defined simultaneously.

Definition 3.8 Let t be a subterm of a formula A. t is *subordinate* to an epsilon term $\varepsilon x.A$ if the variable x occurs in t, i.e., εx binds occurrences of x in t. Otherwise the subterm t *resides* in $\varepsilon x.A$.

The ε-*rank* of an epsilon term is maximal nesting of subordinated subterms, and is defined recursively.

Definition 3.9 1. $\mathrm{rk}_\varepsilon(\varepsilon x.A) = r + 1$ where r denotes the maximal rank of proper ε-subterms subordinate to $\varepsilon x.A$ if such an epsilon term occurs in $\varepsilon x.A$. Otherwise $r = 0$, i.e., $\mathrm{rk}_\varepsilon(\varepsilon x.A) = 1$.

2. The *ε-degree* $\mathrm{dg}_\varepsilon(t)$ of terms t is the maximal nesting of residing ε-subterms, and defined recursively as follows.

   a. $\mathrm{dg}_\varepsilon(t) = 0$ for variables and constants t.
   b. $\mathrm{dg}_\varepsilon(f(t_0, \ldots, t_{n-1})) = \max\{\mathrm{dg}_\varepsilon(t_i) : i < n\}$ for function symbols f.
   c. $\mathrm{dg}_\varepsilon(\varepsilon x.A) = \max\{\mathrm{dg}_\varepsilon(t) : t$ is an ε-subterm residing in $\varepsilon x.A\} + 1$.

Proposition 3.3 *Let $F \equiv (B(t) \to B(\varepsilon y.B))$ be an ε-axiom. For an ε-term $\varepsilon x.A$, assume that $\langle \mathrm{rk}_\varepsilon(\varepsilon y.B), \mathrm{dg}_\varepsilon(\varepsilon y.B)\rangle \leq_{lx} \langle \mathrm{rk}_\varepsilon(\varepsilon x.A), \mathrm{dg}_\varepsilon(\varepsilon x.A)\rangle$ lexicographically. Let F' denote the result of replacing every occurrence of the ε-term $\varepsilon x.A$ by a term s in F.*

If $\varepsilon y.B \equiv \varepsilon x.A$, then $F' \equiv (A(t') \to A(s))$ for the result t' of replacing $\varepsilon x.A$ by s in t.

If $\varepsilon y.B \not\equiv \varepsilon x.A$, then F' is again an ε-axiom $F' \equiv (B'(t') \to B'(\varepsilon y.B'))$ such that $\mathrm{rk}_\varepsilon(\varepsilon y.B') = \mathrm{rk}_\varepsilon(\varepsilon y.B)$, *and* $\mathrm{rk}_\varepsilon(\varepsilon y.B) = \mathrm{rk}_\varepsilon(\varepsilon x.A) \Rightarrow \varepsilon y.B' \equiv \varepsilon y.B$.

Proof First suppose $\varepsilon y.B \equiv \varepsilon x.A$. Then $F \equiv (A(t) \to A(\varepsilon x.A))$, and since $\varepsilon x.A$ is not a proper subterm of itself, $\varepsilon x.A$ does not reside in $A(x)$. Hence $F' \equiv (A(t') \to A(s))$.

Next suppose $\varepsilon y.B \not\equiv \varepsilon x.A$. Since $\mathrm{rk}_\varepsilon(\varepsilon y.B) \leq \mathrm{rk}_\varepsilon(\varepsilon x.A)$, $\varepsilon x.A$ is not subordinate to $\varepsilon y.B$. It is not the case that $\varepsilon x.A$ occurs in F in such a way that either t or $\varepsilon y.B$ is a proper subterm of $\varepsilon x.A$. This means that $\varepsilon x.A$ can occur either in t and/or reside in $B(y)$, and we can write $F \equiv (B(t(\varepsilon x.A), \varepsilon x.A) \to B(\varepsilon y.B(y, \varepsilon x.A), \varepsilon x.A))$. Hence $F' \equiv (B(t(s), s) \to B(\varepsilon y.B(y, s), s))$ is an ε-axiom, and $\mathrm{rk}_\varepsilon(\varepsilon y.B(y, s)) = \mathrm{rk}_\varepsilon(\varepsilon y.B(y, \varepsilon x.A))$ since ranks are unchanged under replacements of residing terms by other terms. Finally suppose $\mathrm{rk}_\varepsilon(\varepsilon y.B) = \mathrm{rk}_\varepsilon(\varepsilon x.A)$. Then $\mathrm{dg}_\varepsilon(\varepsilon y.B) \leq \mathrm{dg}_\varepsilon(\varepsilon x.A)$, and $\varepsilon x.A$ does not reside in $\varepsilon y.B$. In other words $\varepsilon x.A$ can occur in F as a subterm of t, i.e., $F \equiv (B(t(\varepsilon x.A)) \to B(\varepsilon y.B(y))$. Hence $\varepsilon y.B' \equiv \varepsilon y.B$ and $F' \equiv (B(t(s)) \to B(\varepsilon y.B(y))$. □

In the calculus $\boldsymbol{G}_\varepsilon$, $\Gamma, \bar{L}, L$ is an *axiom* for any sequent Γ and any literal L. Inference rules are propositional rules $(\vee)$, $(\wedge)$, and the following inference rule (ε) for epsilon terms and non-empty lists $t_1, \ldots, t_n$ of terms.

$$\frac{\Gamma, A(t_1), \ldots, A(t_n) \quad \neg A(\varepsilon x.A), \Gamma}{\Gamma}\ (\varepsilon)$$

The epsilon term $\varepsilon x.A$ is the *principal term* of the (ε). The epsilon axiom (2.15), $A(t) \to A(\varepsilon x.A(x))$ is provable in $\boldsymbol{G}_\varepsilon$.

$\boldsymbol{G}_\varepsilon \vdash^{\mathbf{a}}_{c} \Gamma$ designates that there exists a proof P of Γ in $\boldsymbol{G}_\varepsilon + (cut)$ such that c is the maximal rank of the principal terms of inferences (ε) in P, and $\mathbf{a} = (a_c, a_{c-1}, \ldots, a_1)$ such that the number of different principal terms of rank r in P is at most a_r. $\boldsymbol{G}_\varepsilon \vdash^{\mathbf{a}}_{0} \Gamma$ iff there is a proof of Γ in which no (ε) occurs.

A $\vee$*-expansion* of a sequent Γ with respect to an ε-term $\varepsilon x.A$ is a sequent $\Gamma_1, \ldots, \Gamma_n$, where each Γ_i is obtained from Γ by renaming free variables by fresh ones,[4] and substituting a term t_i for the ε-term $\varepsilon x.A$. We say that a sequent Δ is a $\vee$-expansion of a sequent Γ if Δ is obtained from Γ by successive expansions of some ε-terms.

Lemma 3.21 *Assume* $\mathbf{G}_\varepsilon \vdash^{\mathbf{a}}_{c} \Gamma_0$ *with* $\mathbf{a} = (a_c, a_{c-1}, \dots, a_1)$ *and* $c > 0$. *Then there exists a* $\vee$*-expansion* $\Gamma_0' = \Gamma_0 \cup \Gamma_1 \cup \cdots \cup \Gamma_n$ *of* Γ_0 *with respect to an* ε*-term, and* $\mathbf{a}' = (a'_c, a'_{c-1}, \dots, a'_1)$, c' *such that* $\mathbf{G}_\varepsilon \vdash^{\mathbf{a}'}_{c'} \Gamma_0'$ *and* $\langle c', a'_{c'}\rangle <_{lx} \langle c, a_c\rangle$ *lexicographically.*

Proof Let P be a proof witnessing the assumption $\mathbf{G}_\varepsilon \vdash^{\mathbf{a}}_{c} \Gamma_0$. Let $\varepsilon x.A$ be a principal term of an (ε) in P such that $\mathrm{rk}_\varepsilon(\varepsilon x.A) = c$ and its ε-degree is maximal among the principal terms of the highest ε-rank. This means that for any principal term $\varepsilon y.B$ occurring in P, $\langle \mathrm{rk}_\varepsilon(\varepsilon y.B), \mathrm{dg}_\varepsilon(\varepsilon y.B)\rangle \leq_{lx} \langle \mathrm{rk}_\varepsilon(\varepsilon x.A), \mathrm{dg}_\varepsilon(\varepsilon x.A)\rangle$ lexicographically.

First let us transform the proof P preliminarily. Transform the left to the right:

$$\dfrac{\Gamma, A(\mathbf{t}) \qquad \dfrac{\dfrac{\Delta, \neg A(\varepsilon x.A), A(\mathbf{s}) \quad \neg A(\varepsilon x.A), \Delta, \neg A(\varepsilon x.A)}{\Delta, \neg A(\varepsilon x.A)}\,(\varepsilon)}{\vdots \atop \neg A(\varepsilon x.A), \Gamma}}{\Gamma}\,(\varepsilon) \quad \rightsquigarrow \quad \dfrac{\Gamma, A(\mathbf{t}) \qquad \dfrac{\dfrac{\neg A(\varepsilon x.A), \Delta, \neg A(\varepsilon x.A)}{\Delta, \neg A(\varepsilon x.A)}}{\vdots \atop \neg A(\varepsilon x.A), \Gamma}}{\Gamma}\,(\varepsilon)$$

and

$$\dfrac{\dfrac{\dfrac{\Delta, A(\mathbf{t} * \mathbf{s}) \quad \neg A(\varepsilon x.A), \Delta}{\Delta, A(\mathbf{t})}\,(\varepsilon)}{\vdots \atop \Gamma, A(\mathbf{t})} \qquad \neg A(\varepsilon x.A), \Gamma}{\Gamma}\,(\varepsilon) \quad \rightsquigarrow \quad \dfrac{\dfrac{\dfrac{\Delta, A(\mathbf{t} * \mathbf{s})}{\Delta, A(\mathbf{t} * \mathbf{s})}}{\vdots \atop \Gamma, A(\mathbf{t} * \mathbf{s})} \quad \neg A(\varepsilon x.A), \Gamma}{\Gamma}\,(\varepsilon)$$

where $A(\mathbf{t}) = A(t_1), \dots, A(t_n)$, $A(\mathbf{s}) = A(s_1), \dots, A(s_m)$ and $A(\mathbf{t} * \mathbf{s}) = A(t_1), \dots, A(t_n), A(s_1), \dots, A(s_m)$. The resulting proof still witnesses $\mathbf{G}_\varepsilon \vdash^{\mathbf{a}}_{c} \Gamma_0$.

Hence we can assume that there occur no nested applications of inference rules (ε) with the same principal term $\varepsilon x.A$ in P, and any such inference is of the form for the same list $t_1, \dots, t_n$ of terms:

$$P = \dfrac{\dfrac{{\vdots\, Q_0 \atop \Delta, A(t_1), \dots, A(t_n)} \qquad {\vdots\, Q \atop \neg A(\varepsilon x.A), \Delta}}{\Delta}\,(\varepsilon)}{\vdots \atop \Gamma_0}$$

[4]No renaming is needed here, but we need it to deal with a second-order ε-calculus in the Exercise 3.3.

where there is no (ε) with the principal term $\varepsilon x.A$ in Q_0, Q nor below the inference rule (ε).

For each $i = 1, \ldots, n$, substitute the term t_i for $\varepsilon x.A$, and rename free variables in Q. From Proposition 3.3 we see that the resulting figure is a proof Q_i of $\neg A(t_i), \Delta_i$, where Δ_i is obtained from Δ by replacing $\varepsilon x.A$ by t_i. Moreover the maximal rank of principal terms in Q_i is at most c, and if it is c, then the number of different principal terms of rank c is unchanged. Delete the inference rule (ε) with the principal term $\varepsilon x.A$ to get the proof P_i, and combining these proofs with the proof Q_0 by a series of (cut)'s, we obtain a proof P':

$$P_i = \begin{array}{c} \vdots\ Q_i \\ \neg A(t_i), \Delta_i \\ \hline \neg A(t_i), \Delta_i \\ \vdots \\ \neg A(t_i), \Gamma_i \end{array} \quad P' = \begin{array}{c} \dfrac{\begin{array}{c}\vdots\ Q_0 \\ \Delta, A(t_1), \ldots, A(t_n)\end{array} \quad \begin{array}{c}\vdots\ P_1 \\ \neg A(t_1), \Gamma_1\end{array} \quad \cdots \quad \begin{array}{c}\vdots\ P_n \\ \neg A(t_n), \Gamma_n\end{array}}{\Delta, \Gamma_1, \ldots, \Gamma_n} \\ \vdots \\ \Gamma_0, \Gamma_1, \ldots, \Gamma_n \end{array}$$

Note here that $\Gamma_i = \Gamma_0(t_i, \mathbf{a}_i)$ for $\Gamma_0 = \Gamma_0(\varepsilon x.A, \mathbf{a})$, free variables $\mathbf{a}$ and fresh ones $\mathbf{a}_i$.

P' witnesses $\boldsymbol{G}_\varepsilon \vdash^{\mathbf{a}'}_{c'} \Gamma'_0$ for a $\vee$-expansion $\Gamma'_0 = \Gamma_0, \Gamma_1, \ldots, \Gamma_n$ of Γ_0 and some $\mathbf{a}' = (a'_c, a'_{c-1}, \ldots, a'_1)$, c' such that $\langle c', a'_{c'} \rangle <_{lx} \langle c, a_c \rangle$.

Specifically if there is only one principal term of rank c in P, then $c' < c \,\&\, \forall r(c' < r \leq c \to a'_r = 0)$. Otherwise $c' = c \,\&\, a'_c = a_c - 1$. In each case $a'_r \leq a_r \cdot (n+1)$ for $1 \leq r < c$, where n is the length of the list $t_1, \ldots, t_n$ of terms in (ε). □

Theorem 3.10 *If $\boldsymbol{G}_\varepsilon \vdash \Gamma$, then there exists a $\vee$-expansion Γ' of Γ such that $\bigvee \Gamma'$ is a tautology and Γ' is ε-free.*

Proof Assume $\boldsymbol{G}_\varepsilon \vdash \Gamma$. From Lemma 3.21 we see that there exists a $\vee$-expansion Γ_0 of Γ such that $\boldsymbol{G}_\varepsilon \vdash^{\emptyset}_{0} \Gamma_0$. Namely there is a $\boldsymbol{G}_\varepsilon + (cut)$-proof P_0 of Γ_0 in which no inference (ε) occurs. Replace every ε-term occurring in P_0 by a constant, we obtain a $\vee$-expansion Γ' of Γ in which ε does no occur. □

Exercises

3.1 In this exercise let us show that there is a non-elementary speed up of the predicate logic over the cut-free calculus. For an expression E, e.g., a sequent or a proof, the *size* of the expression E, $size(E)$ denotes the total number of occurrences of symbols in E.

Theorem 3.11 *There is no elementary recursive function E for which the following holds: for any proof P in $\boldsymbol{G}_1 + (cut)$, there exists a cut-free proof P' of the same end sequent such that $size(P') \leq E(size(P))$ for the size of the proof P, $size(P)$.*

Let $\mathscr{L} = \{0, S, f, =, \neq, N, \bar{N}\}$ be the first-order language, where 0 is an individual constant, S a unary function, f a binary one and N a unary predicate. We write $x \in N$ for $N(x)$, $x \notin N$ for $\bar{N}(x)$ and Sx for $S(x)$ when no confusion likely occurs. Let $\text{Hyp}_N = \{0 \in N, \forall x \in N(Sx \in N), \forall x \forall y[x = y \wedge y \in N \to x \in N]\}$, and Hyp denote the set of the universal closures of the equality axioms (stating that $=$ is a congruence relation) for the language $\{0, S, f\}$ and the following formulas:

$$\begin{cases} f(y, 0) = Sy \\ f(y, Sx) = f(f(y, x), x) \end{cases} \tag{3.6}$$

Note that Hyp is N-free. Let $\text{Hyp}^+ := \text{Hyp}_N \cup \text{Hyp}$, and $\neg\text{Hyp}^+ = \neg\text{Hyp}_N \cup \neg\text{Hyp}$, where $\neg\text{Hyp}_N = \{0 \notin N, \neg\forall x \in N(Sx \in N), \neg\forall x \forall y[x = y \wedge y \in N \to x \in N]\}$. The intended model of Hyp^+ is the model $\mathbb{N}_\omega$ whose universe is the set ω of natural numbers and in which N denotes $\mathbb{N}_\omega := \omega$, 0 is the zero, $Sx = x + 1$ and $f(y, x) = y + 2^x$. In particular $f(0, x) = 2^x$.

A formula is said to be *N-positive* if the predicate N occurs only positively in it, i.e., $\bar{N}$ does not occur in it. A sequent is said to be *N-positive* if it consists solely of N-positive formulas.

For a positive integer k, $\mathbb{N}_k$ denotes an $\mathscr{L}$-model in which the predicate N denotes the set $\mathbb{N}_k := \{n \in \omega : n < k\}$.

For natural numbers k, define terms $f^{(k)}(y)$ inductively by $f^{(0)}(y) :\equiv y$ and $f^{(k+1)}(y) :\equiv f(y, f^{(k)}(y))$. Let $t^{\mathbb{N}}$ denote the value of closed terms t in the model $\mathbb{N}_\omega$. For example $(f^{(k)}(0))^{\mathbb{N}} = 2_k(0)$.

Let us introduce a new axiom

$$\text{(zero)}\ \Gamma, 0 \in N$$

and two new inference rules (S) and (eq_N): for any terms t, s

$$\frac{\Gamma, t \in N, S(t) \in N}{\Gamma, S(t) \in N}\ (S)\ ; \quad \frac{\Gamma, s = t \quad \Gamma, t \in N}{\Gamma, s \in N}\ (eq_N)$$

Let $(N) \vdash^\alpha_c \Gamma$ denote the provability in the extended calculus. Then it is easy to see that $(N) \vdash^4_0 \forall x \in N(Sx \in N)$ and $(N) \vdash^7_0 \forall x \forall y[x = y \wedge y \in N \to x \in N]$.

1. Show that the calculus (N) admits the cut-elimination theorem:

$$(N) \vdash^n_c \Gamma \Rightarrow (N) \vdash^{2_c(n)}_0 \Gamma\ (c < \omega)$$

2. Show the following fact: Let Δ be an N-positive sequent and $k \geq m$. Under an assignment of free variables, if Δ holds in the model $\mathbb{N}_m$, then so does in $\mathbb{N}_k$.
3. For an N-positive sequent Δ, show that $(N) \vdash^k_0 \Delta \Rightarrow \mathbb{N}_{1+k} \models \Delta$.
4. Show that $\boldsymbol{G}_1 \vdash^n_0 \Gamma_k \Rightarrow n \geq 2_{k-5}(0) - 8$ for $\Gamma_k := \neg\text{Hyp}^+ \cup \{f^{(k)}(0) \in N\}$ and $k \geq 5$.

Conclude that no elementary recursive function bounds the function $F(k) := \min\{n \in \omega : G_1 \vdash_0^n \neg\text{Hyp}^+, f^{(k)}(0) \in N\}$. Namely $\forall c \exists k[F(k) > 2_c(k+c)]$.

5. For a sequence $\{\Delta_k\}_k$ of sequents Δ_k, $G_1 + (cut) \vdash^{*k} \Delta_k$ designates that there exist an elementary function E, and proofs P_k of Δ_k in $G_1 + (cut)$ such that $size(P_k) \leq E(k)$, and both the depths and cut degrees of P_k are bounded by a linear function of k.

   Let $A_n(x)$ be formulas recursively defined by:

$$A_0(x) :\equiv (x \in N) \text{ and}$$
$$A_{n+1}(x) :\equiv \forall y[A_n(y) \to A_n(f(y, x))] \tag{3.7}$$

   Show that $G_1 + (cut) \vdash^{*n} \neg\text{Hyp}^+, \forall x \forall y[x = y \wedge A_n(y) \to A_n(x)]$.

6. Show $G_1 + (cut) \vdash^{*n} \neg\text{Hyp}^+, A_n(0)$.
7. Show that there are proofs of $\neg\text{Hyp}^+, f^{(k)}(0) \in N$ in the predicate logic $G_1 + (cut)$ of linear depths: $\forall k\{G_1 + (cut) \vdash^{*k} \neg\text{Hyp}^+, f^{(k)}(0) \in N\}$.
8. Conclude that there is no constant c such that $\forall a \forall \Gamma[G_1 \vdash_a^a \Gamma \Rightarrow G_1 \vdash_0^{2_c(a+size(\Gamma))} \Gamma]$.

3.2 G_1^m denotes the sequent calculus for *minimal logic* obtained from G_1^i by dropping the initial sequents $\Gamma, \bot \Rightarrow C$ and $\Gamma \Rightarrow \top$.

In the exercise PA denotes the classical first-order arithmetic in the language with function symbols for primitive recursive functions. HA denotes the intuitionistic first-order arithmetic obtained from PA by dropping the excluded middle.

1. (Double negation shift, Gödel–Gentzen translation)
   The *negative translation* A^g of a formula A is defined recursively as follows.

   a. $P^g :\equiv \neg\neg P$ for atomic formulas other than $\bot, \top$.
   b. $\bot^g :\equiv \bot$, $\top^g :\equiv \top$, $(A \wedge B)^g :\equiv A^g \wedge B^g$, $(A \to B)^g :\equiv A^g \to B^g$ and $(\forall x A)^g :\equiv \forall x A^g$.
   c. $(A \vee B)^g :\equiv \neg(\neg A^g \wedge \neg B^g)$ and $(\exists x A)^g :\equiv \neg \forall x \neg A^g$.

   For sets Γ of formulas, $\Gamma^g :\equiv \{A^g : A \in \Gamma\}$. Show that if $G_1 \vdash \Gamma$, then $G_1^m \vdash \Rightarrow \Gamma^g$.
2. Show that PA $\vdash A$ implies HA $\vdash A^g$. First show that HA $\vdash \neg\neg(x = y) \to x = y$.
3. (H. Friedman's A-translation)
   Let A be a fixed formula. The *A-translation* $[B]_A$ of a formula B is defined recursively as follows.

   a. $[P]_A :\equiv (P \vee A)$ for atomic formulas other than $\bot, \top$.
   b. $[\bot]_A :\equiv A$ and $[\top]_A :\equiv (A \to A)$.
   c. $[B \circ C]_A :\equiv [B]_A \circ [C]_A$ for $\circ \in \{\vee, \wedge, \to\}$.
   d. $[QxB]_A :\equiv Qx[B]_A$ for $Q \in \{\exists, \forall\}$, where bound variables are renamed to avoid clashes if necessary.

For sets Γ of formulas, $[\Gamma]_A :\equiv \{[B]_A : B \in \Gamma\}$. Show that if $\boldsymbol{G}_1^i \vdash \Gamma \Rightarrow B$, then $\boldsymbol{G}_1^m \vdash [\Gamma]_A \Rightarrow [B]_A$.

4. Let $A \equiv (\exists x P)$ for an atomic formula P other than $\bot, \top$. Show first $\boldsymbol{G}_1^m \vdash [A]_A \Rightarrow A$, and conclude that $\boldsymbol{G}_1^i \vdash\Rightarrow A$ implies $\boldsymbol{G}_1^m \vdash\Rightarrow A$.
5. Show that $\mathsf{PA} \vdash \exists x P$ implies $\mathsf{HA} \vdash \exists x P$ for atomic formulas P.

3.3 $\boldsymbol{2\varepsilon}$ is an extension of the first-order logic calculus G_1 in a language $\mathscr{L}_1 \cup \{X_i^n : n, i < \omega\} \cup \{\varepsilon\}$ with n-ary relation variables X_i^n. In $\boldsymbol{2\varepsilon}$ one can introduce an n-ary relation $\varepsilon X^n.F[X^n]$ (*second-order epsilon term*) for each formula $F[X^n]$ with an n-ary relation variable X^n. For terms $t_1, \ldots, t_n$, $(\varepsilon X^n.F[X^n])(t_1, \ldots, t_n)$ and $(\varepsilon X^n.F[X^n])(t_1, \ldots, t_n)$ are then formulas.

By a *predicate* in $\boldsymbol{2\varepsilon}$ we mean either a relation symbol or a relation variable, or a second-order epsilon term. A second-order epsilon axiom is any formula of the following form:

$$F[R] \to F[\varepsilon X.F[X]] \text{ where } R \text{ is a predicate in } \boldsymbol{2\varepsilon} \tag{3.8}$$

The operation $F[X] \mapsto \varepsilon X.F[X]$ can be iterated, e.g., X may occur in another second-order epsilon term $\varepsilon Y.G[X, Y]$ in $F[X]$. While quantifications in $\boldsymbol{2\varepsilon}$ are restricted to first-order, $\exists x A, \forall x A$, no first-order epsilon term $\varepsilon x.A$ is introduced.

In what follows, let us restrict $\boldsymbol{2\varepsilon}$ to unary ones, i.e., relation symbols, relation variables X as well as second-order epsilon terms we are considering are unary.

A sequent calculus $\boldsymbol{G}_{2\varepsilon}$ is obtained from $\boldsymbol{G}_1$ by modifying the axiom to $\Gamma, \neg A, A$ for any formula A, and adding an inference rule (2ε) for second-order epsilon terms and non-empty lists $R_1, \ldots, R_n$ of (unary) predicates:

$$\frac{\Gamma, A(R_1) \quad \cdots \quad \Gamma, A(R_n) \quad \neg A(\varepsilon X.A), \Gamma}{\Gamma} \ (2\varepsilon)$$

where $\varepsilon X.A$ is the *principal predicate* of the inference (2ε).

A $\vee$*-expansion* of a sequent Γ with respect to an ε-predicate $\varepsilon X.A$ is a sequent $\Gamma_1 \cup \cdots \cup \Gamma_n$, where each Γ_i is obtained from Γ by renaming free variables by fresh ones, substituting a predicate R_i for the ε-predicate $\varepsilon X.A$, and quantifying some first-order variables occurring in R_i existentially. We say that a sequent Δ is a $\vee$-expansion of a sequent Γ if Δ is obtained from Γ by successive expansions of some ε-predicates.

Definition 3.8 is modified for subpredicates in formulas. A predicate R in an epsilon term $\varepsilon X.A$ is *subordinate* to $\varepsilon X.A$ if the variable X occurs in R. Otherwise the subpredicate R *resides* in $\varepsilon X.A$.

The ε-rank $\mathrm{rk}_{2\varepsilon}(R)$ and the ε-degree $\mathrm{dg}_{2\varepsilon}(R)$ of predicates are defined as in Definition 3.9.

$\boldsymbol{G}_{2\varepsilon} \vdash_c^{\mathbf{a}} \Gamma$ designates that there exists a proof P of Γ in $\boldsymbol{G}_{2\varepsilon} + (cut)$ such that c is the maximal rank of the principal predicates of inferences (2ε) in P, and $\mathbf{a} = (a_c, a_{c-1}, \ldots, a_1)$ such that the number of different principal predicates of rank r in P is at most a_r.

We say that $\varepsilon X.A'$ is a *variant* of $\varepsilon X.A$ if it is obtained from $\varepsilon X.A$ by replacing some first-order free variables by bound variables. The result B' of replacing an ε-predicate $\varepsilon X.A$ by a predicate R in a formula B is obtained from B by replacing every occurrence of a variant $\varepsilon X.A'$ of $\varepsilon X.A$ in B by R. In particular $(\exists x\, C)' \equiv \exists x\, (C)'$.

In the proof of Lemma 3.21 a preparatory transformation is made to unify nested inference rules (ε). In the calculus $\boldsymbol{G}_{2\varepsilon}$, the inference rules $(\forall)$ with eigenvariables prevent the transformation. Let us delete all of the inference rules $(\forall)$ from the given proof. Let P be a $\boldsymbol{G}_{2\varepsilon}$-proof of a sequent Γ_0. Delete a lowest inference $(\forall)$ occurring in P to get a proof P_1 of $\exists x\, A(x) \land \neg A(a), \Gamma_0$:

$$P = \begin{array}{c} \dfrac{\neg A(a), \forall x\, \neg A(x), \Gamma}{\forall x\, \neg A(x), \Gamma}\,(\forall) \\ \vdots \\ \Gamma_0 \end{array} \qquad P_1 = \dfrac{\begin{array}{c} \dfrac{}{\exists x\, A(x), \forall x\, \neg A(x), \Gamma}\,(Ax) \\ \vdots \\ \exists x\, A(x), \Gamma_0 \end{array} \quad \begin{array}{c} \dfrac{\neg A(a), \forall x\, \neg A(x), \Gamma}{\neg A(a), \forall x\, \neg A(x), \Gamma} \\ \vdots \\ \neg A(a), \Gamma_0 \end{array}}{\exists x\, A(x) \land \neg A(a), \Gamma_0}\,(\land)$$

Iterate this deletions, we obtain a $(\forall)$-free proof P' of Φ, Γ_0 for a sequent $\Phi = \{\exists x\, A_i(x) \land \neg A_i(a_i) : i < k\}$ such that the free variable a_i does not occur in $\exists x\, A_j(x) \land \neg A_j(a_j)$ for any $j < i$.

Let us denote $\boldsymbol{G}_{2\varepsilon}(\forall)^-$ a calculus obtained from $\boldsymbol{G}_{2\varepsilon}$ by deleting the inference rule $(\forall)$.

1. Proposition 3.3 holds for second-order ε-terms mutatis mutandis. Let $F \equiv (B(R) \to B(\varepsilon Y.B))$ be a second-order ε-axiom. Assume that $\langle \mathrm{rk}_{2\varepsilon}(\varepsilon Y.B), \mathrm{dg}_{2\varepsilon}(\varepsilon Y.B)\rangle \leq_{lx} \langle \mathrm{rk}_{2\varepsilon}(\varepsilon X.A), \mathrm{dg}_{2\varepsilon}(\varepsilon X.A)\rangle$ lexicographically for an ε-predicate $\varepsilon X.A$. Let F' denote the result of replacing every occurrence of the ε-predicate $\varepsilon X.A$ by a predicate S in F. Show the following: If $\varepsilon Y.B \equiv \varepsilon X.A$, then $F' \equiv (A(R') \to A(S))$ for the result R' of replacing $\varepsilon X.A$ by S in R.
   If $\varepsilon Y.B \not\equiv \varepsilon X.A$, then F' is again a second-order ε-axiom $F' \equiv (B'(R') \to B'(\varepsilon Y.B'))$ such that $\mathrm{rk}_{2\varepsilon}(\varepsilon Y.B') = \mathrm{rk}_{2\varepsilon}(\varepsilon Y.B)$, and if $\mathrm{rk}_{2\varepsilon}(\varepsilon Y.B) = \mathrm{rk}_{2\varepsilon}(\varepsilon X.A)$, then $\varepsilon Y.B' \equiv \varepsilon Y.B$.
2. Assume $\boldsymbol{G}_{2\varepsilon}(\forall)^- \vdash^{\mathbf{a}}_{c} \Gamma_0$ with $\mathbf{a} = (a_c, a_{c-1}, \ldots, a_1)$ and $c > 0$. Show that there exists a $\lor$-expansion $\Gamma_0' = \Gamma_0 \cup \Gamma_1 \cup \cdots \cup \Gamma_n$ of Γ_0 with respect to an ε-predicate, and $\mathbf{a}' = (a'_c, a'_{c-1}, \ldots, a'_1), c'$ such that $\boldsymbol{G}_{2\varepsilon}(\forall)^- \vdash^{\mathbf{a}'}_{c'} \Gamma_0'$ and $\langle c', a'_{c'}\rangle <_{lx} \langle c, a_c\rangle$ lexicographically.
3. Conclude the following theorem.

Theorem 3.12 *If P is a $\boldsymbol{G}_{2\varepsilon}$-proof of a sequent Γ_0, then we can find a $\boldsymbol{G}_1$-proof $2\varepsilon(P)$ of an ε-free $\lor$-expansion Γ_0' of Γ_0.*

3.4 Let $A(u, X_0, X_1)$ be a first-order formula with a first-order free variable u, a k_0-ary predicate variable X_0 and a k_1-ary one X_1. Expand the language $\mathcal{L}_2$ by introducing a symbol F_A, which is intended to denote a functional $X_0 \mapsto F_A(u, X_0) = X_1$ such that $A(u, X_0, X_1)$. Then formulas and (atomic) second-order terms are generated simultaneously as follows.

1. Each n-ary predicate variable is an n-ary second-order term.

2. If t is a (first-order) term and V is a k_0-ary second-order term, then $F_A(t, V)$ is a k_1-ary second-order term.
3. If $t_1, \dots, t_n$ are terms and V is an n-ary second-order term, then $V(t_1, \dots, t_n)$ and $\neg V(t_1, \dots, t_n)$ are *atomic* formulas.
4. If B is an *atomic* formula, then $\{(x_1, \dots, x_n)\}B$ is an n-ary second-order term.
5. Formulas are generated from atomic formulas by means of propositional connectives $\vee$, $\wedge$ and (first-order and second-order) quantifications $\exists$, $\forall$.

A second-order sequent calculus $F_A + \boldsymbol{G}'_{2at}$ is obtained from $\boldsymbol{G}'_2$ by adding initial sequents

$$\Gamma, A(t, V, F_A(t, V))$$

for terms t and k_0-ary second-order terms V, and restricting the inference rule $(\exists^2)$ to the following:

$$\frac{\Gamma, B(V)}{\Gamma} \ (\exists^{2at})$$

where $(\exists X\, B(X)) \in \Gamma$, and either V is a second-order term and B is first-order, or V is a variable.

An extension $F_A + \boldsymbol{G}'_{2at}(\mathrm{AC})$ is obtained from $F_A + \boldsymbol{G}'_{2at}$ by adding an inference rule

$$\frac{\Gamma, \exists Y\, C(x, Y) \quad \exists x \neg C(x, (Z)_x), \Gamma}{\Gamma} \ (\mathrm{AC})$$

where C is a first-order formula in $\mathcal{L}_2$, x is an eigenvariable, Y is an n-ary predicate variable, Z is an $(n+1)$-ary predicate variable not occurring in $\Gamma \cup \{C\}$ (eigenvariable), and $(Z)_x = \{(y_1, \dots, y_n)\}Z(y_1, \dots, y_n, x)$. The inference rule (AC) says that $\forall x \exists Y\, C(x, Y) \to \exists Z \forall x\, C(x, (Z)_x)$.

Show the following theorem.

Theorem 3.13 *Assume $F_A + \boldsymbol{G}'_{2at}(\mathrm{AC}) \vdash \exists Y\, B(Y)$ for a first-order formula B in $\mathcal{L}_2$. Then there exist second-order terms $\{W_i\}_{i<p}$ such that $F_A + \boldsymbol{G}_1 \vdash \{\exists B(W_i) : i < p\}$, where $\exists B(W_i)$ denotes a formula obtained from $B(W_i)$ by existentially quantifying some first-order variables.*

3.5 Notes

3.5.1 Section 3.1

Gentzen [6] formulated and proved the cut-elimination theorem. Our proof of Theorem 3.1 by maximal-cut-rank and topmost-first strategy with inversion is found in Tait [16]. Theorem 3.5 for classical propositional logic is implicit in Sato [13].

3.5.2 Section 3.2

Asymmetric interpretation is due to Cantini [4], who attribute the interpretation to Girard [8]. Theorem 3.7 is in [1], where it is shown that there is non-elementary speed-up of FiX over the first-order logic.

3.5.3 Section 3.3

A parallel cut-elimination procedure in Theorems 3.8 and 3.9 is in [2]. The proof is inspired from Mints [10], in which it is shown that monotone (no $\neg$ nor $\rightarrow$) cut formulas are quickly eliminated.

3.5.4 Section 3.4

For a readable account of a better numeric bound in elimination of epsilon symbols, Theorem 3.10, see Moser and Zach [11].

3.5.5 Exercises

Theorem 3.11 in Exercise 3.1 is due to [12], which is a finitary miniature of Gentzen's result for PA in Chap. 4. Orevkov proves the theorem after knowing the result in Statman [15], who shows the the number of disjuncts in Herbrand's theorem for purely existential formulas is not bounded by any elementary function of the size of proofs of the formulas.

The double negation shift in Exercise 1 is due to Gödel–Gentzen [7, 9]. Exercise 3 on A-translation is due to H. Friedman [5]. For a generalization of the translation, see Berger, Buchholz and Schwichtenberg [3, 14].

Theorem 3.12 in Exercise 3.3 is in [1].

References

1. Arai, T.: Non-elementary speed-ups in logic calculi. Math. Logic Quat. **54**, 629–640 (2008)
2. Arai, T.: Quick cut-elimination for strictly positive cuts. Ann. Pure Appl. Logic **162**, 807–815 (2011)
3. Berger, U., Buchholz, W., Schwichtenberg, H.: Refined program extraction from classical proofs. Ann. Pure Appl. Logic **114**, 3–25 (2002)
4. Cantini, A.: On the relationship between choice and comprehension principles in second order arithmetic. J. Symb. Logic **52**, 360–373 (1986)

5. Friedman, H.: Classically and intuitionistically provable recursive functions. In: Scott, D., Müllerm, G. H. (eds.) Higher Set Theory, pp. 21–28. Lecture Notes in Mathematics, vol. 669. Springer, Berlin (1978)
6. Gentzen, G.: Untersuchungen über das logische Schließen. Math. Zeitschr. **39**(I), 176–210: II, 405–431 (1934/35)
7. Gentzen, G.: Über das Verhältnis zwischen intuitionistischer und klassischer Logik. Arch. Math. Logik Grundl. **16**, 119–132 (1974)
8. Girard, J.-Y.: A survey of Π^1_2-logic. In: Pfeiffer, H., Los, J., Cohen, L.J. (eds.) Logic, Methodology and Philosophy of Sciences VI, pp. 89–107 North-Holland (1986)
9. Gödel, K.: Zur intuitionistischen Arithmetik und Zahlentheorie. Ergebnisse eines mathematischen Kolloquiums **4**, 34–38 (1933)
10. Mints, G.E.: Quick cut-elimination for monotone cuts. In: Mints, G., Muskens, R. (Eds.), Games, Logic, and Constructive Sets, Stanford, CA, 2000, pp. 75–83, CSLI Lecture Notes, vol.161, CSLIPubl., Stanford (2003)
11. Moser, G., R. Zach, R., The epsilon calculus and Herbrand complexity. Studia Logica, vol. 82, pp. 133–155 (2006)
12. Orevkov, V.P. : Lower bounds for the lengthening of proofs after cut-elimination (Russian), Zapiski Nauchnykh Seminarov Leningradskago Otdeleniya ONena Lenina Mathematicheskogo Instituta imeni V. A. Steklova Akademii Nauk SSSR (LOMI), vol. 88, pp. 137–162, 242–243 (1979). Translated in Journal of Soviet Mathematics, vol. 20, 2337–2350 (1982)
13. Sato, K.: Ordinal analyses for monotone and cofinal transfinite inductions. Arch. Math. Logic. **59**, 277–291 (2020)
14. Schwichtenberg, S., Wainer, S.S.: Proofs and Computations. Perspective in Logic, ASL. Cambridge University Press, Cambridge (2012)
15. Statman, R.: Lower bounds on Herbrand's theorem. Proc. AMS **75**, 104–107 (1979)
16. Tait, W.W.: Normal derivability in classical logic. In: Barwise. J. (ed.) Syntax and semantics of infinitary languages, Lecture Notes in Mathematics, vol. 72, pp. 204–236 (1968)
17. Troelstra, A.S., Schwichtenberg, H.: Basic Proof Theory, 2nd edn. Cambridge Tracts in Theoretical Computer Science, vol. 43. Cambridge University Press, Cambridge (2000)

Chapter 4
Epsilon Numbers

In this chapter let us begin with the celebrated result by G. Gentzen stating that the proof-theoretic ordinal of the first-order arithmetic PA is equal to the first epsilon number $|\mathsf{PA}| = \varepsilon_0 = \min\{\alpha > \omega : 2^\alpha = \alpha\}$. Our proof of the fact $|\mathsf{PA}| \leq \varepsilon_0$ is based on an elimination of first-order cut formulas. When we lower the cut degree by one, the tree-height of the resulting proof increases by one exponential. Thus the ordinal $\alpha = |\mathsf{PA}|$ needs to be a fixed point $2^\alpha = \alpha$ of an exponential function. Moreover $|\mathsf{PA}| > \omega$ due to the presence of complete induction schema. The main result in this chapter is a slight generalization of Gentzen's.

$\mathsf{PA}(U)$ denotes the first order arithmetic in a language $\mathcal{L}(U)$ with unary predicate U. Although for the result in this chapter it does not matter which function (symbol) and/or relation (symbol) is in the language $\mathcal{L}(U)$, let us specify $\mathcal{L} = \{=, \neq\} \cup \{\mathsf{f} : f \in \mathcal{E}^3\}$, i.e., the equality $=$ and its complement $\neq$ are the only relation symbols, and for each definition of an elementary recursive function f, a function symbol f is in $\mathcal{L}(U)$. Then for each elementary recursive relation R, $R(a_1, \ldots, a_n) :\Leftrightarrow \chi_R(a_1, \ldots, a_n) = 1$ and its complement $\overline{R}(a_1, \ldots, a_n) :\Leftrightarrow \chi_R(a_1, \ldots, a_n) = 0$ for the characteristic function χ_R. In what follows let us identify the function symbol f with the function f denoted by it. Moreover $\mathcal{L}(U)$ contains a distinguished, unary relation symbol U and its complement $\bar{U}$. Induction axiom schema $A(0) \wedge \forall x(A(x) \to A(S(x))) \to \forall x\, A(x)$ is available for any formula $A(x)$ (possibly containing the predicate variable $U, \bar{U}$) in the language $\mathcal{L}(U)$.

$\mathsf{HA}(U)$ denotes the *Heyting arithmetic* (intuitionistic arithmetic) with the unary relation symbol U, which is obtained from $\mathsf{PA}(U)$ by changing the underlying logic to the intuitionistic logic (Heyting predicate logic), or equivalently by deleting the law of the excluded middle.

Definition 4.1 By a *standard epsilon order* we mean a relation $\prec$ on $\mathbb{N}$, which enjoys the following conditions:

1. All of the following items are elementary recursive: the relation $\prec$, its field $fld(\prec) := \{\alpha \in \mathbb{N} : \exists \beta \in \mathbb{N}(\alpha \prec \beta \vee \beta \prec \alpha)\}$, the functions $(\alpha, \beta) \mapsto \alpha + \beta$ (addition) and $(\alpha, n) \mapsto \omega^\alpha \cdot n$ $(\alpha \in fld(\prec), n \in \mathbb{N})$.

© The Editor(s) (if applicable) and The Author(s), under exclusive license
to Springer Nature Singapore Pte Ltd. 2020

T. Arai, *Ordinal Analysis with an Introduction to Proof Theory*, Logic in Asia:
Studia Logica Library, https://doi.org/10.1007/978-981-15-6459-8_4

$\alpha, \beta, \gamma, \dots$ range over $fld(\prec)$. Let $\omega^\alpha := \omega^\alpha \cdot 1$, and $1 := \omega^0$.

2. All of the following elementary algebraic properties on $(\prec, \alpha + \beta, \omega^\alpha \cdot n)$ are provable in the fragment $\mathsf{EA} = I\Sigma_0(\mathcal{E}^3)$ of the first-order arithmetic.

   a. $\prec$ is a linear ordering on $fld(\prec)$.
   b. 0 is the least element of $\prec$.
   c. $+$ is associative, $(\alpha + \beta) + \gamma = \alpha + (\beta + \gamma)$.
   d. $\alpha + 0 = 0 + \alpha = \alpha$.
   e. $\omega^\alpha \cdot 0 = 0$ and $\omega^\alpha \cdot (n+1) = \omega^\alpha \cdot n + \omega^\alpha$.
   f. $\alpha \prec \beta + 1 (:= \beta + \omega^0) \Rightarrow \alpha \preceq \beta (:\Leftrightarrow \alpha \prec \beta \lor \alpha = \beta)$.
   g. $0 \prec \alpha \,\&\, \gamma \prec \beta + \omega^\alpha \to \exists \delta \prec \alpha \exists n \in \mathbb{N}(\gamma \prec \beta + \omega^\delta \cdot n)$.
   This means that $\lambda \in Lim \,\&\, \gamma \prec \beta + \omega^\lambda \Rightarrow \exists \alpha \prec \lambda(\gamma \prec \beta + \omega^\alpha)$ for $\alpha \in Lim :\Leftrightarrow 0 \prec \alpha \,\&\, \forall \beta \prec \alpha(\beta + 1 \prec \alpha)$, and $\gamma \prec \beta + \omega^{\alpha+1} \Rightarrow \exists n \in \mathbb{N}(\gamma \prec \beta + \omega^\alpha \cdot n)$.
   h. $\forall \alpha > 0 \exists !(\alpha_0 \succ \cdots \succ \alpha_n), (k_0, \dots, k_n) \in {}^{<\omega}\mathbb{N}^+[\alpha_0 \leq \alpha \land \alpha = \omega^{\alpha_0} k_0 + \cdots + \omega^{\alpha_n} k_n]$ where $\mathbb{N}^+ = \mathbb{N} \setminus \{0\}$.
   i. Let $\alpha_0 \succ \cdots \succ \alpha_n$, $\beta_0 \succ \cdots \succ \beta_m$ and $(k_0, \dots, k_n), (\ell_0, \dots, \ell_m) \in {}^{<\omega}\mathbb{N}^+$. Then $\omega^{\alpha_0} k_0 + \cdots + \omega^{\alpha_n} k_n < \omega^{\beta_0} \ell_0 + \cdots + \omega^{\beta_m} \ell_m$ iff either $n < m \,\&\, \forall i \leq n[(\alpha_i, k_i) = (\beta_i, \ell_i)]$, or there exists a $j \leq \min\{n, m\}$ such that $\forall i < j[(\alpha_i, k_i) = (\beta_i, \ell_i)]$ and $\alpha_j \prec \beta_j \lor (\alpha_j = \beta_j \land k_j < \ell_j)$.

A *standard epsilon order with base* Ω is a standard epsilon order such that for an $\Omega \in fld(\prec)$, $\forall \alpha \in fld(\prec) \exists n(\alpha \prec \omega_n(\Omega + 1))$, where $\omega_0(\alpha) = \alpha$ and $\omega_{n+1}(\alpha) = \omega^{\omega_n(\alpha)}$.

Let us write $<$ for $\prec$ when no confusion likely occurs. A *standard* ε_0*-order* is a standard epsilon order with base 0, and of type ε_0.

In the following Theorem 4.1, $<$ denotes a standard epsilon order. Let us write $\alpha < \Lambda :\Leftrightarrow \alpha \in fld(<)$, where Λ intends to denote the order type of $<$ when $<$ is well-founded. $\beta <_\alpha \gamma :\Leftrightarrow \beta < \gamma < \alpha$ its initial segments determined by $\alpha < \Lambda$. $\Pi^1_0(U)$ denotes the set of first-order formulas in the arithmetic language with a unary predicate U, $\mathrm{TI}(\Lambda, U) = \{\mathrm{TI}[<, F] : F \in \Pi^1_0(U)\}$, and $\mathrm{TI}(< \Lambda, U) = \{\mathrm{TI}[<_\alpha, F] : \alpha < \Lambda, F \in \Pi^1_0(U)\}$. $\mathrm{TI}(\Lambda) = \{\mathrm{TI}[<, F] : F \in \Pi^1_0\}$ and $\mathrm{TI}(< \Lambda) = \{\mathrm{TI}[<_\alpha, F] : \alpha < \Lambda, F \in \Pi^1_0\}$ denote the transfinite induction schemata without the predicate U, cf. Definition 1.10.

$\mathcal{E}^\omega WDS_\Lambda$ denotes a Π_3-sentence saying that every primitive recursive, weakly descending chain of ordinals $< \Lambda$ has a limit, and $\mathcal{E}^\omega WDS_{<\Lambda} = \{\mathcal{E}^\omega WDS_\alpha : \alpha < \Lambda\}$. While $\mathcal{E}^\omega DS_\Lambda$ denotes a Π_2-sentence saying that there is no primitive recursive, descending chain of ordinals $< \Lambda$, and $\mathcal{E}^\omega DS_{<\Lambda} = \{\mathcal{E}^\omega DS_\alpha : \alpha < \Lambda\}$. $\mathrm{Con}^{(m)}(T)$ is the mth iterated consistency statement of T, and $(\mathcal{E}^\omega\text{–TI})_\Lambda$ an inference rule for transfinite induction along $< \Lambda$, applied to primitive recursive predicates, and $(\mathcal{E}^\omega\text{–TI})_{<\Lambda} = \{(\mathcal{E}^\omega\text{–TI})_\alpha : \alpha < \Lambda\}$.

A computable, total function is α*-recursive* if the function is defined by recursion along the order $<_\alpha$.

Definition 4.2 $\mathcal{R}^\alpha$ denotes the smallest class of number-theoretic functions such that $\mathcal{E}^3 \subset \mathcal{R}^\alpha$ and it is closed under composition, and the following *α-recursion*: Define a function f from functions g, r, h by α-recursion.

$$f(\mathbf{y}, x) = \begin{cases} g(\mathbf{y}, x, f(\mathbf{y}, r(\mathbf{y}, x))) & \text{if} r(\mathbf{y}, x) < x < \alpha \\ h(\mathbf{y}, x) & \text{otherwise} \end{cases} \tag{4.1}$$

Each function in the class $\mathcal{R}^\alpha$ is said to be an *α-recursive function*. Put $\mathcal{R}^{<\alpha} = \bigcup_{\beta<\alpha} \mathcal{R}^\beta$.

For $\alpha \geq \omega$, it is clear that the class $\mathcal{R}^\alpha$ is closed under primitive recursion.

Intuitively the function $f(\mathbf{y}, x)$ in (4.1) is defined since $\{r^{(n)}(\mathbf{y}, x)\}_n$ is not an infinite descending chain of ordinals$< \alpha$.

Definition 4.3 A function g on $\mathbb{N}$ is *α-limit computable*, denoted $g \in \mathcal{LR}^\alpha$ if there exist primitive recursive functions f and h such that $\{h(\mathbf{c}, w)\}_w$ is a weakly descending chain of ordinals$< \alpha$, $\forall \mathbf{c}, w[h(\mathbf{c}, w+1) \leq h(\mathbf{c}, w) < \alpha]$, $\forall \mathbf{c}, w[f(\mathbf{c}, w) \neq f(\mathbf{c}, w+1) \to h(\mathbf{c}, w) > h(\mathbf{c}, w+1)]$, and $g(\mathbf{c}) = \lim_{w\to\infty} f(\mathbf{c}, w)$, i.e., $g(\mathbf{c}) = a \Leftrightarrow \exists w_0 \forall w \geq w_0[a = f(\mathbf{c}, w) = f(\mathbf{c}, w_0)]$.

Intuitively the function $g(\mathbf{c})$ is defined since the weakly descending chain $\{h(\mathbf{c}, w)\}_w$ of ordinals$< \alpha$ has a limit, i.e., $\exists w_0 \forall w \geq w_0[h(\mathbf{c}, w) = h(\mathbf{c}, w_0)]$.

Remark 4.1 Although we could say that the limit function g is α-limit computable *in* T when two conditions $\forall \mathbf{c}, w[h(\mathbf{c}, w+1) \leq h(\mathbf{c}, w) < \alpha]$ and $\forall \mathbf{c}, w[f(\mathbf{c}, w) \neq f(\mathbf{c}, w+1) \to h(\mathbf{c}, w) > h(\mathbf{c}, w+1)]$ are provable in a theory T, as far as we are concerned with the class $Fnc_{\Sigma_2}(T)$ of provably Σ_2-functions in theories $T \supset I\Sigma_1$ in the following Theorem 4.1.3d, these Π_1-conditions are need not to be provable in T, cf. Proposition 2.4.

Theorem 4.1 *1. Let* Ω *be a base of the standard epsilon order* $<$. *Then* $\mathsf{HA}(U) + \mathrm{TI}(\Omega, U)$ *proves* $\mathrm{TI}(< \Lambda, U)$.

2. *Assume that* $<$ *is well-founded. The proof-theoretic ordinal of the extension of* $\mathsf{PA}(U)$ *by the axiom schema* $\mathrm{TI}(< \Lambda, U)$ *is equal to the ordinal* Λ: $|\mathsf{PA}(U) + \mathrm{TI}(< \Lambda, U)| = \Lambda$.
3. *Each of the following equivalences in 3a, 3b, 3e, and 3h is provable in* $I\Sigma_1$:

   a. *The schema* $\mathrm{TI}(\Lambda)$ *of transfinite induction up to* Λ *is equivalent to the uniform reflection schema* $\{\mathrm{RFN}_{\Sigma_n}(\mathsf{PA} + \mathrm{TI}(< \Lambda))\}_{n<\omega}$.
   b. *The 2-consistency* $\mathrm{RFN}_{\Sigma_2}(\mathsf{PA} + \mathrm{TI}(< \Lambda))$ *of* $\mathsf{PA} + \mathrm{TI}(< \Lambda)$ *is equivalent to* $\mathcal{E}^\omega WDS_\Lambda$.
   c. $\mathsf{PA} + \mathrm{TI}(< \Lambda)$ *is* Π_3*-conservative over* $I\Sigma_1 + \mathcal{E}^\omega WDS_{<\Lambda}$.
   d. *For* Σ_2*-definable functions* f *on* $\mathbb{N}$, f *is* Σ_2*-definable in* $\mathsf{PA} + \mathrm{TI}(< \Lambda)$, $f \in Fnc_{\Sigma_2}(\mathsf{PA} + \mathrm{TI}(< \Lambda))$ *iff* f *is* α*-limit computable for an* $\alpha < \Lambda$, $f \in \mathcal{LR}^{<\Lambda} = \bigcup_{\alpha<\Lambda} \mathcal{LR}^\alpha$.
   e. *The 1-consistency* $\mathrm{RFN}_{\Sigma_1}(\mathsf{PA} + \mathrm{TI}(< \Lambda))$ *of* $\mathsf{PA} + \mathrm{TI}(< \Lambda)$ *is equivalent to* $\mathcal{E}^\omega DS_\Lambda$.

f. $\mathsf{PA} + \mathrm{TI}(< \Lambda)$ *is* Π_2*-conservative over* $I\Sigma_1 + \mathscr{E}^\omega DS_{<\Lambda}$.
g. For computable total function f *on* $\mathbb{N}$, f *is provably computable in* $\mathsf{PA} + \mathrm{TI}(< \Lambda)$, $f \in Fnc_{\Sigma_1}(\mathsf{PA} + \mathrm{TI}(< \Lambda))$ *iff* f *is* α*-recursive for an* $\alpha < \Lambda$, $f \in \mathscr{R}^{<\Lambda} = \bigcup_{\alpha<\Lambda} \mathscr{R}^\alpha$.
h. $\{\mathrm{Con}^{(m)}(\mathsf{PA} + \mathrm{TI}(< \Lambda)) : m < \omega\}$ *is equivalent to* $(\mathscr{E}^\omega\text{–TI})_\Lambda$.
i. $\mathsf{PA} + \mathrm{TI}(< \Lambda)$ *is* Π_1*-conservative over (one application of a rule)* $I\Sigma_1 + (\mathscr{E}^\omega\text{–TI})_{<\Lambda}$.

Note that when $<$ is a standard ε_0-order, we have $\mathsf{PA}(U) = \mathsf{PA}(U) + \mathrm{TI}(< \varepsilon_0, U)$ by Theorem 4.1.1. Therefore we obtain the following for PA.

Corollary 4.1 *Let* $<$ *be a standard* ε_0*-order.*

1. *Assuming the well-foundedness of* $<$, $|\mathsf{PA}(U)| = \varepsilon_0$.
2. *Each of the following equivalences in 2a, 2b, 2e, and 2h is provable in* $I\Sigma_1$*:*

   a. The schema $\mathrm{TI}(\varepsilon_0)$ *of transfinite induction up to* ε_0 *and applied to arithmetical formulas, is equivalent to the uniform reflection schema* $\{\mathrm{RFN}_{\Sigma_n}(\mathsf{PA}\}_{n<\omega}$.
   b. The 2-consistency $\mathrm{RFN}_{\Sigma_2}(\mathsf{PA})$ *of* PA *is equivalent to* $\mathscr{E}^\omega WDS_{\varepsilon_0}$.
   c. PA *is* Π_3*-conservative over* $I\Sigma_1 + \mathscr{E}^\omega WDS_{<\varepsilon_0}$.
   d. For Σ_2*-definable functions* f *on* $\mathbb{N}$, f *is* Σ_2*-definable in* PA, $f \in Fnc_{\Sigma_2}(\mathsf{PA})$ *iff* f *is* α*-limit computable for an* $\alpha < \varepsilon_0$, $f \in \mathscr{L}\mathscr{R}^{<\varepsilon_0} = \bigcup_{\alpha<\varepsilon_0} \mathscr{L}\mathscr{R}^\alpha$.
   e. The 1-consistency $\mathrm{RFN}_{\Sigma_1}(\mathsf{PA})$ *of* PA *is equivalent to* $\mathscr{E}^\omega DS_{\varepsilon_0}$.
   f. PA *is* Π_2*-conservative over* $I\Sigma_1 + \mathscr{E}^\omega DS_{<\varepsilon_0}$.
   g. For computable total function f *on* $\mathbb{N}$, f *is provably computable in* PA, $f \in Fnc_{\Sigma_1}(\mathsf{PA})$ *iff* f *is* α*-recursive for an* $\alpha < \varepsilon_0$, $f \in \mathscr{R}^{<\varepsilon_0} = \bigcup_{\alpha<\varepsilon_0} \mathscr{R}^\alpha$.
   h. $\{\mathrm{Con}^{(m)}(\mathsf{PA}) : m < \omega\}$ *is equivalent to* $(\mathscr{E}^\omega\text{–TI})_{\varepsilon_0}$.
   i. PA *is* Π_1*-conservative over (one application of a rule)* $I\Sigma_1 + (\mathscr{E}^\omega\text{–TI})_{<\varepsilon_0}$.

In Sect. 4.1 the transfinite induction $\mathrm{TI}[<_\alpha, U]$ up to *each* $\alpha < \Lambda$ is shown to be provable in the intuitionistic first-order arithmetic (Heyting arithmetic) $\mathsf{HA}(U) + \mathrm{TI}(\Omega, U)$ with a unary predicate U and the base Ω of $<$.

In Sect. 4.2 we see that for any elementary recursive relation, if it is provably well-founded in $\mathsf{PA}(U) + \mathrm{TI}(< \Lambda, U)$, then its order type is less than Λ assuming that $<$ is well-founded. Two proofs of this fact are given. First we obtain upper bounds for order types of provably well-founded, elementary recursive *strict partial orders* from the depths of almost cut-free derivations of the well-foundedness in the ω-logic. Second cut inferences are eliminated from derivation in an ω-logic with a rule for progressiveness, thereby we obtain an upperbound for order types of provably well-founded, elementary recursive *relations*. The second proof is closer to Gentzen's original proof, and yields a byproduct, which states that from a given proof of the well-foundedness of an elementary recursive *relation*, we can find an ordinal recursive embedding from the relation to an initial segment of a standard epsilon order.

The 2-consistency of $\mathsf{PA} + \mathrm{TI}(< \Lambda)$ is shown in Sect. 4.2.3 to be equivalent to the weak descending chain principle up to Λ, which says that every primitive recursive weakly descending (non-increasing) sequence of ordinals $< \Lambda$ has a limit.

In Sect. 4.3 we first present Gentzen's (second) consistency proof, which shows that the consistency of $\mathsf{PA} + \mathrm{TI}(< \Lambda)$ follows from the fact (descending chain principle up to Λ) that no primitive recursive sequence of ordinals $< \Lambda$ is an infinite descending chain. This finitary and finer proof is applied to Π_2-analyses, i.e., to calibrate the proof-theoretic strength of the 1-consistency of $\mathsf{PA} + \mathrm{TI}(< \Lambda)$ with the descending chain principle, and to identify the provably computable functions in $\mathsf{PA} + \mathrm{TI}(< \Lambda)$ with $< \Lambda$-recursive functions. In Sect. 4.3.2 we give several characterizations of the provably computable functions in PA.

Finally in Sect. 4.4 an intuitionistic fixed point theory over PA [over KP] is shown to be conservative over PA [KP], resp. Our proof is based on finitary analysis of intuitionistic fixed point theories, which is a mixture of Gentzen's consistency proof in Sect. 4.3.1, and a cut-elimination procedure for intuitionistic fixed point logic in Sect. 3.3.2.

In this section $<$ denotes a standard epsilon order unless otherwise stated.

4.1 Provability of Transfinite Induction

In this section we show first Theorem 4.1.1. Let $<$ be a standard epsilon order with base Ω. We show that $\mathsf{HA}(U) + \mathrm{TI}(\Omega, U)$ proves the transfinite induction $\mathrm{TI}[<_\alpha, A]$ up to *each* $\alpha < \Lambda$ and each formula A. Since Ω is a base of $<$, it suffices to show that $\mathsf{HA}(U) + \mathrm{TI}(\Omega, U) \vdash \mathrm{TI}[<_{\omega_n(\Omega+1)}, A]$ for each $n \in \mathbb{N}$ and each formula A.

For a given formula $A(\alpha)$, let $\mathrm{j}[A](\alpha)$ denote the following formula:

$$\mathrm{j}[A](\alpha) :\Leftrightarrow \forall \beta[\forall \gamma < \beta A(\gamma) \to \forall \gamma < \beta + \omega^\alpha A(\gamma)] \tag{4.2}$$

We first show the

Claim 4.1 $\mathsf{HA}(U) \vdash Prg[<, A] \to Prg[<, \mathrm{j}[A]]$.

Proof Let us show Claim 4.1. Assume that $A(\alpha)$ is progressive and

$$\forall \delta < \alpha\, \mathrm{j}[A](\delta) \tag{4.3}$$

We have to show $\mathrm{j}[A](\alpha)$. So assume

$$\forall \gamma < \beta A(\gamma) \tag{4.4}$$

and $\gamma < \beta + \omega^\alpha$. We show $A(\gamma)$.

Case 1. $\alpha = 0$: Then $\gamma < \beta + 1$. By (2f) in Definition 4.1 we have $\gamma \leq \beta$. (4.4) with $Prg[<, A]$ (for the case $\gamma = \beta$) yields $A(\gamma)$.

Case 2. $\alpha > 0$: Then by (2g) in Definition 4.1 we have $\gamma < \beta + \omega^\delta \cdot n$ for some $\delta < \alpha$ and n. Hence by (4.3) we have $\mathrm{j}[A](\delta)$. Therefore by induction on n applied to the formula $B(n) :\equiv (\forall \gamma < \beta + \omega^\delta \cdot n\, A(\gamma))$, we see $\forall n \forall \gamma < \beta + \omega^\delta \cdot n\, A(\gamma)$ from the definition of the formula $\mathrm{j}[A]$, (4.4) and (2e). This shows Claim 4.1. □

Proof We show by *metainduction* on $n \in \mathbb{N}$ that $\mathsf{HA}(U) + \mathrm{TI}(\Omega, U) \vdash \mathrm{TI}[<_{\omega_n(\Omega+1)}, A]$ for any A. Assume that a formula A is progressive. Suppose $Prg[<, B] \to \forall\alpha < \omega_n(\Omega+1)B(\alpha)$ for any formula $B(\alpha)$ as IH. By Claim 4.1 the formula $\mathrm{j}[A]$ is also progressive. IH yields $\forall\alpha < \omega_n(\Omega+1)\mathrm{j}[A](\alpha)$, and hence $\mathrm{j}[A](\omega_n(\Omega+1))$. Putting $\beta := 0$ in the definition of the formula $\mathrm{j}[A]$ we see $\forall\gamma < 0 + \omega^{\omega_n(\Omega+1)}A(\gamma)$, i.e., $\forall\gamma < \omega_{n+1}(\Omega+1)A(\gamma)$ from (2b) and (2d) in Definition 4.1.

For the case $n = 0$, $\mathrm{TI}[<_{\Omega+1}, A]$ follows from $\mathrm{TI}(\Omega)$ and (2f) in Definition 4.1. □

The easy half of Theorem 4.1.3a is seen as follows. Arguing in EA, we have $\forall\alpha < \Lambda\, \mathrm{Pr}_T(\ulcorner Prg[<, A] \to A(\dot{\alpha})\urcorner)$ for a standard provability predicate Pr_T for $T = \mathsf{PA} + \mathrm{TI}(<\Lambda)$. Hence for an n, $\mathrm{RFN}_{\Sigma_n}(\mathsf{PA} + \mathrm{TI}(<\Lambda))$ yields $\forall\alpha < \Lambda(Prg[<, A] \to A(\alpha))$, i.e., $\mathrm{TI}[<, A]$.

Let $\{[e] : e \in Code^{(1)}(\mathscr{E}^\omega)\}$ be an enumeration of unary primitive recursive functions in $\mathscr{E}^\omega$ such that $Code^{(1)}(\mathscr{E}^\omega)$ is a set of codes of unary primitive recursive functions, and the relations $e \in Code^{(1)}(\mathscr{E}^\omega)$ and $\{(e, x, y) : [e](x) = y\}$ are primitive recursive.

For $\alpha \leq \Lambda$, let $\mathscr{E}^\omega DS_\alpha$ be a Π_2-sentence saying that 'there is no primitive recursive infinite descending chain of ordinals $< \alpha$':

$$\mathscr{E}^\omega DS_\alpha :\Leftrightarrow \forall e \in Code^{(1)}(\mathscr{E}^\omega)\{[e](0) < \alpha \to \exists x([e](x+1) \not< [e](x))\] \quad (4.5)$$

Note that $\mathscr{E}^\omega DS_\alpha$ is equivalent over EA to each of $\forall e \in Code^{(1)}(\mathscr{E}^\omega)\{\forall x([e](x) < \alpha) \to \exists x([e](x+1) \not< [e](x))\]$ and $\forall e \in Code^{(1)}(\mathscr{E}^\omega)\forall m\exists x \geq m([e](m) < \alpha \to [e](x+1) \not< [e](x))$: Assume the former, and let $[e](0) < \alpha$. If there exists an x_0 such that $[e](x_0) \not< \alpha$, then let $0 < x \leq x_0$ be the least such number. The existence of x is seen in EA. Then $[e](x) \not< [e](x-1)$.

Next let $\mathscr{E}^\omega WDS_\alpha$ be the following Π_3-sentence saying that 'any primitive recursive weakly descending chain has a limit':

$$\begin{aligned} \mathscr{E}^\omega WDS_\alpha :\Leftrightarrow\ & \forall e \in Code^{(1)}(\mathscr{E}^\omega)\{[e](0) < \alpha \wedge \forall x([e](x+1) \leq [e](x)) \\ & \to \exists x\forall y \geq x([e](y) = [e](x))\} \end{aligned} \quad (4.6)$$

Likewise $\mathscr{E}^3 DS_\alpha$ [$\mathscr{E}^3 WDS_\alpha$] denotes a Π_2-sentence [Π_3-sentence] saying that 'there is no *elementary recursive* infinite descending chain of ordinals $< \alpha$' ['any *elementary recursive* weakly descending chain has a limit'], resp. The following Proposition 4.1 show easy halves in Theorems 4.1.3c, 4.1.3d, 4.1.3f, 4.1.3g, and 4.1.3i.

For $\alpha \leq \Lambda$, $(\mathscr{E}^\omega\text{–TI})_\alpha$ denotes the following inference rule for transfinite induction:

$$\frac{\forall\beta < \alpha((f(\beta) < \beta \to B(f(\beta))) \to B(\beta))}{\forall\beta < \alpha\, B(\beta)}\ (\mathscr{E}^\omega\text{–TI})_\alpha$$

where B is a primitive recursive relation in $\mathscr{E}^{\omega}_{*}$, and f is a primitive recursive function in $\mathscr{E}^{\omega}$. Both B and f may have parameters other than β.

Proposition 4.1 *For each* $\alpha < \Lambda$, $\mathsf{PA} + \mathrm{TI}(< \Lambda) \vdash \mathscr{E}^{\omega} DS_{\alpha} \land \mathscr{E}^{\omega} WDS_{\alpha}$, $\mathscr{R}^{\alpha} \subset Fnc_{\Sigma_1}(\mathsf{PA} + \mathrm{TI}(< \Lambda))$, $\mathscr{L}\mathscr{R}^{\alpha} \subset Fnc_{\Sigma_2}(\mathsf{PA} + \mathrm{TI}(< \Lambda))$, *and* $(\mathscr{E}^{\omega}{-}\mathrm{TI})_{\alpha}$ *is an admissible rule in* $\mathsf{PA} + \mathrm{TI}(< \Lambda)$.

Proof Obviously $(\mathscr{E}^{\omega}{-}\mathrm{TI})_{\alpha}$ is an admissible rule in $\mathsf{PA} + \mathrm{TI}(< \Lambda)$, and $\mathsf{PA} \vdash \mathscr{E}^{\omega} WDS_{\alpha} \to \mathscr{E}^{\omega} DS_{\alpha}$. Let $\alpha < \Lambda$. Given a primitive recursive function f such that $f(0) < \alpha$ and $\{f(y)\}_y$ is a weakly descending chain, $\forall y(f(y+1) \leq f(y))$, there exists a $<$-minimal element m in its range $\{m : \exists x(m = f(x))\}$ by $\mathsf{PA} \vdash TI[<_{\alpha}, \Pi_1]$, i.e., by Theorem 4.1.1, since the range of f is a Σ_1-set containing the element $f(0) < \alpha$. Pick an x such that $m = f(x)$. Then $\forall y(f(y) \not<_{\alpha} f(x)), \forall y \geq x(f(y) = f(x))$, and $\mathscr{E}^{\omega} WDS_{\alpha}$ is shown, which yields $\mathscr{R}^{\alpha} \subset Fnc_{\Sigma_1}(\mathsf{PA} + \mathrm{TI}(< \Lambda))$ and $\mathscr{L}\mathscr{R}^{\alpha} \subset Fnc_{\Sigma_2}(\mathsf{PA} + \mathrm{TI}(< \Lambda))$, cf. Remark 4.1. □

4.1.1 A Standard ε_0-Order

Let us define a standard ε_0-order in EA.

Let $(a_0, \ldots, a_{n-1}) \mapsto \langle a_0, \ldots, a_{n-1} \rangle \in \mathbb{N}$ be an elementary recursive encoding of finite sequences $(a_0, \ldots, a_{n-1})$ of natural numbers with an elementary recursive inverses. Assume that the code $0 = \langle\,\rangle$ of the empty sequence $(\,)$.

First define a superset D of the set fld recursively by: $0 \in D$. $\{a_0, \ldots, a_{n-1}\} \subset D \,\&\, n \geq 2 \Rightarrow \langle 0, a_0, \ldots, a_{n-1} \rangle \in D$. $a \in D \Rightarrow \langle 1, a \rangle \in D$.

It is easy to see that D is elementary recursive. Let $a_0 + \cdots + a_{n-1} := \langle 0, a_0, \ldots, a_{n-1} \rangle$ and $\omega^a := \langle 1, a \rangle$.

Next define a binary relation $\prec$ on D as follows. $0 \prec a$ for any $a \neq 0$. $\omega^a \prec \omega^b \Leftrightarrow a \prec b$. $\omega^a \prec \omega^{b_0} + \cdots + \omega^{b_{m-1}}$ iff $a \preceq b_0 :\Leftrightarrow (a \prec b_0 \lor a = b_0)$. $\omega^{a_0} + \cdots + \omega^{a_{n-1}} \prec \omega^b$ iff $a_0 \prec b$. $\omega^{a_0} + \cdots + \omega^{a_{n-1}} \prec \omega^{b_0} + \cdots + \omega^{b_{m-1}}$ iff either $\exists k < \min(n, m)$ $[\forall i < k(a_i = b_i) \land a_k \prec b_k]$ or $n < m \land \forall i < n(a_i = b_i)$.

We see that $\prec$ is an elementary recursive linear ordering.

Let us define the set $fld \subset D$ recursively as follows. $0 \in fld$. $\{a_0, \ldots, a_{n-1}\} \subset fld \,\&\, n \geq 2 \,\&\, a_{n-1} \preceq \cdots \preceq a_0 \Rightarrow \omega^{a_0} + \cdots + \omega^{a_{n-1}} \in fld$. $a \in fld \Rightarrow \omega^a \in fld$.

Finally $<_{\varepsilon_0}$ is defined to be the restriction of $\prec$ to the set fld.

Let us define recursively $\omega^a \cdot 0 := 0$, and $\omega^a \cdot (n+1) := \omega^a + \cdots + \omega^a$ with $(n+1)$'s ω^a. Also $a + b$ for $a, b \in fld$ is defined as follows. $0 + b := b + 0 := b$, $\langle 1, a \rangle + \langle 1, b \rangle := \langle 0, a, b \rangle$ if $b \preceq a$. $\langle 1, a \rangle + \langle 1, b \rangle := \langle 1, b \rangle$ otherwise. $\langle 1, a \rangle + \langle 0, b_0, \ldots, b_{m-1} \rangle := \langle 0, a, b_0, \ldots, b_{m-1} \rangle$ if $b_0 \preceq a$. $\langle 1, a \rangle + \langle 0, b_0, \ldots, b_{m-1} \rangle := \langle 0, b_0, \ldots, b_{m-1} \rangle$ otherwise.

$\langle 0, a_0, \ldots, a_{n-1} \rangle + \langle 0, b_0, \ldots, b_{m-1} \rangle := \langle 0, a_0, \ldots, a_{i-1}, b_0, \ldots, b_{m-1} \rangle$, where $i = \max(\{0\} \cup \{i > 0 : b_0 \preceq a_{i-1}\})$.

Then it is easy to see that $(<_{\varepsilon_0}, a + b, \omega^a \cdot n)$ is a standard ε_0-order.

4.2 Unprovability of Transfinite Induction

In this section we show Theorem 4.1.2.

Theorem 4.2 *Assume that a standard epsilon order* $<$ *is well-founded with* $\Lambda = |<|$. *For any elementary recursive binary relation* $\prec$ *and a unary predicate symbol* U,

$$\mathsf{PA}(U) + \mathrm{TI}(<\Lambda, U) \vdash \mathrm{TI}[\prec, U] \Rightarrow |\prec| < \Lambda.$$

Theorems 4.2 and 4.1.1 yield the

Theorem 4.3 *Let* $<$ *be a standard epsilon order with base* Ω.
Then $|\mathsf{PA}(U) + \mathrm{TI}(\Omega, U)| = \Lambda$. *In particular* $|\mathsf{PA}(U)| = \varepsilon_0$.

First $\mathsf{PA}(U) + \mathrm{TI}(<\Lambda, U)$ is embedded in the ω-logic $\boldsymbol{G}_\omega + (cut)$. Let $\vdash^\alpha_c \Gamma$ denote the provability in $\boldsymbol{G}_\omega + (cut)$. Recall that in the ω-logic $\boldsymbol{G}_\omega$, we consider only closed formulas, i.e., formulas without first-order free variables, and each closed term t is identified with its value $t^{\mathbb{N}}$ in the standard model.

Moreover let us restrict our attentions to *prenex formulas*, and assume that any cut formula occurring in proofs in $\boldsymbol{G}_\omega + (cut)$ is a closed formula in prenex normal form with bounded matrices. In this section the degree of (closed) formulas is redefined to deal with bounded formulas and unbounded ones separately. These changes are needed to deal with fragments of PA, see Exercises of this chapter and Sect. 3.1.3.

Definition 4.4 We define $\mathrm{dg}_b(A) < \omega + \omega$ recursively for prenex formulas A.

1. $\mathrm{dg}_b(L) = 0$ for literals L.
2. $\mathrm{dg}_b(A_0 \lor A_1) = \mathrm{dg}_b(A_0 \land A_1) = \max\{\mathrm{dg}_b(A_i) : i < 2\} + 1$.
3. $\mathrm{dg}_b(\exists x < t\, A(x)) = \mathrm{dg}_b(\forall x < t\, A(x)) = \max\{\mathrm{dg}_b(A(m)) : m < t^{\mathbb{N}}\} + t^{\mathbb{N}}$.
4. $\mathrm{dg}_b(A) = \omega + n$ if A is either a Σ_{1+n}-formula or a Π_{1+n}-formula. This means that either A or $\neg A$ is of the form $\exists x_{n+1} \forall x_n \cdots Qx_1\, B$ with a bounded matrix B.

We see easily that for any bounded formula A

$$m < n \Rightarrow \max\{\mathrm{dg}_b(A(m)), \mathrm{dg}_b(\exists x < m\, A(x))\} < \mathrm{dg}_b(\exists x < n\, A(x)) \tag{4.7}$$

Furthermore let us introduce two inference rules in the ω-logic $\boldsymbol{G}_\omega$ to deal with bounded quantifications.

$$\frac{\Gamma, \exists x < n\, A(x), A(0), \ldots, A(n \dot{-} 1)}{\Gamma, \exists x < n\, A(x)}\ (b\exists\omega)$$

$$\frac{\Gamma, \forall x < n\, A(x), A(0) \quad \cdots \quad \Gamma, \forall x < n\, A(x), A(n \dot{-} 1)}{\Gamma, \forall x < n\, A(x)}\ (b\forall\omega)$$

and the inference rule $(\lor)_{01}$ for binary disjunctions.

$$\frac{\Gamma, A_0 \vee A_1, A_0, A_1}{\Gamma, A_0 \vee A_1} \ (\vee)_{01}$$

$\vdash^{\alpha}_{c} \Gamma$ then designates that there exists an infinitary derivation of Γ in the above calculus whose depth is at most α, and $\mathrm{dg}_b(A) < c$ for any cut formula A occurring in the proof. The inversion lemma for bounded formulas is stated as follows.

Lemma 4.1 *1. For false literal* L, $\vdash^{\alpha}_{c} \Gamma, L \Rightarrow \vdash^{\alpha}_{c} \Gamma$.
2. $\vdash^{\alpha}_{c} \Gamma, A_0 \vee A_1 \Rightarrow \vdash^{\alpha}_{c} \Gamma, A_0, A_1$.
3. $\vdash^{\alpha}_{c} \Gamma, A_0 \wedge A_1 \Rightarrow \vdash^{\alpha}_{c} \Gamma, A_i$ *for* $i < 2$.
4. $\vdash^{\alpha}_{c} \Gamma, \exists x < 0\, A(x) \Rightarrow \vdash^{\alpha}_{c} \Gamma$.
5. $\vdash^{\alpha}_{c} \Gamma, \exists x < n+1\, A(x) \Rightarrow \vdash^{\alpha}_{c} \Gamma, A(n), \exists x < n\, A(x)$.
6. *If* $\vdash^{\alpha}_{c} \Gamma, \forall x < n+1\, A(x)$, *then* $\vdash^{\alpha}_{c} \Gamma, A(n)$ *and* $\vdash^{\alpha}_{c} \Gamma, \forall x < n\, A(x)$.

Lemma 4.2 *1. If* $\vdash^{\alpha}_{k} \Gamma, \neg C$ *and* $\vdash^{\alpha}_{k} C, \Delta$ *with* $\mathrm{dg}_b(C) \leq k < \omega$ *and* $k > 0$, *then* $\vdash^{\alpha+2}_{k} \Gamma, \Delta$.
2. *If* $\vdash^{\alpha}_{c} \Gamma, \forall x \neg A(x)$ *and* $\vdash^{\beta}_{c} \exists x\, A(x), \Delta$ *with* $\mathrm{dg}_b(\exists x\, A(x)) \leq c$, *then* $\vdash^{\alpha+\beta}_{c} \Gamma, \Delta$.

Proof Lemma 4.2.2 is seen as in Lemma 3.4 by induction on β using the fact $\mathrm{dg}_b(A(n)) < \mathrm{dg}_b(\exists x\, A(x))$ for any $n \in \mathbb{N}$.

Lemma 4.2.1 is seen as in Lemma 3.14 as follows. When C is a literal, then $\mathrm{dg}_b(C) = 0 < k$, and a (cut) yields $\vdash^{\alpha+1}_{k} \Gamma, \Delta$.

The case $C \equiv (A_0 \vee A_1)$ is seen from Lemmas 4.1.3 and 4.1.2 using the fact $\mathrm{dg}_b(A_i) < \mathrm{dg}_b(A_0 \vee A_1)$. Consider the case $C \equiv (\exists x < t\, A(x))$. If $t^{\mathbb{N}} = 0$, then Lemma 4.1.4 yields $\vdash^{\alpha}_{k} \Delta$. Suppose $t^{\mathbb{N}} = n+1 > 0$. Lemma 4.1.9 yields $\vdash^{\alpha}_{k} \Gamma, \neg A(n)$ and $\vdash^{\alpha}_{k} \Gamma, \forall x < n \neg A(x)$, and $\vdash^{\alpha}_{k} A(n), \exists x < n\, A(x), \Delta$ by Lemma 4.1.5. Two (cut)'s yields with (4.7)

$$\frac{\vdash^{\alpha}_{k} \Gamma, \neg A(n) \quad \vdash^{\alpha}_{k} \Gamma, \forall x < n \neg A(x) \quad \vdash^{\alpha}_{k} A(n), \exists x < n\, A(x), \Delta}{\vdash^{\alpha+2}_{k} \Gamma, \Delta} \ (cut)$$

□

We see $\vdash^{\alpha}_{1+n+1} \Gamma \Rightarrow \vdash^{2\alpha}_{1+n} \Gamma$, $\vdash^{\alpha}_{\omega} \Gamma \Rightarrow \vdash^{\omega\alpha}_{1} \Gamma$, and $\vdash^{\alpha}_{\omega+n+1} \Gamma \Rightarrow \vdash^{2^{\alpha}}_{\omega+n} \Gamma$ from Lemma 4.2. We obtain the following lemma.

Lemma 4.3 *1.* $\vdash^{\alpha}_{1+n} \Gamma \Rightarrow \vdash^{2^n\alpha}_{1} \Gamma$.
2. $\vdash^{\alpha}_{\omega+n} \Gamma \Rightarrow \vdash^{\omega \cdot 2_n(\alpha)}_{1} \Gamma$.

Let $\omega \leq \lambda < \Lambda$ be a limit ordinal. $\mathsf{PA}(U) + \mathrm{TI}(\lambda, U)$ is formulated in a sequent calculus obtained from $G_1^{<} + (cut)$ by adding two inference rules with the eigenvariable a and terms t, s:

$$\frac{\Gamma, A(0) \quad \neg A(a), \Gamma, A(a+1) \quad \neg A(t), \Gamma}{\Gamma} \ (VJ)$$

and

$$\frac{\neg\forall x <_\lambda a\, A(x), \Gamma, A(a) \quad s <_\lambda t \wedge \neg A(s), \Gamma}{\Gamma}\ (TI)_\lambda$$

both for *prenex formula* A with a bounded matrix.

Axioms Γ, Δ for equality and function symbols for elementary recursive functions are also added, where Δ consists solely of literals such that the disjunction of each closed instance of it is true in the standard model.

Lemma 4.4 (Embedding) *Let $\Gamma(\mathbf{a})$ be a sequent in the language of* $\mathsf{PA}(U)$ *in which no free variable other than the variables* $\mathbf{a}$ *occurs. For sequences* $\mathbf{n}$ *of numerals let* $\Gamma(\mathbf{n})$ *denote the result of substituting* $\mathbf{n}$ *for* $\mathbf{a}$*. Assume* $\mathsf{PA}(U) + \mathrm{TI}(\lambda, U) \vdash \Gamma(\mathbf{a})$*. Then there exist* $k, m, n < \omega$ *such that for any* $\mathbf{n}$, $\vdash^{\lambda k+m}_{\omega+n} \Gamma(\mathbf{n})$ *holds, assuming that* $<_\lambda$ *is well-founded.*

Proof By induction on the depths of $\mathsf{PA}(U) + \mathrm{TI}(\lambda, U)$-proofs. We can assume that the given proof enjoys the pure variable condition in Definition 1.3, and each cut formula in it is a literal.

Any closed instance $\Gamma(\mathbf{n})$ of an axiom $\Gamma(\mathbf{a})$ in $\mathsf{PA}(U) + \mathrm{TI}(\lambda, U)$ is an axiom in G_ω, and hence $\vdash^0_0 \Gamma(\mathbf{n})$: $\Gamma(\mathbf{a}), s(\mathbf{a}) \neq t(\mathbf{a}), s(\mathbf{a}) \notin U, t(\mathbf{a}) \in U$ turns into an axiom $\Gamma(\mathbf{n}), s(\mathbf{n}) \neq t(\mathbf{n}), s(\mathbf{n}) \notin U, t(\mathbf{n}) \in U$, since when $s(\mathbf{n}) \neq t(\mathbf{n})$ is true, it is an axiom $\Delta, k \neq m$, and another axiom $\Delta, k \notin U, k \in U$ otherwise. Other axioms ($\Gamma, \bar{L}, L$ without U, equality axioms and defining equations for elementary recursive functions) are converted to axioms Γ, L for a true closed literal L.

Consider the inference rule $\dfrac{\Gamma(\mathbf{a}), \forall x A(\mathbf{a}, x), A(\mathbf{a}, b)}{\Gamma(\mathbf{a}), \forall x A(\mathbf{a}, x)}\ (\forall)$. By IH there exist $k, m < \omega$ and $c < \omega + \omega$ such that $\forall \mathbf{n} \forall p\{\vdash^{\lambda k+m}_c \Gamma(\mathbf{n}), \forall x A(\mathbf{n}), A(\mathbf{n}, p)\}$. Thus

$$\frac{\{\vdash^{\lambda k+m}_c \Gamma(\mathbf{n}), \forall x A(\mathbf{n}, x), A(\mathbf{n}, p) : p \in \omega\}}{\vdash^{\lambda k+m+1}_c \Gamma(\mathbf{n}), \forall x A(\mathbf{n}, x)}\ (\forall\omega)$$

Likewise the inference rule $(b\forall)$ turns to $(b\forall\omega)$.

Next consider the case when the proof ends with a (VJ).

$$\frac{\Gamma(\mathbf{a}), A(\mathbf{a}, 0) \quad \neg A(\mathbf{a}, b), \Gamma(\mathbf{a}), A(\mathbf{a}, b+1) \quad \neg A(\mathbf{a}, t(\mathbf{a})), \Gamma(\mathbf{a})}{\Gamma(\mathbf{a})}\ (VJ)$$

By IH we have k, m, c such that for any $\mathbf{n}$ and any p, $\mathrm{dg}_b(A(\mathbf{n}, p)) < c$, $\vdash^{\lambda k+m}_c \Gamma', A(0)$, $\vdash^{\lambda k+m}_c \neg A(p), \Gamma', A(p+1)$ and $\vdash^{\lambda k+m}_c \neg A(p'), \Gamma'$, where $\Gamma' = \Gamma(\mathbf{n})$, $A(p) \equiv A(\mathbf{n}, p)$ and $p' = t(\mathbf{n})^{\mathbb{N}}$ denotes the value of $t(\mathbf{n})$.

We show by induction on the binary length $|p| = \min\{q : p < 2^q\}$ that for $p > 0$ and any r

$$\vdash^{\lambda k+m+2(|p|-1)}_c \Gamma', \neg A(r), A(r+p) \tag{4.8}$$

The case $p = 1$ is one of the IH. Assume $p > 1$ and let $\alpha := \lambda k + m + 2(|p| - 2)$. Let $q := \lfloor p/2 \rfloor$, i.e., $p \in \{2q, 2q+1\}$. Note that $q > 0$. Then $|p| > |q|, |q-1|$.

Hence IH on p yields $\vdash^{\alpha}_{c} \Gamma', \neg A(r), A(r+q)$ and $\vdash^{\alpha}_{c} \Gamma', \neg A(r+q+1), A(r+p)$. Thus two successive (cut)'s yield for $\alpha + 2 = \lambda k + m + 2(|p|-1)$

$$\dfrac{\vdash^{\alpha}_{c} \Gamma', \neg A(r), A(r+q) \quad \vdash^{\alpha}_{c} \neg A(r+p), \Gamma', A(r+p+1) \quad \vdash^{\alpha}_{c} \Gamma', \neg A(r+q+1), A(r+p)}{\vdash^{\alpha+2}_{c} \Gamma', \neg A(r), A(r+p)}\ (cut)$$

We obtain $\vdash^{\beta}_{c} \neg A(0), \Gamma', A(p')$ for $\beta = \lambda k + m + 2(|p'|-1) \geq \lambda k + m$ by (4.8). Thus two successive (cut)'s yield for $\beta + \lambda = \lambda(k+1)$ with $\lambda \geq \omega$, which is independent from p', i.e., from $\mathbf{n}$

$$\dfrac{\dfrac{\vdash^{\beta}_{c} \Gamma', A(0) \quad \vdash^{\beta}_{c} \neg A(0), \Gamma', A(p')}{\vdash^{\beta+1}_{c} \Gamma', A(p')}\ (cut) \qquad \vdash^{\beta+1}_{c} \neg A(p'), \Gamma'}{\vdash^{\beta+\lambda}_{c} \Gamma'}\ (cut)$$

Finally consider the case when the proof ends with a (TI).

$$\dfrac{\neg \forall x <_{\lambda} b\, A(\mathbf{a}, x), \Gamma(\mathbf{a}), A(\mathbf{a}, b) \quad s(\mathbf{a}) <_{\lambda} t(\mathbf{a}) \wedge \neg A(\mathbf{a}, s(\mathbf{a})), \Gamma(\mathbf{a})}{\Gamma(\mathbf{a})}\ (TI)_{\lambda}$$

By IH we have k, m, c such that for any $\mathbf{n}$ and any $\beta < \lambda$, $\mathrm{dg}_b(\forall x <_{\lambda} \beta\, A(\mathbf{n}, x)) < c$ and $\vdash^{\lambda k+m}_{c} \neg\forall x <_{\lambda} \beta\, A(x), \Gamma', A(\beta)$ and $\vdash^{\lambda k+m}_{c} \gamma <_{\lambda} \alpha \wedge \neg A(\gamma), \Gamma'$, where $\Gamma' = \Gamma(\mathbf{n})$, $A(\beta) \equiv A(\mathbf{n}, \beta)$ and $\gamma = s(\mathbf{n})^{\mathbb{N}}$ and $\alpha = t(\mathbf{n})^{\mathbb{N}}$ denote the values of $s(\mathbf{n})$ and of $t(\mathbf{n})$. If $\gamma \not<_{\lambda} \alpha$, then by inversion and eliminating the false $\gamma <_{\lambda} \alpha$ by Lemma 4.1.1, we obtain $\vdash^{\lambda k+m}_{c} \Gamma'$, and $\vdash^{\lambda(k+1)}_{c} \Gamma'$

In what follows assume $\gamma <_{\lambda} \alpha$ holds. We show $\forall \gamma < \lambda[\vdash^{G(\gamma)+1}_{c} \Gamma', A(\gamma)]$ for $G(\gamma) = \lambda k + m + 3\gamma$ by induction on $\gamma < \lambda$. IH yields the following.

$$\dfrac{\vdash^{0}_{0} \beta \not<_{\lambda} \gamma}{\vdash^{1}_{0} \Gamma', \beta <_{\lambda} \gamma \to A(\beta)}\ (\vee) \quad (\beta \not<_{\lambda} \gamma) \qquad \dfrac{\vdash^{G(\beta)+1}_{c} \Gamma', A(\beta)}{\vdash^{G(\beta)+2}_{c} \Gamma', \beta <_{\lambda} \gamma \to A(\beta)}\ (\vee) \quad (\beta <_{\lambda} \gamma)$$

$$\dfrac{\dfrac{\vdash^{G(\beta)+2}_{c} \Gamma', \beta <_{\lambda} \gamma \to A(\beta)}{\vdash^{G(\gamma)}_{c} \Gamma', \forall x <_{\lambda} \gamma\, A(x)}\ (\forall\omega) \qquad \vdash^{G(0)}_{c} \neg\forall x <_{\lambda} \gamma\, A(x), \Gamma', A(\gamma)}{\vdash^{G(\gamma)+1}_{c} \Gamma', A(\gamma)}\ (cut)$$

On the other hand we have $\vdash^{G(0)}_{c} \neg A(\gamma), \Gamma'$ by inversion. Hence for $\gamma < \lambda$ and $G(\lambda) = \lambda(k+1)$,

$$\dfrac{\vdash^{G(\gamma)+1}_{c} \Gamma', A(\gamma) \quad \vdash^{G(0)}_{c} \neg A(\gamma), \Gamma'}{\vdash^{G(\lambda)}_{c} \Gamma'}\ (cut)$$

Other cases are easily seen from IH. □

Combining Lemmas 4.4 and 4.3, we see the following lemma.

Lemma 4.5 *Let $\Gamma(\mathbf{a})$ be a sequent in which no free variable other than the variables* $\mathbf{a}$ *occurs. Assume* $\mathsf{PA}(U) + \mathrm{TI}(\lambda, U) \vdash \Gamma(\mathbf{a})$ *and* $<_\lambda$ *is well-founded. Then there exist an* $n < \omega$ *and an* $\alpha < 2_n(\lambda^2)$ *such that* $\forall \mathbf{m}\{\vdash_1^\alpha \Gamma(\mathbf{m})\}$.

Lemma 4.5 with the partial truth definition for Σ_n-formulas yields the following Theorem 4.4, which is the remaining half of Theorem 4.1.3a.

Theorem 4.4 *Over* EA *the schema* $\mathrm{TI}(\Lambda)$ *implies the uniform reflection schema* $\{\mathrm{RFN}_{\Sigma_n}(\mathsf{PA} + \mathrm{TI}(< \Lambda))\}_{n<\omega}$.

Corollary 4.2 *Let* Γ *be a collection of sentences in a bounded complexity, e.g.,* $\Gamma \subset \Sigma_n$ *for an* n. *Assume* $\mathsf{PA} + \mathrm{TI}(< \Lambda) + \Gamma$ *proves the schema* $\mathrm{TI}(\Lambda)$. *Then* $\mathsf{PA} + \mathrm{TI}(< \Lambda) + \Gamma$ *is inconsistent.*

Proof Assume $\mathsf{PA} + \mathrm{TI}(< \Lambda) + \Gamma$ proves the schema $\mathrm{TI}(\Lambda)$. Then by Theorem 4.4, $\mathsf{PA} + \mathrm{TI}(< \Lambda) + \Gamma$ proves the schema $\{\mathrm{RFN}_{\Sigma_n}(\mathsf{PA} + \mathrm{TI}(< \Lambda))\}_{n<\omega}$. We see the fact that $\mathsf{PA} + \mathrm{TI}(< \Lambda) + \Gamma$ is inconsistent from Kreisel-Lévy's essential unboundedness Theorem 1.1. □

4.2.1 Bounding Order Types of Provably Well-Founded Orders

In this subsection we obtain upper bounds for order types of provably well-founded relations $\prec$ from the depths of almost cut-free derivations of the formula $\mathrm{TI}[\prec, U]$. By ordinals we mean natural numbers in the field $fld(<)$ of a standard epsilon order $<$ in Definition 4.1. The order type Λ of the epsilon order $<$ need not to be the least epsilon number ε_0.

4.2.1.1 Strict Partial Orders in ω-Logic

Let $\prec$ be a *strict partial order* on $\mathbb{N}$. This means that $\prec$ is an irreflexive and transitive relation. For ordinals α and sets $M \subset \mathbb{N}$ of natural numbers, define sets $I_\prec^\alpha(M) \subset \mathbb{N}$ recursively by

$$I_\prec^\alpha(M) = M \cup \{n \in \mathbb{N} : \forall m \prec n(m \in I_\prec^{<\alpha}(M))\} \text{ for } I_\prec^{<\alpha}(M) = \bigcup\{I_\prec^\beta(M) : \beta < \alpha\}$$

Then we see that $M \subset I_\prec^0(M)$, and $\alpha < \beta \Rightarrow I_\prec^\alpha(M) \subset I_\prec^\beta(M)$.

Proposition 4.2 *Let* $\prec$ *be a strict partial order.*

1. $n \prec k \,\&\, n \in I_\prec^\alpha(M \cup \{k\}) \Rightarrow n \in I_\prec^\alpha(M)$.

2. $I^{\alpha}_{\prec}(M \cup \{k\}) \subset I^{\alpha+1}_{\prec}(M) \cup \{k\}$.

Proof By induction on α we show Proposition 4.2.1 first, and then Proposition 4.2.2.

Let $n \in I^{\alpha}_{\prec}(M \cup \{k\})$. First consider the case $n \in M \cup \{k\}$. If $n \prec k$, then $n \neq k$ by the irreflexivity, and $n \in M \subset I^{\alpha}_{\prec}(M)$. Also $M \cup \{k\} \subset I^{\alpha+1}_{\prec}(M) \cup \{k\}$. In what follows assume

$$\forall m \prec n(m \in I^{<\alpha}_{\prec}(M \cup \{k\})) \tag{4.9}$$

Let $n \prec k$. Then $m \prec n \Rightarrow m \prec k$ by the transitivity. By IH we have $\forall m \prec n(m \in I^{<\alpha}_{\prec}(M))$, and $n \in I^{\alpha}_{\prec}(M)$. This shows Proposition 4.2.1.

Next we claim that $k \prec n \Rightarrow k \in I^{\alpha}_{\prec}(M)$ under the assumption (4.9). Suppose $k \prec n$. By the assumption together with the transitivity, we obtain $\forall m \prec k(m \in I^{<\alpha}_{\prec}(M \cup \{k\}))$. Proposition 4.2.1 then yields $\forall m \prec k(m \in I^{<\alpha}_{\prec}(M))$. Hence $k \in I^{\alpha}_{\prec}(M)$, and the claim is shown.

Now IH on Proposition 4.2.2 together with (4.9) yields $\forall m \prec n(m \in I^{<\alpha+1}_{\prec}(M) \cup \{k\})$. This means $\forall m \prec n(m \in I^{<\alpha+1}_{\prec}(M))$ by the claim. Therefore $n \in I^{\alpha+1}_{\prec}(M)$, and Proposition 4.2.2 is shown. □

We see the following from Proposition 4.2.2.

$$k \in I^{\alpha}_{\prec}(M) \,\&\, \beta < \alpha \Rightarrow I^{\beta}_{\prec}(M \cup \{k\}) \subset I^{\alpha}_{\prec}(M) \tag{4.10}$$

In the following Lemma 4.6, by an arithmetically definable strict partial order $\prec$ on $\mathbb{N}$, we mean that $n \prec m$ is a first-order formula $A(n, m)$ in a language of arithmetic without relation variables whose free variables are among n, m, and $\mathbb{N} \models \forall n \neg A(n, n) \land \forall n, m, k[A(n, m) \land A(m, k) \to A(n, k)]$.

Lemma 4.6 (Boundedness lemma for ω-logic) *Let $\prec$ be an arithmetically definable* strict partial order *on* $\mathbb{N}$. *Let $\Delta(U^{+})$ be a U-positive sequent, and $\Gamma = \{\bar{U}(n) : n \in M\}$ for a finite set M of natural numbers. If $\vdash^{\alpha}_{1} \neg Prg[\prec, U], \Gamma, \Delta(U)$, then $\bigvee \Delta(I^{\alpha}_{\prec}(M))$ is true in the standard model* $\mathbb{N}$.

Proof We show Lemma 4.6 by induction on α. Let P be a derivation witnessing the fact $\vdash^{\alpha}_{1} \neg Prg[\prec, U], \Gamma, \Delta(U)$.

Let P be an axiom. If $U(n)$ is in $\Delta(U)$ for an $n \in M$, then $n \in M \subset I^{0}_{\prec}(M)$. Otherwise a true literal is in Δ, and there is nothing to prove.

Next suppose that P ends with an inference rule whose main formula is in $\Delta(U)$. The monotonicity of $I^{\alpha}_{\prec}(U)$ in α together with the positivity of $\Delta(U)$ with respect to U suffices to conclude the lemma from IH.

Third suppose that P ends with a (cut) for a $\beta < \alpha$.

$$\frac{\vdash^{\beta}_{1} \neg Prg[\prec, U], \Gamma, \Delta(U), \neg L \quad \vdash^{\beta}_{1} L, \neg Prg[\prec, U], \Gamma, \Delta(U)}{\vdash^{\alpha}_{1} \neg Prg[\prec, U], \Gamma, \Delta(U)} \,(cut)$$

where $\mathrm{dg}_b(L) = 0$, i.e., L is a literal. If U does not occur in L, then one of $\neg L$ and L is false, and either $\vdash^{\beta}_{1} \neg Prg[\prec, U], \Gamma, \Delta(U)$ or $\vdash^{\beta}_{1} \neg Prg[\prec, U], \Gamma, \Delta(U)$

holds. IH together with the monotonicity yields the lemma. Let L be a literal $U(k)$. By IH we obtain $\bigvee \Delta(I^{\beta}_{\prec}(M \cup \{k\}))$, and either $\bigvee \Delta(I^{\beta}_{\prec}(M))$ or $k \in I^{\beta}_{\prec}(M)$ holds. Consider the case $k \in I^{\beta}_{\prec}(M)$. Then $I^{\beta}_{\prec}(M \cup \{k\}) \subset I^{\alpha}_{\prec}(M)$ by (4.10). Therefore $\bigvee \Delta(I^{\alpha}_{\prec}(M))$.

Finally consider the case when P ends with an inference rule whose main formula is $\neg Prg[\prec, U]$: for a k and a $\beta < \alpha$, P ends with

$$\frac{\vdash^{\beta}_{1} \forall y \prec k(y \in U) \land \bar{U}(k), \neg Prg[\prec, U], \Gamma, \Delta(U)}{\vdash^{\alpha}_{1} \neg Prg[\prec, U], \Gamma, \Delta(U)} \ (\exists)$$

By inversion we obtain $\vdash^{\beta}_{1} \neg Prg[\prec, U], \Gamma, \Delta(U), \forall y \prec k(y \in U)$ and $\vdash^{\beta}_{1}$, $\neg Prg[\prec, U], \Gamma, \bar{U}(k), \Delta(U)$. From IH we see that either $\bigvee \Delta(I^{\beta}_{\prec}(M))$ or $\forall y \prec k(y \in I^{\beta}_{\prec}(M))$ holds. If $\bigvee \Delta(I^{\beta}_{\prec}(M))$, then the monotonicity yields $\bigvee \Delta(I^{\alpha}_{\prec}(M))$. Assume $\forall y \prec k(y \in I^{\beta}_{\prec}(M))$. Then $k \in I^{\alpha}_{\prec}(M)$. (4.10) yields $I^{\beta}_{\prec}(M \cup \{k\}) \subset I^{\alpha}_{\prec}(M)$. On the other hand we have $\bigvee \Delta(I^{\beta}_{\prec}(M \cup \{k\}))$ by IH, and we are done. □

Combining Lemmas 4.5 and 4.6, we conclude the following theorem.

Theorem 4.5 *Assume that the standard epsilon order* $<$ *is well-founded. For any* arithmetically definable strict partial order $\prec$ *on* $\mathbb{N}$,

$$\mathsf{PA}(U) + \mathrm{TI}(< \Lambda) \vdash \mathrm{TI}[\prec, U] \Rightarrow |\prec| < \Lambda.$$

Proof Suppose $\mathsf{PA}(U) + \mathrm{TI}(< \Lambda) \vdash \mathrm{TI}[\prec, U]$. Then $\mathsf{PA}(U) + \mathrm{TI}(< \Lambda) \vdash \neg Prg[\prec, U], U(a)$ for a variable a. By Lemma 4.5 pick an $\alpha < \Lambda$ such that $\forall m\{\vdash^{\alpha}_{1} \neg Prg[\prec, U], U(m)\}$. Lemma 4.6 yields $\forall m(m \in I^{\alpha}_{\prec}(\emptyset))$, which is equivalent to $\forall m(|m|_{\prec} \leq \alpha)$, and hence $|\prec| \leq \alpha + 1 < \Lambda$. □

Proof Let us show Theorem 4.2 for arithmetically definable relations under the *assumption of the consistency* of $\mathsf{PA} + \mathrm{TI}(< \Lambda)$.

Assume $\mathsf{PA}(U) + \mathrm{TI}(< \Lambda, U) \vdash \mathrm{TI}[\prec, U]$ for an *arithmetically definable* binary relation $\prec$. Let $\prec^*$ denote the transitive closure of $\prec$, and U^* the downward closure of U defined by $U^* = \{a : \forall b \prec^* a(b \in U)\}$. Note that both $\prec^*$ and U^* are arithmetically definable. First we show

$$\mathsf{PA}(U) \vdash Prg[\prec^*, U] \to Prg[\prec, U^*] \tag{4.11}$$

Suppose $Prg[\prec^*, U]$ and $\forall b \prec a(b \in U^*)$. Then $\forall b \prec^* a(b \in U)$, and hence $a \in U^*$. This shows (4.11).

Therefore we obtain $\mathsf{PA}(U) + \mathrm{TI}(< \Lambda, U) \vdash \mathrm{TI}[\prec^*, U]$ from $\mathsf{PA}(U) + \mathrm{TI}(< \Lambda, U) \vdash \mathrm{TI}[\prec, U^*]$ by (4.11). Next we claim that the transitive relation $\prec^*$ is irreflexive: Let $a_0 \prec \cdots \prec a_m$ for natural numbers a_i with $m > 0$. From $\mathsf{PA}(U) + \mathrm{TI}(< \Lambda, U) \vdash \mathrm{TI}[\prec, U]$ we see that $\mathsf{PA} + \mathrm{TI}(< \Lambda) \vdash a_0 \neq a_m$ by substituting the complement of the set $\{a_0, \ldots, a_m\}$ for U. Then $a_0 \neq a_m$ follows from the consistency of $\mathsf{PA} + \mathrm{TI}(< \Lambda)$.

Hence $\prec^*$ is an arithmetically definable strict partial order for which $\mathsf{PA}(U) + \mathrm{TI}(< \Lambda, U) \vdash \mathrm{TI}[\prec^*, U]$ holds. Theorem 4.5 yields $|\prec| = |\prec^*| < \Lambda$. □

Combining Theorems 4.5, 4.1.1, we obtain the following theorem. Let $PO(\mathcal{E}^3)$ denote the class of all elementary recursive strict partial orders on $\mathbb{N}$. Also Π^1_0 denotes the class of all arithmetically definable binary relation on $\mathbb{N}$.

Theorem 4.6 *Assume that the standard epsilon order* $<$ *is well-founded, and* $\mathsf{PA} + \mathrm{TI}(< \Lambda)$ *is consistent.*

$$\begin{aligned}\Lambda &= \sup\{|\prec| : \mathsf{PA}(U) + \mathrm{TI}(< \Lambda, U) \vdash \mathrm{TI}[\prec, U] \text{ for a } \prec \textit{ in } PO(\mathcal{E}^3)\}\\ &= \sup\{|\prec| : \mathsf{PA}(U) + \mathrm{TI}(< \Lambda, U) \vdash \mathrm{TI}[\prec, U] \text{ for a } \prec \textit{ in } \Pi^1_0\}\end{aligned}$$

4.2.1.2 ω-Logic with a Rule for Progressiveness

Let us give another proof, which is closer to Gentzen's original proof of Theorem 4.2. We obtain not only an upper bound of order types, but also an embedding from provably well-founded relations to ordinals.

Let us introduce a new inference rule (prg) to $\mathsf{PA}(U)$: for any term t

$$\frac{\Gamma, \forall y \prec t\, U(y), U(t)}{\Gamma, U(t)}\ (prg)$$

From $\mathsf{PA}(U) + (prg) \vdash Prg[\prec, U]$ and $\mathsf{PA}(U) + \mathrm{TI}(< \Lambda, U) \vdash \mathrm{TI}[\prec, U]$ we see that $\mathsf{PA}(U) + \mathrm{TI}(< \Lambda, U) + (prg) \vdash U(a)$ for a variable a. It is clear that $\mathsf{PA}(U) + \mathrm{TI}(< \Lambda, U) + (prg)$ admits a cut-elimination since no formula $\bar{U}(t)$ is a major formula of an inference rule with upper sequent. Specifically we see by induction on b that if $\mathsf{PA}(U) + \mathrm{TI}(< \Lambda, U) + (prg) \vdash^a_0 \Gamma, U(t)$ and $\mathsf{PA}(U) + \mathrm{TI}(< \Lambda, U) + (prg) \vdash^b_0 \bar{U}(t), \Delta$, then $\mathsf{PA}(U) + \mathrm{TI}(< \Lambda, U) + (prg) \vdash^{a+b}_0 \Gamma, \Delta$.

On the other side add the following inference rule to $\mathbf{G}_\omega$: for the value m of closed terms

$$\frac{\Gamma, \forall y \prec m\, U(y), U(m)}{\Gamma, U(m)}\ (prg)$$

In what follows let $(prg) \vdash^\alpha_c \Gamma :\Leftrightarrow \mathbf{G}_\omega + (prg) \vdash^\alpha_c \Gamma$. Now Embedding Lemma 4.4 runs as follows.

Lemma 4.7 *Let* $\omega \le \lambda < \Lambda$ *be a limit ordinal, and* $\Gamma(\mathbf{a})$ *be a sequent in which no free variable other than the variables* $\mathbf{a}$ *occurs. Assume* $\mathsf{PA}(U) + \mathrm{TI}(\lambda, U) + (prg) \vdash \Gamma(\mathbf{a})$ *and the well-foundedness of* $<_\lambda$. *Then there exist* $k, m, n < \omega$ *such that* $\forall \mathbf{n}\{(prg) \vdash^{\lambda k+m}_{\omega+n} \Gamma(\mathbf{n})\}$.

We see as before that if $(prg) \vdash^\alpha_\omega \Gamma$, then $(prg) \vdash^{\omega\cdot\alpha}_1 \Gamma$, and hence $(prg) \vdash^{2^{\omega\cdot\alpha}}_0 \Gamma$. Lemma 4.3 runs as follows.

Lemma 4.8 *1.* $(prg) \vdash^\alpha_n \Gamma \Rightarrow (prg) \vdash^\beta_0 \Gamma$ *with* $\beta = 2^{2^n \alpha}$.

2. $(prg) \vdash^{\alpha}_{\omega+n} \Gamma \Rightarrow (prg) \vdash^{\gamma}_{0} \Gamma$ *with* $\gamma = 2^{\omega \cdot 2_n(\alpha)}$.

Let $\alpha < \lambda^2$. Then $2^{2^n \alpha} < \lambda_2$ and $2^{\omega \cdot 2_n(\alpha)} < \lambda_{n+2}$ for $\lambda_1 = \lambda$ and $\lambda_{n+1} = \lambda^{\lambda_n}$. Hence we obtain the following lemma.

Lemma 4.9 *Let* $\Gamma(\mathbf{a})$ *be a sequent in which no free variable other than the variables* $\mathbf{a}$ *occurs. Assume* $\mathsf{PA}(U) + \mathrm{TI}(\lambda, U) + (prg) \vdash \Gamma(\mathbf{a})$. *Then there exists an* $\alpha < \Lambda$ *such that* $\forall \mathbf{n}\{(prg) \vdash^{\alpha}_{0} \Gamma(\mathbf{n})\}$ *assuming that* $<_\lambda$ *is well-founded.*

Now Theorem 4.2 follows from the following lemma without assuming the consistency of $\mathsf{PA} + \mathrm{TI}(< \Lambda)$ explicitly. In the lemma the binary relation $\prec$ need not to be a strict partial order.

Lemma 4.10 (Boundedness lemma for ω-logic with the inference (prg)) *Let* $\prec$ *be an elementary recursive binary relation on* $\mathbb{N}$. *For any* $\Delta = \{U(n_i) : i \leq k\}$, *if* $(prg) \vdash^{\alpha}_{0} \Delta$, *then* $\bigvee \Delta(I^{\alpha}_{\prec}(\emptyset))$ *is true, i.e.,* $\min\{|n_i|_{\prec} : i \leq k\} \leq \alpha$.

Proof By induction on α. The last inference has to be a (prg) with a major formula $U(n_i)$:

$$\frac{(prg) \vdash^{\beta}_{0} \forall y \prec n_i\, U(y), \Delta}{(prg) \vdash^{\alpha}_{0} \Delta}\ (prg)$$

for a $\beta < \alpha$. For any $m \prec n_i$, first by Inversion Lemma 3.2.3 (for $\mathbf{G}_\omega + (prg)$) we have $(prg) \vdash^{\beta}_{0} m \prec n_i \to U(m), \Delta$, and hence $(prg) \vdash^{\beta}_{0} m \not\prec n_i, U(m), \Delta$. Next eliminate the false literal $m \not\prec n_i$ by Lemma 3.3 to get $(prg) \vdash^{\beta}_{0} U(m), \Delta$. IH yields $\min(\{|m|_{\prec}\} \cup \{|n_i|_{\prec} : i \leq k\}) \leq \beta$. Suppose $\min\{|n_i|_{\prec} : i \leq k\}) > \beta$. Then $|m|_{\prec} \leq \beta < \alpha$ for any $m \prec n_i$. Consequently $|n_i|_{\prec} = \sup\{|m|_{\prec} + 1 : m \prec n_i\} \leq \alpha$. We are done. □

Remark 4.2 Define a relation $n \lhd \alpha$ between natural numbers n and ordinals α by recursion on ordinals α as follows.

$$\exists \beta < \alpha \forall m \prec n (m \lhd \beta) \Rightarrow n \lhd \alpha$$

Then Lemma 4.10 shows that if $(prg) \vdash^{\alpha}_{0} \{U(n_i) : i \leq k\}$, then there exists an $i \leq k$ such that $n_i \lhd \alpha$.

4.2.2 Embeddings

In Lemmas 4.6 and 4.10 the order type of the order $\prec$ is bounded by the depth α of almost cut-free derivations of the well-foundedness of $\prec$, $|\prec| \leq \alpha + 1$. Hence there must exist an embedding f between $\prec$ and ordinals such that $n \prec m \Rightarrow f(n) < f(m)$ for any n, m. In general such an embedding is hyperarithmetical, i.e., Δ^1_1-definable (in $\prec$ and the order $<$ on ordinal terms). In this subsection let us sharpen the boundedness theorems in two directions. We show that there exists a *computable* embedding first, and a boundedness theorem for disjunctions of transfinite inductions second. This is utilized in the next Chap. 5.

Let $\prec$ be an arithmetically definable binary relation, and $\prec^*$ its transitive closure. Let us replace the inference (prg) by

$$\frac{\{\Gamma, U(n), U(m) : n \prec^* m\}}{\Gamma, U(m)} \; (prg)_\omega$$

and add the *repetition rule*

$$\frac{\Gamma}{\Gamma} \; (Rep)$$

In the following Theorem 4.7, $\vdash_0^\alpha \Gamma$ designates that there exists a cut-free derivation of a sequent Γ in the ω-logic with the rules $(prg)_\omega$ and (Rep) in depth α. Let $\mathrm{TI}(\alpha)$ denote the Π_1^1-sentence $\forall X\, \mathrm{TI}[<_\alpha, X]$ for an epsilon order $<_\alpha$ of type α.

Theorem 4.7 The following is provable in $\mathrm{ACA}_0 + \mathrm{TI}(\alpha)$:
Suppose $\vdash_0^\alpha \forall x\, U(x)$. *Then there exists an embedding* f *such that* $n \prec m \Rightarrow f(n) < f(m)$, $f(m) < \omega^\alpha$ *for any* n, m.

Proof In the proof the nth numeral $\bar{n}$ is identified with the number $n \in \mathbb{N}$, $<$ denotes a standard epsilon order, and $<_\omega$ the less than relation on $\mathbb{N}$. First from $\vdash_0^\alpha \forall x\, U(x)$ we see by induction on α that there exists an inference $(\forall\omega)$ in the derivation:

$$\begin{array}{c} \vdots \\ \dfrac{\{\vdash_0^{\alpha_1} \forall x\, U(x), U(m)\}_{m\in\mathbb{N}}}{\vdash_0^{\alpha_0} \forall x\, U(x)} \; (\forall\omega) \\ \vdots \\ \vdash_0^\alpha \forall x\, U(x) \end{array}$$

where $\alpha_1 < \alpha_0 \le \alpha$ and there are some (possibly none) (Rep)'s below the $(\forall\omega)$. By inversion we obtain $\vdash_0^{\alpha_1} U(m)$ for any $m \in \mathbb{N}$.

We can assume that the transitive closure $\prec^*$ of the relation $n \prec m$ is irreflexive. Namely there is no sequence $(n_0, \ldots, n_k)$ $(k \ge 1)$ such that $n = n_0 = n_k$ and $\forall j < k(n_{j+1} \prec n_j)$. Suppose that there exists such a sequence. We obtain $\vdash_0^{\gamma_0} U(n_0)$ for $\gamma_0 = \alpha_1$. Any positive literal $U(n_0)$ is not an axiom. We see by induction on ordinals γ_0 that there must be an inference $(prg)_\omega$ in the witnessed derivation, and we obtain $\vdash^{\gamma_1} U(n_0), U(n_1)$ for an $\gamma_1 < \gamma_0$. Again $U(n_0), U(n_1)$ is not an axiom. In this way we would obtain an infinite descending chain $\{\gamma_m\}_{m<\omega}$ of ordinals such that $\vdash_0^{\gamma_m} \{U(n_j) : j < k\}$.

By induction on m, we define an ordinal $\beta(m) \le \alpha_1$ and a sequent $\Gamma(m) \subset \{U(n) : n \in \mathbb{N}\}$ such that $U(m) \in \Gamma(m)$, $\forall n[U(n) \in \Gamma(m) \Rightarrow m \preceq^* n \le_\omega m]$, $\vdash_0^{\beta(m)} \Gamma(m)$, and

$$\forall n <_\omega m(m \prec^* n \to \beta(m) < \beta(n)) \tag{4.12}$$

If $\neg\exists n <_\omega m(m \prec^* n)$, then $\Gamma(m) = \{U(m)\}$ and $\beta(m) = \alpha_1$.

Otherwise pick a $k <_\omega m$ such that $m \prec^* k$ and $\beta(k) = \min\{\beta(n) : n <_\omega m, m \prec^* n\}$. We have $\vdash_0^{\beta(k)} \Gamma(k)$. The sequent $\Gamma(k)$ is not an axiom. Search the lowest inference $(prg)_\omega$ in the derivation showing the fact $\vdash_0^{\beta(k)} \Gamma(k)$:

$$\frac{\{\vdash_0^{\beta_0} \Gamma(k), U(n) : n \prec^* k'\}}{\vdash_0^{\beta'} \Gamma(k)} \ (prg)_\omega$$

where $\beta_0 < \beta' \leq \beta(k)$, there may be some (Rep)'s below the inference $(prg)_\omega$, and $U(k') \in \Gamma(k)$ is the main formula of the inference $(prg)_\omega$. We have $m \prec^* k \preceq^* k'$, and $m \prec^* k'$. Pick the mth branch in the upper sequents. We obtain $\vdash_0^{\beta(m)} \Gamma(m)$ for $\beta(m) := \beta_0 < \beta(k)$ and $\Gamma(m) = \Gamma(k) \cup \{U(m)\}$.

Now define a function $f(m)$ as follows.

$$f(m) = \max\{\omega^{\beta(m_0)}\# \cdots \#\omega^{\beta(m_k)} : m_0 \prec^* \cdots \prec^* m_k = m, m_0, \ldots, m_{k-1} <_\omega m\}$$

where # denotes the natural sum. Note that the set $\{(m_0, \ldots, m_k) : m_0 \prec^* \cdots \prec^* m_k = m, m_0, \ldots, m_{k-1} <_\omega m\}$ is finite since $\prec^*$ is irreflexive.

We show that the function f is a desired embedding between $\prec^*$ and $<$. Assume $m \prec^* n$, and let $m_0, \ldots, m_k$ be a sequence such that $f(m) = \omega^{\beta(m_0)}\# \cdots \#\omega^{\beta(m_k)}$, with $m_0 \prec^* \cdots \prec^* m_k = m$ and $m_0, \ldots, m_{k-1} <_\omega m$. We obtain $m_i \prec^* n$ for any $i \leq k$. Let us partition the set $\{0, \ldots, k\}$ into two sets $A = \{i \leq k : n <_\omega m_i\}$ and $B = \{i \leq k : m_i <_\omega n\}$. Note that $m_i \neq n$ since $\prec^*$ is irreflexive.

By (4.12) we obtain $\beta(m_i) < \beta(n)$ for each $i \in A$, and hence $\#\{\omega^{\beta(m_i)} : i \in A\} < \omega^{\beta(n)}$, where $\#\{\alpha_1, \ldots, \alpha_n\} = \alpha_1\# \cdots \#\alpha_n$. On the other hand we have $\#\{\omega^{\beta(m_i)} : i \in B\} \leq \max\{\omega^{\beta(n_0)}\# \cdots \#\omega^{\beta(n_{\ell-1})} : n_0 \prec^* \cdots \prec^* n_{\ell-1} \prec^* n, n_0, \ldots, n_{\ell-1} <_\omega n\}$. Therefore we conclude $f(m) < f(n)$. □

Next we examine the least order type of relations such that we have in hand a derivation of the disjunction of transfinite inductions of these relations.

The following Lemma 4.11 gives an upper bound of the least order type. The proof is formalizable only in CWO_0 (Comparability of Well-Orderings), which is equivalent to ATR_0, cf. [54].

For each $j \leq \ell$, let $<_j$ be an arithmetical relation. The progressiveness of the relation $<_j$ is formulated in the following inference:

$$\frac{\{\Gamma, E_j(n), E_j(m) : n <_j m\}}{\Gamma, E_j(m)} \ (prg)_j$$

where the variables E_j $(j \leq \ell)$ differ each other.

$(prg) \vdash_0^\alpha \Gamma$ designates the fact that there exists a derivation of the sequent Γ in the cut-free calculus $\boldsymbol{G}_\omega$ with rules $(prg)_j$ $(j \leq \ell)$ and (Rep).

Lemma 4.11 *For each $j \leq \ell$, let $<_j$ be an arithmetical* transitive *relation. Let $\Gamma = \{E_j(\bar{n}_{ji})\}$ be a finite set of atomic formulas $E_j(\bar{n}_{ji})$ which is a descending* *chain* $n_{jk_j} <_j \cdots <_j n_{j0}$ *for each* j. *Assume that there exists an ordinal* α *for which* $(prg) \vdash^{\alpha}_{0} \Gamma$. *Then* $\min_j |n_{jk_j}|_{<_j} \leq \alpha$.

Proof By induction on ordinals α. Assume $\min_j |n_{jk_j}|_{<_j} > \alpha$. For each j pick an m_j so that $m_j <_j n_{jk_j} \wedge \alpha \leq |m|_{<_j}$. Since each $<_j$ is assumed to be transitive, we have $m_j <_j n_{ji}$ for each $i \leq k_j$. Let $\Gamma_1 = \Gamma \cup \{E_j(m_j)\}_j$. We show that there exists a $\beta < \alpha$ such that $(prg) \vdash^{\beta}_{0} \Gamma_1$ holds. Then IH would yield $\alpha \leq \min_j |m_j|_{<_j} \leq \beta < \alpha$, a contradiction.

Γ is not an axiom. Consider the last inference of the derivation showing $(prg) \vdash^{\alpha}_{0} \Gamma$. The inference can be assumed to be a $(prg)_j$ for a $j \leq \ell$ and an ordinal $\beta < \alpha$.

$$\frac{\{(prg) \vdash^{\beta}_{0} \Gamma, E_j(\bar{n}) : n <_j n_{ji}\}}{(prg) \vdash^{\alpha}_{0} \Gamma} \; (prg)_{<_j}$$

By picking the m_jth branch, we obtain $(prg) \vdash^{\beta}_{0} \Gamma, E_j(\bar{m}_j)$. By weakenings we obtain $(prg) \vdash^{\beta}_{0} \Gamma_1$. □

Let us strengthen Lemma 4.11 as follows.

Theorem 4.8 The following is provable in $\mathsf{ACA}_0 + \mathrm{TI}(\alpha)$:

For each $j \leq \ell$, *let* $<_j$ *be an arithmetical relation. Assume that there exists an ordinal* α *for which* $(prg) \vdash^{\alpha}_{0} \bigcup_{j \leq \ell} \Gamma_j$ *holds for sequents* $\Gamma_j \subset \{\forall x E_j(x)\} \cup \{E_j(n) : n \in \mathbb{N}\}$. *Then there exist a* j *such that* $(prg) \vdash^{\alpha}_{0} \Gamma_j$.

Proof Assume $(prg) \vdash^{\alpha}_{0} \Gamma, \Gamma_\ell$ for $\Gamma = \bigcup_{j<\ell} \Gamma_j$. We show by induction on α that either $(prg) \vdash^{\alpha}_{0} \Gamma$ or $(prg) \vdash^{\alpha}_{0} \Gamma_\ell$ holds. Assume that $(prg) \vdash^{\alpha}_{0} \Gamma$ does not hold. The set $\Gamma \cup \Gamma_\ell$ is not an axiom.

First consider the case when the last inference is a $(\forall\omega)$ with $\beta < \alpha$:

$$\frac{\{(prg) \vdash^{\beta}_{0} \Gamma, \Gamma_\ell, E_j(m) : m \in \mathbb{N}\}}{(prg) \vdash^{\alpha}_{0} \Gamma, \Gamma_\ell} \; (prg)_j$$

where $\forall x E_j(x)$ is in $\Gamma \cup \Gamma_\ell$.

First consider the case $j \neq \ell$. By the assumption we see that there exists an $m \in \mathbb{N}$ such that $(prg) \vdash^{\beta}_{0} \Gamma, E_j(m)$ does not hold. IH yields $(prg) \vdash^{\beta}_{0} \Gamma_\ell$.

Second consider the case $j = \ell$. We see from the assumption that for each $m \in \mathbb{N}$, $(prg) \vdash^{\beta}_{0} \Gamma_\ell, E_\ell(m)$ holds. Then an inference $(prg)_\ell$ yields $(prg) \vdash^{\alpha}_{0} \Gamma_\ell$.

Next consider the case when the last inference is a $(prg)_j$ with $\beta < \alpha$:

$$\frac{\{(prg) \vdash^{\beta}_{0} \Gamma, \Gamma_\ell, E_j(m) : m <_j n\}}{(prg) \vdash^{\alpha}_{0} \Gamma, \Gamma_\ell} \; (prg)_j$$

where $E_j(n)$ is in $\Gamma \cup \Gamma_\ell$.

First consider the case $j \neq \ell$. By the assumption we see that there exists an $m <_j n$ such that $(prg) \vdash^{\beta}_{0} \Gamma, E_j(m)$ does not hold. IH yields $(prg) \vdash^{\beta}_{0} \Gamma_\ell$.

Second consider the case $j = \ell$. We see from the assumption that for each $m <_\ell n$, $(prg) \vdash_0^\beta \Gamma_\ell, E_\ell(m)$ holds. Then an inference $(prg)_\ell$ yields $(prg) \vdash_0^\alpha \Gamma_\ell$. □

4.2.3 2-Consistency

In this subsection we show the harder halves in Theorems 4.1.3b, 4.1.3c and 4.1.3d on Π_3-formulas. The easy half in Theorem 4.1.3b is shown in the next Sect. 4.3, cf. (4.16).

Suppose that $\mathsf{PA}(\mathcal{E}_*^3) + \mathrm{TI}(\lambda) \vdash \exists x \forall y\, B(x, y, c)$ for a $\lambda < \Lambda$ and an elementary recursive $B \in \mathcal{E}_*^3$. In what follows argue in $I\Sigma_1$.

Given a finite proof of $\exists x \forall y\, B(x, y)$ in $\mathsf{PA}(\mathcal{E}_*^3) + \mathrm{TI}(\lambda)$, first eliminate cut inferences partially to get a proof of the same formula in which any cut formula is in prenex normal form.

Next embed the proof into an infinitary derivation of the sentence $\exists x \forall y\, B(x, y, \bar{c})$ with the cth numeral $\bar{c}$ in a sequent calculus $\boldsymbol{G}_\omega + (cut)$ in the language of $\mathsf{PA}(\mathcal{E}_*^3)$ with the inference rule, repetition (Rep):

$$\frac{\Gamma}{\Gamma}\ (Rep)$$

Infinitary derivations here are equipped with additional informations as in [42].

Definition 4.5 An infinitary derivation is a tuple

$$D = (T, Seq, Rule, Mfml, Sfml, ord, K)$$

which enjoys the following conditions. The naked tree of D is denoted $T = T(D)$.

1. $T \subset {}^{<\omega}\omega$ is a tree with its root $\emptyset$ such that $a * \langle n \rangle \in T \;\&\; m < n \Rightarrow a * \langle m \rangle \in T$.
2. $Seq(a)$ for $a \in T$ denotes the sequent situated at the node a.
   If $Seq(a)$ is a sequent Γ, then it is denoted
   $$a : \Gamma.$$
3. $Rule(a)$ for $a \in T$ denotes the name of the inference rule with its lower sequent $Seq(a)$. (Int) is the label of initial sequents (axioms).
4. $Mfml(a)$ for $a \in T$ denotes the main formula of the inference rule $Rule(a)$. When $Rule(a) = (Rep), (cut)$, then $Mfml(a) = \emptyset$.
5. $Sfml(a * \langle n \rangle)$ for $a * \langle n \rangle \in T$ denotes the side formula (minor formula) of the inference rule $Rule(a)$, which is in the nth upper sequent, i.e., $Sfml(a * \langle n \rangle) \in Seq(a * \langle n \rangle)$. When $Rule(a) = (Rep), (Int)$, then $Sfml(a * \langle n \rangle) = \emptyset$.
6. $ord(a)$ for $a \in T$ denotes the ordinal $<_\Lambda K$ attached to a, where $K < \Lambda$.
7. The tuple $(T, Seq, Rule, Mfml, Sfml, ord, K)$ has to be locally correct with respect to inference rules of the infinitary calculus $\boldsymbol{G}_\omega + (cut)$ and for being

well-founded tree T. The latter means that $ord(a) <_\Lambda ord(b)$ if b is a proper initial segment of $a \in T$.

In a derivation each inference rule except (Int) receives the following nodes: Let us omit the main formulas in upper sequents.

$$\frac{a * \langle 0\rangle : \Gamma, B(\bar{n})}{a : \Gamma, \exists x B(x)}\ (\exists)\ ;\quad \frac{\cdots\ a * \langle n\rangle : \Gamma, B(\bar{n})\ \cdots (n \in \omega)}{a : \Gamma, \forall x B(x)}\ (\forall\omega)\ ;\quad \frac{a * \langle 0\rangle : \Gamma}{a : \Gamma}\ (Rep)$$

The ordinals $ord_c(a)$ in the inference $(\forall\omega)$

$$\frac{\cdots\ a * \langle n\rangle : \Gamma, B(\bar{n})\ \cdots (n \in \omega)}{a : \Gamma, \forall x B(x)}\ (\forall\omega)$$

enjoys

$$ord(a) > ord(a * \langle n\rangle) = ord(a * \langle m\rangle) \tag{4.13}$$

for any n, m.

As in Lemma 4.5, eliminate cut inferences from an infinitary derivation of $\exists x \forall y\, B(x, y, \bar{c})$ to get a cut-free derivation P_c of the same sentence.

$$P_c = (T_c, Seq_c, Rule_c, Mfml_c, Sfml_c, ord_c, K)$$

denotes the resulting derivartions, where the depth of P_c is bounded by an ordinal $K < \Lambda$ uniformly, i.e., $\forall c[ord_c(P_c) = ord_c(\Gamma_{end}(P_c)) < K]$, where $\Gamma_{end}(P_c)$ denotes the end sequent $\exists x \forall y\, B(x, y, \bar{c})$ of P_c.

As in [35, 42] we see that the function $c \mapsto P_c$ is primitive recursive. The crux here is a continuity of the cut-eliminating operation $(P, Q) \mapsto Red_C(P, Q)$, where P, Q are infinitary ω-proofs and $Red_C(P, Q)$ a proof of $(\Gamma_P - \{\neg C\}) \cup (\Gamma_Q - \{C\})$ for the end sequents Γ_P of P and the end sequent Γ_Q of Q. This means that it suffices for us to have some finite portions of proofs P, Q to determine the sequents $Seq(a)$, the inference rules $Rule(a)$, etc. at a node a.

4.2.3.1 Searching Witnesses of Σ_2 in Derivations

Let us define a tracing function $\sigma(c, w) \in T_c = T(P_c)$.

The function $\{\sigma(c, w)\}_w$ indicates the trail in the proof tree T_c in which we go through in searching a witness x_a of $\exists x \forall y\, B(x, y, \bar{c})$, and verifying $\forall y\, B(x_a, y, \bar{c})$.

1. $\sigma(c, 0) = \emptyset$ (root).
   In what follows let $a = \sigma(c, w)$.
2. Until $Seq_c(a)$ is an upper sequent of an $(\forall\omega)$, go to the leftmost branch:

$$\sigma(c, w + 1) = a * \langle 0\rangle.$$

For example

$$\frac{a * \langle 0\rangle : \Gamma, \exists x \forall y\, B(x, y, \bar{c}), \forall y\, B(x_a, y, \bar{c})}{a : \Gamma, \exists x \forall y\, B(x, y, \bar{c})}\ (\exists)$$

3. The case when $Rule_c(b) = (\forall\omega)$ with $a = b * \langle n\rangle$. Namely $Seq_c(a)$ is the nth upper sequent of an $(\forall\omega)$.

$$\frac{\cdots\quad a : \Gamma, B(x_a, y_a, \bar{c})\quad \cdots}{\Gamma, \forall y\, B(x_a, y, \bar{c})}\ (\forall\omega)$$

x_a, y_a are closed terms, i.e., numerals.

a. If $B(x_a, y_a, \bar{c})$ is true, $\sigma(c, w+1) = a \oplus 1$, the next right to the a:

$$\frac{\sigma(c, w) : \Gamma, B(x_a, y_a, \bar{c})\quad \sigma(c, w+1) : \Gamma, B(x_a, y_a + 1, \bar{c})}{\Gamma, \forall y\, B(x_a, y, \bar{c})}\ (\forall\omega)$$

where for an $a = (a_0, \ldots, a_{n-2}, a_{n-1}) \in {}^{<\omega}\omega$

$$a \oplus 1 = (a_0, \ldots, a_{n-2}, a_{n-1} + 1)$$

if $lh(a) = n > 0$. $\emptyset \oplus 1$ is defined to be $\emptyset$.

b. Otherwise $\sigma(c, w+1) = a * \langle 0\rangle$, i.e., go to the leftmost branch from a.

$$\frac{\cdots\quad \dfrac{\sigma(c, w+1) : \Delta\quad \cdots}{\sigma(c, w) : \Gamma, B(x_a, y_a, \bar{c})}\quad \cdots}{\Gamma, \forall y\, B(x_a, y, \bar{c})}\ (\forall\omega)$$

It is easy to see that the function $(c, w) \mapsto \sigma(c, w)$ is primitive recursive.

Once $\sigma(c, w)$ is on an $(\forall\omega)$, the tracing function goes through the upper sequents as long as the literals $B(x_a, y_a, \bar{c})$ are true.

It is intuitively clear that after a finite number of steps, the sequence $\{\sigma(c, w)\}_w$ goes through the upper sequents of an $(\forall\omega)$:

$$\frac{\sigma(c, w_0) : \Gamma, B(x_a, 0, \bar{c})\quad \cdots\quad \sigma(c, w_0 + y) : \Gamma, B(x_a, \bar{y}, \bar{c})\quad \cdots}{\Gamma, \forall y\, B(x_a, y, \bar{c})}\ (\forall\omega)$$

since $\forall y\, B(x_a, y, \bar{c})$ is true for an x_a. We will know at the limit the fact $\forall y\, B(x_a, y, \bar{c})$.

Now let us define a primitive recursive function f as follows. $f(c, w) = x_a$ if $Seq_c(\sigma(c, w))$ is an upper sequent of an $(\forall\omega)$ with its minor formula $B(x_a, \bar{n}, \bar{c})$. Otherwise $f(c, w)$ is arbitrary, say $f(c, w) = 0$.

Suppose $\sigma(c, w)$ is on an $(\forall\omega)$. If the tracing function $\sigma(c, w)$ goes through the upper sequents of the $(\forall\omega)$ with its minor formulas $B(x_a, \bar{n}, \bar{c})$, then we obtain $\lim_{w\to\infty} f(c, w) = x_a$. When f changes the value, it is obvious that the ordinal decreases. Let $h(c, w) := ord_c(\sigma(c, w))$.

Proposition 4.3 *$I\Sigma_1$ proves the following three facts for the primitive recursive functions f, h and an ordinal $K < \Lambda$:*

1. $\lim_{w\to\infty} f(c, w) = x \to \forall y\, B(x, y, c)$.
2. $K > h(c, w) \geq h(c, w + 1)$.
3. $f(c, w) \neq f(c, w + 1) \to h(c, w) > h(c, w + 1)$.

Proof Let us show the harder halves in Theorems 4.1.3b, 4.1.3c and 4.1.3d. Argue in $I\Sigma_1$. Suppose $\mathsf{PA}(\mathcal{E}^3_*) + \mathrm{TI}(\lambda) \vdash \exists x \forall y\, B(x, y, c)$ for a $\lambda < \Lambda$ and a literal B. For each c, $\{h(c, w)\}_w$ is a weakly descending chain of ordinals$< \Lambda$ by Proposition 4.3. For Theorem 4.1.3c note that we can find a $K < \Lambda$ for which $\forall c, w(h(c, w) < K)$. By $\mathcal{E}^\omega WDS_\Lambda$ for Theorem 4.1.3b and by $\mathcal{E}^\omega WDS_{<\Lambda}$ for Theorem 4.1.3c, pick a w such that $\forall u \geq w(h(c, u) = h(c, w))$. Then Proposition 4.3 yields $\forall u \geq w(f(c, u) = f(c, w))$, i.e., $x := \lim_{w\to\infty} f(c, w)$. Hence $\forall y\, B(x, y, c)$ is true, and Theorems 4.1.3b and 4.1.3c are shown.

For Theorem 4.1.3d, we see from Proposition 4.3 that the function $g(c) = \lim_{w\to\infty} f(c, w)$ is K-limit computable for a $K < \Lambda$, i.e., $g \in \mathcal{LR}^{<\Lambda}$, and it witnesses $\forall c \exists x \forall y\, B(x, y, c)$, i.e., $\forall c, y\, B(g(c), y, c)$.

4.3 Consistency Strengths Calibrated with Ordinals

For a recursively axiomatizable theory T, $\mathrm{Con}(T) :\Leftrightarrow \forall x\, \neg\mathrm{Prov}_T(x, \ulcorner\bot\urcorner)$ denotes a consistency statement for T, where $\mathrm{Prov}_T(x, y)$ is a standard T-proof predicate such that $Pr_T(y) :\Leftrightarrow \exists x\, \mathrm{Prov}_T(x, y)$ enjoys the three derivability conditions **D1**, **D2** and **D3** provably in EA, cf. Sect. 1.3. Then $\mathrm{Con}^{(n)}(T)$ denotes the iterated consistency of T for $n < \omega$: $\mathrm{Con}^{(0)}(T) :\Leftrightarrow \forall x(0 = 0)$, and $\mathrm{Con}^{(n+1)}(T) :\Leftrightarrow \mathrm{Con}(T + \mathrm{Con}^{(n)}(T))$.

In this section both $<$ and $<_\Lambda$ denote a standard epsilon order of type Λ. For $\alpha \leq \Lambda$, let $(\mathcal{E}^\omega\text{–TI})_\alpha$ denote the following inference rule for transfinite induction:

$$\frac{\forall \beta < \alpha((f(\beta) < \beta \to B(f(\beta))) \to B(\beta))}{\forall \beta < \alpha\, B(\beta)}\ (\mathcal{E}^\omega\text{-TI})_\alpha$$

where B is a primitive recursive relation in $\mathcal{E}^\omega_*$, and f is a primitive recursive function in $\mathcal{E}^\omega$. Both B and f may have parameters other than β.

Proposition 4.4 *Let $\alpha \leq \Lambda$ be an ordinal.*

1. *The following rule $(\mathcal{E}^\omega\text{–oTI})_\alpha$ for an outer transfinite induction is an admissible rule in $I\Sigma_1 + (\mathcal{E}^\omega\text{–TI})_{\omega\alpha}$:*

$$\frac{\forall x \forall \beta < \alpha[(d(\beta, x) < \beta \to o(d(\beta, x), r(x)) \to A(r(x))) \to (o(\beta, x) \to A(x))]}{\forall x \forall \beta < \alpha(o(\beta, x) \to A(x))} \ (\mathscr{E}^{\omega}\text{-oTI})_{\alpha}$$

where A, o are relations in $\mathscr{E}^{\omega}_{*}$, and r, d are functions in $\mathscr{E}^{\omega}$. Each A, o, r, d may have parameters other than x, β.

In particular if $\omega\alpha = \alpha$, i.e., $\alpha = \omega^{\omega}\alpha_0$ for an α_0, then $(\mathscr{E}^{\omega}\text{–oTI})_{\alpha}$ is an admissible rule in $I\Sigma_1 + (\mathscr{E}^{\omega}\text{–TI})_{\alpha}$.

2. *For each $\gamma < \alpha \cdot \omega$, $(\mathscr{E}^{\omega}\text{–TI})_{\gamma}$ is an admissible rule in $I\Sigma_1 + (\mathscr{E}^{\omega}\text{–TI})_{\alpha}$.*

Proof Argue in $I\Sigma_{1_{\alpha}}$.

Proposition 4.4.1. Assume that $\forall x \forall \beta < \alpha[(d(\beta, x) < \beta \to o(d(\beta, x), r(x)) \to A(r(x))) \to (o(\beta, x) \to A(x))]$ for primitive recursive A, o, r, d. Let qt and rm denote the primitive recursive functions such that $\beta = \omega \cdot qt(\beta) + rm(\beta)$ with $rm(\beta) < \omega$. Let $B(\beta) :\Leftrightarrow [o(qt(\beta), rm(\beta)) \to A(rm(\beta))]$, and $f(\beta) = \omega \cdot d(qt(\beta), rm($ $r(rm(\beta))$. Suppose $\neg B(\beta)$ for $\beta < \omega\alpha$, and let $x = rm(\beta)$ and $\beta_0 = qt(\beta)$. Then we have $o(\beta_0, x)$ and $\neg A(x)$. Hence by the assumption we obtain $\beta_1 := d(\beta_0, x) < \beta_0 < \alpha, o(\beta_1, r(x))$ and $\neg A(r(x)))$. Then $f(\beta) = \omega\beta_1 + r(x) < \omega\beta_0 + x = \beta$, and $\neg B(f(\beta))$. Thus we obtain $\forall \beta < \omega\alpha((f(\beta) < \beta \to B(f(\beta))) \to B(\beta))$ for primitive recursive B and f. We conclude $\forall \beta < \omega\alpha\, B(\beta)$ by the rule $(\mathscr{E}^{\omega}\text{–TI})_{\omega\alpha}$, which yields $\forall x \forall \beta < \alpha(o(\beta, x) \to A(x))$.

Proposition 4.4.2. We show by metainduction on $k < \omega$ that $(\mathscr{E}^{\omega}\text{–TI})_{\alpha \cdot k}$ is an admissible rule in $I\Sigma_1 + (\mathscr{E}^{\omega}\text{–TI})_{\alpha}$. Assume $\forall \beta < \alpha \cdot (k+1)((f(\beta) < \beta \to B(f(\beta))) \to B(\beta))$ for primitive recursive f, B. Then $\forall \beta < \alpha \cdot k((f(\beta) < \beta \to B(f(\beta))) \to B(\beta))$. We obtain $\forall \beta < \alpha \cdot k\, B(\beta)$ by IH. Let $C(\beta) :\Leftrightarrow B(\alpha \cdot k + \beta)$, and $g(\beta) := f(\alpha \cdot k + \beta) - \alpha \cdot k$, where $\alpha - \beta = 0$ if $\alpha < \beta$, and $\beta + (\alpha - \beta) = \alpha$ else. For $\beta < \alpha$, suppose $\neg C(\beta)$. Then $f(\alpha \cdot k + \beta) < \alpha \cdot k + \beta$ and $\neg B(f(\alpha \cdot k + \beta))$. Since we have $\forall \beta < \alpha \cdot k\, B(\beta)$, $f(\alpha \cdot k + \beta) \geq \alpha \cdot k$ is the case. This means that $g(\beta) < \beta$ and $\neg C(g(\beta))$. Hence $\forall \beta < \alpha((f(\beta) < \beta \to C(f(\beta))) \to C(\beta))$. By the rule $(\mathscr{E}^{\omega}\text{–TI})_{\alpha}$ we obtain $\forall \beta < \alpha\, C(\beta)$. Therefore $\forall \beta < \alpha \cdot (k+1)\, B(\beta)$. □

In this section we show Theorems 4.1.3h, 4.1.3i, 4.1.3e, 4.1.3f, 4.1.3g.
First consider the easy halves:

$$(\mathscr{E}^{\omega}\text{–TI})_{\Lambda} \text{ is an admissible rule in } I\Sigma_1 + \{\mathrm{Con}^{(m)}(\mathsf{PA} + \mathrm{TI}(<\Lambda)) : m < \omega\} \tag{4.14}$$

$$I\Sigma_1 + \mathrm{RFN}_{\Sigma_1}(\mathsf{PA} + \mathrm{TI}(<\Lambda)) \vdash \mathscr{E}^{\omega} DS_{\Lambda} \tag{4.15}$$

$$I\Sigma_1 + \mathrm{RFN}_{\Sigma_2}(\mathsf{PA} + \mathrm{TI}(<\Lambda)) \vdash \mathscr{E}^{\omega} WDS_{\Lambda} \tag{4.16}$$

From the proof in Sect. 4.1 we see the following Proposition 4.5.

Proposition 4.5 *1. For each formula A, there exists an elementary recursive function f_1 such that* $\mathsf{EA} \vdash \forall \alpha < \Lambda[\mathrm{Prov}_{\mathsf{PA}+\mathrm{TI}(<\Lambda)}(f_1(\alpha), \ulcorner \mathrm{TI}[<_{\dot\alpha}, A]\urcorner)]$.

2. *There exists an elementary recursive function* f_2 *such that* $\mathsf{EA} \vdash \forall\alpha < \varepsilon_0[\text{Prov}_{\mathsf{PA}+\text{TI}(<\Lambda)}(f_2(\alpha), \ulcorner \mathcal{E}^3 DS_{\dot\alpha} \urcorner)]$.
3. *There exists an elementary recursive function* f_3 *such that* $\mathsf{EA} \vdash \forall\alpha < \varepsilon_0[\text{Prov}_{\mathsf{PA}+\text{TI}(<\Lambda)}(f_3(\alpha), \ulcorner \mathcal{E}^3 WDS_{\dot\alpha} \urcorner)]$.

We show (4.14), which means that if $I\Sigma_1 + \text{Con}^{(k)}(\mathsf{PA} + \text{TI}(<\Lambda)) \vdash \forall\beta < \Lambda[(f(\beta) < \beta \to B(f(\beta))) \to B(\beta)]$ for $f, B \in \mathcal{E}^\omega$, then $I\Sigma_1 + \text{Con}^{(m)}(\mathsf{PA} + \text{TI}(<\Lambda)) \vdash \forall\beta < \Lambda\, B(\beta)$ for some m.

Assume that $I\Sigma_1 + \text{Con}^{(k)}(\mathsf{PA} + \text{TI}(<\Lambda)) \vdash \forall\beta < \Lambda[(f(\beta) < \beta \to B(f(\beta))) \to B(\beta)]$ and a fortiori $\mathsf{PA} + \text{TI}(<\Lambda) + \text{Con}^{(k)}(\mathsf{PA} + \text{TI}(<\Lambda)) \vdash \forall\beta < \Lambda[(f(\beta) < \beta \to B(f(\beta))) \to B(\beta)]$. For the Π_0-formula $B(\beta)$, we obtain $\mathsf{PA} + \text{TI}(<\Lambda) + \text{Con}^{(k)}(\mathsf{PA} + \text{TI}(<\Lambda)) \vdash Prg[<_\Lambda, B]$. From Proposition 4.5.1 we see

$$I\Sigma_1 \vdash \forall\beta < \Lambda\, \text{Pr}_{\mathsf{PA}+\text{TI}(<\Lambda)+\text{Con}^{(k)}(\mathsf{PA}+\text{TI}(<\Lambda))}(\ulcorner B(\dot\beta) \urcorner).$$

Hence we conclude

$$I\Sigma_1 + \text{Con}^{(k+1)}(\mathsf{PA} + \text{TI}(<\Lambda)) \vdash \forall\beta < \Lambda\, B(\beta)$$

since for a recursive and Σ_1-complete theory T, the consistency $\text{Con}(T)$ is equivalent to the Π_1-uniform reflection principle $\text{RFN}_{\Pi_1}(T)$ of T.

Next consider (4.15). We see $I\Sigma_1 \vdash \forall\alpha < \Lambda[\text{Pr}_{\mathsf{PA}+\text{TI}(<\Lambda)}(\ulcorner \mathcal{E}^\omega DS_{\dot\alpha} \urcorner)]$ from Proposition 4.5.2. Since $\mathcal{E}^\omega DS_\alpha$ is a Π_2-formula, $\text{RFN}_{\Sigma_1}(\mathsf{PA} + \text{TI}(<\Lambda))$, which is equivalent to $\text{RFN}_{\Pi_2}(\mathsf{PA} + \text{TI}(<\Lambda))$, yields $\mathcal{E}^\omega DS_\Lambda$.

(4.16) is seen similarly from Proposition 4.5.3 using the fact that $\mathcal{E}^\omega WDS_\alpha$ is a Π_3-formula, and $\text{RFN}_{\Sigma_2}(\mathsf{PA} + \text{TI}(<\Lambda))$ is equivalent to $\text{RFN}_{\Pi_3}(\mathsf{PA} + \text{TI}(<\Lambda))$. □

4.3.1 Consistency Proof

Next we show the converses of Theorems 4.1.3e, 4.1.3f, 4.1.3g, 4.1.3h, and 4.1.3i following the Gentzen's consistency proof of PA. Given a proof of a contradiction, we rewrite it to another proof of the contradiction in such a way that the ordinals assigned to proofs decrease. We need to define a rewriting step on proofs and ordinals assigned to proofs.

In this subsection it is convenient for us to restrict the language to one without function symbols except zero 0 and the successor S. In such a language terms are of the form $S(\cdots(S(\xi))\cdots)$ for $\xi \equiv 0$ or variables ξ, and the number of symbols occurring in closed terms, i.e., numerals $\bar{n}$ is equal to $1 + n$. Other function symbols such as addition $+$ and multiplication $\cdot$ are replaced by their graphs, i.e., relation symbols. Furthermore it is convenient for us to have relation symbols by which bounded quantifiers are defined. Thus we consider the language with relation symbols for elementary recursive relations $\mathcal{E}^3_*$ in Definition 1.5.

The language $\mathcal{L}(\mathcal{E}^3_*)$ of $\mathsf{PA}(\mathcal{E}^3_*)$ consists of function symbols 0 and S (successor), and relation symbols R for elementary recursive relations R and their complements $\overline{\mathsf{R}}$. $I\Sigma_n(\mathcal{E}^3_*)$ denotes the fragment of $\mathsf{PA}(\mathcal{E}^3_*)$ in which induction formula is restricted to $\Sigma_n(\mathcal{E}^3_*)$-formula $\exists x_1 \forall x_2 \cdots Q x_n\, L$ whose matrix L is a literal. Note that each $\Sigma_0(\mathcal{E}^3_*)$-formula, i.e., a bounded formula in the language $\mathcal{L}(\mathcal{E}^3_*)$ is equivalent to an equation over $I\Sigma_0(\mathcal{E}^3_*)$. Thus the propositional part is absorbed in the atomic formulas in $\mathcal{E}^3_*$.

Let $\forall x \neg B(x)$ be a closed Π_1-formula with a literal B, and $\lambda < \Lambda$ an arbitrary but fixed limit ordinal. $\mathsf{PA}(\mathcal{E}^3_*) + \mathrm{TI}(\lambda) + \forall x \neg B(x)$ denotes the theory obtained from $\mathsf{PA}(\mathcal{E}^3_*) + \mathrm{TI}(\lambda)$ by adding the extra axiom $\forall x \neg B(x)$. $\mathsf{PA}(\mathcal{E}^3_*) + \mathrm{TI}(\lambda) + \forall x \neg B(x)$ is formulated in a sequent calculus obtained from $\boldsymbol{G}_1 + (cut)$ by adding the inference rules (VJ), $(TI)_\lambda$ for prenex $\forall$-formulas A whose matrices are literals.

$$\frac{\Gamma, A(0) \quad \neg A(a), \Gamma, A(S(a)) \quad \neg A(t), \Gamma}{\Gamma}\ (VJ)$$

$$\frac{s <_\lambda t, \Gamma \quad \neg \forall x <_\lambda a\, A(x), \Gamma, A(a) \quad \neg A(s), \Gamma}{\Gamma}\ (TI)_\lambda$$

where t is the *induction term* and A the *induction formula* of the inferences (VJ), $(TI)_\lambda$.

Also inference rules for introducing formulas $\exists x <_\lambda t \neg A(x)$ and $\forall x <_\lambda t\, A(x)$ are

$$\frac{\Gamma, \exists x <_\lambda t \neg A(x), s <_\lambda t \quad \Gamma, \exists x <_\lambda t \neg A(x), \neg A(s)}{\Gamma, \exists x <_\lambda t \neg A(x)}\ (\exists)_\lambda$$

$$\frac{\Gamma, \forall x <_\lambda t\, A(x), a \not<_\lambda t, A(a)}{\Gamma, \forall x <_\lambda t\, A(x)}\ (\forall)_\lambda$$

Moreover an inference rule (E) is added:

$$\frac{\Gamma}{\Gamma}\ (E)$$

and the following arithmetical axioms.

1. Γ, Δ_R, where Δ_R consists of literals and corresponds to the definition of an elementary relation R.
2. Γ, L for a true closed literal L.
3. $\Gamma, \neg B(t)$ for an arbitrary term t.

A *proof* in the sequent calculus is a finite labelled tree according to the above axioms and inference rules. We assume tacitly that each proof enjoys the pure variable condition in Definition 1.3. $s, t, u, \ldots$ denote the nodes in proof trees. $s : \Gamma$ indicates that the sequent Γ is the label of the node s. The label Γ of s is denoted $Seq(s)$.

Let P be a proof in the sequent calculus, and s a node in the proof tree P. We assign the *height* $h(s; P) < \omega$ recursively as follows.

1. $h(s; P) = 0$ if s is the root of the proof tree.
   In what follows let $Seq(s)$ be an upper sequent of an inference rule J with the lower sequent $Seq(s_0)$.
2. $h(s; P) = h(s_0; P) + 1$ if J is an (E).
3. $h(s; P) = h(s_0; P)$ otherwise.

A proof in the sequent calculus $\mathsf{PA}(\mathscr{E}^3_*) + \mathrm{TI}(\lambda) + \forall x \neg B(x)$ is temporarily said to be a *prenex-proof* if no inference rules $(\vee)$, $(\wedge)$ occurs in it. A cut-elimination theorem yields readily that the inconsistency implies the existence of a prenex-proof of the empty sequent. Note that the cut-elimination theorem is provable in EA^4, but not in EA.

For prenex formulas A, let $\mathrm{dg}_1(A) = \mathrm{dg}_b(A) - \omega$ with the degree in Definition 4.4, and $\mathrm{dg}_1(\exists x <_\lambda t\, A(x)) = \mathrm{dg}_1(\forall x <_\lambda t\, \neg A(x)) = \mathrm{dg}_1(A(0)) + 1$. This means that $\mathrm{dg}_1(A) = n$ iff $A \equiv (Q_1 x_1 \cdots Q_{n+1} x_{n+1}\, A_0)$ such that its matrix A_0 is a literal, and alternating quantifiers $Q_1, \ldots, Q_{n+1}$. Specifically $\mathrm{dg}_1(A) = 0$ if either $A \in \Sigma_1 \cup \Pi_1$ or A is a literal.

Definition 4.6 Let P be a prenex-proof. An assignment of an ordinal term $o(s; P) < \Lambda$ to nodes s in the proof tree P is said to be *ordinal assignment* if it enjoys the followings.

1. $o(s; P) = 1$ if $Seq(s)$ is an axiom.
   In what follows let $Seq(s)$ be the lower sequent of an inference rule J with its upper sequents $\{s_i : Seq(s_i)\}_{i<m}$.
2. $o(s; P) = o(s_0; P)$ if J is either a $(\forall)$ or a $(\forall)_\lambda$.
3. $o(s; P) = o(s_0; P) + 1$ if J is an $(\exists)$.
4. $o(s; P) = \max\{o(s_0; P), o(s_1; P)\} + 1$ if J is an $(\exists)_\lambda$.
5. $o(s; P) = o(s_0; P) + \max\{o(s_1; P), o(s_2; P)\} \cdot \omega$ if J is a (VJ).
6. $o(s; P) = \max\{o(s_0; P), (1 + o(s_1; P) + \max\{o(s_2; P), \mathrm{dg}_1(A) + 2\}) \cdot mj(t)\} + 1$ if J is a $(TI)_\lambda$ with its induction term t, where $mj(t) = \lambda$ if t contains a variable. Let t be a numeral α. If $\alpha \not<_\Lambda \lambda$, then $mj(t) \in \{0, \lambda\}$. Otherwise $mj(t) \in \{\alpha, \lambda\}$.
7. $o(s; P) = o(s_0; P) + o(s_1; P)$ if J is a (cut).
8. $o(s; P) = \omega^{o(s_0; P)}$ if J is an (E).

Set $o(P) = o(s_{end}; P)$ with the root s_{end} in the proof tree P.

There are several ordinal assignments to a prenex-proof P due to the inference $(TI)_\lambda$. This means that $\alpha = o(s; P)$ under an ordinal assignment is a relation $o(\alpha, s, P)$, which is in $\mathscr{E}^4_* \subset \mathscr{E}^\omega_*$ since the truth definition of literals in $\mathscr{L}(\mathsf{EA})$ is in $\mathscr{E}^4_*$. If a variable a occurs in a proof P such that it is not an eigenvariable, then substitute the constant 0 for the variable a. The result P' is a proof such that $h(s; P') = h(s; P)$ and $o(s; P') = o(s; P)$ even if a occurs in the induction term $t(a)$ of an inference $(TI)_\lambda$. By the substitution, the induction term becomes a numeral $t(0)$, but $mj(t(a)) = \lambda$ and $mj(t(0)) = \lambda$ is permissible.

Let P be a prenex-proof of the empty sequent in the sequent calculus for $\mathsf{PA}(\mathscr{E}^3_*) + \mathrm{TI}(\lambda) + \forall x \neg B(x)$. We say that P is a *height-normal* proof if the following condition is fulfilled:

(p1) For any (cut) in P, $\mathrm{dg}_1(A) \leq h(s_1; P) = h(s_0; P)$ holds.

$$\frac{s_0 : \Gamma, \neg A \quad s_1 : A, \Delta}{s : \Gamma, \Delta}\ (cut)$$

Assuming that $\forall x \neg B(x)$ is true, we show the following lemma.

Lemma 4.12 *There exist r, d in $\mathscr{E}^\omega$ such that the following is provable in $I\Sigma_1$: For any height-normal proof P and ordinal $\beta_0 < \Lambda$ such that $\beta_0 = o(P)$, $r(P)$ is a height-normal proof such that $d(\beta_0, P) < \beta_0$ and $d(\beta_0, P) = o(r(P))$.*

Let us prove Lemma 4.12. Argue in $I\Sigma_1$. Let P be a height-normal proof. Let us assume that each (cut) in P is of the form

$$\frac{\Gamma, \neg A \quad A, \Delta}{\Gamma, \Delta}\ (cut)$$

where A is either an existential formula or a literal.

Proposition 4.6 *$I\Sigma_1$ proves the fact: Assume that $\forall x \neg B(x)$ is true. If a prenex-proof P contains none of inference rules (VJ), $(TI)_\lambda$, $(\exists)$, $(\exists)_\lambda$, and its end sequent consists solely of closed $\exists$-formulas and literals, then there exists a (cut) on the rightmost branch whose right cut formula is a true literal, or its end sequent contains a true literal.*

Proof Augue in $I\Sigma_1$. Suppose that P contains none of inference rules (VJ), $(TI)_\lambda$, $(\exists)$, $(\exists)_\lambda$, and its end sequent consists solely of closed $\exists$-formulas and literals. The rightmost branch contains neither of $(\forall)$, $(\forall)_\lambda$, and no variable occurs on the branch. From the assumption that $\forall x \neg B(x)$ is true, we see the assertion. □

Therefore in a prenex-proof P with the empty end sequent $\emptyset$, there occurs one of inferences (VJ), $(TI)_\lambda$, $(\exists)$, $(\exists)_\lambda$. Let I be the lowest and rightmost inference (VJ), $(TI)_\lambda$, $(\exists)$, $(\exists)_\lambda$. This means that I is one of such inferences, there is no such inference below I, and there is no such inference right to I, i.e., when I occurs in the left upper part of a (cut), there is no such inference in the right upper part of the (cut).

Let us denote $s : \Gamma : \alpha$ when $\Gamma = Seq(s)$ and $\alpha = o(s; P)$ in a proof P.

Case 0. I is not on the rightmost branch: Then there exists a (cut) below I such that I occurs in the left upper part of it. We claim that there exists a (cut) on the rightmost branch such that its *left* cut formula is a false literal. Consider the (cut) J on the rightmost branch such that I occurs in the left upper part of it. Note that no free variable occurs in the lower sequent for otherwise the variable has to be the eigenvariable of inferences $(\forall)$, $(\forall)_\lambda$ since we are assuming that P enjoys the pure variable condition, and there must exist another (cut) below it whose cut formula is the main formula of the inference with the eigenvariable.

$$P = \cfrac{\begin{array}{cc} I & \\ \vdots & \vdots\; Q \\ \Gamma, \neg C & C, \Delta \end{array}}{\begin{array}{c} \Gamma, \Delta \\ \vdots \\ \emptyset \end{array}}$$

If the rightmost branch of Q contains such a (cut) or C is a true literal, then we are done.

From Proposition 4.6 we see that Δ contains a true literal D. Therefore P is of the form with a true literal D:

$$P = \cfrac{\begin{array}{cc} & \cfrac{\begin{array}{cc} I & \\ \vdots & \vdots\; Q \\ \Gamma, \neg C & C, \Delta \end{array}}{\Gamma, \Delta} \\ \vdots & \vdots\; R \\ \Phi, \neg D : \alpha & D, \Psi : \beta \end{array}}{\begin{array}{c} \Phi, \Psi : \alpha + \beta \\ \vdots \\ \emptyset \end{array}}$$

Thus the claim is shown.

Eliminating the false literal $\neg D$, we obtain the following proof P':

$$P' = \cfrac{\begin{array}{c} \vdots \\ \Phi : \alpha \end{array}}{\begin{array}{c} \Phi, \Psi : \alpha \\ \vdots \\ \emptyset \end{array}}$$

P' is a height-normal proof with $o(P') < o(P)$ since ordinals decrease on the rightmost branch by $\alpha < \alpha + \beta$, i.e., $\beta > 0$.

In what follows we assume that I is on the rightmost branch. Then no free variable occurs below I nor in the upper sequent of I except the eigenvariable of I if any. Moreover none of of inferences $(\forall)$, $(\forall)_\lambda$ occurs below I.

Case 1. I is a (VJ): Let P be the following.

$$P = \dfrac{s_0 : \Gamma, A(0) : \alpha \quad \begin{array}{c}\vdots\ Q(a) \\ s_1 : \neg A(a), \Gamma, A(S(a)) : \beta\end{array} \quad s_2 : \neg A(t), \Gamma : \gamma}{\begin{array}{c} s : \Gamma : \alpha + \max\{\beta, \gamma\} \cdot \omega \\ \vdots \\ \emptyset \end{array}} \ (VJ)\ I$$

where t is a closed term, i.e., a numeral with $t^{\mathbb{N}} = n$, and the induction formula A is a $\forall$-formula.

Let $P' = r(P)$ be the following.

$$\dfrac{s_0 : \Gamma, A(0) : \alpha \quad \begin{array}{c}\vdots\ Q(0) \\ t_1 : \neg A(0), \Gamma, A(1) : \beta\end{array} \quad \cdots \quad \begin{array}{c}\vdots\ Q(n-1) \\ t_n : \neg A(n-1), \Gamma, A(n) : \beta\end{array} \quad s_2 : \neg A(n), \Gamma : \gamma}{\begin{array}{c} s : \Gamma : \alpha + \beta \cdot n + \gamma \\ \vdots \\ \emptyset \end{array}} \ (cut)'s$$

where each $Q(k)$ $(k < n)$ is obtained from the subproof $Q(a)$ by substituting k for the eigenvariable a, and (cut)'s denote a series of n (cut) inferences in arbitrary order. Let us assign ordinals to sequents in $Q(k)$ as for ones in $Q(a)$. This means that when an inference $(TI)_\lambda$ with the induction term $s(a)$ occurs in $Q(a)$, let $mj(s(k)) = \lambda = mj(s(a))$ in $Q(k)$. Then we have $o(t_{k+1}; P') = \beta = o(s_1; P)$, and $o(s; P) = \alpha + \max\{\beta, \gamma\} \cdot \omega$ for $\alpha = o(s_0; P)$ and $\gamma = o(s_2; P)$. While in P', $o(s; P') = \alpha + \beta \cdot n + \gamma$ for $o(s_0; P') = \alpha$, $o(t_i; P') = \beta$ and $o(s_2; P') = \gamma$. From $\beta \cdot n + \gamma < \max\{\beta, \gamma\} \cdot \omega$ with $\beta, \gamma > 0$, we see $o(s; P') < o(s; P)$. Since $\beta' < \beta \Rightarrow \alpha + \beta' < \alpha + \beta \,\&\, \omega^{\beta'} < \omega^{\beta}$, we conclude $o(P') < o(P)$.

Case 2. I is a $(TI)_\lambda$: Let P be the following.

$$\dfrac{\begin{array}{c}\vdots\ Q_0 \\ s_0 : u <_\lambda t, \Gamma : \alpha_0\end{array} \quad \begin{array}{c}\vdots\ Q(a) \\ s_1 : \neg \forall x <_\lambda a\, A(x), \Gamma, A(a) : \alpha_1\end{array} \quad \begin{array}{c}\vdots\ Q_2 \\ s_2 : \neg A(u), \Gamma : \alpha_2\end{array}}{\begin{array}{c} s : \Gamma : \delta \\ \vdots \\ \emptyset \end{array}} \ (TI)_\lambda\ I$$

where the induction formula A is a $\forall$-formula with $d = \mathrm{dg}_1(A) + 2$, both u and t are numerals, $mj(t) \in \{t, \lambda\}$, and $\delta = \max\{\alpha_0, (1 + \alpha_1 + \max\{\alpha_2, d\}) \cdot mj(t)\} + 1$.

Case 2.1. $u \not<_\lambda t$: Then eliminate the false literal $u <_\lambda t$ from the first subproof Q_0 to get the following $P' = r(P)$ with $o(P') < o(P)$ by $\alpha_0 < \delta$.

$$P' = \begin{array}{c} \vdots\ Q'_0 \\ s : \Gamma : \alpha_0 \\ \vdots \\ \emptyset \end{array}$$

Case 2.2. $\gamma = u <_\lambda t = \beta$: Let Q be the following.

$$Q = \dfrac{b <_\lambda u, b \not<_\lambda u : 1 \quad \begin{array}{c}\vdots\ Q(a) \\ \neg \forall x <_\lambda a\, A(x), \Gamma, A(a) : \alpha_1\end{array} \quad \begin{array}{c}\vdots\ Q'_2 \\ \neg A(b), A(b) : d\end{array}}{b \not<_\lambda u, A(b), \Gamma : \delta_0}\ (TI)_\lambda$$

where Q'_2 is a cut-free proof canonically constructed from logical initial sequents $\Delta, \neg L, L : 1$ by inferences $(\exists)$, $(\forall)$. Then let $P' = r(P)$ be the following.

$$\begin{array}{c} \dfrac{\dfrac{\begin{array}{c}\vdots\ Q \\ b \not<_\lambda u, A(b), \Gamma : \delta_0\end{array}}{s_0 : \forall x <_\lambda u\, A(x), \Gamma}\ (\forall)_\lambda \quad \begin{array}{c}\vdots\ Q(u) \\ s_1 : \neg \forall x <_\lambda u\, A(x), \Gamma, A(u) : \alpha_1\end{array} \quad \begin{array}{c}\vdots\ Q_2 \\ s_2 : \neg A(u), \Gamma : \alpha_2\end{array}}{s : \Gamma : \delta'}\ (cut) \\ \vdots \\ \emptyset \end{array}$$

The induction term of the new inference $(TI)_\lambda$ in Q is u, and let $mj(u) = \gamma$. Then $\delta_0 = \max\{1, (1 + \alpha_1 + \max\{d, d\}) \cdot \gamma\} + 1 = (1 + \alpha_1 + d) \cdot \gamma + 1$, and $\delta' = \delta_0 + \alpha_1 + \alpha_2$. We obtain $\delta' \leq (1 + \alpha_1 + \max\{\alpha_2, d\}) \cdot (\gamma + 1) \leq (1 + \alpha_1 + \max\{\alpha_2, d\}) \cdot \beta < \delta$ by $mj(t) \geq \beta > \gamma$. Therefore $o(P') < o(P)$.

Case 3. I is an $(\exists)$: Let $\exists x\, A(x)$ be the main formula of I, and J the lowest cut such that its cut formula is the formula $\exists x\, A(x)$. Let $c = \mathrm{dg}_1(\exists x\, A(x))$.

Case 3.1. There is an (E) between I and J: Let us interchange $(\exists)$ and (E). Let P be the left in the following, and P' the right:

$$\begin{array}{c} \dfrac{\Gamma, \forall x \neg A(x) \qquad \begin{array}{c} \dfrac{A(n), \exists x\, A(x), \Delta_1 : \alpha_1}{\exists x\, A(x), \Delta_1 : \alpha_1 + 1}\ (\exists)\ I \\ \vdots \\ \dfrac{\exists x\, A(x), \Delta_0 : \alpha_0 + 1}{\exists x\, A(x), \Delta_0 : \omega^{\alpha_0 + 1}}\ (E)\ H \\ \vdots \\ \exists x\, A(x), \Delta : \alpha \end{array}}{\Gamma, \Delta}\ (cut), J \\ \vdots \\ \emptyset \end{array} \qquad \begin{array}{c} \dfrac{\Gamma, \forall x \neg A(x) \qquad \begin{array}{c} \dfrac{A(n), \exists x\, A(x), \Delta_1 : \alpha_1}{A(n), \exists x\, A(x), \Delta_1 : \alpha_1} \\ \vdots \\ \dfrac{\dfrac{A(n), \exists x\, A(x), \Delta_0 : \alpha_0}{A(n), \exists x\, A(x), \Delta_0 : \omega^{\alpha_0}}\ (E)}{\exists x\, A(x), \Delta_0 : \omega^{\alpha_0} + 1}\ (\exists)\ I' \\ \vdots \\ \exists x\, A(x), \Delta : \alpha' \end{array}}{\Gamma, \Delta}\ (cut), J \\ \vdots \\ \emptyset \end{array}$$

where H is the uppermost (E) below I. The formula $\exists x\, A(x)$ is in the upper sequent of H. From $\omega^{\alpha_0} + 1 < \omega^{\alpha_0 + 1}$, we see that $\alpha' < \alpha$. Hence $o(P') < o(P)$.

Case 3.2. There is no (E) between I and J:

Case 3.2.1. $c = \mathrm{dg}_1(\exists x\, A(x)) > 0$: This means that a quantifier occurs in A, and $\mathrm{dg}_1(A(n)) = c - 1$. Let P be the following.

$$P = \begin{array}{c} \dfrac{A(n), \exists x\, A(x), \Delta_1 : \beta_1}{\exists x\, A(x), \Delta_1 : \beta_1 + 1}\ (\exists)\, I \\ \vdots \\ \dfrac{\Gamma, \forall x \neg A(x) : \alpha \quad s_1 : \exists x\, A(x), \Delta : \beta + 1}{s : \Gamma, \Delta : \alpha + \beta + 1}\ (cut)\, J \\ \vdots \\ \dfrac{\Pi : \gamma + 1}{t : \Pi : \omega^{\gamma+1}}\ (E)\, H \\ \vdots \\ \emptyset \end{array}$$

where H is the uppermost inference (E) below I. We have $c \leq h(s_1; P) = h(s; P)$ by the condition **(p1)** for the height-normality.

Let P' be the following.

$$P' = \begin{array}{c} \begin{array}{cc} \begin{array}{c} \dfrac{A(n), \exists x\, A(x), \Delta_1 : \beta_1}{A(n), \exists x\, A(x), \Delta_1 : \beta_1} \\ \vdots \\ \dfrac{\Gamma, \forall x \neg A(x) : \alpha \quad \exists x\, A(x), A(n), \Delta : \beta}{\Gamma, \Delta, A(n) : \alpha + \beta} \\ \vdots \\ \dfrac{\Pi, A(n) : \gamma}{\Pi, A(n) : \omega^{\gamma}}\ (E) \end{array} & \begin{array}{c} \vdots \\ \Gamma, \Delta, \neg A(n) : \alpha \\ \vdots \\ \dfrac{\Pi, \neg A(n) : \gamma'}{\Pi, \neg A(n) : \omega^{\gamma'}} \end{array} \end{array} \\ \hline t : \Pi : \omega^{\gamma} + \omega^{\gamma'} \quad (cut) \\ \vdots \\ \emptyset \end{array}$$

where the subproof ending with $\Gamma, \Delta, \neg A(n)$ is obtained from the subproof ending with $\Gamma, \forall x\, A(x)$ in P by inversion and weakening.

We see $\mathrm{dg}_1(A(n)) = c - 1 \leq h(t; P') = h(t; P) = h(s; P) - 1$ from $c \leq h(s; P)$, and P' is height-normal. Next we see $\gamma' < \gamma$ from $\alpha < \alpha + \beta$. Hence $\omega^{\gamma} + \omega^{\gamma'} < \omega^{\gamma+1}$, and hence $o(P') < o(P)$.

Case 3.2.2. $c = 0$: This means that A is a literal. Let P be the following.

$$\dfrac{\dfrac{A(n), \exists x\, A(x), \Delta_1 : \beta_1}{\exists x\, A(x), \Delta_1 : \beta_1 + 1}\ (\exists)\, I}{}$$

$$P = \dfrac{\Gamma, \forall x \neg A(x) : \alpha \qquad \exists x\, A(x), \Delta : \beta + 1}{\Gamma, \Delta : \alpha + \beta + 1}\ (cut)\, J \quad \vdots \quad \emptyset$$

If $A(n)$ is false, then eliminate the false literal $A(n)$ to get the following proof P'.

$$\exists x\, A(x), \Delta_1 : \beta_1 \quad \vdots$$

$$P' = \dfrac{\Gamma, \forall x \neg A(x) : \alpha \quad \exists x\, A(x), \Delta : \beta}{\Gamma, \Delta : \alpha + \beta} \quad \vdots \quad \emptyset$$

Otherwise eliminate the false $\neg A(n)$ with inversion to get the following proof P'.

$$P' = \begin{array}{c} \Gamma : \alpha \\ \vdots \\ \emptyset \end{array}$$

where a subproof ending with $\Gamma, \neg A(n)$ is obtained by inversion. In each case we see $o(P') < o(P)$ from $\alpha, \alpha + \beta < \alpha + \beta + 1$.

Case 4. I is an $(\exists)_\lambda$: Let $\exists x <_\lambda t\, A(x)$ be the main formula of I, and $A(u)$ its minor formula. Both t and u are closed terms.

$$P = \dfrac{u <_\lambda t, \exists x <_\lambda t\, A(x), \Gamma : \alpha \quad A(u), \exists x <_\lambda t\, A(x), \Gamma : \beta}{s : \exists x <_\lambda t\, A(x), \Gamma : \max\{\alpha, \beta\} + 1}\ (\exists)_\lambda \quad \vdots \quad \emptyset$$

If $u \not<_\lambda t$, then eliminate the false literal $u <_\lambda t$ to get the following $P' = r(P)$.

$$P' = \begin{array}{c} s : \exists x <_\lambda t\, A(x), \Gamma : \alpha \\ \vdots \\ \emptyset \end{array}$$

Suppose that $u <_\lambda t$ is true, and let J be the lowest cut such that its cut formula is the formula $\exists x <_\lambda t\, A(x)$.

Case 4.1. There is an (E) between I and J: As in **Case 3.1** interchange $(\exists)_\lambda$ and (E).

Case 4.2. There is no (E) between I and J: As in **Case 3.2.1** introduce a new (cut) with the cut formula $A(u)$ using the fact $\text{dg}_1(\exists x <_\lambda t\, A(x)) > \text{dg}_1(A(u))$.

This completes a proof of Lemma 4.12.

Now we show the harder halves of Theorem 4.1.3 from Lemma 4.12. Assume that a Π_1-sentence $\forall x\, \neg B(x)$ is true. Let $B^+(p)$ denote the fact that 'p is (the Gödel number of) a height-normal proof (of the empty sequent) in $\mathsf{PA}(\mathcal{E}_*^3) + \text{TI}(\lambda) + \forall x \neg B(x)$' for a $\lambda < \Lambda$. Then by the Lemma 4.12 $I\Sigma_1$ proves the following for $\alpha < \Lambda$:

$$\forall x\, \neg B(x) \to \big(\alpha = o(p) \wedge B^+(p) \to d(\alpha, p) < \alpha \wedge d(\alpha, p) = o(r(p)) \wedge B^+(r(p))\big) \tag{4.17}$$

For Theorem 4.1.3h let us show $I\Sigma_1 + (\mathcal{E}^\omega\text{–TI})_\Lambda \vdash \text{Con}^{(m)}(\mathsf{PA}(\mathcal{E}_*^3) + \text{TI}(< \Lambda))$ by metainduction on m. Put $\forall x \neg B(x) :\equiv \text{Con}^{(m)}(\mathsf{PA}(\mathcal{E}_*^3) + \text{TI}(< \Lambda))$. By IH and (4.17) the hypothesis of $(\mathcal{E}^\omega\text{–oTI})_\Lambda$ is provable in $I\Sigma_1 + (\mathcal{E}^\omega\text{–TI})_\Lambda$ and so is $\forall \alpha < \Lambda(\alpha = o(p) \to \neg B^+(p))$ by $(\mathcal{E}^\omega\text{–oTI})_\Lambda$. Hence by Proposition 4.4 we obtain $\forall \alpha < \Lambda(\alpha = o(p) \to \neg B^+(p))$ by $(\mathcal{E}^\omega\text{–TI})_\Lambda$. This means that for any p, if p is a proof of a contradiction in $\mathsf{PA}(\mathcal{E}_*^3) + \text{TI}(\lambda) + \forall x \neg B(x)$, then $\neg B^+(p)$, i.e., p is not height-normal. From any proof p of a contradiction in $\mathsf{PA}(\mathcal{E}_*^3) + \text{TI}(\lambda) + \forall x \neg B(x)$, we obtain a proof p' of a contradiction, which is height-normal by inserting some (E)'s at the end of p if necessary. Since $\lambda < \Lambda$ is arbitrary, we conclude $I\Sigma_1 + (\mathcal{E}^\omega\text{–TI})_\Lambda \vdash \text{Con}^{(m+1)}(\mathsf{PA}(\mathcal{E}_*^3) + \text{TI}(< \Lambda))$.

Next consider Theorem 4.1.3i. Let $\forall x \neg B(x)$ be a Π_1-sentence for which $\mathsf{PA} + \text{TI}(\lambda) \vdash \forall x B(x)$ for a $\lambda < \Lambda$. Argue in $I\Sigma_1$. For a number n, consider the sequent calculus $\mathsf{PA}(\mathcal{E}_*^3) + \text{TI}(\lambda) + \neg B(\bar{n})$ with the nth numeral $\bar{n}$. Then we can find a height-normal proof P and an ordinal $\alpha_0 < \Lambda$ such that $\alpha_0 = o(P)$. Assume $\neg B(\bar{n})$ is true. By (4.17) and $(\mathcal{E}^\omega\text{–oTI})_{\alpha_0}$ we obtain $\forall \alpha \leq \alpha_0(\alpha = o(p) \to \neg B^+(p))$. Thus over $I\Sigma_1$, one application of the rule $(\mathcal{E}^\omega\text{–TI})_{\omega(\alpha_0+1)}$ yields $\forall \alpha \leq \alpha_0(\alpha = o(p) \to \neg B^+(p))$. In other words the assumption $\neg B(\bar{n})$ is refuted. Hence over $I\Sigma_1$, one application of the rule $(\mathcal{E}^\omega\text{–TI})_{\omega(\alpha_0+1)}$ yields $\forall x B(x)$.

For Theorem 4.1.3e, assume $\mathsf{PA}(\mathcal{E}_*^3) + \text{TI}(< \Lambda) + \forall x \neg B(x)$ is inconsistent for a true Π_1-sentence $\forall x\, \neg B(x)$. We can assume that there is a height-normal proof $p = \ulcorner P \urcorner$ in $\mathsf{PA}(\mathcal{E}_*^3) + \text{TI}(\lambda) + \forall x \neg B(x)$ for a $\lambda < \Lambda$. Then $B^+(p)$. Let $r^{(m)}(x)$ denote the mth-iterate of the operation r, and $d^{(0)}(\alpha, p) = \alpha, d^{(m+1)}(\alpha, p) = d(d^{(m)}(\alpha, p), r^{(m)}(p))$. Both functions $r^{(m)}(x)$ and $d^{(m)}(\alpha, p)$ are primitive recursive. By (4.17) we obtain $o(\alpha, p) \wedge B^+(p) \to \forall m[d^{(m+1)}(\alpha, p) < d^{(m)}(\alpha, p) < \Lambda \wedge d^{(m)}(\alpha, p) = o(r^{(m)}(p)) \wedge B^+(r^{(m)}(p))]$ by induction on m in $I\Sigma_1$. The function $m \mapsto d^{(m)}(\alpha, p)$ is a primitive recursive descending chain of ordinals$< \Lambda$. Since $\lambda < \Lambda$ is arbitrary, we conclude $I\Sigma_1 \vdash \mathcal{E}^\omega DS_\Lambda \to \text{RFN}_{\Sigma_1}(\mathsf{PA}(\mathcal{E}_*^3) + \text{TI}(< \Lambda))$.

For Theorem 4.1.3f, assume that $\mathsf{PA} + \text{TI}(\lambda)$ proves a Π_2-sentence $\forall y \exists x\, B(y, x)$ for a $\lambda < \Lambda$. For an n suppose that $\forall x \neg B(\bar{n}, x)$ is true. Then we can find an ordinal $\alpha_0 < \Lambda$ such that there exists a primitive recursive descending chain of ordinals$< \alpha_0$. Therefore $I\Sigma_1 \vdash \mathcal{E}^\omega DS_{<\Lambda} \to \forall y \exists x\, B(y, x)$.

Next let us show the converse in Theorem 4.1.3g. Let $<_\Lambda$ be a standard epsilon order, and α an ordinal term$\leq_\Lambda \Lambda$. We show that each provably computable function in $\mathsf{PA} + \mathrm{TI}(< \Lambda)$ is defined by transfinite recursion up to an ordinal $< \Lambda$. This leads to independent Π_2-statements. There are several schemata for transfinite recursion. Let us begin with the simplest one, cf. Theorem 4.1.3g.

In Lemma 4.12 we have assumed that a Π_1-sentence $\forall x \neg B(x)$ is true. The assumption is needed to ensure a reduction in Proposition 4.6, i.e., the existence of one of inference rules (VJ), (TI), $(\exists)$, $(\exists)_\lambda$ in a prenex-proof. When we perform the reduction steps $p \mapsto r(p)$ as far as possible, we arrive eventually, by the well-foundedness of $<_\Lambda$, at a proof of contradiction from the axioms $\neg B(n)$ and the axioms for elementary relations, in which there occurs no inference rules (VJ), (TI), $(\exists)$, $(\exists)_\lambda$. This means that some axioms $\neg B(n)$ occurring in the proof are false. In other words, such an n is a witness for Σ_1-sentence $\exists x\, B(x)$. Thus given a $\mathsf{PA} + \mathrm{TI}(< \Lambda)$-proof of a Σ_1-sentence $\exists x\, B(x)$, we can find a witness of it by transfinite recursion.

Definition 4.7 The *counting function* $s = s_r$ for a function r is defined by transfinite recursion as follows.

$$s(\mathbf{y}, x) = \begin{cases} s(\mathbf{y}, r(\mathbf{y}, x)) + 1 & \text{if} r(\mathbf{y}, x) <_\Lambda x \\ 0 & \text{otherwise} \end{cases}$$

Its *cut-off* s^α is defined by α-recursion from r:

$$s^\alpha(\mathbf{y}, x) = \begin{cases} s^\alpha(\mathbf{y}, r(\mathbf{y}, x)) + 1 & \text{if} r(\mathbf{y}, x) <_\Lambda x <_\Lambda \alpha \\ 0 & \text{otherwise} \end{cases}$$

$\mathscr{R}_c^\alpha$ denotes the smallest class such that $\mathscr{E}^3 \subset \mathscr{R}_c^\alpha$ and it is closed under composition, *primitive recursion* and the operation $r \mapsto s_r^\alpha$.

Proposition 4.7 *Let f be defined from g, h, j by primitive recursion with parameter substitution:*

$$f(\mathbf{y}, z, 0) = g(\mathbf{y}, z), \quad f(\mathbf{y}, z, x + 1) = h(\mathbf{y}, z, x, f(\mathbf{y}, j(\mathbf{y}, z, x), x))$$

Then f is primitive recursive in g, h, j.

Proof For simplicity let us suppress the parameters $\mathbf{y}$. First define J by primitive recursion $J(z, x, 0) = z$ and $J(z, x, t + 1) = j(J(z, x, t), x \dot{-} t)$. Next define F by $F(z, x, 0) = g(J(z, x \dot{-} 1, x))$ and $F(z, x, t + 1) = h(J(z, x \dot{-} 1, x \dot{-} (t + 1)), x, F(z, x, t))$. Then we see $F(z, x + t, x) = f(J(z, x + t \dot{-} 1, t), x)$ by induction on x. Putting $t = 0$, we obtain $f(z, x) = F(z, x, x)$. □

In the definition of $\mathscr{R}^\alpha$, α-recursion can be replaced by primitive recursion and the operation $r \mapsto s_r^\alpha$ for $\alpha \geq \omega$.

Proposition 4.8 *For $\alpha \geq \omega$, $\mathscr{R}^\alpha = \mathscr{R}_c^\alpha$.*

Proof If $\alpha \geq \omega$, $\mathscr{R}^\alpha$ is closed under primitive recursion, and hence $\mathscr{R}_c^\alpha \subset \mathscr{R}^\alpha$.

Conversely let f be defined from g, r, h by α-recursion as in (4.1). Let T be the function defined from g, r by primitive recursion with parameter substitution, $T(\mathbf{y}, x, z, 0) = z$ and $T(\mathbf{y}, x, z, t+1) = g(\mathbf{y}, x, T(\mathbf{y}, r(\mathbf{y}, x), z, t))$. Then T is primitive recursive in g, r by Proposition 4.7, and we see by induction on $t = s_r^\alpha(\mathbf{y}, x)$ that $f(\mathbf{y}, x) = T(\mathbf{y}, x, h(\mathbf{y}, x), s_r^\alpha(\mathbf{y}, x))$. Hence $f \in \mathscr{R}_c^\alpha$. □

Proof We prove Theorem 4.1.3g. Let us show $Fnc_{\Sigma_1}(\mathsf{PA} + \mathrm{TI}(< \Lambda)) \subset Fnc_{\Sigma_1}(I\Sigma_1 + \mathscr{E}^\omega \mathrm{DS}_{<\Lambda})$. Assume that $\mathsf{PA}(\mathscr{E}_*^3) + \mathrm{TI}(\lambda) \vdash \forall x \exists y, z\, B(x, y, z)$ for a $\lambda < \Lambda$ and a literal B in $\mathscr{E}_*^3$. Let $Q(a)$ be a proof of $\{\exists y, z\, B(a, y, z)\}$ in the sequent calculus $\mathsf{PA}(\mathscr{E}_*^3) + \mathrm{TI}(\lambda)$. We can assume that each formula in $Q(a)$ is in prenex normal form by a partial cut-elimination. For an m, let $P_0(m)$ be the following proof in $\mathsf{PA}(\mathscr{E}_*^3) + \mathrm{TI}(\lambda) + \forall y, z \neg B(m, y, z)$.

$$P_0(m) = \cfrac{\cfrac{\neg B(m, b, c)}{\forall y, z \neg B(m, y, z) : 0}\,(\forall) \qquad \cfrac{\vdots\ Q(m)}{\exists y, z\, B(m, y, z) : \alpha}}{\emptyset : \alpha}\,(cut)$$

where $Q(m)$ is obtained from $Q(a)$ by substituting m for a, and $\neg B(m, b, c)$ is an axiom in $\mathsf{PA}(\mathscr{E}_*^3) + \mathrm{TI}(\lambda) + \forall y, z \neg B(m, y, z)$.

Let $P(m)$ be a height-normal proof obtained from $P_0(m)$ by inserting (E)'s at the end so that $o(P(m)) = \omega_{n-1}(\alpha) < \Lambda$. Let $p(m) = \ulcorner P(m) \urcorner$.

Let $r(p) = p$ if the proof p contains none of rules (VJ), $(TI)_\lambda$, $(\exists)$, $(\exists)_\lambda$. Also let $d(\alpha, p) = \alpha$ when $r(p) = p$. As we saw in the proof of Theorem 4.1.3e, let $r^{(i)}(p)$ be the ith iterate of r, and $d^{(i)}(\alpha, p) < \omega_{n-1}(\alpha) < \Lambda$ be defined by $d^{(0)}(\alpha, p) = \alpha$, $d^{(i+1)}(\alpha, p) = d(d^{(i)}(\alpha, p), r^{(i)}(p))$ if $r^{(i)}(p) \neq p$, and $d^{(i+1)}(\alpha, p) = d^{(i)}(\alpha, p)$ if $r^{(i)}(p) = p$. Both functions are primitive recursive. By invoking $\mathscr{E}^\omega \mathrm{DS}_{<\Lambda}$, let $I(m)$ denote the least i for which $r^{(i)}(p(m)) = p(m)$, and $g(m) = r^{(I(m))}(p(m))$.

$g(m)$ is a proof of the empty sequent from axioms $\neg B(m, k, l)$ in which none of rules (VJ), $(TI)_\lambda$, $(\exists)$, $(\exists)_\lambda$ occurs. From the proof $g(m)$ one can find a pair (k, l) such that $B(m, k, l)$ is true. Then let $f(m)$ denote such a k for some l. Obviously $f(m) = h(g(m))$ for an elementary h. Hence the inclusion $Fnc_{\Sigma_1}(\mathsf{PA} + \mathrm{TI}(< \Lambda)) \subset Fnc_{\Sigma_1}(I\Sigma_1 + \mathscr{E}^\omega \mathrm{DS}_{<\Lambda})$ is shown.

The inclusion $Fnc_{\Sigma_1}(I\Sigma_1 + \mathscr{E}^\omega \mathrm{DS}_{<\Lambda}) \subset \mathscr{R}^{<\Lambda}$ is seen from Theorem 2.14 since each function $g(n) = \mu m[f(n, m+1) \not<_\lambda f(n, m)]$ $(\lambda < \Lambda)$ is in $\mathscr{R}^{<\Lambda}$ for primitive recursive f.

Finally for the inclusion $\mathscr{R}^{<\Lambda} \subset Fnc_{\Sigma_1}(\mathsf{PA} + \mathrm{TI}(< \Lambda))$, it suffices to show for $\alpha < \Lambda$ that if a function f is defined by α-recursion from provably computable functions g, r, h in $\mathsf{PA} + \mathrm{TI}(< \Lambda)$ as in (4.1), then f is provably computable in $\mathsf{PA} + \mathrm{TI}(< \Lambda)$. $f(\mathbf{y}, x) = z$ iff there exists sequences s, t such that $lh(s) = \ell + 1$, $lh(t) = \ell + 2$, $(t)_0 = x$, $\forall i \leq \ell[(t)_{i+1} = r(\mathbf{y}, (t)_i)]$, $\forall i < \ell[(t)_{i+1} <_\Lambda (t)_i <_\Lambda \alpha]$, $\neg[(t)_{\ell+1} <_\Lambda (t)_\ell <_\Lambda \alpha]$, $(s)_0 = z$, $\forall i < \ell[(s)_i = g(\mathbf{y}, x, (s)_{i+1})]$, and $(s)_\ell = h(\mathbf{y}, (t)_\ell)$. The RHS is a Σ_1-formula $\exists t, s\, A(\mathbf{y}, x, z, t, s)$ by IH. The uniqueness of z is obvious. It remains to show that $\forall \mathbf{y}, x \exists t \exists s, z\, A$, which follows from the existence of a sequence t such that $(t)_0 = x$, $\forall i \leq \ell[(t)_{i+1} = r(\mathbf{y}, (t)_i)]$, $\forall i < \ell[(t)_{i+1} <_\Lambda (t)_i <_\Lambda \alpha]$ and $\neg[(t)_{\ell+1} <_\Lambda (t)_\ell <_\Lambda \alpha]$. For this it suffices to show that $\forall \mathbf{y}, x \exists \ell [r^{(\ell)}(\mathbf{y}, x) = 0]$, where $r^{(0)}(\mathbf{y}, x) = x$ and $r^{(i+1)}(\mathbf{y}, x) = r(\mathbf{y}, r^{(i)}(\mathbf{y}, x))$ if $r(\mathbf{y}, r^{(i)}(\mathbf{y}, x)) <_\Lambda r^{(i)}(\mathbf{y}, x) <_\Lambda \alpha$. Otherwise $r(\mathbf{y}, r^{(i)}(\mathbf{y}, x)) = 0$. This is seen as in the proof of Proposition 4.1 since the range $\{r^{(i)}(\mathbf{y}, x) : i \in \mathbb{N}\}$ of the Σ_1-definable function $i \mapsto r^{(i)}(\mathbf{y}, x)$ (in $\mathsf{PA} + \mathrm{TI}(< \Lambda)$) is Σ_1.

This completes a proof of Theorem 4.1. □

4.3.1.1 No-Counter Example Interpretation

Consider a formula A in prenex normal form, e.g., $A \equiv \exists x \forall y \exists z \forall w\, B(x, y, z, w)$. Under an axiom of choice, 'A is false' is paraphrased as $\neg A \leftrightarrow \forall x \exists y \forall z \exists w\, \neg B(x, y, z, w) \leftrightarrow \exists f, g \forall x, z\, \neg B(x, f(x), z, g(x, z))$ for function variables f, g, which are assumed to be counter examples for A. Then 'A is false' does not hold iff $\neg(\neg A) \leftrightarrow \forall f, g \exists x, z\, B(x, f(x), z, g(x, z))$, which is verified by providing functionals F, G such that $A' :\equiv B(t, f(t), s, g(t, s))$ $(t \equiv F(f, g), s \equiv G(f, g))$ holds for any f, g. These functionals F, G witness the fact that there is no counter examples f, g for A. We can find such functionals from proofs of prenex normal form, and functionals are defined by ordinal recursion as defined below.

Definition 4.8 $\mathscr{R}_1^\alpha$ denotes the class of number-theoretic functionals $F : \mathbb{N}^k \times ({}^{\mathbb{N}}\mathbb{N})^\ell \to \mathbb{N}$ $(k, \ell \in \mathbb{N})$ defined as in Definition 4.2 with *application* $Ap_{i,j}(\mathbf{x}; \mathbf{f}) = f_j(x_i)$. A functional F is defined from functionals G, R, H by α-recursion as follows

$$F(\mathbf{y}, x; \mathbf{f}) = \begin{cases} G(\mathbf{y}, x, F(\mathbf{y}, R(\mathbf{y}, x; \mathbf{f}); \mathbf{f}); \mathbf{f}) & \text{if } R(\mathbf{y}, x; \mathbf{f}) <_\Lambda x <_\Lambda \alpha \\ H(\mathbf{y}, x; \mathbf{f}) & \text{otherwise} \end{cases}$$

Each functional in the class $\mathscr{R}_1^\alpha$ is said to be an *α-recursive functional*. Put $\mathscr{R}_1^{<\alpha} = \bigcup_{\beta <_\Lambda \alpha} \mathscr{R}_1^\beta$.

Theorem 4.9 (Kreisel's no-counter example interpretation) *Assume* $\mathsf{PA} + \mathrm{TI}(< \Lambda)$ *proves a sentence A in prenex normal form. Then there exists a $< \Lambda$-recursive functionals for which the quantifier-free formula A' holds.*

Proof This is seen as in Theorem 4.1.3g. Let $\mathsf{PA} + \mathrm{TI}(< \Lambda) \vdash A$. Expand the arithmetic language $\mathscr{L}(\mathsf{PA})$ to a language $\mathscr{L}(\mathsf{PA}_1)$ with function variable $f, g, \ldots$. Then we obtain $\mathsf{PA}_1 + \mathrm{TI}(< \Lambda) \vdash A^H$ logically for the Herbrand normal form A^H of A, cf. Definition 2.6. In the existential formula A^H, some Herbrand functions $f, g, \ldots$ may occur. Fix arbitrarily an interpretation of variables $f, g, \ldots$, i.e., assign functions $f \mapsto \mathsf{f}, g \mapsto \mathsf{g}, \ldots$. Then as in Theorem 4.1.3g we can find witnesses of existential quantifiers in A^H uniformly, i.e., functionals witnessing A^H, and these functionals are defined by $< \Lambda$ recursion. □

4.3.2 Π_2-Analyses

In this subsection let us restrict our attentions to a standard ε_0-order $<$, $Fnc_{\Sigma_1}(\mathsf{PA}) = \mathscr{R}^{<\varepsilon_0}$ closely in several ways.

In Theorem 4.1.3e it is shown that the 1-consistency $\mathrm{RFN}_{\Sigma_1}(\mathsf{PA})$ is equivalent to $\mathscr{E}^{\omega} DS_{\varepsilon_0}$. Actually an apparently weaker statement is seen to be equivalent to the 1-consistency. A key is the Stretching Lemma 4.13 below.

4.3.2.1 Grzegorczyk Representation of Natural Numbers

Let us represent natural numbers in terms of Grzegorczyk functions F_n in Definition 1.4.

Definition 4.9 Let $k_1 \geq 2$. F_n denotes the nth Grzegorczyk function. We define *F-representation* of natural numbers x *with base* k_1 by induction on $x \dot{-} k_1$ as follows.

First if $x < k_1$, then x itself is the F-representation of x with base k_1. Assume $k_1 \leq x$. Let x_1 be the least natural number such that $k_1 \leq x < F_{x_1+1}(k_1)$, and i_1 the maximal number such that $F_{x_1}^{(i_1)}(k_1) \leq x < F_{x_1}^{(k_1)}(k_1) = F_{x_1+1}(k_1)$. If $x_1 = 0$, i.e., $x = k_1 + i_1 < 2k_1 = F_1(k_1)$, then $[(0, i_1)]_{k_1}$ with $0 = x_1$ is the F-representation of x. Otherwise let $x_2 < x_1$ be the least natural number such that $k_2 \leq x < F_{x_2+1}(k_2)$ for $k_2 = F_{x_1}^{(i_1)}(k_1) \leq x < F_{x_1}(k_2)$. If $x = k_2$, then $[(x_1, i_1)]_{k_1}$ is the F-representation of x with base k_1. Otherwise $[(x_1, i_1), (x_2, i_2), \ldots, (x_\ell, i_\ell)]_{k_1}$ is the F-representation of x with base k_1, where $[(x_2, i_2), \ldots, (x_\ell, i_\ell)]_{k_2} \neq [(0, 0)]_{k_2}$ is the F-representation of x with base k_2.

For the case $k_1 \leq x$, note that $k_1 < F_n(k_1) < F_{n+1}(k_1)$ holds by $k_1 \geq 2$ and Proposition 1.3.1. When $x_1 > 0$, $i_1 > 0$ holds by the minimality of x_1. Hence $k_1 < F_{x_1}^{(i_1)}(k_1) = k_2$.

It is clear that for $x \geq k_1$, $[(0, 0)]_{k_1}$ is the F-representation of x iff $x = k_1$. Let $[(x_1, i_1), (x_2, i_2), \ldots, (x_\ell, i_\ell)]_{k_1} \neq [(0, 0)]_{k_1}$ be the F-representation of x with base k_1 for $2 \leq k_1 < x$. Proposition 1.3.4 yields $x_1 < F_{x_1}(k_1) \leq x$. Hence $x > x_1 > x_2 > \cdots > x_\ell \geq 0$, $\forall p \leq \ell(i_p > 0)$. Let k_ℓ $(1 \leq p \leq \ell + 1)$ denote the integers recursively defined as follows. k_1 is the given number, and $k_{p+1} = F_{x_p}^{(i_p)}(k_p)$. Then $i_p < k_p$, and $k_1 < k_2 < \cdots < k_\ell < k_{\ell+1} = x$, i.e., $x = F_{x_\ell}^{(i_\ell)}(\cdots(F_{x_1}^{(i_1)}(k_1))\cdots)$. Moreover $\forall p \leq \ell(i_p < k_p < x)$. Hence we obtain in the F-representation $[(x_1, i_1), (x_2, i_2), \ldots, (x_\ell, i_\ell)]_{k_1}$ of $x \geq k_1 \geq 2$

$$x > x_1 > x_2 > \cdots > x_\ell \geq 0 \,\&\, \forall p \leq \ell(i_p < k_p < x) \tag{4.18}$$

Conversely when the condition (4.18) is fulfilled with the numbers $k_{p+1} = F_{x_p}^{(i_p)}(k_p)$, then $[(x_1, i_1), (x_2, i_2), \ldots, (x_\ell, i_\ell)]_{k_1}$ is the F-representation of $x = F_{x_\ell}^{(i_\ell)}(\cdots(F_{x_1}^{(i_1)}(k_1))\cdots)$.

Note that the function assigning $x \geq k$ to its F-representation is elementary recursive since the ternary relation $R = \{(n, x, y) \in \mathbb{N}^3 : F_n(x) = y\}$ is elementary recursive. This is seen as follows. By Proposition 1.3.1 we see that $(n, x, y) \in R$ iff there exists a matrix $A = (a_{ij})$ such that its size is at most $n \times y$, and its entry $a_{ij} \leq \max\{x, y\}$ is a number $F_m(y_{ij})$ appearing in the computation of $F^{(p)}_{n-1}(x)$ $(p \leq x)$.

Thus x is represented by

$$[(x_1, i_1), (x_2, i_2), \ldots, (x_\ell, i_\ell)]_{k_1} := F^{(i_\ell)}_{x_\ell}(\cdots(F^{(i_1)}_{x_1}(k_1))\cdots) = x.$$

Let $[(x_1, i_1), (x_2, i_2), \ldots, (x_\ell, i_\ell)]_{k_1}$ and $[(y_1, j_1), (y_2, j_2), \ldots, (y_m, j_m)]_{k_1}$ be the F-representations of $x \geq k_1$ and $y \geq k_1$, resp. Then we see the following from $2 \leq k_1 < F_n(k_1) < F_{n+1}(k_1)$.

$$x < y \Leftrightarrow ((x_1, i_1), (x_2, i_2), \ldots, (x_\ell, i_\ell)) \prec ((y_1, j_1), (y_2, j_2), \ldots, (y_m, j_m)) \tag{4.19}$$

where for the lexicographic order $<_{lx}$ on pairs,

$$((x_1, i_1), (x_2, i_2), \ldots, (x_\ell, i_\ell)) \prec ((y_1, j_1), (y_2, j_2), \ldots, (y_m, j_m))$$

iff either $\exists p \leq \min\{\ell, m\}[\forall q < p\{(x_q, i_q) = (y_q, j_q)\} \wedge (x_p, i_p) <_{lx} (y_p, j_p)]$ or $\ell < m \wedge \forall q \leq \ell\{(x_q, i_q) = (y_q, j_q)\}$.

4.3.2.2 Slowly Well-Foundedness

Definition 4.10 We define integers $|\alpha|$ and $C(\alpha)$ for ordinal terms $\alpha < \varepsilon_0$. In the following let $\alpha = \omega^{\alpha_1} n_1 + \cdots + \omega^{\alpha_k} n_k$ with $\alpha_1 > \cdots > \alpha_k$ and $0 < n_1, \ldots, n_k < \omega$ for $k > 0$.

1. $|\alpha| = \sum_{\ell=1}^{k}(1 + |\alpha_\ell|)n_\ell$.
2. $C(\alpha) = \max\{C(\alpha_\ell), n_\ell : 1 \leq \ell \leq k\}$.

$|\alpha|$ is the total number of occurrences of the symbol ω in the ordinal term α, where $\omega^\alpha n = \omega^\alpha + \cdots + \omega^\alpha$ with n's ω^α. $C(\alpha)$ is the maximal coefficient n_ℓ in the ordinal term α. In particular $|0| = C(0) = 0$.

Fix $n > 0$ and $k_1 \geq 2$. Let $k_1 \leq x < F_n(k_1)$, and $[(x_1, i_1), (x_2, i_2), \ldots, (x_\ell, i_\ell)]_{k_1}$ the F-representation of x with base k_1, where $n > x_1 > x_2 > \cdots > x_\ell \geq 0$. $s(x; n, k_1) := (j_1, j_2, \ldots, j_n)$ denotes the sequence of natural numbers j_q, which is obtained from the sequence $(i_1, i_2, \ldots, i_\ell)$ by filling the gaps with zeros, i.e., $j_{x_p} = i_p$ and $j_q = 0$ else. Moreover let $(m_1, m_2, \ldots, m_n)$ be the sequence defined recursively by $m_1 = k_1$ and $m_{q+1} = F^{(j_q)}_{n-q}(m_q)$. We see that $\{m_1 \leq m_2 \leq \cdots \leq m_n\} = \{k_1 < k_2 < \cdots < k_{\ell+1}\}$, $j_q < m_q$ and $m_n = k_{\ell+1} = x$ from (4.18).

Let y_1, y_2 be integers such that $k_1 \leq y_1, y_2 < F_n(k_1)$ for $n > 0$. For simplicity let us write $s(x)$ for $s(x; n, k_1)$. We see from (4.19) that for $k_1 \geq 2$

$$y_1 < y_2 \Leftrightarrow s(y_1) <_{lx} s(y_2) \tag{4.20}$$

where $<_{lx}$ denotes the lexicographic order on n-tuples.

Now let us flip over the integers i_ℓ. Namely let ${}^t s(x) = (m_1 - j_1, m_2 - j_2, \ldots, m_n - j_n)$ for $s(x) = (j_1, j_2, \ldots, j_n)$. ${}^t s(x)$ is an n-tuple of positive integers $m_q - j_q \leq x$ such that

$$y_1 < y_2 \Leftrightarrow {}^t s(y_2) <_{lx} {}^t s(y_1)$$

This is seen as follows. Let $y_1 < y_2$. Then by (4.20) we obtain $s(y_1) = (j_1, j_2, \ldots, j_n) <_{lx} (\ell_1, \ell_2, \ldots, \ell_n) = s(y_2)$. Let $q \leq n$ be the number such that $\forall p < q (j_p = \ell_p) \,\&\, j_q < \ell_q$. Then we see by induction on $p \leq q$ that the numbers m_p $(p \leq q)$ coincide for $s(y_1)$ and $s(y_2)$: $m_1 = k_1$ and $m_{p+1} = F_{n-p}^{(j_{p-1})}(m_p) = F_{n-p}^{(\ell_{p-1})}(m_p)$. Therefore $m_q - j_q > m_q - \ell_q$.

From this we obtain a descending chain $\{g_n(k_1, x)\}_{x < F_n(k_1)}$ of ordinals $g_n(k_1, x) < \omega^{n+1}$ for $n > 0$ as follows. When $k_1 \leq x < F_n(k_1)$, let

$$g_n(k_1, x) = \omega^{n-1}(m_1 - j_1) + \omega^{n-2}(m_2 - j_2) + \cdots + \omega^0(m_n - j_n) \tag{4.21}$$

for $s(x; n, k_1) = (j_1, j_2, \ldots, j_n)$. When $x < k_1$, let $g_n(k_1, x) = \omega^n(k_1 - x)$.

Let us extend g_n by letting $g_n(k_1, x) = 0$ for $x \geq F_n(k_1)$, and $g_0(k_1, x) = (k_1 + 1) \dot{-} x$. Then it is easy to see that for each n there exists a constant c_n for which the following holds for any k_1, x.

$$|g_n(k_1, x)| \leq c_n(k_1 + x + 1),\ C(g_n(k_1, x)) \leq \max\{n, k_1 + 1, x\}$$

Lemma 4.13 (Stretching lemma (H. Friedman)) *For each unary primitive recursive function f, there exist n, c and a primitive recursive function $g : \mathbb{N}^2 \to \omega^n$ such that $x < f(k) \Rightarrow g(k, x+1) < g(k, x)$, $|g(k, x)| \leq c(k + x + 1)$, and $C(g(k, x)) \leq \max\{c, k+1, x\}$ for any k, x.*

Proof Pick an n such that $f(k) \leq F_n(\max\{2, k\})$ by Lemma 1.4. □

Theorem 4.10 *Let $\varepsilon_0 > \alpha_0 > \alpha_1 > \cdots$ be a primitive recursive descending chain of ordinal terms α_k. We can find primitive recursive descending chains $\{\beta_i\}_i$ and $\{\gamma_i\}_i$ of ordinal terms such that $|\beta_i| \leq c(i+1)$ for a constant c and $C(\gamma_i) \leq i + 1$.*

Proof Consider the primitive recursive functions $f_{|\cdot|}(k) = |\alpha_{k+1}|$ and $f_C(k) = C(\alpha_{k+1})$. By Lemma 4.13, let $g, h : \mathbb{N}^2 \to \omega^n$ be primitive recursive functions and c a constant such that $x < |\alpha_{k+1}| \Rightarrow g(k, x+1) < g(k, x)$, $|g(k, x)| \leq c(k + x + 1)$, and $x < C(\alpha_{k+1}) \Rightarrow h(k, x+1) < h(k, x)$, $C(h(k, x)) \leq \max\{c, k+1, x\}$.

For $i \geq |\alpha_0|$, let k, x be numbers such that $i = |\alpha_0| + \cdots + |\alpha_k| + x$ and $x < |\alpha_{k+1}|$. Then set

$$\beta_i = \omega^n \alpha_k + g(k, x)$$

Note here that $|\alpha_k| > 0$ for $\alpha_k > 0$. For $i < |\alpha_0|$ let $\beta_i = \omega^n \alpha_0 + g(0,0) + |\alpha_0| - i$. Then the primitive recursive sequence $\{\beta_i\}_i$ is descending, and $|\beta_i| \leq c_0(i+1)$ for a constant c_0 depending on n, c, $|\alpha_0|$ and $g(0,0)$.

Next let $\ell = \max\{c, C(\alpha_0)\}$. For $i \geq \ell$, let k, x be numbers such that $i = C(\alpha_0) + \cdots + C(\alpha_k) + x$ and $x < C(\alpha_{k+1})$. Then set

$$\gamma_i = \omega^\omega \alpha_k + h(k, x)$$

Note here that $C(\alpha_k) > 0$ for $\alpha_k > 0$.

Let N be a number such that $\omega_{N-\ell} > \omega^\omega \alpha_0$. For $i < \ell$ let $\gamma_i = \omega_{N-i}$. Then the primitive recursive sequence $\{\gamma_i\}_i$ is descending, and $C(\gamma_i) \leq i + 1$. □

Corollary 4.3 *Over* PRA, *the 1-consistency* RFN_{Σ_1}(PA) *of* PA *is equivalent to each of the following facts:*

1. *There is no primitive recursive and infinite descending chain* $\{\beta_i\}_i$ *of ordinals* $\beta_i < \varepsilon_0$ *such that* $|\beta_i| \leq c(i+1)$ *for a constant* c.
2. *There is no primitive recursive and infinite descending chain* $\{\gamma_i\}_i$ *of ordinals* $\gamma_i < \varepsilon_0$ *such that* $C(\gamma_i) \leq i + 1$.

Proof This follows from Corollary 4.1.2e and Theorem 4.10. □

4.3.2.3 Goodstein and Grzegorczyk Sequences

Let $k \geq 2$. A *complete k-representation* of a natural number x is obtained as follows. 0 is the complete k-representation of 0. Let $x > 0$. First let $x = k^{x_1} \cdot c_1 + \cdots + k^{x_n} c_n$ with $n \geq 1$, $x_1 > \cdots > x_n \geq 0$, $0 < c_1, \ldots, c_n < k$. If each x_i is completely k-represented, then we obtain the one for x.

Now let $T(x)[k := m]$ denote the result of replacing k in the complete k-representation of x by m with $2 \leq m \leq \omega$. This means that $T(0)[k := m] = 0$, and $T(x)[k := m] = m^{x'_1} \cdot c_1 + \cdots + m^{x'_n} c_n$ for $x = k^{x_1} \cdot c_1 + \cdots + k^{x_n} c_n > 0$, and $x'_i = T(x_i)[k := m]$. Define the *Goodstein sequence* $\{x_k\}_k$ recursively by $x_{k+1} = T(x_k)[2 + k := 3 + k] \dot{-} 1$.

Theorem 4.11 PA *does not prove the true* Π_2*-statement* $\forall x \exists k [x_k = 0]$ *for the Goodstein sequence* $\{x_k\}_k$ *defined by* $x_{k+1} = T(x_k)[2 + k := 3 + k] \dot{-} 1$.

Let

$$C_k := \{\alpha < \varepsilon_0 : C(\alpha) < k\}.$$

Definition 4.11 For ordinal terms $\alpha < \varepsilon_0$, $G_k(\alpha)$ denotes the integer obtained from α by replacing ω by k in the Cantor normal form of α.

For $0 < \alpha \in C_k$, $P_k \alpha$ denote the predecessor of α in C_k. Namely $P_k \alpha = \max_{<_{\varepsilon_0}} \{\beta \in C_k : \beta < \alpha\}$. Or equivalently $\beta = P_k \alpha \Leftrightarrow (\beta \in C_k \,\&\, G_k(\beta) = G_k(\alpha) - 1)$ for $\alpha > 0$.

Then we see from the definition of the standard ε_0-order in sect. 4.1 that

$$\forall\alpha, \beta \in C_k[\alpha < \beta \leftrightarrow G_k(\alpha) < G_k(\beta)]$$

In particular the order type of C_k is equal to ω, and this justifies the definition of $P_k\alpha$.

Theorem 4.12 *The statement* $\forall\alpha \in C_2\exists k \geq 2[P_{2+k}P_{2+k-1}\cdots P_3\alpha = 0]$ *is independent from* PA.

Proof It suffices to show that the fact implies the 1-consistency of PA over PA. Argue in PA. Suppose that PA is 1-inconsistent. By Corollary 4.3 let $\{\gamma_k\}_k$ be a primitive recursive and infinite descending chain of ordinals $\gamma_i < \varepsilon_0$ such that $C(\gamma_k) \leq 1 + k$. Then $\gamma_k \in C_{2+k}$.

Let $\alpha = \gamma_0 > 0$, and $\alpha_k = P_{2+k}\cdots P_3\alpha$. We show that $\forall k[\gamma_k \leq \alpha_k]$ by induction on k. Then $\alpha_k > 0$ for any k.

First $\gamma_0 = \alpha = \alpha_0$. Suppose $\gamma_k \leq \alpha_k$. We have $C_{2+k+1} \ni \gamma_{k+1} < \gamma_k \leq \alpha_k \in C_{2+k}$. Hence $\gamma_{k+1} \leq P_{2+k+1}\alpha_k = \alpha_{k+1}$. □

We see readily for $\alpha \in C_k$ and the shift $T(x)[k := m]$ that $G_{k+1}(\alpha) = T(G_k(\alpha))[k := k+1]$. Hence $T(G_k(\alpha))[k := k+1]\dot{-}1 = G_{k+1}P_{k+1}\alpha$. In Theorem 4.12, let $G_2(\alpha) = x$, i.e., $T(x)[2 := \omega] = \alpha \in C_2$. We see inductively that $x_k = G_{2+k}P_{2+k}\cdots P_3\alpha$ for the Goodstein sequence $\{x_k\}_k$. Thus Theorem 4.11 is shown.

Next we define *Grzegorczyk sequences* $\{z_k\}_k$ of natural numbers z by base-shift as follows. Let $x = [(x_1, i_1), (x_2, i_2), \ldots, (x_\ell, i_\ell)]_k$ be the F-representation of $x \geq k$ with base k. Then the shift of base k to m in the representation as well as the representations of x_i hereditarily in the left is defined recursively by $x[k := m] = [(x_1[k := m], i_1), (x_2[k := m], i_2), \ldots, (x_\ell[k := m], i_\ell)]_m$. Let $m > k$. We see from (4.19) inductively that $x < y \Rightarrow x[k := m] < y[k := m]$, and $x \leq x[k := m]$. Hence the condition (4.18) is fulfilled, and we see that the RHS gives an F-representation of a number.

Now let $z_{k+1} = z_k\dot{-}1$ if $z_k < 2 + k$. Let $z_k \geq 2 + k$. Then $z_{k+1} = z_k[2 + k := 3 + k] - 1$.

Since the function $(n, x) \mapsto F_n(x)$ is provably computable in PA (but not primitive recursive), so is the function $(x, k, m) \mapsto x[k := m]$.

Theorem 4.13 PA *does not prove the true* Π_2*-statement* $\forall z\exists k[z_k = 0]$ *for the Grzegorczyk sequence* $\{z_k\}_k$ *of* z.

For $x \geq k \geq 2$, let $x = [(x_1, i_1), (x_2, i_2), \ldots, (x_\ell, i_\ell)]_k$ be the F-representation of x with base k. Then an ordinal $o_k(x) < \varepsilon_0$ is associated recursively by

$$o_k(x) = \omega^{o_k(x_1)}i_1 + \omega^{o_k(x_2)}i_2 + \cdots + \omega^{o_k(x_\ell)}i_\ell$$

From (4.19) and (4.18) we see that for $x, y \geq k \geq 2$, $o_k(x)$ is in Cantor normal form with base ω and

$$x < y \Leftrightarrow o_k(x) < o_k(y) \tag{4.22}$$

Let

$$D_k := \{o_k(x) : x \geq k\}$$

and $L_k(\alpha)$ be the inverse of o_k for $\alpha \in D_k$, $L_k(o_k(x)) = x$.

Proof Let us show Theorem 4.13. First we show the termination of Grzegorczyk sequences $\{z_k\}_k$ of $z \geq 2$. Suppose $\forall k(z_k > 0)$. We have $\forall k(z_k \geq 2 + k)$, for if $z_k = m < 2 + k$, then $z_{k+m} = 0$. Hence we obtain $\forall k(0 < o_{2+k}(z_k) \in D_{2+k})$.

From (4.22) we see that ω is the order type of the set D_k of ordinals$< \varepsilon_0$ when $k \geq 2$. For $0 < \alpha \in D_k$, let $Q_k\alpha = \max_{<_{\varepsilon_0}}\{\beta \in D_k : \beta < \alpha\}$. Then it is easy to see that $z_{k+1} = L_{3+k}Q_{3+k}o_{2+k}(z_k)$ from $o_{2+k}(z_k) \in D_{2+k} \subset D_{3+k}$. Therefore $\{o_{2+k}(z_k)\}_k$ would be an infinite descending chain of ordinals$< \varepsilon_0$. Thus we show the fact that each Grzegorczyk sequences $\{z_k\}_k$ of z eventually terminates.

Next for the independence of the fact from PA, it suffices to show that the fact implies the 1-consistency of PA over PA. Argue in PA. Suppose that PA is 1-inconsistent. By Corollary 4.3 let $\{\gamma_k\}_k$ be a primitive recursive and infinite descending chain of ordinals $\gamma_i < \varepsilon_0$ such that $C(\gamma_k) \leq 1 + k$. Then $\gamma_k \in C_{2+k}$. Now observe that $C_k \subset D_k$ since $k < F_x^{(i)}(k)$ for $i > 0$ and $k \geq 2$. Hence $\{\gamma_k\}_k$ would be a primitive recursive and infinite descending chain of ordinals$< \varepsilon_0$ such that $\gamma_k \in D_{2+k}$. Let $v_k = L_{2+k}\gamma_k$, and $\{z_k\}_k$ be the Grzegorczyk sequence of $z_0 = v_0$. We show that $\forall k(v_k \leq z_k)$ by induction on k. Suppose $v_k \leq z_k$. Then $\gamma_k = o_{2+k}(v_k) \leq o_{2+k}(z_k)$. From $\gamma_k, \gamma_{k+1} \in D_{3+k}$ and $\gamma_{k+1} < \gamma_k \leq o_{2+k}(z_k)$ we obtain $\gamma_{k+1} \leq Q_{3+k}o_{2+k}(z_k)$. Hence $v_{k+1} = L_{3+k}\gamma_{k+1} \leq L_{3+k}Q_{3+k}o_{2+k}(z_k) = z_{k+1}$. $\forall k(v_k \leq z_k)$ is shown. Since $\gamma_k > 0$, we have $v_k > 0$. Thus $\{z_k\}_k$ would be a non-terminating Grzegorczyk sequence of z_0. □

4.3.2.4 Norm Bounding Recursion

Let us introduce a way to define fast growing functions. Functions are defined by bounding complexities of ordinal *terms*, syntactic objects.

Definition 4.12 An elementary recursive function $N : \varepsilon_0 \to \mathbb{N}$ is said to be a *norm function* (in $I\Sigma_1$) if $I\Sigma_1$ proves that $N\alpha = 0 \leftrightarrow \alpha = 0$ and $\forall \alpha, n\exists m[\#\{\beta < \alpha : N\beta < n\} < m]$. $N\alpha$ is the *norm* of ordinal terms α.

For example both of $|\alpha|$ and $C(\alpha)$ in Definition 4.10 are norms.

Let $f : \mathbb{N} \times \varepsilon_0 \ni (i, \alpha) \mapsto f(i, \alpha) \in \mathbb{N}$ be an elementary recursive function for which $I\Sigma_1$ proves $f(i, \alpha) \leq f(i + 1, \alpha)$. For a norm function $N\beta$ let

$$\beta <_i^{N,f} \alpha :\Leftrightarrow \beta < \alpha \,\&\, N\beta \leq f(i, \alpha)$$

Then it is clear that $\{\beta : \beta <_i^{N,f} \alpha\}$ is a finite set for each α, i, and $\beta <_i^{N,f} \alpha \Rightarrow \beta <_{i+1}^{N,f} \alpha$, both of which is provable in $I\Sigma_1$.

Let us define functions $\varphi^{N,f} : (i, \alpha) \mapsto \varphi^{N,f}(i, \alpha) \in \mathbb{N}$ and $\psi^{N,f} : (i, \alpha) \mapsto \psi^{N,f}(i, \alpha) \in \mathbb{N}$ by letting $\varphi^{N,f}(i, 0) = \psi^{N,f}(i, 0) = 0$, and for $\alpha \neq 0$,

$$\begin{aligned} \varphi^{N,f}(i, \alpha) &= \max\{\varphi^{N,f}(i + 1, \beta) : \beta <_i^{N,f} \alpha\} + 1 \\ \psi^{N,f}(i, \alpha) &= \max\{\psi^{N,f}(i, \beta) : \beta <_i^{N,f} \alpha\} + 1 \end{aligned} \tag{4.23}$$

In other words,

$$\varphi^{N,f}(i, \alpha) = \max\{k \in \mathbb{N} : \exists(\alpha_0, \dots, \alpha_k)[\alpha_k <_{i+k-1}^{N,f} \cdots <_{i+1}^{N,f} \alpha_1 <_i^{N,f} \alpha_0 = \alpha]\}$$
$$\psi^{N,f}(i, , \alpha) = \max\{k \in \mathbb{N} : \exists(\alpha_0, \dots, \alpha_k)[\alpha_k <_i^{N,f} \cdots <_i^{N,f} \alpha_1 <_i^{N,f} \alpha_0 = \alpha]\}$$

Both $\varphi^{N,f}$ and $\psi^{N,f}$ are $\mathscr{R}^{\varepsilon_0}$-functions in Definition 4.2, and their restrictions to ordinals$< \varepsilon_0$ are in $\mathscr{R}^{<\varepsilon_0}$, e.g., $\varphi^{N,f} \restriction \alpha : (i, \beta) \mapsto \varphi^{N,f}(i, \beta)\ (\beta < \alpha)$ is provably computable in PA.

$\varphi^{N,f}(i, \alpha)$ denotes the depth of a finitely branching, labelled tree T_i^α such that the label of the root is α, and the immediate subtrees are T_{i+1}^β with $\beta <_i^{N,f} \alpha$.

Proposition 4.9 *Assume that f is independent from the second argument, $f(i, \alpha) = f(i, \beta)$. Then $\varphi^{N,f}(i, \alpha) = \varphi^{N,f}(i + 1, \max_{<_{\varepsilon_0}}\{\beta : \beta <_i^{N,f} \alpha\}) + 1$ and $\psi^{N,f}(i, \alpha) = \psi^{N,f}(i, \max_{<_{\varepsilon_0}}\{\beta : \beta <_i^{N,f} \alpha\}) + 1$ for $\alpha \neq 0$.*

Proof We show for $\alpha \neq 0$, that $\max\{\varphi^{N,f}(i + 1, \beta) : \beta <_i^{N,f} \alpha\} = \varphi^{N,f}(i + 1, \max_{<_{\varepsilon_0}}\{\beta : \beta <_i^{N,f} \alpha\})$. $\max\{\varphi^{N,f}(i + 1, \beta) : \beta <_i^{N,f} \alpha\} \geq \varphi^{N,f}(i + 1, \max_{<_{\varepsilon_0}}\{\beta : \beta <_i^{N,f} \alpha\})$ is obvious. Conversely let $\beta_0 = \max_{<_{\varepsilon_0}}\{\beta : \beta <_i^{N,f} \alpha\}$ and $\beta <_i^{N,f} \alpha$. Then $\beta \leq \beta_0$, and $\forall \gamma <_{i+1}^{N,f} \beta (\gamma <_{i+1}^{N,f} \beta_0)$ by the assumption $f(i + 1, \beta) = f(i + 1, \beta_0)$. Hence $\varphi^{N,f}(i + 1, \beta) \leq \varphi^{N,f}(i + 1, \beta_0)$. The assertion for $\psi^{N,f}$ is similarly seen. □

With norm functions $|\alpha|$ and $C(\alpha)$ in Definition 4.10, let $\varphi_{|\cdot|}(k) = \varphi^{|\cdot|,f}(1, \omega_k)$ for $f(i, \alpha) = c(1 + i)$ with a sufficiently large constant c, and $\varphi_C(k) = \varphi^{C,g}(1, \omega_k)$ for $g(i, \alpha) = 1 + i$ in (4.23).

Let $P_i^{|\cdot|}\alpha = \max_{<_{\varepsilon_0}}\{\beta < \alpha : |\beta| \leq c(1 + i)\}$ and $P_i^C\alpha = \max_{<_{\varepsilon_0}}\{\beta < \alpha : C(\beta) \leq 1 + i\}$. Then $\varphi_{|\cdot|}(k) = \min\{\ell : P_\ell^{|\cdot|} \cdots P_1^{|\cdot|}\omega_k = 0\}$ and $\varphi_C(k) = \min\{\ell : P_\ell^C \cdots P_1^C\omega_k = 0\}$.

Corollary 4.4 *Over* PRA, *the 1-consistency* $\mathrm{RFN}_{\Sigma_1}(\mathsf{PA})$ *of* PA *is equivalent to the totality of the functions $\varphi_{|\cdot|}$ and one of the function φ_C.*

Proof For the function $\varphi_{|\cdot|}$ it suffices to show the following by Corollary 4.3.1: Let $\{\beta\}_i$ be a primitive recursive, descending chain of ordinals$< \varepsilon_0$ such that $|\beta_i| \leq c(i + 1)$. Then for $\gamma_i = P_i^{|\cdot|} \cdots P_1^{|\cdot|}\beta_0$, $\forall i[\beta_i \leq \gamma_i]$ holds. We show this by induction on i. Let $\beta_i \leq \gamma_i$. Then $\beta_{i+1} < \gamma_i$ from $\beta_{i+1} < \beta_i$ and $|\beta_{i+1}| \leq c(1 + i + 1)$. Thus we obtain $\beta_{i+1} \leq \gamma_{i+1} = P_{i+1}^{|\cdot|}\gamma_i$.

The corollary for the function φ_C is seen similarly from Corollary 4.3.3. □

4.3.2.5 Stepping-Down and Hardy Functions

Here fast growing functions are defined through fundamental sequences, a classic approach to the class $Fnc_{\Sigma_1}(\mathsf{PA})$. We write $<$ for $<_{\varepsilon_0}$ when no confusion likely occurs.

Definition 4.13 (Fundamental sequences $\{\lambda[x]\}_x$ associated with limit ordinals $\lambda \leq_{\varepsilon_0} \varepsilon_0$) Let $\alpha \leq_{\varepsilon_0} \varepsilon_0$ be an ordinal (term), and x a natural number. An ordinal $\alpha[x]$ is defined recursively as follows.

1. $0[x] = 0$.
2. $(\alpha + 1)[x] = \alpha$.
   In what follows $\lambda[x]$ is defined for limit ordinals $\lambda \leq \varepsilon_0$.
3. $\omega^{\alpha+1}[x] = \omega^\alpha \cdot x$ for $0 \leq \alpha < \varepsilon_0$.
4. $\omega^\lambda[x] = \omega^{\lambda[x]}$ if $\lambda < \varepsilon_0$ is a limit ordinal.
5. $(\omega^{\alpha_n} + \cdots + \omega^{\alpha_1} + \omega^{\alpha_0})[x] = \omega^{\alpha_n} + \cdots + \omega^{\alpha_1} + (\omega^{\alpha_0}[x])$ where $\varepsilon_0 > \alpha_n \geq \cdots \geq \alpha_1 \geq \alpha_0 > 0$.
6. $\varepsilon_0[x] = \omega_x$.

It is clear that $\lambda[x] < \lambda[x+1]$ and $\lambda = \sup_x \lambda[x]$ for limit ordinals λ.

Lemma 4.14 *The assignment of fundamental sequences $\{\alpha[x]\}_x$ enjoys the Bachmann property, i.e.,*

$$\alpha[x] < \beta \leq \alpha[x+1] \Rightarrow \alpha[x] \leq \beta[1]$$

Proof Let λ, μ be limit ordinals, and $\lambda[x] < \mu \leq \lambda[x+1]$. We show $\lambda[x] \leq \mu[1]$ by induction on $|\lambda|$.

First let $\lambda = \omega^{\alpha+1}$. From $\omega^\alpha \cdot x < \mu \leq \omega^\alpha(x+1)$ we see that $\mu = \omega^\alpha \cdot x + \beta$ with $0 < \beta \leq \omega^\alpha$. Then $\omega^\alpha \cdot x \leq \omega^\alpha \cdot x + \beta[1] = \mu[1]$.

Second let $\lambda = \omega^\sigma$ with a limit σ. From $\omega^{\sigma[x]} < \mu \leq \omega^{\sigma[x+1]}$ we see either $\mu = \omega^\tau$ with $\sigma[x] < \tau \leq \sigma[x+1]$, or $\mu = \omega^\tau + \beta$ with $\sigma[x] \leq \tau < \sigma[x+1]$ and $0 < \beta < \omega^{\tau+1}$. In the former case IH yields $\sigma[x] \leq \tau[1]$, and $\omega^{\sigma[x]} \leq \omega^{\tau[1]} = \mu[1]$. In the latter we obtain $\omega^{\sigma[x]} \leq \omega^\tau \leq \omega^\tau + \beta[1] = \mu[1]$.

Finally let $\lambda = \gamma + \omega^\alpha$ with $\lambda[x] = \gamma + \omega^\alpha[x]$ and $\gamma > 0$. Then $\mu = \gamma + \delta$ with $\omega^\alpha[x] < \delta \leq \omega^\alpha[x+1]$. IH yields $\omega^\alpha[x] \leq \delta[1]$, and $\lambda[x] \leq \gamma + \delta[1] = \mu[1]$. □

Definition 4.14 $\alpha <_n \beta$ denotes the transitive closure of the relation $\{(\alpha, \beta) : \alpha = \beta[n]\}$, i.e., $\alpha <_n \beta$ iff $\exists k > 0 \exists (\alpha_0, \ldots, \alpha_k)[\alpha = \alpha_k \wedge \beta = \alpha_0 \wedge \forall i < k(\alpha_{i+1} = \alpha_i[n])]$. $\alpha \leq_n \beta :\Leftrightarrow \alpha <_n \beta \vee \alpha = \beta$.

It is clear that the relation $<_n$ is transitive. The set $\{k : \alpha[n]^{(k)} \neq 0\}$ is easily seen to be finite, where $\alpha[n]^{(0)} = \alpha$ and $\alpha[n]^{(k+1)} = (\alpha[n]^{(k)})[n]$. Let $S_n(\alpha) := \#\{k : \alpha[n]^{(k)} \neq 0\}$. $S_n(\alpha)$ is a function in $\mathcal{E}^4$.

Corollary 4.5 *For any limit $\lambda < \varepsilon_0$*

$$\lambda[x] <_1 \lambda[x+1].$$

Proof It suffices to show that

$$\lambda[x] < \alpha \leq \lambda[x+1] \Rightarrow \lambda[x] <_1 \alpha$$

by induction on $S_1(\alpha)$. Let $\lambda[x] < \alpha \leq \lambda[x+1]$. Lemma 4.5 yields $\lambda[x] \leq \alpha[1]$. We obtain $\lambda[x] \leq_1 \alpha[1]$ by IH. □

Definition 4.15 We write $\gamma \dot{+} \alpha$ when $\gamma + \alpha = \gamma \# \alpha$. This means that if $\gamma = \omega^{\gamma_1} + \cdots + \omega^{\gamma_n}$ with $\gamma_1 \geq \cdots \geq \gamma_n$ and $\alpha = \omega^{\alpha_1} + \cdots + \omega^{\alpha_m}$ with $\alpha_1 \geq \cdots \geq \alpha_m$, then $\gamma_n \geq \alpha_1$. Also put $0 \dot{+} \alpha = \alpha \dot{+} 0 := \alpha$.

Proposition 4.10 *1.* $0 <_n \beta \wedge 1 \leq_{1+n} \beta$ *for* $\beta > 0$.
2. $\alpha <_n \beta \Rightarrow \gamma \dot{+} \alpha <_n \gamma \dot{+} \beta$, *and* $\gamma \leq_n \gamma \dot{+} \beta$.
3. $\alpha <_n \beta \Rightarrow \omega^\alpha <_n \omega^\beta$ *for* $n > 0$.
4. $\alpha <_n \beta \Rightarrow \alpha <_{n+1} \beta$.
5. $\alpha < \beta \Rightarrow \alpha <_{|\alpha|} \beta$.

Proof Proposition 4.10.1. These are seen by induction on $S_n(\beta)$ or on $S_{1+n}(\beta)$. Note that $\beta[1+n] = 0 \Leftrightarrow \beta = 0, 1$.

Proposition 4.10.2. The first assertion is seen by induction on $S_n(\beta)$ using the fact that $(\gamma \dot{+} \beta)[n] = \gamma \dot{+} \beta[n]$. The second assertion follows from the first and Proposition 4.10.1 when $\beta > 0$.

Proposition 4.10.3. This is seen by induction on $S_n(\beta)$ using the second assertion in Proposition 4.10.2.

Proposition 4.10.4. It suffices to show that $\forall x < n(\beta[x] <_n \beta)$ for $\beta > 0$ and $n > 0$ by induction on $S_n(\beta)$. Let β be a limit ordinal. By Corollary 4.5 we have $\beta[x] <_1 \beta[x+1] <_1 \cdots <_1 \beta[n]$, and hence $\beta[x] <_1 \beta[n]$. IH yields $\alpha[1] <_n \alpha$ for any α with $0 < \alpha \leq_n \beta[n]$. Therefore $\beta[x] <_n \beta[n]$.

Proposition 4.10.5. We show the assertion by induction on $|\alpha| + |\beta|$. Assume that $\alpha > 0$, and let $a = |\alpha|$.

First consider the case when $\alpha = \omega^\gamma$ and $\beta = \omega^\delta$. IH with $\gamma < \delta$ yields $\gamma <_{|\gamma|} \delta$. and $\omega^\gamma <_a \omega^\delta$ by Propositions 4.10.3 and 4.10.4.

Second consider the case when $\alpha = \omega^{\gamma_1} \cdot n_1 + \cdots + \omega^{\gamma_k} n_k$ with $\gamma_1 > \cdots > \gamma_k$, $0 < n_1, \ldots, n_k < \omega$ and $(k = 1 \Rightarrow n_1 > 1)$, and $\beta = \omega^\delta$. We have $\gamma_1 + 1 \leq \delta$ with $|\gamma_1 + 1| < a$. IH with Proposition 4.10.4 yields $\gamma_1 + 1 \leq_a \delta$. Proposition 4.10.3 yields $\omega^{\gamma_1+1} \leq_a \beta$. It suffices to show that $\alpha <_a \omega^{\gamma_1+1}$. If $k = 1$, then we have $\alpha = \omega^{\gamma_1} \cdot n_1 <_a \omega^{\gamma_1+1}$ by $a \geq n_1$. Assume $k > 1$. Then $a > n_1$, and $\omega^{\gamma_1} \cdot (n_1 + 1) <_a \omega^{\gamma_1+1}$. On the other hand we have $|\omega^{\gamma_2} \cdot n_2 + \cdots + \omega^{\gamma_k} n_k| + |\omega^{\gamma_1}| \leq a < a + |\beta|$. IH yields $\omega^{\gamma_2} \cdot n_2 + \cdots + \omega^{\gamma_k} n_k <_a \omega^{\gamma_1}$. We obtain $\alpha <_a \omega^{\gamma_1} \cdot (n_1 + 1)$ by Proposition 4.10.2.

Finally let $\alpha = \omega^{\gamma_1} + \cdots + \omega^{\gamma_k}$ with $\gamma_1 \geq \cdots \geq \gamma_k$ and $k \geq 1$, and $\beta = \omega^{\delta_1} + \cdots + \omega^{\delta_m}$ with $\delta_1 \geq \cdots \geq \delta_m$ and $m > 1$. If $\forall i < \ell(\gamma_i = \delta_i)$ and $\gamma_\ell < \delta_\ell$ for an $\ell \leq \min\{k, m\}$, then IH with Proposition 4.10.4 yields $\omega^{\gamma_\ell} + \cdots + \omega^{\gamma_k} <_a \omega^{\delta_\ell}$. We obtain $\alpha <_a \beta$ by Proposition 4.10.2. Otherwise we have $\forall i \leq k(\gamma_i = \delta_i)$ and $k < m$. We obtain $\alpha <_a \beta$ by the second assertion in Proposition 4.10.2. □

Proposition 4.11 *1. Let $\alpha < \varepsilon_0$ be a limit ordinal, and $0 < x < \omega$. Then $2^{(\omega\alpha)[x]} \leq_x (2^{\omega\alpha})[x]$.*
2. For $0 < x < \omega$, $\beta <_x \alpha \Rightarrow 2^\beta <_{2^x} 2^\alpha$.

Proof Proposition 4.11.1. First consider the case $\alpha = \beta \dot{+} \omega^{\gamma+1}$. Then $(\omega\alpha)[x] = \left(\omega\beta + \omega^{1+\gamma+1}\right)[x] = \omega\beta + \omega^{1+\gamma} \cdot x$, and $2^{(\omega\alpha)[x]} = \omega^{\beta+\omega^\gamma \cdot x}$. On the other hand we have $(2^{\omega\alpha})[x] = \omega^{\beta+\omega^{\gamma+1}[x]} = \omega^{\beta+\omega^\gamma \cdot x}$. Hence $2^{(\omega\alpha)[x]} = (2^{\omega\alpha})[x]$.

Next consider the case $\alpha = \beta \dot{+} \omega^\gamma$ with a limit ordinal γ. Then $(2^{\omega\alpha})[x] = \omega^{\beta+\omega^{\gamma[x]}}$. On the other hand we have $(\omega\alpha)[x] = (\omega\beta + \omega^\gamma)[x] = \omega\beta + \omega^{\gamma[x]}$, and $2^{(\omega\alpha)[x]} = \omega^{\beta+\omega^\delta}$, where $1 + \delta = \gamma[x]$. We see $\delta \leq_x \gamma[x]$ from $\gamma[x] > 0$, i.e., from $x > 0$. Thus $2^{(\omega\alpha)[x]} \leq_x (2^{\omega\alpha})[x]$.

Proposition 4.11.2. Let $k = 2^x$. We show this by induction on α.

If $\alpha = \alpha_0 + 1$, then $\beta \leq_x \alpha_0$. IH yields $2^\beta \leq_k 2^{\alpha_0} <_k 2^{\alpha_0} + 2^{\alpha_0} = 2^\alpha$.

Next let $\alpha = \omega(\alpha_0 + 1)$. Then $\beta \leq_x \omega\alpha + x$. IH yields $2^\beta \leq_k 2^{\omega\alpha+x} = 2^{\omega\alpha} \cdot 2^x$. On the other hand we have $(2^\alpha)[k] = \left(\omega^{\alpha_0+1}\right)[k] = \omega^{\alpha_0} \cdot k = 2^{\omega\alpha} \cdot k$ for $k = 2^x$. We obtain $2^\beta \leq_k (2^\alpha)[k]$.

Finally let $\alpha = \omega\alpha_0$ with a limit ordinal α_0. Then $\beta \leq_x \alpha[x]$. IH with Proposition 4.11.1 yields $2^\beta \leq_k 2^{(\omega\alpha_0)[x]} \leq_x (2^{\omega\alpha_0})[x]$. On the other side $(2^{\omega\alpha_0})[x] <_1 (2^{\omega\alpha_0})[k]$ follows from Corollary 4.5 and $k = 2^x > x$. Thus we obtain $2^\beta \leq_k (2^{\omega\alpha_0})[k]$ by Proposition 4.10.4. □

Definition 4.16 1. The *Hardy functions* H_α on $\mathbb{N}$ are defined by recursion on $\alpha \leq \varepsilon_0$ as follows. $H_0(n) = n$, $H_{\alpha+1}(n) = H_\alpha(n+1)$ and $H_\lambda(n) = H_{\lambda[n]}(n)$ for limit λ.
2. We say that a number theoretic function $f(x_1, \ldots, x_n)$ is *dominated* by a function $g(y)$ if $\exists c \forall x_1, \ldots, x_n[\max\{x_1, \ldots, x_n\} \geq c \Rightarrow f(x_1, \ldots, x_n) < g(\max\{x_1, \ldots, x_n\})]$.

Proposition 4.12 *1. $H_{\alpha \dot{+} \beta} = H_\alpha \circ H_\beta$.*

2. Each H_α is a strictly increasing function, and $\alpha <_n \beta \Rightarrow H_\alpha(n) \leq H_\beta(n)$.
3. H_β dominates H_α for $\alpha < \beta$.
4. $H_\alpha(n) < H_{\omega^\alpha}(n)$ for $n \geq 2$.
5. $H_\alpha(n) \leq H_{\gamma \dot{+} \alpha}(n)$.
6. $H_\alpha(n) < H_{2^\alpha}(2^n)$ for $n > 0$.

Proof Proposition 4.12.1. This is seen by induction on ordinals β using the facts $H_1(n) = n + 1$ and $(\alpha \dot{+} \beta)[n] = \alpha \dot{+} \beta[n]$ for limit β.

Proposition 4.12.2. We show $\forall n(H_\beta(n) < H_\beta(n+1) \wedge H_{\beta[n]}(n) \leq H_\beta(n))$ by induction on ordinals β. If $\beta = \gamma + 1$, then IH yields $H_\beta(n) = H_\gamma(n+1) < H_\gamma(n+2) = H_\beta(n+1)$ and $H_\gamma(n) < H_\gamma(n+1) = H_\beta(n)$ for $\beta[n] = \gamma$. Let β be a limit ordinal. We have $\beta[n] <_{n+1} \beta[n+1]$ by Corollary 4.5 and Proposition 4.10.4. IH yields $H_{\beta[n]}(n) < H_{\beta[n]}(n+1) \leq H_{\beta[n+1]}(n+1)$ for $H_{\beta[n]}(n) = H_\beta(n)$.

Proposition 4.12.3. Let $\alpha < \beta$ and $n \geq |\alpha + 1|$. Then $\alpha + 1 \leq_n \beta$ by Propositions 4.10.4 and 4.10.5. Proposition 4.12.2 yields $H_\alpha(n) < H_\alpha(n+1) = H_{\alpha+1}(n) \leq H_\beta(n)$.

Proposition 4.12.4. We show the assertion by induction on ordinals α. First $H_0(n) = n < n+1 = H_1(n)$. Second let $\alpha = \beta + 1$. We have $n < n+1 = H_1(n) \leq H_{\omega^\beta}(n)$ by Propositions 4.10.1 and 4.12.2. IH with Propositions 4.12.2, 4.12.1 and $n \geq 2$ yields $H_\alpha(n) = H_\beta(n+1) < H_{\omega^\beta}(n+1) \leq H_{\omega^\beta}(H_{\omega^\beta}(n)) \leq H_{\omega^\alpha}(n)$. Finally let α be a limit ordinal. IH yields $H_\alpha(n) = H_{\alpha[n]}(n) < H_{\omega^{\alpha[n]}}(n) = H_{\omega^\alpha}(n)$.

Proposition 4.12.5. We show the assertion by induction on ordinals α. First $H_0(n) = n \leq H_\gamma(n)$ by Proposition 4.12.2. Second let $\alpha = \beta + 1$. IH yields $H_\alpha(n) = H_\beta(n+1) \leq H_{\gamma \dot{+} \beta}(n+1) = H_{\gamma \dot{+} \alpha}(n)$. Finally let α be a limit ordinal. IH yields $H_\alpha(n) = H_{\alpha[n]}(n) \leq H_{\gamma \dot{+} \alpha[n]}(n) = H_{\gamma \dot{+} \alpha}(n)$.

Proposition 4.12.6. We show the assertion by induction on ordinals α. Let $k = 2^n$. First $H_m(n) = n + m < k + 2^m = H_{2^m}(k)$ for $m < \omega$. Next IH yields $H_{\alpha+1}(n) = H_\alpha(n+1) < H_{2^\alpha}(2k)$. Proposition 4.12.2 with $2k = H_\omega(k) \leq H_{2^\alpha}(k)$ and $\omega \leq_1 2^\alpha$ for $2^\alpha \geq \omega$ yields $H_{2^\alpha}(2k) \leq H_{2^\alpha}(H_{2^\alpha}(k))$, and $H_{2^\alpha}(H_{2^\alpha}(2)) = H_{2^{\alpha+1}}(2)$ by Proposition 4.12.1. Finally let α be a limit ordinal. IH yields $H_\alpha(n) = H_{\alpha[n]}(n) < H_{2^{\alpha[n]}}(k)$. On the other hand we have $2^{\alpha[n]} <_k 2^\alpha$ by Proposition 4.11.2 for $n > 0$. We obtain $H_{2^{\alpha[n]}}(k) \leq H_{2^\alpha}(k)$ by Proposition 4.12.2. □

We show the following theorem.

Theorem 4.14 *Each provably computable function in* PA *is dominated by a function H_α for an $\alpha < \varepsilon_0$, and by the function H_{ε_0}.*

We define a derivability relation $\gamma, k \vdash^\alpha_m \Gamma$ relating to the stepping-down relation $\beta <_k \alpha$ and the functions H_γ, where k, m are natural numbers, $\gamma, \alpha < \varepsilon_0$ and Γ a finite set of sentences such that each sentence is in prenex normal form with alternating quantifiers whose matrices are literals in the language with relation symbols in $\mathcal{E}^3_*$, and 0 and the successor S as the only function symbol. Recall that $\mathrm{dg}_1(A) = \min\{m : A \in \Sigma^0_{m+1} \cup \Pi^0_{m+1}\}$ for formulas A.

$\gamma, k \vdash^\alpha_m \Gamma$ iff one of the following cases holds:

(Ax) Γ contains a true closed literal.

(cut) There exist a sentence A and α_0 such that $\alpha_0 + 2 = \alpha$, $\mathrm{dg}_1(A) < m$, and $\gamma, k \vdash^{\alpha_0}_m \Gamma, A$ and $\gamma, k \vdash^{\alpha_0}_m \Gamma, \neg A$.

($\forall$) There exist $\forall x A(x) \in \Gamma$ and α_0 such that $\alpha_0 + 2 = \alpha$ and $\gamma, \max\{k, n\} \vdash^{\alpha_0}_m \Gamma, A(n)$ for any $n \in \mathbb{N}$.

($\exists$) There exist $\exists x A(x) \in \Gamma$, an $n \in \mathbb{N}$ and an α_0 such that $\alpha_0 + 2 = \alpha$, $\gamma, k \vdash^{\alpha_0}_m A(n), \Gamma$ and $n < H_\gamma(k)$.

($<$) There exists an α_0 such that $\alpha_0 <_k \alpha$, $\gamma, k \vdash^{\alpha_0}_m \Gamma$.

The clause ($\exists$) indicates that witnesses of existential quantifiers in a sequent Γ is suspected to be bounded by $H_\gamma(k)$ when $\gamma, k \vdash^\alpha_m \Gamma$ holds, cf. Bounding Lemma 4.18 below.

Lemma 4.15 *1.* (Weakening) *Suppose $\Gamma \subset \Gamma_1$, $k \leq k_1$, $\gamma \leq_{k_1} \gamma_1$, $\alpha \leq_{k_1} \alpha_1$, and $m \leq m_1$. Then $\gamma, k \vdash^\alpha_m \Gamma \Rightarrow \gamma_1, k_1 \vdash^\alpha_{m_1} \Gamma_1$.*

2. (False) *If $\gamma, k \vdash^\alpha_m \Gamma, A$ for a false closed literal A, then $\gamma, k \vdash^\alpha_m \Gamma$.*

3. (Inversion) *If $\gamma, k \vdash^\alpha_m \Gamma, \forall x A(x)$, then $\gamma, \max\{k, n\} \vdash^\alpha_m \Gamma, A(n)$ for any n.*

4. *If* $n < H_\delta(k)$ *and* $\gamma, \max\{k, n\} \vdash^\alpha_m \Gamma$, *then* $\gamma \dot{+} \delta, k \vdash^\alpha_m \Gamma$.

Proof Lemma 4.15.1. If $k \leq k_1$, then $\alpha_0 <_k \alpha \Rightarrow \alpha_0 <_{k_1} \alpha$ and $H_\gamma(k) \leq H_\gamma(k_1)$. Also $\gamma \leq_k \gamma_1 \Rightarrow H_\gamma(k) \leq H_{\gamma_1}(k)$.

Lemma 4.15.3. By induction on α using Propositions 4.10.4 and 4.12.2.

Lemma4.15.4. This is seen from the fact that $H_{\gamma\dot{+}\delta}(k) = H_\gamma(H_\delta(k)) \geq H_\delta(k)$. □

Lemma 4.16 (Reduction) *Let* C *be either a false literal or an existential sentence. Assume* $\gamma, k \vdash^\alpha_m \Gamma, \neg C$ *and* $\delta, k \vdash^\beta_m \Delta, C$ *with* $\mathrm{dg}_1(C) \leq m$ *and* $m > 0$. *Then* $\gamma \dot{+} \delta, k \vdash^{\alpha \dot{+} \beta}_m \Gamma, \Delta$.

Proof We show the lemma by induction on β.

If $\Delta \cup \{C\}$ contains a true literal, then so does Δ. In what follows suppose that $\delta, k \vdash^\beta_m \Delta, C$ follows from an inference rule I.

If C is not the main formula of the inference I, then the assertion follows from Propositions 4.10.2 and 4.12.5.

Suppose that $C \equiv (\exists x A(x))$ is the main formula of $I = (\exists)$. We have $\gamma, k \vdash^\alpha_m \Gamma, \forall x \neg A(x)$, $\delta, k \vdash^{\beta_0}_m \Delta, C, A(n)$, $\beta_0 + 2 = \beta$ and $n < H_\delta(k)$. Inversion Lemma 4.15 yields $\gamma, \max\{k, n\} \vdash^\alpha_m \Gamma, \neg A(n)$, and $\gamma \dot{+} \delta, k \vdash^{\alpha \dot{+} \beta_0}_m \Gamma, \neg A(n)$ by Lemmas 4.15.1 and 4.15.4. On the other side IH yields $\gamma \dot{+} \delta, k \vdash^{\alpha \dot{+} \beta_0}_m \Gamma, \Delta, A(n)$. A (cut) with $\mathrm{dg}_1(A(n)) < m$ yields $\gamma \dot{+} \delta, k \vdash^{\alpha \dot{+} \beta}_m \Gamma, \Delta$ for $\alpha \dot{+} \beta_0 + 2 = \alpha \dot{+} \beta$. □

Lemma 4.17 (Elimination) $\gamma, k \vdash^\alpha_{m+1} \Gamma \Rightarrow 2^{\gamma \dot{+} \alpha}, 2^k \vdash^{2^\alpha}_m \Gamma$ *for* $k, m \geq 1$ *and* $\omega \cdot 2 \leq_1 \gamma$.

Proof By induction on α. Let $k, m \geq 1$.

We can assume that $\gamma, k \vdash^\alpha_{m+1} \Gamma$ follows from an inference rule I.

First suppose that I is an $(\exists)$. We have $\gamma, k \vdash^\beta_{m+1} \Gamma, B(n), \beta + 2 = \alpha, n < H_\gamma(k)$ and $(\exists x B(x)) \in \Gamma$. IH yields $2^{\gamma \dot{+} \beta}, 2^k \vdash^{2^\beta}_m \Gamma, B(n)$. We obtain $2^{\gamma \dot{+} \beta} <_{2^k} 2^{\gamma \dot{+} \alpha}$ and $2^\beta + 2 <_{2^k} 2^\alpha$ by Proposition 4.11.2 for $k \geq 1$. Lemma 4.15.1 yields $2^{\gamma \dot{+} \alpha}, 2^k \vdash^{2^\beta}_m \Gamma, B(n)$. We obtain $H_\gamma(k) < H_{2^{\gamma \dot{+} \alpha}}(2^k)$ by Proposition 4.12.6. $(\exists)$ with $(<)$ yields $2^{\gamma \dot{+} \alpha}, 2^k \vdash^{2^\alpha}_m \Gamma$.

Next suppose that I is a $(<)$. We have $\gamma, k \vdash^\beta_{m+1} \Gamma, \beta <_k \alpha$. IH yields $2^{\gamma \dot{+} \beta}, 2^k \vdash^{2^\beta}_m \Gamma$. Proposition 4.11.2 yields $2^{\gamma \dot{+} \beta} <_{2^k} 2^{\gamma \dot{+} \alpha}$ and $2^\beta <_{2^k} 2^\alpha$. Hence by $(<)$ we obtain $2^{\gamma \dot{+} \alpha}, 2^k \vdash^{2^\alpha}_m \Gamma$.

Third suppose that I is a $(\forall)$. We have $\gamma, \max\{k, n\} \vdash^\beta_{m+1} \Gamma, B(n), \beta + 2 = \alpha$, and $(\forall x B(x)) \in \Gamma$ for each n. IH yields $2^{\gamma \dot{+} \beta}, 2^{\max\{k,n\}} \vdash^{2^\beta}_m \Gamma, B(n)$. We claim that $2^{\gamma \dot{+} \alpha}, \max\{2^k, n\} \vdash^{2^\beta}_m \Gamma, B(n)$ holds for every n. We can assume that $n > k \geq 1$. We have $\omega \cdot 2 \leq_1 \gamma \dot{+} \beta$ and $H_{\omega^2}(n) = 2^n n$. Proposition 4.11.2 yields $\omega^2 = 2^{\omega \cdot 2} \leq_2 2^{\gamma \dot{+} \beta}$, and $2^{\gamma \dot{+} \beta} \dot{+} \omega^2 \leq_2 2^{\gamma \dot{+} \alpha}$ for $\alpha = \beta + 2$. We obtain $H_{2^{\gamma \dot{+} \beta}}(2^n) \leq H_{2^{\gamma \dot{+} \beta} \dot{+} \omega^2}(n) \leq H_{2^{\gamma \dot{+} \alpha}}(n)$ for $n \geq 2$. Thus we obtain $2^{\gamma \dot{+} \alpha}, n \vdash^{2^\beta}_m \Gamma, B(n)$, and the claim is shown. $(\forall)$ with $2^\beta + 2 <_{2^k} 2^\alpha$ and $(<)$ yields $2^{\gamma \dot{+} \alpha}, 2^k \vdash^{2^\alpha}_m \Gamma$.

Finally consider the case when I is a (cut) with a cut formula C of $\mathrm{dg}_1(C) \leq m$. IH together with Reduction Lemma 4.16 yields $2^{\gamma \dot{+} \beta + 1}, 2^k \vdash^{2^{\beta+1}}_m \Gamma$ with $\beta + 2 = \alpha$. We obtain $2^{\gamma \dot{+} \alpha}, 2^k \vdash^{2^\alpha}_m \Gamma$ by $2^{\beta+1} <_{2^k} 2^\alpha$. □

For natural numbers n and a sentence $\exists x A$ with quantifier-free A, $n \models \exists x A :\Leftrightarrow \mathbb{N} \models \exists x < n\, A$. For finite sets Γ of Σ_1-sentences, $n \models \Gamma$ designates that there exists a sentence $B \in \Gamma$ such that $n \models B$. Obviously $n \models \Gamma \,\&\, n \leq m \Rightarrow m \models \Gamma$.

Lemma 4.18 (Bounding) *Let* $\Gamma \subset \Sigma^0_1$ *and* $\gamma, k \vdash^{\alpha}_{1} \Gamma$ *with* $\omega \cdot 2 \leq_1 \gamma$. *Then* $H_{2^{\gamma \dot{+} \alpha}}(2^k) \models \Gamma$ *for* $k \geq 1$.

Proof By induction on α. We can assume that $\gamma, k \vdash^{\alpha}_{1} \Gamma$ follows from an inference rule I.

Suppose that I is a $(<)$. We have $\alpha_0 <_k \alpha, \gamma, k \vdash^{\alpha_0}_{1} \Gamma$. IH yields $H_{2^{\gamma \dot{+} \alpha_0}}(2^k) \models \Gamma$. On the other hand we have $H_{2^{\gamma \dot{+} \alpha_0}}(2^k) \leq H_{2^{\gamma \dot{+} \alpha}}(2^k)$ by Proposition 4.12.6.

Next suppose that I is an $(\exists)$ with the main formula $\exists x A(x)$. We have $\alpha_0 + 2 = \alpha$, $\gamma, k \vdash^{\alpha_0}_{1} A(m), \Gamma$ and $m < H_{\gamma}(k)$. IH yields $H_{2^{\gamma \dot{+} \alpha_0}}(2^k) \models \{A(m)\} \cup \Gamma$. Hence the assertion follows from $m < H_{\gamma}(k) \leq H_{2^{\gamma \dot{+} \alpha}}(2^k)$ and Proposition 4.12.6.

Consider the case when I is a (cut). We have $\beta + 2 = \alpha$, $\gamma, k \vdash^{\beta}_{1} \Gamma, \neg A$ and $\gamma, k \vdash^{\beta}_{1} \Gamma, A$ with $\mathrm{dg}_1(A) = 0$. Suppose that A is a Σ_1-sentence $\exists x\, C(x)$. IH yields $H_{2^{\gamma \dot{+} \beta}}(2^k) \models \Gamma \cup \{\exists x\, C(x)\}$. Assume that $H_{2^{\gamma \dot{+} \beta}}(2^k) \models \exists x\, C(x)$. Let n be a number such that $n < H_{2^{\gamma \dot{+} \beta}}(2^k)$ and $C(n)$ is true. From $\gamma, k \vdash^{\beta}_{1} \Gamma, \forall x \neg C(x)$ and Inversion Lemma 4.15 with False Lemma 4.15.2, we obtain $\gamma, \max\{k, n\} \vdash^{\beta}_{1} \Gamma$ for the false literal $\neg C(n)$. IH yields $H_{2^{\gamma \dot{+} \beta}}(2^{\max\{k,n\}}) \models \Gamma$. It suffices to show $H_{2^{\gamma \dot{+} \beta}}(2^{\max\{k,n\}}) \leq H_{2^{\gamma \dot{+} \alpha}}(2^k)$. We can assume that $n > k \geq 1$. We have $\omega \cdot 2 \leq_1 \gamma \dot{+} \beta$ and $H_{\omega^2}(n) = 2^n n$. Proposition 4.11.2 yields $\omega^2 = 2^{\omega \cdot 2} \leq_2 2^{\gamma \dot{+} \beta}$, and $2^{\gamma \dot{+} \beta} \dot{+} \omega^2 \leq_2 2^{\gamma \dot{+} \beta + 1}$. We obtain $H_{2^{\gamma \dot{+} \beta}}(2^n) \leq H_{2^{\gamma \dot{+} \beta} \dot{+} \omega^2}(n) \leq H_{2^{\gamma \dot{+} \beta + 1}}(n)$ for $n \geq 2$. Moreover we obtain $H_{2^{\gamma \dot{+} \beta + 1}}(n) < H_{2^{\gamma \dot{+} \beta + 1}}(H_{2^{\gamma \dot{+} \beta}}(2^k)) < H_{2^{\gamma \dot{+} \alpha}}(2^k)$ for $\alpha = \beta + 2$. Therefore $H_{2^{\gamma \dot{+} \alpha}}(2^k) \models \Gamma$. □

Lemma 4.19 (Embedding) *If* $FV(\Gamma) \subset \mathbf{x} = \{x_i : i < p\}$ *and* $\mathsf{PA} \vdash \Gamma$, *then there exist natural numbers* c, l, d, m *such that for any natural numbers* $\mathbf{n}$, $\omega \cdot c, 2 \max \mathbf{n} \vdash^{\omega \cdot l + d}_{m} \Gamma(\mathbf{n})$ *holds.*

Proof Let P be a proof of Γ in $\mathsf{PA}(\mathscr{E}^3_*)$. Let m denote $\mathrm{dg}_1(A) + 1$ for induction formulas and cut formulas A in P, which can be assumed to be in prenex normal form, and l be the maximum nesting number of the inference rules (VJ) for complete induction in P.

We omit the subscript m (cut rank). Also we omit $(\mathbf{n})$ indicating substitutions for readability. Let $n' = \max(2\mathbf{n} \cup \{1\})$.

Case 1. Γ follows from an $(\exists)$ with the main formula $\exists x A(x)$ and the instance term t: For some c_1 the instance term $t = S^{(c_1)}(\xi)$ with $\xi \in \{0\} \cup \{x_i : i < p\}$. Assume that $\xi \equiv x \equiv x_i$ for an $i < p$ and denote $n \equiv n_i$. Then $t = n + c_1$. We can assume that $\omega \cdot c, n' \vdash^{\alpha} \Gamma, A(n + c_1)$ holds with $\alpha = \omega \cdot l + d$ for $c_1 + 1 < 2^c$. On the other hand we have $n + c_1 < 2^c n' = H_{\omega \cdot c}(n')$ for $n' \geq 1$. Thus we get the assertion by $(\exists)$.

Case 2. Γ follows from an $(\forall)$ with the main formula $\forall x A(x)$: We have, for all k, $\gamma, \max\{n', k\} \vdash^{\alpha} \Gamma, A(k)$ with $\gamma = \omega \cdot c$ and $\alpha = \omega \cdot l + d$. $(\forall)$ yields $\gamma, n' \vdash^{\alpha + 2} \Gamma$.

Case 3. Γ follows from a (VJ) with the induction formula A and an induction term t: We can assume that $t \equiv x \equiv x_i$ for some $i < p$. Denote $n \equiv n_i$ $\gamma = \omega \cdot c$, and $\alpha = \omega \cdot l + d$. We have $\gamma, n' \vdash^{\alpha} \Gamma, A(0)$, $\gamma, n' \vdash^{\alpha} \neg A(j), \Gamma, A(j + 1)$ for $j < n$

and $\gamma, n' \vdash^{\alpha} \neg A(n), \Gamma$. By induction on $j \leq n$ using cuts, we obtain $\gamma, n' \vdash^{\alpha+2j} \Gamma, A(j)$. By $\alpha + 2n <_{n'} \alpha + \omega$ and Lemma 4.15.1, a $(<)$ yields $\gamma, n' \vdash^{\omega\cdot(l+1)} \Gamma, A(n)$ for $\omega \cdot (l+1) = \alpha + \omega$. One more cut yields $\gamma, n' \vdash^{\omega\cdot(l+1)+1} \Gamma$. □

Proof Let us show Theorem 4.14. Assume $\mathsf{PA} \vdash \exists y A(x, y)$ for a $\exists y A(x, y) \in \Sigma_1$. By Embedding Lemma 4.19 we obtain $\forall n > 0\{\gamma, 2n \vdash^{\beta}_{1+m} \exists y A(n, y)\}$ with ordinals $\gamma = \omega \cdot c \geq \omega \cdot 2$, $\beta = \omega \cdot l + d$. Elimination Lemma 4.17 yields $\forall n > 0\{\gamma_m, 2_m(2n) \vdash^{\alpha}_{1} \exists y A(n, y)\}$ for $\alpha = 2_m(\beta)$, where $\gamma_0 = \gamma = \omega \cdot c$ and $\gamma_{m+1} = 2^{\gamma_m \dot{+} 2_m(\beta)}$. Let $n > 0$. From Bounding Lemma 4.18 we see that there exists an $i < H_{\gamma_{m+1}}(2_{m+1}(2n))$ for which $A(n, i)$ is true. From $2^{2n} < 2^{2^n+n} \cdot n = H_{\omega^2\cdot 2}(n)$ we see that $2_{m+1}(2n) < H_{\omega^2(2m+2)}(n)$. Thus we conclude that $\forall n \geq 1 \exists y < H_{\gamma_{m+1} \dot{+} \omega^2(2m+2)}(n)\, A(n, y)$. □

Note that $\gamma_{m+1} \dot{+} \omega^2(2m+2) < 2_{m+1}(\omega^2)$.

4.4 Intuitionistic Fixed Point Theories

For a theory T in a language $\mathcal{L}$, let $\Phi(X, x)$ be an X-positive formula in the language $\mathcal{L} \cup \{X\}$ with an extra unary predicate symbol X. Introduce a fresh unary predicate symbol I together with the axiom stating that I is a fixed point of $\Phi(X, x)$:

$$\forall x[I(x) \leftrightarrow \Phi(I, x)] \tag{4.24}$$

The resulting extension of T is a conservative extension of T. This is seen from Corollary 3.1, i.e., from a cut-elimination, or from the completeness theorem.

When T has an axiom schema, e.g., $T = \mathsf{PA}$, let us define the fixed point extension FiX(PA)[1] to have the induction schema for any formula with the fixed point predicate I. Then FiX(PA) is stronger than PA, e.g., FiX(PA) proves the consistency of PA since a truth definition of first-order formulas in negation normal form can be defined as a fixed point in FiX(PA), and an easy induction with the truth definition yields the consistency of PA.

As contrasted with the proof-theoretic strength of FiX(PA), it turns out that the *intuitionistic* fixed point theory FiX^i(PA) over PA is a conservative extension of PA. This follows from the fact that FiX^i(HA) is a conservative extension of the Heyting arithmetic HA, cf. Theorem 4.15.1.

Let $\prec$ be a primitive recursive well ordering on $\mathbb{N}$. We assume that the order type Ω of $\prec$ is an epsilon number, and $\prec$ is a standard epsilon order as described in Sect. 4.1. Then $\mathsf{HA}(U) + \{\mathrm{TI}(\prec\restriction n, U) : n \in \mathbb{N}\}$ denotes an extension of HA with a unary predicate symbol U by the axioms $\mathrm{TI}(\prec\restriction n, U)$ for transfinite induction schema

$$\forall x \prec n(\forall y \prec x F(y) \to F(x)) \to \forall x \prec n F(x) \tag{4.25}$$

[1]The theory FiX(PA) is also denoted by $\widehat{ID}$ or $\widehat{ID}$(PA) in Sect. 5.4 below.

for any formula F in the expanded language $\mathscr{L}(\mathsf{HA}) \cup \{U\}$. When $\prec$ is a standard ε_0-ordering, $\mathsf{HA}(U) + \{\mathrm{TI}(\prec\restriction n, U) : n \in \mathbb{N}\} = \mathsf{HA}(U)$.

$\mathrm{FiX}^i(\mathsf{HA}(U) + \{\mathrm{TI}(\prec\restriction n, U) : n \in \mathbb{N}\})$ is the intuitionistic fixed point theory over $\mathsf{HA}(U) + \{\mathrm{TI}(\prec\restriction n, U) : n \in \mathbb{N}\}$, in which the complete induction schema as well as the transfinite induction schema (4.25) is available for any formula with the predicates U and I for fixed points. Then $\mathrm{FiX}^i(\mathsf{HA}(U) + \{\mathrm{TI}(\prec\restriction n, U) : n \in \mathbb{N}\})$ is seen to be a conservative extension of $\mathsf{HA}(U) + \{\mathrm{TI}(\prec\restriction n, U) : n \in \mathbb{N}\}$.

The same holds also for the intuitionistic fixed point theory over set theories T. Let T be a set theory in the language $\{\in, =, U\}$.

Fix an X-strictly positive formula $\Phi(X, x)$ in the language $\{\in, =, U, X\}$ with an extra unary predicate symbol X. In $\Phi(X, x)$ the predicate symbol X occurs only strictly positive. Namely the predicate symbol X does not occur in the antecedent A of implications $A \to B$ nor in the scope of negations $\neg$. The language of $\mathrm{FiX}^i(T)$ is $\{\in, =, U, I\}$ with a fresh unary predicate symbol I. The axioms in $\mathrm{FiX}^i(T)$ consist of the following:

1. All provable sentences in T (in the language $\{\in, =, U\}$).
2. Foundation schema for any formula A in the language $\{\in, =, U, I\}$:

$$\forall x(\forall y \in x\, A(y) \to A(x)) \to \forall x\, A(x) \tag{4.26}$$

3. Fixed point axiom (4.24).

The underlying logic in $\mathrm{FiX}^i(T)$ is defined to be the intuitionistic (first-order predicate) logic (with equality). $\forall x, y(x = y \to I(x) \to I(y))$ is an axiom.

Theorem 4.15 *1.* $\mathrm{FiX}^i(\mathsf{HA}(U) + \{\mathrm{TI}(\prec\restriction n, U) : n \in \mathbb{N}\})$ *is a conservative extension of* $\mathsf{HA}(U) + \{\mathrm{TI}(\prec\restriction n, U) : n \in \mathbb{N}\}$, *and* $\mathrm{FiX}^i(\mathsf{PA}(U) + \{\mathrm{TI}(\prec\restriction n, U) : n \in \mathbb{N}\})$ *is a conservative extension of* $\mathsf{PA}(U) + \{\mathrm{TI}(\prec\restriction n, U) : n \in \mathbb{N}\}$.
2. Let $T \supset \mathsf{KP}(U)$ *be a set theory comprising the Kripke-Platek set theory without the axiom of infinity.*
Then $\mathrm{FiX}^i(T)$ *is a conservative extension of* T.

Theorem 4.15.2 holds also for a slightly weaker set theories T than KP, but we need to assume that T can manipulate finite sequences and partially define truth.

As for the construction of a standard epsilon order in Sect. 4.1, we can define a Δ_1-class ON_ε and a Δ_1-relation $<_\varepsilon$ inside KP. ON_ε is the class of codes of ordinals less than the next epsilon number $\varepsilon_{\Omega+1}$ to the order type Ω of the class of ordinals in the universe V, and $<_\varepsilon$ is a standard epsilon order with base Ω. Here it is convenient to have an operation sending codes a, b of ordinals to the code of ordinal $\Omega^a \cdot b$ with the code $b = \langle 0, \beta\rangle$ of ordinals $\beta < \Omega$.

Let Ω_n be the code of the ordinal tower of n's Ω. $\Omega_0 = 1$ and $\Omega_{n+1} = \Omega^{\Omega_n}$.

Let $\mathsf{KP}(U)$ be obtained from KP by extending the Foundation schema to

$$\forall x[\forall y \in x A(y, U) \to A(x, U)] \to \forall x\, A(x, U) \tag{4.27}$$

for any formula A in the language $\{\in, =, U\}$ with a unary predicate variable U, and the equality axiom $\forall x, y[x = y \to U(x) \to U(y)]$ for the predicate U. U is intended to range over definable classes (first order formulas). The Δ_0-formulas in Δ_0-Separation and Δ_0-Collection remain to be set-theoretic bounded formulas. In other words, $a \cap U = \{x \in a : U(x)\}$ is not assumed to be a set.

Proposition 4.13 *For any formula* A *in* $\{\in, =, U\}$ *and* each $n < \omega$, $\mathsf{KP}(U) \vdash \mathrm{TI}[<_{\Omega_n}, A]$.

Proof This is seen as in Theorem 4.1.1 by metainduction on n. The case $n = 1$ follows from the Foundation schema (4.27). □

4.4.1 Finitary Analysis of Intuitionistic Fixed Points Theories

Let us prove Theorem 4.15.2. Theorem 4.15.1 is seen similarly. We could prove Theorem 4.15.2 through infinitary derivations as follows. First the finite proofs of set-theoretic sentences B_0 in $\mathrm{FiX}^i(T)$ are embedded to infinitary derivations of a sequent $C_0 \Rightarrow B_0$ for a provable sentence C_0 in T, then partial cut-elimination is possible. This results in a Δ_1-definable infinitary derivation of the same sequent $C_0 \Rightarrow B_0$ in which there occur no fixed point formulae. The depth of the derivation is bounded by an exponential ordinal tower. Then transfinite induction shows that $C_0 \Rightarrow B_0$ is true. By formalizing the infinitary arguments in T we would see that the end formula B_0 is true in T. However in the case $T = \mathsf{ZFC}$, the infinitary derivations are not sets, but proper classes. This forces us a careful formalization of the proof. Let us take another route in terms of Gentzen-Takeuti's finitary analyses of finite proofs as in Sect. 4.3.1 since its formalization is a trivial matter.

In what follows we work in a set theory $T \supset \mathsf{KP}(U)$. $\alpha, \beta, \gamma, \ldots$ range over codes in the domain of $<_\varepsilon$, while $a, b, c, \ldots$ over sets in the universe V. $A, B, C, \ldots$ denote formulas in the language $\mathcal{L}_V := \{\in, =, U, I\} \cup \{\bar{a} : a \in V\}$, where $\bar{a} := \langle 0, a\rangle$ is the name (individual constant) for the set a. A term is either a name or a variable. $\iota, \nu, \ldots$ denote terms.

A sequent calculus for $\mathrm{FiX}^i(T)$ is obtained from FiX^i in Sect. 3.3.2 by adding the following inference rules $(chain)$, $(fund)$, (Rep), (E). Recall that the inference rules for the fixed point predicate I are followings:

$$\frac{\Gamma, I(\iota), \Phi(I, \iota) \Rightarrow C}{\Gamma, I(\iota) \Rightarrow C}\,(LI)\;;\quad \frac{\Gamma \Rightarrow \Phi(I, \iota)}{\Gamma \Rightarrow I(\iota)}\,(RI)$$

$\bot$ stands ambiguously for false atomic sentences $\bar{a} \in \bar{b}$ for $a \notin b$, and $\bar{a} = \bar{b}$ for $a \neq b$. The *initial sequents* are the following two for arbitrary formulas A:

$$\Gamma, \iota = \nu, A(\iota) \Rightarrow A(\nu)\,; \qquad \Gamma, \bot \Rightarrow A$$

$$\frac{\Gamma_k \Rightarrow A_k \quad \cdots \quad \Gamma_1 \Rightarrow A_1 \quad \Delta, A_k, \ldots, A_1 \Rightarrow C}{\Delta, \Gamma_k, \ldots, \Gamma_1 \Rightarrow C}\ (chain)$$

where $A_k, \ldots, A_1$ ($k > 0$) is a non-empty list of *strictly positive* formulas.

The inference rule $(chain)$ is a series of several (cut)'s with the strictly positive *cut formulas* $A_k, \ldots, A_1$.

$$\frac{\Gamma, \forall y \in x\, A(y) \Rightarrow A(x) \quad A(\iota), \Gamma \Rightarrow C \quad \Gamma \Rightarrow \iota \in \nu}{\Gamma \Rightarrow C}\ (fund)$$

The *eigenvariable* x does not occur in the lower sequent $\Gamma \Rightarrow C$.

$$\frac{\Gamma \Rightarrow A}{\Gamma, \Delta \Rightarrow A}\ (Rep)\ ;\ \frac{\Gamma \Rightarrow A}{\Gamma \Rightarrow A}\ (E)$$

A *proof* in this sequent calculus is a finite labelled tree according to the above initial sequents and inference rules. $s, t, u, \ldots$ denote the nodes in proof trees. $s : \Gamma \Rightarrow A$ indicates that the sequent $\Gamma \Rightarrow A$ is the label of the node s. The label $\Gamma \Rightarrow A$ of s is denoted $Seq(s)$.

Suppose that a $\{\in, =, U\}$-sentence B_0 is provable in $\mathrm{FiX}^i(T)$. Then there exists a T-provable sentence C_0 such that the sequent $C_0 \Rightarrow B_0$ is provable in the sequent calculus. In what follows fix C_0, B_0 and a proof P_0 of $C_0 \Rightarrow B_0$.

Definition 4.17 The *end-piece* of a proof tree P is a collection of nodes in P such that any inference rule below it is one of (cut), $(chain)$, (Rep) and (E).

If a proof enjoys the pure variable condition in Definition 1.3, and its end sequent consists solely of sentences, no free variable occurs in its end-piece.

Definition 4.18 The *I-degree* $\mathrm{dg}_I(A) < \omega$ of a formula A is defined as follows, cf. Definitions 3.5 and 3.7.

1. $\mathrm{dg}_I(A) = 0$ if A is I-free, i.e., the fixed point predicate I does not occur in A.
   In what follows consider the case when I occurs in A.
2. $\mathrm{dg}_I(A) = 2$ if A is strictly positive (with respect to I).
   In what follows consider the case when I occurs in A, and A is not strictly positive.
3. $\mathrm{dg}_I(A) = \max\{\mathrm{dg}_I(A_0), \mathrm{dg}_I(A_1)\} + 1$ if $A \equiv (A_0 \lor A_1), (A_0 \land A_1), (A_0 \to A_1)$.
4. $\mathrm{dg}_I(A) = \mathrm{dg}_I(A_0) + 1$ if $A \equiv (\exists x\, A_0), (\forall x\, A_0)$.

Note that $\mathrm{dg}_I(A) \neq 1$.

Let P be a proof in the sequent calculus, and s a node in the proof tree P. We assign the *height* $h(s; P) < \omega$ recursively as follows.

Definition 4.19 1. $h(s; P) = 0$ if s is the root of the proof tree P.
In what follows let $Seq(s)$ be an upper sequent of an inference rule J with the lower sequent $Seq(s_0)$.
2. $h(s; P) = h(s_0; P) + 1$ if J is an (E).

3. $h(s; P) = \max\{h(s_0; P), 2\}$ if J is a $(chain)$ with its *rightmost* upper sequent $Seq(s)$.

$$\frac{s_k : \Gamma_k \Rightarrow A_k \quad \cdots \quad s_1 : \Gamma_1 \Rightarrow A_1 \quad s : \Delta, A_k, \ldots, A_1 \Rightarrow C}{s_0 : \Delta, \Gamma_k, \ldots, \Gamma_1 \Rightarrow C} \ (chain)$$

4. $h(s; P) = h(s_0; P)$ in all other cases.

Note that for upper sequents s_i of a $(chain)$ other than the rightmost one s, $h(s_i; P) = h(s_0; P)$, i.e., the height is the same.

A proof P is said to be *height-normal* if the following four conditions hold.

1. For any $(chain)$ occurring in P

$$\frac{s_k : \Gamma_k \Rightarrow A_k \quad \cdots \quad s_1 : \Gamma_1 \Rightarrow A_1 \quad s : \Delta, A_k, \ldots, A_1 \Rightarrow C}{s_0 : \Delta, \Gamma_k, \ldots, \Gamma_1 \Rightarrow C} \ (chain)$$

   $h(s_0; P) = 0$, in other words there is neither (E) nor no rightmost upper sequent of $(chain)$ below any $(chain)$. Thus $h(s_i; P) = 0$, while $h(s; P) = 2$ in height-normal proof P.
2. For any (cut) occurring in P

$$\frac{\Gamma \Rightarrow A \quad \Delta, A \Rightarrow C}{s : \Gamma, \Delta \Rightarrow C} \ (cut)$$

   $h(s; P) \geq \mathrm{dg}_I(A)$.
3. For any $(fund)$ occurring in P

$$\frac{\Gamma, \forall y \in x\, A(y) \Rightarrow A(x) \quad A(\iota), \Gamma \Rightarrow C \quad \Gamma \Rightarrow \iota \in \nu}{s : \Gamma \Rightarrow C} \ (fund)$$

   $h(s; P) \geq \mathrm{dg}_I(\forall y \in \nu\, A(y))$.
4. Any $(chain)$ and (E) in P is in the end-piece.

Without loss of generality we can assume that the given sequent calculus proof P_0 of $C_0 \Rightarrow B_0$ does not contain any $(chain)$, and is height-normal. Otherwise add some inference rules (E) at the end of the proof.

Let P be a height-normal proof in the sequent calculus, and s be a node in the proof tree P. We assign an ordinal $o(s; P) <_\varepsilon \varepsilon_{\Omega+1}$ recursively as follows. $\alpha \# \beta$ denotes the *natural sum* or commutative sum of ordinals α, β, and $\alpha \times \beta$ the *natural product* or commutative product, cf. Definition 1.12.

Definition 4.20 1. $o(s; P) = \bar{2}$ if $Seq(s)$ is an axiom.

In what follows let $Seq(s)$ be the lower sequent of an inference rule J with its upper sequents $\{s_i : Seq(s_i)\}_{i<m}$.

2. $o(s; P) = o(s_0; P)\#\bar{1}$ if J is one of the inference rules (LI), (RI), $(R\vee)$, $(L\wedge)$, $(R\to)$, $(L\exists)$, $(R\exists)$, $(L\forall)$, and $(R\forall)$ with a single upper sequent.
3. $o(s; P) = o(s_0; P)\#o(s_1; P)$ if J is one of the inference rules $(L\vee)$, $(R\wedge)$, $(L\to)$ and (cut) with two upper sequents.
4. $o(s; P) = \beta \times \Omega_2(\alpha) := \beta \times \Omega^{\Omega^{\alpha}}$ if J is a $(chain)$.

$$\frac{s_0 : \Gamma_0 \Rightarrow A_0 \quad \cdots \quad s_{m-2} : \Gamma_{m-2} \Rightarrow A_{m-2} \quad s_{m-1} : \Delta, A_0, \ldots, A_{m-2} \Rightarrow C}{s : \Delta, \Gamma_0, \ldots, \Gamma_{m-2} \Rightarrow C}\ (chain)\ J$$

where $\alpha = o(s_{m-1}; P)$ and $\beta = o(s_0; P)\# \cdots \#o(s_{m-2}; P)$.
5. $o(s; P) = ((o(s_0; P)\#\bar{6}) \times mj(\nu))\#o(s_1; P)\#o(s_2; P)$ if J is an $(fund)$:

$$\frac{s_0 : \Gamma, \forall y \in x\, A(y) \Rightarrow A(x) \quad s_1 : A(\iota), \Gamma \Rightarrow C \quad s_2 : \Gamma \Rightarrow \iota \in \nu}{s : \Gamma \Rightarrow C}\ (fund)\ J$$

where for terms ν,

$$mj(\nu) := \begin{cases} \mathrm{rk}(a) & \text{if } \nu = \bar{a} \text{ with a} \in V \\ \Omega & \text{if } \nu \text{ is a variable} \end{cases}$$

with $\mathrm{rk}(a) = \sup\{\mathrm{rk}(b) + 1 : b \in a\}$.
6. $o(s; P) = o(s_0; P)$ if J is a (Rep).
7. $o(s; P) = \Omega^{o(s_0; P)}$ if J is an (E).

Finally let $o(P) = o(s_{end}; P)$ for the root (end sequent) s_{end} of P.

The rôle of operations #, $\times$ and $\beta \cdot \Omega_2(\alpha)$ in ordinal assignment $o(s; P)$ are as follows. The sum $\alpha\#\beta$ collects two subproofs together, and $\times$ is needed to multiply ν in transfinite induction $(fund)$ up to ν, cf. **Case 2** below. Exponentiation is used first in the rule (E), i.e., to measure an increase of ordinal depths in lowering cut rank, and second in the rule $(chain)$. The assignment $(\beta_k\# \cdots \#\beta_1) \times \Omega^{\Omega^{\alpha}}$ in $(chain)$ comes from Theorem 3.8 and Lemma 3.20 for the fixed point logic FiX^i. Lexicographic comparing, i.e., multiplication of $\beta_k\# \cdots \#\beta_1$ and $\Omega^{\Omega^{\alpha}}$ is used in **Case 9**, and a doubly exponential $\Omega^{\Omega^{\alpha}}$ is needed in **Cases 6** and **7**, once multiplications are introduced. Note that when exponent α decreases, one can duplicate multiplier β in $\beta \cdot \Omega_2(\alpha)$.

A formula in $\mathcal{L}_V$ is said to be an *instance* of a formula A if it is obtained from A by substituting terms for free variables.

Definition 4.21 $ISbfml(P_0)$ denotes the class of all instances of subformulas of formulas occurring in P_0.

Call a proof *restricted* (with respect to P_0) if it is height-normal, enjoys the pure variable condition, any formula occurring in it is in $ISbfml(P_0)$, and its end sequent consists solely of I-free sentences.

For $\alpha <_\varepsilon \varepsilon_{\Omega+1}$ let $\tau(\alpha)$ denote the formula stating that for any restricted proof P if $o(P) \leq_\varepsilon \alpha$, then its end sequent is true. Note here that the satisfaction relation for the I-free formulas in $Sbfml(P_0)$ (the set of subformulas of formulas occurring in

P_0) or equivalently the partial truth definition for the I-free sentences in $ISbfml(P_0)$ is T-definable with $T \supset \mathsf{KP}(U)$.

We show the following Lemma 4.20.

Lemma 4.20 *T proves that $\tau(\alpha)$ is progressive, i.e.,*
$T \vdash \forall \alpha <_\varepsilon \varepsilon_{\Omega+1}[\forall \beta <_\varepsilon \alpha\, \tau(\beta) \to \tau(\alpha)]$.

Then Theorem 4.15.2 is seen as follows. Proposition 4.13 and Lemma 4.20 yield $\tau(o(P_0))$, and hence the end sequent $C_0 \Rightarrow B_0$ of P_0 is true in T. Therefore $T \vdash B_0$.

Let us show Lemma 4.20. We work in T. Let P be a restricted proof of a sequent $\Gamma_0 \Rightarrow A_0$. Suppose as the IH that the end sequents of restricted proofs with smaller ordinals are true. We need to show that $\Gamma_0 \Rightarrow A_0$ is true. It suffices to show that there are restricted proofs P_i ($i \in J$) of sequents S_i such that $o(P_i) <_\varepsilon o(P)$ for any $i \in J$ and if all of S_i are true, then so is $\Gamma_0 \Rightarrow A_0$.

Case 1. The case when there exists an initial sequent in the end-piece of P.

Since there are no free variables in the end-piece, any initial sequent in it is either $\Lambda, \bot \Rightarrow A$ or $\Lambda, A \Rightarrow A$.

If the end sequent $\Gamma_0 \Rightarrow A_0$ itself is an initial sequent, i.e., $\{\bot, A_0\} \cap \Gamma_0 \neq \emptyset$, then there is nothing to prove. In what follows assume that this is not the case.

Consider first the case that an initial sequent $\Lambda, \bot \Rightarrow A$ is in the end-piece. Then the formula $\bot$ in the antecedent has to vanish somewhere as a cut formula. Let P be the following.

$$\dfrac{\Gamma_i \Rightarrow A_i\ (i = 1, \ldots, k) \quad \begin{array}{c}\vdots\, Q \\ s_0 : \Gamma \Rightarrow \bot\end{array} \quad \begin{array}{c}\Lambda, \bot \Rightarrow A \\ \vdots \\ \Delta, A_k, \ldots, A_1, \bot \Rightarrow C\end{array}}{\begin{array}{c} s : \Delta, \Gamma_k, \ldots, \Gamma_1, \Gamma \Rightarrow C \\ \vdots \\ \Gamma_0 \Rightarrow A_0 \end{array}}\ (chain)$$

Let P' be the following, where Q_C is obtained from the subproof Q of $s_0 : \Gamma \Rightarrow \bot$ in P by replacing $\bot$ by C in the succedents of sequents $\Gamma' \Rightarrow \bot$ in Q.

$$\dfrac{\begin{array}{c}\vdots\, Q_C \\ s_0 : \Gamma \Rightarrow C\end{array}}{\begin{array}{c} s : \Delta, \Gamma_k, \ldots, \Gamma_1, \Gamma \Rightarrow C \\ \vdots \\ \Gamma_0 \Rightarrow A_0 \end{array}}\ (Rep)$$

Then it is clear that P' is restricted. Moreover we see $o(s; P') = o(s_0; P') = o(s_0; P) <_\varepsilon o(s; P)$ from $h(s; P) = h(s_0; P) = h(s; P') = h(s_0; P') = 0$. Hence $o(P') <_\varepsilon o(P)$. From IH we see that $\Gamma_0 \Rightarrow A_0$ is true.

The case when $\bot$ vanishes at a (cut) is similar.

Next consider the case that an initial sequent $\Lambda, A \Rightarrow A$ is in the end-piece. Then one of the formulas A has to vanish somewhere as a cut formula of J, which is either a $(chain)$ or a (cut). Suppose J is a $(chain)$, and let P be one of the followings:

$$\dfrac{\Gamma_i \Rightarrow A_i\ (i=1,\ldots,k) \quad \begin{array}{c} \vdots\, Q \\ s_0 : \Gamma \Rightarrow A \end{array} \quad \begin{array}{c} \Lambda, A \Rightarrow A \\ \vdots \\ s_1 : \Delta, A_k, \ldots, A_1, A \Rightarrow A \end{array}}{s : \Delta, \Gamma_k, \ldots, \Gamma_1, \Gamma \Rightarrow A}\, J$$
$$\vdots$$
$$\Gamma_0 \Rightarrow A_0$$

$$\dfrac{\Gamma_i \Rightarrow A_i\ (i=1,\ldots,k) \quad \begin{array}{c} \Lambda, A \Rightarrow A \\ \vdots \\ s_1 : \Gamma, A \Rightarrow A \end{array} \quad \begin{array}{c} \vdots\, Q \\ s_0 : \Delta, A_k, \ldots, A_1, A \Rightarrow C \end{array}}{s : \Delta, \Gamma_k, \ldots, \Gamma_1, \Gamma, \Lambda \Rightarrow C}\, J$$
$$\vdots$$
$$\Gamma_0 \Rightarrow A_0$$

Let P' be the followings, resp.:

$$\dfrac{\begin{array}{c} \vdots\, Q \\ s_0 : \Gamma \Rightarrow A \end{array}}{s : \Delta, \Gamma_k, \ldots, \Gamma_1, \Gamma \Rightarrow A}\,(Rep) \qquad \dfrac{\Gamma_i \Rightarrow A_i\ (i=1,\ldots,k) \quad \begin{array}{c} \vdots\, Q \\ s_0 : \Delta, A_k, \ldots, A_1, A \Rightarrow C \end{array}}{s : \Delta, \Gamma_k, \ldots, \Gamma_1, \Gamma, A \Rightarrow C}\, J$$
$$\vdots \qquad\qquad\qquad\qquad \vdots$$
$$\Gamma_0 \Rightarrow A_0 \qquad\qquad \Gamma_0 \Rightarrow A_0$$

In the right hand side J denotes two consecutive (E)'s if $k = 0$, and an $(chain)$ otherwise. In each case P' is restricted. Moreover $o(s_0; P') = o(s_0; P)$ and $o(s_1; P) \neq \bar{0}, \bar{1}$. Hence $o(s; P') <_\varepsilon o(s; P)$ when $k = 0$ in the right hand side, and $o(P') <_\varepsilon o(P)$. From IH we see that $\Gamma_0 \Rightarrow A_0$ is true.

The case when A vanishes at a (cut) is similar.

Case 2. The case when there exists a lower sequent of a $(fund)$ in the end-piece of P. Let P be the following:

$$\dfrac{\begin{array}{c} \vdots\, Q_0(x) \\ s_0 : \Gamma, \forall y \in x\, A(y) \Rightarrow A(x) \end{array} \quad \begin{array}{c} \vdots\, Q_1 \\ s_1 : A(\bar{a}), \Gamma \Rightarrow C \end{array} \quad s_2 : \Gamma \Rightarrow \bar{a} \in \bar{b}}{s : \Gamma \Rightarrow C}\,(fund)$$
$$\vdots$$
$$\Gamma_0 \Rightarrow A_0$$

If the formula $\bar{a} \in \bar{b}$ is false, i,e., $a \notin b$, then replace $\bar{a} \in \bar{b}$ by C in the succedents of the proof of $s_2 : \Gamma \Rightarrow \bar{a} \in \bar{b}$:

$$\dfrac{s_2 : \Gamma \Rightarrow C}{s : \Gamma \Rightarrow C}\ (Rep)$$
$$\vdots$$
$$\Gamma_0 \Rightarrow A_0$$

We have $o(s;\, P) = (\gamma_0 \# \bar{6}) \times \mathrm{rk}(b) \# \gamma_1 \# \gamma_2$ for $\gamma_i = o(s_i;\, P)$. Since $o(s;\, P') = o(s_2;\, P') = o(s_2;\, P) = \gamma_2 <_\varepsilon o(s;\, P)$, we obtain $o(P') <_\varepsilon o(P)$.

Assume $\bar{a} \in \bar{b}$ is true. Then $\mathrm{rk}(a) < \mathrm{rk}(b)$ holds. Let P' be the following:

$$\dfrac{\dfrac{\dfrac{\overset{\vdots\ Q_0(x)}{s_0 : \Gamma, \forall y \in x\, A(y) \Rightarrow A(x)} \quad A(z), \Gamma \Rightarrow A(z) \quad \Gamma, z \in \bar{a} \Rightarrow z \in \bar{a}}{s' : \Gamma, z \in \bar{a} \Rightarrow A(z)}\,(fund)}{\Gamma \Rightarrow \forall y \in \bar{a}\, A(y)}\,(R \to, R\forall) \quad \overset{\vdots\ Q_0(a)}{s_a : \Gamma, \forall y \in \bar{a}\, A(y) \Rightarrow A(\bar{a})}}{\Gamma \Rightarrow A(\bar{a})} \quad \overset{\vdots\ Q_1}{s_1 : A(\bar{a}), \Gamma \Rightarrow C}$$
$$\dfrac{\Gamma \Rightarrow A(\bar{a}) \qquad s_1 : A(\bar{a}), \Gamma \Rightarrow C}{s : \Gamma \Rightarrow C}$$
$$\vdots$$
$$\Gamma_0 \Rightarrow A_0$$

where the proof $Q_0(a)$ is obtained from the subproof $Q_0(x)$ of P by substituting the constant $\bar{a}$ for the eigenvariable x, and renaming free variables for the pure variable condition for P'. The last two inference rules leading to $s : \Gamma \Rightarrow C$ are (cut)'s.

It is easy to see that $\gamma_0' = o(s_a;\, P') \le_\varepsilon o(s_0;\, P) = \gamma_0$ from $\mathrm{rk}(a) <_\varepsilon mj(x) = \Omega$ for $a \in V$. We have $o(s';\, P') = (\gamma_0 \# \bar{6}) \times \mathrm{rk}(a) \# \bar{4}$, and $(\gamma_0 \# \bar{6}) \times \mathrm{rk}(a) \# \bar{6} \# \gamma_0' \le_\varepsilon (\gamma_0 \# \bar{6}) \times \mathrm{rk}(b)$. Hence we obtain by $\gamma_2 \neq \bar{0}$, $o(s;\, P') = (\gamma_0 \# \bar{6}) \times \mathrm{rk}(a) \# \bar{6} \# \gamma_0' \# \gamma_1 <_\varepsilon (\gamma_0 \# \bar{6}) \times \mathrm{rk}(b) \# \gamma_1 \# \gamma_2 = o(s;\, P)$. This yields $o(P') <_\varepsilon o(P)$.

In the following two cases inference rules introducing I-free formulas and (cut) with I-free cut formulas are pushed down to the end of proofs.

Case 3. The case when there exists a lower sequent of an explicit inference rule in the end-piece of P, where an inference rule J is explicit in P iff its major (principal) formula is in the antecedents (succedents) of any sequent below it when the major formula is in the antecedent (succedent) of the lower sequent of J, resp.

Let J be such an inference rule. J is one of the inference rules $(L\vee)$, $(R\vee)$, $(L\wedge)$, $(R\wedge)$, $(L \to)$, $(R \to)$, $(L\exists)$, $(R\exists)$, $(L\forall)$, and $(R\forall)$, but neither of (LI) and (RI), since the fixed point predicate I does not occur in the end sequent of P.

Consider the cases when J is either an $(R\forall)$ or an $(L \to)$. For the first case let P be the left in the following, and P_a in the right for each $a \in V$:

$$\dfrac{\overset{\vdots\ Q(y)}{s_0 : \Gamma \Rightarrow A(y)}}{s : \Gamma \Rightarrow \forall x\, A(x)}\ (R\forall) \qquad \dfrac{\overset{\vdots\ Q(a)}{s_a : \Gamma \Rightarrow A(\bar{a})}}{s : \Gamma \Rightarrow A(\bar{a})}\ (Rep)$$
$$\vdots \qquad\qquad\qquad\qquad \vdots$$
$$\Gamma_0 \Rightarrow \forall x\, A(x) \qquad\qquad \Gamma_0 \Rightarrow A(\bar{a})$$

Since $o(s;\, P_a) = o(s_a;\, P_a) \le_\varepsilon o(s_0;\, P) <_\varepsilon o(s;\, P)$, we obtain $o(P_a) <_\varepsilon o(P)$. By IH $\Gamma_0 \Rightarrow A(\bar{a})$ is true for any $a \in V$. Hence so is $\Gamma_0 \Rightarrow \forall x\, A(x)$.

For the second case let P be the following:

$$\dfrac{\Gamma, B \to C \Rightarrow B \quad \Gamma, B \to C, C \Rightarrow A_1}{s : \Gamma, B \to C \Rightarrow A_1}\,(L \to)$$
$$\vdots\, Q$$
$$\Gamma_0 \Rightarrow A_0$$

where $(B \to C) \in \Gamma_0$.

Let P_C be the left in the following, and P_B the right:

$$\dfrac{\Gamma, B \to C, C \Rightarrow A_1}{s : \Gamma, B \to C, C \Rightarrow A_1}\,(Rep) \qquad \dfrac{\Gamma, B \to C \Rightarrow B}{s : \Gamma, B \to C \Rightarrow B}\,(Rep)$$
$$\vdots \qquad\qquad\qquad\qquad \vdots\, Q_B$$
$$\Gamma_0, C \Rightarrow A_0 \qquad\qquad \Gamma_0 \Rightarrow B$$

Since $o(s; P_C) <_\varepsilon o(s; P)$, we obtain $o(P_C) <_\varepsilon o(P)$, and $\Gamma_0, C \Rightarrow A_0$ is true by IH.

In the P_B, the trunk Q_B is obtained from the trunk Q of P as follows. If A_1 vanishes as a cut formula in Q, then the part

$$s : \Gamma, B \to C \Rightarrow A_1$$
$$\vdots$$
$$\dfrac{\Gamma_i \Rightarrow A_i\ (i = 2, \dots, k) \quad \Gamma_1, B \to C \Rightarrow A_1 \quad \Delta, A_k, \dots, A_2, A_1 \Rightarrow D}{\Delta, \Gamma_k, \dots, \Gamma_2, \Gamma_1, B \to C \Rightarrow D}\,(chain)$$

turns to the following:

$$s : \Gamma, B \to C \Rightarrow B$$
$$\vdots$$
$$\dfrac{\Gamma_1, B \to C \Rightarrow B}{\Delta, \Gamma_k, \dots, \Gamma_2, \Gamma_1, B \to C \Rightarrow B}\,(Rep)$$

This pruning step is iterated when D vanishes below. Clearly we have $o(P_B) <_\varepsilon o(P)$, and $\Gamma_0 \Rightarrow B$ is true by IH.

Since both $\Gamma_0, C \Rightarrow A_0$ and $\Gamma_0 \Rightarrow B$ are true, and $(B \to C) \in \Gamma_0$, so is $\Gamma_0 \Rightarrow A_0$.

Case 4. The case when there exists a cut formula A_1 in the end-piece of P such that A_1 is an I-free formula.

Let P be the following:

$$\dfrac{\Gamma_i \Rightarrow A_i\ (i = 2, \dots, k) \quad \Gamma_1 \Rightarrow A_1 \quad \Delta, A_k, \dots, A_2, A_1 \Rightarrow C}{\Delta, \Gamma_k, \dots, \Gamma_2, \Gamma_1 \Rightarrow C}\,(chain)$$
$$\vdots$$
$$\Gamma_0 \Rightarrow A_0$$

Let P_ℓ be the left in the following which is obtained from P as for P_B in the **Case 3**, and P_r the right:

$$\dfrac{\Gamma_1 \Rightarrow A_1}{\Delta, \Gamma_k, \dots, \Gamma_2, \Gamma_1 \Rightarrow A_1}\,(Rep) \qquad \dfrac{\Gamma_i \Rightarrow A_i\ (i=2,\dots,k) \quad \Delta, A_k, \dots, A_2, A_1 \Rightarrow C}{\Delta, \Gamma_k, \dots, \Gamma_2, \Gamma_1, A_1 \Rightarrow C}\,J$$
$$\vdots \qquad\qquad\qquad\qquad \vdots$$
$$\Gamma_0 \Rightarrow A_1 \qquad\qquad\qquad \Gamma_0, A_1 \Rightarrow A_0$$

where in P_r, J denotes two consecutive (E)'s if $k = 1$ and a $(chain)$ otherwise.

Obviously both P_ℓ and P_r are restricted, and $o(P_\ell), o(P_r) <_\varepsilon o(P)$. IH says that both $\Gamma_0 \Rightarrow A_1$ and $\Gamma_0, A_1 \Rightarrow A_0$ are true. Hence so is $\Gamma_0 \Rightarrow A_0$.

The case when A_1 is a cut formula of a (cut) is similar.

Case 5. The case when there exists a (cut) J_0 in the end-piece of P such that for its lower sequent $s : \Gamma, \Delta \Rightarrow C$ and cut formula A, $h(s; P) > d := \mathrm{dg}_I(A)$ holds. Due to **Case 4** we can assume that the predicate I occurs in A, i.e., $\mathrm{dg}_I(A) > 0$. Let J be the uppermost (E) below J_0. Note that there is no $(chain)$ between J_0 and J since P is height-normal. Let P be the left in the following, and P' the right, which is obtained from P by lowering the (cut) J_0 below the (E) J:

$$\dfrac{s_1 : \Gamma \Rightarrow A \quad s_2 : \Delta, A \Rightarrow C}{s : \Gamma, \Delta \Rightarrow C}\,(cut)\ J_0 \qquad\qquad \dfrac{s_1 : \Gamma \Rightarrow A}{s : \Gamma, \Delta \Rightarrow A}\,(Rep) \quad \dfrac{s_2 : \Delta, A \Rightarrow C}{s : \Gamma, \Delta, A \Rightarrow C}\,(Rep)$$
$$\vdots \qquad\qquad\qquad\qquad \vdots \qquad\qquad \vdots$$
$$\dfrac{t : \Gamma_1 \Rightarrow C_1}{u : \Gamma_1 \Rightarrow C_1}\,(E)\ J \qquad\qquad \dfrac{\dfrac{t_1 : \Gamma_1 \Rightarrow A}{u_1 : \Gamma_1 \Rightarrow A}\,(E) \quad \dfrac{t_2 : \Gamma_1, A \Rightarrow C_1}{u_2 : \Gamma_1, A \Rightarrow C_1}\,(E)}{u : \Gamma_1 \Rightarrow C_1}\,(cut)$$
$$\vdots \qquad\qquad\qquad\qquad \vdots$$
$$\Gamma_0 \Rightarrow A_0 \qquad\qquad\qquad \Gamma_0 \Rightarrow A_0$$

Let $\alpha_i = o(s_i; P) = o(s_i; P')$ for $i = 1, 2$. Then for some β, $o(t; P) = \beta\#\alpha_1\#\alpha_2$, and $o(u; P) = \Omega^{\beta\#\alpha_1\#\alpha_2}$. On the other side for some $\beta' \leq_\varepsilon \beta$, $o(t_1; P') = \beta'\#\alpha_1$. The case $\beta' <_\varepsilon \beta$ happens when a pruning is performed. Also $o(t_2; P') = \beta\#\alpha_2$. Hence $o(u_1; P') \leq_\varepsilon \Omega^{\beta\#\alpha_1}$ and $o(u_2; P') = \Omega^{\beta\#\alpha_2}$. From $\alpha_i \neq \bar{0}$, we see that $o(u; P') \leq_\varepsilon \Omega^{\beta\#\alpha_1}\#\Omega^{\beta\#\alpha_2} <_\varepsilon \Omega^{\beta\#\alpha_1\#\alpha_2} = o(u; P)$. Hence $o(P') <_\varepsilon o(P)$, and $\Gamma_0 \Rightarrow A_0$ is true from IH.

In the following cases, adjacent (cut)'s are first collected into $(chain)$, **Case 6**. This as well as the analysis of strictly positive cut formula in **Case 9** prolongs $(chain)$. In **Case 7**, (cut) with strictly positive cut formula is replaced by $(chain)$, thereby $(chain)$ is introduced in proofs.

Case 6. The case when there exists a (cut) J_0 in the end-piece of P such that its lower sequent $\Delta, A_k, \dots, A_1 \Rightarrow C$ is the rightmost upper sequent of a $(chain)$ J. Let P be the following with $\Delta = \Delta_0 \cup \Delta_1$:

$$\dfrac{s_i : \Gamma_i \Rightarrow A_i \ (i = 1, \dots, k) \quad \dfrac{s_0 : \Delta_0, A_k, \dots, A_1 \Rightarrow A_0 \quad t : \Delta_1, A_k, \dots, A_1, A_0 \Rightarrow C}{\Delta, A_k, \dots, A_1 \Rightarrow C}\ (cut)\, J_0}{\dfrac{s : \Delta, \Gamma_k, \dots, \Gamma_1 \Rightarrow C}{\vdots \atop \Gamma_0 \Rightarrow A_0}}\ (chain)\, J$$

Since P is height-normal, we have $2 = h(t; P) \geq \mathrm{dg}_I(A_0) \geq 2$ by **Case 4**. Hence $\mathrm{dg}_I(A_0) = 2$, i.e., the predicate I occurs in A_0 and A_0 is strictly positive.

Let P' be the following with $i = 1, \dots, k$:

$$\dfrac{s_i : \Gamma_i \Rightarrow A_i \quad \dfrac{s'_i : \Gamma_i \Rightarrow A_i \quad s_0 : \Delta_0, A_k, \dots, A_1 \Rightarrow A_0}{\Delta_0, \Gamma_k, \dots, \Gamma_1 \Rightarrow A_0}\ (chain) \quad \dfrac{t : \Delta_1, A_k, \dots, A_1, A_0 \Rightarrow C}{\Delta_1, A_k, \dots, A_1, A_0 \Rightarrow C}\ (Rep)}{\dfrac{s : \Delta, \Gamma_k, \dots, \Gamma_1 \Rightarrow C}{\vdots \atop \Gamma_0 \Rightarrow A_0}}\ (chain)$$

Observe that $2 = h(s_0; P') = h(s_0; P) = h(t; P) = h(t; P')$ and $0 = h(s_i; P') = h(s'_i; P') = h(s_i; P)$. Let $\alpha_i = o(s_i; P) = o(s_i; P') = o(s'_i; P')$, $\alpha_0 = o(s_0; P) = o(s_0; P')$ and $\beta = o(t; P) = o(t; P')$. Then $o(s; P) = \alpha \times \Omega_2(\alpha_0 \# \beta)$ with $\alpha = \alpha_k \# \cdots \# \alpha_1$, and $o(s; P') = (\alpha \# (\alpha \times \Omega_2(\alpha_0))) \times \Omega_2(\beta) = \alpha \times (\Omega_2(\alpha_0) \times \Omega_2(\beta) \# \Omega_2(\beta))$. We see $o(s; P') <_\varepsilon o(s; P)$ from $\alpha_0, \beta \neq \bar{0}$, i.e., $\Omega_2(\alpha_0) \times \Omega_2(\beta) \# \Omega_2(\beta) <_\varepsilon \Omega_2(\alpha_0 \# \beta)$. Hence $o(P') <_\varepsilon o(P)$, and we see that $\Gamma_0 \Rightarrow A_0$ is true from IH.

Case 7. The case when there exists a (cut) with a strictly positive cut formula A in the end-piece of P. Let J be a lowest such (cut). By virtue of **Case 5** we have $h(t; P) = \mathrm{dg}_I(A) = 2$, and by **Case 6** there is no rightmost upper sequent of a $(chain)$ below J. Hence there are two consecutive (E)'s below J by **Cases 4** and **5**. Furthermore the two consecutive (E)'s is immediately below the lowest J, i.e., there is no left upper sequent of any $(chain)$ between J and (E)'s since P is height-normal. Let P be the left in the following, and P' the right:

$$\dfrac{\dfrac{{\vdots \atop u_0 : \Gamma \Rightarrow A} \quad {\vdots \atop u_1 : \Delta, A \Rightarrow C}}{t : \Gamma, \Delta \Rightarrow C}\ (cut)\, J}{\dfrac{s : \Gamma, \Delta \Rightarrow C}{\vdots \atop \Gamma_0 \Rightarrow A_0}}\ (E)^2 \qquad \dfrac{\dfrac{\dfrac{\vdots \atop u'_0 : \Gamma \Rightarrow A}{t_0 : \Gamma, \Delta \Rightarrow A}\ (Rep)}{s_0 : \Gamma, \Delta \Rightarrow A}\ (E)^2 \quad \dfrac{\vdots \atop u'_1 : \Delta, A \Rightarrow C}{t_1 : \Gamma, \Delta, A \Rightarrow C}\ (Rep)}{\dfrac{s : \Gamma, \Delta \Rightarrow C}{\vdots \atop \Gamma_0 \Rightarrow A_0}}\ (chain)$$

We see $h(s; P) = h(s; P') = h(s_0; P') = 0$ and $h(t_0; P') = h(t_1; P') = h(t; P) = 2$. Let $\alpha_i = o(u_i; P)$ for $i = 0, 1$. Then $o(u'_0; P') = \alpha_0$, $o(t_1; P') = o(u'_1; P') = \alpha_1$, and $o(s_0; P') = \Omega_2(\alpha_0)$. Hence $o(s; P') = \Omega_2(\alpha_0) \times \Omega_2(\alpha_1) <_\varepsilon \Omega_2(\alpha_0 \# \alpha_1) = o(s; P)$. Therefore $o(P') <_\varepsilon o(P)$, and by IH $\Gamma_0 \Rightarrow A_0$ is true.

By virtue of **Case 1–Case 3** we can assume that any topmost sequent in the end-piece of P is a lower sequent of an implicit inference rule other than $(fund)$, (cut), $(chain)$, (Rep) and (E) such that the fixed point predicate I occurs in its major formula. Call temporarily such an inference rule *boundary* of P if its lower sequent is in the end-piece, but not its upper sequents. We see that there is an inference J such that J is either a (cut) or a $(chain)$, and one of its cut formula A comes from major formulas of boundaries. Pick one of the lowest such inference. Then no formula in its lower sequent comes from major formulas of boundaries. Let J be one of the topmost inference such that one of its cut formula comes from major formulas of boundaries, but no formula in its lower sequent does. Then we see that both of cut formulas come from major formulas of boundaries, cf. [59] (the existence of a suitable cut).

$$\dfrac{\Gamma_i \Rightarrow A_i\ (i=1,\ldots,k) \quad \begin{array}{c}\overline{\Gamma_\ell \Rightarrow A}\ J_\ell \\ \vdots \\ \Gamma \Rightarrow A\end{array} \quad \begin{array}{c}\overline{\Delta_1, A \Rightarrow C_1}\ J_r \\ \vdots \\ \Delta, A_k, \ldots, A_1, A \Rightarrow C\end{array}}{\begin{array}{c}\Delta, \Gamma_k, \ldots, \Gamma_1, \Gamma \Rightarrow C \\ \vdots \\ \Gamma_0 \Rightarrow A_0\end{array}}\ J$$

where both J_ℓ and J_r are boundaries, A in their lower sequents are their major formulas, and the formula A is in the succednets [antecedents] of any sequents between J_ℓ and J [between J_r and J], resp.

In what follows pick such rules J, J_ℓ and J_r with the formula A, which is a cut formula of J. By virtue of **Case 7**, J is a (cut) iff $\mathrm{dg}_I(A) > 2$.

Case 8. The case when $\mathrm{dg}_I(A) > 2$ and J is a (cut). For example consider the case when A is a formula $\forall x\, D(x)$. Let P be the following:

$$\dfrac{\begin{array}{c}\dfrac{\Gamma_1 \Rightarrow D(y)}{\Gamma_1 \Rightarrow \forall x\, D(x)}\ (R\forall)\ J_\ell \\ \vdots \\ u_0 : \Gamma \Rightarrow \forall x\, D(x)\end{array} \quad \begin{array}{c}\dfrac{\Delta_1, \forall x\, D(x), D(a) \Rightarrow C_1}{\Delta_1, \forall x\, D(x) \Rightarrow C_1}\ (L\forall)\ J_r \\ \vdots \\ u_1 : \Delta, \forall x\, D(x) \Rightarrow C\end{array}}{\begin{array}{c}s : \Gamma, \Delta \Rightarrow C \\ \vdots \\ \dfrac{u : \Gamma_2 \Rightarrow B}{t : \Gamma_2 \Rightarrow B}\ (E)\ J_0 \\ \vdots \\ \Gamma_0 \Rightarrow A_0\end{array}}\ (cut)\ J$$

By virtue of **Case 5** we can assume that $h(s; P) = \mathrm{dg}_I(\forall x\, D(x)) = d + 1$ with $d = \mathrm{dg}_I(D(a)) > 2$. J_0 denotes the uppermost (E) below J with $h(t; P) = d$.

Let P' be the following:

$$
\begin{array}{c}
\dfrac{
\begin{array}{c}
\dfrac{\Gamma_1 \Rightarrow D(a)}{\Gamma_1 \Rightarrow D(a)}\,(Rep) \\
\vdots \\
\dfrac{u_0' : \Gamma \Rightarrow D(a)}{s_\ell : \Gamma, \Delta \Rightarrow D(a)}\,(Rep) \\
\vdots \\
\dfrac{u_\ell : \Gamma_2 \Rightarrow D(a)}{t_\ell : \Gamma_2 \Rightarrow D(a)}\,(E)
\end{array}
\qquad
\begin{array}{c}
\dfrac{
\begin{array}{cc}
\vdots & \begin{array}{c} \dfrac{\Delta_1, \forall x\, D(x), D(a) \Rightarrow C_1}{\Delta_1, \forall x\, D(x), D(a) \Rightarrow C_1}\,(Rep) \\ \vdots \end{array} \\
u_0 : \Gamma \Rightarrow \forall x\, D(x) & u_1' : \Delta, \forall x\, D(x), D(a) \Rightarrow C
\end{array}
}{s_r : \Gamma, \Delta, D(a) \Rightarrow C}\,(cut) \\
\vdots \\
\dfrac{u_r : \Gamma_2, D(a) \Rightarrow B}{t_r : \Gamma_2, D(a) \Rightarrow B}\,(E)
\end{array}
}{t' : \Gamma_2 \Rightarrow B}\,(cut) \\
\vdots \\
\Gamma_0 \Rightarrow A_0
\end{array}
$$

We have $o(s; P) = \alpha_0 \# \alpha_1$ where $\alpha_i = o(u_i; P)$ for $i = 0, 1$. On the other hand we have $o(s_\ell; P') = \alpha_0' = o(u_0'; P') <_\varepsilon \alpha_0 = o(u_0; P') <_\varepsilon o(s_r; P')$ and $\alpha_1' = o(u_1'; P') <_\varepsilon \alpha_1$. Hence $o(s_\ell; P') <_\varepsilon o(s_r; P') <_\varepsilon o(s; P)$, and $o(u_\ell; P') <_\varepsilon o(u_r; P') <_\varepsilon o(u; P)$. Thus for $o(t_\ell; P') = \Omega^{o(u_\ell; P')}$, $o(t_r; P') = \Omega^{o(u_r; P')}$, and $\Omega^{o(u; P)} = o(t; P)$, we obtain $o(t'; P') = o(t_\ell; P') \# o(t_r; P') <_\varepsilon o(t; P)$. Therefore $o(P') <_\varepsilon o(P)$, and by IH $\Gamma_0 \Rightarrow A_0$ is true.

The other cases are seen similarly.

Case 9. The case when $\mathrm{dg}_I(A) = 2$ and J is a $(chain)$.

First consider the case when A is an implicational formula $D \to E$, where E is strictly positive and D is I-free. Let P be the following:

$$
\begin{array}{c}
\dfrac{
\begin{array}{c} (i = 1, \ldots, k) \\ t_i : \Gamma_i \Rightarrow A_i \end{array}
\quad
\begin{array}{c}
\dfrac{s_4 : \Gamma_R, D \Rightarrow E}{s_3 : \Gamma_R \Rightarrow D \to E}\,(R \to)\, J_\ell \\
\vdots \\
s_1 : \Gamma \Rightarrow D \to E
\end{array}
\quad
\begin{array}{c}
\dfrac{s_6 : \Delta_1, D \to E \Rightarrow D \quad s_7 : \Delta_1, D \to E, E \Rightarrow C_1}{s_5 : \Delta_1, D \to E \Rightarrow C_1}\,(L \to)\, J_r \\
\vdots \\
s_2 : \Delta, A_k, \ldots, A_1, D \to E \Rightarrow C
\end{array}
}{s_0 : \Delta, \Gamma_k, \ldots, \Gamma_1, \Gamma \Rightarrow C}\,(chain)\, J \\
\vdots \\
\Gamma_0 \Rightarrow A_0
\end{array}
$$

Let P_ℓ be the following:

$$
\begin{array}{c}
\dfrac{
\begin{array}{c} (i = 1, \ldots, k) \\ \Gamma_i \Rightarrow A_i \end{array}
\quad
\begin{array}{c} \vdots \\ \Gamma \Rightarrow D \to E \end{array}
\quad
\begin{array}{c}
\dfrac{s_6 : \Delta_1, D \to E \Rightarrow D}{\Delta_1, D \to E \Rightarrow D}\,(Rep) \\
\vdots \\
s_{2\ell} : \Delta, A_k, \ldots, A_1, D \to E \Rightarrow D
\end{array}
}{s_\ell : \Delta, \Gamma_k, \ldots, \Gamma_1, \Gamma, \Rightarrow D}\,(chain) \\
\vdots \\
\Gamma_0 \Rightarrow D
\end{array}
$$

Let P_r be the following:

$$\dfrac{s_4 : \Gamma_R, D \Rightarrow E}{\Gamma_R, D \Rightarrow E}\,(Rep) \qquad \dfrac{s_7 : \Delta_1, D \to E, E \Rightarrow C_1}{\Delta_1, D \to E, E \Rightarrow C_1}\,(Rep)$$

$$\vdots \qquad\qquad \vdots$$

$$\dfrac{\begin{matrix}(i = 1, \ldots, k) \\ \Gamma_i \Rightarrow A_i\end{matrix} \quad \Gamma \Rightarrow D \to E \quad s_{1r} : \Gamma, D \Rightarrow E \qquad s_{2r} : \Delta, A_k, \ldots, A_1, D \to E, E \Rightarrow C}{s_r : \Delta, \Gamma_k, \ldots, \Gamma_1, \Gamma, D \Rightarrow C}\,(chain)$$

$$\vdots$$

$$\Gamma_0, D \Rightarrow A_0$$

Let $\alpha_i = o(s_i; P)$ for $i = 4, 6, 7$. In P, $o(s_3; P) = \alpha_4 \# \bar{1}$, $o(s_5; P) = \alpha_6 \# \alpha_7$, and $o(s_0; P) = (\beta \# o(s_1; P)) \times \Omega_2(o(s_2; P))$ for $\beta_i = o(t_i; P)$ and $\beta = \beta_k \# \cdots \# \beta_1$. On the other side in P_ℓ and P_r, $\alpha_6 = o(s_6; P_\ell)$, $\alpha_4 = o(s_4; P_r)$ and $\alpha_7 = o(s_7; P_r)$, and hence $o(s_{2\ell}; P_\ell) <_\varepsilon o(s_2; P)$, $o(s_{1r}; P_r) <_\varepsilon o(s_1; P)$ and $o(s_{2r}; P_r) <_\varepsilon o(s_2; P)$. Moreover $o(s_\ell; P_\ell) = (\beta \# o(s_1; P)) \times \Omega_2(o(s_{2\ell}; P_\ell))$ and $o(s_r; P_r) = (\beta \# o(s_1; P) \# o(s_{1r}; P_r)) \times \Omega_2(o(s_{2r}; P_r))$.

We see $o(s_\ell; P_\ell), o(s_r; P_r) <_\varepsilon o(s_0; P)$. From these we see that $o(P_\ell), o(P_r) <_\varepsilon o(P)$, and by IH both $\Gamma_0 \Rightarrow D$ and $\Gamma_0, D \Rightarrow A_0$ are true. Therefore $\Gamma_0 \Rightarrow A_0$ is true.

Next consider the case when $A \equiv I(a)$ for the fixed point predicate I. Let P be the following:

$$\dfrac{\Gamma_R \Rightarrow \Phi(I, a)}{\Gamma_R \Rightarrow I(a)}\,(RI)\, J_\ell \qquad \dfrac{\Delta_1, I(a), \Phi(I, a) \Rightarrow C_1}{\Delta_1, I(a) \Rightarrow C_1}\,(LI)\, J_r$$

$$\vdots \qquad\qquad \vdots$$

$$\dfrac{\begin{matrix}(i = 1, \ldots, k) \\ t_i : \Gamma_i \Rightarrow A_i\end{matrix} \quad s_1 : \Gamma \Rightarrow I(a) \qquad s_2 : \Delta, A_k, \ldots, A_1, I(a) \Rightarrow C}{s_0 : \Delta, \Gamma_k, \ldots, \Gamma_1, \Gamma \Rightarrow C}\,(chain)\, J$$

$$\vdots$$

$$\Gamma_0 \Rightarrow A_0$$

Let P' be the following:

$$\dfrac{\Gamma_1 \Rightarrow \Phi(I, a)}{\Gamma_1 \Rightarrow \Phi(I, a)}\,(Rep) \qquad \dfrac{\Delta_1, I(a), \Phi(I, a) \Rightarrow C_1}{\Delta_1, I(a), \Phi(I, a) \Rightarrow C_1}\,(Rep)$$

$$\vdots \qquad \vdots \qquad\qquad \vdots$$

$$\dfrac{\begin{matrix}(i = 1, \ldots, k) \\ t_i : \Gamma_i \Rightarrow A_i\end{matrix} \quad s_1 : \Gamma \Rightarrow I(a) \quad s_1' : \Gamma \Rightarrow \Phi(I, a) \qquad s_2 : \Delta, A_k, \ldots, A_1, I(a), \Phi(I, a) \Rightarrow C}{s_0 : \Delta, \Gamma_k, \ldots, \Gamma_1, \Gamma \Rightarrow C}\,(chain)$$

$$\vdots$$

$$\Gamma_0 \Rightarrow A_0$$

We have $o(s_0; P) = (\beta \# o(s_1; P)) \times \Omega_2(o(s_2; P))$ for $\beta_i = o(t_i; P)$ and $\beta = \beta_k \# \cdots \# \beta_1$. Also $o(t_i; P') = o(t_i; P)$, $o(s_1'; P') <_\varepsilon o(s_1; P) = o(s_1; P')$, $o(s_2; P') <_\varepsilon o(s_2; P)$, and $o(s_0; P') = (\beta \# o(s_1; P) \# o(s_1'; P')) \times \Omega_2(o(s_2; P'))$. Hence $o(s_0; P') <_\varepsilon o(s_0; P)$. Therefore $o(P') <_\varepsilon o(P)$, and $\Gamma_0 \Rightarrow A_0$ is true by IH.

The other cases are seen similarly. This completes a proof of Lemma 4.20, and of Theorem 4.15.

Exercises

4.1 Show the following theorem.

Theorem 4.16 *1. For each* $\alpha < \omega^2$ *and* $\Pi_0(U)$*-formulas A*

$$I\Sigma_0(U) \vdash \mathrm{TI}[<_\alpha, A].$$

2. Let $n > 0$*, and* $m \leq n$*. For each* $\alpha < \omega_{n+1-m}$ *and* $\Pi_{m+1}(U)$*-formulas A*

$$I\Sigma_n(U) \vdash \mathrm{TI}[<_\alpha, A].$$

4.2 Let $n > 0$. Show that for *each* $\alpha < \omega_{n+1}$, $I\Sigma_n \vdash \mathcal{E}^\omega DS_\alpha \wedge \mathcal{E}^\omega WDS_\alpha$.

4.3 In this exercise let us consider a restriction $<^1$ of a standard ε_0-order $<_{\varepsilon_0}$. The domain of the relation $<^1$ is defined to be one of $<_{\varepsilon_0}$. $\alpha <^1 \beta$ holds iff one of the following cases occurs.

1. $\alpha <^1 \alpha + 1$.
2. $\alpha + \omega^\beta \cdot n <^1 \alpha + \omega^{\beta+1}$ for an $n \in \omega$.
3. $\alpha + \omega^\delta \cdot n <^1 \alpha + \omega^\lambda$ for an $n \in \omega$ and $\delta <^1 \lambda \in Lim$.

It is clear that $<^1$ is elementary recursive, and $<_{\varepsilon_0}$ is the transitive closure of $<^1$. For a given formula $A(\alpha)$, let $\mathrm{i}[A](\alpha)$ denote the following formula:

$$\mathrm{i}[A](\alpha) :\Leftrightarrow \forall\beta[A(\beta) \rightarrow A(\beta + \omega^\alpha)]$$

Let $n \geq 0$.

1. Show that $I\Sigma_n(U) \vdash Prg[<^1, A] \rightarrow Prg[<^1, \mathrm{i}[A]]$ for $\Pi_n(U)$-formulas A.
2. Conclude the following theorem, cf. Theorem 4.16.2 in Exercise 4.1.

Theorem 4.17 *For each* $k < \omega$ *and* $\Pi_m(U)$*-formula A*

$$I\Sigma_n(U) \vdash Prg[<^1, A] \rightarrow \forall\alpha < \omega_{n+1-m}(\omega^0 \cdot k)\, A(\alpha)$$

4.4 Show the following, cf. Theorem 4.5: For any arithmetically definable strict partial order $\prec$ on ω, if $I\Sigma_n(U) \vdash \mathrm{TI}[\prec, U]$, then $|\prec| < 2_n(\omega^2)$. Conclude that, cf. Definition 1.11 and Theorem 4.16 in Exercise 4.1, the proof-theoretic ordinal $|I\Sigma_n(U)| = 2_n(\omega^2)$ for $n \geq 0$.

4.5 Assuming the consistency of $I\Sigma_n$, show the following: For any elementary recursive binary relation $\prec$ on ω, if $I\Sigma_n(U) \vdash \mathrm{TI}[\prec, U]$, then $|\prec| < \omega_{n+2}$.

Conclude that for each $n \geq 0$, cf. (1.8) in Definition 1.11
$\sup\{|\prec| : I\Sigma_n(U) \vdash \mathrm{TI}[\prec, U]$ for some computable irreflexive relation $\prec\} = \omega_{n+2}$.

4.6 For each $n \geq 0$, show that $2_n(\omega^2) = \sup\{|\prec| : I\Sigma_n(U) \vdash \mathrm{TI}[\prec, U]$ for a $\prec$ in $PO(\mathcal{E}^3)\} = \sup\{|\prec| : I\Sigma_n(U) \vdash \mathrm{TI}[\prec, U]$ for a $\prec$ in $PO(\Pi_\infty)\}$ for *strict partial orders*.

4.7 For each $n \geq 0$, show that $2_{n+1}(\omega^2) = \omega_{n+2} = \sup\{|\prec| : I\Sigma_n(U) \vdash \mathrm{TI}[\prec, U]$ for a $\prec$ in $\mathcal{E}^3_*\}$, where $\mathcal{E}^3_*$ denotes the class of all elementary recursive binary *relations* on $\mathbb{N}$.

4.8 Show the following equivalence for provably Δ^0_2-sets in $\mathsf{PA} + \mathrm{TI}(< \Lambda)$, where $<$ is a standard epsilon order of type Λ, cf. Exercise 2.9 and Definition 4.3:

For Σ_2-formulas A^+, A^-, $\mathsf{PA} + \mathrm{TI}(< \Lambda) \vdash \forall c[A^+(c) \leftrightarrow \neg A^-(c)]$ iff there exist a binary primitive recursive predicate f, an ordinal $K < \Lambda$ and a primitive recursive function $h : \mathbb{N} \times \mathbb{N} \to K$ such that $\mathsf{PA} + \mathrm{TI}(< \Lambda)$ proves (weakly descending) $\forall \mathbf{c}, w[h(c, w+1) \leq h(\mathbf{c}, w) < K]$, (lowering) $\forall \mathbf{c}, w[f(c, w) \neq f(c, w+1) \to h(c, w) > h(c, w+1)]$, (reduction) $\lim_{w\to\infty} f(c, w) = 0 \to A^+(c)$, $\lim_{w\to\infty} f(c, w) = 1 \to \neg A^-(c)$, and $A^+(c) \to \neg A^-(c)$.

4.9 Show the following equivalences over $I\Sigma_1$ for each $n > 0$.

1. $\{\mathrm{Con}^{(m)}(I\Sigma_n(\mathcal{E}^3_*)) : m < \omega\}$ is equivalent to $(\mathcal{E}^\omega{-}\mathrm{TI})_{\omega_{n+1}}$.
2. The 1-consistency $\mathrm{RFN}_{\Sigma_1}(I\Sigma_n(\mathcal{E}^3_*))$ of $I\Sigma_n(\mathcal{E}^3_*)$ is equivalent to $\mathcal{E}^\omega DS_{\omega_{n+1}}$.
3. The 2-consistency $\mathrm{RFN}_{\Sigma_2}(I\Sigma_n(\mathcal{E}^3_*))$ of $I\Sigma_n(\mathcal{E}^3_*)$ is equivalent to $\mathcal{E}^\omega WDS_{\omega_{n+1}}$.

4.10 Let us extend the Grzegorczyk hierarchy $\{F_n\}_{n<\omega}$ in Definition 1.4 to the transfinite level.

Definition 4.22 (*Schwichtenberg-Wainer hierarchy*)

1. *Fast growing functions* F_α $(\alpha \leq \varepsilon_0)$ are defined by recursion on ordinals α by $F_0(x) = x + 1$, $F_{\alpha+1}(x) = F^{(x)}_\alpha(x)$ and $F_\lambda(x) = F_{\lambda[x]}(x)$ for limits λ.
2. $\mathcal{E}^\alpha$ denotes the elementary closure of functions $\{F_\beta\}_{\beta<\alpha}$.

For $\alpha, \lambda < \varepsilon_0$ with limit λ show that $F_\alpha = H_{\omega^\alpha}$ for Hardy functions H_α in Definition 4.16.

4.11 Show that the functions $G_k(\alpha)$ and $P_k\alpha$ in Definition 4.11 can be defined alternatively by the following equations: $G_k(0) = 0$, $G_k(\alpha+1) = G_k(\alpha) + 1$ and $G_k(\lambda) = G_k(\lambda[k])$, and $P_k 0 = 0$, $P_k(\alpha+1) = \alpha$ and $P_k\lambda = P_k(\lambda[k])$ for $\alpha + 1, \lambda \in C_k$.

4.12 The *flat Goodstein sequence* $\{y_k\}_k$ of y is defined by $y_0 = y$, and $y_{k+1} = (3+k)^{x_1} \cdot c_1 + \cdots + (3+k)^{x_n} c_n - 1$ if $y_k = (2+k)^{x_1} \cdot c_1 + \cdots + (2+k)^{x_n} c_n > 0$ with $n \geq 1, x_1 > \cdots > x_n \geq 0, 0 < c_1, \ldots, c_n < 2+k$. If $y_k = 0$, then $y_{k+1} = 0$.

Show that $I\Sigma_1$ does not prove the true Π_2-statement $\forall y \exists k[y_k = 0]$ for the flat Goodstein sequence $\{y_k\}_k$ of y.

4.13 Let us introduce a class of relations $\beta <_k \alpha$, which seem to be inspired from the collapsing technique in Chap. 6. Let $<$ be a standard ε_0-order.

Definition 4.23 Let $\beta <_k \alpha$ denote a primitive recursive ternary relation for a natural number k and ordinal terms α and β. If $I\Sigma_1$ proves the following conditions on the relation, then the relation is said to be a *Weiermann relation*. $\alpha \# \beta$ denotes the natural sum of α and β.

(W0) $\alpha <_k \beta \to \alpha < \beta, \alpha \neq 0 \to 0 <_k \alpha$ and $\forall \alpha, k \exists m [\#\{\beta : \beta <_k \alpha\} \leq m]$.
(W1) $\beta <_k \alpha \to \gamma \# \beta <_k \gamma \# \alpha \wedge \beta <_k \gamma \# \alpha \wedge \omega^\beta <_k \omega^\alpha \wedge \beta <_k \omega^\alpha$.
(W2) $\alpha_0, \alpha_1 <_k \alpha \to \omega^{\alpha_0} \# \omega^{\alpha_1} <_k \omega^\alpha$.
(W3) $\forall n < \omega (n <_n \omega \wedge n + 1 <_n \omega)$.
(W4) $\beta <_n \alpha \to \beta + n <_k \alpha + n$.

Note that the Weiermann relation need not to be transitive.

By condition **(W0)** the function

$$\psi_n(\alpha) := \psi(<_n, \alpha) := \max\{k : \exists (\alpha_0, \ldots, \alpha_k)[\alpha_k <_n \cdots <_n \alpha_0 = \alpha]\}$$

is a total computable function, and its restrictions to ordinals$< \varepsilon_0$ are provably computable in PA.

Here are some examples of Weiermann relations, each of which enjoys $\beta <_k \alpha \to \beta <_{k+1} \alpha$ and $\beta < \alpha \to \beta <_{p(|\beta|)} \alpha$ for an elementary function p.

1. $\beta <_k^{|\cdot|} \alpha$ iff $\beta < \alpha$ and $|\beta| \leq f_0(|\alpha|)(k+1)$, where $f_0(0) = 0$ and $f_0(n+1) = 2(f_0(n)+1)$, i.e., $f_0(n) = 2^{1+n} - 2$. Let $\psi_n^{|\cdot|}(\alpha) := \psi(<_n^{|\cdot|}, \alpha)$. Note that $\psi_n^{|\cdot|}(\alpha) = \psi^{|\cdot|, f}(n, \alpha)$ in (4.23) for $f(n, \alpha) = f_0(|\alpha|)(n+1)$.
2. $\beta <_k^C \alpha$ iff $\beta < \alpha$ and $C(\beta) \leq |\alpha| \cdot \max\{C(\alpha), k\}$. Let $\psi_n^C(\alpha) := \psi(<_n^C, \alpha)$. Note that $\psi_n^C(\alpha) = \psi^{C,f}(n, \alpha)$ in (4.23) for $f(n, a) = |\alpha| \cdot \max\{C(\alpha), n\}$.

We define a derivability relation $k \vdash_m^\alpha \Gamma$ relating to a Weiermann relation $\beta <_k \alpha$, where k, m are natural numbers, $\alpha < \varepsilon_0$ and Γ a finite set of sentences such that each sentence is in prenex normal form with alternating quantifiers whose matrices are literals in the language with relation symbols in $\mathcal{E}_*^3$, and 0 and the successor S as the only function symbol. Recall that $\mathrm{dg}_1(A) := \min\{m : A \in \Sigma_{m+1} \cup \Pi_{m+1}\}$ for formulas.

$k \vdash_m^\alpha \Gamma$ iff one of the following cases holds:

(Ax) Γ contains a true closed literal.
($\exists$) There exist $\exists x A(x) \in \Gamma$, an $n \in \omega$ and an α_0 such that $k \vdash_m^{\alpha_0} A(n), \Gamma, \alpha_0 <_k \alpha$ and $n <_k \alpha$.
($\forall$) There exist $\forall x A(x) \in \Gamma$ and α_n such that $k \vdash_m^{\alpha_n} \Gamma, A(n)$ and $\alpha_n <_n \alpha$ for any $n \in \mathbb{N}$.
(cut) There exist a sentence A and α_0, α_1 such that $k \vdash_m^{\alpha_0} \Gamma, A$ and $k \vdash_m^{\alpha_1} \Gamma, \neg A$ with $\mathrm{dg}_1(A) < m$ and $\alpha_0, \alpha_1 <_k \alpha$.
($<_k$) There exists an α_0 such that $k \vdash_m^{\alpha_0} \Gamma$ and $\alpha_0 <_k \alpha$.

1. Show the following facts.

   a. (Weakening) $k \vdash_m^\alpha \Gamma \;\&\; \Gamma \subset \Gamma_1 \;\&\; m \leq m_1 \Rightarrow k \vdash_{m_1}^\alpha \Gamma_1$.
   b. (False) If $k \vdash_m^\alpha \Gamma, A$ for a false closed literal A, then $k \vdash_m^\alpha \Gamma$.
   c. (Inversion) If $k \vdash_m^\alpha \Gamma, \forall x A(x)$, then $k \vdash_m^{\alpha+n} \Gamma, A(n)$ for any n.

2. Show that the (Reduction) holds: Assuming, $k \vdash^{\alpha}_{m} \Gamma, \neg A$ and $k \vdash^{\beta}_{m} \Delta, A$ for a sentence A with $\mathrm{dg}_1(A) \leq m$, $k \vdash^{\alpha\#\beta}_{m} \Gamma, \Delta$ holds.
3. Show the (Elimination) holds: Assuming $k \vdash^{\alpha}_{m+1} \Gamma$, $k \vdash^{\omega^\alpha}_{m} \Gamma$ holds.
4. Show the (Collapsing) holds: Assuming $k \vdash^{\alpha}_{0} \exists x A(x)$ for $\exists x A(x) \in \Sigma_1$, there exists an $m < \psi_k(\alpha)$ for which $A(m)$ s true.
5. Show the (Embedding) holds: Assuming $FV(\Gamma) \subseteq \{x_i : i < p\}$ and $\mathsf{PA} \vdash \Gamma$, there exist natural numbers l, c, m such that for any natural numbers k and $\mathbf{n}$, $k \vdash^{\omega \cdot l + c + \sum \mathbf{n}}_{m} \Gamma(\mathbf{n})$ holds.
6. Conclude the following theorem.

Theorem 4.18 *Let $\beta <_k \alpha$ be a Weiermann relation. Then for any provable Π_2-sentence $\forall x \exists y A(x, y)$ in* PA *there exists an ordinal $\alpha < \varepsilon_0$ such that $\forall n \exists m < \psi_n(\alpha) A(n, m)$.*

4.14 Let $|\varepsilon_0| = C(\varepsilon_0) := 1$. Then $\omega_n <^{|\cdot|}_n \varepsilon_0$ and $\omega_n <^{C}_n \varepsilon_0$. Show that each provably computable function in PA is dominated by the functions $n \mapsto \psi^{|\cdot|}_n(\varepsilon_0)$ and $n \mapsto \psi^{C}_n(\varepsilon_0)$, and each of the statements $\forall n \exists k[\psi^{|\cdot|}_n(\varepsilon_0) = k]$ and $\forall n \exists k[\psi^{C}_n(\varepsilon_0) = k]$ is independent from PA.

4.15 (*Bounds on provably well-founded relations in set theories*) For a set theory $T \supset \mathsf{KP}$, $T(U)$ denotes the set theory T augmented with a unary predicate variable U as for $\mathsf{KP}(U)$. Specifically the Foundation schema is available for any formula with the variable U in $T(U)$, and the equality axiom for U is an axiom in $T(U)$. U does not occur in other axiom schema, e.g., in Separation and Collection even for $T = \mathsf{ZFC}$. Let $<_\varepsilon$ denote a standard epsilon order with base Ω, and of type $\varepsilon_{\Omega+1}$ for the order type Ω of the class of ordinals in the universe V, cf. the Δ_1-class ON_ε and the Δ_1-relation $<_\varepsilon$ in Sect. 4.4. In this exercise let us show the following theorem.

Theorem 4.19 *Let $T \supset \mathsf{KP}$. Let $\prec$ be a set-theoretically definable relation which is provably well-founded in $T(U)$, i.e., $T(U) \vdash \mathrm{TI}[\prec, U]$. Also assume that there exists a definable class $I^{\alpha}_{\prec}$ such that*

$$T \vdash \alpha <_\varepsilon \beta \to I^{\alpha}_{\prec} \subset I^{\beta}_{\prec} \land (\forall a \prec b(a \in I^{\alpha}_{\prec}) \to b \in I^{\beta}_{\prec}) \tag{4.28}$$

Then there exists an $n < \omega$ such that $T \vdash \forall a(a \in I^{\omega_n(\Omega+1)}_{\prec})$.

In particular $T(U) \nvdash \mathrm{TI}[<_\varepsilon, U]$.

When $\prec$ is a standard epsilon order $<_\varepsilon$, let $a \in I^{\alpha}_{<_\varepsilon} :\Leftrightarrow a \leq_\varepsilon \alpha$.

Argue in the intuitionistic fixed point theory $\mathrm{FiX}^i(T)$ over the set theory T. $T(U)$ is embedded in an infinitary calculus $\boldsymbol{G}_V + (cut)$.

The language of the calculus is defined to be $\{\in, =\} \cup \{\bar{c} : c \in V\} \cup \{U\}$ for (the individual constant corresponding to) each set c in the universe V of a transitive and well-founded model of T. For a set-theoretic sentence A in the language $\{\in, =\} \cup \{\bar{c} : c \in V\}$ we say that A is *true* iff $V \models A$.

Axioms in the calculus $\boldsymbol{G}_V + (cut)$ are $\Gamma, \bar{L}, L$ for literals L, and Γ, A for true (U-free) sentences A including the T-axioms other than Foundation. Inference rules are $(\vee)$, $(\wedge)$, $(\exists)$, (cut) and the following inference rule:

$$\frac{\{\Gamma, A(\bar{c}) : c \in V\}}{\Gamma, \forall x A(x)} \ (\forall V)$$

For $\alpha <_{\varepsilon} \varepsilon_{\Omega+1}$ and $d < \omega$, $\vdash^{\alpha}_{d} \Gamma$ is intended to designate that there exists a $\boldsymbol{G}_V + (cut)$-derivation of Γ whose depth is at most α, and whose cut degree is less than d. However due to the infinitary rule $(\forall V)$, derivations in the calculus may be a proper class, and an inductive definition of the relation $\vdash^{\alpha}_{d} \Gamma$ along the 'ordinals' $\alpha <_{\varepsilon} \varepsilon_{\Omega+1}$ may go beyond ZFC. Formally the relation $\vdash^{\alpha}_{d} \Gamma$ should be understood as a *fixed point* of a strictly positive operator. (Actually it is a strongly positive operator.)

1. (Tautology) For any Γ and sentence A, show $\vdash^{2d}_{0} \Gamma, \neg A, A$ with $d := \text{dg}(A)$.
2. (Foundation) For any set $c \in V$, sequent Γ and formula $A(x)$, show $\vdash^{2d+4\alpha+2}_{0} \Gamma, \Theta, A(\bar{c})$, where $d := \max\{\text{dg}(A), 1\}$, $\alpha := \text{rk}(c) = \min\{\alpha : c \in V_{\alpha+1}\}$ and $\Theta := \neg\forall x[\forall y \in x A(y) \to A(x)]$.
3. (Embedding) Let $\Gamma(x_1, \dots, x_n; U)$ be a sequent in $T(U)$ in which no free variable other than the variables $x_1, \dots, x_n$ occurs. For sequences $c_1, \dots, c_n$ of sets let $\Gamma(\bar{c}_1, \dots, \bar{c}_n; U)$ denote the result of substituting $\bar{c}_i$ for each x_i

   Assuming $T(U) \vdash \Gamma(x_1, \dots, x_n; U)$, show that there exist $m, d < \omega$ such that $\forall c_1, \dots, c_n \in V\{\vdash^{\Omega+m}_{d} \Gamma(\bar{c}_1, \dots, \bar{c}_n; U)\}$.
4. Introduce a new inference rule $(prg)_V$: for any set $c \in V$

$$\frac{\Gamma, \forall y \prec \bar{c}\, U(y), U(\bar{c})}{\Gamma, U(\bar{c})} \ (prg)_V$$

   Let $(prg)_V \vdash^{\alpha}_{d} \Gamma$ denote the derivability in the calculus with the inference rule $(prg)_V$. Let $\Delta = \{U(\bar{c}_i) : i = 0, 1, \dots m\}$. Show that for each $k < \omega$, the following is provable in $\text{FiX}^i(T)$: Suppose that there exists a witnessing proof of the fact $(prg)_V \vdash^{\alpha}_{0} \Delta$ such that every formula occurring in the proof is in Π_k. Then $\bigvee \Delta(I^{\alpha}_{\prec})$ holds.
5. Conclude Theorem 4.19.

4.16 Prove Theorem 4.15.1.

4.5 Notes

4.5.1 Section 4.1

Provability of transfinite induction schema of initial segments of a standard ϵ_0-order is proved in Gentzen [32].

4.5.2 Section 4.2

Unprovability of transfinite induction schema up to ε_0 is also proved in [32]. The proof of Lemma 4.10 is closer to the Gentzen's original proof, in which finite proof figures with a rule (prg) for progressiveness of a computable relation $\prec$ are transformed to a normal form. Schütte [50] eliminates cut inferences in the ω-derivations without the extra rule for progressiveness. The set (reachability operator) $I^{\alpha}_{\prec}(M)$ in the proof of Theorem 4.5 is introduced in Beckmann's dissertation [17], cf. [18]. In the proof we don't need to eliminate cut inferences completely, and it suffices to lower cut ranks to 1. The price to pay is that we have to assume that the relation $\prec$ for transfinite induction is a strict partial order. Note that proving the transfinite induction schema of non-transitive relations is easier than for strict partial orders, cf. Exercise 4.3.

An involved Definition 4.4 is due to Sato [48] as in Theorem 3.5, and to compute proof-theoretic ordinals of fragments in Exercise 4.4. 'Proof-theoretic ordinals' of fragments depends on its definition, cf. Exercises 4.4 and 4.5.

Corollary 4.2 is due to Kreisel-Lévy [41].

Theorem 4.7 is due to Takeuti [58, 59]. Under the assumption there exists an order preserving map f elementarily recursive in the ordering, cf. [4]. Both proofs of the stronger result and Theorem 4.7 follows the Takeuti's proof. Theorem 4.8 for multiple relations is took from [15].

Theorems 4.1.3b, 3c and 3d for Σ_2-provable formulas and weak descending chain principle are took from [11]. Exercise 4.8 on provably Δ^0_2-sets is also from [11]. See Stephan, Yang and Yu [55] for moe on hierarchies of Δ^0_2-sets.

4.5.3 Section 4.3

Gentzen had three consistency proofs of PA [30, 31, 33]. The aim of the galley proof [33] is to give a finitistic interpretation of PA, not just to prove its consistency. Very roughly speaking, a formula is true in the interpretation, if it has a cut-free ω-derivation. See Tait [56] for subtle differences between the bar theorem and the arguments used in [33]. Reference [33] received a criticism of a use of the fan theorem, and it was withdrawn. Thanks to the false criticism, the transfinite ordinals enters seriously in proof theory by the first consistency proof since a derivation, i.e., a well-founded tree receives an ordinal height. Before Gentzen, who could imagine the ordinal (structure) ε_0 is tied with the first-order arithmetic PA? For an account of [30], see Buchholz [22]. Gentzen [31] published a streamlined proof. As Buchholz [20] reveals the secret, the second consistency proof [31] transforms finite proof figures as preimages in the embedding of PA into ω-arithmetic.

Our proof of Lemma 4.12 follows the second consistency proof, and is adapted from [5]. In essence it shows that the descending chain principle $\mathcal{E}^{\omega}DS_{\varepsilon_0}$ yields a normalization theorem for proof figures in PA with Σ_1-end formulas although sequent calculi lack canonical rewriting steps as contrasted with natural deductions. Here a proof figure in PA is normal if it is cut-free, enjoys a pure variable condition in Definition 1.3, and every induction term t in the inferences (VJ) is a variable:

$$\frac{\Gamma, A(0) \quad \neg A(a), \Gamma, A(S(a)) \quad \neg A(t), \Gamma}{\Gamma}\ (VJ)$$

It is easy to modify the proof of Lemma 4.12 to show the normalization theorem in PA from $\mathcal{E}^{\omega}DS_{\varepsilon_0}$. Cf. Jervell [38] for normalization theorems of first-order arithmetics in natural deduction.

Takeuti [57] proved a normalization theorem of a second-order logic calculus, which implies the 1-consistency $\mathrm{RFN}_{\Sigma_1}(\mathsf{PA})$ of PA. Let us state the theorem in a simplified form as formulated in [7]. The calculus is obtained from the predicative second order logic $\boldsymbol{G}_2$ in Sect. 2.1.3 by adding the inference rule

$$\frac{\Gamma, \exists X\, A(X), A(V)}{\Gamma, \exists X\, A(X)}$$

where V is an arbitrary abstract as long as A is a first-order formula. Actually $\mathrm{RFN}_{\Sigma_1}(\mathsf{PA})$ is equivalent to the normal form theorem (cut-elimination) with Σ_1-end formulas.

As seen in the proof of Theorem 4.1.3g, we can extract readily a witness of a Σ_1-sentence from a normal proof of the sentence, and the proof of this fact is modified to yield the no-counter example interpretation in Kreisel [40], in which the class $Fnc_{\Sigma_1}(\mathsf{PA})$ of provably computable functions in PA is identified with the class $\mathcal{R}^{<\varepsilon_0}$ of functions defined by ordinal recursion of ε_0, Corollary 4.1.2g. The proof in [40] is based on Ackermann's epsilon substitution method in [2], cf. [9].

Having characterized the class $Fnc_{\Sigma_1}(\mathsf{PA})$ in terms of ordinal recursion, a hierarchy theory emerged in Schwichtenberg [51] with fast growing functions F_α, and Wainer [60] with Hardy functions H_α. The class splits into hierarchies $\mathcal{R}^{<\varepsilon_0} = \mathcal{E}^{\varepsilon_0}$, cf. Exercise 4.10 and Definition 4.16, and hence $Fnc_{\Sigma_1}(\mathsf{PA}) = \mathcal{E}^{\varepsilon_0}$. The Schwichtenberg–Wainer hierarchy $\mathcal{E}^{\varepsilon_0}$ is also called the extended Grzegorczyk hierarchy since it extends the Grzegorczyk hierarchy $\mathsf{PRIM} = \mathcal{E}^{\omega}$, Corollary 1.1 into the transfinite level. The Bachmann property in Lemma 4.14 with Corollary 4.5 is a key to prove the monotonicity of the functions H_α, F_α, and due to Schmidt [49].

Having established $Fnc_{\Sigma_1}(\mathsf{PA}) = \mathcal{E}^{\varepsilon_0}$ via $\mathcal{R}^{<\varepsilon_0}$, Buchholz and Wainer [26] obtain a direct proof of the fact that each provably computable function in PA is dominated by a fast growing function. Reference [26] is a base case of the results in Buchholz [19] for ID_n $(n \leq \omega)$. Our proof of Theorem 4.14 using a derivability relation $\gamma, k \vdash^{\alpha}_{m} \Gamma$ is modified from Fairtlough and Wainer [28].

Norm bounding recursion is introduced in Buchholz, Cichon and Weiermann [23], and inspired from the collapsing technique in Chap. 6. Weiermann [63] proves that each provably computable function in PA is dominated by a function defined by norm-bounding recursion. The proof is modified in Exercise 4.13 with a general class of Weiermann relations in [6].

Goodstein sequence is due to Goodstein [37], and the independence of its termination from PA is proved in Kirby-Paris [39]. Cichon [27] establishes $G_x P_x(\alpha) = P_x G_x(\alpha)$, where P_x, G_x are defined below Theorem 4.11. Our proof of Theorem 4.12 is due to Rathjen [45], which is based on a technique by which infinite sequences are slowed, cf. Stretching lemma 4.13 and Theorem 4.10. The technique is due to Friedman [53], who shows an independence of a Π_2-statement that slowly growing sequences of finite trees are well-quasi ordered in the sense of the Kruskal's tree theorem. The technique is used also in Corollary 4.4. Some slow well-orderings are ingredients in A. Weiermann's phase transitions, e.g., see [8, 64]. Since Stretching lemma 4.13 is obtained by flipping over integers i_ℓ in Grzegorczyk representations of integers, Grzegorczyk sequences arise. Theorem 4.13 with the sequence seems to be new. The flat Goodstein sequence in Exercise 4.12 is due to Abrusci, Girard and Van de Wiele [1].

On the other side, Goodstein sequence in [37] is based on the representation of integers in terms of plus, times and exponentiation together with a base shift. Recently A. Weiermann et al. introduce another Goodstein sequences relative to a ternary Ackermann function $A_a(k, b)$ with base k, and [65] shows that the termination of the resulting sequences is independent from PA. A usual binary Ackermann function is defined by double recursion as follows. $A(0, b) = b + 1$ and $A(a + 1, b) = A_a^{(1+b)}(1)$, where $A_a : b \mapsto A_a(b)$. Then it is easy to see that $A(a + 1, b) = A_a^{(1+b)}(1)$, each function A_a is primitive recursive, and for each primitive recursive function $f(x_1, \ldots, x_n)$, there exists an a such that $f(x_1, \ldots, x_n) \leq A_a(\max(\{2\} \cup \{x_1, \ldots, x_n\})$ holds for any $x_1, \ldots, x_n$, cf. Lemma 1.4. A ternary Ackermann function $A_a(k, b)$ is defined as follows. $A_0(k, b) = b + 1$ and $A_{a+1}(k, b) = A_a(k, \cdot)^{(k(1+b))}(1)$, where $A_a(k, \cdot) : b \mapsto A_a(k, b)$. Thus $A_a(1, b) = A(a, b)$. Fixing a k, positive integers m are represented by the functions $A_a(k, \cdot)$ through a sandwiching procedure, i.e., iterated approximations of m. It is shown in [16] that another ternary Ackermann function starting with $A_0(k, b) = k^b$ yields an independence result for much stronger theory ATR_0 defined in Chap. 5.

For $G_k(\alpha)$ in Definition 4.11 the function $k \mapsto G_k(\alpha)$ is called a *slow growing function*, since it is elementary recursive for each $\alpha < \varepsilon_0$. $n \mapsto G_n(\omega_n)$ is elementary recursive in the superexponential or tower function F_3 and vice versa. J.-Y. Girard [34] showed that the Hardy function H_{ε_0} is elementary recursive in $k \mapsto G_k(\eta)$ and vice versa, where $\eta = \psi_{\Omega_1}(\varepsilon_{\Omega_1+1})$ is the Bachmann–Howard ordinal, which is shown to be the proof-theoretic ordinal of an impredicative theory ID_1 in Chap. 6. In Theorem 4.14 it is shown that the function H_{ε_0} dominates every provably computable function in PA. Thus we need the much bigger ordinal η to capture Π_2-theorems in PA in terms of slow growing functions. Reference [3] gives a proof-theoretic explanation of this hierarchy comparison theorem. For more on slow growing versus fast growing and hierarchy comparison, see Wainer [61] and Weiermann [62].

For more on subrecursive functions and Π_2-analyses, see Rose [46], Fairtlough and Wainer [28], and Schwichtenberg and Wainer [52].

Exercise 4.15 on bounds on set theories should be a folklore.

4.5.4 Section 4.4

The theory ID_ν of νth times iterated positive inductive definitions over natural numbers defined in Chap. 6, has the same prof-theoretic strengths as its intuitionistic counterpart ID^i_ν. This is shown in Pohlers' Habilitationsschrift [44] and Buchholz–Pohlers [25], cf. [24].

Without a serious thinking, I supposed that an intuitionistic counterpart of the fixed point theory has the same proof-theoretic strength as the classical fixed point theory FiX(PA) over PA until the appearance of Buchholz [21], in which it is shown that the intuitionistic fixed point theory over HA with strongly positive operators is conservative over HA with respect to almost negative formulas. The proof is based on a realizability interpretation. In particular the intuitionistic fixed point theory does not prove the consistency of HA.

On the other side FiX(PA) is stronger than PA since the truth definition of arithmetic formulas is defined as a fixed point. In particular FiX(PA) proves the consistency of PA. Feferman [29] interprets $\text{FiX}(\mathsf{PA}) = \widehat{\mathsf{ID}}_1$ in a second-order arithmetic Σ^1_1-AC, Σ^1_1-Axiom of Choice with complete induction schema, whose proof-theoretic ordinal is known to be equal to $\varphi_{\varepsilon_0}(0) > \varepsilon_0$, and conversely the transfinite induction of initial segments of the ordinal is provable in FiX(PA), cf. Chap. 5. Therefore the intuitionistic counterpart of FiX(PA) with strongly positive operators is proof-theoretically weaker than FiX(PA), and the situation differs between inductive definitions and fixed points with respect to the underlying logics.

An account of this difference is given in [4], where the intuitionistic fixed point theory with strongly positive operators is shown to be conservative over HA with respect to all arithmetic formulas by interpreting the intuitionistic fixed point theory in the intuitionistic Σ^1_1-AC^i, and then invoking the Goodman's theorem in [36], stating that the choice schema over intuitionistic elementary analysis is a conservative extension of HA. The intuitionistic fixed point theory over $\mathsf{HA} + \text{TI}(< \Lambda)$ for an ordinal Λ, suffices to formalize proof-theoretic analyses through infinitary derivations with the ω-rule since the derivability relation $\vdash^\alpha_c \Gamma$ in ω-logic can be defined as a fixed point of a strongly positive formula.

The problem remains to extend the conservation for the intuitionistic fixed point theory FiX^i(HA) with strictly positive formulas. Such an extension is done in Rüede and Strahm [47], where it is shown that FiX^i(HA) is conservative over HA with respect to almost negative formulas. The proof is based again on a realizability interpretation. Finally [12] proves the full conservation that FiX^i(HA) is conservative over HA with respect to all arithmetic formulas. The proof is done through a parallel cut-elimination in infinitary derivations, and a formalization of it in HA. In the elimination procedure we first transform the cut inference, which is least with respect to the Kleene–Brouwer ordering of the derivation tree as described in [10]. Such a procedure is given in Mints[43], also cf. [13]. Since the whole proof involves a non-trivial formalization of arguments for infinitary derivations, [14] as well as in Sect. 4.4, avoids it, and gives a proof by transformations of finite proof figures.

Once we know that $\mathrm{FiX}^i(\mathsf{HA})$ is a conservative extension of HA, we obtain instantly the same result between $\mathrm{FiX}^i(\mathsf{PA})$ and PA since the exclude middle $A \vee \neg A$ for arithmetic formulas A is again an arithmetic formula. Thus when a classical theory T is proof-theoretically analyzed through operator controlled derivations and ordinals Λ, we see that T is a conservative extension of $\mathrm{FiX}^i(\mathsf{PA} + \mathrm{TI}(< \Lambda))$, and hence of $\mathsf{PA} + \mathrm{TI}(< \Lambda)$.

References

1. Abrusci, V.M., Girard, J.-Y., Van de Wiele, J.: Some uses of dilators in combinatorial problems, part I. In: Simpson, S.G. (ed.) Logic and Combinatorics. Contemporary Mathematics, vol. 65, pp. 25–54. AMS, Providence (1987)
2. Ackermann, W.: Zur Widerspruchsfreiheit der Zahlentheorie. Math. Ann. **117**, 162–194 (1940)
3. Arai, T.: Slow growing analogue to Buchholz' proof. Ann. Pure Appl. Logic **54**, 101–120 (1991)
4. Arai, T.: Some results on cut-elimination, provable well-orderings, induction and reflection. Ann. Pure Appl. Logic **95**, 93–184 (1998)
5. Arai, T.: Consistency proof via pointwise induction. Arch. Math. Logic **37**, 149–165 (1998)
6. Arai, T.: Variations on a theme by Weiermann. J. Symb. Logic **63**, 897–925 (1998)
7. Arai, T.: Introduction to finitary analyses of proof figures. In: Cooper, S.B., Truss, J.K. (eds.) Sets and Proofs. London Mathematical Society Lecture Notes, vol. 258, pp. 1–25. Cambridge University Press, Cambridge (1999)
8. Arai, T.: On the slowly well orderedness of ε_0. Math. Logic Quart. **48**, 125–130 (2002)
9. Arai, T.: Epsilon substitution method for theories of jump hierarchies. Arch. Math. Logic **41**, 123–153 (2002)
10. Arai, T.: Intuitionistic fixed point theories over Heyting arithmetic. In: Feferman, S., Sieg, W.(eds.) Proofs, Categories and Computations. Essays in honor of Grigori Mints, pp. 1–14. College Publications, King's College London (2010)
11. Arai, T.: Provably Δ^0_2 and weakly descending chains. In Arai, T. Feng, Q., Kim, B., Wu, G., Yang, Y. (eds.) Proceedings of the 11th Asian Logic Conference, pp. 1–21, World Scientific Publishing (2011)
12. Arai, T.: Quick cut-elimination for strictly positive cuts. Ann. Pure Appl. Logic **162**, 807–815 (2011)
13. Arai, T.: Nested PLS. Arch. Math. Logic **50**, 395–409 (2011)
14. Arai, T.: Intuitionistic fixed point theories over set theories. Arch. Math. Logic **54**, 531–553 (2015)
15. Arai, T.: Proof-theoretic strengths of the well ordering principles. Arch. Math. Logic. **59**, 257–275 (2020)
16. Arai, T., Fernández-Duque, D., Wainer, S., Weiermann, A.: Predicatively unprovable termination of the Ackermannian Goodstein process. Proc. Amer. Math. Soc. **148**, 3567–3582 (2020)
17. Beckmann, A.: Separating fragments of bounded arithmetic. Ph.D. thesis, Westfälische Wilhelms-Universität Münster (1996)

18. Beckmann, A.: Dynamic ordinal analysis. Arch. Math. Logic **43**, 303–334 (2003)
19. Buchholz, W.: An independence result for $(\Pi^1_1 - CA) + BI$. Ann. Pure Appl. Logic **33**, 131–155 (1987)
20. Buchholz, W.: Explaining Gentzen's consistency proof within infinitary proof theory. In: Gottlob, G., Leitsch, A., Mundici, D.(eds), Computational Logic and Proof Theory. 5th Kurt Gödel Colloquium, KGC'97. Lecture Notes in Computer Science, vol. 1298, pp. 4–17, Springer, Berlin (1997)
21. Buchholz, W.: An intuitionistic fixed point theory. Arch. Math. Logic **37**, 21–27 (1997)
22. Buchholz, W.: On Gentzen's first consistency proof for arithmetic. In: Kahle, R., Rathjen, M.(eds.) Gentzen's Centenary. The Quest for Consistency, pp. 63–87. Springer, Berlin (2015)
23. Buchholz, W., Cichon, E.A., Weiermann, A.: A uniform approach to fundamental sequences and hierarchies. Math. Logic Q. **40**, 273–286 (1994)
24. Buchholz, W., Feferman, S., Sieg, W., Pohlers, W.: Iterated Inductive Definitions and Subsystems of Analysis: Recent Proof-Theoretical Studies. Lecture Notes in Mathematics, vol. 897. Springer, Berlin (1981)
25. Buchholz, W., Pohlers, W.: Provable well orderings of formal theories for transfinitely iterated inductive definitions. J. Symb. Logic **43**, 118–125 (1978)
26. Buchholz, W., Wainer, S.S.: Provably computable functions and the fast growing hierarchy, In: Simpson, S.G. (ed.) Logic and Combinatorics. Contemporary Mathematics, vol. 65, pp. 179–198. AMS (1987)
27. Cichon, E.A.: A short proof of two recently discovered independence proofs using recursion theoretic methods. Proc. AMS **87**, 704–706 (1983)
28. Fairtlough, M., Wainer, S.S.: Hierarchies of provably recursive functions. In: Buss, S.R. (ed.) Handbook of Proof Theory, pp. 149–207. Elsevier (1998)
29. Feferman, S.: Iterated inductive fixed-point theories: applications to Hancock's conjecture. In: Metakides, G. (ed.) Patras Logic Symposion, pp. 171–196. North-Holland, Amsterdam (1982)
30. Gentzen, G.: Die Widerspruchsfreiheit der reinen Zahlentheorie. Math. Ann. **112**, 493–565 (1936)
31. Gentzen, G.: Neue Fassung des Widerspruchsfreiheitsbeweises für die reine Zahlentheorie, Forschungen zur Logik und Grundlegung der exakten Wissenschaften. Neue Folge **4**, 19–44 (1938)
32. Gentzen, G.: Beweisbarkeit und Unbeweisbarkeit von Anfangsfällen der transfiniten Induktion in der reinen Zahlentheorie. Math. Ann. **119**, 143–161 (1943)
33. Gentzen, G.: Der erste Widerspruchsfreiheitsbeweis für die klassische Zahlentheorie. Arch. Math. Logik Grundl. **16**, 97–118 (1974)
34. Girard, J.-Y.: Π^1_2-logic, Part 1: Dilators. Ann. Math. Logic **21**, 75–219 (1981)
35. Girard, J.-Y.: Proof Theory and Logical Complexity, vol. 1. Bibliopolis, Napoli (1987)
36. Goodman, N.: Relativized realizability in intuitionistic arithmetic of all finite types. J. Symb. Logic **43**, 23–44 (1978)
37. Goodstein, R.L.: On the restricted ordinal theorem. J. Symb. Logic **9**, 33–41 (1944)
38. Jervell, H.: A normalization in first order arithmetic, In: Fenstad, J.E. (ed) Proceedings of 2nd Scandinavian Logic Symposium, pp. 93–108. North-Holland (1971)
39. Kirby, L.A.S., Paris, J.B.: Accessible independence results for Peano Arithmetic. Bull. Lond. Math. Soc. **14**, 285–293 (1982)
40. Kreisel, G.: On the interpretation of non-finitist proofs II. J. Symb. Logic **17**, 43–58 (1952)
41. Kreisel, G., Lévy, A.: Reflection principles and their use for establishing the complexity of axiomatic systems. Z. Math. Logik Grundlagen Math. **14**, 97–142 (1968)
42. Mints, G.E., Finite investigations of transfinite derivations, In: Selected Papers in Proof Theory, pp. 17–72. Bibliopolis, Napoli (1992)
43. Mints, G.E.: Quick cut-elimination for monotone cuts, in: Mints, G., Muskens, R. (Eds.), Games, Logic, and Constructive Sets, Stanford, CA, 2000. CSLI Lecture Notes, vol. 161, pp.75–83. CSLI Publishing, Stanford (2003)
44. Pohlers, W.: Beweistheorie der iterierten induktiven Definitionen. Habilitattionsschrift, München (1977)

45. Rathjen, M.: Goodstein's theorem revisited. In: Kahle, R., Rathjen, M.(eds.) Gentzen's Centenary. The Quest for Consistency, pp. 225–242. Springer (2015)
46. Rose, H.E.: Subrecursion: Functions and hierarchies. Oxford Logic Guides, vol. 9. Oxford University Press, Oxford (1984)
47. Rüede, C., Strahm, T.: Intuitionistic fixed point theories for strictly positive operators. Math. Log. Q. **48**, 195–202 (2002)
48. Sato, K.: Ordinal analyses for monotone and cofinal transfinite inductions. Arch. Math. Logic. **59**, 277–291 (2020)
49. Schmidt, D.: Built-up systems of fundamental sequences and hierarchies of number-theoretic functions. Arch. Math. Logik Grundl. **18**, 47–53 (1976)
50. Schütte, K.: Beweistheoretische Erfassung der unendlichen Induktion in der Zahlentheorie. Math. Ann. **122**, 369–389 (1951)
51. Schwichtenberg, H.: Eine Klassifikation der ε_0-rekursiven Funktionen. Zeitsch. Math. Logik Grundl. Math. **17**, 61–74 (1971)
52. Schwichtenberg, S., Wainer, S.S.: Proofs and Computations. Perspective in Logic, ASL, Cambridge UP (2012)
53. Simpson, S.G.: Nichtbeweisbarkeit von gewissen kombinatorischen Eigenschaften endlicher Bäume. Arch. math. Logik Grundl. **25**(1985), 45–65 (1985)
54. Simpson, S.G.: Subsystems of second order arithmetic, 2nd edn. Perspectives in Logic, Cambridge UP (2009)
55. Stephan, F., Yang, Y., L. Yu, Turing degrees and the Ershov hierarchy. In: Arai, T., Brendle, J., Chong, C. T. R. Downey, R., Q. Feng, G., Kikyo, T., Ono, H. (eds.), Proceedings of the 10th Asian Logic Conference, 2009, pp. 300–321. World Scientific, Singapore (2009)
56. Tait, W.W.: Gentzen's original consistency proof and the bar theorem. In: Kahle, R., Rathjen, M.(eds.) Gentzen's Centenary. The Quest for Consistency, pp. 213–228. Springer (2015)
57. Takeuti, G.: On the fundamental conjecture of GLC I. J. Math. Soc. Jpn. **7**, 249–275 (1955)
58. Takeuti, G.: A remark on Gentzen's paper "Beweibarkeit und Unbeweisbarkeit von Anfangsfällen der transfiniten Induktion in der reinen Zahlentheorie". Proc. Jpn. Acad. **39**, 263–269 (1963)
59. Takeuti, G.: Proof Theory, 2nd edn. North-Holland, Amsterdam (1987). reprinted from Dover Publications (2013)
60. Wainer, S.S.: Ordinal recursion and a refinement of the extended Grzegorczyk hierarchy. J. Symb. Logic **38**, 281–292 (1972)
61. Wainer, S.S.: Slow growing versus fast growing. J. Symb. Logic **54**, 608–614 (1989)
62. Weiermann, A.: Investigations on slow versus fast growing: How to majorize slow growing functions nontrivially by fast growing ones. Arch. Math. Logic **34**, 313–330 (1995)
63. Weiermann, A.: How to characterize provably total functions by local predicativity. J. Symb. Logic **61**, 52–69 (1996)
64. Weiermann, A.: Analytic combinatorics, proof-theoretic ordinals, and the phase transitions for independence results. Ann. Pure Appl. Logic **136**, 189–218 (2005)
65. Weiermann, A.: Ackermannian Goodstein principles for first order Peano arithmetic. In: Friedman, S-D., Raghavan, D., Yang, Y. (eds.) Lecture Notes Series, Institute for Mathematical Sciences, National University of Singapore, Sets and Computations, pp. 157–181 (2017)

Chapter 5
Iterations

In this chapter we discuss straightforward extensions of results in Chap. 4, which are obtained by iterating cut-elimination procedures for first-order arithmetic. The main result in this chapter is stated in Theorem 5.8: $\mathsf{ATR}_0 = \mathsf{FP}_0 = \mathrm{WOP}(\lambda X.\varphi X0)_0$ and the proof-theoretic ordinal of these theories is equal to the Feferman–Schütte ordinal, the least strongly critical number $\Gamma_0 := \min\{\alpha > 0 : \forall\beta, \gamma < \alpha(\varphi_\beta(\gamma) < \alpha)\}$, i.e., the first fixed point of the normal function $\alpha \mapsto \varphi_\alpha(0)$ for the binary Veblen function $\varphi_\alpha(\beta)$, cf. Sect. 5.1 below.

ATR_0 is an SOA, one of the big five in the reverse mathematics, whose main axiom is the Arithmetical Transfinite Recursion admitting a jump hierarchy of sets along a well ordering. FP_0 is another SOA whose main axiom states that a fixed point of a positive formula exists as a set. The main axiom of the SOA $\mathrm{WOP}(\lambda X.\varphi X0)_0$ is the well ordering principle for the normal function $\alpha \mapsto \varphi_\alpha(0)$, which states that if X is a well ordering, then a linear ordering $\varphi X0$ is well founded.

It is convenient for us to analyze proof-theoretically the theories $(\Pi^{0-}_1\text{-CA})_\alpha$ of the absolute jump hierarchy up to α in Sect. 5.3. Proving a cut-elimination Theorem 5.3 for $(\Pi^{0-}_1\text{-CA})_\alpha$ is a straightforward extension of Lemma 3.5 in Chap. 3. In the next Sect. 5.4 classical fixed point theories $\widehat{ID}$ are reduced to the theories of the jump hierarchy via asymmetric interpretations as for fixed point logic in Sect. 3.2. We show by a proof search method in Sect. 2.1, the fact that the well ordering principle $\mathrm{WOP}(\lambda X.\varphi X0)_0$ implies the existence of a fixed point for positive formulas, cf. Theorem 5.5.

Finally we extend proof-theoretic analyses for predicative theories to a metapredicative theory ATR_0^+ in the disguise of the well-ordering principle. A theory is said to be *metapredicative* if its proof-theoretic ordinal is larger than the limit Γ_0 of predicativity, but we can analyze it through a straightforward extension of analyses for predicative theories.

© The Editor(s) (if applicable) and The Author(s), under exclusive license to Springer Nature Singapore Pte Ltd. 2020

T. Arai, *Ordinal Analysis with an Introduction to Proof Theory*, Logic in Asia: Studia Logica Library, https://doi.org/10.1007/978-981-15-6459-8_5

Predicativity

For foundations of mathematics, theories in Theorem 5.8 are thought to codify predicative proofs, and identified with the limit of predicatively provable formulas. Let us begin with a discussion of the notion of predicativity in this context.

The dichotomy, predicative versus impredicative, concerns with predicates $P(x)$ and definitions of sets (or in general definitions of objects) $S = \{x \in X : P(x)\}$ by predicates $P(x)$. Here sets are assumed to be given by comprehension. The definition of sets $S = \{x \in X : P(x)\}$ by comprehension is said to be *predicative* if the meaning of the predicate $P(x)$ is determined independently of the existence of the set S. If we understand that the existence of sets S is assumed to be equivalent to the definiteness of its elements, the condition to hold $P(x)$ should be independent from the set S for any given object x.

For example, let us define a set $S = \{n \in \mathbb{N} : \forall X \subset \mathbb{N}\, B(X, n)\}$ of natural numbers by a Π^1_1-formula $\forall X \subset \mathbb{N}\, B(X, n)$. To determine the meaning of the predicate $\forall X \subset \mathbb{N}\, B(X, n)$, we need to determine the meaning of 'arbitrary sets $X \subset \mathbb{N}$ of natural numbers' in advance. However the set $S \subset \mathbb{N}$ to be defined is a set of natural numbers, and the definition of the set S is in circle provided that 'the set of all sets of natural numbers $\mathscr{P}(\mathbb{N})$' is not assumed to exist independently of our constructions, rather sets are assumed to be constructed or defined.

Although the difference was introduced to avoid vicious circle (Poincaré, Russell, Weyl), we are interested in delineating the line between predicative definitions and impredicative ones, and which part of mathematics are developed predicatively.

If definitions and constructions are to be predicative in a strict sense, it is hard for us to define, e.g., a natural number n by saying that 'n is the least natural number enjoying a predicate' involving 'for any natural number $\forall m \in \mathbb{N}$' or its dual $\exists m \in \mathbb{N}$. However we could accept the set $\mathbb{N}$ of natural numbers to exist as a totality since the generation of all natural numbers 0, 1, 2, ... is intuitively clear. Then, the quantifications $\forall n \in \mathbb{N}, \exists n \in \mathbb{N}$ over natural numbers have a definite meaning as well. In what follows we consider the notion of a predicativity relatively on this ground of the existence of $\mathbb{N}$.

If a definition of a set of natural numbers is absolute, then it has a definite meaning, and is predicative. In other words, if a predicate $A[n]$ on natural numbers n enjoys the condition $\langle \mathbb{N}; M\rangle \models A[n] \Leftrightarrow \langle \mathbb{N}; N\rangle \models A[n]$ for any $M, N \subset \mathscr{P}(\mathbb{N})$ then the definition $\{n \in \mathbb{N} : A[n]\}$ of sets is to be predicative. Therefore there is no problem in accepting predicatively Δ^1_1-Comprehension Axiom, Δ^1_1-CA, $\forall y(\neg A(y) \leftrightarrow B(y)) \to \exists X \forall y[y \in X \leftrightarrow A(y)]$ for Σ^1_1-formulas A, B. Still, it is conceivable that there is a set which is predicatively defined, but not defined by Δ^1_1-CA.

Following Russell's ramified type theory let us construct a family of sets of natural numbers, *ramified analytic hierarchy*, each of which is defined predicatively. First let $<$ be a computable well ordering on $\mathbb{N}$. Define $R_\alpha \subset \mathscr{P}(\mathbb{N})$ recursively on (codes of) ordinals α as follows. $R_0 = \emptyset$, $R_{\alpha+1} = Df(\mathscr{R}_\alpha)$, and $R_\lambda = \bigcup_{\alpha<\lambda} R_\alpha$ for limit ordinals, where $S \in Df(\mathscr{R}_\alpha)$ with the ω-model $\mathscr{R}_\alpha = \langle \mathbb{N}; R_\alpha\rangle$ iff S is defined on $\mathscr{R}_\alpha$ by a second-order formula $A(x, X)$: $S = \{n \in \mathbb{N} : \mathscr{R}_\alpha \models A[n, \mathscr{X}]\}$ for an $\mathscr{X} \in R_\alpha$. For example R_1 is the set of arithmetically definable sets in the arithmetic hierarchy.

$\{R_\alpha\}_\alpha$ is said to be the *ramified analytic hierarchy* (relative to the computable well ordering $<$). Besides the predicativity of each set $\mathcal{X} \in R_\alpha$, if the family R_α of sets has a definite meaning, then so do the quantifications $\forall X \in R_\alpha, \exists X \in R_\alpha$. Hence the next one $R_{\alpha+1}$ has also a definite meaning. Can we accept the whole hierarchy $\{R_\alpha\}_\alpha$ of sets as predicative? The problem here lies in the notion of 'ordinal' or 'well ordering'. It is defined by a Π^1_1-formula, and hard for us to accept the general notion as predicative.

Thus we need to concern about the 'proof' of the fact that a definition is well-defined besides the predicativity of the definition. To be specific, an ordinal is predicative if the transfinite induction $I(\alpha) :\Leftrightarrow \forall X[\forall x(\forall y < x\, X(y) \to X(x)) \to \forall x < \alpha\, X(x)]$ up to α has been proved predicatively, where a proof of $I(\alpha)$ is predicative if the proof is carried out in a system, which has been accepted as predicative before the αth stage.

To formulate the above idea formally, let us expand a language for the first-order arithmetic PA by adding variables X^β_i $(i < \omega)$ ranging over sets in R_β for each β. For a formula A in the language of second-order arithmetic, let A^β denote the result of replacing (free and bound) variables X by X^β. A system $\overline{RA}$ is obtained from PA in the expanded language by adding the axioms $\exists X^\alpha \forall z(X^\alpha(z) \leftrightarrow A^\beta(z))$ $(\beta < \alpha)$. The *ramified analysis* RA_α of level α is defined as follows. For ordinals α, a formula is said to be a formula in RA_α if $\beta \leq \alpha$ holds for each variable X^β occurring in it. Moreover a proof in the system $\overline{RA}$ is a proof in RA_α if every formula occurring in the proof is in RA_α. Now a set RA of formulas, each of which is predicatively provable, is defined by $RA_0 \subset RA, \exists\beta < \alpha(RA_\beta \vdash I^1(\alpha)) \Rightarrow RA_\alpha \subset RA$. Since RA_0 is essentially the same as PA, the first $RA_0 \subset RA$ says that each PA-provable formula is predicatively provable. The second says that if the transfinite induction up to α is proved in RA_β for a smaller $\beta < \alpha$, then each RA_α-provable formula is predicatively provable. Roughly RA_α corresponds to the theory $(\Pi^{0-}_1\text{-CA})_{<\omega\alpha} = \bigcup_{\beta<\omega\alpha}(\Pi^{0-}_1\text{-CA})_\beta$ of jump hierarchy in Definition 5.6 below.

It turns out that the proof-theoretic ordinal of RA is equal to an ordinal Γ_0, the least strongly critical ordinal defined in the next Sect. 5.1, $|RA| = \Gamma_0$, and $RA = RA_{<\Gamma_0} = \bigcup_{\alpha<\Gamma_0} RA_\alpha$ gives the limit of predicativity when the set $\mathbb{N}$ is assumed to exist.

5.1 Binary Veblen Functions and Club Sets

In this section we work in the fragment $\mathsf{KP}\omega_{\Pi_2}$ of Kripke–Platek set theory with the axiom of Infinity, $\mathsf{KP}\omega$ in Definition 1.17. In $\mathsf{KP}\omega_{\Pi_2}$, the foundation (transfinite induction) schema is restricted to Π_2-formulas. Ω denotes the order type of $<$ on the class of ordinals (in a well founded model of $\mathsf{KP}\omega_{\Pi_2}$). In other words, $\alpha < \Omega$ means $\alpha \in ON$. For a function f on Ω and a natural number n, f^n denotes the nth *iterate* of f: $f^0(\alpha) = \alpha$, $f^{n+1}(\alpha) := f(f^n(\alpha))$.

Definition 5.1 Let f be a function on Ω, and X a subclass of Ω.

1. $\mathrm{rng}(f)$ denotes the *range* of f.
2. f is said to be *continuous* if $f(\lambda) = \sup\{f(\alpha) : \alpha < \lambda\}$ for limit ordinals λ.
3. A continuous and strictly increasing function on Ω is called a *normal function*. A Σ*-normal function* is a Σ-definable normal function.
4. $\alpha > 0$ is a *limit point* of X if $\alpha = \sup(X \cap \alpha)$, i.e., $\forall\beta < \alpha\exists\gamma \in X \cap \alpha(\beta < \gamma)$. Any limit point is a limit ordinal.
5. X is said to be *closed* if $\lambda \in X$ holds for any limit point λ of X.
6. A closed and unbounded class is called *club*. A Δ*-club* class is a Δ-definable club class.

Lemma 5.1 *The range* $\mathrm{rng}(f)$ *of strictly increasing function on* Ω *is unbounded.*

Proof This is seen from $\alpha \leq f(\alpha)$. □

Remark 5.1 Let Ω^* denote the projectum of Ω: Ω^* denotes the least ordinal such that there exists an Ω-recursive injection from Ω to Ω^*.

Lemma 5.1 does not mean $\Omega^* = \Omega$. In fact the projectum of ω_1^{CK} is equal to ω: For recursive ordinal α, let $e = f(\alpha) < \omega$ denotes the least code of recursive well ordering of type α. Then f is an ω_1^{CK}-recursive injection into ω.

Lemma 5.2 *1. The range* $\mathrm{rng}(f)$ *of a* Σ*-normal function* f *is* Δ*-club. Conversely the enumerating function* $Enum(X)(\alpha)$*(=*α*th point) of a* Δ*-club* X *is a (totally defined)* Σ*-normal function.*

2. *The fixed points* $FX(f) := \{\alpha < \Omega : f(\alpha) = \alpha\}$ *of a* Σ*-normal function is* Δ*-club. Its enumerating function is said to be the* derivative *of* f*, and denoted* $f' := Enum(FX(f))$.
3. *The intersection* $\bigcap_{\beta<\alpha} C_\beta$ $(\alpha < \Omega)$ *of* Δ*-club family* $\{C_\beta : \beta < \alpha\}$ *is again* Δ*-club, where by a* Δ*-club family* $\{C_\beta : \beta < \alpha\}$*, we mean* $\{(\gamma, \beta) : \gamma \in C_\beta\}$ *is* Δ*, and each* C_β *is club.*

Proof Lemma 5.2.1. Let f be a Σ-function, which is normal, and put $X = \mathrm{rng}(f)$. Clearly X is Δ: $\beta \in X \Leftrightarrow \exists\alpha \leq \beta[f(\alpha) = \beta]$.

Next we show X is closed. Assume $\delta > 0$ is a limit point of X, $\delta = \sup(X \cap \delta)$. By Lemma 5.1 $Y := \{\alpha : f(\alpha) < \delta\}$ is bounded, and transitive, i.e., $Y = \lambda < \Omega$ for an ordinal λ. Hence $f(\lambda) = \sup(X \cap \delta) = \delta$ by $X \cap \delta = \{f(\alpha) : \alpha \in Y\}$.

Conversely assume that X is Δ-club, and let $f = Enum(X)$. Then $f(\alpha) = \inf\{\beta \in X : \forall\gamma < \alpha(f(\gamma) < \beta)\}$. This gives a Σ-definition of f, and we see immediately that f is totally defined strictly increasing function. Continuity of f follows from the assumption that X is closed.

Lemma 5.2.2. We have $\alpha \in FX(f) \Leftrightarrow f(\alpha) = \alpha \Leftrightarrow \alpha \in \mathrm{rng}(f) \wedge \forall\beta < \alpha[f(\beta) < \alpha]$. Hence $FX(f)$ is Δ. $FX(f)$ is closed since f is normal.

Next we show $FX(f)$ is unbounded. For any given β, if $\beta + 1 \in FX(f)$, then there is nothing to prove. Assume $f(\beta + 1) > \beta + 1$. The series $\{f^n(\beta + 1)\}_{n\in\omega}$ with the nth iterate f^n of f, is Σ, and increasing. Let $\alpha = \sup\{f^n(\beta + 1) : n \in \omega\}$. Then $\alpha < \Omega$ by **Σ-Collection** 1.3 and $\omega < \Omega$. We obtain $FX(f) \ni f(\alpha) = \alpha > \beta$.

Lemma 5.2.3 by induction on α applied to a Π_2-formula for unboundedness.

For the Δ-predicate $\{(\gamma,\beta):\gamma\in C_\beta\}$, $\bigcap_{\beta<\alpha} C_\beta$ is also Δ. It is easy to see that the intersection is closed.

Next we show the intersection is unbounded. First consider the case when $\alpha=\beta+1$. By IH $D_0=\bigcap_{\gamma<\beta} C_\gamma$ is club, and $D_1=C_\beta$ is also club. Define recursively an increasing series $\{\delta_n\}_{n\in\omega}$ as follows. First pick a $\delta_0\in D_0$ so that $\delta_0>\delta_{-1}$ for a given δ_{-1}. Then assuming $\delta_n\in D_m$ $(n\equiv m \pmod 2)$ let $\delta_{n+1}=\min\{\delta\in D_{1\dot{-}m}:\delta>\delta_n\}$. Then the series $\{\delta_n\}$ is Σ, and hence $\Omega>\delta=\sup\{\delta_n:n\in\omega\}\in D_0\cap D_1$.

Second consider the case when α is limit. By IH we can assume that $\{C_\beta:\beta<\alpha\}$ is decreasing: $\gamma<\beta<\alpha\Rightarrow C_\gamma\supset C_\beta$. Define recursively an increasing function $\{f(\beta):\beta<\alpha\}$ by $f(\beta)=\min\{\delta\in C_\beta:\forall\gamma<\beta[\delta>f(\gamma)]\,\&\,\delta>\delta_{-1}\}$ for a given δ_{-1}. Then the function f is Σ, and hence $\Omega>\delta=\sup\{f(\beta):\beta<\alpha\}\in\bigcap_{\beta<\alpha} C_\beta$. □

Let C be a Δ-club class. By Lemma 5.2.1, its enumerating function $f=Enum(C)$ is Σ-normal. Then its derivative $f'=Enum(FX(f))$ is again Σ-normal by Lemma 5.2.2. Hence its range $rng(f')$ is Δ-club. The Δ-club class $C'=rng((Enum(FX(Enum(C)))))=FX(Enum(C))$ is the *derivative* of the Δ-club class C. $\alpha\in C'$ iff α is the αth element of C.

Lemma 5.3 *The* diagonal intersection

$$\Delta_{\alpha<\Omega}C_\alpha:=\{\alpha>0:\forall\beta<\alpha(\alpha\in C_\beta)\}$$

of a Δ-club family $\{C_\alpha:\alpha<\Omega\}$ is Δ-club.

Proof It is easy to see that the diagonal intersection $X:=\Delta_{\alpha<\Omega}C_\alpha$ is Δ. Assume $\alpha=\sup(X\cap\alpha)$, and let $\beta<\alpha$. Then $\alpha=\sup(C_\beta\cap\alpha)$, and hence $\alpha\in C_\beta$. Therefore X is closed.

By Lemma 5.2.3 we can assume that $\{C_\alpha:\alpha<\Omega\}$ is decreasing. Define recursively an increasing function $\{f(\beta):\beta<\Omega\}$ by $f(\beta)=\min\{\delta\in C_\beta:\forall\gamma<\beta[\delta>f(\gamma)]\}$. Then the function f is Σ. By Π_2-**Reflection** 1.13 on ordinals pick an $\alpha>\delta_{-1}$ for a given δ_{-1} so that $\forall\beta<\alpha[f(\beta)<\alpha]$. Then $\forall\beta<\alpha[\alpha=\sup(C_\beta\cap\alpha)]$, and hence $\delta_{-1}<\alpha\in X$. □

Definition 5.2 Let g be a Σ-normal function on Ω such that

$$0<\mathsf{g}(0)\wedge\forall\beta(\beta+1<\mathsf{g}(\beta+1)) \tag{5.1}$$

Let us build the *binary Veblen hierarchy* $\{\varphi[\mathsf{g}]_\alpha\}_{\alpha<\Omega}$ starting with g. Let $C[\mathsf{g}]_\alpha=rng(\varphi[\mathsf{g}]_\alpha)$ denote the range of the function $\varphi[\mathsf{g}]_\alpha$. We see that each $\varphi[\mathsf{g}]_\alpha$ is a Σ-normal function on Ω, and each $C[\mathsf{g}]_\alpha$ is a Δ-club class. The definition is based on induction on the ordinals α.

1. $\varphi[\mathsf{g}]_0=\mathsf{g}$, i.e., $C[\mathsf{g}]_0=rng(\mathsf{g})$.

2. For $\beta > 0$,

$$C[\mathsf{g}]_\beta = \bigcap_{\beta' < \beta} (C[\mathsf{g}]_{\beta'})' \tag{5.2}$$

This means that $\varphi[\mathsf{g}]_\beta(\gamma)$ is the γth common fixed point of the functions $\varphi[\mathsf{g}]_{\beta'}$ $(\beta' < \beta)$.

Write $\varphi[\mathsf{g}]\beta\gamma := \varphi[\mathsf{g}]_\beta(\gamma)$. The binary function $\varphi[\mathsf{g}]$ is called the binary *Veblen function* starting with g. Let $Lim = \{\alpha < \Omega : \alpha \text{ is a limit ordinal}\}$.

$$\begin{aligned}
\varphi[\mathsf{g}]_0(\gamma) &:= \mathsf{g}(\gamma) \\
\varphi[\mathsf{g}]_\alpha(\gamma) &:= \sup\{\varphi[\mathsf{g}]_\alpha(\gamma') : \gamma' < \gamma\} \, (\gamma \in Lim) \\
\varphi[\mathsf{g}]_{\beta+1}(0) &:= \sup\{(\varphi[\mathsf{g}]_\beta)^n(0) : n < \omega\} \\
\varphi[\mathsf{g}]_\beta(0) &:= \sup\{\varphi[\mathsf{g}]_{\beta'}(0) : \beta' < \beta\} \, (\beta \in Lim) \\
\varphi[\mathsf{g}]_{\beta+1}(\gamma+1) &:= \sup\{(\varphi[\mathsf{g}]_\beta)^n(\varphi[\mathsf{g}]_{\beta+1}(\gamma)+1) : n < \omega\} \\
\varphi[\mathsf{g}]_\beta(\gamma+1) &:= \sup\{\varphi[\mathsf{g}]_{\beta'}(\varphi[\mathsf{g}]_\beta(\gamma)+1) : \beta' < \beta\} \, (\beta \in Lim)
\end{aligned} \tag{5.3}$$

Theorem 5.1 *The above definition (5.3) determines a unique binary Σ-function $\varphi[\mathsf{g}] : (\alpha, \gamma) \mapsto \varphi[\mathsf{g}]_\alpha(\gamma)$ in $\mathsf{KP}\omega_{\Pi_2}$.*

Proof By the Second Recursion Theorem 1.12 pick a Σ-predicate $\varphi[\mathsf{g}]_\alpha(\gamma) = \delta$ defining the graph of the binary function $\varphi[\mathsf{g}]$. We show $\forall\alpha\forall\gamma\exists!\delta(\varphi[\mathsf{g}]_\alpha(\gamma) = \delta)$ by main induction on ordinals α with subsidiary induction on γ. The uniqueness of the function is easily seen by induction.

The existence $\exists\delta(\varphi[\mathsf{g}]_\alpha(\gamma) = \delta)$ is seen by main induction on α with subsidiary induction on γ. For example in showing $\exists\delta(\varphi[\mathsf{g}]_{\beta+1}(\gamma+1) = \delta)$, we have $\exists!\sigma\,(\varphi[\mathsf{g}]_{\beta+1}(\gamma) + 1 = \sigma)$. Then we obtain $\forall n < \omega\exists!\delta_n((\varphi[\mathsf{g}]_{\beta+1})^n(\sigma) = \delta_n)$. By Corollary 1.5, ($\Sigma$-Replacement) $\{\delta_n\}_{n<\omega}$ is a function, and hence $\exists\delta(\delta = \sup\{\delta_n : n < \omega\})$. □

Lemma 5.4 *Assume g is a Σ-normal function enjoying (5.1).*

1. *$\forall\gamma < \alpha\{\varphi[\mathsf{g}]_\gamma(\varphi[\mathsf{g}]_\alpha(\beta)) = \varphi[\mathsf{g}]_\alpha(\beta)\}$.*
2. *Each $\varphi[\mathsf{g}]_\alpha$ is normal.*
3. *$\varphi[\mathsf{g}]_{\alpha_0}(\beta_0) < \varphi[\mathsf{g}]_{\alpha_1}(\beta_1)$ iff one of the following holds:*
   a. *$\alpha_0 < \alpha_1$ & $\beta_0 < \varphi[\mathsf{g}]_{\alpha_1}(\beta_1)$.*
   b. *$\alpha_0 = \alpha_1$ & $\beta_0 < \beta_1$.*
   c. *$\alpha_0 > \alpha_1$ & $\varphi[\mathsf{g}]_{\alpha_0}(\beta_0) \leq \beta_1$.*
4. *Each $\varphi[\mathsf{g}]_\alpha$ enjoys (5.1): $0 < \varphi[\mathsf{g}]_\alpha(0)$ and $\forall\beta(\beta + 1 < \varphi[\mathsf{g}]_\alpha(\beta+1))$.*
5. *$\alpha \mapsto \varphi[\mathsf{g}]_\alpha(0)$ is a normal function.*
6. *The function $\varphi[\mathsf{g}]_\alpha$ enjoys (5.2) for $C[\mathsf{g}]_\alpha = rng(\varphi[\mathsf{g}]_\alpha)$.*
7. *Let $\gamma \in rng(\mathsf{g})$ be such that $\gamma < \Gamma[\mathsf{g}](0) := \min\{\gamma > 0 : \forall\alpha, \beta < \gamma(\varphi[\mathsf{g}]_\alpha(\beta) < \gamma)$. Then there are unique α and β such that $\alpha, \beta < \varphi[\mathsf{g}]_\alpha(\beta) = \gamma$.*

Proof Continuity of $\varphi[\mathsf{g}]_\alpha$ is seen from the definition (5.3).

Lemmas 5.4.1 and 5.4.2. Simultaneously by main induction on α with subsidiary induction on β show Lemma 5.4.1 and $\forall\gamma < \beta(\varphi[\mathsf{g}]_\alpha(\gamma) < \varphi[\mathsf{g}]_\alpha(\beta))$ using (5.3).

Lemma 5.4.3 is seen from Lemmas 5.4.1 and 5.4.2.

Lemma 5.4.4 is seen by induction on α using (5.1) for g and Lemma 5.4.2.

Lemma 5.4.5. Continuity is seen from (5.3). From $0 < \varphi[\mathsf{g}]_\alpha(0)$ in Lemma 5.4.4 we see $(\varphi[\mathsf{g}]_\alpha)^n(0) < (\varphi[\mathsf{g}]_\alpha)^{n+1}(0)$ for any $n < \omega$. Hence $\varphi[\mathsf{g}]_\alpha(0) < \varphi[\mathsf{g}]_{\alpha+1}(0)$.

Lemma 5.4.6. We show that for $\alpha > 0$, $\varphi[\mathsf{g}]_\alpha$ is the enumerating function of common fixed points of $\varphi[\mathsf{g}]_\beta$ $(\beta < \alpha)$, $\varphi[\mathsf{g}]_\alpha = Enum(\bigcap\{FX(\varphi[\mathsf{g}]_\beta) : \beta < \alpha\})$ and $\mathrm{rng}(\varphi[\mathsf{g}]_\alpha) = \bigcap\{\mathrm{rng}(\varphi[\mathsf{g}]'_\beta) : \beta < \alpha\}$.

$\mathrm{rng}(\varphi[\mathsf{g}]_\alpha) \subset \bigcap\{FX(\varphi[\mathsf{g}]_\beta) : \beta < \alpha\}$ is shown in Lemma 5.4.1.

The fact that $\varphi[\mathsf{g}]_\alpha(\gamma) =$ the γ-th element of $\bigcap\{FX(\varphi[\mathsf{g}]_\beta) : \beta < \alpha\}$ is seen from (5.3) and Lemma 5.4.5.

For example, we see the fact that there is no fixed point of $\varphi[\mathsf{g}]_\alpha$ below $\varphi[\mathsf{g}]_{\alpha+1}(0)$ from $(\varphi[\mathsf{g}]_\alpha)^n(0) < (\varphi[\mathsf{g}]_\alpha)^{n+1}(0)$. Similarly we see the fact that there is no fixed point of $\varphi[\mathsf{g}]_\alpha$ between $\varphi[\mathsf{g}]_{\alpha+1}(\beta)$ and $\varphi[\mathsf{g}]_{\alpha+1}(\beta+1)$ from $(\varphi[\mathsf{g}]_\alpha)^n(\varphi[\mathsf{g}]_{\alpha+1}(\beta)+1) < (\varphi[\mathsf{g}]_\alpha)^{n+1}(\varphi[\mathsf{g}]_{\alpha+1}(\beta)+1)$, which follows from $\varphi[\mathsf{g}]_{\alpha+1}(\beta)+1 < \varphi[\mathsf{g}]_\alpha(\varphi[\mathsf{g}]_{\alpha+1}(\beta)+1)$ in Lemma 5.4.4.

Lemma 5.4.7. Let $rng(\mathsf{g}) \ni \gamma < \Gamma[\mathsf{g}](0)$. By Lemma 5.4.5 and $\gamma < \Gamma[\mathsf{g}](0)$ we obtain $\gamma < \varphi[\mathsf{g}]_\gamma(0)$, and $\gamma \notin rng(\varphi[\mathsf{g}]_\gamma)$. Let $\alpha_1 = \min\{\alpha \leq \gamma : \gamma \notin rng(\varphi[\mathsf{g}]_\alpha)\}$. Since $rng(\varphi[\mathsf{g}]_\lambda) = \bigcap_{\beta<\lambda} rng(\varphi[\mathsf{g}]_\beta)$ and $\gamma \in rng(\mathsf{g})$, α_1 is a successor ordinal. Let $\alpha_1 = \alpha + 1$ and $\gamma = \varphi[\mathsf{g}]_\alpha(\beta)$. We claim that $\alpha, \beta < \gamma$. $\alpha + 1 = \alpha_1 \leq \gamma$ yields $\alpha < \gamma$. If $\beta = \gamma$, then we would have $\gamma \in rng(\varphi[\mathsf{g}]_\alpha)' = rng(\varphi[\mathsf{g}]_{\alpha+1})$. Thus $\beta < \gamma$. □

The derivative of the normal function $\alpha \mapsto \varphi[\mathsf{g}]_\alpha(0)$ is denoted $\Gamma[\mathsf{g}]$. Thus the ordinal $\Gamma[\mathsf{g}](\beta)$ is the βth fixed point of $\alpha \mapsto \varphi[\mathsf{g}]_\alpha(0)$, and a *$\mathsf{g}$-strongly critical ordinal*. Obviously $\Gamma[\mathsf{g}]$ enjoys (5.1).

Lemma 5.5 *The followings are mutually equivalent each other for ordinals α:*

1. *α is g-strongly critical.*
2. *$\alpha > 0$ and $\forall\beta, \gamma < \alpha(\varphi[\mathsf{g}]_\beta(\gamma) < \alpha)$.*
3. *α is an limit ordinal and $\alpha \in \Delta_{\alpha<\Omega}\mathrm{rng}(\varphi[\mathsf{g}]_\alpha)$.*

Namely $\Gamma[\mathsf{g}] = Enum(Lim \cap \Delta_{\alpha<\Omega}\mathrm{rng}(\varphi[\mathsf{g}]_\alpha)) = (\alpha \mapsto \varphi[\mathsf{g}]_\alpha(0))'$ for the class Lim of limit ordinals.

Proof (2)$\Rightarrow$ (3). Assume $\alpha > 0$ and $\forall\beta, \gamma < \alpha(\varphi[\mathsf{g}]_\beta(\gamma) < \alpha)$. Then α is a limit ordinal since if $\alpha = \beta + 1$, then we would have $\beta \leq \varphi[\mathsf{g}]_\beta(0) \leq \varphi[\mathsf{g}]_\beta(\beta) \leq \beta$. Namely $\beta = 0$. However $0 < \mathsf{g}(0) = \varphi[\mathsf{g}]_0(0)$.

Let $\beta < \alpha$. Then $\alpha \geq \sup\{\varphi[\mathsf{g}]_\beta(\gamma) : \gamma < \alpha\} = \varphi[\mathsf{g}]_\beta(\alpha)$. Therefore $\alpha = \varphi[\mathsf{g}]_\beta(\alpha) \in \mathrm{rng}(\varphi[\mathsf{g}]_\beta)$.

(3)$\Rightarrow$ (1). Assume $\alpha \in \Delta_{\alpha<\Omega}\mathrm{rng}(\varphi[\mathsf{g}]_\alpha)$ for a limit ordinal α. Then $\varphi[\mathsf{g}]_\alpha(0) = \sup\{\varphi[\mathsf{g}]_\beta(0) : \beta < \alpha\} \leq \alpha$ since $\alpha \in \mathrm{rng}(\varphi[\mathsf{g}]_\beta)$ for any $\beta < \alpha$. Therefore $\varphi[\mathsf{g}]_\alpha(0) = \alpha$.

(1)$\Rightarrow$ (2). Assume $\alpha = \varphi[\mathsf{g}]_\alpha(0)$, and let $\beta, \gamma < \alpha$. Then $\alpha > 0$ and $\varphi[\mathsf{g}]_\beta(\gamma) < \varphi[\mathsf{g}]_\alpha(0) = \alpha$ is seen from Lemma 5.4.3. □

The standard choice for the starting function g is $\mathsf{g}_0(\alpha) = \omega^\alpha$, which enjoys (5.1). Then the hierarchy $\{\varphi[\mathsf{g}_0]_\alpha\}_{\alpha<\Omega}$ is denoted $\{\varphi_\alpha\}_{\alpha<\Omega}$, the *binary Veblen hierarchy*. Putting $\varphi\alpha\beta := \varphi_\alpha(\beta)$ $(\alpha, \beta < \Omega)$, the binary function φ is the *binary Veblen function*. $\Gamma_\alpha := \Gamma[\mathsf{g}_0](\alpha)$ is said to be the αth *strongly critical number*.

The least strongly critical number $\Gamma_0 = \Gamma[\mathsf{g}_0](0) = \min\{\lambda < \Omega : 0 < \lambda \;\&\; \forall\alpha, \beta < \lambda(\varphi\alpha\beta < \lambda)\}$, *Feferman–Schütte ordinal*, is known to be the limit of the predicativity. From Lemmas 5.4.3 and 5.4.7 we see that each ordinal$< \Gamma_0$ is denoted uniquely from 0 by means of the functions $+, \varphi$, and this yield a computable notation system of ordinals$< \Gamma_0$.

Let us do it once again from the next starting function $\mathsf{g}_1(\alpha) = \Gamma_\alpha$. Then the hierarchy $\{\varphi[\mathsf{g}_1]_\alpha\}_{\alpha<\Omega}$ is denoted $\{\varphi_{(1,\alpha)}\}_{\alpha<\Omega}$. This means that $\varphi_{(1,0)}(\beta) = \Gamma_\beta$, and for $\alpha > 0$, $\varphi_{(1,\alpha)}(\beta)$ is the βth common fixed point of the functions $\{\varphi_{(1,\alpha_0)}\}_{\alpha_0<\alpha}$. Putting $\Phi\alpha\beta := \varphi_{(1,\alpha)}(\beta)$ $(\alpha, \beta < \Omega)$, the binary function Φ is the *next binary Veblen function*. These functions are needed to describe proof-theoretic ordinals of metapredicative theories, cf. Sect. 5.5. For the Veblen hierarchy $\{\varphi_\alpha\}_\alpha = \{\varphi[\mathsf{g}_0]_\alpha\}_\alpha$ with $\mathsf{g}_0(\beta) = \omega^\beta$, we write $\varphi_{(0,\alpha)}(\beta) = \varphi_\alpha(\beta)$.

5.2 Axiom Schemata in Second Order Arithmetic

$\mathscr{L}_2(\mathsf{EA})$ denotes a language for second-order arithmetic. The first-order variables or *number variables* are denoted by $n, m, \ldots, x, y, z$, the second-order variables or *set variables* by $X, Y, Z, \ldots$. Set variables are assumed to be unary, and $X(t)$ or $t \in X$ is an atomic formula for number terms t. Other atomic formulas are $t = s$ and $t < s$ for number terms t, s. Number terms are generated from number variables and the constant 0 by function symbols for elementary recursive functions. A *set term* is an expression of the form $\{x : A(x)\}$ or $\{x\}A(x)$ or $\lambda x.A(x)$ for a formula $A(x)$ with a variable x. For a set term $T \equiv \{x : A(x)\}$, $t \in T :\equiv (A(t))$, and $F(T)$ denotes the result of replacing each atomic formula $t \in X$ by $t \in T$ in a formula $F(X)$. $t \in T$ and $F(T)$ are defined modulo α-conversion, i.e., modulo renaming bound variables. $(Y)_n$ denotes the set term $(Y)_n :\equiv \{x : \langle n, x\rangle \in Y\}$ with a bijective pairing function $\langle x, y\rangle$. For a formula $m \prec n$, let $(Z)_{\prec n} := \sum_{m\prec n}(Z)_m := \{\langle m, x\rangle : x \in (Z)_m, m \prec n\}$.

Our base theory is the second-order elementary recursive arithmetic $\mathsf{EA}^2 = \mathsf{EA} + \Delta^0_0\text{-IND} + \Delta^0_0\text{-CA}$ in the second order language $\mathscr{L}_2(\mathsf{EA})$. Its axioms are the defining axioms for elementary recursive functions, $\forall x(0 \neq x + 1)$, axioms for the discrete linear order $<$, and the induction axiom $\forall X[X(0) \land \forall y(X(y) \to X(y+1)) \to \forall x\, X(x)]$ and the comprehension axiom schema $\exists X\forall y[y \in X \leftrightarrow A(y)]$ for bounded formulas A in $\mathscr{L}_2(\mathsf{EA})$.

In the following Definitions 5.3 and 5.4 $<_0$ denotes a linear order on ω such that $x <_0 y$ is given by a bounded formula $\theta_{<_0}(x, y)$ in the language $\mathscr{L}_2(\mathsf{EA})$ (possibly with a second-order parameter). The domain of the relation $<_0$ is also assumed to be given by a bounded formula. For such a linear order $<_0$, let us construct canonically a linear order $<_1$ (*epsilon order over* $<_0$) whose order type is ε_α, and a linear order

$<_2$ (*Veblen order over* $<_0$) whose order type is $\varphi_\alpha(0)$ when $<_0$ is a well-order of type α. Small Greek letters $\alpha, \beta, \gamma, \ldots$ range over elements in the field of the relations $<_1, <_2$, while $u, v, w, \ldots$ range over elements in the field of $<_0$.

Definition 5.3 (*Epsilon order over* $<_0$) Let $<_0$ be a linear order with its field $fld(<_0) = \{n : \exists m(n <_0 m \vee m <_0 n)\}$. Let $\omega^\alpha := \langle 0, \alpha \rangle$, $\varepsilon_\alpha := \langle 1, \alpha \rangle$, and $\alpha_1 + \cdots + \alpha_n := \langle 2, \langle \alpha_1, \ldots, \alpha_n \rangle \rangle$. The field $fld(<_1)$ of the relation $<_1$, its subset P and the relation $<_1$ are simultaneously defined as follow.

1. $0 \in fld(<_1)$, and $0 <_1 \alpha$ for any $\alpha \neq 0$ in $fld(<_1)$.
2. If $\alpha_1, \ldots, \alpha_n \in P$ with $n > 1$, and $\alpha_n \leq_1 \cdots \leq_1 \alpha_1$, then $\alpha_1 + \cdots + \alpha_n \in fld(<_1)$.
   For $\alpha_1 + \cdots + \alpha_n, \beta_1 + \cdots + \beta_m \in fld(<_1)$ with $\alpha_i, \beta_j \in P$ and $n + m > 2$, $\alpha_1 + \cdots + \alpha_n <_1 \beta_1 + \cdots + \beta_m$ iff either $\exists i \leq \min\{n, m\}[\alpha_i <_1 \beta_i \wedge \forall j < i(\alpha_i = \beta_i)]$ or $n < m \wedge \forall i < n(\alpha_i = \beta_i)$.
3. Let $\alpha \in fld(<_1)$, and it is not the case that $\alpha = \varepsilon_\beta$. Then $\omega^\alpha \in P \subset fld(<_1)$.
   For $\omega^\alpha, \omega^\beta \in fld(<_1)$, $\omega^\alpha <_1 \omega^\beta$ iff $\alpha <_1 \beta$.
4. Let $u \in fld(<_0)$. Then $\varepsilon_u \in P \subset fld(<_1)$.
   For $\varepsilon_u, \varepsilon_v, \omega^\alpha \in fld(<_1)$, $\varepsilon_u <_1 \varepsilon_v$ iff $u <_0 v$. $\varepsilon_u <_1 \omega^\beta$ iff $\varepsilon_u <_1 \beta$. $\omega^\beta <_1 \varepsilon_u$ iff $\beta <_1 \varepsilon_u$.

When $<_0$ is given by a set X as $n <_0 m \leftrightarrow \langle n, m \rangle \in X$, we write ε_X for $fld(<_1)$.

Definition 5.4 (*Veblen order over* $<_0$) Let $<_0$ be a linear order with its field $fld(<_0) = \{n : \exists m(n <_0 m \vee m <_0 n)\}$. Let $\varphi\alpha\beta := \langle 0, \langle \alpha, \beta \rangle \rangle$, and $\alpha_1 + \cdots + \alpha_n := \langle 1, \langle \alpha_1, \ldots, \alpha_n \rangle \rangle$. The field $fld(<_2)$ of the relation $<_2$, its subset P and the relation $<_2$ are simultaneously defined as follow.

1. $0 \in fld(<_2)$, and $0 <_2 \alpha$ for any $\alpha \neq 0$ in $fld(<_2)$.
2. If $\alpha_1, \ldots, \alpha_n \in P$ with $n > 1$, and $\alpha_n \leq_2 \cdots \leq_2 \alpha_1$, then $\alpha_1 + \cdots + \alpha_n \in fld(<_2)$.
   For $\alpha_1 + \cdots + \alpha_n, \beta_1 + \cdots + \beta_m \in fld(<_2)$ with $\alpha_i, \beta_j \in P$ and $n + m > 2$, $\alpha_1 + \cdots + \alpha_n <_2 \beta_1 + \cdots + \beta_m$ iff either $\exists i \leq \min\{n, m\}[\alpha_i <_2 \beta_i \wedge \forall j < i(\alpha_i = \beta_i)]$ or $n < m \wedge \forall i < n(\alpha_i = \beta_i)$.
3. Let $u \in fld(<_0)$ and $\alpha \in fld(<_2)$, and it is not the case that $\alpha = \varphi v \beta$ with $u <_0 v$. Then $\varphi u \alpha \in P \subset fld(<_2)$.
   For $\varphi u \alpha, \varphi v \beta \in fld(<_2)$, $\varphi u \alpha <_2 \varphi v \beta$ iff $u <_0 v \wedge \alpha <_2 \varphi v \beta$ or $u = v \wedge \alpha <_2 \beta$ or $v <_0 u \wedge \varphi u \alpha <_2 \beta$.

When $<_0$ is given by a set X as $n <_0 m \leftrightarrow \langle n, m \rangle \in X$, we write $\varphi X0$ for $fld(<_2)$.

It is clear that when $<_0$ is a linear order, then so are $<_1, <_2$. Also it is easy to see that $(fld(<_1), <_1)$ and $(fld(<_2), <_2)$ are elementary recursive in $(fld(<_0), <_0)$.

Let us consider the following axioms and axiom schemata.

Definition 5.5 IND $:\Leftrightarrow \forall X \forall z[X(0) \wedge \forall y(X(y) \rightarrow X(y+1)) \rightarrow X(z)]$.
Let Φ be a class of formulas.

1. Φ – IND denotes the collection of the universal closures of formulas

$$\forall z[A(0) \wedge \forall y(A(y) \rightarrow A(y+1)) \rightarrow A(z)]\ (A \in \Phi)$$

2. Φ – CA denotes the collection of the universal closures of formulas

$$\exists X \forall y[y \in X \leftrightarrow A(y)]\ (A \in \Phi)$$

3. Φ – AC denotes the collection of the universal closures of formulas

$$\forall n \exists X\, A(n, X) \rightarrow \exists Y \forall n\, A(n, (Y)_n)\ (A \in \Phi)$$

4. Φ – DC denotes the collection of the universal closures of formulas

$$\forall n \forall X \exists Y\, A(n, X, Y) \rightarrow \exists Z \forall n\, A(n, (Z)_{<n}, (Z)_n)\ (A \in \Phi)$$

5. FP denotes the collection of the formulas

$$\forall X \exists Y \forall n(n \in Y \leftrightarrow A(n, Y, X))$$

   for *arithmetic positive operators* $A(n, Y, X) \in \Pi^1_0$ such that Y occurs only positively, and free variables occurring in it are among n, Y, X.
6. ATR denotes the collection of the universal closures of formulas

$$WO(\prec) \rightarrow \exists Y \forall x, n(x \in (Y)_n \leftrightarrow A(x, (Y)_{\prec n}))$$

   for set variables $\prec$ and arithmetic formulas, i.e, first-order formulas $A(x, X) \in \Pi^1_0$, where $\mathrm{WO}(\prec) :\Leftrightarrow \mathrm{LO}(\prec) \wedge \forall Y\, \mathrm{TI}[\prec, Y]$ and $\mathrm{LO}(\prec) :\Leftrightarrow \forall n, m, k \in fld(\prec)[(n \not\prec n) \wedge (n \prec m \vee n = m \vee m \prec n) \wedge (n \prec m \wedge m \prec k \rightarrow n \prec k)]$ with $n \in fld(\prec) :\Leftrightarrow \exists m(n \prec m \vee m \prec n)$.
7. Each $X \subset \mathbb{N}$ is viewed as a binary relation $<_X := \{(n, m) : \langle n, m\rangle \in X\}$. Then $\mathrm{LO}(X) :\Leftrightarrow \mathrm{LO}(<_X)$ and $\mathrm{WO}(X) :\Leftrightarrow \mathrm{WO}(<_X)$.

   The *well-ordering principle* for a definable functional $f : \mathcal{P}(\mathbb{N}) \rightarrow \mathcal{P}(\mathbb{N})$,

$$\mathrm{WOP}(f) :\Leftrightarrow \forall X\, (\mathrm{WO}(X) \rightarrow \mathrm{WO}(f(X)))$$

8. When $<_0 = <_X$, $\mathrm{WOP}(\lambda X.\varphi X0)$ denotes the well-ordering principle $\mathrm{WOP}(f)$ for the Veblen ordering $f(X) = \varphi X0$ over $<_X$.

For one of these axioms and axiom schemata T, $(T)_0$ denotes the second-order arithmetic extending EA^2 by the axiom schema T. (T) is obtained from $(T)_0$ by adding the full induction schema Π^2_0-IND. $(\Pi^1_0\text{-CA})_0$ is denoted ACA_0.

Also for axiom schemata T and S, $(T+S)_0$ is an extension of EA^2 by the axiom schemata T and S. $(T+S)$ is obtained from $(T+S)_0$ by adding the full induction schema.

Let Δ^1_1-CA denote the collection of the universal closures of formulas

$$\forall y(\neg A(y) \leftrightarrow B(y)) \to \exists X \forall y[y \in X \leftrightarrow A(y)]$$

for Σ^1_1-formulas A, B.

5.3 Theories of Jump Hierarchies

In this section $<$ denotes a standard epsilon order of type Γ_0. Small Greek letters $\alpha, \beta, \gamma, \delta, \ldots$ range over the domain of the relation, which is also assumed to be elementary recursive.

5.3.1 *Transfinite Inductions in the Theories of Jump Hierarchies*

Definition 5.6 Let U be a fixed set variable (parameter).

1. $(\Pi^{0-}_1\text{-CA})_\alpha$ denotes a first-order theory for the Turing jump hierarchy $\{H^U_\delta\}_{\delta \le \alpha}$, where $H^U_0 = U$ and $H^U_\delta = (\sum_{\gamma<\delta} H^U_\gamma)'$ for $\delta > 0$ with the Turing jump $X' = \{n : \{n\}^X(n) \downarrow\}$.
Specifically $(\Pi^{0-}_1\text{-CA})_\alpha$ denotes a first-order theory in the language $\mathscr{L}_H := \mathscr{L}(\mathsf{PA}) \cup \{U, H\}$, where U is a fixed set parameter, and H a unary predicate symbol. Axioms in $(\Pi^{0-}_1\text{-CA})_\alpha$ are those of PA in the expanded language including the complete induction schema, which is applied to arbitrary formulas in the language, and the axioms $H_0 = U$ and for $\beta > 0$, $\forall \beta \le \alpha[H_\beta = (H_{<\beta})']$ for the predicate H, where $H_{<\beta} = \sum_{\gamma<\beta} H_\gamma = \{\langle \gamma, x\rangle : \gamma < \beta, x \in H_\gamma\}$, and $X' := \{x : \{x\}^X(x) \downarrow\}$, i.e., $x \in X' \Leftrightarrow \exists y\, T^X(x, x, y)$ for the Kleene's T-predicate. Moreover the transfinite induction schema $\mathrm{TI}(<_\alpha) = \{\mathrm{TI}[<_\alpha, B]\}_B$ with formulas B in the language, along the well-ordering $<_\alpha$ up to α, is an axiom in $(\Pi^{0-}_1\text{-CA})_\alpha$.
2. $(Y \in R_c) :\Leftrightarrow (Y = U) \vee \exists d < c \exists e[\forall x\, \{e\}^{H_d}(x) \downarrow \wedge Y = \{x : \{e\}^{H_d}(x) \simeq 0\}]$.
3. $I^c(\gamma) :\Leftrightarrow \forall Y \in R_c\, I(\gamma, Y)$, where $I(\gamma, Y)$ denotes the transfinite induction up to γ applied to Y.

Let with $\alpha | \beta :\Leftrightarrow \exists \gamma > 0(\beta = \alpha \cdot \gamma)$

$$A_\alpha(a) :\Leftrightarrow \forall \beta \forall c[c + 2\omega^a \le \alpha \wedge 2\omega^a | c \to I^{c+2\omega^a}(\beta) \to I^c(\varphi_a(\beta))].$$

Lemma 5.6 $(\Pi^{0-}_1\text{-}CA)_\alpha \vdash Prg[<, A_\alpha]$.

Proof Argue in $(\Pi^{0-}_1\text{-CA})_\alpha$. Assume $\forall b < a\, A_\alpha(b)$. We show $A_\alpha(a)$. Suppose $2\omega^a|c$ and $I^{c+2\omega^a}(\beta)$ for $c + 2\omega^a \leq \alpha$. We show $I^c(\varphi_a(\beta))$.
Case 0. $a = 0$: Let $Y \in R_c$, and assume $Prg[<, Y]$. Then by Claim 4.1 we have $Prg[<, \mathrm{j}[Y]]$ for the Π_2-formula $\mathrm{j}[Y]$ in Y, cf. (4.2). Then $\mathrm{j}[Y] \in R_{c+2}$. By $I^{c+2}(\beta)$ we obtain $I(\beta, \mathrm{j}[Y])$, which yields $\forall\gamma < \beta\, \mathrm{j}[Y](\gamma)$. Therefore $\forall\gamma < \omega^\beta(Y(\gamma))$.

In what follows assume $a > 0$. Let $B(\beta) :\Leftrightarrow I^c(\varphi_a(\beta))$. It suffices to show $Prg[<, B]$ by $I^{c+\omega}(\beta)$ and $B \in R_{c+\omega}$. When λ is a limit number, we see $\forall\beta < \lambda\, B(\beta) \to B(\lambda)$ easily from the continuity of the function φ_a.
Case 1. $a = b + 1$: Assuming $B(\beta) \leftrightarrow I^c(\varphi_a(\beta))$, let us show $B(\beta + 1)$. From $B(\beta)$ we obtain $I^c(\varphi_a(\beta) + 1)$. We have $\varphi_a(\beta + 1) = \sup_n \varphi^n_b(\varphi_a(\beta) + 1)$, and $c = \sup\{d < c : 2\omega^b|d\}$. It suffices to show $I^d(\varphi^n_b(\varphi_a(\beta) + 1))$ for any $n < \omega$ and any $d < c$ with $2\omega^b|d$. Let $n < \omega$ and $d < c$ such that $2\omega^b|d$. Then $2\omega^b|(d + 2\omega^b n)$. From $I^c(\varphi_a(\beta) + 1)$ and $d + 2\omega^b n < c$ we obtain $I^{d+2\omega^b n}(\varphi_a(\beta) + 1)$. $A_\alpha(b)$ yields $I^{d+2\omega^b(n-m)}(\varphi^m_b(\varphi_a(\beta) + 1))$ by induction on $m \leq n$. Thus we obtain $I^c(\varphi_a(\beta + 1))$.

$B(0)$ is seen similarly from $\varphi_a(0) = \sup_n \varphi^n_b(0)$.
Case 2. a is a limit number: Assuming $B(\beta)$, let us show $B(\beta + 1)$. We have $\varphi_a(\beta + 1) = \sup\{\varphi_b(\varphi_a(\beta) + 1) : b < a\}$. Let $b < a$. Then $c = \sup\{d < c : 2\omega^b|d\}$. Let $d < c$ with $2\omega^b|d$. From $I^c(\varphi_a(\beta))$ we obtain $I^c(\varphi_a(\beta) + 1)$, which yields $I^{d+2\omega^b}(\varphi_a(\beta) + 1)$ by $d + 2\omega^b < c$. $A_\alpha(b)$ yields $I^d(\varphi_b(\varphi_a(\beta) + 1))$. $I^c(\varphi_a(\beta + 1))$ follows.

$B(0)$ is seen similarly. □

Lemma 5.7 $|(\Pi^{0-}_1\text{-CA})_\alpha| \geq \varphi(\alpha)$, *where*
$\varphi(\alpha) = \varphi_{a_n}(\cdots(\varphi_{a_1}(\varepsilon(\alpha))\cdots))$ *for* $\alpha = \omega^{a_n} + \cdots + \omega^{a_1}$ *with* $a_n \geq \cdots \geq a_1 > 0$ $(n \geq 0)$, *and* $\varepsilon(\alpha)$ *denotes the least epsilon number greater than* α.

Proof We can assume $n > 0$ by Theorem 4.2 since $(\Pi^{0-}_1\text{-CA})_0$ is an extension of PA. Argue in $(\Pi^{0-}_1\text{-CA})_\alpha$.

By Lemma 5.6 and the transfinite induction $\mathrm{TI}[<_\alpha, A_\alpha]$ we have $\forall a \leq \alpha\, A_\alpha(a)$. Recall that

$$A_\alpha(a) \Leftrightarrow \forall\beta\forall c[c + 2\omega^a \leq \alpha \wedge 2\omega^a|c \to I^{c+2\omega^a}(\beta) \to I^c(\varphi_a(\beta))]$$

Let $c_i = \omega^{a_n} + \cdots + \omega^{a_{i+1}}$ for $i \leq n$. First we obtain $I^{c_0}(\gamma)$ for $\gamma < \varepsilon(\alpha)$ by the transfinite induction schema $\mathrm{TI}(<_\alpha)$. Putting successively $\begin{array}{c|ccc} a & a_1 & \cdots & a_n \\ c & c_1 & \cdots & c_n \end{array}$, we obtain from $I^{c_0}(\gamma)\,(\gamma < \varepsilon(\alpha))$ that $I^{c_1}(\varphi_{a_1}(\gamma)), \cdots, I^{c_n}(\varphi_{a_n}(\cdots(\varphi_{a_1}(\gamma))\cdots))$. In the last $I^{c_n}(\varphi_{a_n}(\cdots(\varphi_{a_1}(\gamma))\cdots))$, we have $c_n = 0$ with $R_0 = \{U\}$. Therefore we conclude $I(< \varphi_{a_n}(\cdots(\varphi_{a_1}(\varepsilon(\alpha)))\cdots), U)$. □

Theorem 5.2 $\mathsf{ATR}_0 \vdash \mathrm{WOP}(\lambda X.\varphi X0)$.

Proof Argue in ATR_0. Assume that $<_X$ is a well-ordering. Let $<$ in Lemma 5.6 denote the Veblen ordering $<_2$ over $<_X$. For any $\alpha \in fld(<_X)$ the subtheory $(\Pi^{0-}_1\text{-CA})_\alpha$ of ATR_0 proves $Prg[<_X, A_\alpha]$. Hence we obtain $\mathrm{WO}(\varphi\alpha 0)$. □

5.3.2 Predicative Cut Elimination

Fix an ordinal (natural number) $\Lambda < \Gamma$. Let $A(X, x)$ be a first-order formula whose free variables are among the first-order one x, a binary predicate variable X and a fixed unary predicate symbol U. Introduce a unary predicate symbol H^A_α ($\alpha \leq \Lambda$) and a binary one $H^A_{<\alpha}$ ($\alpha \leq \Lambda$) for each such formula $A(x, X)$. Consider an expanded language $\mathcal{L}(\Lambda)$ obtained from the language $\mathcal{L}_2(\mathsf{EA})$ by adding H^A_α ($\alpha \leq \Lambda$), $H^A_{<\alpha}$ ($\alpha \leq \Lambda$), and their complements $\bar{H}^A_\alpha$, $\bar{H}^A_{<\alpha}$ for each such formula $A(x, X)$.

We are going to introduce a one-sided infinitary sequent calculus $\boldsymbol{G}(\Lambda; \mathcal{L})$. A closed term t is identify with its value $t^{\mathbb{N}}$. For simplicity let us denote the nth numeral $\bar{n}$ by n. $\boldsymbol{G}(\Lambda; \mathcal{L})$ is obtained from the ω-logic $\boldsymbol{G}_\omega$ by adding an initial sequent and four new inference rules for the predicate constants H^A_α, $H^A_{<\alpha}$. These says that

$$\forall \alpha \leq \Lambda \forall x \{H^A_\alpha(x) \leftrightarrow A(H^A_{<\alpha}, x)\}$$

and

$$\forall \alpha \leq \Lambda \forall x, \beta \{H^A_{<\alpha}(\beta, x) \leftrightarrow \beta < \alpha \land H^A_\beta(x)\}.$$

Namely

$$\forall \alpha \leq \Lambda [H^A_\alpha = \{x : A(H^A_{<\alpha}, x)\} \land H^A_{<\alpha} = \sum_{\beta<\alpha} H^A_\beta] \tag{5.4}$$

A new initial sequent: for $m \not< \alpha$

$$\Gamma, \bar{H}^A_{<\alpha}(m, n)$$

New inference rules: for $\alpha \leq \Lambda$

$$\frac{\Gamma, H^A_\alpha(n), A(H^A_{<\alpha}, n)}{\Gamma, H^A_\alpha(n)}\ (H^A_\alpha) \qquad \frac{\Gamma, \bar{H}^A_\alpha(n), \neg A(H^A_{<\alpha}, n)}{\Gamma, \bar{H}^A_\alpha(n)}\ (\bar{H}^A_\alpha)$$

$$\frac{\Gamma, H^A_{<\alpha}(\beta, n), H^A_\beta(n)}{\Gamma, H^A_{<\alpha}(\beta, n)}\ (H^A_{<\alpha})\ \text{if } \beta < \alpha \qquad \frac{\Gamma, \bar{H}^A_{<\alpha}(\beta, n), \bar{H}^A_\beta(n)}{\Gamma, \bar{H}^A_{<\alpha}(\beta, n)}\ (\bar{H}^A_{<\alpha})$$

Definition 5.7 The *degree* $\mathrm{dg}'(A)$ of a formula A in the language $\mathcal{L}(\Lambda)$.

1. $\mathrm{dg}'(L) = 0$ for a literal L in $\mathcal{L}_2(\mathsf{EA})$.
2. $\mathrm{dg}'(A_0 \lor A_1) = \mathrm{dg}'(A_0 \land A_1) = \max\{\mathrm{dg}'(A_i) : i = 0, 1\} + 1$.
3. $\mathrm{dg}'(\exists x A(x)) = \mathrm{dg}'(\forall x A(x)) = \mathrm{dg}'(A(0)) + 1$.
4. $\mathrm{dg}'([\neg]H^A_{<\alpha}(\beta, n)) = (n_A + 2)\alpha$, where $n_A < \omega$ denotes the number such that $\mathrm{dg}'(A(U, n)) = n_A$. Then[1] $\mathrm{dg}'([\neg]A(H^A_{<\alpha}, n)) \leq (n_A + 2)\alpha + n_A$.
5. $\mathrm{dg}'([\neg]H^A_\alpha(n)) = (n_A + 2)\alpha + n_A + 1$.

[1]Provided that X occurs in $A(X, x)$.

The degrees are defined so that

$$\mathrm{dg}'(H^A_\alpha(n)) > \mathrm{dg}'(A(H^A_\alpha, n)) \,\&\, \forall\beta < \alpha[\mathrm{dg}'(H^A_{<\alpha}(\beta, n)) > \mathrm{dg}'(H^A_\beta(n))] \quad (5.5)$$

Definition 5.8 $G(\Lambda; \mathscr{L}) \vdash^\alpha_c \Gamma$ iff there exists a derivation of Γ in $G(\Lambda; \mathscr{L}) + (cut)$ such that its tree-height is at most α and the degree $\mathrm{dg}'(A)$ of any cut formula A in it is less than c.

In what follows we write $\vdash^\alpha_c \Gamma$ for $G(\Lambda; \mathscr{L}) \vdash^\alpha_c \Gamma$.

The following Lemmas 5.8, 5.9, 5.10 and 5.11 are seen as in the previous chapters.

Lemma 5.8 (Weakening Lemma) *Assume* $\beta \le \alpha$ *and* $d \le c$. *Then* $\vdash^\beta_d \Gamma \Rightarrow \vdash^\alpha_c \Gamma, \Delta$.

Lemma 5.9 (Inversion Lemma)

1. *If* $\vdash^\alpha_c \Gamma, A_0 \wedge A_1$, *then* $\vdash^\alpha_c \Gamma, A_i$ *for* $i = 0, 1$.
2. *If* $\vdash^\alpha_c \Gamma, \forall x A(x)$, *then* $\vdash^\alpha_c \Gamma, A(n)$ *for any* n.
3. *For* $\alpha < \Lambda$ *if* $\vdash^\gamma_c \Gamma, \bar{H}^A_\alpha(n)$, *then* $\vdash^\gamma_c \Gamma, \neg A(H^A_{<\alpha}, n)$.
4. *For* $\alpha \le \Lambda$ *if* $\vdash^\gamma_c \Gamma, \bar{H}^A_{<\alpha}(n, \beta)$, *then* $\vdash^\gamma_c \Gamma, \bar{H}^A_\beta(n)$.

Lemma 5.10 (Eliminating false arithmetic literals) *Let* L *be a false arithmetic literal in* $\mathscr{L}_2(\mathsf{EA})$. *If* $\vdash^\alpha_c \Gamma, L$, *then* $\vdash^\alpha_c \Gamma$.

Definition 5.9 A formula is said to be a $\forall$-*formula*, if it is either a literal in the language $\mathscr{L}_2(\mathsf{EA})$ or a conjunction $A_0 \wedge A_1$ or a universal formula $\forall x B(x)$ or $\bar{H}^A_\alpha(n)$ or $\bar{H}^A_{<\alpha}(n, \beta)$.

Lemma 5.11 *For a* $\forall$-*formula* C, *if* $\vdash^\alpha_c \Gamma, C$ *and* $\vdash^\beta_c \neg C, \Delta$ *with* $\mathrm{dg}'(C) \le c$, *then* $\vdash^{\alpha+\beta}_c \Gamma, \Delta$.

Proof By induction on β using (5.5) as in Lemma 3.4 in Chap. 3. □

Theorem 5.3 (Predicative cut-elimination theorem) $\vdash^\beta_{c+\omega^\alpha} \Gamma \Rightarrow \vdash^{\varphi\alpha\beta}_c \Gamma$.

Proof By main induction on α with subsidiary induction on β.

Since $\beta \mapsto \varphi\alpha\beta$ is strictly increasing, it suffices to consider the case when Γ is the lowersequent of a (cut):

$$\frac{\vdash^\gamma_{c+\omega^\alpha} \Psi, C \quad \vdash^\gamma_{c+\omega^\alpha} \neg C, \Delta}{\vdash^\beta_{c+\omega^\alpha} \Psi, \Delta(=\Gamma)}$$

for a $\forall$-cut formula C with $\mathrm{dg}'(C) < c + \omega^\alpha$ and a $\gamma < \beta$. By SIH and Lemma 5.11, we obtain for $c' = \max\{c, \mathrm{dg}'(C)\}$

$$\frac{\vdash^{\varphi\alpha\gamma}_c \Psi, C \quad \vdash^{\varphi\alpha\gamma}_c \neg C, \Delta}{\vdash^{(\varphi\alpha\gamma)\cdot 2}_{c'} \Psi, \Delta}$$

Suppose $\mathrm{dg}'(C) \geq c$, and let $\mathrm{dg}'(C) = c + \omega^{\alpha_n} + \cdots + \omega^{\alpha_0}$ for $\alpha > \alpha_n \geq \cdots \geq \alpha_0$. By MIH we, then, obtain

$$\vdash_c^{\varphi\alpha_n(\cdots(\varphi\alpha_0((\varphi\alpha\gamma)\cdot 2))\cdots)} \Psi, \Delta$$

and by Lemma 5.4.3 $\varphi\alpha_n(\cdots(\varphi\alpha_0((\varphi\alpha\gamma)\cdot 2))\cdots) < \varphi\alpha\beta$. □

Theorem 5.4 *$|(\Pi^{0-}_1\text{-CA})_\alpha| = \varphi(\alpha)$ and $(\Pi^{0-}_1\text{-CA})_\alpha$ is a conservative extension of $\mathsf{PA} + \mathrm{TI}(< \varphi(\alpha))$, where $\varphi(\alpha) = \varphi_{a_n}(\cdots(\varphi_{a_1}(\varepsilon(\alpha))\cdots))$ for $\alpha = \omega^{a_n} + \cdots + \omega^{a_1}$ with $a_n \geq \cdots \geq a_1 > 0\,(n \geq 0)$, and $\varepsilon(\alpha)$ denotes the least epsilon number greater than α.*

Proof We can assume $\alpha \geq \omega$ by Theorem 4.2 since $(\Pi^{0-}_1\text{-CA})_k$ is include in ACA_0 with $|\mathsf{ACA}_0| = \varepsilon_0 = \varepsilon(k)$ for $k < \omega$. By Lemma 5.7 it suffices to show $|(\Pi^{0-}_1\text{-CA})_\alpha| \leq \varphi(\alpha)$. Assume that $(\Pi^{0-}_1\text{-CA})_\alpha$ proves $\mathrm{TI}[\prec, U]$ for a computable strict partial order $\prec$. We show $|\prec| < \varphi(\alpha)$. Let $m < \omega$ be such that $\mathrm{dg}'(A) < \alpha + m$ for any formula A occurring in the proof of $\mathrm{TI}[\prec, U]$ in $(\Pi^{0-}_1\text{-CA})_\alpha$. Then we see as in Embedding Lemma 4.4 that $\boldsymbol{G}(\alpha; \mathscr{L}) \vdash^{\alpha\cdot\omega}_{\alpha+m} \mathrm{TI}[\prec, U]$ for the calculus $\boldsymbol{G}(\alpha; \mathscr{L})$ with $\Lambda = \alpha$. Theorem 5.3 yields successively that $\boldsymbol{G}(\alpha; \mathscr{L}) \vdash^{<\varepsilon(\alpha)}_{\alpha} \mathrm{TI}[\prec, U]$, $\boldsymbol{G}(\alpha; \mathscr{L}) \vdash^{<\varphi_{a_1}(\varepsilon(\alpha))}_{\omega^{a_n}+\cdots+\omega^{a_2}} \mathrm{TI}[\prec, U], \ldots,$ and $\boldsymbol{G}(\alpha; \mathscr{L}) \vdash^{<\varphi(\alpha)}_0 \mathrm{TI}[\prec, U]$. The last $\boldsymbol{G}(\alpha; \mathscr{L}) \vdash^{<\varphi(\alpha)}_0 \mathrm{TI}[\prec, U]$ means that $\boldsymbol{G}_\omega \vdash^{<\varphi(\alpha)}_0 \mathrm{TI}[\prec, U]$, which yields $|\prec| < \varphi(\alpha)$ by Lemma 4.6.

Next assume $(\Pi^{0-}_1\text{-CA})_\alpha$ proves a first-order formula A. In the same vein we see that $\boldsymbol{G}_\omega \vdash^{<\varphi(\alpha)}_0 A$. Hence $\mathsf{PA} + \mathrm{TI}(< \varphi(\alpha))$ proves A. □

5.4 Classical Fixed Point Theories

Definition 5.10 Let T be a first-order, recursively enumerable theory extending $\mathsf{PA}(U)$ possibly with a unary predicate U such that its countable language $\mathscr{L}(T)$ is obtained from the arithmetic language of $\mathsf{PA}(U)$ by adding some predicate constants.

A first-order theory $\widehat{ID}(T)$ (*fixed point theory over* T) is then defined as follows:

1. The language $\mathscr{L}(\widehat{ID}(T))$ of $\widehat{ID}(T)$ is obtained from the language $\mathscr{L}(T)$ of T by adding a unary predicate constant I^A for each X-positive formula $A(X, x)$ in the language $\mathscr{L}(T) \cup \{X\}$ with $X \notin \mathscr{L}(T)$.
2. Axioms of $\widehat{ID}(T)$ are obtained from those of T in the expanded language $\mathscr{L}(\widehat{ID}(T))$, i.e., the complete induction schema for $\mathscr{L}(\widehat{ID}(T))$, and the following axioms for each X-positive formula $A(X, x)$

$$\forall x \left(x \in I^A \leftrightarrow A(I^A, x)\right) \tag{5.6}$$

Let $\widehat{ID}_0(T) = T$, and $\widehat{ID}_{n+1}(T) = \widehat{ID}(\widehat{ID}_n(T))$. Also let $\widehat{ID}_n = \widehat{ID}_n(\mathsf{PA})$.

For example in $\widehat{ID}_2$, one can introduce first a fixed point predicate $I^A = \{x | A(I^A, x)\}$ for arithmetic positive formulas $A(X, x)$, and then introduce another fixed point $I^B = \{x | B(I^B, I^A, x)\}$ for X-positive formula $B(X, I^A, x)$ in the language $\mathcal{L}(\mathsf{PA}) \cup \{I^A\}$.

5.4.1 Eliminating Fixed Points

We are going to introduce a one-sided infinitary sequent calculi $\widehat{ID}^{\infty}(T)$. A closed term t is identify with its value $t^{\mathbb{N}}$. For simplicity let us denote the mth numeral $\bar{m}$ by m. $\widehat{ID}_0^{\infty}(T)$ is obtained from the ω-logic $\mathbf{G}_{\omega}$ in the language $\mathcal{L}(T)$ by adding initial sequents Γ, A for axioms A in T. $\widehat{ID}^{\infty}(T)$ is obtained from the ω-logic $\widehat{ID}_0^{\infty}(T)$ by adding two new inference rules for the predicate constants I^A, saying that

$$\forall x\{I^A(x) \leftrightarrow A(I^A, x)\}.$$

New inference rules: for closed terms t

$$\frac{\Gamma, I^A(t), A(I^A, t)}{\Gamma, I^A(t)}\ (I^A) \quad \frac{\Gamma, \bar{I}^A(t), \neg A(I^A, t)}{\Gamma, \bar{I}^A(t)}\ (\bar{I}^A)$$

Let $\mathcal{POS}$ $[\mathcal{NEG}]$ denote the set of formulas in which the predicate constants I^A occurs only positively $[I^A$ occurs only negatively$]$, resp. Put $\mathcal{PN} = \mathcal{POS} \cup \mathcal{NEG}$. Note that each formula in $\mathcal{L}(T)$ is in $\mathcal{POS} \cap \mathcal{NEG} \subset \mathcal{PN}$.

The *$\mathcal{PN}$-degree* $\mathrm{dg}_{PN}(A)$ of a formula A is defined as in Definition 1.1 by letting $\mathrm{dg}_{PN}(A) := 0$ for any $A \in \mathcal{PN}$.

Definition 5.11 $\widehat{ID}_0^{\infty}(T) \vdash^{\alpha} \Gamma$ iff there exists a derivation of Γ in $\widehat{ID}_0^{\infty}(T) + (cut)$ such that its tree-height is at most α.

$\widehat{ID}^{\infty}(T) \vdash_c^{\alpha} \Gamma$ iff there exists a derivation of Γ in $\widehat{ID}^{\infty}(T) + (cut)$ such that its tree-height is at most α and $\mathcal{PN}$-degree of any cut formula in it is less than c.

Fix an interpretation of predicates in $\mathcal{L}(T) \setminus \mathcal{L}(\mathsf{PA})$. The X-positive formula $A(X, x) \in \mathcal{L}(T)$ determines a monotone operator $\mathcal{A} : \mathcal{X} \mapsto \{m \in \mathbb{N} : \mathbb{N} \models A(\mathcal{X}, m)\}$. From this operator $\mathcal{A}$, sets $I_{\beta}^A = \{m \in \mathbb{N} : \mathbb{N} \models A(I_{<\beta}^A, m)\}$ with $I_{<\beta}^A = \bigcup_{\gamma<\beta} I_{\gamma}^A$ are inductively generated. Then $I_{<\infty}^A = \bigcup\{I_{\beta}^A : \beta \text{ is an ordinal}\}$ is the *least* fixed point of the operator $\mathcal{A}$.

Now we apply an asymmetric interpretation. Namely replace an arbitrary fixed point I^A of $\mathcal{A}$ by a set (constant) I_{β}^A where the ordinal β indicating the stage of inductively generated set I_{β}^A depends on the context of occurrences of I^A. Specifically if a formula B in a restricted form has an infinitary proof of depth α_0 and we replace negative occurrences of I^A (premisses) by an I_{β}^A, then we can control increases of ordinals β' by using the depth α_0 so that the result holds when we replace further positive occurrences of I^A (conclusions) by an $I_{\beta'}^A$. In this way we can embed $\widehat{ID}^{\infty}(T)$ into an infinitary system $(I^{<\alpha}(T))$ with the set constants $\{I_{\beta}^A : \beta < \alpha\}$ and the latter admits a cut elimination. Furthermore if I^A does not occur in a formula B, then in the resulting cut-free proof of B, no new constant I^A_β occurs.

Let $\alpha < \Gamma_0$. A one-side sequent calculus $(I^{<\alpha}(T))$ is obtained in the language $\mathscr{L}^{<\alpha}(T) = \mathscr{L}(T) \cup \{I^A_\beta, I^A_{<\beta} : \beta < \alpha, A(X, x) \in \mathscr{L}(T),\ X\text{-positive}\}$ from $\widehat{ID}^\infty_0(T)$ by adding the following inference rules (I^A_β), $(\bar{I}^A_\beta)$ and $(I^A_{<\beta})$, $(\bar{I}^A_{<\beta})$ for each $\beta < \alpha$,

$$\frac{\Gamma, I^A_\beta(m), A(I^A_{<\beta}, m)}{\Gamma, I^A_\beta(m)}\ (I^A_\beta) \qquad \frac{\Gamma, \bar{I}^A_\beta(m), \neg A(I^A_{<\beta}, m)}{\Gamma, \bar{I}^A_\beta(m)}\ (\bar{I}^A_\beta)$$

$$\frac{\Gamma, I^A_{<\beta}(m), I^A_\gamma(m)}{\Gamma, I^A_{<\beta}(m)}\ (I^A_{<\beta})\ \text{for } \gamma < \beta \qquad \frac{\{\Gamma, \bar{I}^A_{<\beta}(m), \bar{I}^A_\gamma(m) : \gamma < \beta\}}{\Gamma, \bar{I}^A_{<\beta}(m)}\ (\bar{I}^A_{<\beta})$$

The *degree* $\mathrm{dg}'(A)$ of a formula A in the language $\mathscr{L}^{<\alpha}(T)$ is defined as in Definition 5.7 by letting $\mathrm{dg}'(B) := 0$ for any formula B in the language $\mathscr{L}(T)$, $\mathrm{dg}'([\neg]I^A_{<\alpha}(m)) = (n_A + 2)\alpha$, and $\mathrm{dg}'([\neg]I^A_\alpha(m)) = (n_A + 2)\alpha + n_A + 1$ so that

$$\mathrm{dg}'(I^A_\alpha(m)) > \mathrm{dg}'(A(I^A_\alpha, m))\ \&\ \forall\beta < \alpha[\mathrm{dg}'(I^A_{<\alpha}(m)) > \mathrm{dg}'(I^A_\beta(m))] \tag{5.7}$$

holds.

Definition 5.12 $(I^{<\alpha}(T)) \vdash^\alpha_c \Gamma$ iff there exists a derivation of Γ in $(I^{<\alpha}(T)) + (cut)$ such that its tree-height is at most α and degree $\mathrm{dg}'(A)$ of any cut formula A in it is less than c.

For $B \in \mathscr{P}\mathscr{N}$, $B^{(\beta,\gamma)}$ denotes the result of replacing each negative occurrence I^A by $I^A_{<\beta}$ and each positive occurrence I^A by $I^A_{<\gamma}$. For $\Gamma \subset \mathscr{P}\mathscr{N}$, $\Gamma^{(\beta,\gamma)} = \{B^{(\beta,\gamma)} : B \in \Gamma\}$.

Lemma 5.12 *1. For $\Gamma \subset \mathscr{P}\mathscr{N}$, assume $\widehat{ID}^\infty(T) \vdash^{\alpha_0}_1 \Gamma$ for $\alpha_0 < \alpha$. Then $(I^{<\alpha}(T)) \vdash^{2\alpha_0}_{\omega(\beta+2^{\alpha_0}+1)} \Gamma^{(\beta,\beta+2^{\alpha_0})}$ for any $\beta < \alpha$.*
2. Assume $(I^{<\alpha}(T)) \vdash^\beta_{c+\omega^a} \Gamma$ for $c > 0$. Then $(I^{<\alpha}(T)) \vdash^{\varphi_a(\beta)}_c \Gamma$.

Proof Cf. Sect. 3.2. Lemma 5.12.1 is seen by induction on α_0 using the fact that if $(I^{<\alpha}(T)) \vdash^\beta_c \Gamma, I^A_{<\gamma}$, then $(I^{<\alpha}(T)) \vdash^\beta_c \Gamma, I^A_{<\gamma+\delta}$. Note that every formula occurring in the derivation witnessing the fact $\widehat{ID}^\infty(T) \vdash^{\alpha_0}_1 \Gamma$ for $\Gamma \subset \mathscr{P}\mathscr{N}$, is in $\mathscr{P}\mathscr{N}$. Lemma 5.12.2 is seen as in Theorem 5.3. □

Let $\varepsilon(a) = \sup\{\omega_k(a+1) : k < \omega\}$ denote the least epsilon number larger than a. Let $\vdash^{<\alpha}_c \Gamma :\Leftrightarrow \exists\beta < \alpha \vdash^\beta_c \Gamma$, and $\vdash^{<\alpha}_{<\alpha} \Gamma :\Leftrightarrow \exists\beta < \alpha \vdash^\beta_\beta \Gamma$.

Corollary 5.1 *Let Γ be a sequent in the language $\mathscr{L}(T)$.*
If $\widehat{ID}^\infty(T) \vdash^{<\varepsilon(a)}_c \Gamma$ for $c < \omega$, then $\widehat{ID}^\infty_0(T) \vdash^{<\varphi_{\varepsilon(a)}(0)} \Gamma$.

Proof Assume $\widehat{ID}^{\infty}(T) \vdash_{c}^{<\varepsilon(a)} \Gamma$ for $c < \omega$. Then $\widehat{ID}^{\infty}(T) \vdash_{1}^{<\varepsilon(a)} \Gamma$. Lemma 5.12.1 yields $(I^{<\varepsilon(a)}(T)) \vdash_{<\varepsilon(a)}^{<\varepsilon(a)} \Gamma$ with $\Gamma^{(0,\alpha)} \equiv \Gamma$. Then by Lemma 5.12.2 we obtain $(I^{<\varepsilon(a)}(T)) \vdash_{1}^{<\varphi_{\varepsilon(a)}(0)} \Gamma$. Every cut formula B occurring in a witnessing derivation is $\mathrm{dg}'(B) = 0$, i.e., B is a formula in $\mathcal{L}(T)$. This means that the derivation is one in the infinitary calculus $\widehat{ID}_0^{\infty}(T)$. Hence we get $\widehat{ID}_0^{\infty}(T) \vdash^{<\varphi_{\varepsilon(a)}(0)} \Gamma$. □

5.4.2 Proving the Fixed Point Axiom from the Well-Ordering Principle

Theorem 5.5 *Over* ACA_0, $\mathrm{WOP}(\lambda X.\varphi X0)$ *implies the fixed point axiom* FP.

Our proof of Theorem 5.5 is based on a proof search method. Let $A(X, x) \equiv A(X, x, Y)$ be an X-positive formula with a second-order parameter Y. Our aim is to prove $\forall Y \exists Z \forall x[x \in Z \leftrightarrow A(Z, x, Y)]$ from the well-ordering principle $\mathrm{WOP}(\lambda X.\varphi X0)$.

Augue in ACA_0. Fix a set $\mathcal{Y} \subset \mathbb{N}$ interpreting the variable Y. Let $\widehat{ID}^{\infty}(\mathcal{Y})$ denote an infinitary calculus in the language $\mathcal{L}(\mathsf{PA}) \cup \{Y, I\}$ with two unary predicates Y, I. $\widehat{ID}^{\infty}(\mathcal{Y})$ is obtained from $\widehat{ID}^{\infty} = \widehat{ID}^{\infty}(\mathsf{PA})$ in Definition 5.11 by adding initial sequents for atomic diagram of $\mathcal{Y}$: $\Gamma, n \in Y$ if $n \in \mathcal{Y}$, and $\Gamma, n \notin Y$ if $n \notin \mathcal{Y}$, and the repetition rule (Rep).

By searching a derivation of a contradiction, let us test the consistency of $\widehat{ID}^{\infty}(\mathcal{Y})$. If it is consistent, then we can find a set $\mathcal{I}^A$, which is a fixed point. Otherwise the search procedure yields a derivation of the empty sequent.

Modify the construction of the refutation tree $\mathcal{T}$ in Sect. 2.1.5 as follows: First put the empty sequent at the root $\emptyset$. **Leaf condition** is literally the same as before: If $Seq(\sigma)$ is an axiom in $\widehat{ID}^{\infty}(\mathcal{Y})$, then σ is a leaf in $\mathcal{T}$. The construction is divided to two. Suppose that the tree $\mathcal{T}$ has been constructed up to a node $\sigma \in {}^{<\omega}\omega$.
Case 0. $lh(\sigma)$ is even: Apply one of inferences $(\vee)$, $(\wedge)$, $(\exists)$, $(\forall\omega)$, (I^A), $(\bar{I}^A)$ if it is possible. Otherwise repeat.
Case 1. $lh(\sigma) = 2n + 1$ for $n < \omega$: Apply the inference (cut) with the cut formula $I^A(n)$.

$$\frac{\Gamma, I^A(n) \quad \bar{I}^A(n), \Gamma}{\Gamma} \ (cut)$$

If the tree $\mathcal{T}$ is not well-founded, then let $\mathcal{P}$ be an infinite path through $\mathcal{T}$. Let $n \in \mathcal{I}^A$ iff $\bar{I}^A(n)$ is on the path $\mathcal{P}$. Due to the **Case 1** exactly one of formulas $I^A(n)$ and $\bar{I}^A(n)$ occurs on $\mathcal{P}$ for each n, and the same for formulas $A(I^A, n)$ and $\neg A(I^A, n)$. Then we see by induction on degrees $\mathrm{dg}_I(B)$ with $\mathrm{dg}_I(I^A(n)) = 0$ that each formula B on $\mathcal{P}$ is false in the model $\langle \mathbb{N}; \mathcal{Y}, \mathcal{I}^A \rangle$. In particular we see that $A(\mathcal{I}^A, n) \leftrightarrow n \in \mathcal{I}^A$ for any n. Since the path $\mathcal{P}$ through $\mathcal{T}$ is arithmetical in $\mathcal{Y}$, $\mathcal{I}^A \in \Pi^1_0(\mathcal{P})$ exists as a set in ACA_0.

In what follows assume that $\mathcal{T}$ is well-founded. Let Λ denote a limit ordinal greater than the order type $otp(<_{KB})$ of the Kleene-Brouwer ordering $<_{KB}$ on $\mathcal{T}$. ACA_0 proves that $<_{KB}$ is a well-ordering, cf. Proposition 1.10.

For $\beta < \Lambda$ let us write $\widehat{ID}^{\infty}(\mathcal{Y}) \vdash^{\beta} \Gamma$ when there exists a derivation of Γ in $\widehat{ID}^{\infty}(\mathcal{Y})$ whose depth is bounded by $\beta < \Lambda$, and each cut formula in the derivation is a formula $I^A(n)$. Note that each formula occurring in a derivation witnessing the fact $\widehat{ID}^{\infty}(\mathcal{Y}) \vdash^{\beta} \Gamma$ is either positive or negative with respect to the predicate I^A if each formula in Γ is either positive or negative.

On the other side, an infinitary calculus $(I^{<\Lambda}(\mathcal{Y}))$ is obtained from $(I^{<\Lambda})$ by adding initial sequents for the atomic diagram of $\mathcal{Y}$. Let $(I^{<\Lambda}(\mathcal{Y})) \vdash^{\alpha}_{c} \Gamma$ iff there exists a derivation of Γ in $(I^{<\Lambda}(\mathcal{Y})) + (cut)$ such that its tree-height is at most α and degree of any cut formula in it is less than c, where the degree is defined as in (5.7).

Then we see the following as in Lemma 5.12 from $\mathrm{WO}(\Lambda)$. Note that the condition $c > 0$ was needed in the case of Lemma 5.12.2, since cut formulas in $\mathcal{L}(T)$ are left.

Lemma 5.13 *1. Assume* $\widehat{ID}^{\infty}(\mathcal{Y}) \vdash^{\alpha_0} \Gamma$ *for* $\alpha_0 < \Lambda$. *Then* $(I^{<\Lambda}(\mathcal{Y})) \vdash^{2\alpha_0}_{\omega(\beta+2^{\alpha_0}+1)} \Gamma^{(\beta,\beta+2^{\alpha_0})}$ *for any* $\beta < \Lambda$.
2. Assume $(I^{<\Lambda}(\mathcal{Y})) \vdash^{\beta}_{c+\omega^a} \Gamma$. *Then* $(I^{<\Lambda}(\mathcal{Y})) \vdash^{\varphi_a(\beta)}_{c} \Gamma$.

From this lemma and the assumption we obtain for the empty sequent $\emptyset$, $(I^{<\Lambda}(\mathcal{Y})) \vdash^{\varphi_a(0)}_{0} \emptyset$ with $a = \omega^{\Lambda}$.

On the other hand we have $\mathrm{WO}(\Lambda) \to \mathrm{WO}(\omega^{\Lambda})$ in ACA_0, cf. Theorem 4.1.1. We obtain $\mathrm{WO}(\varphi\omega^{\Lambda}0)$ by $\mathrm{WOP}(\lambda X.\varphi X0)$, and from this we see that there is no cut-free derivation of $\emptyset$ in depth $\varphi_a(0)$. Therefore the tree $\mathcal{T}$ is not well-founded.

5.4.3 Simulating Jump Hierarchies by Fixed Points

Proposition 5.1 (Simultaneous inductive definition) *For any given* $A_0[X_0, X_1, n_0]$ *and* $A_1[X_0, X_1, n_1]$ *in which both* X_0 *and* X_1 *occur only positively, there exists a positive* B *such that simultaneous fixed points* P_i *for* A_i $(i < 2)$ *are definable from any fixed point* P *for* B.

$$n_0 \in P_0 \leftrightarrow A_0[P_0, P_1, n_0],\ n_1 \in P_1 \leftrightarrow A_1[P_0, P_1, n_1].$$

Proof Let B be the X-positive formula

$$B[X, m, n_0, n_1] :\Leftrightarrow \bigvee_{i<2} \left(m = i \wedge A_i[\{n_0' : X(0, n_0', 0)\}, \{n_1' : X(1, 1, n_1')\}, n_i]\right).$$

Let P be a fixed point for B. We obtain $n_0 \in P_0 \leftrightarrow (0, n_0, 0) \in P \leftrightarrow B[P, 0, n_0, 0] \leftrightarrow A_0[P_0, P_1, n_0]$ and $n_1 \in P_1 \leftrightarrow A_1[P_0, P_1, n_1]$. □

Let $\alpha < \Gamma_0$. We interprete $(\Pi^{0-}_1\text{-CA})_\alpha$ in $\text{TI}(\alpha, \mathcal{L}(\widehat{ID}_1)) + \widehat{ID}_1$ as follows, where $\text{TI}(\alpha, \mathcal{L}(\widehat{ID}_1))$ denotes the transfinite induction schema up to α, applied to any formula in the language $\mathcal{L}(\widehat{ID}_1)$: Leave H-free formulas unchanged. Consider the unary abstracts

$$V^+(X, \gamma) :\Leftrightarrow \{z : (z)_0 < \gamma \wedge z \in X\}$$
$$V^-(X, \gamma) :\Leftrightarrow \{z : (z)_0 < \gamma \rightarrow z \in X\}$$

where $(z)_i$ $(i = 0, 1)$ denote inverses of a pairing function such that $\langle (z)_0, (z)_1 \rangle = z$. Then $\neg V^{\pm}(X, \gamma) \equiv V^{\mp}(\neg X, \gamma)$. Note that $H_{<\gamma} = V^+(H, \gamma)$.

By distinguishing positive and negative occurrences of X let $J_0(x, X, Y)$ denote the formula such that X and Y occur only positively in it and

$$J_0(x, X, \neg X) \leftrightarrow J(x, X) \leftrightarrow (x \in X')$$

Put

$$J^+(x, X, Y, \gamma) :\Leftrightarrow J_0(x, V^+(X, \gamma), V^-(Y, \gamma))$$
$$J^-(x, X, Y, \gamma) :\Leftrightarrow \neg J_0(x, \neg V^-(Y, \gamma), \neg V^+(X, \gamma))$$

Note that both X and Y occur only positively in $J^{\pm}(x, X, Y, \gamma)$.

Define simultaneously fixed points P^+_α and P^-_α so that

$$\forall \gamma, x \left(P^+_\alpha(\langle \gamma, x \rangle) \leftrightarrow (\gamma \leq \alpha \rightarrow J^+(x, P^+_\alpha, P^-_\alpha, \gamma))\right)$$
$$\forall \gamma, x \left(P^-_\alpha(\langle \gamma, x \rangle) \leftrightarrow (\gamma \leq \alpha \wedge J^-(x, P^+_\alpha, P^-_\alpha, \gamma))\right) \tag{5.8}$$

For each B with the predicate H let $B^{\pm}$ denote the result of replacing the positive H by P^+_α and negative H by P^-_α. Also let B^+ denote the result of replacing all (positive and negative) occurrences of H by P^+_α.

Lemma 5.14 $(\Pi^{0-}_1\text{-CA})_\alpha \vdash B \Rightarrow \text{TI}(\alpha, \mathcal{L}(\widehat{ID}_1)) + \widehat{ID}_1 \vdash B^+$.

Proof $\text{TI}(\alpha, \mathcal{L}(\widehat{ID}_1)) + \widehat{ID}_1$ proves the transfinite induction $\text{TI}(\alpha, B^+)$ for every formula B in the language of $(\Pi^{0-}_1\text{-CA})_\alpha$. It suffices to show that

$$\text{TI}(\alpha, \mathcal{L}(\widehat{ID}_1)) + \widehat{ID}_1 \vdash \forall \gamma, x(P^+_\alpha(\langle \gamma, x \rangle) \leftrightarrow \neg P^-_\alpha(\langle \gamma, x \rangle)).$$

For $\gamma > \alpha$, $P^+_\alpha(\langle \gamma, x \rangle)$ is true and $P^-_\alpha(\langle \gamma, x \rangle)$ is false by the definition (5.8). We show

$$\gamma \leq \alpha \rightarrow \forall x \left(P^+_\alpha(\langle \gamma, x \rangle) \leftrightarrow \neg P^-_\alpha(\langle \gamma, x \rangle)\right) \tag{5.9}$$

by transfinite induction on $\gamma \leq \alpha$ applied to the formula with fixed point predicates $P^{\pm}_\alpha$. By IH we have $\forall \delta < \gamma \forall y \left(P^+_\alpha(\langle \delta, y \rangle) \leftrightarrow \neg P^-_\alpha(\langle \delta, y \rangle)\right)$. Hence for any δ and any y

$$\langle\delta, y\rangle \in V^+(P^+_\alpha, \gamma) \leftrightarrow \delta < \gamma \wedge P^+_\alpha(\langle\delta, y\rangle) \leftrightarrow \delta < \gamma \wedge \neg P^-_\alpha(\langle\delta, y\rangle) \leftrightarrow \langle\delta, y\rangle \notin V^-(P^-_\alpha, \gamma)$$

That is to say,

$$V^+(P^+_\alpha, \gamma) = \neg V^-(P^-_\alpha, \gamma)$$

By this and the definition (5.8) we have for $\gamma \le \alpha$

$$P^+_\alpha(\langle\gamma, x\rangle) \leftrightarrow J^+(x, P^+_\alpha, P^-_\alpha, \gamma) \leftrightarrow J_0(x, V^+(P^+_\alpha, \gamma), V^-(P^-_\alpha, \gamma)) \quad (5.10)$$
$$\leftrightarrow J_0(x, \neg V^-(P^-_\alpha, \gamma), \neg V^+(P^-_\alpha, \gamma)) \leftrightarrow \neg J^-(x, P^+_\alpha, P^-_\alpha, \beta) \leftrightarrow \neg P^-_\alpha(\langle\gamma, x\rangle)$$

This shows (5.9), which yields $\mathrm{TI}(\alpha, \mathcal{L}(\widehat{ID}_1)) + \widehat{ID}_1 \vdash B^\pm \leftrightarrow B^+$ for any formula B. Hence $\mathrm{TI}(\alpha, \mathcal{L}(\widehat{ID}_1)) + \widehat{ID}_1 \vdash \left(\forall\gamma \le \alpha\forall x(x \in H_\gamma \leftrightarrow J(x, H_{<\gamma}))\right)^+$. □

Let $(a| - 1) = 0$, $(a|0) = \varepsilon(a)$, the least epsilon number larger than a, and $(a|n + 1) = \varphi_{(a|n)}(0)$.

Lemma 5.15 *For* $n \ge 0$ *and* $\alpha < \Gamma_0$,

1. $(\Pi^{0-}_1\text{-CA})_{<(\alpha|n-1)} \vdash B \Rightarrow \mathrm{TI}(\alpha, \mathcal{L}(\widehat{ID}_n)) + \widehat{ID}_n \vdash B^+$.
2. $\mathrm{TI}(\alpha, \mathcal{L}(\widehat{ID}_n)) + \widehat{ID}_n \vdash \mathrm{TI}(< (\alpha|n), U)$, *where* $\mathrm{TI}(< (\alpha|n), U) = \{\mathrm{TI}(\beta, U) : \beta < (\alpha|n)\}$, *the collection of the transfinite induction* $\mathrm{TI}(\beta, U)$ *up to* β *applied to the fixed predicate* U.

Proof By simultaneous induction on n. For $n = 0$, Lemma 5.15.1 is trivial, and Lemma 5.15.2 follows from Theorem 4.1.1 with $(\alpha|0) = \varepsilon(\alpha)$.

Let $n \ge 1$. By Theorem 5.4 we have $(\Pi^{0-}_1\text{-CA})_{<(\alpha|n-1)} \vdash \mathrm{TI}(< (\alpha|n), U)$ with $(\alpha|n) = \varphi_{(\alpha|n-1)}(0) = \sup\{\varphi_\beta(0) : \beta < (\alpha|n-1)\}$. Lemma 5.15.1 for n yields $\mathrm{TI}(\alpha, \mathcal{L}(\widehat{ID}_n)) + \widehat{ID}_n \vdash \mathrm{TI}(< (\alpha|n), U)(\equiv (\mathrm{TI}(< (\alpha|n), U))^+)$, i.e., Lemma 5.15.2 for n.

Next we show Lemma 5.15.1 for $n + 1$ from Lemma 5.15.2 for n. Suppose $(\Pi^{0-}_1\text{-CA})_{<(\alpha|n)} \vdash B$. By Lemma 5.14 we obtain $\mathrm{TI}(< (\alpha|n), \mathcal{L}(\widehat{ID}_1)) + \widehat{ID}_1 \vdash B^+$, where $\mathrm{TI}(< (\alpha|n), \mathcal{L}(\widehat{ID}_1))$ is the collection of transfinite induction up to $\beta < (\alpha|n)$ applied to formulas in the language of $\widehat{ID}_1$. On the other hand we have an $\mathrm{TI}(\alpha, \mathcal{L}(\widehat{ID}_n)) + \widehat{ID}_n$-proof of $\mathrm{TI}(< (\alpha|n), U)$. By substituting formulas in the language of $\widehat{ID}_1$ for the set parameter U in the proof, we get an $\mathrm{TI}(\alpha, \mathcal{L}(\widehat{ID}_{n+1})) + \widehat{ID}_{n+1}$-proofs of $\mathrm{TI}(< (\alpha|n), \mathcal{L}(\widehat{ID}_1))$. Therefore we obtain $\mathrm{TI}(\alpha, \mathcal{L}(\widehat{ID}_{n+1})) + \widehat{ID}_{n+1} \vdash B^+$. □

Theorem 5.6 *For any arithmetical formula* $C \in \mathcal{L}(\mathsf{PA}) \cup \{U\}$, $\widehat{ID}_n \vdash C$ *iff* $(\Pi^{0-}_1\text{-CA})_{<(1|n-1)} \vdash C$, *and* $|\widehat{ID}_n| = (1|n)$ *for* $0 \le n < \omega$.

Proof Lemma 5.15.1 shows that every $(\Pi^{0-}_1\text{-CA})_{<(1|n-1)}$-provable arithmetical formula is provable in $\widehat{ID}_n$, and Lemma 5.15.2 shows $|\widehat{ID}_n| \ge (1|n)$.

Conversely assume that $\widehat{ID}_n$ proves a formula C in the language $\mathcal{L}(\mathsf{PA}) \cup \{U\}$. Then we see easily for the infinitary calculus $\widehat{ID}^\infty_n$ that $\widehat{ID}^\infty_n \vdash^{<\omega^2}_{<\omega} C$. Corollary 5.1 yields $\widehat{ID}^\infty_0 \vdash^{<(1|n)}_1 C$. Hence C has a fixed point free derivation in the ω-logic so that $\boldsymbol{G}_\omega \vdash^{<(1|n)}_0 C$. By a partial truth definition we see that C is true from transfinite induction $\mathrm{TI}(<(1|n), \Pi^1_0)$ up to an ordinal$<(1|n)$ applied to an arithmetical formula. By Theorem 5.4 we have $(\Pi^{0-}_1\text{--CA})_{<(1|n-1)} \vdash \mathrm{TI}(<(1|n), U)$. Therefore $(\Pi^{0-}_1\text{--CA})_{<(1|n-1)} \vdash C$.

When $C \equiv (\mathrm{TI}(\prec, U))$ for a recursive strict partial order $\prec$, we obtain $|\prec| < (1|n)$ by Lemma 4.6. □

Theorem 5.7 FP_0 *proves the axiom* ATR *of arithmetic transfinite recursion.*

Proof Let $\prec$ be a well ordering, and $A(x, X)$ be a first-order formula. As sbove, let $A_0(x, X, Y)$ be a positive formula with respect to X and Y such that $A_0(x, X, \neg X) \leftrightarrow A(x, X)$. As in (5.8) define simultaneously fixed points P^+ and P^- so that

$$\forall\gamma, x\left(P^+(\langle\gamma, x\rangle) \leftrightarrow A^+(x, P^+, P^-, \gamma)\right)$$
$$\forall\gamma, x\left(P^-(\langle\gamma, x\rangle) \leftrightarrow A^-(x, P^+, P^-, \gamma)\right)$$

where $V^+(X, \gamma) \Leftrightarrow \{z : (z)_0 \prec \gamma \land z \in X\}$, $V^-(X, \gamma) \Leftrightarrow \{z : (z)_0 \prec \gamma \to z \in X\}$, $A^+(x, X, Y, \gamma) :\Leftrightarrow A_0(x, V^+(X, \gamma), V^-(Y, \gamma))$ and $A^-(x, X, Y, \gamma) :\Leftrightarrow \neg A_0(x, \neg V^-(Y, \gamma), \neg V^+(X, \gamma))$.

Then we see as in Lemma 5.14 that $\forall\gamma, x(P^+(\langle\gamma, x\rangle) \leftrightarrow \neg P^-(\langle\gamma, x\rangle))$ from $\mathrm{WO}(\prec)$. This yields $\forall x, \gamma(P^+(\langle\gamma, x\rangle) \leftrightarrow A(x, (P^+)_{\prec\gamma}))$ for $(P^+)_{\prec\gamma} = V^+(P^+, \gamma)$. □

Lemma 5.16 FP_0 *is a conservative extension of* $\widehat{\mathrm{ID}}_{<\omega}$.

Proof Let $\mathsf{FP}_0(\widehat{\mathrm{ID}}_{<\omega})$ denote a join of FP_0 and $\widehat{\mathrm{ID}}_{<\omega}$. Its language obtained from the first-order language of $\widehat{\mathrm{ID}}_{<\omega}$ with a unary predicate U by adding a countable list $\{X_i\}_i$ of unary second-order variables together with second-order quantifications $\exists X, \forall X$. Its axioms are obtained from those of $\widehat{\mathrm{ID}}_{<\omega}$ in the expanded language by adding the axioms of FP_0 again in the expanded language. We show that $\mathsf{FP}_0(\widehat{\mathrm{ID}}_{<\omega}) \vdash A \Rightarrow \widehat{\mathrm{ID}}_{<\omega} \vdash A$ for any first-order A, i.e., any formula A in the language of $\widehat{\mathrm{ID}}_{<\omega}$.

Let us formulate $\mathsf{FP}_0(\widehat{\mathrm{ID}}_{<\omega})$ in the predicative second-order logic $\boldsymbol{G}_2$ in Sect. 2.1.3 with unary variables. Complete induction schema for first-order formulas A is replaced by the inference rule.

$$\frac{\Gamma, A(0) \quad \neg A(x), \Gamma, A(S(x)) \quad \neg A(t), \Gamma}{\Gamma}\ (VJ)$$

and for the axiom FP introduce the following inference rule.

$$\frac{\neg\forall x(x \in Y \leftrightarrow A(x, Y, V)), \Gamma}{\Gamma}\ (FP) \tag{5.11}$$

where V is a unary abstract $\{y\}F(y, x)$ with a first-order F, in which Y does not occur, and the eigenvariable Y occurs only positively in a first-order $A(x, Y, X)$, but not in Γ. The arithmetical comprehension axiom is replaced by the inference rule $(\exists^2_{1st})$

$$\frac{\Gamma, B(V)}{\Gamma, \exists X\, B(X)}\ (\exists^2_{1st})$$

for a first-order abstract $V \equiv (\{x\}F(x))$.

Now suppose $\mathsf{FP}_0(\widehat{\mathrm{ID}}_{<\omega}) \vdash A$ for first-order A. Then there exists a cut-free proof of $\Delta = \Delta_0 \cup \{A\}$ in the calculus defined above, where Δ_0 denotes a finite set of negations of axioms $\widehat{\mathrm{ID}}_{<\omega}$, cf. Theorem 2.2. Since Δ is first-order, each sequent occurring in the cut-free proof is also first-order. In other words, no inference rules $(\exists^2_{1st})$, $(\forall)^2$ for second-order quantifications occur in it. In the sequent Δ, no second-order variables except the parameter U occurs.

Consider one of the lowest inference (5.11), (FP). Let $A'(x, Y) \equiv A(x, Y, V)$ in which Y occurs only positively and no second-order variables except Y and U occurs. Substitute the predicate constant $I^{A'}$ for the eigenvariable Y. We obtain a proof of $\neg\forall x(x \in I^{A'} \leftrightarrow A'(x, I^{A'})(\leftrightarrow A(x, I^{A'}, V))), \Gamma$, where $\forall x(x \in I^{A'} \leftrightarrow A'(x, I^{A'}))$ is an axiom in $\widehat{\mathrm{ID}}_{<\omega}$. Iterating this substitutions from below to above we obtain a proof of Δ in $\widehat{\mathrm{ID}}_{<\omega}$. □

Theorem 5.8 *Over* ACA_0, *the equivalence* $\mathsf{ATR}_0 \leftrightarrow \mathsf{FP}_0 \leftrightarrow \mathrm{WOP}(\lambda X.\varphi X0)_0$ *holds.* $|\mathsf{ATR}_0| = |\mathsf{FP}_0| = |\mathrm{WOP}(\lambda X.\varphi X0)_0| = \Gamma_0$, *and these theories are conservative extensions of* $\mathsf{PA} + \mathrm{TI}(< \Gamma_0)$.

Proof $\mathsf{ATR}_0 = \mathsf{FP}_0 = \mathrm{WOP}(\lambda X.\varphi X0)_0$ follows from Theorems 5.2, 5.5 and 5.7. Theorem 5.6 with Lemma 5.16 yields $|\mathsf{FP}_0| = \Gamma_0$, and we see from Theorem 5.4 that FP_0 is a conservative extension of $\mathsf{PA} + \mathrm{TI}(< \Gamma_0)$. □

From Theorems 5.8 and 4.1 we see for example the following.

Corollary 5.2 *1. For* Σ^0_2*-definable functions* f *on* $\mathbb{N}$, $f \in Fnc_{\Sigma_2}(\mathsf{ATR}_0)$ *iff* $f \in \mathscr{LR}^{<\Gamma_0}$.
2. For computable total function f *on* $\mathbb{N}$, $f \in Fnc_{\Sigma_1}(\mathsf{ATR}_0)$ *iff* $f \in \mathscr{R}^{<\Gamma_0}$.

5.5 Proof-Theoretic Strengths of the Well-Ordering Principles

In the next Chap. 6 ordinal analyses are given for some impredicative theories such as the theory ID for positive inductive definitions over $\mathbb{N}$ and the SOA $(\Pi^1_1\text{-CA})_0$. In the analysis finite proofs are embedded to infinitary proofs in uncountable depths, and after a partial cut-elimination, a *collapsing* procedure is carried through to get countable proofs from uncountable ones. Then a boundedness theorem is obtained to bound witnesses for unbounded existential quantifiers. Actually, these two (collapsing and boundedness) are tied each other.

However a variety of impredicative theories are found whose proof-theoretic analysis is obtained similarly for predicative theories. Such theories are called *metapredicative*. Here a theory is to be impredicative if its proof-theoretic ordinal is larger than the Feferman–Scütte ordinal Γ_0, and a proof-theoretic analysis for metapredicative theories is obtained through a straightforward extension of proof theory for predicative theories. In doing it, methods for impredicative theories such as collapsings are dispensable.

In this section as a sample example of metapredicative theories, we analyze an SOA ATR_0^+, which we are going to introduce.

Definition 5.13 A *countable coded ω-model* of an SOA T is a set $Q \subset \mathbb{N}$ such that $M(Q) \models T$, where $M(Q) = \langle \mathbb{N}, \{(Q)_n\}_{n\in\mathbb{N}}, +, \cdot, 0, 1, < \rangle$ with $(Q)_n = \{m \in \mathbb{N} : \langle n, m \rangle \in Q\}$.

Let $X \in_\omega Y :\Leftrightarrow (\exists n[X = (Y)_n])$ and $X =_\omega Y :\Leftrightarrow (\forall Z(Z \in_\omega X \leftrightarrow Z \in_\omega Y))$.

Definition 5.14 T^+ denotes the extension of an SOA T by the axiom stating that

$$\text{`there exists an arbitrarily large countable coded } \omega\text{-model of } \mathsf{ACA}_0 + T' \quad (5.12)$$

Namely for any set X there exists a countable coded ω-model Y of $\mathsf{ACA}_0 + T$ such that $X \in_\omega Y$.

Note that when T is axiomatized by a Π^1_2-sentence over RCA_0, T^+ is axiomatized by the Π^1_2-sentence (5.12) over RCA_0.

We first show that ATR_0^+ is equivalent to a well-ordering principle.

Theorem 5.9 *The following two are mutually equivalent over* ACA_0*:*

1. $\mathrm{WOP}(\lambda X.\Gamma_X)$.
2. $(\mathrm{WOP}(\lambda X.\varphi_X(0)))^+ :\Leftrightarrow \forall X \exists Y[X \in_\omega Y \wedge M(Y) \models \mathsf{ACA}_0 + \mathrm{WOP}(\lambda X.\varphi_X(0))]$.
   Namely there exists an arbitrarily large countable coded ω-model of $\mathsf{ACA}_0 + \mathrm{WOP}(\lambda X.\varphi_X(0))$.

We obtain the following Corollary 5.3 by Theorems 5.8 and 5.9.

Corollary 5.3 *Over* ACA_0*, the following equivalences hold:*
$\mathrm{WOP}(\lambda X.\Gamma_X) \leftrightarrow (\mathrm{WOP}(\lambda X.\varphi_X(0)))^+ \leftrightarrow \mathsf{ATR}_0^+$.

Next the SOA $\mathrm{WOP}(\lambda X.\Gamma_X)$ is analyzed proof-theoretically.

Theorem 5.10 *The proof-theoretic ordinal of the SOA's* $\mathrm{WOP}(\lambda X.\Gamma_X)$, $(\mathrm{WOP}(\lambda X.\varphi_X(0)))^+$*, and* ATR_0^+ *is equal to the least fixed point of the Γ-function.*
$|\mathrm{WOP}(\lambda X.\Gamma_X)| = |\,(\mathrm{WOP}(\lambda X.\varphi_X(0)))^+\,| = |\mathsf{ATR}_0^+| = \min\{\alpha : \Gamma_\alpha = \alpha\}$.

Before proving these theorems we need first introduce the Γ-order over a given order. In Definition 5.4 a linear order $<_2$ (Veblen order) is introduced over a linear order $<_0$ on ω. The order type of $<_2$ is $\varphi_\alpha(0)$ when $<_0$ is a well-ordering of type α. Here we need to extend $<_2$ to an order $<_3$ whose order type is Γ_α when $<_0$ is a well-ordering of type α. Small Greek letters $\alpha, \beta, \gamma, \ldots$ range over elements in the field of the relation $<_3$, while $u, v, w, \ldots$ range over elements in the field of $<_0$.

Definition 5.15 (*Γ-order over* $<_0$) Let $<_0$ be a linear order with its field $fld(<_0) = \{n : \exists m(n <_0 m \vee m <_0 n)\}$. Let $\varphi\alpha\beta := \langle 0, \langle\alpha, \beta\rangle\rangle$, $\alpha_1 + \cdots + \alpha_n := \langle 1, \langle\alpha_1, \ldots, \alpha_n\rangle\rangle$, and $\Gamma_\alpha := \langle 2, \alpha\rangle$. The field $fld(<_3)$ of the relation $<_3$, its subsets P, SC and the relation $<_3$ are simultaneously defined as follow.

1. $0 \in fld(<_3)$, and $0 <_3 \alpha$ for any $\alpha \neq 0$ in $fld(<_3)$.
2. If $\alpha_1, \ldots, \alpha_n \in P$ with $n > 1$, and $\alpha_n \leq_3 \cdots \leq_3 \alpha_n$, then $\alpha_1 + \cdots + \alpha_n \in fld(<_2)$.
   For $\alpha_1 + \cdots + \alpha_n, \beta_1 + \cdots + \beta_m \in fld(<_3)$ with $\alpha_i, \beta_j \in P$ and $n + m > 2$, $\alpha_1 + \cdots + \alpha_n <_3 \beta_1 + \cdots + \beta_m$ iff either $\exists i \leq \min\{n, m\}[\alpha_i <_3 \beta_i \wedge \forall j < i(\alpha_i = \beta_i)]$ or $n < m \wedge \forall i < n(\alpha_i = \beta_i)$.
3. Let $\alpha, \beta \in fld(<_3)$, $\neg\exists\delta(\beta = \varphi\gamma\delta)$ with $\alpha <_3 \gamma$ and $\{\alpha, \beta\} \cap SC = \emptyset$. Then $\varphi\alpha\beta \in P \subset fld(<_3)$.
   For $\varphi\alpha_0\beta_0, \varphi\alpha_1\beta_1 \in fld(<_3)$, $\varphi\alpha_0\beta_0 <_3 \varphi\alpha_1\beta_1$ iff $\alpha_0 <_3 \alpha_1 \wedge \beta_0 <_3 \varphi\alpha_1\beta_1$ or $\alpha_0 = \alpha_1 \wedge \beta_0 <_3 \beta_1$ or $\alpha_1 <_3 \alpha_0 \wedge \varphi\alpha_0\beta_0 <_3 \beta_1$.
4. Let $u \in fld(<_0)$. Then $\Gamma_u \in SC \subset fld(<_3)$.
   For $\Gamma_u, \Gamma_v, \varphi\alpha\beta \in fld(<_3)$, $\Gamma_u <_3 \Gamma_v$ iff $u <_0 v$. $\varphi\alpha\beta <_3 \Gamma_u$ iff $\alpha, \beta <_3 \Gamma_u$. $\Gamma_u <_3 \varphi\alpha\beta$ iff $\Gamma_u <_3 \alpha$ or $\Gamma_u <_3 \beta$.

When $<_0$ is given by a set X as $n <_0 m \leftrightarrow \langle n, m\rangle \in X$, we write $n <_X m$ for $n <_0 m$, $n <_{\Gamma_X} m$ for $n <_3 m$, and Γ_X for $fld(<_3)$.

It is clear that when $<_0$ is a linear order, then so is $<_3$. Also it is easy to see that $(fld(<_3), <_3)$ is elementary recursive in $(fld(<_0), <_0)$.

5.5.1 *Derivative and Countable Coded ω-Models*

In this subsection we show Theorem 5.9, and we write $\mathsf{g}(\alpha)$ for $\varphi_\alpha(0)$, and $\mathsf{g}'(\alpha)$ for Γ_α.

First let us show the easy half 2⇒1. Suppose $(\text{WOP}(\lambda X.\varphi_X(0)))^+$. We need to show $\text{WOP}(\lambda X.\Gamma_X)$. Argue in ACA_0.

Let sets X, U be given such that $\text{WO}(<_0)$ for $<_0 = <_X$. We have $\text{LO}(<_{\mathsf{g}'(X)})$. Pick a countable coded ω-model M of $\mathsf{ACA}_0 + \text{WOP}(\mathsf{g})$ such that $X, U \in M$. Then $\mathsf{g}(X), \mathsf{g}'(X) \in M$. Let $<_{top}$ be obtained from $<_0$ by adding the largest element α. This means that $a <_{top} \alpha$ for any a in the field of $<_0$. We have $\text{WO}(<_{top})$ by $\text{WO}(<_0)$. We show $Prg[<_{top}, C(a)]$ for an arithmetical formula

$$C(a) :\Leftrightarrow M \models \forall Y \left(Prg[<_3, Y] \rightarrow \forall x <_3 \mathsf{g}'(a)\, Y(x)\right)$$

for $<_3 = <_{\mathsf{g}'(<_{top})}$, i.e., $<_3$ is the Γ-order over $<_{top}$ in Definition 5.15. This yields $C(\alpha)$. Since $x <_3 \mathsf{g}'(\alpha)$ for any x in the field of $<_{\mathsf{g}'(X)} = <_{\mathsf{g}'(<_0)}$, we obtain $M \models \forall Y \left(Prg[<_{\mathsf{g}'(X)}, Y] \rightarrow \forall x \in \text{fld}(\mathsf{g}'(X))\, Y(x)\right)$. Hence we obtain $M \models \left(Prg[<_{\mathsf{g}'(X)}, U] \rightarrow \forall x \in \text{fld}(\mathsf{g}'(X))\, U(x)\right)$, i.e., $\text{TI}(<_{\mathsf{g}'(X)}, U)$. Since U is an arbitrary set, we conclude $\text{WO}(<_{\mathsf{g}'(X)})$.

It remains to show that $Prg[<_{top}, C(a)]$. When a is a limit element, this follows from the continuity of the function $\mathsf{g}'(a) = \Gamma_a$. Assuming $C(a)$, let us show $C(a+1)$. Argue in the model M. Suppose $Prg[<_3, Y]$ and $x <_3 \mathsf{g}'(a+1) = \Gamma_{a+1} = \sup_n \mathsf{g}^n(\mathsf{g}'(a)+1)$, where $\mathsf{g}^0(\mathsf{g}'(a)+1) = \Gamma_a + 1$ and $\mathsf{g}^{n+1}(\mathsf{g}'(a)+1) = \varphi_{\mathsf{g}^n(\mathsf{g}'(a)+1)}(0)$. By induction on $n < \omega$ we see that $\forall x <_3 \mathsf{g}^n(\mathsf{g}'(a)+1)\, Y(x)$ using $\mathrm{WOP}(\mathsf{g})$ and $C(a)$, i.e., $\mathrm{WO}(<_3\restriction (\mathsf{g}'(a)+1))$. Hence we obtain $C(a+1)$. $C(0)$ is seen similarly.

Conversely assume $\mathrm{WOP}(\mathsf{g}')$. We need to find a countable coded ω-model of $\mathsf{ACA}_0 + \mathrm{WOP}(\mathsf{g})$. The idea is to search a derivation of the negation of $\mathrm{WOP}(\mathsf{g})$ in ω-logic as in the proof of Theorem 5.5. Construct a locally correct ω-branching tree in a canonical way. If the search results in a fail, i.e., if the constructed tree is not well-founded, then we can find a countable coded ω-model of $\mathsf{ACA}_0 + \mathrm{WOP}(\mathsf{g})$ from an infinite path through the tree. Otherwise the tree is well-founded, i.e., a derivation in a depth α. It turns out that the derivation can be converted to a cut-free deduction with the empty sequent at its root, and in depth bounded by $\mathsf{g}'(\alpha) = \Gamma_\alpha$. Then by our assumption $\mathrm{WOP}(\mathsf{g}')$, the deduction is well-founded, i.e., a derivation of the empty sequent. We see that this is not the case by transfinite induction up to $\mathsf{g}'(\alpha)$. This shows the consistency of $\mathsf{ACA}_0 + \mathrm{WOP}(\mathsf{g})$ in ω-logic based on $\mathrm{WOP}(\mathsf{g}')$.

5.5.1.1 Epsilon Function and the ωth Jump

Before proving Theorem 5.9, let us show an easier case for illustration. Moreover it is convenient for us to have the simplest case in hand.

Theorem 5.11 *The following two are mutually equivalent over* ACA_0*:*

1. $\mathrm{WOP}(\lambda X.\varepsilon_X)$.
2. ACA_0^+.

Assuming ACA_0^+, we see $\mathrm{WOP}(\lambda X.\varepsilon_X)$ as for $\mathrm{WOP}(\lambda X.\Gamma_X)$ using the facts $\varepsilon_{a+1} = \sup_n \omega_n(\varepsilon_a + 1)$ and $\mathrm{WOP}(\lambda X.\omega^X)$, which follows from ACA_0, cf. Claim 4.1.

Definition 5.16 Let $\mathcal{Q} \subset \mathbb{N}$ be a subset of $\mathbb{N}$. Let

$$\mathrm{D}_{\mathcal{Q}}(i,n) = \begin{cases} X_i(n) & \text{if } n \in (\mathcal{Q})_i \\ \bar{X}_i(n) & \text{if } n \notin (\mathcal{Q})_i \end{cases} \tag{5.13}$$

and $\mathrm{Diag}(\mathcal{Q}) = \{\mathrm{D}_{\mathcal{Q}}(i,n) : i, n \in \mathbb{N}\}$.

Assuming $\mathrm{WOP}(\lambda X.\varepsilon_X)$, we need to show the existence of a countable coded ω-model $\mathcal{Q}$ of ACA_0 for a given set $(\mathcal{Q})_0 \subset \mathbb{N}$.

Let us search a proof of the contradiction $\emptyset$ in the following calculus $\boldsymbol{G}_{0\omega}((\mathcal{Q})_0) + (ACA)$. Let $X_i, \bar{X}_i$ be a countable list of variables X_i and its complement $\bar{X}_i$. The first variable X_0 is one for the set $(\mathcal{Q})_0$. A *true literal* is either an arithmetic literal true in $\mathbb{N}$ or a literal $D_{\mathcal{Q}}(0, n)$ for the atomic diagram of the set $(\mathcal{Q})_0$ as in (5.13). Note that only the variable X_0 is interpreted.

Axioms in $\mathbf{G}_{0\omega}((\mathcal{Q})_0) + (ACA)$ are

$$\Gamma, \bar{X}_i(n), X_i(n)$$

and

$$\Gamma, L$$

for true literals L.

Inference rules in $\mathbf{G}_{0\omega}((\mathcal{Q})_0) + (ACA)$ are obtained from those of the infinitary propositional calculus $\mathbf{G}_{0\omega}$ in Sect. 3.1.3 by adding the following inference (ACA):

$$\frac{X_j \neq A, \Gamma}{\Gamma}\ (ACA)$$

where A is a first-order formula, X_j is the eigenvariable not occurring freely in $\Gamma \cup \{A\}$, and $X_j \neq A :\Leftrightarrow \neg\forall x[X_j(x) \leftrightarrow A(x)]$.

A tree $\mathcal{T} \subset {}^{<\omega}\mathbb{N}$ is constructed recursively as follows. At the empty sequence, we put the empty sequent. Suppose that the tree $\mathcal{T}$ has been constructed up to a node $a \in {}^{<\omega}\mathbb{N}$. Let $\{A_i\}_i$ be an enumeration of all first-order formulas (abstracts).

Case 0. $lh(a) = 2i$: Apply one of inferences $(\bigvee)$, $(\bigwedge)$ if it is possible. Otherwise repeat, i.e., apply an inference (Rep).

Case 1. $lh(a) = 2i + 1$: Apply the inference (ACA) backwards with the first-order $A \equiv A_i$.

If the tree $\mathcal{T}$ is not well-founded, then let $\mathcal{P}$ be an infinite path through $\mathcal{T}$. We see for any i, n that at most one of $X_{1+i}(n)$ or $\bar{X}_{1+i}(n)$ is on $\mathcal{P}$, and $[(\bar{X}_0(n)) \in \mathcal{P} \Rightarrow n \in (\mathcal{Q})_0]$ & $[(X_0(n)) \in \mathcal{P} \Rightarrow n \notin (\mathcal{Q})_0]$ due to the axioms Γ, $D_{\mathcal{Q}}(0, n)$. Let $(\mathcal{Q})_{1+i}$ be the set defined by $(\bar{X}_{1+i}(n)) \in \mathcal{P} \Leftrightarrow n \in (\mathcal{Q})_{1+i}$.

$\mathcal{Q}$ is shown to be a countable coded ω-model of ACA_0 as follows. The search procedure is fair, i.e., each formula is eventually analyzed on every path. To ensure fairness, formulas in sequents Γ are assumed to stand in a queue. The head of the queue is analyzed in **Case 0**, and the analyzed formula moves to the end of the queue in the next stage. We see from the fairness that $\mathrm{Diag}(\mathcal{Q}) \not\models A$ by induction on the number of occurrences of logical connectives in formulas A on the path $\mathcal{P}$, cf. Sects. 2.1.3 and 3.1.2. Moreover $\mathrm{Diag}(\mathcal{Q}) \models \mathsf{ACA}_0$ since the inference rules (ACA) are analyzed for every A_i.

In what follows assume that the tree $\mathcal{T}$ is well-founded. Since we are working in ACA_0, we know that the Kleene-Brouwer ordering $<_{KB}$ on $\mathcal{T}$ is a well-ordering, cf. Proposition 1.10. Let $\Lambda = otp(<_{KB})$ denote the order type of the Kleene-Brouwer ordering $<_{KB}$. We have $\mathrm{WO}(\varepsilon_{\omega+\Lambda})$ by $\mathrm{WOP}(\lambda X.\varepsilon_X)$ and $\mathrm{WO}(\omega + \Lambda)$.

For $b < \Lambda$ let us write $\vdash^b \Gamma$ when there exists a derivation of Γ in $\mathbf{G}_{0\omega}((\mathcal{Q})_0) + (ACA)$ whose depth is bounded by b. The inferences (ACA) are replaced by cut inferences:

$$\dfrac{\begin{array}{c}\vdots\\ X_j \neq A, \Gamma\end{array}}{\Gamma}\,(ACA) \leadsto \dfrac{\begin{array}{c}\vdots\, \pi_A \\ A = A\end{array} \quad \begin{array}{c}\vdots\, X_j := A \\ A \neq A, \Gamma\end{array}}{\Gamma}\,(cut)$$

where in the right, π_A denotes a canonical cut-free derivation of the tautology $A = A$, the first-order formula A is substituted for the eigenvariable X_j, and append the derivations of $\neg A(n), A(n), \Delta'$ at the top $\neg X_j(n), X_j(n), \Delta$. Thus we obtain $\boldsymbol{G}_{0\omega}((\mathcal{Q})_0) \vdash^{\omega+b}_{\omega} \emptyset$, where subscripts ω indicates that in the witnessing derivation, cut inferences occur with first-order formulas. Then by Predicative cut-elimination Theorems 5.3 and 3.6 we obtain $\boldsymbol{G}_{0\omega}((\mathcal{Q})_0) \vdash^{\varepsilon_{\omega+b}}_{0} \emptyset$, but we see that this is not the case by $\mathrm{WO}(\varepsilon_{\omega+b})$ for $\varepsilon_{\omega+b} < \varepsilon_{\omega+\Lambda}$. Therefore the tree $\mathcal{T}$ is not well-founded. Thus Theorem 5.11 is proved.

5.5.2 Elimination of the Inference for Well-Ordering Principle

Now let us prove Theorem 5.9. Each first-order formula A defines a binary relation $n <_A m :\Leftrightarrow A(\langle n, m\rangle)$. Let $n <_{\mathsf{g}_A} m :\Leftrightarrow \mathsf{g}(A)(\langle n, m\rangle)$. Let us add a countable list $\{E_i\}_i$ of second-order (unary) variables. Each variable E_i is used solely for the inference rules of the well-foundedness of the relation $<_A$, where $i = \ulcorner A \urcorner$ is the Gödel number of the first-order formula A. We write E_A for E_i with $i = \ulcorner A \urcorner$. For a finite set Γ of first-order formulas, $Var(\Gamma) = \bigcup\{Var(A) : A \in \Gamma\}$ denotes the set of second-order variables E_i occurring in a formula A in Γ.

Let us search a proof of the contradiction $\emptyset$ in the calculus $\boldsymbol{G}_{0\omega}((\mathcal{Q})_0) + (prg)^\infty + (WP)^\infty + (ACA)$, which is obtained from the calculus $\boldsymbol{G}_{0\omega}((\mathcal{Q})_0) + (ACA)$ in the expanded language by adding the following inference rules $(prg)^\infty$, $(WP)^\infty$, and $(\exists^2_{1st})$ for each first-order formula A, $E_A \equiv E_i$ with the Gödel number $i = \ulcorner A \urcorner$, ordinals $\beta_0 < \beta$ and $\alpha_0 < \alpha$:

$$\frac{\{\vdash^{\beta_0}_{\alpha} \Gamma, E_A(m), n \not<^*_A m, E_A(n) : n \in \mathbb{N}\}}{\vdash^{\beta}_{\alpha} \Gamma, E_A(m)}\,(prg)^\infty$$

where $<^*_A$ denotes the transitive closure of the relation $<_A$ and $Var(A) \subset Var(\Gamma)$.

$$\frac{\{\vdash^{\beta_0}_{\alpha_0} \Gamma, E_A(n) : n \in \mathbb{N}\} \quad \vdash^{\beta_0}_{\alpha_0} \Gamma, \mathrm{LO}(<_A) \quad \vdash^{\beta_0}_{\alpha_0} \neg\mathrm{TI}[<_{\mathsf{g}_A}], \Gamma}{\vdash^{\beta}_{\alpha} \Gamma}\,(WP)^\infty$$

where the variable E_A does not occur in Γ, and $\mathrm{TI}[<] :\Leftrightarrow \forall Y\, \mathrm{TI}[<, Y]$.

The inference rule $(\exists^2_{1st})$ is the same as for the predicative second-order logic $\boldsymbol{G}_2$ in Sect. 2.1.3. For $\gamma < \beta$ we have

$$\frac{\vdash^{\gamma}_{\alpha} F(A), \exists X F(X), \Gamma}{\vdash^{\beta}_{\alpha} \exists X F(X), \Gamma} \; (\exists^2_{1st})$$

Definition 5.17 Let π be a tree of sequents, which is locally correct with respect to axioms and inference rules in $\mathbf{G}_{0\omega}((\mathscr{Q})_0) + (prg)^{\infty} + (WP)^{\infty} + (ACA)$, and $T(\pi) \subset {}^{<\omega}\mathbb{N}$ the underlying tree of π. The tree $T(\pi)$ need not to be well-founded. Let us assign recursively a family $\mathscr{E}^X(\sigma) = \mathscr{E}^X(\sigma; \pi)$ of *finite* sets $\mathscr{E}^X_i(\sigma)$ of natural numbers to each node $\sigma \in T(\pi)$ in a bottom-up way as follows. $n \in \mathscr{E}^X_i(\sigma)$ iff the positive literal $E_i(n)$ in the sequent at the node σ is traceable either to a minor formula of one of $(WP)^{\infty}$, $(prg)^{\infty}$ or to a formula in the end-sequent.

In the definition, $\mathscr{E}^X(\sigma) \vdash \Gamma$ designates that $\mathscr{E}^X(\sigma)$ is assigned to the node σ at which the sequent Γ is placed. In this case we write $\sigma : \Gamma$.

To the bottom sequent $\emptyset : \Gamma_0$, assign the set $\mathscr{E}^X_i(\emptyset) = \{n : E_i(n) \in \Gamma_0\}$.

Suppose that finite sets $(\mathscr{E}^X_j(\sigma))_{j \neq i}$ are assigned to the lower sequent $\sigma : \Gamma$ of a rule $(WP)^{\infty}$ for the relation $<_A$ with $i = \ulcorner A \urcorner$. For the nth left upper sequents $\sigma * (n) : \Gamma, E_A(n)$, assign the family $((\mathscr{E}^X_j(\sigma))_{j \neq i}, \{n\})$ with $\mathscr{E}^X_i(\sigma * (n)) = \{n\}$. For the middle and the right upper sequents $\sigma * (\omega) : \Gamma, \mathrm{LO}(<_A)$ and $\sigma * (\omega + 1) : \neg \mathrm{TI}[<_{\mathsf{g}_A}], \Gamma$, assign the family $(\mathscr{E}^X_j(\sigma))_{j \neq i}$.

$$\frac{\{((\mathscr{E}^X_j(\sigma))_{j \neq i}, \{n\}) \vdash \Gamma, E_A(n) : n \in \mathbb{N}\} \quad (\mathscr{E}^X_j(\sigma))_{j \neq i} \vdash \Gamma, \mathrm{LO}(<_A) \quad (\mathscr{E}^X_j(\sigma))_{j \neq i} \vdash \neg \mathrm{TI}[<_{\mathsf{g}_A}], \Gamma}{(\mathscr{E}^X_j(\sigma))_{j \neq i} \vdash \Gamma} \; (WP)^{\infty}$$

where the variable E_A with $i = \ulcorner A \urcorner$ does not occur in Γ.

Next suppose that a family $((\mathscr{E}^X_j(\sigma))_{j \neq i}, \mathscr{E}^X_i(\sigma))$ $(i = \ulcorner A \urcorner)$ is assigned to the lower sequent $\sigma : \Gamma, E_A(m)$ of the rule $(prg)^{\infty}$. For each number n, assign the family $((\mathscr{E}^X_j(\sigma))_{j \neq i}, \mathscr{E}^X_i(\sigma) \cup \{n\})$ to the nth upper sequent $\sigma * (n) : \Gamma, E_A(m), n \not<^*_A m, E_A(n)$ with $\mathscr{E}^X_i(\sigma * (n)) = \mathscr{E}^X_i(\sigma) \cup \{n\}$.

$$\frac{\{((\mathscr{E}^X_j(\sigma))_{j \neq i}, \mathscr{E}^X_i(\sigma) \cup \{n\}) \vdash \Gamma, E_A(m), n \not<^*_A m, E_A(n) : n \in \mathbb{N}\}}{((\mathscr{E}^X_j(\sigma))_{j \neq i}, \mathscr{E}^X_i(\sigma)) \vdash \Gamma, E_A(m)} \; (prg)^{\infty}$$

where $E_A \equiv E_i$ with the Gödel number $i = \ulcorner A \urcorner$ of the formula A.

For rules other than $(WP)^{\infty}$, $(prg)^{\infty}$, the upper sequents receive the same family as the lower sequent receives. For example

$$\frac{\mathscr{E}^X(\sigma) \vdash F(A), \exists X F(X), \Gamma}{\mathscr{E}^X(\sigma) \vdash \exists X F(X), \Gamma} \; (\exists^2_{1st}) \qquad \frac{\mathscr{E}^X(\sigma) \vdash X_j \neq A, \Gamma}{\mathscr{E}^X(\sigma) \vdash \Gamma} \; (ACA)$$

A family $\mathscr{E}^X(\sigma)$ has been assigned to each node $\sigma \in T(\pi)$ in the tree.

A tree $\mathscr{T} \subset {}^{<\omega}\mathbb{N}$ is constructed recursively as follows. At each node σ, a sequent and a family $\mathscr{E}^X(\sigma)$ of finite sets are assigned. At the empty sequence, we put the empty sequent. Suppose that the tree $\mathscr{T}$ has been constructed up to a node $\sigma \in {}^{<\omega}\mathbb{N}$. Let $\{A_i\}_i$ be an enumeration of all first-order formulas (abstracts).

Case 0. $lh(\sigma) = 3i$: Apply one of inferences $(\bigvee)$, $(\bigwedge)$, $(\exists^2_{1st})$ and $(prg)^\infty$ if it is possible. Otherwise repeat, i.e., apply an inference (Rep).

When $(\exists^2_{1st})$ is applied backwards, the first-order $A \equiv A_j$ is chosen so that j is the least such that A_j has not yet been tested for the major formula $\exists X\, F(X)$ of the $(\exists^2_{1st})$, and $Var(A_j) \subset Var(\Gamma)$ with the lower sequent Γ.

When $(prg)^\infty$ is applied backwards to a main formula $E_A(m)$ with $j = \lceil A \rceil$, $Var(A) \subset Var(\Gamma)$ and the condition

$$m \in \mathscr{E}^X_j(\sigma) \tag{5.14}$$

have to be met.

Case 1. $lh(\sigma) = 3\langle i, n\rangle + 1$: Apply the inference (ACA) backwards with the first-order $A \equiv A_i$ and an eigenvariable Y_j if $Var(A) \subset Var(\Gamma)$, where j is the least number such that Y_j does not occur in $\Gamma \cup \{A\}$.

$$\frac{Y_j \neq A, \Gamma}{\Gamma}\ (ACA)$$

Otherwise repeat

Case 2. $lh(\sigma) = 3i + 2$: Apply the inference $(WP)^\infty$ backwards with the relation $<_A$ for $i = \lceil A \rceil$.

If the tree $\mathscr{T}$ is not well-founded, then let $\mathscr{P}$ be an infinite path through $\mathscr{T}$. As in Theorem 5.11 an infinite path yields a countable coded ω-model of ACA_0 as follows. $(\mathscr{Q})_0$ is the given set of natural numbers. Define $n \in (\mathscr{Q})_{2i+1} \Leftrightarrow (E_i(n)) \notin \mathscr{P}$ and $n \in (\mathscr{Q})_{2(1+i)} \Leftrightarrow (X_i(n)) \notin \mathscr{P}$. We show $\mathrm{Diag}(\mathscr{Q}) \models \mathrm{WOP}(\mathsf{g})$. Assume that $\mathrm{Diag}(\mathscr{Q}) \models \mathrm{WO}(<_A)$ for a first-order A. Let $n <^{*,\mathscr{Q}}_A m :\Leftrightarrow \mathrm{Diag}(\mathscr{Q}) \models n <^*_A m$.

The path $\mathscr{P}$ passes through an inference $(WP)^\infty$ for the relation $<_A$. If $\mathscr{P}$ passes through the rightmost upper sequent of $\neg\mathrm{TI}[<_{\mathsf{g}_A}]$, then $\mathrm{Diag}(\mathscr{Q}) \not\models \neg\mathrm{TI}[<_{\mathsf{g}_A}]$. This means that $\mathrm{Diag}(\mathscr{Q}) \not\models \neg\mathrm{TI}[<_{\mathsf{g}_A}, B]$ for any first-order B. We obtain $\mathrm{Diag}(\mathscr{Q}) \models \mathrm{TI}[<_{\mathsf{g}_A}]$, and we are done.

$\mathscr{P}$ does not pass through the middle upper sequent of $\mathrm{LO}(<_A)$ since we are assuming that $\mathrm{Diag}(\mathscr{Q}) \models \mathrm{LO}(<_A)$.

Suppose that $\mathscr{P}$ passes through an n_0th upper sequent $((\mathscr{E}^X_j(\sigma_0))_{j\neq i}, \mathscr{E}^X_i(\sigma_0)) \vdash \Gamma_0, E_A(n_0)$ and $E_A = E_i$ with $i = \lceil A \rceil$. Since the condition (5.14), $n_0 \in \mathscr{E}^X_i(\sigma_0) = \{n_0\}$ is met, the formula $E_A(n_0)$ is analyzed after a number of steps at a $(prg)^\infty$, and $\mathscr{P}$ passes through an n_1th branch $((\mathscr{E}^X_j(\sigma_1))_{j\neq i}, \mathscr{E}^X_i(\sigma_1)) \vdash \Gamma_1, n_1 \not<^*_A n_0, E_A(n_1), E_A(n_0)$.

We obtain $\mathrm{Diag}(\mathscr{Q}) \not\models n_1 \not<^*_A n_0$, i.e., $n_1 <^{*,\mathscr{Q}}_A n_0$. Also $\{n_0, n_1\} \subset \mathscr{E}^X_i(\sigma_1)$. In this way we obtain an infinite descending chain $\cdots <^{*,\mathscr{Q}}_A n_2 <^{*,\mathscr{Q}}_A n_1 <^{*,\mathscr{Q}}_A n_0$ from $\mathscr{P}$, contradicting the assumption $\mathrm{WO}(<^{\mathscr{Q}}_A)$.

In what follows assume that the tree $\mathcal{T}$ is well-founded. Let $\Lambda = otp(<_{KB})$ denote the order type of the Kleene-Brouwer ordering $<_{KB}$. We have $\mathrm{WO}(\mathsf{g}'(\Lambda))$, i.e., $\mathrm{WO}(\Gamma_\Lambda)$ by $\mathrm{WOP}(\mathsf{g}')$ and $\mathrm{WO}(\Lambda)$.

For $b < \Lambda$ let us write $\vdash^b_c \Gamma$ when there exists a derivation of Γ in $\mathbf{G}_{0\omega}((\mathcal{Q})_0) + (prg)^\infty + (WP)^\infty + (ACA)$ whose depth is bounded by b, the depth of nested applications of the rules $(WP)^\infty$ is bounded by c, and the condition (5.14) is enjoyed for each inference $(prg)^\infty$ in the derivation, where a family $\mathcal{E}^X(\sigma)$ of finite sets is assigned to each node σ in the derivation tree, cf. Definition 5.17.

Since the Γ-order over $<_0$ contains an ε-order over $<_0$, $\mathrm{WOP}(\mathsf{g}') = \mathrm{WOP}(\lambda X.\Gamma_X)$ yields $\mathrm{WOP}(\lambda X.\varepsilon_X)$. By Theorem 5.11 we obtain ACA_0^+.

Proposition 5.2 ACA_0^+ *proves the existence of the* ω*th jump of any set:* $\forall X \exists Y[(Y)_0 = X \wedge \{(Y)_{n+1} = ((Y)_n)'\}]$.

Proof For a given set $(\mathcal{Q})_0$, pick a countable coded ω-model $\mathcal{Q}$ of ACA_0. Let $\langle n, m\rangle \in Z :\Leftrightarrow \langle \mathbb{N}; \mathcal{Q}\rangle \models \exists Y[(Y)_0 = (\mathcal{Q})_0 \wedge \forall i < n\{(Y)_{i+1} = ((Y)_i)' \wedge m \in (Y)_n\}]$. Such a set Z exists by ACA_0, and Z is the ωth jump of $(\mathcal{Q})_0$. □

From Proposition 5.2 we see that given a family $\mathcal{Q} = \{(\mathcal{Q})_i\}_i$ of sets, there exists a set $\{\ulcorner A \urcorner : \mathrm{Diag}(\mathcal{Q}) \models A\}$ for the satisfaction relation $\mathrm{Diag}(\mathcal{Q}) \models A$ for first-order formulas A.

For the inference $\dfrac{Y_j \neq A, \Gamma}{\Gamma}\,(ACA)$ substitute A for the eigenvariable Y_j. Axioms $\Gamma, \bar{Y}_j(n), Y_j(n)$ turns to another valid sequent $\Gamma', \neg A(n), A(n)$. Deduce it logically in a finite number of steps. In $(WP)^\infty$, if Y_j occurs in $B(Y_j)$, then the variable $E_{B(Y_j)} \equiv E_i$ with $i = \ulcorner B(Y_j) \urcorner$ should be renamed to $E_{B(A)} \equiv E_k$ with $k = \ulcorner B(A) \urcorner$.

$$\frac{\Gamma(Y_j), E_{B(Y_j)}(n) \quad \Gamma(Y_j), \mathrm{LO}(<_{B(Y_j)}) \quad \neg\mathrm{TI}[<_{\mathsf{g}_{B(Y_j)}}], \Gamma(Y_j)}{\Gamma(Y_j)}$$

turns to

$$\frac{\Gamma(A), E_{B(A)}(n) \quad \Gamma(A), \mathrm{LO}(<_{B(A)}) \quad \neg\mathrm{TI}[<_{\mathsf{g}_{B(A)}}], \Gamma(A)}{\Gamma(A)}$$

Moreover eliminate the false formula $A \neq A$. Here the condition (5.14) is forced in the search. Then we obtain $\mathbf{G}_{0\omega}((\mathcal{Q})_0) + (prg)^\infty + (WP)^\infty \vdash^{\omega+b}_b \emptyset$ from $\mathbf{G}_{0\omega}((\mathcal{Q})_0) + (prg)^\infty + (WP)^\infty + (ACA) \vdash^b_b \emptyset$.

In the proof of the following Theorem 5.12 we need to extend an embedding f between $<_A$ and $<$, to an embedding F from $\mathsf{g}(<_A)$ to $\mathsf{g}(<)$.

Let $X = fld(<_X)$ for a linear order $<_X$. It is easy to see that $\langle u : u \in \{0\} \cup X\rangle$ is an indiscernible sequence for Veblen orders $\langle \mathsf{g}(X), <_{\mathsf{g}(X)}\rangle$ over $<_X$: Let $\alpha[0, u_1, \ldots, u_n], \beta[0, u_1, \ldots, u_n] \in \mathsf{g}(X)$ be terms such that constants occurring in them are among the list $0, u_1, \ldots, u_n$. Then for any increasing sequences $u_1 <_X \cdots <_X u_n$ and $v_1 <_X \cdots <_X v_n$, the following holds.

$$\alpha[0, u_1, \ldots, u_n] <_{\mathsf{g}(X)} \beta[0, u_1, \ldots, u_n] \Leftrightarrow \alpha[0, v_1, \ldots, v_n] <_{\mathsf{g}(X)} \beta[0, v_1, \ldots, v_n] \tag{5.15}$$

Proposition 5.3 *The following is provable in* RCA_0 *for* $\mathsf{g}(X) = \varphi_X(0)$*: Let both* X *and* Y *be linear orderings.*

Let $f : \{0\} \cup X \to \{0\} \cup Y$ *be an order preserving map,* $u <_X v \Rightarrow f(u) <_Y f(v)$ $(u, v \in \{0\} \cup X)$*. Then there is an order preserving map* $F : \mathsf{g}(X) \to \mathsf{g}(Y)$*,* $n <_{\mathsf{g}(X)} m \Rightarrow F(n) <_{\mathsf{g}(Y)} F(m)$*, which extends* f *in the sense that* $F(\mathsf{g}(n)) = \mathsf{g}(f(n))$*.*

Proof Let $F(0) = 0$. Let $\alpha[0, u_1, \ldots, u_n] \in \mathsf{g}(X)$ be a term such that constants occurring in it are among the list $0, u_1, \ldots, u_n$ for $u_i \in \{0\} \cup X$. Define $F(\alpha[0, u_1, \ldots, u_n]) = \alpha[0, f(u_1), \ldots, f(u_n)]$. From (5.15) on $\mathsf{g}(X + Y)$, we see that F is an order preserving map from $\mathsf{g}(X)$ to $\mathsf{g}(Y)$. Moreover we see that if $\alpha[0, u_1, \ldots, u_n] = \beta[0, u_1, \ldots, u_n]$, then $F(\alpha[0, u_1, \ldots, u_n]) = F(\beta[0, u_1, \ldots, u_n])$. □

For normal function $\mathsf{g}(\alpha) = \varphi_\alpha(0)$ and ordinals β, α, let us define ordinals $F(\beta, \alpha)$ recursively on α as follows. $F(\beta, 0) = \omega^{1+\beta}$, $F(\beta, \lambda) = \sup\{F(\beta, \alpha) + 1 : \alpha < \lambda\}$ for limit ordinals λ, and $F(\beta, \alpha + 1) = F\left(\mathsf{g}(\omega^{F(\beta,\alpha)+\beta+1}), \alpha\right) + 1$.

Proposition 5.4 *1.* $\gamma < \beta \Rightarrow F(\gamma, \alpha) \le F(\beta, \alpha)$, *and* $\gamma < \alpha \Rightarrow F(\beta, \gamma) < F(\beta, \alpha)$.
2. If $\beta < \mathsf{g}'(\alpha)$ *and* $\gamma < \omega(1 + \alpha)$*, then* $F(\beta, \gamma) < \mathsf{g}'(\alpha)$*.*
3. $F(\beta, \omega(1 + \alpha)) = \mathsf{g}'(\alpha)$ *for* $\beta < \mathsf{g}'(\alpha)$*.*

Proof Proposition 5.4.1. This follows from the fact that each of functions $\beta \mapsto \alpha + \beta$, $\beta \mapsto \omega^\beta$ and $\beta \mapsto \mathsf{g}(\beta)$ is strictly increasing.
Propositions 5.4.2 and 5.4.3. These are seen simultaneously by induction on α using the facts that $\mathsf{g}'(\alpha)$ is closed under g, addition and exponentiation. □

Let $\mathrm{Diag}((\mathcal{Q})_0, \emptyset) = \mathrm{Diag}(\mathcal{Q})$ with $(\mathcal{Q})_{1+i} = \emptyset$ for any i. $\boldsymbol{G}_{0\omega}((\mathcal{Q})_0, \emptyset)$ denotes the calculus in which each literal $D_{\mathcal{Q}}(0, n) \in \{X_0(n), \bar{X}_0(n)\}$ for the atomic diagram of the set $(\mathcal{Q})_0$ in (5.13) is true, and each negative literal $\bar{E}_i(n)$ as well as $\bar{X}_{1+i}(n)$ is defined to be true.

$\boldsymbol{G}_{0\omega}((\mathcal{Q})_0, \emptyset) + (prg)^{\emptyset}$ denotes the calculus obtained from the calculus $\boldsymbol{G}_{0\omega}((\mathcal{Q})_0, \emptyset)$ by adding the following inference $(prg)^{\emptyset}$. Let A be a first-order formula with the Gödel number $i = \ulcorner A \urcorner$. $n <_A^{*,\emptyset} m$ denotes the transitive closure of the relation $n <_A^{\emptyset} m :\Leftrightarrow \mathrm{Diag}((\mathcal{Q})_0, \emptyset) \models A(\langle n, m \rangle)$. Only when

$$m \in \mathcal{E}_i^X \tag{5.14}$$

holds, the inference $(prg)^{\emptyset}$ can be applied for $\beta_0 < \beta$:

$$\frac{\{((\mathcal{E}_j^X)_{j \neq i}, \mathcal{E}_i^X \cup \{n\}) \vdash^{\beta_0} \Gamma, E_A(m), E_A(n) : n <_A^{*,\emptyset} m\}}{((\mathcal{E}_j^X)_{j \neq i}, \mathcal{E}_i^X) \vdash^{\beta} \Gamma, E_A(m)} \; (prg)^{\emptyset}$$

where we assume that the variable $E_A \equiv E_i$ does not occur in A, $Var(A) \subset Var(\Gamma)$, and a family $\mathscr{E}^X = \mathscr{E}^X(\sigma)$ of finite sets is assigned to each node σ as in Definition 5.17.

For a sequent Γ and a family $\mathscr{E}^X$ of *finite* sets $\mathscr{E}_i^X$, let

$$\Delta(\mathscr{E}^X; \Gamma) := \{E_i(n) : n \in \mathscr{E}_i^X, E_i \in Var(\Gamma), i \in \mathbb{N}\}. \tag{5.15}$$

Theorem 5.12 (Elimination of $(WP)^\infty$) *Let π be a derivation of $\vdash^{\beta_1}_{\alpha_1} \Gamma_1$ in the calculus $\mathbf{G}_{0\omega}((\mathscr{Q})_0) + (prg)^\infty + (WP)^\infty$ for $\Gamma_1 \subset \{E_\prec(n) : n \in \mathbb{N}\}$ with an arithmetical relation $n \prec m$, where the condition (5.14) is enjoyed for each rule $(prg)^\infty$ occurring in the derivation π. $\mathscr{E}^X(\sigma; \pi)$ denotes the family of finite sets $\mathscr{E}_i^X(\sigma; \pi)$ attached to the node σ in the derivation tree, cf. Definition 5.17.*

In the derivation π, suppose that for a finite set Φ of Σ^1_1-formulas, $\vdash^\beta_\alpha \Phi, \Gamma$ holds at a node $\sigma \in T(\pi)$ with $\sigma : \Phi, \Gamma$. Moreover assume that $\Gamma \subset \Delta(\mathscr{E}^X(\sigma; \pi); \Phi, \Gamma)$, cf. (5.15), and Diag$((\mathscr{Q})_0, \emptyset) \not\models B$ *for any $B \in \Phi$.*

Then $\vdash^{F(\beta,\alpha)+\beta} \Delta(\mathscr{E}^X(\sigma; \pi); \Phi, \Gamma)$ holds in the calculus $\mathbf{G}_{0\omega}((\mathscr{Q})_0, \emptyset) + (prg)^\emptyset$.

Proof By induction on β. In the calculus $\mathbf{G}_{0\omega}((\mathscr{Q})_0) + (prg)^\infty + (WP)^\infty$, suppose that $\vdash^\beta_\alpha \Phi, \Gamma$ holds in a derivation π for a sequent $\sigma : \Phi, \Gamma$ such that Φ is a Σ^1_1-formulas with Diag$((\mathscr{Q})_0, \emptyset) \not\models \bigvee \Phi$ and $\Gamma \subset \Delta(\mathscr{E}^X(\sigma); \Phi, \Gamma)$. Let $\mathscr{E}^X = \mathscr{E}^X(\sigma)$.

Let Φ, Γ be an axiom in $\mathbf{G}_{0\omega}((\mathscr{Q})_0) + (prg)^\infty + (WP)^\infty$. Since Γ contains positive literals $E_i(m)$ only and Φ consists of false formulas only, we may assume $\bar{E}_i(m) \in \Phi$ and $E_i(m) \in \Gamma$. However from Diag$((\mathscr{Q})_0, \emptyset) \models \bar{E}_i(m)$ we see that this is not the case. Consider the last inference in the derivation showing $\vdash^\beta_\alpha \Phi, \Gamma$.

Case 1. The last inference is a $(prg)^\infty$. For $\gamma < \beta$ and $i = \ulcorner A \urcorner$, we have for an $E_i(m) \in \Phi \cup \Gamma$

$$\frac{\{((\mathscr{E}_j^X)_{j \neq i}, \mathscr{E}_i^X \cup \{n\}) \vdash^\gamma_\alpha \Phi, n \not\prec^*_A m, \Gamma, E_i(n) : n \in \mathbb{N}\}}{((\mathscr{E}_j^X)_{j \neq i}, \mathscr{E}_i^X) \vdash^\beta_\alpha \Phi, \Gamma} \; (prg)^\infty$$

IH yields $\vdash^{F(\gamma,\alpha)+\gamma} \Delta_n$ for each $n <^{*,\emptyset}_A m$, where $E_i(n) \in \Delta_n = \Delta((\mathscr{E}_j^X)_{j \neq i}, \mathscr{E}_i^X \cup \{n\}; \Phi, n \not\prec^*_A m, \Gamma, E_i(m), E_i(n))$, and $\Delta((\mathscr{E}_j^X)_{j \neq i}, \mathscr{E}_i^X \cup \{n\}; \Phi, \Gamma, E_i(m)) \cup \{E_i(n)\} = \Delta_n$. We have (5.14), $m \in \mathscr{E}_i^X$. An inference $(prg)^\emptyset$ with $F(\gamma, \alpha) + \gamma < F(\beta, \alpha) + \beta$ yields $\vdash^{F(\beta,\alpha)+\beta} \Delta((\mathscr{E}_j^X)_{j \neq i}, \mathscr{E}_i^X; \Phi, \Gamma, E_i(m))$.

Case 2. The last inference is a $(WP)^\infty$. For $\gamma < \beta$, $\alpha_0 < \alpha$, $Var(A) \subset Var(\Gamma)$, $i = \ulcorner A \urcorner$, and the variable E_i not occurring in Γ, we have

$$\frac{\{((\mathscr{E}_j^X)_{j \neq i}, \{n\}) \vdash^\gamma_{\alpha_0} \Phi, \Gamma, E_i(n) : n \in \mathbb{N}\} \quad \mathscr{E}^X \vdash^\gamma_{\alpha_0} \Phi, \mathrm{LO}(<_A), \Gamma \quad \mathscr{E}^X \vdash^\gamma_{\alpha_0} \neg \mathrm{TI}[<_{g_A}], \Phi, \Gamma}{(\mathscr{E}_j^X)_{j \neq i} \vdash^\beta_\alpha \Phi, \Gamma} \; (WP)^\infty$$

For the left upper sequent we have for each $n \in \mathbb{N}$

$$((\mathscr{E}_j^X)_{j \neq i}, \{n\}) \vdash^\gamma_{\alpha_0} \Phi, \Gamma, E_i(n)$$

By IH we obtain $\vdash^{F(\gamma,\alpha_0)+\gamma} \Delta((\mathcal{E}_j^X)_{j\neq i}; \Phi, \Gamma), E_i(n)$. Here note that $\Delta((\mathcal{E}_j^X)_{j\neq i}; \Phi, \Gamma) \cup \{E_i(n)\} = \Delta((\mathcal{E}_j^X)_{j\neq i}, \{n\}; \Phi, \Gamma, E_i(n))$. From Theorem 4.8 we see that either $\vdash^{F(\gamma,\alpha_0)+\gamma} \Delta(\mathcal{E}^X; \Phi, \Gamma)$ or $\vdash^{F(\gamma,\alpha_0)+\gamma} E_i(n)$ holds. If $\vdash^{F(\gamma,\alpha_0)+\gamma} \Delta(\mathcal{E}^X; \Phi, \Gamma)$, then we are done.

Assume $\vdash^{F(\gamma,\alpha_0)+\gamma} E_i(n)$ for every n. If $<_A^{\emptyset}$ is not a linear ordering, i.e., if $\mathrm{Diag}((\mathcal{Q})_0, \emptyset) \not\models \mathrm{LO}(<_A)$, then IH yields $\vdash^{F(\gamma,\alpha_0)+\gamma} \Delta(\mathcal{E}^X; \Phi, \Gamma)$ with $Var(A) \subset Var(\Phi, \Gamma)$. In what follows assume that $<_A^{\emptyset}$ is a linear ordering. By Theorem 4.7 we obtain an embedding f from $<_A^{\emptyset}$ to $\omega^{F(\gamma,\alpha_0)+\gamma+1}$, which yields an embedding from $<_{\mathsf{g}(A)}^{\emptyset}$ to $\delta := \mathsf{g}(\omega^{F(\gamma,\alpha_0)+\gamma+1})$ by Proposition 5.3. Hence we see from $\mathrm{WO}(\delta)$ that $\mathrm{Diag}((\mathcal{Q})_0, \emptyset) \models \mathrm{TI}[<_{\mathsf{g}_A}, C]$ for any first-order formulas C. Therefore $\mathrm{Diag}((\mathcal{Q})_0, \emptyset) \not\models \neg\mathrm{TI}[<_{\mathsf{g}_A}]$.

Second consider the right upper sequent. IH yields

$$\vdash^{F(\gamma,\alpha_0)+\gamma} \Delta(\mathcal{E}^X; \Phi, \Gamma).$$

On the other side Proposition 5.4.1 yields $F(\gamma, \alpha_0) + \gamma \leq F(\gamma, \alpha) + \gamma \leq F(\beta, \alpha) + \beta$. Hence the assertion $\vdash^{F(\beta,\alpha)+\beta} \Delta(\mathcal{E}^X; \Phi, \Gamma)$ follows.

Case 3. The last inference is other than $(prg)^{\infty}$ and $(WP)^{\infty}$.

Consider first the case when the last inference is a rule for existential second-order quantifier.

$$\frac{(\mathcal{E}_j^X)_{j\neq i} \vdash_{\alpha}^{\gamma} \neg\mathrm{TI}[<_{\mathsf{g}_A}], \neg\mathrm{TI}[<_{\mathsf{g}_A}, C], \Phi, \Gamma}{(\mathcal{E}_j^X)_{j\neq i} \vdash_{\alpha}^{\beta} \neg\mathrm{TI}[<_{\mathsf{g}_A}], \Phi, \Gamma} \; (\exists^2_{1st})$$

where $\gamma < \beta$ and C is a first-order formula such that $Var(C) \subset Var(A, \Gamma)$. IH yields $\vdash^{F(\gamma,\alpha)+\gamma} \Delta(\mathcal{E}^X; \Phi, \Gamma)$ for $\Delta(\mathcal{E}^X; \Phi, \Gamma) = \Delta(\mathcal{E}^X; \neg\mathrm{TI}[<_{\mathsf{g}_A}, C], \Phi, \Gamma)$ by $Var(A, C) \subset Var(\Phi, \Gamma)$.

Second consider the case when the last inference is a rule $(\bigwedge)$. For $\gamma < \beta$ we have

$$\frac{\{\mathcal{E}^X \vdash_{\alpha}^{\gamma} A_n, \Phi, \Gamma : n \in \mathbb{N}\}}{\mathcal{E}^X \vdash_{\alpha}^{\beta} \Phi, \Gamma} \; (\bigwedge)$$

where $\bigwedge_n A_n$ is in the set Φ. Let n be the least number such that $\mathrm{Diag}((\mathcal{Q})_0, \emptyset) \not\models A_n$. IH yields $\vdash^{F(\gamma,\alpha)+\gamma} \Delta(\mathcal{E}^X; \Phi, \Gamma)$.

Other cases are similarly seen. □

Now suppose $\mathbf{G}_{0\omega}((\mathcal{Q})_0) + (prg)^{\infty} + (WP)^{\infty} \vdash_b^{\omega+b} \emptyset$. We obtain by Theorem 5.12 that $\vdash^{F(\omega+b,b)+\omega+b} \emptyset$ holds in the calculus $\mathbf{G}_{0\omega}((\mathcal{Q})_0, \emptyset) + (prg)^{\emptyset}$, where $\Delta(\mathcal{E}^X(\emptyset; \pi); \emptyset) = \emptyset$. On the other side we see $F(\omega + b, b) + \omega + b < \mathsf{g}'(\Lambda)$ from Proposition 5.4.2 and $b < \Lambda$. The whole of the supposed derivation consists solely in the repetition rule (Rep). We see by induction up to the ordinal $\mathsf{g}'(\Lambda)$ that this is not the case. Therefore the tree $\mathcal{T}$ is not well-founded.

Thus our proof of Theorem 5.9 is completed.

5.5.3 Proof-Theoretic Ordinals of the Well-Ordering Principles

In this subsection we write $\mathsf{g}(X)$ for $\Gamma_X = fld(<_3)$, with $<_{\mathsf{g}}=<_3$ over $<_X=<_0$. Next we show Theorem 5.10. First consider the easy half. Let $<$ be a standard order of type $\mathsf{g}'(0)$. A series of ordinals $\{\gamma_n\}_n < \mathsf{g}'(0)$ is defined recursively by $\gamma_0 = 0$ and $\gamma_{n+1} = \mathsf{g}(\gamma_n) = \Gamma_{\gamma_n}$. Then WOP($\mathsf{g}$) yields inductively TI[$<_{\gamma_n}$] for initial segments of type γ_n, where TI[$<$] $:\Leftrightarrow \forall Y$ TI[$<, Y$]. Hence $|\text{WOP}(\mathsf{g})| \geq \mathsf{g}'(0)$.

Conversely assume that TI[$\prec$] is provable from WOP(g) in ACA_0, where $\prec$ is an arithmetical relation. Let us introduce a finitary calculus for the SOA $\mathsf{ACA}_0 +$ WOP(g). It is obtained from the predicative second-order logic G_2 in Sect. 2.1.3 by adding the following inference rules (prg), (WP) and (VJ). For first-order formulas A, we have

$$\frac{\Gamma, E_A(t), x \not<^*_A t, E_A(x)}{\Gamma, E_A(t)}\ (prg) \qquad \frac{\Gamma, E_A(x) \quad \Gamma, \text{LO}(<_A) \quad \neg\text{TI}[<_{\mathsf{g}_A}], \Gamma}{\Gamma}\ (WP)$$

where $E_A \equiv E_i$ with $i = \ulcorner A \urcorner$, in (prg), x is an eigenvariable not occurring freely in Γ, $E_A(t)$. In (WP), the variable E_A does not occur in Γ (nor in A).

$$\frac{\Gamma, A(0) \quad \neg A(x), \Gamma, A(S(x)) \quad \neg A(t), \Gamma}{\Gamma}\ (VJ)$$

where x is an eigenvariable not occurring freely in Γ, $A(0)$.

We can assume that in a finitary proof, a variable E occurs in an upper sequent of an inference, but not in the lower sequent only when the inference is either a $(\forall^2)$ or a (WP), and the variable E is the eigenvariable of the inference. The axiom of arithmetic comprehension is deduced from the inference rule $(\exists^2_{1st})$, and the axiom WOP(g) for the well-ordering principle of g is deduced from the inference rules (prg) and (WP).

Let Δ_0 denote a set of negations of axioms for first-order arithmetic except complete induction. By eliminating (cut)'s we obtain a cut-free proof of $\Delta_0, E_\prec(x)$ in $G_2 + (VJ) + (prg) + (WP)$, where $E_\prec \equiv E_i$ with $i = \ulcorner x_0 \prec x_1 \urcorner$. Note that we can eliminate cut inferences in a standard way since each of rules (VJ) and (WP) has no main formula, and there is no inference rule with negative main formulas $\bar{E}_A(t)$ for which $E_A(t)$ can be a main formula of the rule (prg). In the cut-free proof, each formula is either a first-order formula or a Σ^1_1-formula. In particular there occurs no universal second-order quantifier nor inference $(\forall^2)$.

Let us embed the finitary calculus $G_2 + (VJ) + (prg) + (WP)$ to an intermediate infinitary calculus $(prg)^\infty + (WP)^\infty + (cut)_{1st}$. In the embedding it is convenient for us to replace first-order quantifiers by infinitary disjunctions and conjunctions. Each formula in the calculus is a translation A^∞ of a formula A without free first-order variables in the language of SOA. The translation is defined recursively as follows. For an arithmetic literal L, $L^\infty \equiv \top$ if L is true in the standard model $\mathbb{N}$,

$L^\infty \equiv \bot$ otherwise. For a closed terms t and $R \in \{E_i, \bar{E}_i, X_i, \bar{X}_i : i \in \mathbb{N}\}$, $R(t)^\infty \equiv R(n)$ with the value n of the closed term t in $\mathbb{N}$. $(A_0 \lor A_1)^\infty \equiv (A_0^\infty \lor A_1^\infty)$, and similarly for conjunctions. $(\exists x\, A(x))^\infty \equiv \bigvee_n A(\bar{n})^\infty$ for the nth numeral $\bar{n}$. $(\forall x\, A(x))^\infty$ is defined to be an infinitary conjunction similarly. $(\exists X\, A(X))^\infty \equiv (\exists X\, A(X)^\infty)$, and similarly for the second-order universal quantifiers. Let $\text{dg}(A^\infty) := \text{dg}_{0\omega}(A^\infty) = \text{dg}(A)$.

The calculus $(prg)^\infty + (WP)^\infty + (cut)_{1st}$ is obtained from $\mathbf{G}_{0\omega}$ in Sect. 3.1.3 by adding the inference rules $(prg)^\infty$ and $(WP)^\infty$, and the cut inference $(cut)_{1st}$ with a first-order cut formula A:

$$\frac{\Gamma, \neg A^\infty \quad A^\infty, \Delta}{\Gamma, \Delta}\ (cut)_{1st}$$

Let $\Gamma(x, \ldots)$ be a sequent possibly with free first-order variables $x, \ldots$. Assuming $\mathbf{G}_2 + (VJ) + (prg) + (WP) \vdash \Gamma(x, \ldots)$, we see as in Lemma 4.4 that there exist $d, p, k, m < \omega$ such that $(prg)^\infty + (WP)^\infty + (cut)_{1st} \vdash^{\omega k+m}_{d,p} \Gamma(n, \ldots)^\infty$ holds for any natural numbers $n, \ldots$, where the first subscript d indicates that the number of nested applications of the rule (WP) is bounded by d, and the second p designates that any (first-order) cut-formula A^∞ occurring in the witnessing derivation has the depth $\text{dg}(A^\infty) < p$. Note that each variable E occurring in the induction formula A of a (VJ) can be assumed to occur also in the lower sequent Γ. We see that there exist $d, p < \omega$ such that $(prg)^\infty + (WP)^\infty + (cut)_{1st} \vdash^{\omega^2}_{d,p} \Delta_0, E_\prec(n)$ holds for any natural number n. Eliminating the false arithmetic Δ_0, we obtain $(prg)^\infty + (WP)^\infty + (cut)_{1st} \vdash^{\omega^2}_{d,p} E_\prec(n)$. Let $2_0(\beta) = \beta$ and $2_{p+1}(\beta) = 2^{2_p(\beta)}$ for $p < \omega$.

Proposition 5.5 *Suppose* $(prg)^\infty + (WP)^\infty + (cut)_{1st} \vdash^{\beta}_{d,p} \Gamma$.
Then $(prg)^\infty + (WP)^\infty \vdash^{2_p(\beta)}_{2_p(d),0} \Gamma$.

Proof Let A be one of formulas $\bigvee_n B_n$, $\bar{E}_i(n)$ and $\bot$. As in Lemma 3.15 we see by induction on α that if $(prg)^\infty + (WP)^\infty + (cut)_{1st} \vdash^{\beta}_{d,p} \Gamma, \neg A^\infty$ and $(prg)^\infty + (WP)^\infty + (cut)_{1st} \vdash^{\alpha}_{e,p} A^\infty, \Delta$ with $\text{dg}(A) \le p$, then $(prg)^\infty + (WP)^\infty + (cut)_{1st} \vdash^{\beta+\alpha}_{d+e,p} \Gamma, \Delta$. From the fact we see the proposition by induction on $p < \omega$. □

By Proposition 5.5 we obtain a $\beta < \varepsilon_0$ and a $c < \omega$ for which $(prg)^\infty + (WP)^\infty \vdash^{\beta}_{c} E_\prec(n)$ holds for every n.

In a witnessing derivation π of the fact $(prg)^\infty + (WP)^\infty \vdash^{\beta}_{c} E_\prec(n)$, the condition (5.14) may be violated. Let us convert the derivation π to a derivation $\pi^\top$ as follows.

Definition 5.18 For a formula A and a family $\mathcal{E} = (\mathcal{E}_i)_i$ of sets, $A(\mathcal{E})$ denotes the result of replacing each literal $E_i(m)$ by $\top$ when $m \notin \mathcal{E}_i$. $A(\mathcal{E})$ is defined recursively as follows. Let $i = \ulcorner A \urcorner$.

$$\left((E_A(m))(\mathcal{E}), (\bar{E}_A(m))(\mathcal{E})\right) \equiv \begin{cases} (\top, \bot) & \text{if } m \notin \mathcal{E}_i \\ (E_{A(\mathcal{E})}(m), \bar{E}_{A(\mathcal{E})}(m)) & \text{if } m \in \mathcal{E}_i \end{cases}$$

$L(\mathcal{E}) \equiv L$ when $L \in \{\top, \bot, X_i(n), \bar{X}_i(n) : i, n \in \mathbb{N}\}$. $(\bigvee_n A_n)(\mathcal{E}) \equiv \bigvee_n (A_n(\mathcal{E}))$ and $(\bigwedge_n A_n)(\mathcal{E}) \equiv \bigwedge_n (A_n(\mathcal{E}))$. $(\exists X\, F(X))(\mathcal{E}) \equiv \exists X(F(X)(\mathcal{E}))$ and $(\forall X\, F(X))(\mathcal{E}) \equiv \forall X(F(X)(\mathcal{E}))$. For a sequent Γ, let $\Gamma(\mathcal{E}) = \{A(\mathcal{E}) : A \in \Gamma\}$.

For each node $\sigma : \Gamma$ in the derivation π, let for the sets $\mathcal{E}^X(\sigma)$ in Definition 5.17

$$A^\sigma :\equiv A(\mathcal{E}^X(\sigma)),\ \Gamma^\sigma := \{A^\sigma : A \in \Gamma\}.$$

Lemma 5.17 *Let π be a derivation of $\mathcal{E}^X_\prec(\emptyset; \pi) \vdash^{\beta_1}_{\alpha_1} \Gamma_1$ in $(prg)^\infty + (WP)^\infty$, where $\Gamma_1 \subset \{E_\prec(n) : n \in \mathbb{N}\}$ with an arithmetical relation $n \prec m$ in which no E_i occurs, and $\mathcal{E}^X_\prec(\emptyset; \pi) = \{n : E_\prec(n) \in \Gamma_1\}$. Then there exists a derivation $\pi^\top$ witnessing the same fact in $(prg)^\infty + (WP)^\infty$ such that $\mathcal{E}^X_{A^\sigma}(\sigma; \pi^\top) = \mathcal{E}^X_A(\sigma; \pi)$ for $\sigma \in T(\pi^\top) \subset T(\pi)$, and the condition (5.14) is enjoyed for each rule $(prg)^\infty$ occurring in $\pi^\top$.*

Proof This is seen by induction on the tree order on the well-founded tree $T(\pi)$. Each axiom $\sigma : \Gamma, \bar{E}_A(m), E_A(m)$ turns either to $\sigma : \Gamma^\sigma, \bar{E}_{A^\sigma}(m), E_{A^\sigma}(m)$ or to $\sigma : \Gamma^\sigma, \bot, \top$.

Consider a rule $(prg)^\infty$ in π.

$$\frac{\{((\mathcal{E}^X_j(\sigma;\pi))_{j\neq i}, \mathcal{E}^X_i(\sigma;\pi) \cup \{n\}) \vdash \Gamma, E_A(m), n \not\prec^*_A m, E_A(n) : n \in \mathbb{N}\}}{((\mathcal{E}^X_j(\sigma;\pi))_{j\neq i}, \mathcal{E}^X_i(\sigma;\pi)) \vdash \Gamma, E_A(m)}\ (prg)^\infty$$

where $E_A \equiv E_i$ with the Gödel number $i = \ulcorner A \urcorner$ of the formula A. If $m \in \mathcal{E}^X_A(\sigma; \pi)$, then $m \in \mathcal{E}^X_{A^\sigma}(\sigma; \pi^\top) = \mathcal{E}^X_A(\sigma; \pi)$, and

$$\frac{\{((\mathcal{E}^X_j(\sigma))_{j\neq i}, \mathcal{E}^X_i \cup \{n\}) \vdash \Gamma^\sigma, E_{A^\sigma}(m), n \not\prec^*_{A^\sigma} m, E_{A^\sigma}(n) : n \in \mathbb{N}\}}{((\mathcal{E}^X_j(\sigma))_{j\neq i}, \mathcal{E}^X_i(\sigma)) \vdash \Gamma^\sigma, E_{A^\sigma}(m)}\ (prg)^\infty$$

Otherwise $(E_A(m))^\sigma \equiv \top$. $\Gamma^\sigma, \top$ is an axiom. Discard the upper part.

From the construction of $\pi^\top$ we see easily that $\mathcal{E}^X_{A^\sigma}(\sigma; \pi^\top) = \mathcal{E}^X_A(\sigma; \pi)$ for each node $\sigma \in T(\pi^\top) \subset T(\pi)$, and the condition (5.14) is enjoyed for each rule $(prg)^\infty$ occurring in $\pi^\top$. □

From the fact $(prg)^\infty + (WP)^\infty \vdash^\beta_c E_\prec(n)$, Lemma 5.17 and Theorem 5.12 we see that $\vdash^\alpha_0 E_\prec(n)$ holds for any n in the calculus $\mathbf{G}_{0\omega}(\emptyset) + (prg)^\emptyset$, where each negative literal $\bar{E}_i(n)$ as well as $\bar{X}_i(n)$ is defined to be true, $\alpha = F(\beta, c) + \beta$, and $\Delta(\{n\}, \emptyset; E_\prec(n)) = \{E_\prec(n)\}$. Theorem 4.7 yields an embedding f such that $n \prec m \Rightarrow f(n) < f(m) < \omega^{\alpha+1}$. On the other hand we have $\omega^{\alpha+1} = \omega^{F(\beta,c)+\beta+1} < \mathsf{g}'(0)$ by Proposition 5.4.2 and $\beta < \varepsilon_0 \leq \mathsf{g}'(0)$. Thus Theorem 5.10 is proved.

Exercises

5.1 In Theorems 5.2 and 5.5 we have shown that the fixed point axiom FP is provable in ATR_0 via $\mathrm{WOP}(\lambda X.\varphi X0)$. In this exercise let us show the fact directly through a pseudohierarchy. Argue in ATR_0.

Given an X-positive formula $A(X, x)$, let

$$A'(X, x) :\Leftrightarrow (A(\{y : \exists c\, X(\langle c, y\rangle)\}, x) \vee \exists c\, X(\langle c, x\rangle)) .$$

Then A' is X-positive, and if Y enjoys $\forall b\,\big((Y)_b = \{x : A'((Y)_{\prec b}, x)\}\big)$ with $(Y)_{\prec b} = \sum_{c\prec b}(Y)_c$, then $\forall b\,\big((Y)_b = \{x : A(\bigcup_{c\prec b}(Y)_c, x)\} \cup \bigcup_{c\prec b}(Y)_c\big)$.

Let $C(\prec)$ iff $\mathrm{LO}(\prec)$ and

$$\exists Y \left[\forall b \left((Y)_b = \{x : A(\bigcup_{c\prec b}(Y)_c, x)\} \cup \bigcup_{c\prec b}(Y)_c\right) \wedge \right.$$
$$\left. \forall a, x \left(x \in (Y)_a \to \exists b \preceq a (x \in (Y)_b \wedge x \notin \bigcup_{c\prec b}(Y)_c)\right)\right] \tag{5.16}$$

1. Show the existence of a set $\prec$ such that $C(\prec)$ and $\neg\mathrm{WO}(\prec)$.
2. Let D be a set such that $\forall b \in D \exists c \in D(c \prec b)$, and $E = \{a : \forall b \in D(a \prec b)\}$. On the other let Y be a set enjoying (5.16). Y is said to be a pseudohierarchy. Show that $Z_u = Z_l$ for $Z_u = \bigcap_{b\in D}(Y)_b$ and $Z_l = \bigcup_{b\in E}(Y)_b$.
3. Show that $\forall x(x \in Z_l \to A(Z_l, x))$ and $\forall x(A(Z_u, x) \to x \in Z_u)$.
4. Conclude that $Z_l = Z_u = \{x : A(Z_l, x)\}$ is a fixed point, and a set.

5.2 Show that $(\Sigma^1_1\text{-AC})_0 = (\Sigma^1_0\text{-AC})_0$ and $(\Sigma^1_1\text{-DC})_0 = (\Sigma^1_0\text{-DC})_0$.

5.3 Show that $(\Sigma^1_1\text{-AC})_0$ proves Δ^1_1-CA.

5.4 Show that $(\Sigma^1_1\text{-DC})_0$ proves Σ^1_1-AC, Σ^1_1-IND, and proves $\forall n \forall X \exists Y\, A(n, X, Y) \to \forall U \exists Z[(Z)_0 = U \wedge \forall n\, A(n, (Z)_n, (Z)_{n+1})]$ for Σ^1_1-formulas A.

5.5 **Definition 5.19.** Let $\alpha < \Gamma_0$. $<$ denotes a standard epsilon order of type Γ_0.

1. Π^1_0-DC$_\alpha$ denotes the collection of the universal closures of formulas

$$\forall\beta, X \exists Y\, A(\beta, X, Y) \to \exists Z \forall \beta < \alpha\, A(\beta, (Z)_{<\beta}, (Z)_\beta)\ (A \in \Pi^1_0)$$

   Σ^1_1-DC$_\alpha$ denotes the dependent choice schema for Σ^1_1-matrix A.
2. Π^1_0-DC!$_\alpha$ denotes the collection of the universal closures of formulas

$$\forall\beta, X \exists ! Y\, A(\beta, X, Y) \to \exists Z \forall \beta < \alpha\, A(\beta, (Z)_{<\beta}, (Z)_\beta)\ (A \in \Pi^1_0)$$

Let T_α be one of the above two axiom schemata. Then $T_{<\beta} := \bigcup_{\alpha<\beta} T_\alpha$.

Let T_α be one of the above two axiom schemata with set parameters.

It is clear that $(T_\alpha)_0 = (T_{<\alpha\cdot\omega})_0$.

For a Π^1_0-formula $A(\beta, X, Y)$, let

$$\mathscr{A}(X,\gamma) :\Leftrightarrow \forall\beta < \gamma\, A(\beta, (X)_{<\beta}, (X)_\beta).$$

Let ξ be a limit ordinal, and $\mathrm{TI}[<_\xi] :\Leftrightarrow \forall X(Prg[<, X] \to \xi \subset X)$.

1. Show that $(\mathrm{TI}[<_\xi] + \Sigma^1_1\text{-DC}_\xi)_0 \vdash \forall\beta, X\exists Y A(\beta, X, Y) \to Prg[<, B]$ for the formula

$$B(\alpha) :\Leftrightarrow (\forall\gamma\forall X\exists Y[\mathscr{A}(X,\gamma) \to (X)_{<\gamma} = (Y)_{<\gamma} \wedge \mathscr{A}(Y, \gamma + \xi^\alpha)]).$$

   For limit ordinal λ, show $\forall n\, B(\lambda_n) \to B(\lambda)$ for a fundamental sequence $\{\lambda_n\}_n$ such that $\forall n(\lambda_n < \lambda_{n+1} < \lambda)$ and $\lambda = \sup_n \lambda_n$.
2. Show that $(TI[<_\xi] + \Sigma^1_1\text{-DC}_\xi)_0 \vdash \Pi^1_0\text{-DC}_{<\xi^\omega}$. In other words $(TI[<_\xi] + \Sigma^1_1\text{-DC}_\xi)_0 \vdash \forall\beta, X\exists Y A(\beta, X, Y) \to \exists Z\mathscr{A}(Z, \xi^k)$ for each $k < \omega$.
3. Show that $(TI[<_\xi] + \Sigma^1_1\text{-DC}_\xi) \vdash \Pi^1_0\text{-DC}_{<\xi^{\varepsilon_0}}$. In other words $(TI[<_\xi] + \Sigma^1_1\text{-DC}) \vdash \forall\beta, X\exists Y A(\beta, X, Y) \to \exists Z\mathscr{A}(Z, \alpha)$ for each $\alpha < \xi^{\varepsilon_0}$.

5.6 Show that $(\Sigma^1_1\text{-DC})_0 \vdash \Pi^1_0\text{-CA}_{<\omega^\omega}$, and $(\Sigma^1_1\text{-DC}) \vdash \Pi^1_0\text{-CA}_{<\varepsilon_0}$.

5.7 Show that $\forall\beta, X\exists! Y\, A(\beta, X, Y) \to Prg[<, H]$ in $(\Delta^1_1\text{-CA})$ for a Π^1_0-formula A, where $H(\alpha) :\Leftrightarrow \alpha \le \alpha_0 \to \exists Z\mathscr{A}(Z,\alpha) \wedge \forall Z, W[\mathscr{A}(Z,\alpha) \wedge \mathscr{A}(W,\alpha) \to (Z)_{<\alpha} = (W)_{<\alpha}]$ for an $\alpha_0 < \varepsilon_0$ and the formula $\mathscr{A}$ in Exercise 5.5. Conclude that $(\Delta^1_1\text{-CA}) \vdash \Pi^1_0\text{-DC}!_{<\varepsilon_0}$.

5.8 Show that $(\Delta^1_1\text{-CA}) \vdash \Pi^1_0\text{-CA}_{<\varepsilon_0}$.

5.9 Definition 5.20. Let $\alpha < \Gamma_0$, and U a set parameter.

1. For a first-order formula $A(X, Y)$ in the language $\mathscr{L}_2(\mathsf{EA})$ with set variables X, Y, introduce a new binary predicate symbol D^U_A.
   $D[A]_\alpha$ denotes the universal closures of formulas

$$(D^U_A)_0 = U \wedge \forall\beta < \alpha\, A((D^U_A)_{<1+\beta}, (D^U_A)_{1+\beta})$$

   where $(D^U_A)_\beta = \{x : D^U_A(\beta, x)\}$ and $(D^U_A)_{<\beta} = \sum_{\gamma<\beta}(D^U_A)_\gamma$.
2. For a set Φ of formulas $A(X, Y)$, $D[\Phi]_\alpha$ denotes the extension of PA in the language with the axioms $D[A]_\alpha$ for $A \in \Phi$.
3. Let Δ^U_1 denote the set of codes of total computable functions in a set U, $e \in \Delta^U_1 :\Leftrightarrow \forall x(\{e\}^U(x)\downarrow)$.
   For $e \in \Delta^U_1$, $Set(e) := \{x : \{e\}^U(x) \simeq 0\}$ and $Set(\Delta^U_1) = \{Set(e) : e \in \Delta^U_1\}$.
4. $\forall y \in \Delta^U_1 C(y)$ denotes a formula obtained from a formula $\forall Y\, C(Y)$ by replacing each atomic formula $Y(t)$ by $\{y\}^U(t) \simeq 0$.
   $\exists y \in \Delta^U_1 C(y)$ is defined similarly.

5. For ordinals α, $\mathscr{X}^{(\alpha)}$ denotes the αth Turing jump of sets $\mathscr{X} \subset \mathbb{N}$: $\mathscr{X}^{(0)} = \mathscr{X}$ and $\mathscr{X}^{(\alpha)} = (\sum_{\beta<\alpha} \mathscr{X}^{(\beta)})'$ for $\alpha > 0$.
6. For ordinals β, let

$$\mathscr{D}_A(\beta) := Set(\Delta_1^{(D_A^U)_{<1+\beta}}).$$

7. For ordinals α, β, $B[\alpha; \beta]$ is obtained from a formula B by replacing each occurrence of a universal quantifier $\forall X$ by $\forall X \in \mathscr{D}_A(\alpha)$, and replacing each occurrence of an existential quantifier $\exists Y$ by $\exists Y \in \mathscr{D}_A(\alpha + \beta)$. For sequents Γ, $\Gamma[\alpha]$ denotes the set of formulas $X \notin \mathscr{D}_A(\alpha)$ for set variables X occurring freely in Γ. Let $\Gamma[\alpha; \beta] := (\Gamma[\alpha]) \cup \{B[\alpha; \beta] : B \in \Gamma\}$.

   It is clear that

$$\mathsf{EA}^2 \vdash \forall \beta_0 < \beta[\mathscr{D}_A(\beta_0) \subset \mathscr{D}_A(\beta)] \tag{5.17}$$

and hence we have for $\Gamma \subset \Pi_1^1 \cup \Sigma_1^1$

$$\mathsf{EA}^2 \vdash \bigvee \Gamma[\alpha + \gamma; \beta] \to \bigvee \Gamma[\alpha; \gamma + \beta + \delta] \tag{5.18}$$

Let Φ be a set of Π_2^1-sentences $\forall X \exists Y A(X, Y)$ with Π_0^1-matrix A. Assume the following for Φ:

(a) $J(X, Y) \in \Phi$ for $J(X, Y) :\Leftrightarrow (X' = Y)$.
(b) if $A(X, Y) \in \Phi$, then

$$A'(U, Y) :\Leftrightarrow \exists e \in \Delta_1^U A(Set(\{e\}^U), Y) \tag{5.19}$$

   is in Φ.
(c) Φ is closed under positive boolean combinations $\vee, \wedge$ with arithmetic atomic formulas.
   Show that $(D[\Phi]_{<\omega})_0 \subset \{\forall X \exists Y A(X, Y) : A \in \Phi\}$, $(D[\Phi]_{<\omega^\omega})_0 \subset \{\forall X \exists Y A(X, Y) : A \in \Phi\} + (\Sigma_1^1\text{-DC})_0$, and $(D[\Phi]_{\varepsilon_0})_0 \subset \{\forall X \exists Y A(X, Y) : A \in \Phi\} + (\Sigma_1^1\text{-DC})$.
   In the following we show the converse directions.

5.10 Show that $\{\forall X \exists Y A(X, Y) : A \in \Phi\} + (\Sigma_1^1\text{-AC})_0$ is Π_2^1-conservative over $(D[\Phi]_{<\omega})_0$: if $\{\forall X \exists Y A(X, Y) : A \in \Phi\} + (\Sigma_1^1\text{-AC})_0 \vdash \exists Z\, C(U, Z)$, then there exists an $m < \omega$ such that $(D[\Phi]_{<\omega})_0 \vdash \exists Z \in \mathscr{D}_A(m) C(U, Z)$ for $C \in \Pi_0^1$ with a set parameter U.

5.11 Show that $\{\forall X \exists Y A(X, Y) : A \in \Phi\} + (\Sigma_1^1\text{-DC})_0$ is Π_2^1-conservative over $(D[\Phi]_{<\omega^\omega})_0$: if $\{\forall X \exists Y A(X, Y) : A \in \Phi\} + (\Sigma_1^1\text{-DC})_0 \vdash \exists Z\, C(U, Z)$, then there exists a $k < \omega$ such that $(D[\Phi]_{<\omega^\omega})_0 \vdash \exists Z \in \mathscr{D}_A(\omega^k) C(U, Z)$ for $C \in \Pi_0^1$ with a set parameter U.

5.12 Show that $\{\forall X \exists Y A(X, Y) : A \in \Phi\} + (\Sigma_1^1\text{-DC})$ is Π_2^1-conservative over $(D[\Phi]_{<\varepsilon_0})_0$: if $\{\forall X \exists Y A(X, Y) : A \in \Phi\} + (\Sigma_1^1\text{-DC}) \vdash \exists Z\, C(U, Z)$, then there exists an $\alpha < \varepsilon_0$ such that $(D[\Phi]_{<\varepsilon_0})_0 \vdash \exists Z \in \mathcal{D}_A(\alpha)C(U, Z)$ for $C \in \Pi^1_0$ with a set parameter U.

5.13 Conclude the following corollary.

Corollary 5.4 *1.* $(\Sigma^1_1\text{-AC})_0$ *is* Π^1_2*-conservative over* $(\Pi^{1-}_0\text{-CA}_{<\omega})_0 = \mathsf{ACA}_0$, *and* $|(\Sigma^1_1\text{-AC})_0| = \varepsilon_0$.

2. $(\Sigma^1_1\text{-DC})_0$ *is* Π^1_2*-conservative over* $(\Pi^{1-}_0\text{-CA}_{<\omega^\omega})_0$, *and* $|(\Sigma^1_1\text{-DC})_0| = \varphi\omega 0$.
3. $(\Sigma^1_1\text{-DC})$ *is* Π^1_2*-conservative over* $(\Pi^{1-}_0\text{-CA}_{<\varepsilon_0})_0$, *and* $|(\Sigma^1_1\text{-DC})| = \varphi\varepsilon_0 0$.

5.14 Show the converse of Proposition 5.2. Over RCA_0, the existence of the ωth jump of any set yields ACA_0^+.

5.15 Let g be one of the normal functions $\mathsf{g}(a) = \varphi_{(i,\alpha)}(a)$ and $\mathsf{g}(a) = \varphi_{(i,a)}(0)$ for $i = 0, 1$, cf. the end of Sect. 5.1. Show the followings.

1. WOP(g') is equivalent to (WOP(g))$^+$ over ACA_0, cf. Theorem 5.9.
2. The proof-theoretic ordinal $|\mathsf{ACA}_0 + \text{WOP}(\mathsf{g})| = \mathsf{g}'(0)$, cf. Theorem 5.10.
3. $|\mathsf{ACA} + \text{WOP}(\mathsf{g})| = \mathsf{g}'(\varepsilon_0)$.

5.6 Notes

Feferman [6] and Schütte [19] identified the first strongly critical ordinal Γ_0 with the limit of the predicativity on the ground $\mathbb{N}$. For more on predicative proof theory, see Schütte [20] and Jäger's Habilitationsschrift [10]. Jäger [10] discusses predicatively reducible set theories. In the recent article [18], K. Sato determines the proof-theoretic ordinals of combinations of iterated comprehension axioms and transfinite inductions thoroughly.

5.6.1 Section 5.2

For more on ATR_0 and other SOA's, see Simpson [21].

5.6.2 Section 5.3

Lemma 5.7 is due to Feferman [6]. Predicative cut-elimination Theorem 5.3 is due to Tait [24].

5.6.3 Section 5.4

Theorem 5.6 is due to Feferman [7]. The asymmetric interpretation for $\widehat{ID}^{\infty}$ in Lemma 5.12 is due to Jäger and Primo [12]. The equivalence between FP_0 and ATR_0 is proved by Avigad [4]. The proof utilizes a pseudohierarchy as reproduced in Exercise 5.1. We employ a proof search method in a direct proof of Theorem 5.5 showing that a well-ordering principle for the Veblen function implies the fixed point axiom. Such an application of the search method is due to Afshari and Rathjen [1], in which Theorem 5.11 is proved proof-theoretically.

5.6.4 Section 5.5

Let us mention some works done metapredicatively. Jäger [9] opens up proof-theoretic studies of set theories without foundation. It is shown that a set theory KPi^0 is proof-theoretically equivalent to ATR_0, where KPi^0 is obtained from the set theory KPi for recursively inaccessible universes by restricting the complete induction to Δ_0-formulas (or equivalently to sets) and omitting the foundation schema. Jäger, Kahle, Setzer and Strahm [11] computes the proof-theoretic ordinals of the transfinitely iterated fixed point theories $\widehat{ID}_\alpha$ in terms of the ternary Veblen function $(\alpha, \beta, \gamma) \mapsto \varphi\alpha\beta\gamma$. For example they show that $|\widehat{ID}_\omega| = \Gamma_{\varepsilon_0} = \varphi_{(1,\varepsilon_0)}(0)$. Strahm [22] discusses an explicit mathematics EMU, and shows that it is proof-theoretically equivalent to $\widehat{ID}_{<\varepsilon_0} = \bigcup_{\alpha<\varepsilon_0} \widehat{ID}_\alpha$. Then Jäger and Strahm [13] establish proof-theoretic equivalences between the transfinitely iterated fixed point theories and ATR with the Σ^1_1-Dependent Choice. Jäger and Strahm [14] and Strahm [23] investigate a set theory KPm^0 without foundation. KPm^0 is obtained from a set theory KPm for recursively Mahlo universes by restricting the complete induction to sets and omitting the foundation schema. They show that $|\mathsf{KPm}^0| = \varphi\omega 00$.

Theorem 5.11 is due to Marcone and Montalbán [15]. Their proof is computability theoretic. For more on ACA_0^+, see [21]. Theorem 5.9 is took from [2]. Actually for normal functions g on ordinals with the condition (5.15) on indiscernibility, the well-ordering principle WOP(g') for the derivative g' is equivalent to (WOP(g))$^+$ over ACA_0. For more on the proof-theoretic studies on the well-ordering principles, see [1, 16, 17]. Theorem 5.10 on the proof-theoretic ordinal of the well-ordering principle is took from [3], in which a flaw in [2] is corrected. Under a mild condition on normal functions g, the proof-theoretic ordinal $|\mathsf{ACA}_0 + \mathrm{WOP}(\mathsf{g})|$ is seen to be equal to the least fixed point $\mathsf{g}'(0)$ of g, cf. Exercise 5.15.

5.6.5 *Exercises 5.5.3*

Corollary 5.4 in Exercise 5.13 is due to Friedman [8]. Its proof-theoretic proof via asymmetric interpretations is obtained by Cantini [5].

References

1. Afshari, B., Rathjen, M.: Reverse mathematics and well-ordering principles: a pilot study. Ann. Pure Appl. Log. **160**, 231–237 (2009)
2. Arai, T.: Derivatives of normal functions and ω-models. Arch. Math. Log. **57**, 649–664 (2017)
3. Arai, T.: Proof-theoretic strengths of the well ordering principles. Arch. Math. Log. **59**, 257–275 (2020)
4. Avigad, J.: On the relationship between ATR_0 and $\widehat{ID}_{<\omega}$. Jour. Symb. Log. **61**, 768–779 (1996)
5. Cantini, A.: On the relationship between choice and comprehension principles in second order arithmetic. Jour. Symb. Log. **52**, 360–373 (1986)
6. Feferman, S.: Systems of predicative analysis. Jour. Symb. Log. **29**, 1–30 (1964)
7. Feferman, S.: Iterated inductive fixed-point theories: applications to Hancock's conjecture. In: Metakides, G. (ed.) Patras Logic Symposion, pp. 171–196. North-Holland, Amsterdam (1982)
8. Friedman, H.: Iterated inductive definitions and Σ^1_2-AC. In: Kino, A., Myhill, J., Vesley, R.E. (eds.) Intuitionism and Proof Theory, Proceedings of the Summer Conference at Buffalo, N.Y (1968), pp. 435–442. North-Holland, Amsterdam (1970)
9. Jäger, G.: The strength of admissibility without foundation. Jour. Symb. Log. **49**, 867–879 (1984)
10. Jäger, G.: Theories for Admissible Sets. A Unifying Approach to Proof Theory. Studies in Proof Theory Lecture Notes, vol. 2. Bibliopolis, Napoli (1986)
11. Jäger, G., Kahle, R., Setzer, A., Strahm, T.: The proof-theoretic analysis of transfinitely iterated fixed point theories. Jour. Symb. Log. **64**, 53–67 (1999)
12. Jäger, G., Primo, B.: About the proof-theoretic ordinals of weak fixed point theories. Jour. Symb. Log. **57**, 1108–1119 (1992)
13. Jäger, G., Strahm, T.: Fixed point theories and dependent choice. Arch. Math. Log. **39**, 493–508 (2000)
14. Jäger, G., Strahm, T.: Upper bounds for metapredicative Mahlo in explicit mathematics and admissible set theory. Jour. Symb. Log. **66**, 935–958 (2001)
15. Marcone, A., Montalbán, A.: The Veblen functions for computability theorists. Jour. Symb. Log. **76**, 575–602 (2011)
16. Rathjen, M.: ω-models and well-ordering principles. In: Tennant, N. (ed.) Foundational Adventures, vol. 22, pp. 179–212, Tributes. Colloquium Publications, London (2014)
17. Rathjen, M., Weiermann, A.: Reverse mathematics and well-ordering principles. In: Cooper, S., Sorbi, A. (eds.) Computability in Context, pp. 351–370. World Scientific, Singapore (2011)
18. Sato, K.: A note on predicative ordinal analysis I: Iterated comprehension and transfinite induction. Jour. Symb. Log. **84**, 226–265 (2019)
19. Schütte, K.: Predicative well-orderings. In: Crossley, J.N., Dummett, M. (eds.) Formal Systems and Recursive Functions, pp. 280–303. North-Holland, Amsterdam (1965)
20. Schütte, K.: Proof Theory. Translated from the revised German edition by J. N. Crossley. Grundlehren der Mathematischen Wissenschaften, Band 225. Springer, Berlin (1977)
21. Simpson, S.G.: Subsystems of second order arithmetic. Perspectives in Logic, 2nd edn. Cambridge University Press, Cambridge (2009)
22. Strahm, T.: First steps into metapredicativity in explicit mathematics. In: Cooper, S.B., Truss, J. K. (eds.) Sets and Proofs. London Mathematical Society Lecture Notes, vol. 258, pp. 383–402. Cambridge University Press, Cambridge (1999)

23. Strahm, T.: Wellordering proofs for metapredicative Mahlo. Jour. Symb. Log. **67**, 260–278 (2002)
24. Tait, W.W.: Normal derivability in classical logic. In: Barwise, J. (ed.) Syntax and Semantics of Infinitary Languages. Lecture Notes in Mathematics, vol. 72, pp. 204–236 (1968)

Chapter 6
Collapsings

In this chapter we analyze impredicative theories proof-theoretically. To extract computational (or countable) contents we employ a technique, *collapsings*, by which uncountable infinitary derivations and uncountable ordinals are collapsed down to countable ones. This is done through Mostowski collapsings of Skolem hulls as in the Condensation lemma, which is a key to prove the fact that the GCH (Generalized Continuum Hypothesis) holds in the constructible universe L.

In Sect. 6.1 we introduce for each computable well-order of type ν, theories ID_ν for iterated positive elementary inductive definitions over natural numbers, and set theories KP_ν for iterated admissibility. The intended model of KP_ν is the constructible set L_{Ω_ν}, where $0 < \alpha \mapsto \Omega_\alpha$ denotes the continuous closure of the function $0 < \alpha \mapsto \tau_\alpha$ for the αth admissible ordinal τ_α. This means that $\Omega_{\alpha+1}$ is the least admissible ordinal above Ω_α with $\Omega_0 = \omega$, and $\Omega_\lambda = \sup\{\Omega_\alpha : \alpha < \lambda\}$ for limit ordinals λ.

In Sect. 6.2 an iterated Skolem hull $\mathcal{H}_\alpha(X)$ of sets X of ordinals and a collapsing function $(\sigma, \alpha) \mapsto \psi_\sigma(\alpha)$ are introduced simultaneously, where σ is a recursively regular ordinal. Roughly $\psi_\sigma(\alpha)$ is defined to be the αth collapse$< \sigma$ of σ in $\mathcal{H}_\alpha(\psi_\sigma(\alpha))$ in such a way that $\mathcal{H}_\alpha(\psi_\sigma(\alpha)) \cap \psi_\sigma(\alpha) = \psi_\sigma(\alpha)$. It turns out that $\mathcal{H}_{\varepsilon_{\Omega_\nu+1}}(\{0\})$ is isomorphic to a computable set of ordinal terms, thereby yielding a notation system of ordinals. The theory ID_ν is shown to prove the well-foundedness of the notation system up to each ordinal term in Sect. 6.3.

In Sect. 6.4 we consider the simplest case to illustrate the ideas in cut-elimination procedures for impredicative theories. Namely a theory $\mathsf{ID}_1^{\mathbb{O}}$, which is ID_1 with ordinals, is analyzed through the *operator controlled derivations*, and ID_1 through the *Ω-rule*. Also we establish proof-theoretic equivalences of ID_1, and the light-face Π^1_1-comprehension axiom. The general case, i.e., an ordinal analysis of the set theory KP_ν is treated in Sect. 6.5.

In Sect. 6.6 we give two applications of the method of the operator controlled derivations. The first one is a relativized ordinal analysis. An operator to control derivations is a relativized Skolem hull $\mathcal{H}_\alpha^\theta$ relative to a function f_θ on ordinals. In the second, a set theory $\mathsf{KP}\Pi_{N+1}$ for Π_{N+1}-reflections is proof-theoretically reduced to a set theory of iterations of Π_N-recursively Mahlo operations. A transitive and well-founded model of $\mathsf{KP}\omega$ controls derivations in the second.

© The Editor(s) (if applicable) and The Author(s), under exclusive license to Springer Nature Singapore Pte Ltd. 2020

T. Arai, *Ordinal Analysis with an Introduction to Proof Theory*, Logic in Asia: Studia Logica Library, https://doi.org/10.1007/978-981-15-6459-8_6

6.1 Theories ID_ν, Π^1_1-CA and KP_ν

For a recursive ordinal $\nu < \omega_1^{CK}$, let us introduce theories ID_ν for ν-times iterated positive elementary inductive definitions over $\mathbb{N}$. Actually the theory ID_ν depends on a specific elementary recursive well ordering $<_\nu$ on $\mathbb{N}$ of type ν. Let us write $<$ for $<_\nu$ when no confusion likely occurs. We assume that both the relation $<$ and its field are elementary recursive. $a < \nu$ designates that a natural number a is in the field of the ordering $<$, i.e., $<_\nu$. Moreover we assume that 0 is the least element when $\nu > 0$, and there is an elementary recursive function $a + 1$ such that $a + 1$ is the successor of $a < \nu$ with respect to the ordering $<$ unless a is the largest element in $<$. When a is the largest, we set $a + 1 := \nu$. Furthermore we assume that all of the above facts on $<, 0, \lambda a.a + 1$ are provable in a weak fragment of arithmetic, e.g., in EA for suitable definitions of elementary recursive $<, \lambda a.a + 1$. To be specific, assume that EA proves $\forall a, b, c < \nu[(a \not< a) \land (a < b \lor a = b \lor b < a) \land (a < b < c \to a < c)]$, $\forall a, b(a < b \to a, b < \nu)$, $\forall a < \nu(0 \leq a)$, and $\forall a, b < \nu(a < b \to a < a + 1 \land a + 1 \leq b)$, where $a \leq b :\Leftrightarrow (a < b \lor a = b)$.

Let X be a unary predicate symbol, and Y a binary one. A formula $\mathscr{A}[X, n, b, Y]$ in the language $\mathscr{L}(\mathsf{PA}) \cup \{X, Y\}$ is *X-positive elementary* if the unary predicate symbol X occurs only positively in it. The *language* $\mathscr{L}(\mathsf{ID})$ of ID_ν is obtained from the language $\mathscr{L}(\mathsf{PA})$ by adding binary predicate symbols $P_\mathscr{A}$ for X-positive elementary formulas $\mathscr{A}[X, n, b, Y]$.

The (first-order) theory ID_ν is an extension of PA in the language $\mathscr{L}(\mathsf{ID})$. This means that the complete induction schema is available for arbitrary formula in the language $\mathscr{L}(\mathsf{ID})$. ID_ν is obtained from the extended PA by adding the following axiom $(P_\mathscr{A}.1)$ and the axiom schema $(P_\mathscr{A}.2)$ for positive elementary $\mathscr{A}$, and the transfinite induction schema (TI_ν) for $<_\nu$: Let $(P_\mathscr{A})_c = \{n : P_\mathscr{A}(c, n)\}$, $P_{\mathscr{A}_{<b}} := \sum_{c<b}(P_\mathscr{A})_c$ and $\mathscr{A}_b[X] = \{n : \mathscr{A}[X, n, b, P_{\mathscr{A}_{<b}}]\}$. Also $n \in (P_\mathscr{A})_b :\Leftrightarrow P_\mathscr{A}(b, n)$. A formula $F(n)$ with a free variable n is identified with the class $\{n : F(n)\}$. For example $G \subset F :\Leftrightarrow (\forall n(G(n) \to F(n)))$.

$(P_\mathscr{A}.1)$ $\forall b < \nu\{\mathscr{A}_b[(P_\mathscr{A})_b] \subset (P_\mathscr{A})_b\}$.
Namely $\forall b < \nu\forall n \left(\mathscr{A}[(P_\mathscr{A})_b, n, b, P_{\mathscr{A}_{<b}}] \to n \in (P_\mathscr{A})_b\right)$.

$(P_\mathscr{A}.2)$ $\forall b < \nu(\mathscr{A}_b[F] \subset F \to (P_\mathscr{A})_b \subset F)$ for arbitrary formula F in the language $\mathscr{L}(\mathsf{ID})$.
Namely $\forall b < \nu\left[\forall n \left(\mathscr{A}[F, n, b, P_{\mathscr{A}_{<b}}] \to F(n)\right) \to \forall n\, (n \in (P_\mathscr{A})_b \to F(n))\right]$.

(TI_ν) $Prg[<_\nu, F] \to \forall n\, F(n)$ for arbitrary formula F in the language $\mathscr{L}(\mathsf{ID})$.

$P_\mathscr{A}$ is intended to denote a hierarchy $\{(P_\mathscr{A})_b\}_{b<\nu}$ of sets $(P_\mathscr{A})_b$ of natural numbers inductively defined on 'ordinals' b. Each set $(P_\mathscr{A})_b$ is the least fixed point of the monotonic operator $\mathscr{A}_b : X \mapsto \mathscr{A}_b[X]$ on $\mathbb{N}$, $X \in \mathscr{P}(\mathbb{N})$. $(P_\mathscr{A}.1)$ states that $(P_\mathscr{A})_b$ is closed under the operator $\mathscr{A}_b$, and $(P_\mathscr{A}.2)$ says that $(P_\mathscr{A})_b$ is the least such set at least in definable sets.

$\mathsf{ID}_{<\nu}$ denotes the union $\bigcup_{\mu<\nu} \mathsf{ID}_\mu$. Specifically, in $\mathsf{ID}_{<\nu}$, the $(P_\mathscr{A}.1)$ denotes the collection $\{\forall b < \mu\{\mathscr{A}_b[(P_\mathscr{A})_b] \subset (P_\mathscr{A})_b\} : \mathbb{N} \ni \mu < \nu\}$, and $(P_\mathscr{A}.2)$ the collection $\{\forall b < \mu(\mathscr{A}_b[F] \subset F \to (P_\mathscr{A})_b \subset F) : \mathbb{N} \ni \mu < \nu, F \in \mathscr{L}(\mathsf{ID})\}$.

6.1.1 Kripke–Platek Set Theory for Iterated Admissibility

Next we are going to introduce a set theory KP_ν, in which ID_ν in interpreted.

KP_ν denotes a Kripke–Platek set theory with ν admissible sets. It involves sets and natural numbers through an elementary recursive well-ordering $<_\nu$ of type ν. It is convenient for us to formulate KP_ν as a set theory with *urelements*, i.e., natural numbers.

The language of KP_ν is obtained from the language $\mathcal{L}(\mathsf{PA})$ of the first-order arithmetic with function symbols for elementary recursive functions by adding unary predicate symbol $\mathbb{N}$, a binary relation $\in$, and a unary function symbol M. Terms are generated from variables and the constant 0 (zero in $\mathbb{N}$) by applying function symbols for elementary recursive functions and M. Atomic formulas are $s = t, s \in t$ and $\mathbb{N}(t)$ for terms s, t. We write $t \in \mathbb{N}$ for $\mathbb{N}(t)$, M_t for $M(t)$, and $t \in \mathbb{S}$ for $t \notin \mathbb{N} :\equiv \neg\mathbb{N}(t)$. $\mathbb{S}$ denotes the class of all sets. $a, b, n, m, \ldots$ are variables varying through $\mathbb{N}$, and $x, y, z, u, v, \ldots$ for sets. We sometimes write $\forall n \in \mathbb{N}(\cdots)$ for $\forall n(n \in \mathbb{N} \to \cdots)$, and similarly for $\exists n \in \mathbb{N}$.

The axioms in KP_ν are classified in the following five groups.

1. (PA) KP_ν is an extension of PA in the expanded language.

   a. If A is an axiom in PA, then $A^{\mathbb{N}}$ is an axiom in KP_ν, where $A^{\mathbb{N}}$ is obtained from A by relativizing the quantifiers Qn to $Qn \in \mathbb{N}$.
   b. $0 \in \mathbb{N}$, $\forall n \in \mathbb{N}(n + 1 \in \mathbb{N})$.
   c. The complete induction schema $F(0) \to \forall n \in \mathbb{N}(F(n) \to F(n+1)) \to \forall n \in \mathbb{N}\, F(n)$ is an axiom for arbitrary formula F in the expanded language.

   For example $\forall n, m \in \mathbb{N}((n + m) + 1 = n + (m + 1))$ is an axiom. For each elementary recursive function symbol f, $\forall n_1, \ldots, n_k \in \mathbb{N}(f(n_1, \ldots, n_k) \in \mathbb{N})$ follows from the above axioms.
2. (Ontological and equality axioms) $\forall x, y(x \in y \to y \in \mathbb{S})$, $\forall x(M_x \in \mathbb{S})$, $\forall x(x = x)$ and $\forall x, y(x = y \to A(x) \to A(y))$ for each atomic formula A. For example $\forall x, y(x = y \to x \in \mathbb{N} \to y \in \mathbb{N})$ is an (equality) axiom.
3. (well-ordering $<_\nu$) The following (Lin_M) are axioms in KP_ν.

(Lin_M) $\forall a, b \in \mathbb{N}(a, b < \nu \to (a <_\nu b \leftrightarrow M_a \in M_b))$ and $\forall a \in \mathbb{N}(a < \nu \to \emptyset \neq M_a$ is a transitive set), where $a <_\nu b$ denotes $f(a, b) = 1$ for the characteristic function (symbol) f of the relation $<_\nu$, and 'x is a transitive set' denotes $\forall y \in x \forall z \in y(z \in x)$.

$(TI_\nu)^{\mathbb{N}}$ for arbitrary formulas F follows from the axiom (Lin_M) with the Foundation axiom schema.

4. (Universe) Each axiom in KP except Δ_0-Collection is an axiom in KP_ν. Namely (extensionality) $\forall x, y \in \mathbb{S}[\forall z(z \in x \leftrightarrow z \in y) \to x = y]$, (pair) $\forall x, y \exists z \in \mathbb{S}(x, y \in z)$, (union) $\forall x \in \mathbb{S} \exists y \in \mathbb{S} \forall z \in x(z \subset y)$, ($\Delta_0$-Separation) for each Δ_0-formula A in the expanded language, i.e., a bounded formula, $\forall u, v \in \mathbb{S} \exists y \in \mathbb{S}(y = \{x \in u : A(x, v)\})$, and the Foundation axiom schema $\forall x \in \mathbb{S}(\forall y \in x\, F(y) \to F(x)) \to \forall x \in \mathbb{S}\, F(x)$ for arbitrary formula F.

Moreover when ν is a limit ordinal, then $V = \bigcup_{a<\nu} M_a$, i.e., $\forall x \in \mathbb{S}\exists a \in \mathbb{N}(a < \nu \land x \in M_a)$ is an axiom. Otherwise Δ_0-Collection for the universe with Δ_0-formulas A, $\forall u \in \mathbb{S}\,(\forall x \in u \exists y \in \mathbb{S}\, A(x, y) \to \exists z \in \mathbb{S}\forall x \in u \exists y \in z\, A(x, y))$ is an axiom schema in KP_ν.

5. (admissibility of M_a) Let $a \in Lim :\Leftrightarrow (a \leq \nu \land \forall b <_\nu a(b + 1 <_\nu a))$, $a \in Suc :\Leftrightarrow (\exists b \in \mathbb{N}(b < \nu \land a = b + 1))$ for the successor $b + 1$ with respect to $<_\nu$.

   a. (zero and limit) $\mathbb{N} \subset M_0$, i.e., $\forall n \in \mathbb{N}(n \in M_0)$, and $\forall a \in \mathbb{N}(a \in Lim \to M_a = \bigcup_{b<_\nu a} M_b)$, where $M_a = \bigcup_{b<_\nu a} M_b :\Leftrightarrow (\forall x \in M_a \exists b <_\nu a(x \in M_b))$.
   b. (successor) The relativized axioms (pair), (union), (Δ_0-Separation), and (Δ_0-Collection) to M_a is an axiom for $a \in Suc$.
   c. (sequence) $\forall b < \nu\left((M_c)_{c\leq_\nu b} \in M_{b+1}\right)$ for the sequence $(M_c)_{c\leq_\nu b}$ with $c \mapsto M_c$.

For example the following is an axiom for arbitrary Δ_0-formula A.

$$\forall a \in \mathbb{N}[a \in Suc \land a < \nu \to$$
$$\forall u, v \in M_a(\forall x \in u \exists y \in M_a\, A(x, y, v) \to \exists z \in M_a \forall x \in u \exists y \in z\, A(x, y, v))]$$

Let $\mathscr{A}[X, n, b, Y]$ be an X-positive elementary formula in the language of arithmetic. $\mathscr{A}^{\mathbb{N}}$ denotes the result of restricting each quantifier Qm to $Qm \in \mathbb{N}$. For $a < \nu$, Ω_a denotes the order type of ordinals in M_a: $\xi < \Omega_a :\Leftrightarrow \xi \in M_a \cap ON$, where $\xi \in ON$ denotes a Δ_0-formula saying that ξ is an ordinal, i.e., transitive and linearly ordered by $\in$. When $a = \nu$, $\xi < \Omega_a :\Leftrightarrow \xi \in ON$.

From (TI_ν) and the Foundation we see that the lexicographic ordering on $(b, \xi) \in \sum_{b\in\mathbb{N}} \Omega_{b+1}$, $(c, \zeta) <_{lx} (b, \xi) \Leftrightarrow c <_\nu b \lor (c = b \land \zeta < \xi)$ is well-founded, and set-like, i.e., each initial segment $\{(c, \zeta) \in \sum_{b\in\mathbb{N}} \Omega_{b+1} : (c, \zeta) <_{lx} (b, \xi)\}$ is a set. Then by Δ-Recursion, Corollary 1.6, define a Δ-predicate $I^{<\xi}_{\mathscr{A},b}$ by

$$n \in I^{<\xi}_{\mathscr{A},b} \leftrightarrow n, b \in \mathbb{N} \land b < \nu \land \xi < \Omega_{b+1} \land \exists \zeta < \xi\, \mathscr{A}^{\mathbb{N}}\left[I^{<\zeta}_{\mathscr{A},b}, n, b, \sum_{c<_\nu b} I^{<\Omega_{c+1}}_{\mathscr{A},c}\right]$$

where $\sum_{c<_\nu b} I^{<\Omega_{c+1}}_{\mathscr{A},c}$ is the direct sum of $\{I^{<\Omega_{c+1}}_{\mathscr{A},c}\}_{c<_\nu b}$ with $m \in I^{<\Omega_{c+1}}_{\mathscr{A},c} :\Leftrightarrow \exists \zeta < \Omega_{c+1}(m \in I^{<\zeta}_{\mathscr{A},c})$.

A' is obtained from a sentence A in the language $\mathscr{L}(\mathsf{ID})$ by restricting each quantifier Qm to $Qm \in \mathbb{N}$, and replacing $P_{\mathscr{A}}(c, n)$ by the Σ-formula $n \in I^{<\Omega_{c+1}}_{\mathscr{A},c}$.

Proposition 6.1 *For a sentence A in the language $\mathscr{L}(\mathsf{ID})$, if $\mathsf{ID}_\nu \vdash A$, then $\mathsf{KP}_\nu \vdash A'$.*

Proof The axiom $(P_{\mathscr{A}}.1)$ is translated to $\forall b, n \in \mathbb{N}\left(b < \nu \to \mathscr{A}^{\mathbb{N}}[I^{<\Omega_{b+1}}_{\mathscr{A},b}, n, b, \sum_{c<_\nu b} I^{<\Omega_{c+1}}_{\mathscr{A},c}] \to n \in I^{<\Omega_{b+1}}_{\mathscr{A},b}\right)$. Assume $b < \nu$ and $\mathscr{A}^{\mathbb{N}}[I^{<\Omega_{b+1}}_{\mathscr{A},b}, n, b, \sum_{c<_\nu b} I^{<\Omega_{c+1}}_{\mathscr{A},c}]$

for natural numbers b, n. This is a Σ-formula on M_{b+1} by the axiom (sequence), $(M_c)_{c\le_\nu b} \in M_{b+1}$. By Σ-Reflection Theorem 1.10 on M_{b+1} we obtain $\mathscr{A}^{\mathbb{N}}[I^{<\xi}_{\mathscr{A},b}, n, b, \sum_{c<_\nu b} I^{<\Omega_{c+1}}_{\mathscr{A},c}]$ for a $\xi < \Omega_{b+1}$. This means that $n \in I^{<\xi+1}_{\mathscr{A},b}$.

$\forall b \in \mathbb{N}\left(b < \nu \to \mathscr{A}^{\mathbb{N}}_b[F] \subset F \to \forall \xi < \Omega_{b+1}(I^{<\xi}_{\mathscr{A},b} \subset F)\right)$ is the translation of the axiom ($P_{\mathscr{A}}.2$), which is seen by induction on ordinals $\xi < \Omega_{b+1}$. □

6.2 Higher Ordinals with Collapsing Functions

In this section we work in KP_ν with $\nu > 0$.

For the class ON of ordinals let $ON \times ON \ni (\alpha, \beta) \mapsto \langle\alpha, \beta\rangle \in ON$ denote a recursive (Δ_1-definable) pairing function on ordinals with recursive projections (inverses). The coding is extended to finite sequences of ordinals:
${}^{<\omega}ON \ni (\alpha_1, \dots, \alpha_n) \mapsto \langle\alpha_1, \dots, \alpha_n\rangle \in ON$.

Let $<_\Gamma$ denote a Γ-order in Definition 5.15 whose order type is the next strongly critical number $\Gamma_{\Omega_\nu+1}$ to the order type Ω_ν of ON. Specifically let $e : \Gamma_{\Omega_\nu+1} \to \Omega$ denote the encoding defined by

1. $e(\alpha) = \langle 0, \alpha\rangle$ for $\alpha < \Omega_\nu :\Leftrightarrow \alpha \in ON$.
2. $e(\Omega_\nu) = \langle 1, 0\rangle$.
3. $e(\alpha_0 + \cdots + \alpha_n) = \langle 2, e(\alpha_0), \dots, e(\alpha_n)\rangle$ for $\alpha_0 + \cdots + \alpha_n > \Omega_\nu$, $\alpha_0 \ge \cdots \ge \alpha_n$ and $n > 0$.
4. $e(\varphi\alpha\beta) = \langle 3, e(\alpha), e(\beta)\rangle$ for $\varphi\alpha\beta > \Omega_\nu$.

Then a recursive well order $<_\Gamma$ can be defined on the recursive class ON_Γ of the codes (=the range of e) so that the addition and the Veblen function on the codes are recursive. Observe that, in KP_ν, each initial segment $\{x : x <_\Gamma e(\alpha)\}$ $(\alpha < \Omega_\nu)$ is a set isomorphic to α.

In what follows let us identify the code $e(\alpha)$ with $\alpha < \Gamma_{\Omega_\nu+1}$ and drop the subscript from $<_\Gamma$, when no confusion likely occurs.

α^+ denotes the least admissible ordinal above $\alpha < \Omega_\nu$. Let Ω_a denote the recursive analogue of ω_a, i.e., the continuous closure of the class of admissible ordinals. Namely $\Omega_0 = \omega$, $\Omega_{a+1} = (\Omega_a)^+$ and $\Omega_\lambda = \sup\{\Omega_a : a < \lambda\}$ for limit ordinals λ. We see from Σ-recursion Theorem 1.11 that the map $\nu \ge a \mapsto \Omega_a$ is a provably total Σ_1-function on the field $fld(<_\nu) \subset \mathbb{N}$ in KP_ν when ν is a successor, i.e., Δ_0-Collection for the universe is assumed. This is seen from the fact that there is a Π_3-sentence ad such that ad^x holds iff x is an admissible set, cf. Exercise 6.1.

$\sigma, \kappa, \rho, \dots$ denote the recursively regular ordinals Ω_{a+1} $(a < \nu)$ below or equal to the order type Ω_ν of the class ON of ordinals.

Let $\mathsf{KP}_\nu(U)$ denote a theory obtained from KP_ν by adding a unary predicate symbol U. U is intended to range over definable classes (first-order formulas), and $\{x \in a : x \in U\}$ need not to be a set. Only the (Foundation) axiom schema (and equality axiom) is extended to $\forall x[\forall y \in x F(y) \to F(x)] \to \forall x F(x)$ for arbitrary formula F possibly with the unary predicate U. Then the following Proposition 6.2 is easily seen as in Exercise 4.15.

Proposition 6.2 *For any definable relation $\prec$ in which U does not occur, if $\prec$ is provably well-founded in $\mathsf{KP}_\nu(U)$, i.e., $\mathsf{KP}_\nu(U) \vdash \mathrm{TI}[\prec, U]$, then its order type is less than the next epsilon number $\varepsilon_{\Omega_\nu+1}$ to Ω_ν: $|\prec| < \varepsilon_{\Omega_\nu+1}$.*

Conversely $\mathsf{KP}_\nu(U) \vdash \mathrm{TI}[<_\Gamma\restriction \alpha, U]$ for each $\alpha < \varepsilon_{\Omega_\nu+1}$.

We are in a position to introduce a collapsing function $\psi_\sigma(\alpha) < \sigma$ (even if $\alpha \geq \sigma$). The following definition is due to Buchholz [7].

Definition 6.1 Define simultaneously by recursion on 'ordinals' $\alpha < \Gamma_{\Omega_\nu+1}$ the classes $\mathcal{H}_\alpha(X)$ ($X \subset \Omega_\nu$) and the ordinals $\psi_\sigma(\alpha)$ as follows.

$\mathcal{H}_\alpha(X)$ is the Skolem hull of $\{0\} \cup \{\Omega_a : 0 < a \leq \nu\} \cup X$ under the functions $+, \varphi$, and $(\sigma, \beta) \mapsto \psi_\sigma(\beta)$ ($\beta < \alpha$) for $\sigma = \Omega_{a+1}$ ($a + 1 \leq \nu$).

1. $\mathcal{H}_\alpha^0(X) = \{0\} \cup \{\Omega_a : 0 < a \leq \nu\} \cup X$.
2. $\gamma, \delta \in \mathcal{H}_\alpha^n(X) \Rightarrow \gamma + \delta, \varphi\gamma\delta \in \mathcal{H}_\alpha^{n+1}(X)$.
3. $\gamma \in \mathcal{H}_\alpha^n(X) \,\&\, \gamma < \alpha \Rightarrow \psi_\sigma(\gamma) \in \mathcal{H}_\alpha^{n+1}(X)$ for $\sigma = \Omega_{a+1}$ and $a + 1 \leq \nu$.
4. $\mathcal{H}_\alpha(X) = \bigcup\{\mathcal{H}_\alpha^n(X) : n \in \omega\}$.

Finally let for $\sigma = \Omega_{a+1}$ ($a + 1 \leq \nu$)

$$\psi_\sigma(\alpha) = \min\{\beta < \sigma : \mathcal{H}_\alpha(\beta) \cap \sigma \subset \beta\} \tag{6.1}$$

Let us interpret $\Omega_a = \omega_a = \aleph_a$ as cardinals. Then we see readily that if the cardinality of the set X is less than σ, then so is $\mathcal{H}_\alpha(X)$ for any regular cardinals $\sigma > \omega$.

To see that the ordinal $\psi_\sigma(\alpha)$ could be defined, it suffices to show the existence of an ordinal $\beta < \sigma$ such that $\mathcal{H}_\alpha(\beta) \cap \sigma \subset \beta$ for $\sigma = \Omega_{a+1}$: let $\beta = \sup\{\beta_n : n \in \omega\}$ with $\beta_{n+1} = \min\{\beta < \sigma : \mathcal{H}_\alpha(\beta_n) \cap \sigma \subset \beta\}$ and $\beta_0 = 0 < \sigma$. Then $\mathcal{H}_\alpha(\beta) \cap \sigma \subset \beta$ since $\mathcal{H}_\alpha(\beta) = \bigcup_n \mathcal{H}_\alpha(\beta_n)$, and $\beta < \sigma$ since $\sigma > \omega$ is regular.

This cardinality argument can not be performed within KP_ν. We show that we can mimic the argument within KP_ν when ν is a successor ordinal $\nu = \mu + 1$.

Theorem 6.1 *For each $n < \omega$, Definition 6.1 defines sets $\mathcal{H}_\alpha(z)$ for any $\alpha < \omega_n(\Omega_{\mu+1} + 1)$ and sets $z \subset ON$ of ordinals, and a recursive map $\psi : (a, \alpha) \mapsto \psi_{\Omega_{a+1}}(\alpha)$ ($\alpha < \omega_n(\Omega_{\mu+1} + 1), a \leq \mu$) in $\mathsf{KP}_{\mu+1}$ (uniformly in the elementary recursive well orderings $<_{\mu+1}$ on ω).*

Proof Using the Second Recursion Theorem 1.12 let $H(x, \alpha, z) \leftrightarrow x = \mathcal{H}_\alpha(z)$ and $P(\alpha, \beta, a) \leftrightarrow \psi_{\Omega_{a+1}}(\alpha) = \beta$ denote Σ-predicates for $a \leq \mu$ and $\sigma = \Omega_{a+1}$ such that

$$x = \mathcal{H}_\alpha(z) \leftrightarrow \text{there exists a function } f \text{ such that } \mathrm{dom}(f) = \omega \land$$
$$\forall n \in \omega \left(f(n) = \mathcal{H}_\alpha^n(z)\right) \land x = \bigcup_n f(n) \subset \mathrm{ON}_\Gamma$$
$$\psi_\sigma(\alpha) = \beta \leftrightarrow \beta < \sigma \land \exists x[x = \mathcal{H}_\alpha(\beta) \land x \cap \sigma \subset \beta]$$
$$\land \forall \gamma < \beta \exists y[y = \mathcal{H}_\alpha(\gamma) \land y \cap \sigma \not\subset \gamma]$$

where $f(0) = \mathcal{H}_\alpha^0(z) :\Leftrightarrow f(0) = \{0\} \cup \{\Omega_{b+1} : b \le \mu\} \cup z$ and $f(n+1) = \mathcal{H}_\alpha^{n+1}(z)$ iff $f(n) \subset f(n+1)$, $\forall \gamma, \delta \in f(n)(\{\gamma + \delta, \varphi\gamma\delta\} \subset f(n+1))$, $\forall \gamma \in f(n) \cap \alpha \forall b \le \mu \exists \delta (\psi_{\Omega_{b+1}}(\gamma) = \delta \in f(n+1))$, and $\forall \eta \in f(n+1)[\eta \in f(n) \lor \exists \gamma, \delta \in f(n)(\eta \in \{\gamma + \delta, \varphi\gamma\delta\}) \lor \exists \gamma \in f(n) \cap \alpha \exists b \le \mu(\psi_{\Omega_{b+1}}(\gamma) = \eta)$.

We show that $A(\alpha) :\Leftrightarrow \forall z \subset ON \exists x[x = \mathcal{H}_\alpha(z)] \land \forall \sigma \exists \beta < \sigma[\psi_\sigma(\alpha) = \beta]$ is progressive. Suppose $\forall \gamma < \alpha\, A(\gamma)$ as the IH.

First we show $\forall z \subset ON \exists x[x = \mathcal{H}_\alpha(z)]$. Let $z \subset ON$ be a set of ordinals. Using Σ-Recursion Theorem 1.11 define a recursive function f by $f(0) = \{0\} \cup \{\Omega_{b+1} : b \le \mu\} \cup z$ and $f(n+1) = f(n) \cup \{\gamma + \delta, \varphi\gamma\delta : \gamma, \delta \in f(n)\} \cup \{\psi_{\Omega_{b+1}}(\gamma) : b \le \mu, \gamma \in f(n) \cap \alpha\}$. From IH we see $\forall n \in \omega\{f(n) = \mathcal{H}_\alpha^n(z)\}$, and hence $x = \bigcup_n f(n) = \mathcal{H}_\alpha(z)$ is a desired set by Δ_0-Collection.

Second to see $\exists \beta < \sigma[\psi_\sigma(\alpha) = \beta]$ for recursively regular $\sigma \le \Omega_{\mu+1}$, it suffices to show $\exists \beta < \sigma[\mathcal{H}_\alpha(\beta) \cap \sigma \subset \beta]$. Again using Σ-Recursion Theorem 1.11 define a recursive sequence $\{\beta_n\}$ by $\beta_0 = 0$ and $\beta_{n+1} = \min\{\beta < \sigma : \mathcal{H}_\alpha(\beta_n) \cap \sigma \subset \beta\} = \sup\{\gamma + 1 : \exists x[x = \mathcal{H}_\alpha(\beta_n) \land \gamma \in x \cap \sigma]$. Finally let $\beta = \sup\{\beta_n : n \in \omega\}$. Then $\beta < \sigma$ since σ is recursively regular, and $\mathcal{H}_\alpha(\beta) = \bigcup_n \mathcal{H}_\alpha(\beta_n)$ yields $\mathcal{H}_\alpha(\beta) \cap \sigma \subset \beta$. □

The ordinal $\psi_{\Omega_1}(\varepsilon_{\Omega_1+1})$ is called the *Bachmann–Howard ordinal*.

In the rest of this section, ordinals α in $\mathcal{H}_\alpha(X)$ or $\psi_\sigma(\alpha)$ should be understood $\alpha < \omega_n(\Omega_\nu + 1)$ for a fixed $n < \omega$.

Proposition 6.3 *1.* $\alpha_0 \le \alpha_1 \land X_0 \subset X_1 \Rightarrow \mathcal{H}_{\alpha_0}(X_0) \subset \mathcal{H}_{\alpha_1}(X_1)$.

2. $\mathcal{H}_\alpha(\psi_\sigma(\alpha)) \cap \sigma = \psi_\sigma(\alpha)$ *and* $\psi_\sigma(\alpha) \notin \mathcal{H}_\alpha(\psi_\sigma(\alpha))$.
3. $\alpha_0 \le \alpha \Rightarrow \psi_\sigma(\alpha_0) \le \psi_\sigma(\alpha) \land \mathcal{H}_{\alpha_0}(\psi_\sigma(\alpha_0)) \subset \mathcal{H}_\alpha(\psi_\sigma(\alpha))$.
4. $\alpha_0 \in \mathcal{H}_\alpha(\psi_\sigma(\alpha)) \cap \alpha \Rightarrow \psi_\sigma(\alpha_0) < \psi_\sigma(\alpha)$. *Therefore* $\alpha_0 \in \mathcal{H}_{\alpha_0}(\psi_\sigma(\alpha_0)) \land \alpha \in \mathcal{H}_\alpha(\psi_\sigma(\alpha)) \Rightarrow (\alpha_0 < \alpha \leftrightarrow \psi_\sigma(\alpha_0) < \psi_\sigma(\alpha))$.
5. $\psi_{\Omega_{b+1}}(\alpha)$ *is a strongly critical number such that* $\Omega_b < \psi_{\Omega_{b+1}}(\alpha) < \Omega_{b+1}$.
6. $\gamma \in \mathcal{H}_\alpha(\beta) \Leftrightarrow \mathsf{SC}(\gamma) \subset \mathcal{H}_\alpha(\beta)$, *where* $\mathsf{SC}(0) = \mathsf{SC}(\Omega_\alpha) = \emptyset$, $\mathsf{SC}(\gamma) = \{\gamma\}$ *if* $\gamma \notin \{\Omega_\alpha : \alpha \le \nu\}$ *is strongly critical, and* $\mathsf{SC}(\varphi\gamma\delta) = \mathsf{SC}(\gamma + \delta) = \mathsf{SC}(\gamma) \cup \mathsf{SC}(\delta)$.
7. $\mathcal{H}_\alpha(\psi_{\Omega_{b+1}}(\alpha)) = \mathcal{H}_\alpha(\Omega_b)$ *and* $\psi_{\Omega_{b+1}}(\alpha) = \min\{\xi : \xi \notin \mathcal{H}_\alpha(\Omega_b) \cap \Omega_{b+1}\}$.

Proof Proposition 6.3.3. $\mathcal{H}_{\alpha_0}(\psi_\sigma(\alpha)) \cap \sigma \subset \psi_\sigma(\alpha)$ yields $\psi_\sigma(\alpha_0) \le \psi_\sigma(\alpha)$.

Proposition 6.3.6 is seen from $\mathsf{SC}(\gamma) \le \gamma$.

Proposition 6.3.7 by induction on α. Let $\xi = \min\{\xi : \xi \notin \mathcal{H}_\alpha(\Omega_b) \cap \Omega_{b+1}\}$. Then $\Omega_b < \xi \subset \mathcal{H}_\alpha(\Omega_b) \cap \Omega_{b+1}$, and hence $\mathcal{H}_\alpha(\Omega_b) = \mathcal{H}_\alpha(\xi)$. We show by induction on n that

$$\mathcal{H}_\alpha^n(\Omega_b) \cap \Omega_{b+1} \subset \xi \tag{6.2}$$

If $\gamma + \delta \in \mathcal{H}_\alpha^{n+1}(\Omega_b) \cap \Omega_{b+1}$ with $\{\gamma, \delta\} \subset \mathcal{H}_\alpha^n(\Omega_b)$ is not strongly critical, then $\gamma, \delta < \xi$ by IH on n and $\gamma + \delta < \xi$ since ξ is strongly critical. $\varphi\gamma\delta \in \mathcal{H}_\alpha^{n+1}(\Omega_b) \cap \Omega_{b+1}$ is similar. Assume $\gamma \in \mathcal{H}_\alpha(\Omega_b) \cap \alpha$. Then by IH on α we obtain $\psi_{\Omega_{b+1}}(\gamma) = \mathcal{H}_\gamma(\Omega_b) \cap \Omega_{b+1} \subset \mathcal{H}_\alpha(\Omega_b) \cap \Omega_{b+1}$. On the other hand we have $\psi_{\Omega_{b+1}}(\gamma) \in \mathcal{H}_\alpha(\Omega_b) \cap \Omega_{b+1}$, and hence $\psi_{\Omega_{b+1}}(\gamma) < \xi$.

Equation (6.2) yields $\mathcal{H}_\alpha(\xi) \cap \Omega_{b+1} = \mathcal{H}_\alpha(\Omega_b) \cap \Omega_{b+1} \subset \xi$. Therefore $\psi_{\Omega_{b+1}}(\alpha) \le \xi$, which in turn implies $\mathcal{H}_\alpha(\Omega_b) \subset \mathcal{H}_\alpha(\psi_{\Omega_{b+1}}(\alpha)) \subset \mathcal{H}_\alpha(\xi) = \mathcal{H}_\alpha(\Omega_b)$. From $\psi_{\Omega_{b+1}}(\alpha) \notin \mathcal{H}_\alpha(\psi_{\Omega_{b+1}}(\alpha)) \cap \Omega_{b+1} = \mathcal{H}_\alpha(\Omega_b) \cap \Omega_{b+1}$, we conclude $\psi_{\Omega_{b+1}}(\alpha) = \xi$. □

Proposition 6.3.7 means that $\psi_{\Omega_{b+1}}(\alpha)$ is the Mostowski's collapse of the point Ω_{b+1} in the iterated Skolem hull $\mathcal{H}_\alpha(\Omega_b)$ of ordinals $\Omega_b \cup \{\Omega_a : a \le \nu\}$ under addition $+$ and the binary Veblen function φ. This suggests us that the ordinal $\psi_{\Omega_{b+1}}(\alpha)$ could be a substitute for Ω_{b+1} in a restricted situation.

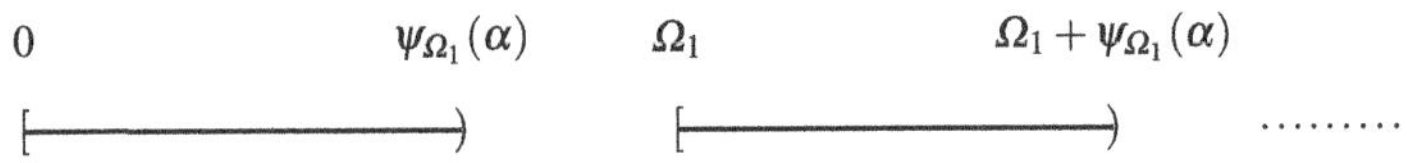

6.2.1 Recursive Notation System $T(\Omega_\nu)$ of Ordinals

By Proposition 6.3.7 we have $\mathcal{H}_{\varepsilon_{\Omega_\nu+1}}(0) = \mathcal{H}_{\varepsilon_{\Omega_\nu+1}}(\omega) = \mathcal{H}_{\varepsilon_{\Omega_\nu+1}}(\psi_{\Omega_1}(\varepsilon_{\Omega_\nu+1}))$ with $\omega = \Omega_0$, and hence each ordinal below $\psi_{\Omega_1}(\varepsilon_{\Omega_\nu+1})$ can be denoted by terms built up from $0, \Omega_a$ $(a \le \nu), +, \varphi, \psi$. Although the representation is not uniquely determined from ordinals, e.g., $\psi_{\Omega_1}(\psi_{\Omega_1}(\Omega_1)) = \psi_{\Omega_1}(\Omega_1)$ by Exercise 6.2, α can be determined from the ordinal $\psi_{\Omega_{b+1}}(\alpha)$ if $\alpha \in \mathcal{H}_\alpha(\Omega_b)$, cf. Propositions 6.3.4 and 6.3.7. In this subsection we devise a recursive notation system $T(\Omega_\nu)$ of ordinals with this restriction.

Let $T(\varepsilon_{\Omega_\nu+1}, 0)$ denote the set of terms built up from $0, \Omega_a$ $(a \le \nu), +, \varphi, \psi$, where both of φ and ψ are binary function symbols. Each term α represents a construction of an ordinal $o(\alpha) \in \mathcal{H}_{\varepsilon_{\Omega_\nu+1}}(0)$. $T(\Omega_\nu)$ is defined to be a subset of $T(\varepsilon_{\Omega_\nu+1}, 0)$.

Definition 6.2 For terms $\alpha \in T(\varepsilon_{\Omega_\nu+1}, 0)$ define finite sets $G_\kappa(\alpha) \subset T(\varepsilon_{\Omega_\nu+1}, 0)$ as follows:

1. $G_\kappa(\psi_\sigma(\alpha)) = \begin{cases} \{\alpha\} \cup G_\kappa(\alpha) & \text{if} \kappa \le \sigma \\ \emptyset & \text{if} \kappa > \sigma \end{cases}$
2. $G_\kappa(\alpha) = \bigcup\{G_\kappa(\beta) : \beta \in \mathrm{SC}(\alpha)\}$ otherwise.

Proposition 6.4 *For any term* $\beta \in T(\varepsilon_{\Omega_\nu+1}, 0)$

$$o(G_{\Omega_{c+1}}(\beta)) < \alpha [:\Leftrightarrow \forall \delta \in G_{\Omega_{c+1}}(\beta)(o(\delta) < \alpha)] \Leftrightarrow o(\beta) \in \mathcal{H}_\alpha(\Omega_c).$$

Proof By induction on the length of terms β. □

Definition 6.3 Define simultaneously sets $P \subset T(\Omega_\nu)$ of terms, and a relation $<$ on $T(\Omega_\nu)$ as follows:

1. $0 \in T(\Omega_\nu)$ and $\Omega_a \in P$ for $0 < a \leq_\nu \nu$.
2. $\alpha_0, \dots, \alpha_n \in P$ $(n > 0) \wedge \alpha_0 \geq \cdots \geq \alpha_n \Rightarrow \alpha_0 + \cdots + \alpha_n \in T(\Omega_\nu)$.
3. Assume $\alpha, \beta \in T(\Omega_\nu)$. Then $\alpha, \beta < \Omega_\nu \Rightarrow \bar{\varphi}\alpha\beta \in P$, and $\beta \geq \Omega_\nu \Rightarrow \bar{\varphi}0\beta \in P$, where $\bar{\varphi}$ is the fixed-point free Veblen function:
$$\bar{\varphi}\alpha\beta := \begin{cases} \varphi\alpha(\beta+1) & \text{if } \exists n < \omega(\beta = \gamma + n \wedge \varphi\alpha\gamma = \gamma) \\ \varphi\alpha\beta & \text{otherwise} \end{cases}$$
and $n = 1 + \cdots + 1$ with $1 = \bar{\varphi}00$.
4. $\alpha \in T(\Omega_\nu) \wedge G_{\Omega_{a+1}}(\alpha) < \alpha \Rightarrow \psi_{\Omega_{a+1}}(\alpha) \in P$ for $a < \nu$.
5. $\Omega_a < \Omega_b :\Leftrightarrow a <_\nu b$.
6. $\psi_{\Omega_{a+1}}\alpha < \Omega_b :\Leftrightarrow a + 1 \leq_\nu b$.
7. $a <_\nu b \Rightarrow \psi_{\Omega_{a+1}}(\alpha) < \psi_{\Omega_{b+1}}(\beta)$ for $\psi_{\Omega_{a+1}}(\alpha), \psi_{\Omega_{b+1}}(\beta) \in T(\Omega_\nu)$.
8. $\psi_{\Omega_{a+1}}(\alpha) < \psi_{\Omega_{a+1}}(\beta) :\Leftrightarrow \alpha < \beta$ for $\psi_{\Omega_{a+1}}(\alpha), \psi_{\Omega_{a+1}}(\beta) \in T(\Omega_\nu)$.
9. Other items for defining the relation $<$ are obvious by setting terms $\psi_{\Omega_{a+1}}(\alpha)$, Ω_{1+b} to be strongly critical numbers.

It is easy to see the following demonstrably in a weak arithmetic, e.g., in EA.

Proposition 6.5 *If $<_\nu$ is an elementary recursive linear order, then so is $(T(\Omega_\nu), <)$. Specifically* EA *proves that if $<_\nu$ is a linear order, then so is $(T(\Omega_\nu), <)$.*

In what follows $\alpha, \beta, \gamma, \delta, \dots$ range over ordinal terms in $T(\Omega_\nu)$, and $<$ denotes the relation between ordinal terms defined in Definition 6.3. An ordinal term α is identified with the set $\{\beta \in T(\Omega_\nu) : \beta < \alpha\}$. $\sigma, \kappa, \rho, \dots$ range over ordinal terms of the form Ω_{a+1} with $a < \nu$, which denote recursively regular ordinals. For ordinal terms α, β, ordinal terms $\alpha + \beta$ and ω^α are defined trivially.

6.3 Well-Foundedness Proof

Although Theorem 6.1 yields a well-foundedness proof of the notation system $T(\Omega_{\mu+1})$ of ordinals up to each $\alpha < \psi_{\Omega_1}(\varepsilon_{\Omega_{\mu+1}+1})$ in $\mathsf{KP}_{\mu+1}$, it is worth to prove the fact arithmetically even for limit ν.

In this section we show that the theory ID_ν defined in Sect. 6.1 proves the fact that the relation $<$ on $T(\Omega_\nu)$ is well-founded up to each $\alpha < \psi_{\Omega_1}(\varepsilon_{\Omega_\nu+1})$.

Theorem 6.2 *For* each $n < \omega$
$$\mathsf{ID}_\nu \vdash \mathrm{TI}[<\upharpoonright \psi_{\Omega_1}(\omega_n(\Omega_\nu + 1)), B]$$
for any formula B in the language $\mathcal{L}(\mathsf{ID})$.

Acc denotes the accessible part of $<$ in $T(\Omega_\nu)$, which is defined in ID_1 as the least fixed point $P_{\mathscr{A}}$ of the operator $\mathscr{A}(X,\alpha) :\Leftrightarrow \alpha \subset X \Leftrightarrow (\forall \beta < \alpha(\beta \in X))$. It suffices to show the following, which is equivalent to Theorem 6.2.

Theorem 6.3 *For each* $\alpha < \psi_{\Omega_1}(\varepsilon_{\Omega_\nu+1})$, $\mathsf{ID}_\nu \vdash \alpha \in Acc$.

Let us consider the simplest case $\nu = 1$ and the set $T(\Omega_1)$ of ordinal terms. The least fixed point Acc enjoys $\forall\alpha(\alpha \subset Acc \to \alpha \in Acc)$, and $\forall\alpha(\alpha \subset F \to \alpha \in F) \to Acc \subset F$. From these we see easily that Acc is closed under $+, \bar{\varphi}$ besides $0 \in Acc$. Hence we obtain $\Gamma_0 = \psi_{\Omega_1}(0) \in Acc$. Likewise $\Gamma_1 = \psi_{\Omega_1}(1) \in Acc$ follows. To prove $\psi_{\Omega_1}(\Omega) \in Acc$, we need to show $\psi_{\Omega_1}(\alpha) \in Acc$ for any $\alpha < \Omega$ such that $\psi_{\Omega_1}(\alpha)$ is an ordinal term, i.e., $G_{\Omega_1}(\alpha) < \alpha$. This means that when $\psi_{\Omega_1}(\beta)$ occurs in α, then $\beta < \alpha$ holds. Thus we have a chance to prove inductively that $\psi_{\Omega_1}(\alpha) \in Acc$. The ordinal term α is built from 0, Ω_1 and some ordinal terms $\psi_{\Omega_1}(\beta)$ with $\beta < \alpha$ by $+, \bar{\varphi}$. Let us assume that each of ordinals $\psi_{\Omega_1}(\beta)$ occurring in α is in Acc, and denote the set of such ordinals α by M_1. Though we don't have $\Omega_1 \in Acc$ in hand (since this means that $T(\Omega_1) \cap \Omega$ is well-founded, which is the fact we are going to prove), Ω_1 is in the accessible part of the set M_1. Then let $\alpha \in W_1 :\Leftrightarrow \psi_{\Omega_1}(\alpha) \in Acc$ for ordinal terms $\psi_{\Omega_1}(\alpha)$. W_1 is first-order definable set from Acc. It turns out that W_1 is progressive on M_1, and $\Omega_1 \in W_1$. Moreover $\omega^{\Omega_1+1} \in W_1$ is seen as in the jump set for epsilon numbers in Sect. 4.1. In this way we see that $\alpha \in W_1$, i.e., $\psi_{\Omega_1}(\alpha) \in Acc$ for each $\alpha < \varepsilon_{\Omega_1+1}$.

For the general case $\nu > 1$, we need to define W_1 to be the accessible part of the set M_1. Then it turns out that $W_1 \cap \Omega_2$ is an end extension of $Acc \cap \Omega_1$, and so on.

Let $\mathsf{SC}(\alpha)$ denote the set of strongly critical parts of α defined in Proposition 6.3.6.

Definition 6.4 1. For $\alpha \in T(\Omega_\nu)$ and $a \leq \nu$, a finite set $K_a(\alpha)$ of subterms of α is defined recursively as follows. $K_a(\alpha) = \bigcup\{K_a(\beta) : \beta \in \mathsf{SC}(\alpha)\}$ when α is not strongly critical. $K_a(\Omega_b) = \{\Omega_b\}$ if $a \geq b > 0$. $K_a(\Omega_b) = \emptyset$ if $a < b$. $K_a(\psi_\sigma(\alpha)) = K_a(\alpha)$ if $\Omega_{a+1} < \sigma$. $K_a(\psi_\sigma(\alpha)) = \{\psi_\sigma(\alpha)\}$ if $\Omega_{a+1} \geq \sigma$.
2. Let us define $\{W_a\}_{a<\nu}$ by an iterated inductive definition as follows. Let

$$M_a = \{\alpha \in T(\Omega_\nu) \cap \Omega_{a+1} : \forall b < a(K_b(\alpha) \subset W_b)\}\, (a \leq \nu).$$

W_a is the least fixed point of the operator $X \mapsto \{\alpha \in M_a : \forall \beta <_a \alpha(\beta \in X)\}$ with $\beta <_a \alpha :\Leftrightarrow \beta < \alpha \land \{\beta, \alpha\} \subset M_a$.

This means that W_a is the accessible part of $(M_a, <)$. In particular $M_0 = \Omega_1$ and $Acc \cap \Omega_1 = W_0$ for the least element 0 in the ordering $<_\nu$. By the definition we have the following.

$(W.1)$ $\forall a < \nu\, (\forall \alpha \in M_a(M_a \cap \alpha \subset W_a \to \alpha \in W_a))$.
$(W.2)$ $\forall a < \nu\, (\forall \alpha \in M_a(M_a \cap \alpha \subset F \to \alpha \in F) \to W_a \subset F)$ for any formula F.

From $(W.1)$ and $(W.2)$ we see for any $a < \nu$ that $\alpha \in W_a \to M_a \cap \alpha \subset W_a$ since $\forall \alpha \in M_a(M_a \cap \alpha \subset F \to \alpha \in F)$ for $F(\alpha) \Leftrightarrow M_a \cap \alpha \subset W_a$. This yields for any formula F that $\forall\alpha \in W_a(M_a \cap \alpha \subset F \to \alpha \in F) \to W_a \subset F$ since supposing $\forall\alpha \in W_a(M_a \cap \alpha \subset F \to \alpha \in F)$ we see $\forall\alpha \in M_a(M_a \cap \alpha \subset F' \to \alpha \in F')$ with $F'(\alpha) :\Leftrightarrow (\alpha \in W_a \to F(\alpha))$.

Proposition 6.6 *1.* $G_\kappa(\alpha) \subset G_\sigma(\alpha)$ *if* $\kappa > \sigma$.
2. $K_b(K_a(\alpha)) := \bigcup\{K_b(\beta) : \beta \in K_a(\alpha)\} = K_b(\alpha)$ *if* $b \leq a$.
3. $G_\sigma(\beta) < \alpha \Rightarrow \forall b \geq a(K_b(\beta) < \psi_{\Omega_{b+1}}(\alpha))$ *for* $\psi_\sigma(\alpha) \in T(\Omega_\nu)$ *with* $\sigma = \Omega_{a+1}$.

Proof Propositions 6.6.1 and 6.6.2. are seen by induction on the length of ordinal terms α.

Proposition 6.6.3 is shown by induction on the length of ordinal terms β. Assume $G_\sigma(\beta) < \alpha$ and $b \geq a$. Then by Proposition 6.6.1 we have $G_{\Omega_{b+1}}(\alpha) < \alpha$. By IH we can assume either $\beta = \Omega_c$ or $\beta = \psi_\kappa(\gamma)$. For $0 < c \leq b$, we have $K_b(\Omega_c) = \{\Omega_c\} < \psi_{\Omega_{b+1}}(\alpha)$ by Proposition 6.3.5. In what follows let $\beta = \psi_\kappa(\gamma)$.

If $\Omega_{b+1} \geq \kappa$, then $K_b(\beta) = \{\beta\}$. If $\kappa < \Omega_{b+1}$, then $\beta < \kappa < \psi_{\Omega_{b+1}}(\alpha)$. Suppose $\kappa = \Omega_{b+1} \geq \sigma$. Then $G_\sigma(\beta) = \{\gamma\} \cup G_\sigma(\gamma) < \alpha$. Hence $\beta = \psi_\kappa(\gamma) < \psi_\kappa(\alpha)$. Suppose $\sigma \leq \Omega_{b+1} < \kappa$. Then $K_b(\beta) = K_b(\gamma)$ and $G_\sigma(\beta) = \{\gamma\} \cup G_\sigma(\gamma) < \alpha$. IH yields $K_b(\gamma) < \psi_{\Omega_{b+1}}(\alpha)$. □

In what follows we work in ID_ν except otherwise stated.

Proposition 6.7 *For any* $a < \nu$*, the following hold.*

1. $W_a \subset M_a, \{\gamma, \delta\} \subset M_a \to \{\gamma + \delta, \bar{\varphi}\gamma\delta\} \subset M_a, \gamma + \delta \in M_a \to \delta \in M_a, \bar{\varphi}\gamma\delta \in M_a \to \{\gamma, \delta\} \subset M_a$ *and* $\gamma \in W_a \to M_a \cap \gamma \subset W_a$.
2. $0 \in W_a$.
3. $\{\gamma, \delta\} \subset W_a \to \gamma + \delta \in W_a$.
4. $\{\gamma, \delta\} \subset W_a \to \bar{\varphi}\gamma\delta \in W_a$.
5. $\alpha \in W_a \leftrightarrow \alpha < \Omega_{a+1} \wedge K_a(\alpha) \subset W_a$.

Proof Proposition 6.7.3. Assume $\gamma \in W_a$, $\delta \in M_a$, and $\forall\beta <_a \delta(\gamma + \beta \in W_a)$. We then see from Proposition 6.7.1 that $\gamma + \delta \in M_a \wedge M_a \cap (\gamma + \delta) \subset W_a$. Hence $\gamma + \delta \in W_a$ by $(W.1)$. Therefore $\gamma \in W_a \to \delta \in W_a \to \gamma + \delta \in W_a$ by $(W.2)$.

Proposition 6.7.4. Assume $\gamma \in W_a$, $\forall\alpha <_a \gamma\forall\beta \in W_a(\bar{\varphi}\alpha\beta \in W_a)$, $\delta \in W_a$, and $\forall\beta <_a \delta(\bar{\varphi}\gamma\beta \in W_a)$. We obtain $\bar{\varphi}\gamma\delta \in M_a$ by Proposition 6.7.1.

We show $\alpha_0 \in M_a \cap (\bar{\varphi}\gamma\delta) \to \alpha_0 \in W_a$ by induction on the length of ordinal terms α_0. When α_0 is strongly critical, then $\alpha_0 \leq \max\{\gamma, \delta\}$, and $\alpha_0 \in W_a$. Suppose that α_0 is not strongly critical. By Propositions 6.7.1, 6.7.2 and 6.7.3 we can assume that $\alpha_0 = \bar{\varphi}\alpha\beta$ with $\{\alpha, \beta\} \subset M_a$. By IH and $\beta < \alpha_0$ we obtain $\beta \in W_a$. If $\alpha < \gamma$, then $\alpha_0 \in W_a$ by the second assumption. If $\alpha = \gamma$, then $\beta <_a \delta$ and $\alpha_0 \in W_a$ by the fourth assumption. Finally let $\alpha > \gamma$. Then $\alpha_0 \leq \delta$, and we obtain $\alpha_0 \in W_a$ by $\delta \in W_a$. Thus $M_a \cap (\bar{\varphi}\gamma\delta) \subset W_a$ is shown.

By $(W.1)$ we obtain $\gamma, \delta \in W_a \to \forall\alpha <_a \gamma\forall\beta \in W_a(\bar{\varphi}\alpha\beta \in W_a) \to \forall\beta <_a \delta(\bar{\varphi}\gamma\beta \in W_a) \to \bar{\varphi}\gamma\delta \in W_a$. $(W.2)$ yields $\gamma \in W_a \to \forall\alpha <_a \gamma\forall\beta \in W_a(\bar{\varphi}\alpha\beta \in W_a) \to \forall\delta \in W_a(\bar{\varphi}\gamma\delta \in W_a)$. Once again by $(W.2)$ we obtain $\gamma \in W_a \to \forall\delta \in W_a(\bar{\varphi}\gamma\delta \in W_a)$.

Proposition 6.7.5. We show the assertion by induction on the length of ordinal terms α. By Propositions 6.7.1–6.7.4 we can assume that α is strongly critical. Then $K_a(\alpha) = \{\alpha\}$ for $\alpha < \Omega_{a+1}$. □

Lemma 6.1 *1. For $a < b < \nu$, $W_a \subset W_b$ and $\forall\beta \in W_b \forall\alpha \in W_a(\beta < \alpha \to \beta \in W_a)$. Namely W_b is an end extension of W_a, $W_a \subset_e W_b$.*
2. $M_\nu \cap \Omega_\nu = \bigcup_{a<\nu} W_a$.

Proof Lemma 6.1.1. Let $W_b \ni \beta < \alpha \in W_a$ for $a < b$. Then $\beta \in M_b \subset M_a$, and $\beta \in M_a \cap \alpha$. Hence $\beta \in W_a$.

By induction on $b < \nu$, we show $\forall a < b(W_a \subset W_b)$. Let $a < b$ and $\alpha \in W_a$. Then $\alpha \in M_a$, and IH yields $\forall c(a \leq c < b \to \alpha \in W_c)$. Hence $\forall c < b(K_c(\alpha) \subset W_c)$ by Proposition 6.7.5, i.e., $\alpha \in M_b$. Next assume $M_a \cap \alpha \subset W_b$. Then $M_b \cap \alpha \subset M_a \cap \alpha \subset W_b$, and hence $\alpha \in W_b$. Thus we obtain $\forall\alpha \in W_a(M_a \cap \alpha \subset W_b \to \alpha \in W_b)$. Therefore $W_a \subset W_b$ by $(W.2)$.

Lemma 6.1.2. First let $\alpha \in W_a$ for $a < \nu$. Then $\alpha < \Omega_{a+1} \leq \Omega_\nu$, and $\alpha \in W_b$ for any b with $a \leq b < \nu$ by Lemma 6.1.1. Hence $\forall b < \nu(K_b(\alpha) \subset W_b)$ by Proposition 6.7.5, i.e., $\alpha \in M_\nu$.

Conversely assume $\alpha \in M_\nu \cap \Omega_\nu$. Let $a < \nu$ be such that $\Omega_a \leq \alpha < \Omega_{a+1}$. Then $K_a(\alpha) \subset W_a$, and we obtain $\alpha \in W_a$ by Proposition 6.7.5. □

Proposition 6.8 $\forall a < \nu(\Omega_a \in W_a)$.

Proof Let $a < \nu$. We have $\forall b < a(K_b(\Omega_a) = \emptyset)$, and $\Omega_a \in M_a$. It remains to show $M_a \cap \Omega_a \subset W_a$. Assume $\alpha \in M_a \cap \Omega_a$. Let $b < a$ be such that $\Omega_b \leq \alpha < \Omega_{b+1}$. Then $K_b(\alpha) \subset W_b$, which yields $\alpha \in W_b \subset W_a$ by Proposition 6.7.5 and Lemma 6.1.1. □

Let

$$\mathcal{A}_\nu(X) := \{\alpha \in M_\nu : M_\nu \cap \alpha \subset X\}.$$

Proposition 6.9 *For each formula F, $\mathcal{A}_\nu(F) \subset F \to \Omega_\nu \in F$.*

Proof Assuming $\mathcal{A}_\nu(F) \subset F$, we show $\Omega_\nu \in \mathcal{A}_\nu(F)$. We have $\forall b < \nu(K_b(\Omega_\nu) = \emptyset)$, and $\Omega_\nu \in M_\nu$. On the other hand we have $M_\nu \cap \Omega_\nu = \bigcup_{a<\nu} W_a$ by Lemma 6.1.2. Hence it suffices to show $\forall a < \nu(W_a \subset F)$. Let $M_a \cap \alpha \subset F$ and $\alpha \in W_a$ for $a < \nu$. Then $\alpha \in M_\nu$, and $M_\nu \cap \alpha \subset F$ by $M_\nu \subset M_a$. Hence $\alpha \in \mathcal{A}_\nu(F)$, and $\alpha \in F$ by the assumption. Therefore $\forall\alpha \in W_a(M_a \cap \alpha \subset F \to \alpha \in F)$. $(W.2)$ yields $W_a \subset F$. □

Lemma 6.2 *For each formula F, $\mathcal{A}_\nu(F) \subset F \to \mathcal{A}_\nu(\mathrm{j}_\nu[F]) \subset \mathrm{j}_\nu[F]$, where $\mathrm{j}_\nu[F] := \{\beta \in T(\Omega_\nu) : \forall\alpha(M_\nu \cap \alpha \subset F \to M_\nu \cap (\alpha + \omega^\beta) \subset F)\}$.*

Proof This is seen as in Claim 4.1.

Assume $\mathcal{A}_\nu(F) \subset F$, $\beta \in \mathcal{A}_\nu(\mathrm{j}_\nu[F])$, $M_\nu \cap \alpha \subset F$, and $\gamma \in M_\nu \cap (\alpha + \omega^\beta)$. We need to show $\gamma \in F$. If $\gamma < \alpha$, then $\gamma \in F$ by $M_\nu \cap \alpha \subset F$. If $\gamma = \alpha$, then $\alpha \in F$ by $\mathcal{A}_\nu(F) \subset F$ and $M_\nu \cap \alpha \subset F$. Let $\alpha < \gamma < \alpha + \omega^\delta \cdot n$ for a $\delta < \beta$ and $n < \omega$. From $\gamma \in M_\nu$ we can assume $\delta \in M_\nu$. From $\beta \in \mathcal{A}_\nu(\mathrm{j}_\nu[F])$ we see that $\delta \in \mathrm{j}_\nu[F]$. By induction on $n < \omega$ using $M_\nu \cap \alpha \subset F$, we obtain $M_\nu \cap (\alpha + \omega^\delta \cdot n) \subset F$. Hence $\gamma \in F$. □

Lemma 6.3 *For each formula F and* each $n < \omega$, $\mathscr{A}_\nu(F) \subset F \to \omega_n(\Omega_\nu + 1) \in F$.

Proof We show the assertion by meta-induction on $n < \omega$. Assume $\mathscr{A}_\nu(F) \subset F$. Then $\mathscr{A}_\nu(\mathrm{j}_\nu[F]) \subset \mathrm{j}_\nu[F]$ by Lemma 6.2. By Proposition 6.9 we have $\Omega_\nu \in F$. From this we see that $\Omega_\nu + 1 \in \mathscr{A}_\nu(F)$, and hence $\Omega_\nu + 1 \in F$. By IH we have $\omega_n(\Omega_\nu + 1) \in \mathrm{j}_\nu[F]$, and hence $M_\nu \cap \omega_{n+1}(\Omega_\nu + 1) \subset F$. The assumption $\mathscr{A}_\nu(F) \subset F$ yields $\omega_{n+1}(\Omega_\nu + 1) \in F$. □

Let

$$\alpha \in W_\nu :\Leftrightarrow \forall a < \nu \left(\psi_{\Omega_{a+1}}(\alpha) \in T(\Omega_\nu) \to \psi_{\Omega_{a+1}}(\alpha) \in W_a\right).$$

Lemma 6.4 $\mathscr{A}_\nu(W_\nu) \subset W_\nu$.

Proof Assume $\alpha \in \mathscr{A}_\nu(W_\nu)$ and $\psi_{\Omega_{a+1}}(\alpha) \in T(\Omega_\nu)$ for $a < \nu$. Then $\alpha \in M_\nu$ and $M_\nu \cap \alpha \subset W_\nu$. For any $b < a$ we have $K_b(\psi_{\Omega_{a+1}}(\alpha)) = K_b(\alpha) \subset W_b$ by $\alpha \in M_\nu$. Hence $\psi_{\Omega_{a+1}}(\alpha) \in M_a$.

Next we show

$$\forall b \geq a \left(\gamma \in M_b \cap (\psi_{\Omega_{b+1}}(\alpha)) \to \gamma \in W_b\right) \tag{6.3}$$

by induction on the length of ordinal terms γ.

By Propositions 6.7.5, 6.6.2 and 6.8 with IH, and Lemma 6.1.1 we can assume that $\gamma = \psi_\sigma(\beta) \in M_b \cap (\psi_{\Omega_{b+1}}(\alpha))$ for a $b \geq a$. If $\sigma = \Omega_{c+1} < \Omega_{b+1}$, then $K_c(\gamma) = \{\gamma\} \subset W_c \subset W_b$. Suppose $\sigma = \Omega_{b+1}$. Then $\beta < \alpha$. From $\gamma \in M_b$ and $\forall c < b(K_c(\gamma) = K_c(\beta))$, we see $\beta \in M_b$.

Now we show that $\beta \in M_\nu$, i.e., $\forall c < \nu(K_c(\beta) \subset W_c)$ by induction on $c < \nu$. Let $c \geq b$. We have $G_\sigma(\beta) < \beta$. Proposition 6.6.3 yields $\forall c \geq b(K_c(\beta) < \psi_{\Omega_{c+1}}(\beta) < \psi_{\Omega_{c+1}}(\alpha))$. Moreover we have $K_c(\beta) \subset M_c$ by Proposition 6.6.2 and IH on c. Thus $K_c(\beta) \subset M_c \cap (\psi_{\Omega_{c+1}}(\alpha))$, and IH on the length yields $K_c(\beta) \subset W_c$.

Therefore $\beta \in M_\nu \cap \alpha \subset W_\nu$, which yields $\gamma = \psi_\sigma(\beta) \in W_b$. (6.3) is shown. In particular we obtain $M_a \cap (\psi_{\Omega_{a+1}}(\alpha)) \subset W_a$. We conclude $\psi_{\Omega_{a+1}}(\alpha) \in W_a$. □

Proof Let us show Theorem 6.3. We show that ID_ν proves $\psi_{\Omega_1}(\omega_n(\Omega_\nu + 1)) \in W_0$ for each $n < \omega$. By Lemmas 6.3 and 6.4 we obtain $\omega_n(\Omega_\nu + 1) \in W_\nu$. Thus $\psi_{\Omega_1}(\omega_n(\Omega_\nu + 1)) \in W_0$ by the definition of W_ν.

6.4 Impredicative Cut Elimination

In this section we expound cut-elimination procedures in impredicative theories. To illustrate ideas, we consider first the simplest case, i.e., analyze proof-theoretically a theory $\mathsf{ID}_1^{\mathbb{O}}$ through the *operator controlled derivations* due to Buchholz [8]. ID_1 is embedded in $\mathsf{ID}_1^{\mathbb{O}}$. We show the Bachmann–Howard ordinal $\psi_{\Omega_1}(\varepsilon_{\Omega_1+1})$ is an upperbound for the proof-theoretic ordinal of $\mathsf{ID}_1^{\mathbb{O}}$. Then ID_1 is analyzed proof-theoretically through the *Ω-rule* also due to Buchholz [6]. Moreover we establish proof-theoretic equivalences of ID_1, and the light-face Π^1_1-comprehension axiom over weak SOA's.

The *language* $\mathcal{L}(\mathsf{ID}_1)$ of ID_1 is obtained from the language $\mathcal{L}(\mathsf{PA})$ by adding a *unary* predicate $P_{\mathcal{A}}$ for each positive elementary formula $\mathcal{A}[X,n]$. Its axioms are those of PA in the expanded language, $(P_{\mathcal{A}}.1)$ $\mathcal{A}[P_{\mathcal{A}}] \subset P_{\mathcal{A}}$, and the schema $(P_{\mathcal{A}}.2)$ $\mathcal{A}[F] \subset F \to P_{\mathcal{A}} \subset F$ for each positive elementary $\mathcal{A}$ and formulas F in $\mathcal{L}(\mathsf{ID}_1)$, where $\mathcal{A}[X] = \{n : \mathcal{A}[X,n]\}$.

Intuitively these axioms state that $P_{\mathcal{A}}$ is the least fixed point of the operator $X \mapsto \mathcal{A}[X]$. There are two ways to define the least fixed point. First it is the union of stages: to stratify the set into stages, $P_{\mathcal{A}} = \bigcup_{\xi<\Omega_1} I^{<\xi}_{\mathcal{A}}$, where $I^{\xi}_{\mathcal{A}} = \mathcal{A}[I^{<\xi}_{\mathcal{A}}]$ with $I^{<\xi}_{\mathcal{A}} = \bigcup_{\eta<\xi} I^{\eta}_{\mathcal{A}}$. Second it is the intersection of all closed sets, $P_{\mathcal{A}} = \bigcap\{X \subset \mathbb{N} : \mathcal{A}[X] \subset X\}$, i.e., $n \in P_{\mathcal{A}} \Leftrightarrow \forall X \subset \mathbb{N}\{\mathcal{A}[X] \subset X \to n \in X\}$. The first way is formulated naturally in a theory $\mathcal{L}(\mathsf{ID}^{\mathbb{O}})$ with stages $I^{\xi}_{\mathcal{A}}$, which is analyzed through the operator controlled derivations in Sect. 6.4.1. The second way is analyzed through the Ω-rule in Sect. 6.4.2.

6.4.1 Operator Controlled Derivations

The *language* $\mathcal{L}(\mathsf{ID}^{\mathbb{O}})$ of $\mathsf{ID}^{\mathbb{O}}_1$ is a two sorted language (one sort $\mathbb{N}$ for natural numbers and the other $\mathbb{O}$ for ordinals), and is obtained from the language $\mathcal{L}(\mathsf{PA})$ by adding the following symbols:

1. The $\mathbb{O}$-variables $\xi, \zeta, \eta, \ldots$ ranging over ordinals, and the predicate constants $=^{\iota}$, $<^{\iota}$ for equality and less than relation on each sort $\iota \in \{\mathbb{N}, \mathbb{O}\}$.
2. Two binary predicate constants $I_{\mathcal{A}}, I^{<}_{\mathcal{A}}$ and a unary one $I^{<\Omega_1}_{\mathcal{A}}$ for each positive elementary formula $\mathcal{A}[X,n]$.

The (first order) theory $\mathsf{ID}^{\mathbb{O}}_1$ is obtained from PA in the language $\mathcal{L}(\mathsf{ID}^{\mathbb{O}})$ by adding the following axioms. We write $<$ for $<^{\mathbb{O}}$ when no confusion likely occurs.

Let $I^{<\xi}_{\mathcal{A}} = \{n : I^{<}_{\mathcal{A}}(\xi, n)\}$, and $I^{\xi}_{\mathcal{A}} := \{n : I_{\mathcal{A}}(\xi, n)\}$. The quantifier $\forall\xi$ on sort $\mathbb{O}$ is denoted $\forall\xi < \Omega_1$, and similarly for the existential quantifiers $\exists\xi$.

$(I_{\mathcal{A}})$ $\forall\xi < \Omega_1 \left(\mathcal{A}[I^{<\xi}_{\mathcal{A}}] = I^{\xi}_{\mathcal{A}}\right)$. Namely $\forall\xi < \Omega_1 \forall n \left(\mathcal{A}[I^{<\xi}_{\mathcal{A}}, n,] \leftrightarrow n \in I^{\xi}_{\mathcal{A}}\right)$.

$(I^{<}_{\mathcal{A}})$ $\forall\xi \leq \Omega_1 \left(I^{<\xi}_{\mathcal{A}} = \bigcup_{\eta<\xi} I^{\eta}_{\mathcal{A}}\right)$, i.e., $\forall\xi \leq \Omega_1 \forall n \left(n \in I^{<\xi}_{\mathcal{A}} \leftrightarrow \exists\eta <^{\mathbb{O}} \xi (n \in I^{\eta}_{\mathcal{A}})\right)$.

(Cl) Closure axiom: $\mathcal{A}[I^{<\Omega_1}_{\mathcal{A}}] \subset I^{<\Omega_1}_{\mathcal{A}}$. Namely $\forall n \left(\mathcal{A}[I^{<\Omega_1}_{\mathcal{A}}, n] \to n \in I^{<\Omega_1}_{\mathcal{A}}\right)$.

$(TI_{\mathbb{O}})$ Transfinite induction schema: $\forall\xi(\forall\zeta < \xi F(\zeta) \to F(\xi)) \to \forall\xi F(\xi)$ for any formula F.

$I^{<\Omega_1}_{\mathcal{A}} = \bigcup_{\xi<\Omega_1} I^{\xi}_{\mathcal{A}}$ denotes the least fixed point of the positive elementary operator $\mathcal{A}$, where $I^{\xi}_{\mathcal{A}}$ is the ξth stage of the inductive definition.

For any formula $B \equiv B[P_{\mathcal{A}}, \ldots]$ in $\mathcal{L}(\mathsf{ID}_1)$ let B' denote the formula in $\mathcal{L}(\mathsf{ID}^{\mathbb{O}})$ resulted from B by replacing $P_{\mathcal{A}}(n)$ by $n \in I^{<\Omega_1}_{\mathcal{A}}$.

Proposition 6.10 $\mathsf{ID}_1 \vdash B \Rightarrow \mathsf{ID}_1^{\mathbb{O}} \vdash B'$, *and* $\mathsf{ID}_1^{\mathbb{O}}$ *is interpreted in* KP_1 *canonically.*

Proof The translated $(P_{\mathscr{A}}.1)$ follows from the Closure axiom (Cl), while the translation $\mathscr{A}[F] \subset F \to \forall\xi < \Omega_1 \left(I_{\mathscr{A}}^{\xi} \subset F\right)$ of $(P_{\mathscr{A}}.2)$, is shown by transfinite induction on ordinals ξ using the positivity of $\mathscr{A}$.

A canonical interpretation of $\mathsf{ID}_1^{\mathbb{O}}$ in KP_1 is given in Proposition 6.1. □

The translation (Cl) $\forall x \left(\mathscr{A}[I_{\mathscr{A}}^{<\Omega_1}, x] \to \exists\xi < \Omega_1(x \in I_{\mathscr{A}}^{\xi})\right)$ of the closure axiom $(P_{\mathscr{A}}.1)$, $\mathscr{A}[P_{\mathscr{A}}] \subset P_{\mathscr{A}}$ is the crucial axiom to be analyzed. Since X occurs only positively in $\mathscr{A}[X, x]$, the formula $\mathscr{A}[I_{\mathscr{A}}^{<\Omega_1}, x]$ is a Σ_1-formula in the language of set theory, and the translation follows from Σ-Reflection, Theorem 1.10. Roughly the axiom is analyzed as follows. Suppose that we have an infinitary derivation of the sequent $\Gamma, \mathscr{A}[I_{\mathscr{A}}^{<\Omega_1}, n]$ in depth α. We show that the derivation can be collapsed to a derivation in a countable $\xi = \psi_{\Omega_1}(\hat{\alpha})$ when the derivation is almost cut-free, and Γ is a positive sequent in which $P_{\mathscr{A}}$ occurs only positively, i.e., Σ_1-formulas in the language of set theory, cf. Collapsing Theorem 6.4 below. Then we see easily that $\Gamma, \mathscr{A}[I_{\mathscr{A}}^{\xi}, n]$ holds, and $\Gamma, n \in I_{\mathscr{A}}^{\xi+1}$ follows, cf. Boundedness Lemma 6.7.

In what follows we work in the intuitionistic fixed point theory $\mathrm{FiX}^i(\mathsf{PA} + \{\mathrm{TI}(T(\Omega_1), <)\})$ over the first-order arithmetic PA extended by the axiom schema $\mathrm{TI}(T(\Omega_1), <)$ for the transfinite induction with respect to the order $(T(\Omega_1), <)$.

The language of an infinitary calculus for $\mathsf{ID}_1^{\mathbb{O}}$ is obtained from the language of $\mathsf{ID}_1^{\mathbb{O}}$ by adding (the individual constant corresponding to) each ordinal term $\alpha \in T(\Omega_1) \cap (\Omega_1 + 1)$. We consider sentences, i.e., closed formulas. A closed term t in sort $\mathbb{N}$ is identify with the numeral $\bar{n}$, or even with the number n where $n = \mathrm{val}(t)$ (the value of t in the standard model). In what follows $A, B, \ldots$ denote the sentences in the language with ordinal terms.

For simplicity predicate constants in the language $\mathscr{L}(\mathsf{PA})$ of arithmetic are restricted to $=^{\mathbb{N}}$ and $<^{\mathbb{N}}$. Then an atomic sentence is one of the form $n =^{\mathbb{N}} m, n <^{\mathbb{N}} m$, $\alpha =^{\mathbb{O}} \beta, \alpha <^{\mathbb{O}} \beta$, and $n \in I_{\mathscr{A}}^{\xi}, n \in I_{\mathscr{A}}^{<\xi}$ for $n, m \in \omega$ and $\alpha, \beta, \xi \in T(\Omega_1) \cap (\Omega_1 + 1)$. A literal is either an atomic sentence or its negation. Let us specify *true* literals.

An atomic sentence of the form $n =^{\mathbb{N}} m, n <^{\mathbb{N}} m$ and $\alpha =^{\mathbb{O}} \beta, \alpha <^{\mathbb{O}} \beta$ is defined to be *true* if it is true in the standard model, where $\alpha <^{\mathbb{O}} \beta$ is defined to be true iff $\alpha < \beta$ in $T(\Omega_1)$. Otherwise its negation is *true*. These are *prime literal*. A prime literal is defined to be *false* iff its negation is true. Note that no atomic sentence of the form $[\neg]n \in I_{\mathscr{A}}^{\xi}, [\neg]n \in I_{\mathscr{A}}^{<\xi}$ is defined to be true nor false.

Definition 6.5 We assign disjunctions or conjunctions to sentences as follows. When a disjunction $\bigvee(A_i)_{i\in J}$ [a conjunction $\bigwedge(A_i)_{i\in J}$] is assigned to A, we denote $A \simeq \bigvee(A_i)_{i\in J}$ [$A \simeq \bigwedge(A_i)_{i\in J}$], resp. In each case J is an ordinal.

1. For a prime literal A, $A \simeq \begin{cases} \bigvee(A_i)_{i\in J} & A \text{ is false} \\ \bigwedge(A_i)_{i\in J} & A \text{ is true} \end{cases}$ with $J = 0$
2. $(A_0 \vee A_1) \simeq \bigvee(A_i)_{i\in J}$ and $(A_0 \wedge A_1) \simeq \bigwedge(A_i)_{i\in J}$ with $J = 2$.
3. $(\exists x\, A(x)) \simeq \bigvee(A(n))_{n\in J}$ and $(\forall x\, A(x)) \simeq \bigwedge(A(n))_{n\in J}$ with $J = \omega$ for variables x of sort $\mathbb{N}$.

4. $(\exists\xi\, A(\xi)) \simeq \bigvee(A(\zeta))_{\zeta\in J}$ and $(\forall\xi\, A(\xi)) \simeq \bigwedge(A(\zeta))_{\zeta\in J}$ with $J = T(\Omega_1) \cap \Omega_1$ for variables ξ of sort $\mathbb{O}$.
5. $(n \in I^{\xi}_{\mathscr{A}}) \simeq \bigvee(A_i)_{i\in J}$ and $(n \notin I^{\xi}_{\mathscr{A}}) \simeq \bigwedge(\neg A_i)_{i\in J}$ with $A_0 \equiv \mathscr{A}[I^{<\xi}_{\mathscr{A}}, n]$ and $J = 1$.
6. $(n \in I^{<\xi}_{\mathscr{A}}) \simeq \bigvee(A_\zeta)_{\zeta\in J}$ and $(n \notin I^{<\xi}_{\mathscr{A}}) \simeq \bigwedge(\neg A_\zeta)_{\zeta\in J}$ with $A_\zeta \equiv (n \in I^{\zeta}_{\mathscr{A}})$ and $J = T(\Omega_1) \cap \xi$.

Definition 6.6 (*Cf. Definition* 5.7) For a formula B in the language $\mathscr{L}(\mathsf{PA}) \cup \{X\}$, $n_B < \omega$ denotes the number defined recursively as follows. $n_L = 0$ for arithmetic literals L. $n_B = 1$ for atomic formulas $t \in X$. $n_{\neg B} = n_B$. $n_{B_0\vee B_1} = \max\{n_{B_i} : i = 0, 1\} + 1$. $n_{\exists x B(x)} = n_{B(0)} + 1$.

The *degree* $\mathrm{dg}(A) < \Omega_1 + \omega$ of a sentence A is defined recursively.

1. $\mathrm{dg}(L) = 0$ for any prime literal L, and $\mathrm{dg}(\neg A) = \mathrm{dg}(A)$.
2. $\mathrm{dg}(A_0 \vee A_1) = \max\{\mathrm{dg}(A_i) : i = 0, 1\} + 1$.
3. $\mathrm{dg}(\exists x A(x)) = \mathrm{dg}(A(0)) + 1$.
4. $\mathrm{dg}(\exists\xi A(\xi)) = \max\{\Omega_1 + 1, \mathrm{dg}(A(0)) + 1\}$.
5. $\mathrm{dg}(t \in I^{<\xi}_{\mathscr{A}}) = (n_{\mathscr{A}} + 2)\xi$, $\mathrm{dg}(t \in I^{\xi}_{\mathscr{A}}) = (n_{\mathscr{A}} + 2)\xi + n_{\mathscr{A}} + 1$ for $\xi \leq \Omega_1$.

Definition 6.7 For a sentence A let $\mathsf{k}(A)$ denote the set of individual constants $\alpha \leq \Omega_1$ occurring in A, In particular $\mathsf{k}(n \in I^{\xi}_{\mathscr{A}}) = \mathsf{k}(n \in I^{<\xi}_{\mathscr{A}}) = \{\xi\}$. $\mathsf{k}(\Gamma) := \bigcup\{\mathsf{k}(A) : A \in \Gamma\}$.

The degrees are defined so that the followings hold for any formula A.

Proposition 6.11 *1.* $\mathrm{dg}(A) < \Omega_1 + \omega$.
2. $\mathsf{SC}(\mathsf{dg}(\mathsf{A})) \subset \mathsf{SC}(\mathsf{k}(\mathsf{A}))$.
3. *Let* $A \simeq \bigvee(A_i)_{i\in J}$ *for a sentence* A*. Then* $\forall i \in J(\mathrm{dg}(A_i) < \mathrm{dg}(A))$.
4. $\beta < \alpha \leq \Omega_1 \Rightarrow \mathrm{dg}(A(\beta)) \leq \mathrm{dg}(A(\alpha))$.

Proof Proposition 6.11.3. First we show $\forall\xi \leq \Omega_1 \left(\mathrm{dg}(n \in I^{\xi}_{\mathscr{A}}) > \mathrm{dg}(\mathscr{A}[I^{<\xi}_{\mathscr{A}}, n])\right)$. We see inductively on formulas $\mathscr{A}$ that $\mathrm{dg}(\mathscr{A}[I^{<\xi}_{\mathscr{A}}, n]) \leq (n_{\mathscr{A}} + 2)\xi + n_{\mathscr{A}}$ for any n and $\xi \leq \Omega_1$. We see easily that $\forall\xi \leq \Omega_1 \forall\zeta < \xi \left(\mathrm{dg}(n \in I^{<\xi}_{\mathscr{A}}) > \mathrm{dg}(n \in I^{\zeta}_{\mathscr{A}})\right)$.

We see by induction on A that $\mathrm{dg}(A(0)) \geq \Omega_1 \Rightarrow \mathrm{dg}(A(\zeta)) = \mathrm{dg}(A(0))$ and $\mathrm{dg}(A(0)) < \Omega_1 \Rightarrow \mathrm{dg}(A(\zeta)) < \Omega_1$ for any $\zeta < \Omega_1$. These yield $\mathrm{dg}(\exists\xi A(\xi)) > \mathrm{dg}(A(\zeta))$ for any $\zeta < \Omega_1$. □

Definition 6.8 1. A formula is said to be a $\Sigma(\Omega_1)$-*formula* iff the predicate $I^{<\Omega_1}_{\mathscr{A}}$ occurs only positively, and universal quantifier $\forall\xi$ on sort $\mathbb{O}$ does not occur in it. $\Sigma(\Omega_1)$ denote the set of $\Sigma(\Omega_1)$-formulas.
2. For $C \in \Sigma(\Omega_1)$ and an ordinal $\alpha < \Omega_1$, let $C^{(\alpha)}$ denote the result of replacing *some* positive literals $n \in I^{<\Omega_1}_{\mathscr{A}}$ by the restricted $n \in I^{\alpha}_{\mathscr{A}}$, and *some* existential quantifier $\exists\xi(\cdots)$ by the restricted $\exists\xi < \alpha(\cdots) :\equiv (\exists\xi(\xi < \alpha \wedge \cdots))$. For $\Gamma \subset \Sigma(\Omega_1)$, $\Gamma^{(\alpha)} := \{C^{(\alpha)} : C \in \Gamma\}$.

Proposition 6.12 *1.* $\text{dg}(C) < \Omega_1 \Rightarrow C \in \Sigma(\Omega_1)$ *for sentences* C.
2. *Let* $A \simeq \bigvee(A_i)_{i\in J}$ *or* $A \simeq \bigwedge(A_i)_{i\in J}$, *and* $A \in \Sigma(\Omega_1)$. *Then* $\{A_i\}_{i\in J} \subset \Sigma(\Omega_1)$.

Definition 6.9 1. A *Skolem hull operator* is a map

$$\mathcal{H} : \mathcal{P}(ON) \to \mathcal{P}(ON)$$

such that $\forall X \in \mathcal{P}(ON)[X \subset \mathcal{H}(X)]$ and $\forall X, Y \in \mathcal{P}(ON)[X \subset \mathcal{H}(Y) \Rightarrow \mathcal{H}(X) \subset \mathcal{H}(Y)]$ for the class ON of ordinals. For our purpose we can set $ON := T(\Omega_1)$.
2. Let us introduce the abbreviations for an operator $\mathcal{H}$, an ordinal α and a set $X \in \mathcal{P}(ON)$ of ordinals:

$$\alpha \in \mathcal{H} :\Leftrightarrow \alpha \in \mathcal{H}(\emptyset)$$
$$X \subset \mathcal{H} :\Leftrightarrow X \subset \mathcal{H}(\emptyset)$$

3. An operator $\mathcal{H}$ is said to be *closed* under a function $f : ON^n \to ON$ if for any $X \in \mathcal{P}(ON)$ and any $(\alpha_1, \ldots, \alpha_n) \in ON^n$

$$\{\alpha_1, \ldots, \alpha_n\} \subset \mathcal{H}(X) \Rightarrow f(\alpha_1, \ldots, \alpha_n) \in \mathcal{H}(X).$$

4. A set $M \in \mathcal{P}(ON)$ induces a new Skolem hull operator $\mathcal{H}[M]$ from a Skolem hull operator $\mathcal{H}$ by

$$\mathcal{H}[M](X) := \mathcal{H}(M \cup X).$$

For example, $\mathcal{H}_\alpha(X)$ in Definition 6.1 with $\Omega_1 \in \mathcal{H}_\alpha(X)$ is a Skolem hull operator closed under addition, exponentiation to base ω, and the Veblen function below Ω_1.

Proposition 6.13 *Let* $\mathcal{H}$ *be a Skolem hull operator, and* $M \subset ON$.

1. $\mathcal{H}$ *is monotonic in the sense that* $\forall X, Y \in \mathcal{P}(ON)[X \subset Y \Rightarrow \mathcal{H}(X) \subset \mathcal{H}(Y)]$.
2. $M \subset \mathcal{H} \Rightarrow \mathcal{H}[M] = \mathcal{H}$.

Let $\mathcal{H}$ be a Skolem hull operator, Γ a sequent, $\alpha < \varepsilon_{\Omega_1+1}$(, i.e., $\alpha \in T(\Omega_1)$) and $d < \Omega_1 + \omega$. We define a relation $\mathcal{H} \vdash^\alpha_d \Gamma$ (read: there exists an $\mathcal{H}$-controlled derivation of Γ such that its tree-height is at most α and the degree of any cut formula in it is less than d.).

The relation $\mathcal{H}_\gamma[\Theta] \vdash^\alpha_d \Gamma$ for finite sets $\Theta \subset T(\Omega_1)$ is defined as a fixed point of a strictly (strongly) positive formula H

$$H(\gamma, \Theta, \alpha, d, \Gamma) \Leftrightarrow \mathcal{H}_\gamma[\Theta] \vdash^\alpha_d \Gamma$$

in an intuitionistic fixed point theory over first-order arithmetic.

Definition 6.10 $\mathcal{H} \vdash_d^\alpha \Gamma$ holds if

$$\{\alpha\} \cup \mathsf{k}(\Gamma) \subset \mathcal{H} \tag{6.4}$$

and one of the following cases holds:

($\bigvee$) There are an $\Gamma \ni A \simeq \bigvee(A_i)_{i\in J}$ and $\alpha(i) < \alpha$ for an $i \in J$ such that $\mathcal{H} \vdash_d^{\alpha(i)} \Gamma, A_i$ and

$$i < \alpha \tag{6.5}$$

Let us depict it as follows.

$$\frac{\mathcal{H} \vdash_d^{\alpha(i)} \Gamma, A_i}{\mathcal{H} \vdash_d^\alpha \Gamma} \ (\bigvee)$$

($\bigwedge$) There are an $\Gamma \ni A \simeq \bigwedge(A_i)_{i\in J}$ and $\alpha(i) < \alpha$ such that $\mathcal{H}[\{i\}] \vdash_d^{\alpha(i)} \Gamma, A_i$ holds for each $i \in J$.

$$\frac{\{\mathcal{H}[\{i\}] \vdash_d^{\alpha(i)} \Gamma, A_i : i \in J\}}{\mathcal{H} \vdash_d^\alpha \Gamma} \ (\bigwedge)$$

(Cl) There are $(n \in I_{\mathcal{A}}^{<\Omega_1}) \in \Gamma$ and an $\alpha_0 < \alpha$ such that $\mathcal{H} \vdash_d^{\alpha_0} \Gamma, \mathcal{A}[I_{\mathcal{A}}^{<\Omega_1}, n]$ holds.

$$\frac{\mathcal{H} \vdash_d^{\alpha_0} \Gamma, \mathcal{A}[I_{\mathcal{A}}^{<\Omega_1}, n]}{\mathcal{H} \vdash_d^\alpha \Gamma} \ (Cl)$$

(cut) There are a formula C and an $\alpha_0 < \alpha$ such that $\mathrm{dg}(C) < d$, $\mathcal{H} \vdash_d^{\alpha_0} \Gamma, \neg C$ and $\mathcal{H} \vdash_d^{\alpha_0} C, \Gamma$ hold.

$$\frac{\mathcal{H} \vdash_d^{\alpha_0} \Gamma, \neg C \quad \mathcal{H} \vdash_d^{\alpha_0} C, \Gamma}{\mathcal{H} \vdash_d^\alpha \Gamma} \ (cut)$$

When $A \simeq \bigwedge(A_i)_{i\in J}$ with $J = 0$, ($\bigwedge$) is an axiom with the empty set of upper sequents. This means that if Γ contains a true literal, then Γ is an axiom.

Inferences ($\bigvee$), ($\bigwedge$) are denoted by specifying the main formula or the logical connective. For example an inference with the main formula $n \in I_{\mathcal{A}}^{<\xi}$ is written by $(I_{\mathcal{A}}^{<})$.

The condition (6.5) for ($\bigvee$) is needed to prove Boundedness Lemma 6.7, which is one of a key to show Theorem 6.5 below. Actually we need the condition (6.5) only for the inferences $(I_{\mathcal{A}}^{<})$: For $\xi \leq \Omega_1$, $(n \in I_{\mathcal{A}}^{<\xi}) \in \Gamma, \alpha(\zeta) < \alpha$ and $\zeta < \xi$ such that

$$\frac{\mathcal{H} \vdash_d^{\alpha(\zeta)} \Gamma, n \in I_{\mathcal{A}}^{\zeta}}{\mathcal{H} \vdash_d^{\alpha} \Gamma} \; (I_{\mathcal{A}}^{<}) \text{ where } \zeta < \alpha \tag{6.5}$$

If you want to bound the existential quantifiers $\exists \xi$ of ordinal sort (and a boundedness lemma for it), then the condition (6.5) is relevant also for inferences $(\exists \boldsymbol{O})$: For $\exists \xi \, A(\xi) \in \Gamma$, $\alpha(\zeta) < \alpha$ and $\zeta < \Omega_1$ such that

$$\frac{\mathcal{H} \vdash_d^{\alpha(\zeta)} \Gamma, A(\zeta)}{\mathcal{H} \vdash_d^{\alpha} \Gamma} \; (\exists \boldsymbol{O}) \text{ where } \zeta < \alpha \tag{6.5}$$

In what follows $\mathcal{H}$ denotes a Skolem hull operator closed under addition and exponentiation to base ω. First let us embed $\mathsf{ID}_1^{\mathbb{O}}$ in the operator controlled derivations.

Lemma 6.5 (Weakening) *Assume $\beta \leq \alpha \in \mathcal{H}'$, $d \leq c$ and $\mathsf{k}(\Delta) \subset \mathcal{H}'$ for a Skolem hull operator $\mathcal{H}'$ such that $\forall X \in \mathcal{P}(ON)[\mathcal{H}(X) \subset \mathcal{H}'(X)]$. Then*

$$\mathcal{H} \vdash_d^{\beta} \Gamma \Rightarrow \mathcal{H}' \vdash_c^{\alpha} \Gamma, \Delta.$$

Proof This is seen by induction on $\beta \in T(\Omega_1)$. □

Lemma 6.6 *1. $\mathcal{H} \vdash_d^{\alpha} \Gamma, A \Rightarrow \forall i \in J(\mathcal{H}[\{i\}] \vdash_d^{\alpha} \Gamma, A_i)$ for $A \simeq \bigwedge(A_i)_{i \in J}$.*

2. Let $C(I_{\mathcal{A}}^{<\xi})$ denote a formula in which $I_{\mathcal{A}}^{<\xi}$ occurs only positively for $\xi < \Omega_1$, and let $C(I_{\mathcal{A}}^{<\zeta})$ denote the result of replacing every occurrence of $I_{\mathcal{A}}^{<\xi}$ by $I_{\mathcal{A}}^{<\zeta}$. Then $\mathcal{H} \vdash_d^{\alpha} \Gamma, C(I_{\mathcal{A}}^{<\xi})$ & $\xi < \zeta \in \mathcal{H} \Rightarrow \mathcal{H} \vdash_d^{\alpha} \Gamma, C(I_{\mathcal{A}}^{<\zeta})$.

3. $\mathcal{H} \vdash_d^{\alpha} \Gamma, n \in I_{\mathcal{A}}^{\xi}$ & $\xi \leq \zeta \in \mathcal{H} \Rightarrow \mathcal{H} \vdash_d^{\alpha} \Gamma, n \in I_{\mathcal{A}}^{\zeta}$.

4. Let $C(I_{\mathcal{A}}^{\xi})$ denote a formula in which $I_{\mathcal{A}}^{\xi}$ occurs only positively for $\xi < \Omega_1$, and let $C(I_{\mathcal{A}}^{<\zeta})$ denote the result of replacing every occurrence of $I_{\mathcal{A}}^{\xi}$ by $I_{\mathcal{A}}^{<\zeta}$ for a $\zeta > \xi$. Then

$$\mathcal{H} \vdash_d^{\alpha} \Gamma, C(I_{\mathcal{A}}^{\xi}) \; \& \; \{\xi, \zeta\} \subset \mathcal{H} \Rightarrow \mathcal{H} \vdash_d^{\xi+2\alpha} \Gamma, C(I_{\mathcal{A}}^{<\zeta}).$$

Proof Lemma 6.6.3 is seen from Lemmas 6.6.1 and 6.6.2.

We show Lemma 6.6.4 by induction on α.

Assume for an $\alpha_0 < \alpha$

$$\frac{\mathcal{H} \vdash_d^{\alpha_0} \Gamma, n \in I_{\mathcal{A}}^{\xi}, \mathcal{A}[I_{\mathcal{A}}^{<\xi}, n]}{\mathcal{H} \vdash_d^{\alpha} \Gamma, n \in I_{\mathcal{A}}^{\xi}} \; (I_{\mathcal{A}})$$

IH yields $\mathcal{H} \vdash_d^{\xi+2\alpha_0} \Gamma, n \in I_{\mathcal{A}}^{<\zeta}, \mathcal{A}[I_{\mathcal{A}}^{<\xi}, n]$, and by the inferences $(I_{\mathcal{A}})$ and $(I_{\mathcal{A}}^{<})$ for $\xi < \xi + 2\alpha$, cf. (6.5)

$$\dfrac{\dfrac{\mathcal{H} \vdash_d^{\xi+2\alpha_0} \Gamma, n \in I_{\mathcal{A}}^{<\zeta}, \mathcal{A}[I_{\mathcal{A}}^{<\xi}, n]}{\mathcal{H} \vdash_d^{\xi+2\alpha_0+1} \Gamma, n \in I_{\mathcal{A}}^{<\zeta}, n \in I_{\mathcal{A}}^{\xi}}\ (I_{\mathcal{A}})}{\mathcal{H} \vdash_d^{\xi+2\alpha} \Gamma, n \in I_{\mathcal{A}}^{<\zeta}}\ (I_{\mathcal{A}}^{<})$$

□

Lemma 6.7 (Boundedness)

$$\mathcal{H} \vdash_d^{\alpha} \Gamma, \Lambda \,\&\, \alpha \leq \beta < \Omega_1 \,\&\, \beta \in \mathcal{H} \,\&\, \Lambda \subset \Sigma(\Omega_1) \Rightarrow \mathcal{H} \vdash_d^{3^\alpha} \Gamma, \Lambda^{(\beta)}.$$

Proof By induction on α. For simplicity consider first the case $\Lambda = \{n \in I_{\mathcal{A}}^{<\Omega_1}\}$.

The case when the last inference is an $(I_{\mathcal{A}}^{<})$ for an $\alpha(\xi) < \alpha$ and $\xi < \Omega_1$

$$\dfrac{\mathcal{H} \vdash_d^{\alpha(\xi)} \Gamma, n \in I_{\mathcal{A}}^{<\Omega_1}, n \in I_{\mathcal{A}}^{\xi}}{\mathcal{H} \vdash_d^{\alpha} \Gamma, n \in I_{\mathcal{A}}^{<\Omega_1}}\ (I_{\mathcal{A}}^{<})$$

We have $\xi < \min\{\Omega_1, \alpha\} = \alpha$ by (6.5). By IH, Lemma 6.6.3, $\xi < \alpha \leq \beta < \Omega_1$ and Weakening Lemma 6.5 we obtain

$$\dfrac{\mathcal{H} \vdash_d^{3^{\alpha(\xi)}} \Gamma, n \in I_{\mathcal{A}}^{\beta}, n \in I_{\mathcal{A}}^{\xi}}{\mathcal{H} \vdash_d^{3^\alpha} \Gamma, n \in I_{\mathcal{A}}^{\beta}}$$

The case when the last inference is a (Cl) for an $\alpha_0 < \alpha \leq \beta$

$$\dfrac{\mathcal{H} \vdash_d^{\alpha_0} \Gamma, n \in I_{\mathcal{A}}^{<\Omega_1}, \mathcal{A}[I_{\mathcal{A}}^{<\Omega_1}, n]}{\mathcal{H} \vdash_d^{\alpha} \Gamma, n \in I_{\mathcal{A}}^{<\Omega_1}}\ (Cl)$$

By IH, Lemmas 6.6.3 and 6.6.4 we obtain

$$\dfrac{\dfrac{\mathcal{H} \vdash_d^{3^{\alpha_0}} \Gamma, n \in I_{\mathcal{A}}^{\alpha_0}, \mathcal{A}[I_{\mathcal{A}}^{\alpha_0}, n]}{\mathcal{H} \vdash_d^{\alpha_0+2\cdot 3^{\alpha_0}} \Gamma, n \in I_{\mathcal{A}}^{\beta}, \mathcal{A}[I_{\mathcal{A}}^{<\beta}, n]}}{\mathcal{H} \vdash_d^{3^\alpha} \Gamma, n \in I_{\mathcal{A}}^{\beta}}\ (I_{\mathcal{A}})$$

Second consider the case

$$\dfrac{\mathcal{H} \vdash_d^{\alpha_0} \Gamma, \exists\zeta\, A(\zeta), A(\xi)}{\mathcal{H} \vdash_d^{\alpha} \Gamma, \exists\zeta\, A(\zeta)}\ (\exists\mathbb{O})$$

with $\alpha_0 < \alpha$, $\xi < \alpha \leq \beta$. By IH we obtain

$$\dfrac{\dfrac{\mathcal{H} \vdash^0_d \xi < \beta \quad \mathcal{H} \vdash^{3^{\alpha_0}}_d \Gamma, \exists \zeta < \beta\, A^{(\beta)}(\zeta), A^{(\beta)}(\xi)}{\mathcal{H} \vdash^{3^{\alpha_0}+1}_d \Gamma, \exists \zeta < \beta\, A^{(\beta)}(\zeta), \xi < \beta \land A^{(\beta)}(\xi)}\,(\land)}{\mathcal{H} \vdash^{3^{\alpha}}_d \Gamma, \exists \zeta < \beta\, A^{(\beta)}(\zeta)}\,(\exists\mathbb{O})$$

Other cases are easily seen from IH using Proposition 6.12.2. □

Lemma 6.8 (Tautology) $\mathsf{k}(\{A\} \cup \Gamma) \subset \mathcal{H} \Rightarrow \mathcal{H} \vdash^{2d}_0 \Gamma, \neg A, A$ *with* $d = \mathrm{dg}(A)$.

Proof By induction on $\mathrm{dg}(A)$ using Proposition 6.11. First we have $\mathsf{k}(A) \subset \mathcal{H} \Rightarrow 2\mathrm{dg}(A) \in \mathcal{H}$ by Proposition 6.11.2.

Consider the case when A is an atomic sentence $n \in I^{<\xi}_{\mathcal{A}}$ with $\xi \leq \Omega_1$. For $d = \mathrm{dg}(A) = (n_{\mathcal{A}} + 2)\xi$ and $d_\zeta = \mathrm{dg}(n \in I^{\zeta}_{\mathcal{A}}) = (n_{\mathcal{A}} + 2)\zeta + n_{\mathcal{A}} + 1$, we obtain $2d > 2d_\zeta + 1$ for $\zeta < \xi$.

$$\dfrac{\cdots \quad \dfrac{\mathcal{H}[\{\zeta\}] \vdash^{2d_\zeta}_0 \Gamma, n \in I^{\zeta}_{\mathcal{A}}, n \notin I^{\zeta}_{\mathcal{A}}}{\mathcal{H}[\{\zeta\}] \vdash^{2d_\zeta+1}_0 \Gamma, n \in I^{<\xi}_{\mathcal{A}}, n \notin I^{\zeta}_{\mathcal{A}}}\,(I^{<}_{\mathcal{A}}) \quad (\zeta < \xi)}{\mathcal{H} \vdash^{2d}_0 \Gamma, n \in I^{<\xi}_{\mathcal{A}}, n \notin I^{<\xi}_{\mathcal{A}}}\,(\neg I^{<}_{\mathcal{A}})$$

with $2d_\zeta + 1 > \zeta$ for (6.5).

Next consider the case when A is an atomic sentence $n \in I^{\xi}_{\mathcal{A}}$. For $d = \mathrm{dg}(A) = (n_{\mathcal{A}} + 2)\xi + n_{\mathcal{A}} + 1$ and $d_0 = \mathrm{dg}(\mathcal{A}[I^{<\xi}_{\mathcal{A}}, n])$, we have $d > d_0$ by Proposition 6.11.3, and $2d > 2d_0 + 1$.

$$\dfrac{\dfrac{\mathcal{H} \vdash^{2d_0}_0 \Gamma, \mathcal{A}[I^{<\xi}_{\mathcal{A}}, n], \neg\mathcal{A}[I^{<\xi}_{\mathcal{A}}, n]}{\mathcal{H} \vdash^{2d_0+1}_0 \Gamma, n \in I^{\xi}_{\mathcal{A}}, \neg\mathcal{A}[I^{<\xi}_{\mathcal{A}}, n]}\,(I_{\mathcal{A}})}{\mathcal{H} \vdash^{2d}_0 \Gamma, n \in I^{\xi}_{\mathcal{A}}, n \notin I^{\xi}_{\mathcal{A}}}\,(\neg I_{\mathcal{A}})$$

The case when A is a sentence $\exists\xi\, B(\xi)$ is seen from IH using Proposition 6.11.3. □

Lemma 6.9 (Induction)

$$\forall\alpha < \Omega_1 \left[\mathsf{k}(\{F\} \cup \Gamma) \cup \{\alpha\} \subset \mathcal{H} \Rightarrow \mathcal{H} \vdash^{f(\alpha)}_0 \Gamma, \Theta, F(\alpha)\right]$$

for $\Theta = \{\neg\forall\xi[\forall\eta <^{\mathbb{O}} \xi\, F(\eta) \to F(\xi)]\}$ *and* $f(\alpha) = 2(1 + \mathrm{dg}(F(\alpha)) + 2\alpha + 1)$.

Proof By induction on $\alpha < \Omega_1$. Suppressing the side sequent Γ, assume $\mathsf{k}(F) \cup \{\alpha\} \subset \mathcal{H}$. Let $d = \mathrm{dg}(F(\alpha))$ and $f(\alpha) - 2 = 2 + 2d + 4\alpha$. Tautology Lemma 6.8 yields $\mathcal{H} \vdash^{2d}_0 \neg F(\alpha), F(\alpha)$. Let $\beta < \alpha$. We have $\mathcal{H}[\{\beta\}] \vdash^{f(\beta)}_0 \Theta, F(\beta)$ by IH, and $\mathrm{dg}(F(\beta)) \leq d$ by Proposition 6.11.4. Hence $f(\beta) + 1 < f(\alpha) - 2$. On the other hand we have $\mathcal{H}[\{\beta\}] \vdash^0_0 \Theta, \beta \not<^{\mathbb{O}} \alpha$ with the true literal $\beta \not<^{\mathbb{O}} \alpha$ when $\beta \geq \alpha$. Hence we obtain

$$\dfrac{\dfrac{\mathcal{H}[\{\beta\}] \vdash_0^{f(\beta)} \Theta, F(\beta)}{\mathcal{H}[\{\beta\}] \vdash_0^{f(\beta)+1} \Theta, \beta \not<^{\mathbb{O}} \alpha \vee F(\beta)\ (\beta < \alpha)} \quad \dfrac{\mathcal{H}[\{\beta\}] \vdash_0^{0} \Theta, \beta \not<^{\mathbb{O}} \alpha}{\mathcal{H}[\{\beta\}] \vdash_0^{1} \Theta, \beta \not<^{\mathbb{O}} \alpha \vee F(\beta)\ (\beta \geq \alpha)}\ (\vee)}{\mathcal{H} \vdash_0^{f(\alpha)-2} \Theta, \forall \eta <^{\mathbb{O}} \alpha F(\eta)}\ (\forall \mathbb{O})$$

and

$$\dfrac{\dfrac{\mathcal{H} \vdash_0^{f(\alpha)-2} \Theta, \forall \eta <^{\mathbb{O}} \alpha F(\eta) \quad \mathcal{H} \vdash_0^{2d} \neg F(\alpha), F(\alpha)}{\mathcal{H} \vdash_0^{f(\alpha)-1} \Theta, \forall \eta <^{\mathbb{O}} \alpha F(\eta) \wedge \neg F(\alpha), F(\alpha)}\ (\wedge)}{\mathcal{H} \vdash_0^{f(\alpha)} \Theta, F(\alpha)}\ (\exists \mathbb{O})$$

□

From Tautology Lemma 6.8 and Induction Lemma 6.9 with Weakening Lemma 6.5 we conclude the following as in Lemma 4.4.

Lemma 6.10 (Embedding) *Let* $\Gamma' = \Gamma[x_1 := n_1, \dots, x_p := n_p, \xi_1 := \alpha_1, \dots, \xi_q := \alpha_q]$ $(\alpha_1, \dots, \alpha_q < \Omega_1)$ *denote a closed instance of a sequent* Γ *in* $\mathcal{L}(\mathsf{ID}^{\mathbb{O}})$. *Assume* $\mathsf{ID}_1^{\mathbb{O}} \vdash \Gamma$. *Then*

$$\exists m, l < \omega \forall n_1, \dots, n_p < \omega \forall \alpha_1, \dots, \alpha_q < \Omega_1 \forall \mathcal{H} \left(\mathcal{H}[\{\alpha_1, \dots, \alpha_q\}] \vdash_{\Omega_1+m}^{\Omega_1+l} \Gamma' \right)$$

where $\mathcal{H}$ *ranges over Skolem hull operators closed under addition and exponentiation to base* ω.

Proof By induction on the depths of $\mathsf{ID}_1^{\mathbb{O}}$-proofs. We can assume that the given proof enjoys the pure variable condition in Definition 1.3.

First consider the axioms in $\mathsf{ID}_1^{\mathbb{O}}$. The closed instances of the axiom schema $(TI_{\mathbb{O}})$ follows from Induction Lemma 6.9.

The axiom $(I_{\mathcal{A}})$, $\forall \xi < \Omega_1 \left(\mathcal{A}[I_{\mathcal{A}}^{<\xi}] = I_{\mathcal{A}}^{\xi} \right)$ follows from the inference rules $(I_{\mathcal{A}})$ and $(\neg I_{\mathcal{A}})$. The Closure axiom, $\mathcal{A}[I_{\mathcal{A}}^{<\Omega_1}] \subset I_{\mathcal{A}}^{<\Omega_1}$ follows from the inference rule (Cl). For the axiom $(I_{\mathcal{A}}^{<})$, $\forall \xi \leq \Omega_1 \left(I_{\mathcal{A}}^{<\xi} = \bigcup_{\eta<\xi} I_{\mathcal{A}}^{\eta} \right)$ we have for $\eta < \xi \leq \Omega_1$, $d_\eta = \mathrm{dg}(n \in I_{\mathcal{A}}^{\eta}) < \mathrm{dg}(n \in I_{\mathcal{A}}^{<\xi}) = d$ and $2d_\eta + 1 > \eta$ for (6.5),

$$\dfrac{\dfrac{\mathcal{H}[\{\eta\}] \vdash_0^{2d_\eta} n \notin I_{\mathcal{A}}^{\eta}, n \in I_{\mathcal{A}}^{\eta}}{\mathcal{H}[\{\xi, \eta\}] \vdash_0^{2d_\eta+1} n \notin I_{\mathcal{A}}^{\eta}, n \in I_{\mathcal{A}}^{<\xi}}\ (I_{\mathcal{A}}^{<})}{\mathcal{H}[\{\xi\}] \vdash_0^{2d+1} \neg \exists \eta < \xi (n \in I_{\mathcal{A}}^{\eta}), n \in I_{\mathcal{A}}^{<\xi}}\ (\vee, \bigwedge)$$

and

$$\dfrac{\dfrac{\mathcal{H}[\{\eta\}] \vdash_0^{2d_\eta} n \notin I_{\mathcal{A}}^{\eta}, n \in I_{\mathcal{A}}^{\eta}}{\mathcal{H}[\{\xi, \eta\}] \vdash_0^{2d_\eta+2} n \notin I_{\mathcal{A}}^{\eta}, \exists \eta < \xi (n \in I_{\mathcal{A}}^{\eta})}\ (\wedge, \bigvee)}{\mathcal{H}[\{\xi\}] \vdash_0^{2d+1} n \notin I_{\mathcal{A}}^{<\xi}, \exists \eta < \xi (n \in I_{\mathcal{A}}^{\eta})}\ (\neg I_{\mathcal{A}}^{<})$$

Consider the case when Γ is the lower sequent of an inference such that a closed instance of its upper sequent might contain ordinal constants other than $\alpha_1, \ldots, \alpha_q$. This can happen only when a variable of ordinal sort occurs in one of upper sequent but not in the lower sequent. In other words the inference is either a rule for introducing quantifiers of ordinal sort or a (cut). By the pure variable condition we can assume that the inference introduces a universal quantifier and the variable is the eigenvariable. IH yields the assertion for the lower sequent. □

Second cut inferences are eliminated from operator controlled derivations.

Lemma 6.11 (Reduction) *Let* $C \simeq \bigvee(C_i)_{i\in J}$ *with* $\Omega_1 \neq \mathrm{dg}(C) \leq d$. *Then* $\mathcal{H} \vdash^{\alpha}_{d} \Gamma, \neg C$ and $\mathcal{H} \vdash^{\beta}_{d} C, \Lambda \Rightarrow \mathcal{H} \vdash^{\alpha+\beta}_{d} \Gamma, \Lambda$.

Proof By induction on β. Note that $\mathrm{dg}(n \in I^{<\Omega_1}_{\mathcal{A}}) = \Omega_1$ for the main formula $n \in I^{<\Omega_1}_{\mathcal{A}}$ of an inference (Cl). Consider the case

$$\frac{\mathcal{H} \vdash^{\beta_0}_{d} C, C_i, \Lambda}{\mathcal{H} \vdash^{\beta}_{d} C, \Lambda}\ (\bigvee)$$

for some $i \in J \cap \beta$ and $\beta_0 < \beta$. By IH we have $\mathcal{H} \vdash^{\alpha+\beta_0}_{d} C_i, \Gamma, \Lambda$. On the other hand we can assume $i \in \mathsf{k}(C_i) \subset \mathcal{H}$ by (6.4). Hence by Inversion Lemma 6.6.1 we have $\mathcal{H} \vdash^{\alpha}_{d} \Gamma, \neg C_i$. We obtain for $\mathrm{dg}(C_i) < \mathrm{dg}(C) \leq d$

$$\frac{\mathcal{H} \vdash^{\alpha}_{d} \Gamma, \neg C_i \quad \mathcal{H} \vdash^{\alpha+\beta_0}_{d} C_i, \Gamma, \Lambda}{\mathcal{H} \vdash^{\alpha+\beta}_{d} \Gamma, \Lambda}\ (cut)$$

□

Lemma 6.12 (Predicative Cut-elimination) *Let* $\mathcal{H}$ *be a Skolem operator closed under the Veblen function, and assume* $\neg(d \leq \Omega_1 < d + \omega^{\alpha})$. *Then* $\mathcal{H} \vdash^{\beta}_{d+\omega^{\alpha}} \Gamma \Rightarrow \mathcal{H} \vdash^{\varphi\alpha\beta}_{d} \Gamma$.

Proof By main induction on α with subsidiary induction on β as in the proof of Theorem 5.3.

Consider the case for a $\beta_0 < \beta$ and $\mathrm{dg}(C) < d + \omega^{\alpha}$:

$$\frac{\mathcal{H} \vdash^{\beta_0}_{d+\omega^{\alpha}} \Gamma, \neg C \quad \mathcal{H} \vdash^{\beta_0}_{d+\omega^{\alpha}} C, \Gamma}{\mathcal{H} \vdash^{\beta}_{d+\omega^{\alpha}} \Gamma}\ (cut)$$

By SIH we have $\mathcal{H} \vdash^{\varphi\alpha\beta_0}_{d} \Gamma, \neg C$ and $\mathcal{H} \vdash^{\varphi\alpha\beta_0}_{d} C, \Gamma$. If $\mathrm{dg}(C) < d$, then $\mathcal{H} \vdash^{\varphi\alpha\beta_0+1}_{d} \Gamma$ by a (cut), where $\varphi\alpha\beta_0 + 1 < \varphi\alpha\beta$. Suppose $\mathrm{dg}(C) \geq d$, and let $d' = \mathrm{dg}(C) = d + \omega^{\alpha_n} + \cdots + \omega^{\alpha_0}$ for $\alpha > \alpha_n \geq \cdots \geq \alpha_0$. We obtain $\mathcal{H} \vdash^{\varphi\alpha\beta_0\cdot 2}_{d'} \Gamma$ by Reduction Lemma 6.11 for $\mathrm{dg}(C) \neq \Omega_1$. By MIH we obtain $\mathcal{H} \vdash^{\varphi\alpha_n(\cdots(\varphi\alpha_0((\varphi\alpha\beta_0\cdot 2))\cdots)}_{d} \Gamma$ for $\varphi\alpha_n(\cdots(\varphi\alpha_0((\varphi\alpha\beta_0 \cdot 2))\cdots) < \varphi\alpha\beta$. □

Theorem 6.4 (Collapsing) *Suppose* $\gamma \in \mathcal{H}_\gamma[\Theta]$ *and*

$$\Theta \subset \mathcal{H}_\gamma(\psi_{\Omega_1}(\gamma)) \tag{6.6}$$

for a finite set Θ *of ordinals. Moreover assume* $\Gamma \subset \Sigma(\Omega_1)$. *Then for* $\hat{\alpha} = \gamma + \omega^\alpha$

$$\mathcal{H}_\gamma[\Theta] \vdash^{\alpha}_{\Omega_1+1} \Gamma \Rightarrow \mathcal{H}_{\hat{\alpha}+1}[\Theta] \vdash^{\psi_{\Omega_1}(\hat{\alpha})}_{\psi_{\Omega_1}(\hat{\alpha})} \Gamma.$$

Proof By induction on α.

First note that $\psi_{\Omega_1}(\hat{\alpha}) \in \mathcal{H}_{\hat{\alpha}+1}[\Theta]$ for (6.17) since $\hat{\alpha} = \gamma + \omega^\alpha \in \mathcal{H}_\gamma[\Theta]$ by the assumption $\{\gamma, \alpha\} \subset \mathcal{H}_\gamma[\Theta]$ by (6.17). Assume $\mathcal{H}_\gamma[\Theta][\Lambda] \vdash^{\alpha_0}_{\Omega_1+1} \Gamma_0$ with $\alpha_0 < \alpha$ and $\Lambda \subset \mathcal{H}_\gamma(\psi_{\Omega_1}(\gamma))$. Then by $\gamma \leq \hat{\alpha}$ and (6.6) we have $\widehat{\alpha_0} \in \mathcal{H}_\gamma[\Theta][\Lambda] \subset \mathcal{H}_\gamma(\psi_{\Omega_1}(\gamma)) \subset \mathcal{H}_{\hat{\alpha}}(\psi_{\Omega_1}(\hat{\alpha}))$. This yields, by Proposition 6.3.4, that $\alpha_0 < \alpha \Rightarrow \psi_{\Omega_1}(\widehat{\alpha_0}) < \psi_{\Omega_1}(\hat{\alpha})$.

Second observe that $\mathsf{k}(\Gamma) \subset \mathcal{H}_\gamma[\Theta] \subset \mathcal{H}_{\hat{\alpha}+1}[\Theta]$ by $\gamma < \hat{\alpha} + 1$.

Case 1. First consider the case for $\zeta < \min\{\xi, \alpha\}$ and $\xi \leq \Omega_1$

$$\frac{\mathcal{H}_\gamma[\Theta] \vdash^{\alpha(\zeta)}_{\Omega_1+1} \Gamma, n \in I^{<\xi}_{\mathcal{A}}, n \in I^{\zeta}_{\mathcal{A}}}{\mathcal{H}_\gamma[\Theta] \vdash^{\alpha}_{\Omega_1+1} \Gamma, n \in I^{<\xi}_{\mathcal{A}}}\ (I^{<}_{\mathcal{A}})$$

We claim for (6.5)

$$\zeta < \psi_{\Omega_1}(\hat{\alpha}) \tag{6.7}$$

Then IH yields for $\widehat{\alpha(\zeta)} = \gamma + \omega^{\alpha(\zeta)}$

$$\frac{\mathcal{H}_{\widehat{\alpha(\zeta)}+1}[\Theta] \vdash^{\psi_{\Omega_1}(\widehat{\alpha(\zeta)})}_{\psi_{\Omega_1}(\widehat{\alpha(\zeta)})} \Gamma, n \in I^{<\xi}_{\mathcal{A}}, n \in I^{\zeta}_{\mathcal{A}}}{\mathcal{H}_{\hat{\alpha}+1}[\Theta] \vdash^{\psi_{\Omega_1}(\hat{\alpha})}_{\psi_{\Omega_1}(\hat{\alpha})} \Gamma, n \in I^{<\xi}_{\mathcal{A}}}\ (I^{<}_{\mathcal{A}})$$

Now we show (6.7). We have $(n \in I^{<\xi}_{\mathcal{A}}) \in \Sigma(\Omega_1)$ for $\xi \leq \Omega_1$, and hence $\zeta < \xi \leq \Omega_1$. We obtain $\Omega_1 > \zeta \in \mathsf{k}(n \in I^{\zeta}_{\mathcal{A}}) \subset \mathcal{H}_\gamma[\Theta] \subset \mathcal{H}_\gamma(\psi_{\Omega_1}(\gamma))$ by (6.4) and the assumption (6.6). Hence $\zeta < \psi_{\Omega_1}(\gamma) < \psi_{\Omega_1}(\hat{\alpha})$ by Proposition 6.3.4.

Case 2. Second consider the case

$$\frac{\{\mathcal{H}_\gamma[\Theta \cup \{\zeta\}] \vdash^{\alpha(\zeta)}_{\Omega_1+1} \Gamma, n \notin I^{<\xi}_{\mathcal{A}}, n \notin I^{\zeta}_{\mathcal{A}} : \zeta < \xi\}}{\mathcal{H}_\gamma[\Theta] \vdash^{\alpha}_{\Omega_1+1} \Gamma, n \notin I^{<\xi}_{\mathcal{A}}}\ (\neg I^{<}_{\mathcal{A}})$$

where $\alpha(\zeta) < \alpha$ and $\xi \leq \Omega_1$. From $(n \notin I^{<\xi}_{\mathcal{A}}) \in \Sigma(\Omega_1)$ we see $\xi < \Omega_1$.

We claim

$$\forall \zeta < \xi \left(\zeta \in \mathcal{H}_\gamma(\psi_{\Omega_1}(\gamma))\right) \tag{6.8}$$

Then IH yields

$$\frac{\{\mathcal{H}_{\widehat{\alpha(\zeta)}+1}[\Theta\cup\{\zeta\}]\vdash^{\psi_{\Omega_1}(\widehat{\alpha(\zeta)})}_{\psi_{\Omega_1}(\widehat{\alpha(\beta)})}\Gamma, n\notin I^{<\xi}_{\mathcal{A}}, n\notin I^{\zeta}_{\mathcal{A}} : \zeta<\xi\}}{\mathcal{H}_{\hat{\alpha}+1}[\Theta]\vdash^{\psi_{\Omega_1}(\hat{\alpha})}_{\psi_{\Omega_1}(\hat{\alpha})}\Gamma, n\notin I^{<\xi}_{\mathcal{A}}}\ (\neg I^{<}_{\mathcal{A}})$$

for $\widehat{\alpha(\zeta)} = \gamma + \omega^{\alpha(\zeta)}$, since $\psi_{\Omega_1}(\widehat{\alpha(\beta)}) < \psi_{\Omega_1}(\hat{\alpha})$ by Proposition 6.3.4. Note that $\mathcal{H}_{\widehat{\alpha(\zeta)}+1}(X) \subset \mathcal{H}_{\hat{\alpha}+1}(X)$ and hence the derivability relation $\mathcal{H}_{\widehat{\alpha(\zeta)}+1}\vdash$ is included in $\mathcal{H}_{\hat{\alpha}+1}\vdash$ by Weakening Lemma 6.5.

Now we show (6.8). Assume $\zeta<\xi$. We have $\Omega_1>\xi\in \mathsf{k}(n\notin I^{<\xi}_{\mathcal{A}})\subset\mathcal{H}_\gamma[\Theta]\subset\mathcal{H}_\gamma(\psi_{\Omega_1}(\gamma))$ by (6.4) and the assumption (6.6). Hence $\zeta<\xi\in\mathcal{H}_\gamma(\psi_{\Omega_1}(\gamma))\cap\Omega_1=\psi_{\Omega_1}(\gamma)$ by Proposition 6.3.2, and $\zeta<\psi_{\Omega_1}(\gamma)\subset\mathcal{H}_\gamma(\psi_{\Omega_1}(\gamma))$. This shows (6.8).

Case 3. Third consider the case for an $\alpha_0<\alpha$ and a C

$$\frac{\mathcal{H}_\gamma[\Theta]\vdash^{\alpha_0}_{\Omega_1+1}\Gamma,\neg C \quad \mathcal{H}_\gamma[\Theta]\vdash^{\alpha_0}_{\Omega_1+1}C,\Gamma}{\mathcal{H}_\gamma[\Theta]\vdash^{\alpha}_{\Omega_1+1}\Gamma}\ (cut)$$

Case 3.1. $\mathrm{dg}(C)<\Omega_1$.

We claim

$$\mathrm{dg}(C)<\psi_{\Omega_1}(\hat{\alpha}) \tag{6.9}$$

Then IH yields for $\widehat{\alpha_0}=\gamma+\omega^{\alpha_0}$

$$\frac{\mathcal{H}_{\widehat{\alpha_0}+1}[\Theta]\vdash^{\psi_{\Omega_1}(\widehat{\alpha_0})}_{\psi_{\Omega_1}(\widehat{\alpha_0})}\Gamma,\neg C \quad \mathcal{H}_{\widehat{\alpha_0}+1}[\Theta]\vdash^{\psi_{\Omega_1}(\widehat{\alpha_0})}_{\psi_{\Omega_1}(\widehat{\alpha_0})}C,\Gamma}{\mathcal{H}_{\hat{\alpha}+1}[\Theta]\vdash^{\psi_{\Omega_1}(\hat{\alpha})}_{\psi_{\Omega_1}(\hat{\alpha})}\Gamma}\ (cut)$$

Now we show (6.9). We have, by Proposition 6.11.2, $\mathsf{SC}(\mathrm{dg}(\mathsf{C}))\subset\mathsf{SC}(\mathsf{k}(\mathsf{C}))$. On the other hand we have $\mathsf{k}(C)\subset\mathcal{H}_\gamma[\Theta]\subset\mathcal{H}_\gamma(\psi_{\Omega_1}(\gamma))$ by (6.4) and (6.6). We obtain $\mathsf{SC}(\mathsf{k}(\mathsf{C}))\subset\mathcal{H}_\gamma(\psi_1(\gamma))$. Therefore $\mathsf{SC}(\mathrm{dg}(\mathsf{C}))\subset\mathcal{H}_\gamma(\psi_1(\gamma))$, and $\mathrm{dg}(C)\in\mathcal{H}_\gamma(\psi_{\Omega_1}(\gamma))\cap\Omega_1=\psi_{\Omega_1}(\gamma)$. Hence $\mathrm{dg}(C)<\psi_{\Omega_1}(\gamma)\le\psi_{\Omega_1}(\hat{a})$.

Case 3.2. $\Omega_1=\mathrm{dg}(C)$.

Then $C\equiv(n\in I^{<\Omega_1}_{\mathcal{A}})$ for an n and an $\mathcal{A}$.

$$\frac{\mathcal{H}_\gamma[\Theta]\vdash^{\alpha_0}_{\Omega_1+1}\Gamma, n\notin I^{<\Omega_1}_{\mathcal{A}} \quad \mathcal{H}_\gamma[\Theta]\vdash^{\alpha_0}_{\Omega_1+1}n\in I^{<\Omega_1}_{\mathcal{A}},\Gamma}{\mathcal{H}_\gamma[\Theta]\vdash^{\alpha}_{\Omega_1+1}\Gamma}\ (cut)$$

We have $\{n\in I^{<\Omega_1}_{\mathcal{A}}\}\cup\Gamma\subset\Sigma(\Omega_1)$. From the right upper sequent, IH yields for $\widehat{\alpha_0}=\gamma+\omega^{\alpha_0}$ and $\beta_0=\psi_{\Omega_1}(\widehat{\alpha_0})$

$$\mathcal{H}_{\widehat{\alpha_0}+1}[\Theta]\vdash^{\beta_0}_{\beta_0}n\in I^{<\Omega_1}_{\mathcal{A}},\Gamma$$

Then by Boundedness Lemma 6.7 with $\beta_0 = 3^{\beta_0}$ and $\beta_0 \in \mathcal{H}_{\widehat{\alpha_0}+1}$, we obtain

$$\mathcal{H}_{\widehat{\alpha_0}+1}[\Theta] \vdash^{\beta_0}_{\beta_0} n \in I^{\beta_0}_{\mathcal{A}}, \Gamma$$

On the other hand we have by Lemma 6.6.1 from the left uppersequent

$$\mathcal{H}_{\widehat{\alpha_0}+1}[\Theta] \vdash^{\alpha_0}_{\Omega_1+1} \Gamma, n \notin I^{\beta_0}_{\mathcal{A}}$$

IH with $\Gamma \cup \{n \notin I^{\beta_0}_{\mathcal{A}}\} \subset \Sigma(\Omega_1)$ yields for $\beta_1 = \psi_{\Omega_1}(\widehat{\alpha_1})$ and $\widehat{\alpha_1} = \widehat{\alpha_0} + 1 + \omega^{\alpha_0} = \gamma + \omega^{\alpha_0} + \omega^{\alpha_0} < \gamma + \omega^{\alpha} = \hat{\alpha}$

$$\mathcal{H}_{\widehat{\alpha_1}+1}[\Theta] \vdash^{\beta_1}_{\beta_1} \Gamma, n \notin I^{\beta_0}_{\mathcal{A}}$$

On the other hand we have $\widehat{\alpha_i} \in \mathcal{H}_{\gamma}[\Theta]$ and $\widehat{\alpha_0} < \widehat{\alpha_1}$. We obtain $\beta_0 = \psi_{\Omega_1}(\widehat{\alpha_0}) < \psi_{\Omega_1}(\widehat{\alpha_1}) = \beta_1$. Also $\mathrm{dg}(n \in I^{\beta_0}_{\mathcal{A}}) = (n_{\mathcal{A}} + 2)\beta_0 + n_{\mathcal{A}} + 1 < \beta_1 < \psi_{\Omega_1}(\hat{\alpha})$. Consequently

$$\dfrac{\mathcal{H}_{\widehat{\alpha_1}+1}[\Theta] \vdash^{\beta_1}_{\beta_1} \Gamma, n \notin I^{\beta_0}_{\mathcal{A}} \quad \mathcal{H}_{\widehat{\alpha_0}+1}[\Theta] \vdash^{\beta_0}_{\beta_0} n \in I^{\beta_0}_{\mathcal{A}}, \Gamma}{\mathcal{H}_{\hat{\alpha}+1}[\Theta] \vdash^{\psi_{\Omega_1}(\hat{\alpha})}_{\psi_{\Omega_1}(\hat{\alpha})} \Gamma}\ (cut)$$

Other cases are seen from IH. The case when the last inference is an $(\exists\mathbb{O})$ is treated similarly as **Case 1**. Since $\Gamma \subset \Sigma(\Omega_1)$, the last inference is not a $(\forall\mathbb{O})$. □

$\models \Gamma$ designates that $\bigvee \Gamma$ is true in the standard model by interpreting the predicate $<^{\mathbb{O}}$ by $<$ in $T(\Omega_1)$. The following Lemma 6.13.2 and Theorem 6.5.2 are proved *outside* the theory $\mathrm{FiX}^i(\mathsf{PA} + \{\mathrm{TI}(T(\Omega_1), <)\})$, while Lemma 6.13.1 and Theorem 6.5.1 are proved in $\mathrm{FiX}^i(\mathsf{PA} + \{\mathrm{TI}(T_n, <) : n \in \omega\})$, where $T_n = \{\alpha \in T(\Omega_1) \cap \omega_n(\Omega_1 + 1) : G_{\Omega_1}(\alpha) < \omega_n(\Omega + 1)\}$.

Lemma 6.13 (Truth)

1. $(\mathrm{FiX}^i(\mathsf{PA} + \{\mathrm{TI}(T_n, <) : n \in \omega\}))$
For each arithmetic *sequent* Γ *in which no quantifier on sort* $\mathbb{O}$ *nor predicates* $I_{\mathcal{A}}, I^{<}_{\mathcal{A}}$ *occur,* $\mathcal{H}_{\gamma} \vdash^{\alpha}_{0} \Gamma \Rightarrow \mathbb{N} \models \Gamma$ *if* $\alpha \in T_n$ *for an* $n < \omega$.

2. *If* $\mathcal{H} \vdash^{\alpha}_{\Omega_1} \Gamma$ *with* $\mathrm{dg}(\Gamma) := \max\{\mathrm{dg}(A) : A \in \Gamma\} < \Omega_1$, *then* $\models \Gamma$.

Proof By induction on α. For Lemma 6.13.1 use a partial truth definition for arithmetic formulas. □

Theorem 6.5 *1. For* each arithmetic *sequent* Γ, *if* $\mathsf{ID}^{\mathbb{O}}_1 \vdash \Gamma$, *then* $\mathrm{FiX}^i(\mathsf{PA} + \{\mathrm{TI}(T(\Omega_1) \cap \psi_{\Omega_1}(\omega_n(\Omega_1 + 1)), <) : n \in \omega\}) \vdash \Gamma$.

2.

$$\mathsf{ID}^{\mathbb{O}}_1 \vdash \Gamma \text{ and } \Gamma \subset \Sigma(\Omega_1) \Rightarrow \exists m < \omega[\models \Gamma^{(\psi_{\Omega_1}(\omega_m(\Omega_1+1)))}].$$

In particular

$$\mathsf{ID}_1^{\mathbb{O}} \vdash n \in I_{\mathscr{A}}^{<\Omega_1} \Rightarrow \exists m < \omega[|n|_{\mathscr{A}} \leq \psi_{\Omega_1}(\omega_m(\Omega_1 + 1))].$$

Proof Assume $\mathsf{ID}_1^{\mathbb{O}} \vdash \Gamma$. By Embedding Lemma 6.10 we have $\mathscr{H}_0 \vdash_{\Omega_1+1+m}^{\omega^{\Omega_1+1}} \Gamma$ for $\omega^{\Omega_1+1} = \Omega_1 \cdot \omega$ and an $m < \omega$.

Predicative Cut-elimination Lemma 6.12 yields $\mathscr{H}_0 \vdash_{\Omega_1+1}^{\omega_{m+1}(\Omega_1+1)} \Gamma$, which in turn implies by Collapsing Theorem 6.4, $\mathscr{H}_{\omega_{1+m+1}(\Omega_1+1)+1} \vdash_{\beta}^{\beta} \Gamma$ for $\beta = \psi_{\Omega_1}(\omega_{1+m+1}(\Omega_1 + 1))$ and $\omega_{1+m+1}(\Omega_1 + 1) = 0 + \omega^{\Omega_1+\omega_{m+1}(\Omega_1+1)}$.

Theorem 6.5.1. Let Γ be an arithmetic sequent. Predicative Cut-elimination Lemma 6.12 yields $\mathscr{H}_{\omega_{1+m+1}(\Omega_1+1)+1} \vdash_0^{\gamma} \Gamma$ for $\gamma = \varphi\beta\beta$. We see in $\mathrm{FiX}^i(\mathsf{PA} + \{\mathrm{TI}(T_n \cap \psi_{\Omega_1}(\omega_n(\Omega_1 + 1)), <))$ that Γ holds by Truth Lemma 6.13.1. Finally it suffices to show that $\mathrm{FiX}^i(\mathsf{PA} + \{\mathrm{TI}(T(\Omega_1) \cap \psi_{\Omega_1}(\omega_{n+1}(\Omega_1 + 1)), <))$ is an extension of $\mathrm{FiX}^i(\mathsf{PA} + \{\mathrm{TI}(T_n \cap \omega_n(\Omega_1 + 1), <))$. This is seen as follows. We see $G_{\Omega_1}(\omega_n(\Omega_1 + 1) + \alpha) < \omega_n(\Omega_1 + 1)$ for ordinal terms $\alpha \in T_n \cap \omega_n(\Omega_1 + 1)$. Hence $\psi_{\Omega_1}(\omega_n(\Omega_1 + 1) + \alpha) \in T(\Omega_1) \cap \psi_{\Omega_1}(\omega_{n+1}(\Omega_1 + 1))$, and $\alpha < \beta \leftrightarrow \psi_{\Omega_1}(\omega_n(\Omega_1 + 1) + \alpha) < \psi_{\Omega_1}(\omega_n(\Omega_1 + 1) + \beta)$ for $\alpha, \beta \in T_n \cap \omega_n(\Omega_1 + 1)$.

Theorem 6.5.2. Let $\Gamma \subset \Sigma(\Omega_1)$. Boundedness Lemma 6.7 yields $\mathscr{H}_{\omega_{1+m+1}(\Omega_v+1)+1} \vdash_{\beta}^{\beta} \Gamma^{(\beta)}$. We conclude $\models \Gamma^{(\beta)}$ by Truth Lemma 6.13.2. □

Corollary 6.1 *Both* ID_1 *and* $\mathsf{ID}_1^{\mathbb{O}}$ *are conservative extensions of* $\mathsf{PA} + \{\mathrm{TI}(T(\Omega_1) \cap \psi_{\Omega_1}(\omega_n(\Omega_1 + 1)), <) : n \in \omega\}$. *Moreover* $|\mathsf{ID}_1| = |\mathsf{ID}_1^{\mathbb{O}}| = \psi_{\Omega_1}(\varepsilon_{\Omega_1+1})$.

Proof By Theorem 6.2 ID_1 is an extension of $\mathsf{PA} + \{\mathrm{TI}(T(\Omega_1) \cap \psi_{\Omega_1}(\omega_n(\Omega_1 + 1)), <) : n \in \omega\}$, and $|\mathsf{ID}_1| \geq \psi_{\Omega_1}(\varepsilon_{\Omega_1+1})$.

Conversely let $\mathsf{ID}_1 \vdash A$ for an arithmetic sentence A. Proposition 6.10 yields $\mathsf{ID}_1^{\mathbb{O}} \vdash A$. By Theorem 6.5.1 we obtain $\mathrm{FiX}^i(\mathsf{PA} + \{\mathrm{TI}(T(\Omega_1) \cap \psi_{\Omega_1}(\omega_n(\Omega_1+1)), <) : n \in \omega\}) \vdash A$, and Theorem 6.5.2 yields $|\mathsf{ID}_1^{\mathbb{O}}| \leq \psi_{\Omega_1}(\varepsilon_{\Omega_1+1})$. Theorem 4.15.1 yields $\mathsf{PA} + \{\mathrm{TI}(T(\Omega_1) \cap \psi_{\Omega_1}(\omega_n(\Omega_1 + 1)), <) : n \in \omega\} \vdash A$. □

6.4.1.1 How the Method of the Operator Controlled Derivations Works?

Let us try to expound the ideas in the operator controlled derivations and its interplay with the iterated Skolem hulls $\mathscr{H}_\alpha(X)$. In what follows let $\Omega := \Omega_1$ and $\psi\alpha := \psi_{\Omega_1}(\alpha)$.

Let $(T, <)$ be a computable well ordering with a distinguished epsilon number Ω, which is assumed to be a substitute for the least recursively regular ω_1^{CK}. Embed $\mathsf{ID}_1^{\mathbb{O}}$ into an infinitary calculus $\vdash_{\rho}^{a} \Gamma$, in which we interpret the predicate $<^{\mathbb{O}}$ by $<$ in $(T, <)$. $\vdash_{\rho}^{a} \Gamma$ is defined by suppressing $\mathscr{H}$ and conditions (6.4) and (6.5) in Definition 6.9. Then Truth Lemma 6.13, Embedding Lemma 6.10 and Predicative Cut-elimination Lemma 6.12 go through.

The problem is how to eliminate cut inferences

$$\frac{\vdash^{\alpha_0}_{\Omega+1} \Gamma, n \notin I^{<\Omega}_{\mathcal{A}} \quad \vdash^{\alpha_0}_{\Omega+1} n \in I^{<\Omega}_{\mathcal{A}}, \Gamma}{\vdash^{\alpha}_{\Omega+1} \Gamma} \ (cut)$$

In other words, cf. the proof of Collapsing Theorem 6.4,

> how can we extract effectively an ordinal bound $\beta := f(\alpha; \mathcal{H}) < \Omega$ from the witnessing derivation (Herleitung) $\mathcal{H}$ of $\vdash^{\alpha}_{\Omega+1} \Gamma$ and its depth α such that $\vdash^{\alpha'}_{\Omega} \Gamma^{(\beta)}$ holds for an $\alpha' < \Omega$?

The bound $f(\alpha; \mathcal{H})$ has to be larger than (or equal to the maximum of) ordinals β in the inferences

$$\frac{\vdash^{\alpha_1}_{\Omega} \Gamma_0, n \in I^{\beta}_{\mathcal{A}}}{\vdash^{\alpha_0}_{\Omega} \Gamma_0, n \in I^{<\Omega}_{\mathcal{A}}} \ (I^{<}_{\mathcal{A}})$$

occurring in $\mathcal{H}$. Therefore the relation $\vdash^{\alpha}_{d} \Gamma$ has to be enriched with a data $\mathcal{H}$ to bound such ordinals β.

Moreover, cf. the proof of Boundedness Lemma 6.7, $f(\alpha; \mathcal{H})$ should be monotonic in the depths α (or in $\mathcal{H}$) in view of the inferences

$$\frac{\vdash^{\alpha_1}_{\Omega} \Gamma_0, \mathcal{A}[I^{<\Omega}_{\mathcal{A}}, n]}{\vdash^{\alpha_0}_{\Omega} \Gamma_0, n \in I^{<\Omega}_{\mathcal{A}}} \ (Cl)$$

However ordinal terms $f(\alpha; \mathcal{H})$ need to be smaller than its subterm $\Omega > f(\alpha; \mathcal{H})$. $\alpha \geq \Omega$ happens mainly because of the transfinite induction on $<^{\mathbb{O}}$, cf. Induction Lemma 6.9. This means that $f(\alpha; \mathcal{H})$ has to be a collapsing function, and we need to collapse not only the positive predicates $I^{<\Omega}_{\mathcal{A}}$ down to $f(\alpha; \mathcal{H}) < \Omega$ but also its derivation depths.

Let us direct our attentions to ordinal constants occurring in derivations. First consider the embedded derivations. Let

$$\frac{\vdash^{\alpha_0} \Gamma_0}{\vdash^{\alpha} \Gamma}$$

be an inference occurring in the derivation. Then we can assume by the pure variable condition, that any epsilon numbers $\mathcal{E}(\Gamma_0)$ occurring in an uppersequent Γ_0 occur already in the lowersequent Γ, i.e.,

$$\mathcal{E}(\Gamma_0) \subset \mathcal{E}(\Gamma) \tag{6.10}$$

except the inferences $(\forall\mathbb{O})$ and $(\neg I^{<}_{\mathcal{A}})$, which have eigenvariables of ordinal sort. This observation yields that

$$\mathcal{E}(\alpha) \subset \mathcal{E}(\Gamma) \tag{6.11}$$

again except ($\forall\mathbb{O}$) and ($\neg I^{<}_{\mathcal{A}}$). Moreover these extra conditions are preserved under Predicative Cut-elimination procedure. For example, let C be a sentence such that $\mathrm{dg}(C) \le d$. Given derivations witnessing $\vdash^{\alpha}_{d} \Gamma, \neg C$ and $\vdash^{\beta}_{d} C, \Lambda$ ($d \neq \Omega + 1$) which enjoy the conditions (6.10) and (6.11), and assume $\mathscr{E}(C) \subset \mathscr{E}(\Gamma) \cup \mathscr{E}(\Lambda)$, then we can construct a derivation witnessing $\vdash^{\alpha+\beta}_{d} \Gamma, \Lambda$ enjoying the same conditions.

Call a (cut) with its cut degree Ω, $(cut)^{\Omega}$ temporarily. First consider the rightmost and uppermost $(cut)^{\Omega}$. We can assume $\vdash^{\alpha_0}_{\Omega} n_0 \in I^{<\Omega}_{\mathcal{A}}, \Gamma_0$ and $\Gamma_0 \subset \Sigma^{\Omega}$, where the rightmost and uppermost $(cut)^{\Omega}$ means that there is no $(cut)^{\Omega}$ in the derivation $\mathscr{H}_0$ of its right upper sequent, and there is no left upper sequent of $(cut)^{\Omega}$ below it.

$$
\dfrac{\dfrac{\Gamma_1, n_1 \notin I^{<\Omega}_{\mathcal{A}} \quad \begin{matrix} \vdots\, \mathscr{H}_1(\Omega := \beta_0) \\ \vdash^{\alpha_1}_{\Omega} n_1 \in I^{<\Omega}_{\mathcal{A}}, \Gamma_1 \end{matrix}}{\Gamma_1}\,(cut)^{\Omega} \\ \vdots \\ \Gamma_0, n_0 \notin I^{<\Omega}_{\mathcal{A}} \qquad \begin{matrix} \vdots\, \mathscr{H}_0 \\ \vdash^{\alpha_0}_{\Omega} n_0 \in I^{<\Omega}_{\mathcal{A}}, \Gamma_0 \end{matrix}}{\begin{matrix}\Gamma_0 \\ \vdots \end{matrix}}\,(cut)^{\Omega}
$$

Now consider the ordinal constants $\beta < \Omega$ occurring in the derivation $\mathscr{H}_0$. Since Γ_0 is the lower sequent of the rightmost and uppermost $(cut)^{\Omega}$, and there occurs no ordinal constant (other than $0, \Omega$) in the end sequent, we can assume that there occurs no ordinal constant in $\mathscr{H}_0$. Therefore we could further assume $\mathsf{SC}(\alpha_0) = \emptyset$ for the derivation depth $\alpha_0 < \varepsilon_{\Omega+1}$. This means that in the ordinal terms α we can replace Ω by ω, or collapse Ω down to ω. Thus set $\beta_0 := f(\alpha_0; \mathscr{H}_0) = \varepsilon_0$ when there occurs no ordinal constant in $\mathscr{H}_0$, where $f(\alpha; \mathscr{H})$ are assumed to be epsilon numbers for mild manipulations involved with the proof of Boundedness Lemma 6.7.

Next consider the rightmost and uppermost $(cut)^{\Omega}$ in the derivation of $\Gamma_0, n_0 \notin I^{\beta_0}_{\mathcal{A}}$, which is obtained from the derivation of the left upper sequent $\Gamma_0, n_0 \notin I^{<\Omega}_{\mathcal{A}}$ by inversion. Let $\mathscr{H}_1$ denote the derivation of the right upper sequent $n_1 \in I^{<\Omega}_{\mathcal{A}}, \Gamma_1$ of the $(cut)^{\Omega}$: $\mathscr{H}_1 \vdash^{\alpha_1}_{\Omega} n_1 \in I^{<\Omega}_{\mathcal{A}}, \Gamma_1$. Then β_0 may occur in $\mathscr{H}_1$, and hence $f(\alpha_1; \mathscr{H}) > \beta_0 = \varepsilon_0$ for any subderivations $\mathscr{H}$ of $\mathscr{H}_1$. Also note that once an ordinal constant β occurs in $\mathscr{H}_1$, then so does any ordinal $\gamma < \beta$ because of the inferences ($\neg I^{<}_{\mathcal{A}}$). We can assume that the derivation depths α of the subderivations of $\mathscr{H}_1$ are constructed from $\{\Omega\} \cup \{\gamma : \gamma \le \beta_0\}$ by $+$ and $\gamma \mapsto \omega^{\gamma}$. Therefore we could replace Ω by an ordinal$> \beta_0$ in the ordinal terms α. Thus $f(\alpha_1; \mathscr{H}_1)$ could be the next epsilon number$(= \varepsilon_1)$ to β_0 when ordinal constants occurring in $\mathscr{H}_1$ is smaller than $\beta_0 + 1$.

$$
\dfrac{\dfrac{\cdots \quad \Gamma_1, n_1 \notin I^{\beta_1}_{\mathcal{A}} \quad \cdots}{\vdash^{\alpha_1}_{\Omega+1} \Gamma_1, n_1 \notin I^{<\Omega}_{\mathcal{A}}} \qquad \begin{array}{c} \vdots\ \mathcal{H}_1 \\ \vdash^{\alpha_1}_{\Omega} n_1 \in I^{<\Omega}_{\mathcal{A}}, \Gamma_1 \end{array}}{\vdash_{\Omega+1} \Gamma_1}
$$

$$
\vdots
$$

$$
\dfrac{\dfrac{\cdots \qquad \Gamma_0, n_0 \notin I^{\beta_0}_{\mathcal{A}} \qquad \cdots}{\vdash^{\alpha_0}_{\Omega+1} \Gamma_0, n_0 \notin I^{<\Omega}_{\mathcal{A}}} \qquad \begin{array}{c} \vdots\ \mathcal{H}_0 \\ \vdash^{a_0}_{\Omega} n_0 \in I^{<\Omega}_{\mathcal{A}}, \Gamma_0 \end{array}}{\vdash_{\Omega+1} \Gamma_0}
$$

This collapsing procedure could be iterated transfinitely, i.e., α-fold iteration for $\mathcal{H} \vdash^{\alpha}_{\Omega+1} \Gamma$. Namely $f(a_\alpha; \mathcal{H}_\alpha)$ is the αth collapse of the point Ω with the Skolem hull of $\{0, \Omega\} \cup \{f(a_\beta; \mathcal{H}_\beta) : \beta < \alpha\}$ under $+$ and exponentiation. Thus ψ-function and the hull $\mathcal{H}_\alpha(\beta)$ emerged.

The condition (6.4) when $\mathcal{H}_\gamma \vdash^{\alpha}_{\rho} \Gamma$ tells you that the ordinal constants occurring in α or in Γ are in the Skolem hull $\mathcal{H}_\gamma$, and this guarantees that the ordinal $\psi\gamma$ is larger than any ordinals β in the inferences $(I^{<}_{\mathcal{A}})$. Also $\alpha \mapsto \psi(\gamma + \omega^{\alpha})$ is monotonic in α if $\gamma \in \mathcal{H}_\gamma$ and (6.4), as we saw in the proof of Collapsing Theorem 6.4. Thus the enriched data γ in $\mathcal{H}_\gamma \vdash^{\alpha}_{\rho} \Gamma$ together with (6.4) tells us that we are in the γth collapsing procedure.

Then what is the rôle of the condition (6.5) for the inferences $(I^{<}_{\mathcal{A}})$? The condition is dispensable to prove Theorem 6.5, but is needed to state Boundedness Lemma 6.7 separately. We could show simultaneously Collapsing Theorem 6.4 and Boundedness Lemma 6.7.

The reason why $\mathcal{H}_\alpha(\beta)$ is defined to be closed under the Veblen function φ is to have Predicative Cut-elimination theorem 6.12 in a complete form, i.e., to eliminate cuts completely from $\Sigma(\Omega_1)$-endsequent. This will be needed below but not for Theorem 6.5, which is stated with $\mathsf{ID}^{\mathbb{O}}_1$: Let $\gamma \in \mathcal{H}_\gamma$ and $\Gamma \subset \Sigma(\Omega_1)$. Then $\mathcal{H}_\gamma \vdash^{a}_{\Omega+1} \Gamma \Rightarrow \mathcal{H}_{\hat{a}+1} \vdash^{\psi\hat{a}}_{\psi\hat{a}} \Gamma$ for $\hat{a} = \gamma + \omega^{a}$. For the **Case 3.1** in the proof of Collapsing Theorem 6.4, namely the case when the last inference is a (cut) with a cut degree $\mathrm{dg}(C) < \Omega$, cf. (6.9), it suffices for $\psi\gamma$ to be epsilon numbers.

6.4.2 *Ω-Rule*

In the case of the local predicativity method in Sect. 6.4.1 the crucial axiom to be analyzed is the closure axiom $(P_{\mathcal{A}}.1)$, $\mathcal{A}[P_{\mathcal{A}}] \subset P_{\mathcal{A}}$.

Let us define the least fixed point $P_{\mathcal{A}}$ as the intersection $P_{\mathcal{A}} = \bigcap\{X : \mathcal{A}[X] \subset X\}$. Then the closure axiom $(P_{\mathcal{A}}.1)$ follows logically: Assume $\mathcal{A}[P_{\mathcal{A}}, n]$ and $\mathcal{A}[X] \subset X$. We need to show $n \in X$. We obtain $P_{\mathcal{A}} \subset X$ by the definition of the intersection $P_{\mathcal{A}}$. By the positivity we obtain $\mathcal{A}[P_{\mathcal{A}}] \subset \mathcal{A}[X]$. This yields $\mathcal{A}[X, n]$ by the first assumption, and then $n \in X$ by the second assumption. To prove the transfinite induction axiom ($P_{\mathscr{A}}.2$), we need a logical 'axiom' of the form $\forall X\, G(X) \to G(F)$, i.e., $\forall X(\mathscr{A}[X] \subset X \to X(n)) \to (\mathscr{A}[F] \subset F \to F(n))$. This is obviously impredicative since the formula F may contain the formula $\forall X\, G(X)$ itself.

In the case of the first-order arithmetic PA, the crucial axiom is the complete induction schema $F(0) \wedge \forall y(F(y) \to F(S(y))) \to \forall x\, F(x)$. In chapter 4 we have 'proved' it using the ω-rule. Then the cut inferences in the resulting infinitary derivations are eliminated as for the first-order logic. We now ask: how to 'prove' the axiom $\mathscr{A}[F] \subset F \to (P_{\mathscr{A}}(n) \to F(n))$ in such a way that a cut-elimination procedure could be performed? Recall that in the BHK(Brouwer-Heyting-Kolmogorov) interpretation of the logical connectives, a 'proof' of an implication $A \to B$ is an operation π which transforms each proof d of A to a proof $\pi(d)$ of B. Inspired from this, a 'proof' of the implication $P_{\mathscr{A}}(n) \to F(n)$ is understood as an operation π which transforms each proof d of $P_{\mathscr{A}}(n)$ to a proof $\pi(d)$ of $F(n)$. Let us agree to understand that a proof of $P_{\mathscr{A}}(n)$ is an infinitary derivation d of $P_{\mathscr{A}}(n)$ in a calculus ID_0^∞, which is obtained from the ω-logic by adding the inference rule

$$\frac{\Gamma, \mathscr{A}[P_{\mathscr{A}}, n], P_{\mathscr{A}}(n)}{\Gamma, P_{\mathscr{A}}(n)}\ (P)$$

for the axiom ($P_{\mathscr{A}}.1$). Note that only a positive formula $P_{\mathscr{A}}(n)$ can be a major formula in the calculus ID_0^∞, and hence we see easily that the calculus admits a cut-elimination. Then a proof π of $P_{\mathscr{A}}(n) \to F(n)$ is an operation, which transforms a derivation d of $P_{\mathscr{A}}(n)$ in ID_0^∞ to a derivation $\pi(d)$ of $F(n)$. In eliminating cut inferences, it is convenient for us to allow positive side formulas Δ_d with $P_{\mathscr{A}}(n)$. Let $\mathscr{D}_n$ denote the set of cut-free derivations d of sequents $\Delta_d, P_{\mathscr{A}}(n)$ for positive sequents Δ_d, in which predicates $P_{\mathscr{A}}$ occur only positively. Here is a $\mathscr{D}_n$-branching inference rule for introducing *negative* formula $\neg P_{\mathscr{A}}(n)$:

$$\frac{\cdots \quad \overset{\vdots\, \pi(d)}{\Delta_d, \Gamma} \quad \cdots\ (d \in \mathscr{D}_n)}{\neg P_{\mathscr{A}}(n), \Gamma}$$

where for each derivation $d \in \mathscr{D}_n$ of a positive sequent $\Delta_d, P_{\mathscr{A}}(n)$, a derivation $\pi(d)$ of Δ_d, Γ is the dth branch. It is convenient for us to incorporate the following cut inference with an inference.

$$\frac{\Gamma, P_{\mathscr{A}}(n) \qquad \dfrac{\cdots \quad \overset{\vdots\, \pi(d)}{\Delta_d, \Gamma} \quad \cdots\ (d \in \mathscr{D}_n)}{\neg P_{\mathscr{A}}(n), \Gamma}}{\Gamma}\ (cut)$$

Thus we arrive at the following *Ω-rule*:

$$\frac{\Gamma, P_{\mathscr{A}}(n) \quad \cdots \quad \begin{array}{c} \vdots\ \pi(d) \\ \Delta_d, \Gamma \end{array} \quad \cdots (d \in \mathscr{D}_n)}{\Gamma} \ (\Omega)$$

Let ID_1^∞ denote the infinitary calculus obtained from ID_0^∞ by adding the Ω-rule. We restrict our attentions to closed formulas in the infinitary calculus ID_1^∞, and each closed term t is identified with its value $t^{\mathbb{N}}$ in the standard model. The nth numeral is denoted by n.

The *degree* $\mathrm{dg}(A) < \omega$ of formulas A is defined exactly as in Definition 1.1. Specifically $\mathrm{dg}(P_{\mathscr{A}}(n)) = \mathrm{dg}(\neg P_{\mathscr{A}}(n)) = 0$.

To define the relation $\mathsf{ID}_1^\infty \vdash_c^\alpha \Gamma$, let us specify what ordinal terms α are. Let $T_\vartheta(\Omega)$ be a set of ordinal terms built from $0, \Omega$ by applying the addition $+$, exponentiation $\alpha \mapsto \omega^\alpha$ and a function $\alpha \mapsto \vartheta(\alpha)$ defined in Exercise 6.3.

Epsilon numbers in $T_\vartheta(\Omega)$ are Ω and $\vartheta(\alpha) < \Omega$. $E(\alpha)$ denotes the set of epsilon numbers$< \Omega$ occurring in ordinal terms α. Let $E(\alpha) < \vartheta(\beta) :\Leftrightarrow \forall\gamma \in E(\alpha)(\gamma < \vartheta(\beta))$, and $\vartheta(\alpha) \leq E(\beta) :\Leftrightarrow \exists\delta \in E(\beta)(\vartheta(\alpha) \leq \delta)$. Then $\vartheta(\alpha) < \vartheta(\beta)$ iff either $E(\alpha) < \vartheta(\beta)\,\&\,\alpha < \beta$, or $\vartheta(\alpha) \leq E(\beta)$. Thus $(T_\vartheta(\Omega), <)$ is elementary recursive. Let $\alpha \ll \beta :\Leftrightarrow \alpha < \beta\,\&\,E(\alpha) < \vartheta(\beta)$.

Next let us define a set $T_\vartheta(\Omega, *)$ of ordinal terms with a placeholder $*$ recursively as follows. $*$ occurs only once in each term. Moreover the occurrence of $*$ in $\alpha[*]$ is not in the scope of ϑ.

1. $2* \in T_\vartheta(\Omega, *)$.
2. If $\alpha[*] \in T_\vartheta(\Omega, *)$, then so is $\omega^{\alpha[*]}$.
3. If $\alpha[*] \in T_\vartheta(\Omega, *)$ and $\beta \in T_\vartheta(\Omega)$, then so is $\beta\#(\alpha[*])$.

For $\alpha[*] \in T_\vartheta(\Omega, *)$ and $\Omega \geq z \in T_\vartheta(\Omega)$, $\alpha[z]$ denotes the result of replacing the placeholder $*$ by the ordinal term z. For example if $\alpha[*] = 2*$, then $\alpha[z] = 2z$.

Proposition 6.14 *1.* $E(\alpha) < \vartheta(\alpha)$.
2. $\alpha \ll \beta \Leftrightarrow \alpha < \beta\, \vartheta(\alpha) < \vartheta(\beta)$.
3. For $\alpha, \beta < \Omega, \alpha \ll \beta \Leftrightarrow \alpha < \beta$.
4. Let $\alpha \ll \beta$. *Then* $\gamma\#\alpha \ll \gamma\#\beta$. *Let* $\alpha_0, \alpha_1 \ll \beta$. *Then* $\omega^{\alpha_0}\#\omega^{\alpha_1} \ll \omega^\beta$.
5. For $\alpha[*] \in T_\vartheta(\Omega, *)$, $z < w \leq \Omega \Rightarrow \alpha[z] < \alpha[w]$.

Proof Proposition 6.14.1 follows from $\gamma \leq E(\alpha)$ for $\gamma \in E(\alpha)$. Propositions 6.14.2, 6.14.3 and 6.14.4 follow from Proposition 6.14.1 and the fact $E(\alpha) \leq \alpha$.

Proposition 6.14 is seen by induction on the construction of $\alpha[*]$. □

Definition 6.11 For $i = 0, 1$, ordinal terms $\alpha \in T_\vartheta(\Omega)$, $c < \omega$ and sequents Γ, let us define relations $\mathsf{ID}_i^\infty \vdash_c^\alpha \Gamma$ (Γ has a derivation in ID_i^∞ such that the depth of the derivation is at most α and its cut rank is less than c), where $\alpha \in T_\vartheta(\Omega) \cap \Omega$ when $i = 0$, and $\alpha \in T_\vartheta(\Omega)$ for $i = 1$. Let us write $\vdash_{i,c}^\alpha \Gamma$ for $\mathsf{ID}_i^\infty \vdash_c^\alpha \Gamma$.

$\vdash^{\alpha}_{0,c} \Gamma$ is defined as for ω-logic $\boldsymbol{G}_{\omega}$. Initial sequents are the sequents Γ, L for true arithmetic literals L, and $\Gamma, \neg L, L$ for literals L including the case $L \equiv P_{\mathscr{A}}(n)$. Thus $\vdash^{\alpha}_{i,c} \Gamma, \neg P_{\mathscr{A}}(n), P_{\mathscr{A}}(n)$ holds for any $\alpha \in T_{\vartheta}(\Omega)$ with $i = 1$, and any $\alpha \in T_{\vartheta}(\Omega) \cap \Omega$ when $i = 0$.

1. For the inference (P), if $\vdash^{\beta}_{i,c} \Gamma, \mathscr{A}[P_{\mathscr{A}}(n), n]$ with $(P_{\mathscr{A}}(n)) \in \Gamma$ and $\beta \ll \alpha$, then $\vdash^{\alpha}_{i,c} \Gamma$, where $\alpha \in T_e(\Omega) \cap \Omega$ if $i = 0$, and $\beta, \alpha \in T_{1,e}(\Omega)$ for $i = 1$.

$$\frac{\vdash^{\beta}_{i,c} \Gamma, \mathscr{A}[P_{\mathscr{A}}, n], P_{\mathscr{A}}(n)}{\vdash^{\alpha}_{i,c} \Gamma, P_{\mathscr{A}}(n)} \; (P)$$

2. For the Ω-rule, we define as follows. Let $\alpha[*] \in T_{\vartheta}(\Omega, *)$, for which $\vdash^{\alpha[0]}_{1,c} \Gamma, P_{\mathscr{A}}(n)$ holds. Moreover assume that for any positive sequent Δ and any $z \in T_e(\Omega) \cap \Omega$ if $\vdash^{z}_{0,0} \Delta, P_{\mathscr{A}}(n)$ holds, then $\vdash^{\alpha[z]}_{1,c} \Delta, \Gamma$ holds.
Then we conclude $\vdash^{\alpha}_{1,c} \Gamma$ for $T_{\vartheta}(\Omega) \ni \alpha = \alpha[\Omega]$ by the Ω-rule. Pos denotes the set of positive sequents.

$$\frac{\vdash^{\alpha[0]}_{1,c} \Gamma, P_{\mathscr{A}}(n) \quad \vdash^{\alpha[z]}_{1,c} \Delta, \Gamma \; (\Delta \subset \mathrm{Pos}, z < \Omega, \vdash^{z}_{0,0} \Delta, P_{\mathscr{A}}(n))}{\vdash^{\alpha}_{1,c} \Gamma} \; (\Omega)$$

Note that there is no major formula of the Ω-rule.
3. For other inferences $(\vee)$, $(\wedge)$, $(\exists)$, $(\forall\omega)$, (cut), if $\vdash^{\beta}_{i,c} \Gamma, C_k$ and $\beta \ll \alpha$, then $\vdash^{\alpha}_{i,c} \Gamma$, where a major formula is in Γ, and $\{C_k\}_k$ are minor formulas, $\alpha \in T_{\vartheta}(\Omega) \cap \Omega$ if $i = 0$, and $\beta, \alpha \in T_{\vartheta}(\Omega)$ for $i = 1$.

Lemma 6.14 (Tautology) $\vdash^{2d}_{i,0} \Gamma, \neg A, A$ *with* $d = \mathrm{dg}(A)$.

Proof This is seen by induction on $\mathrm{dg}(A)$. □

Lemma 6.15 (Embedding) *Let $\Gamma(\mathbf{a})$ be a sequent in* ID_1 *in which no free variable other than the variables $\mathbf{a} = (a_1, \ldots, a_p)$ occurs. For sequences $\mathbf{n} = (n_1, \ldots, n_p)$ of numerals let $\Gamma(\mathbf{n})$ denote the result of substituting $\mathbf{n}$ for $\mathbf{a}$. Assume* $\mathsf{ID}_1 \vdash \Gamma(\mathbf{a})$. *Then there exist $k, m, c < \omega$ such that for any $\mathbf{n}$, $\vdash^{\Omega+\omega k+m}_{1,c} \Gamma(\mathbf{n})$ holds with $\Omega + \omega k + m \in T_{\vartheta}(\Omega)$.*

Proof By induction on the depths of ID_1-proofs. It suffices to consider axioms $(P_{\mathscr{A}}.1)$ and $(P_{\mathscr{A}}.2)$. For $k = \mathrm{dg}(\mathscr{A}[P_{\mathscr{A}}, n])$, we have $\vdash^{2k}_{1,0} \Gamma, \neg\mathscr{A}[P_{\mathscr{A}}, n], \mathscr{A}[P_{\mathscr{A}}, n], P_{\mathscr{A}}(n)$ by Tautology Lemma 6.14. We obtain $\vdash^{2k+1}_{1,0} \Gamma, \neg\mathscr{A}[P_{\mathscr{A}}, n], P_{\mathscr{A}}(n)$ by the inference rule (P), and hence the axiom $(P_{\mathscr{A}}.1)$, $\vdash^{2k+4}_{1,0} \Gamma, \forall x(\mathscr{A}[P_{\mathscr{A}}, x] \to P_{\mathscr{A}}(x))$ follows.

Next consider the axiom $(P_{\mathscr{A}}.2)$, $\Gamma = \{\exists x(\mathscr{A}[F, x] \wedge \neg F(x)), \neg P_{\mathscr{A}}(n), F(n)\}$. We claim that for any $\Delta \subset \mathrm{Pos}$ and $z \in T_{\vartheta}(\Omega) \cap \Omega$

$$\vdash^{z}_{0,0} \Delta, P_{\mathscr{A}}(n) \Rightarrow \vdash^{\alpha[z]}_{1,0} \Delta, \Gamma \tag{6.12}$$

where $\alpha[*] = 2k\#2*$ for $k = \text{dg}(F)$.

Suppose that we have a derivation d witnessing the fact $\vdash^{z}_{0,0} \Delta, P_{\mathscr{A}}(n)$ for positive Δ. Note that every sequent occurring in the cut-free d is positive. In particular no initial sequent $\Pi, \neg P_{\mathscr{A}}(m), P_{\mathscr{A}}(m)$ occurs in d. Replace (some occurrences of) the predicate $P_{\mathscr{A}}$ by the formula F, and add the sequent Γ at each sequent. This results in an invalid derivation of Δ, Γ with $(F(n)) \in \Gamma$ since an inference (P) with its major formula $P_{\mathscr{A}}(m)$ becomes illegal. To remedy it, add a canonical cut-free derivation of $\neg F(m), F(m)$, and two inference rules $(\wedge), (\exists)$ as follows.

$$\dfrac{\vdash^{w}_{0,0} \Pi, P^{\mathscr{A}}(m), \mathscr{A}(P^{\mathscr{A}}, m)}{\vdash^{z}_{0,0} \Pi, P^{\mathscr{A}}(m)}\ (P) \quad \rightsquigarrow \quad \dfrac{\dfrac{\vdash^{2k\#2w}_{1,0} \Pi', \Gamma, F(m), \mathscr{A}(F, m) \quad \vdash^{2k}_{1,0} \neg F(m), F(m)}{\vdash^{2k\#2w+1}_{1,0} \Pi', \Gamma, F(m), \mathscr{A}(F, m) \wedge \neg F(m)}\ (\wedge)}{\vdash^{2k\#2z}_{1,0} \Pi', \Gamma, F(m)}\ (\exists)$$

Thus the claim (6.12) is shown. On the other hand we have $\vdash^{\alpha[0]}_{1,0} \Gamma, P_{\mathscr{A}}(n)$ for $\alpha[0] = 2k$. An Ω-rule yields $\vdash^{\alpha[\Omega]}_{1,0} \Gamma$ with $\alpha[\Omega] = 2k\#2\Omega = \Omega + 2k$. Therefore $\vdash^{\Omega+2k+5}_{1,0} \mathscr{A}[F] \subset F \to P_{\mathscr{A}} \subset F$ follows. □

Lemma 6.16 (Inversion)

1. *If* $\vdash^{\alpha}_{i,c} \Gamma, \forall x\, F(x)$ *holds, then* $\vdash^{\alpha}_{i,c} \Gamma, F(n)$ *holds for any* $n \in \mathbb{N}$.
2. *If* $\vdash^{\alpha}_{i,c} \Gamma, F_0 \wedge F_1$ *holds, then* $\vdash^{\alpha}_{i,c} \Gamma, F_n$ *holds for* $n = 0, 1$.

Lemma 6.17 (Cut-elimination) *If* $\vdash^{\alpha}_{1,c} \Gamma$, *then* $\vdash^{\omega_c(\alpha)}_{1,0} \Gamma$.

Proof This is seen by induction on $c < \omega$ using the fact that if $\vdash^{\alpha}_{1,c+1} \Gamma$, then $\vdash^{\omega^{\alpha}}_{1,c} \Gamma$. The fact in turn follows from the following fact

$$\vdash^{\alpha}_{1,c} \Gamma, \neg C \text{ and } \vdash^{\beta}_{1,c} C, \Delta \Rightarrow \vdash^{\alpha\#\beta}_{1,c} \Gamma, \Delta$$

where $\alpha, \beta \in T_{1,e}(\Omega)$, and C is a formula of the form $C_0 \vee C_1, \exists x\, C_0(x), \neg P_{\mathscr{A}}(n)$ and arithmetic true literals, and $\text{dg}(C) \leq c$. The fact is seen by induction on β.

If C is a formula $\neg P_{\mathscr{A}}(n)$, then eliminate the formula from $\vdash^{\beta}_{1,c} \neg P_{\mathscr{A}}(n), \Delta$, and add the sequent Γ. For initial sequents $\vdash^{\gamma}_{1,c} \Pi, \neg P_{\mathscr{A}}(n), P_{\mathscr{A}}(n)$, graft the derivation witnessing the fact $\vdash^{\alpha}_{1,c} \Gamma, P_{\mathscr{A}}(n)$ to obtain $\vdash^{\alpha\#\gamma}_{1,c} \Pi, \Gamma, P_{\mathscr{A}}(n)$. Note that there is no inference with the major formula $\neg P_{\mathscr{A}}(n)$.

Suppose that C, Δ is obtained by an inference rule. When C is a major formula of an inference, then use Inversion Lemma 6.16 and IH as usual. Otherwise lift the left derivation to the upper sequents. For example when the inference is an Ω-rule with $\beta = \beta[\Omega]$,

$$\dfrac{\vdash^{\beta[0]}_{1,c} C, \Delta, P_{\mathscr{A}}(n) \quad \vdash^{\beta[z]}_{1,c} \Delta_0, C, \Delta\ (\Delta_0 \subset \text{Pos}, z < \Omega, \vdash^{z}_{0,0} \Delta_0, P_{\mathscr{A}}(n))}{\vdash^{\beta}_{1,c} C, \Delta}\ (\Omega)$$

then this turns to the following with $(\alpha\#\beta)[*] = \alpha\#(\beta[*]) \in T_\vartheta(\Omega, *)$ and $\alpha\#\beta = \alpha + \beta[\Omega]$

$$\frac{\vdash^{\alpha\#\beta[0]}_{1,c} \Gamma, \Delta, P_{\mathscr{A}}(n) \quad \vdash^{\alpha\#\beta[z]}_{1,c} \Delta_0, \Gamma, \Delta\,(\Delta_0 \subset \mathrm{Pos}, z < \Omega, G_\Omega(z) \leq \beta[0], \vdash^z_{0,0} \Delta_0, P_{\mathscr{A}}(n))}{\vdash^{\alpha\#\beta}_{1,c} \Gamma, \Delta}\ (\Omega)$$

□

Lemma 6.18 (Collapsing) *For a positive sequent* Γ, *if* $\vdash^\alpha_{1,0} \Gamma$, *then* $\vdash^{\vartheta(\alpha)}_{0,0} \Gamma$.

Proof By induction on α using Proposition 6.14.2. Consider the case when Γ is a conclusion of an Ω-rule with $\alpha = \alpha[\Omega]$.

$$\frac{\vdash^{\alpha[0]}_{1,0} \Gamma, P_{\mathscr{A}}(n) \quad \vdash^{\alpha[z]}_{1,0} \Delta, \Gamma\,(\Delta \subset \mathrm{Pos}, z < \Omega, \vdash^z_{0,0} \Delta, P_{\mathscr{A}}(n))}{\vdash^\alpha_{1,0} \Gamma}\ (\Omega)$$

IH yields first $\vdash^{\vartheta(\alpha[0])}_{0,0} \Gamma, P_{\mathscr{A}}(n)$ for positive sequent $\Gamma \cup \{P_{\mathscr{A}}(n)\}$. For positive sequent $\Delta = \Gamma$ and $z = \vartheta(\alpha[0]) < \Omega$ we obtain $\vdash^{\alpha[z]}_{1,0} \Delta, \Gamma$ for $\Delta \cup \Gamma = \Gamma$ for $\alpha[z] \in T_{1,e}(\Omega)$. Again IH yields $\vdash^{\vartheta(\alpha[z])}_{0,0} \Gamma$. We see $\vartheta(\alpha[z]) = \vartheta(\alpha[\vartheta(\alpha[0])) < \vartheta(\alpha[\Omega]) = \psi_\Omega(\alpha)$ from $z < \Omega$ and Propositions 6.14.1 and 6.14.5.

For other inferences,

$$\frac{\{\vdash^\beta_{1,0} \Gamma, C_k\}_k}{\vdash^\alpha_{1,0} \Gamma}$$

we have $\vdash^{\vartheta(\beta)}_{0,0} \Gamma, C_k$ by IH. We obtain $\vartheta(\beta) < \vartheta(\alpha)$. Hence we conclude $\vdash^{\vartheta(\alpha)}_{0,0} \Gamma$.

□

Theorem 6.6 *Assume* ID_1 *proves a positive sentence* A. *Then* $\vdash^\alpha_{0,0} A$ *for an* $\alpha < \vartheta(\varepsilon_{\Omega+1})$. *In particular if* $\mathsf{ID}_1 \vdash P_{\mathscr{A}}(n)$, *then* $|n|_{\mathscr{A}} < \vartheta(\varepsilon_{\Omega+1})$.

Proof Suppose $\mathsf{ID}_1 \vdash A$. By Embedding Lemma 6.15 we have $\vdash^\beta_{1,c} A$ for some $\beta = \Omega + \omega k + m \ll \Omega \cdot \omega = \omega^{\Omega+1}$ and $c < \omega$. Cut-elimination Lemma 6.17 yields $\vdash^{\omega_c(\beta)}_{1,0} A$. Collapsing Lemma 6.18 yields $\vdash^\alpha_{0,0} A$ for $\alpha = \vartheta(\omega_c(\beta)) < \vartheta(\varepsilon_{\Omega+1})$. □

6.4.3 Interpretations

In this subsection by giving mutual interpretations, we establish proof-theoretic equivalences of ID_1, and the light-face Π^1_1-comprehension axiom over weak SOA's.

Π^1_1-Comprehension Axiom schema without second-order parameters is denoted by Π^{1-}_1-CA, and for a Π^{1-}_1-formula, i.e., Π^1_1-formula without second-order parameters $A(y)$, $\exists X \forall y[y \in X \leftrightarrow A(y)]$ is its instance. $T + \Pi^{1-}_1$-CA denotes the SOA obtained from an SOA T by adding the axiom schema Π^{1-}_1-CA. Recall that EA^2 is our base SOA with complete induction and comprehension for Δ^0_0-formulas, cf. Sect. 5.2.

Proposition 6.15 ID_1 *is interpreted in* $\mathsf{EA}^2 + \Pi^{1-}_1$*-CA.*

Proof For a given positive formula $\mathscr{A}(X, y)$, let $I_{\mathscr{A}} = \bigcap\{X : \mathscr{A}(X) \subset X\}$ with $\mathscr{A}(X) = \{y : \mathscr{A}(X, y)\}$. $I_{\mathscr{A}}$ exists as a set by Π^{1-}_1-CA. For formulas B in the language $\mathscr{L}(\mathsf{ID})$, let B^I denote the result of replacing $P_{\mathscr{A}}$ by $I_{\mathscr{A}}$. We show that $\mathsf{EA}^2 + \Pi^{1-}_1$-CA proves B^I for complete induction axiom B and for axioms $(P_{\mathscr{A}}.1)$ and $(P_{\mathscr{A}}.2)$. Note that each formula $C(a, P_{\mathscr{A}}, P_{\mathscr{B}}, \ldots, z)$ in $\mathscr{L}(\mathsf{ID})$ is first-order in predicates $P_{\mathscr{A}}, P_{\mathscr{B}}, \ldots$.

First consider the complete induction. Let for a first-order formula $C(a, X, z)$

$$N_C(a, z) :\Leftrightarrow \forall X[C(0, X, z) \wedge \forall y(C(y, X, z) \rightarrow C(S(y), X, z)) \rightarrow C(a, X, z)]$$

$N_C(a, z)$ is a Π^{1-}_1-formula and the class $\{\langle a, z\rangle : N_C(a, z)\}$ exists as a set by the axiom Π^{1-}_1-CA. It is obvious that $N_C(0, z)$ and $\forall a[N_C(a, z) \rightarrow N_C(a + 1, z)]$. Therefore by Δ^0_0-IND we obtain $\forall a\, N_C(a, z)$, i.e., $\forall X[C(0, X, z) \wedge \forall y(C(y, X, z) \rightarrow C(S(y), X, z)) \rightarrow \forall a\, C(a, X, z)]$. Let I be the disjoint union of finitely many sets $I_{\mathscr{A}}, I_{\mathscr{B}}, \ldots$, which is again a set by Δ^0_0-CA. $C(0, I, z) \wedge \forall y(C(y, I, z) \rightarrow C(S(y), I, z)) \rightarrow \forall a\, C(a, I, z)$ follows.

Next let $\mathscr{A}(X, y), \mathscr{B}(X, y)$ be positive formulas. The translation $\mathscr{A}(I_{\mathscr{A}}) \subset I_{\mathscr{A}}$ of the axiom $(P_{\mathscr{A}}.1)$ is seen logically, cf. the beginning of Sect. 6.4.2.

Let $C(X, y)$ be a first-order formula. We show the translated $(P_{\mathscr{A}}.2)$:

$$\mathscr{A}(C(I_{\mathscr{B}})) \subset C(I_{\mathscr{B}}) \rightarrow I_{\mathscr{A}} \subset C(I_{\mathscr{B}}) \tag{6.13}$$

Let

$$B(y) :\Leftrightarrow \forall X[\mathscr{A}(C(X)) \subset C(X) \rightarrow C(X, y)].$$

We claim that

$$\mathscr{A}(B) \subset B \tag{6.14}$$

Assume $\mathscr{A}(B, y)$ and $\mathscr{A}(C(X)) \subset C(X)$. We need to show $C(X, y)$. We first show $B \subset C(X)$. Suppose $B(z)$. Then by the assumption $\mathscr{A}(C(X)) \subset C(X)$ we obtain $C(X, z)$. Hence $B \subset C(X)$, and $\mathscr{A}(B, y) \rightarrow \mathscr{A}(C(X), y)$ by the positivity of $\mathscr{A}(X)$. The assumption $\mathscr{A}(B, y)$ yields $\mathscr{A}(C(X), y)$, and we conclude $C(X, y)$ by $\mathscr{A}(C(X)) \subset C(X)$. This shows (6.14).

Since the class $\{y : B(y)\}$ exists as a set by Π^{1-}_1−CA, we obtain $I_{\mathscr{A}} \subset B$ by (6.14). On the other hand we have $B(y) \rightarrow \mathscr{A}(C(I_{\mathscr{B}})) \subset C(I_{\mathscr{B}}) \rightarrow C(I_{\mathscr{B}}, y)$ since $I_{\mathscr{B}}$ is a set. Therefore $\mathscr{A}(C(I_{\mathscr{B}})) \subset C(I_{\mathscr{B}}) \rightarrow B \subset C(I_{\mathscr{B}})$. This together with $I_{\mathscr{A}} \subset B$ yields (6.13). □

Conversely let us show that $\mathsf{ACA}_0 + \Pi^{1-}_1$-CA is Π^1_1-conservative over ID_1. First $\mathsf{ACA}_0 + \Pi^{1-}_1$-CA is shown to be equivalent to an auxiliary SOA $\mathsf{ACA}_0 + W$-CA for the set W of codes of computable well-founded trees in Definition 1.8. Its language is obtained from the language $\mathcal{L}_2$ of the SOA by adding a unary predicate constant W. $\Pi^1_0(W)$ $[\Pi^1_1(W)]$ denote the class of first-order formulas [Π^1_1-formulas] in the expanded language, resp. $\mathsf{ACA}_0 + W$-CA is obtained from $\mathsf{ACA}(W)_0$, i.e., ACA_0 in the expanded language by adding the defining axiom of W:

$$W = \{e \in Rtree : \forall f \exists n[\bar{f}(n) \notin Set(e)]\},$$

where $Rtree$ denotes the set of codes of total computable functions defining trees, i.e., $e \in Rtree \Rightarrow \forall s \subset_e t \in Set(e)[s \in Set(e)]$ with $t \in Set(e) :\Leftrightarrow \{e\}(t) \simeq 0$.

Proposition 6.16 *For any formula A in the language of the SOA,* $\mathsf{ACA}_0 + \Pi^{1-}_1$*–CA* $\vdash A$ *iff* $\mathsf{ACA}_0 + W$*–CA* $\vdash A$.

Proof It suffices to show that $\mathsf{ACA}_0 + W$–CA proves each instance of Π^{1-}_1–CA. Argue in ACA_0. We obtain Theorem 1.2 for Π^1_1-normal form, and Theorem 1.3. Thus W is Π^{1-}_1-complete, and hence $\mathsf{ACA}_0 + W$-CA $\vdash \Pi^{1-}_1$-CA. □

To interpret W-CA in ID_1 we need a basis theorem for Π^1_1-predicates, which states that each non well-founded recursive tree has an infinite path recursive in W. Let $T_s := \{t \in {}^{<\omega}\omega : s * t \in T\}$. $\mathscr{W}$ denotes the positive operator defined by

$$\mathscr{W}[X, e] :\Leftrightarrow e \in Rtree \wedge [Set(e) = \emptyset \vee \forall n(e \restriction \langle n\rangle \in X)] \tag{6.15}$$

where $e \restriction \langle n\rangle$ denotes the number such that $\{e \restriction \langle n\rangle\}(s) \simeq \{e\}(\langle n\rangle * s)$, i.e., $Set(e \restriction \langle n\rangle) = Set(e)_{\langle n\rangle}$. The function $f(e, n) = e \restriction \langle n\rangle$ is seen to be primitive recursive by the S-m-n Theorem. It is clear that the least fixed point $P_{\mathscr{W}}$ of the operator $\mathscr{W}$ is equal to the set W.

Lemma 6.19 *In* ID_1 *the followings are provable.*

1.
$$e_0 \in P_{\mathscr{W}} \wedge F \in Fnc \to \exists x[\bar{F}(x) \notin Set(e_0)]$$

for any formula F in $\mathcal{L}(\mathsf{ID})$, where $F \in Fnc :\Leftrightarrow \forall x \exists ! y\, F(x, y)$, and $\bar{F}(x) = t \Leftrightarrow t \in {}^{<\omega}\omega \wedge lh(t) = x \wedge \forall i < x\, F(i, (t)_i)$.

2.
$$e_0 \in Rtree \wedge \forall e \in \Delta^{P_{\mathscr{W}}}_1\, \exists x[\overline{\{e\}^{P_{\mathscr{W}}}}(x) \notin Set(e_0)] \to e_0 \in P_{\mathscr{W}},$$

where $\Delta^{P_{\mathscr{W}}}_1$ denotes the set of codes of total recursive unary functions in the predicate $P_{\mathscr{W}}$.

Proof The defining axioms for $P_{\mathscr{W}}$ are the following.

($P_{\mathscr{W}}$.1) $\forall e \in Rtree[Set(e) = \emptyset \vee \forall n(e \restriction \langle n\rangle \in P_{\mathscr{W}}) \to e \in P_{\mathscr{W}}]$.
($P_{\mathscr{W}}$.2) $\forall e \in Rtree[Set(e) = \emptyset \vee \{\forall n\, B(e \restriction \langle n\rangle) \to B(e)\}] \to P_{\mathscr{W}} \subset B$.

Let $\mathscr{T}$ denote the formula

$$s \in \mathscr{T}[X; e_0] :\Leftrightarrow Set(e_0)_s = \emptyset \vee \forall m[s * \langle m\rangle \in X]. \tag{6.16}$$

and put

$$s \in \text{Sec}_{e_0} :\Leftrightarrow (e_0 \upharpoonright s) \in P_{\mathscr{W}} \text{ (read: } s \text{ is } Set(e_0)\text{-securable).}$$

We see immediately from $(P_{\mathscr{W}}.1)$ and $(P_{\mathscr{W}}.2)$ that

(Sec.1) $e_0 \in Rtree \to \mathscr{T}[\text{Sec}_{e_0}; e_0] \subset \text{Sec}_{e_0}$.
(Sec.2) $e_0 \in Rtree \wedge \mathscr{T}[B; e_0] \subset B \to \text{Sec}_{e_0} \subset B$.

Lemma 6.19.1. Assume $e_0 \in Rtree$, $F \in Fnc$ and $s = \bar{F}(lh(s))$. Since $\emptyset \in \text{Sec}_{e_0} \leftrightarrow e_0 \in P_{\mathscr{W}}$, it suffices to show $\text{Sec}_{e_0} \subset B$ for $B(s) :\Leftrightarrow \big(\exists x \geq lh(s)[\bar{F}(x) \notin Set(e_0)]\big)$. We see $\mathscr{T}[B; e_0] \subset B$, and (Sec.2) yields $\text{Sec}_{e_0} \subset B$.

Lemma 6.19.2. Assume $e_0 \in Rtree$. It suffices to show

$$\forall e \in \Delta_1^{P_{\mathscr{W}}} \{s = \overline{\{e\}^{P_{\mathscr{W}}}}(lh(s)) \to \exists x \geq lh(s)[\overline{\{e\}^{P_{\mathscr{W}}}}(x) \notin Set(e_0)]\} \to s \in \text{Sec}_{e_0}.$$

Suppose $s \notin \text{Sec}_{e_0}$. Then by (Sec.1) we obtain $s \notin \mathscr{T}[\text{Sec}_{e_0}; e_0]$, i.e., $Set(e_0)_s \neq \emptyset (\leftrightarrow s \in Set(e_0))$ and $\exists m[s * \langle m\rangle \notin \text{Sec}_{e_0}]$. Choosing the smallest such m for extending s, we see $s * \langle m\rangle \in Set(e_0)$. Proceeding recursively one can define a recursive function $e \in \Delta_1^{P_{\mathscr{W}}}$ such that $s = \overline{\{e\}^{P_{\mathscr{W}}}}(lh(s))$ and $\forall x[\overline{\{e\}^{P_{\mathscr{W}}}}(x) \in Set(e_0)]$. □

Definition 6.12 For a formula $A \equiv A[W; X, \ldots]$ in the language of the SOA possibly with the predicate W and set parameters X, let A^r denote the formula in $\mathscr{L}(\mathsf{ID})$ obtained from A as follows:

1. Replace W by $P_{\mathscr{W}}$.
2. Replace any atomic formula $t \in X$ by $\{x\}^{P_{\mathscr{W}}}(t) \simeq 0$.
3. Restrict second order quantifiers QX $(Q \in \{\exists, \forall\})$ to sets in $\Delta_1^{P_{\mathscr{W}}}$, i.e., $Qx \in \Delta_1^{P_{\mathscr{W}}}$.
4. Append the assumptions $x \in \Delta_1^{P_{\mathscr{W}}}$ for each set parameter X in A.

Corollary 6.2 $\mathsf{RCA} + W{-}\mathrm{CA}$ *is interpreted to* ID_1*: if* $\mathsf{RCA}_0 + W{-}\mathrm{CA} \vdash A$*, then* $\mathsf{ID}_1 \vdash A^r$ *for any* A.

Proof This follows from Lemma 6.19. □

In the presence of the arithmetical comprehension axiom, we need to restrict formulas A to Π_1^1-formulas.

Lemma 6.20 *For any* $A \in \Pi_1^1(W)$*, if* $\mathsf{ACA}_0 + W{-}\mathrm{CA} \vdash A$*, then* $\mathsf{ID}_1 \vdash A^r$.

Proof Let $\boldsymbol{G}_2(W)$ denote a calculus obtained from the predicative second order logic $\boldsymbol{G}_2$ in Sect. 2.1.3, by adding the inference rules for the predicate W:

$$\frac{\Gamma, t \in Rtree \wedge \forall f \exists x[\bar{f}(x) \notin Set(t)], t \in W}{\Gamma, t \in W}\ (W)$$

$$\frac{\Gamma, t \notin Rtree, F \in Fnc \wedge \forall x[\bar{F}(x) \in Set(t)], t \notin W}{\Gamma, t \notin W}\ (\neg W) \text{ for } F \in \Pi^1_0(W)$$

We see easily that for any formula A, if $\mathsf{ACA}_0 + W\text{-CA} \vdash A$, then $\boldsymbol{G}_2(W) + (cut) \vdash \neg Eq, \neg IA, \neg B, A$, where $Eq :\Leftrightarrow \forall X \forall x \forall y[x = y \to (X(x) \leftrightarrow X(y))]$, $IA :\Leftrightarrow \forall X[X(0) \wedge \forall y(X(y) \to X(y+1)) \to \forall x X(x)]$, and for a conjunction B of arithmetical axioms for constants in the first-order arithmetic. For a sequent Γ, $\Gamma^r := \{A^r : A \in \Gamma\}$. It suffices to show the following Claim 6.4.3.

Claim For any $\Gamma_0 \subset \Pi^1_1(W)$,

$$\boldsymbol{G}_2(W) + (cut) \vdash \neg Eq, \neg IA, \neg B, \Gamma_0 \Rightarrow \mathsf{ID}_1 \vdash \Gamma_0^r.$$

Let us show Claim 6.4.3. Eliminate cut inferences from the given derivation of $\neg Eq, \neg IA, \neg B, \Gamma_0$ by defining the degrees of any $\Pi^1_0(W)$-formulas to be 0. Any sequent in the resulting derivation is of the form $\neg Eq, \neg IA, \neg B, \Gamma$ for a $\Gamma \subset \Pi^1_1(W)$. Then proceed inductively on the depth of such derivations to show $\mathsf{ID}_1 \vdash \Gamma^r$.

Consider first the case when the last inference introduces one of $\neg Eq$ and $\neg IA$ as its major formula. For example, for an $F \in \Pi^1_0(W)$

$$\frac{\neg Eq, \neg[F(0) \wedge \forall y(F(y) \to F(y+1)) \to \forall x F(x)], \neg IA, \neg B, \Gamma}{\neg Eq, \neg IA, \neg B, \Gamma}\ (\exists^2)$$

By IH we have $\mathsf{ID}_1 \vdash \neg[F(0) \wedge \forall y(F(y) \to F(y+1)) \to \forall x F(x)]^r, \Gamma^r$. On the other hand we have $\mathsf{ID}_1 \vdash [F(0) \wedge \forall y(F(y) \to F(y+1)) \to \forall x F(x)]^r$.

Second consider the case when the last inference is a (W).

$$\frac{\neg Eq, \neg IA, \neg B, \Gamma, t \in W, t \in Rtree \wedge \forall f \exists x[\bar{f}(x) \notin Set(t)]}{\neg Eq, \neg IA, \neg B, \Gamma, t \in W}\ (W)$$

By IH we have $\mathsf{ID}_1 \vdash \Gamma^r, t \in P_{\mathcal{W}}, t \in Rtree \wedge (\forall f \exists x[\bar{f}(x) \notin Set(t)])^r$. $\mathsf{ID}_1 \vdash \Gamma^r, t \in P_{\mathcal{W}}$ is seen from Lemma 6.19.2 and the fact that if $e \in \Delta_1^{P_{\mathcal{W}}}$ then its graph $\{\langle x, y \rangle : \{e\}^{P_{\mathcal{W}}}(x) \simeq y\}$ is also recursive in $P_{\mathcal{W}}$.

Finally consider the case when the last inference is a $(\neg W)$.

$$\frac{\neg Eq, \neg IA, \neg B, \Gamma, t \notin W, t \notin Rtree, F \in Fnc \wedge \forall x[\bar{F}(x) \in Set(t)]}{\neg Eq, \neg IA, \neg B, \Gamma, t \notin W}\ (\neg W)$$

for an $F \in \Pi^1_0(W)$.

By IH we have $\mathsf{ID}_1 \vdash \Gamma^r, t \notin P_{\mathcal{W}}, t \notin Rtree, (F \in Fnc \wedge \forall x[\bar{F}(x) \in Set(t)])^r$. On the other hand we have $\mathsf{ID}_1 \vdash t \in P_{\mathcal{W}} \wedge (F \in Fnc)^r \to \exists x[\bar{F}(x) \notin Set(t)]^r$ by Lemma 6.19.1, and $t \in Rtree$ from $t \in P_{\mathcal{W}}$. Therefore $\mathsf{ID}_1 \vdash \Gamma^r, t \notin P_{\mathcal{W}}$.

This shows Claim 6.4.3, and hence our proof of Lemma 6.20 is completed. □

We obtain the following equivalence by Lemma 6.20, Propositions 6.15 and 6.16, and Corollary 6.1.

Corollary 6.3 *For each arithmetic (first-order) formula A,* $\mathsf{ID}_1 \vdash A$ *iff* $\mathsf{ID}_1^{\mathbb{O}} \vdash A$ *iff* $\mathsf{EA}^2 + \Pi^{1-}_1\text{–CA} \vdash A$ *iff* $\mathsf{ACA}_0 + \Pi^{1-}_1\text{–CA} \vdash A$ *iff* $\mathsf{PA} + \{\mathrm{TI}(T(\Omega_1) \cap \psi_{\Omega_1}(\omega_n(\Omega_1 + 1)), <) : n \in \omega\} \vdash A$.

Furthermore $\mathsf{ACA}_0 + \Pi^{1-}_1\text{–CA}$ *is* Π^1_1*-conservative over* $\mathsf{EA}^2 + \Pi^{1-}_1\text{–CA}$.

In the exercises at the end of this chapter, further proof-theoretic equivalences between ID_ν and SOA's are established.

6.5 Ordinal Analysis of Kripke–Platek Set Theory KP_ν

In this section we consider the set theory KP_ν in which ID_ν is embedded.

6.5.1 Ramified Set Theory

Definition 6.13 *RS-terms t* and their *levels* $|t|$ are defined recursively as follows.

1. Each natural number n is an RS-term of level $|n| = 0$.
2. For each ordinal $\alpha \in T(\Omega_\nu) \cap (\Omega_\nu + 1)$, L_α is an RS-term of level $|\mathsf{L}_\alpha| = \alpha$.
3. Let $\theta(x, y_1, \ldots, y_n)$ be a formula in the language of KP_ν, and $s_1, \ldots, s_n$ be RS-terms such that $\max\{|s_i| : 1 \leq i \leq n\} < \alpha$. Then the formal expression $[x \in \mathsf{L}_\alpha : \theta^{\mathsf{L}_\alpha}(x, s_1, \ldots, s_n)]$ is an RS-term of level $|[x \in \mathsf{L}_\alpha : \theta^{\mathsf{L}_\alpha}(x, s_1, \ldots, s_n)]| = \alpha$.

RS denotes the set of all RS-terms. RS-terms L_α and $[x \in \mathsf{L}_\alpha : \theta^{\mathsf{L}_\alpha}(x, s_1, \ldots, s_n)]$ are *set terms*.

Terms $f(t_1, \ldots, t_i)$ with a function symbol f for an elementary recursive function on $\mathbb{N}$ is identified with 0, when one of t_i is a set term. Each arithmetic closed term is identified with its value. Terms M_t with a set term t is also identified with L_0.

Let $\theta(x_1, \ldots, x_n)$ be a formula in the language of KP_ν such that each quantifier is bounded by a variable y, $Qx \in y$ or bounded by $\mathbb{N}$, $Qx \in \mathbb{N}$, all free variables occurring in θ are among the list $x_1, \ldots, x_n$, and each x_i occurs freely in θ. An *RS-formula* is obtained from such a formula $\theta(x_1, \ldots, x_n)$ by substituting RS-terms t_i for each x_i.

Let $\mathsf{k}(a) := \{|a|\}$ for set terms a, $\mathsf{k}(n) := \emptyset$ for natural numbers n, and

$$\mathsf{k}(\theta(t_1, \ldots, t_n)) := \{|t_1|, \ldots, |t_n|\},\ |\theta(t_1, \ldots, t_n)| := \max\{|t_1|, \ldots, |t_n|, 0\}.$$

The bound $\mathsf{L}_{\Omega_\nu} = M_\nu$ in $\exists x \in \mathsf{L}_{\Omega_\nu}$ and $\forall x \in \mathsf{L}_{\Omega_\nu}$ is the replacements of the unbounded quantifiers $\exists$ and $\forall$, resp. Set $M_a := \mathsf{L}_{\Omega_a}$ for $a \leq \nu$.

Definition 6.14 Let s, t be RS-terms with $|s| < |t|$.

$$(s\dot{\in}t) :\equiv \begin{cases} B(s) & t \equiv [x \in \mathsf{L}_\alpha : B(x)] \\ \top & t \equiv \mathsf{L}_\alpha \end{cases}$$

where $\top$ denotes a true literal, e.g., $0 = 0$.

We assign disjunctions or conjunctions to sentences as follows. When a disjunction $\bigvee(A_i)_{i\in J}$ [a conjunction $\bigwedge(A_i)_{i\in J}$] is assigned to A, we denote $A \simeq \bigvee(A_i)_{i\in J}$ [$A \simeq \bigwedge(A_i)_{i\in J}$], resp.

Definition 6.15 1. $(A_0 \vee A_1) :\simeq \bigvee(A_i)_{i\in J}$ and $(A_0 \wedge A_1) :\simeq \bigwedge(A_i)_{i\in J}$ with $J := 2$.

2. $(a \in b) :\simeq \bigvee(t\dot{\in}b \wedge t = a)_{t\in J}$ and $(a \notin b) :\simeq \bigwedge(t\dot{\in}b \to t \neq a)_{t\in J}$ with $J := \{t \in RS : |t| < |b|\}$.
3. a. Let a, b be set terms.
   $(a \neq b) :\simeq \bigvee(\neg A_i)_{i\in J}$ and $(a = b) :\simeq \bigwedge(A_i)_{i\in J}$ with $J := 2$ and $A_0 :\equiv (\forall x \in a(x \in b))$, $A_1 :\equiv (\forall x \in b(x \in a))$.
   b. For natural numbers n, m,
   $$(n = m, n \neq m) :\simeq \begin{cases} (\bigwedge(A_i)_{i\in J}, \bigvee(A_i)_{i\in J}) & \text{if } n = m \\ (\bigvee(A_i)_{i\in J}, \bigwedge(A_i)_{i\in J}) & \text{if } n \neq m \end{cases} \text{ with } J := 0.$$
   c. Let a be a set term, and n a natural number.
   $(a = n), (n = a) :\simeq \bigvee(A_i)_{i\in J}$ and $(a \neq n), (n \neq a) :\simeq \bigwedge(A_i)_{i\in J}$ with $J := 0$.
4. $\exists x \in b\, A(x) :\simeq \bigvee(t\dot{\in}b \wedge A(t))_{t\in J}$ and $\forall x\in b\, A(x) :\simeq \bigwedge(t\dot{\in}b \to A(t))_{t\in J}$ with $J := \{t \in RS : |t| < |b|\}$.
5. $$(\mathbb{N}(a), \neg\mathbb{N}(a)) :\simeq \begin{cases} (\bigwedge(A_i)_{i\in J}, \bigvee(A_i)_{i\in J}) & \text{if } a \text{ is a natural number} \\ (\bigvee(A_i)_{i\in J}, \bigwedge(A_i)_{i\in J}) & \text{if } a \text{ is a set term} \end{cases} \text{ with } J := 0.$$
6. $\exists x \in \mathbb{N}\, A(x) :\simeq \bigvee(A(n))_{n\in J}$ and $\forall x \in \mathbb{N}\, A(x) :\simeq \bigwedge(A(n))_{n\in J}$ with $J := \omega$.

Lemma 6.21 $\forall i \in J\, (\mathsf{k}(i) \subset \mathsf{k}(A_i) \subset \mathsf{k}(A) \cup \mathsf{k}(i))$ *for* $A \simeq \bigvee(A_i)_{i\in J}$.

Definition 6.16 The *degree* $\mathrm{dg}(A), \mathrm{dg}(a) < \Omega_\nu + \omega$ of RS-formulas A and RS-terms a are defined simultaneously as follows.

1. $\mathrm{dg}(n) = \mathrm{dg}(\mathbb{N}(a)) = \mathrm{dg}(\neg\mathbb{N}(a)) = 0$ for natural numbers n.
2. $\mathrm{dg}(\mathsf{L}_\alpha) = \omega\alpha$.
3. $\mathrm{dg}([x \in \mathsf{L}_\alpha : B(x)]) = \max\{\omega\alpha, \mathrm{dg}(B(\mathsf{L}_0)) + 1\}$.
4. $\mathrm{dg}(a \in b) = \mathrm{dg}(a \notin b) = \max\{\mathrm{dg}(a) + 6, \mathrm{dg}(b) + 1\}$.
5. $\mathrm{dg}(A_0 \vee A_1) = \mathrm{dg}(A_0 \wedge A_1) = \max\{\mathrm{dg}(A_i) : i < 2\} + 1$.
6. a. $\mathrm{dg}(a = b) = \mathrm{dg}(a \neq b) = \max\{\mathrm{dg}(\forall x \in a(x \in b)), \mathrm{dg}(\forall x \in b(x \in a))\} + 1$ for set terms a, b.
   b. $\mathrm{dg}(a = b) = \mathrm{dg}(a \neq b) = 0$ if one of a and b is a natural number.

7. $\text{dg}(\exists x \in b\, B(x)) = \text{dg}(\forall x \in b\, B(x)) = \max\{\text{dg}(b) + 1, \text{dg}(B(\mathsf{L}_0)) + 2\}$.
8. $\text{dg}(\exists x \in \mathbb{N}\, B(x)) = \text{dg}(\forall x \in \mathbb{N}\, B(x)) = \text{dg}(B(0)) + 1$.

The degrees are defined so that the followings hold for any formula A.

Proposition 6.17 *1.* $\text{dg}(\mathscr{A}) \in \{\omega|\mathscr{A}| + n : n \in \omega\}$ *for RS-terms and RS-formulas* $\mathscr{A}$.
2. $\text{dg}(B(t)) \in \{\omega|t| + n : n \in \omega\} \cup \{\text{dg}(B(\mathsf{L}_0))\}$.
3. $\text{dg}(t\dot{\in}b) < \text{dg}(b)$ *if* $|t| < |b|$.
4. $\text{dg}(t = a) = \max\{6, \text{dg}(t), \text{dg}(a)\} + 4$ *for set terms* t, a.

Proof Proposition 6.17.1. These are seen simultaneously by induction on the constructions of RS-terms and RS-formulas.

Proposition 6.17.2 is seen from Proposition 6.17.1.

Proposition 6.17.3. Let $|t| < |b|$. Then $\text{dg}(b) \geq \omega > \text{dg}(0 = 0)$. Let $b \equiv [x \in \mathsf{L}_\alpha : B(x)]$. Then $\text{dg}(t\dot{\in}b) = \text{dg}(B(t))$ and $\text{dg}(b) = \max\{\omega\alpha, \text{dg}(B(\mathsf{L}_0)) + 1\}$. Proposition 6.17.2 with $|t| < |b| = \alpha$ yields $\text{dg}(t\dot{\in}b) < \text{dg}(b)$.

Proposition 6.17.4 is seen from the definition. □

Lemma 6.22 *Let* $A \simeq \bigvee(A_i)_{i\in J}$. *Then* $\forall i \in J(\text{dg}(A_i) < \text{dg}(A))$.

Proof We show for set terms b, a that $\text{dg}(t\dot{\in}b \wedge t = a) < \text{dg}(a \in b)$ and $\text{dg}(t\dot{\in}b \wedge B(t)) < \text{dg}(\exists x \in b\, B(x))$ when $|t| < |b|$. Let $|t| < |b|$. Then $\forall n \in \omega(\text{dg}(t) + n < \text{dg}(b))$. We compute $\text{dg}(t\dot{\in}b \wedge t = a) = \max\{\text{dg}(t\dot{\in}b) + 1, \text{dg}(t) + 5, \text{dg}(a) + 5, 11\} \leq \max\{\text{dg}(b), \text{dg}(a) + 5\} < \max\{\text{dg}(b) + 1, \text{dg}(a) + 6\} = \text{dg}(a \in b)$ using Propositions 6.17.4 and 6.17.3. Also $\text{dg}(t\dot{\in}b \wedge B(t)) = \max\{\text{dg}(t\dot{\in}b) + 1, \text{dg}(B(t)) + 1\} \leq \max\{\text{dg}(b), \text{dg}(B(t)) + 1\} < \max\{\text{dg}(b) + 1, \text{dg}(B(\mathsf{L}_0)) + 2\} = \text{dg}(\exists x \in b\, B(x))$. □

Definition 6.17 1. Let $B(x_1, \ldots, x_n)$ be a Δ_0-formula in the language $\{\in, =\}$, and $a_1, \ldots, a_n \in RS$ be $|a_i| < \Omega_{b+1}$. Then $B(a_1, \ldots, a_n)$ is a *$\Delta(\Omega_{b+1})$-formula*.
2. Let $A(x_1, \ldots, x_n)$ be a Σ-formula in the language $\{\in, =\}$, and $a_1, \ldots, a_n \in RS$ be $|a_i| < \Omega_{b+1}$. Then $A^{(\mathsf{L}_{\Omega_{b+1}})}(a_1, \ldots, a_n)$ is a *$\Sigma(\Omega_{b+1})$-formula*, where for RS-terms c, $A^{(c)}$ denotes the result of replacing unbounded existential quantifiers $\exists x(\cdots)$ by $\exists x \in c(\cdots)$.
3. Let $B \equiv A^{(\mathsf{L}_{\Omega_{b+1}})}$ be a $\Sigma(\Omega_{b+1})$-formula, and $\alpha \in T(\Omega_\nu) \cap \Omega_\nu$. Then $B^{(\alpha, \Omega_{b+1})} \equiv A^{(\mathsf{L}_\alpha)}$. For $\Gamma \subset \Sigma(\Omega_{b+1})$, $\Gamma^{(\alpha, \Omega_{b+1})} := \{B^{(\alpha, \Omega_{b+1})} : B \in \Gamma\}$.

Proposition 6.18 *1.* $\text{dg}(C) < \Omega_{b+1} \Rightarrow C \in \Delta(\Omega_{b+1})$ *for* $b < \nu$ *and an RS-formula* C.
2. Let $A \simeq \bigvee(A_i)_{i\in I}$ *and* $A \in \Sigma(\Omega_{b+1})$. *Then* $\{A_i\}_{i\in I} \subset \Sigma(\Omega_{b+1})$.

Let us define a relation $\mathscr{H} \vdash^\alpha_d \Gamma$ for Skolem hull operators $\mathscr{H} : \mathscr{P}(T(\Omega_\nu)) \to \mathscr{P}(T(\Omega_\nu)), \alpha < \varepsilon_{\Omega_\nu+1}, d < \Omega_\nu + \omega$ and RS-sequents, i.e., finite sets of RS-formulas Γ. The relation $\mathscr{H}_\gamma[\Theta] \vdash^\alpha_d \Gamma$ for finite sets Θ of ordinals is defined as a fixed point of a strictly (strongly) positive formula H

$$H(\gamma, \Theta, \alpha, d, \Gamma) \Leftrightarrow \mathcal{H}_\gamma[\Theta] \vdash^\alpha_d \Gamma$$

in an intuitionistic fixed point theory over a first-order arithmetic.

Definition 6.18 $\mathcal{H} \vdash^\alpha_d \Gamma$ holds if

$$\{\alpha\} \cup \mathsf{k}(\Gamma) \subset \mathcal{H} \tag{6.17}$$

and one of the following cases holds:

($\bigvee$) There are $A \in \Gamma$ such that $A \simeq \bigvee(A_i)_{i \in J}$, an $i \in J$ with

$$|i| < \alpha \tag{6.18}$$

and an $\alpha(i) < \alpha$ for which $\mathcal{H} \vdash^{\alpha(i)}_d \Gamma, A_i$ holds.

($\bigwedge$) There is an $A \in \Gamma$ such that $A \simeq \bigwedge(A_i)_{i \in J}$, and for any $i \in J$, there is an $\alpha(i)$ such that $\alpha(i) < \alpha$ for which $\mathcal{H}[\mathsf{k}(i)] \vdash^{\alpha(i)}_d \Gamma, A_i$ holds.

(cut) There are C and α_0, α_1 such that $\mathrm{dg}(C) < d, \alpha_0, \alpha_1 < \alpha$, $\mathcal{H} \vdash^{\alpha_0}_d \Gamma, \neg C$ and $\mathcal{H} \vdash^{\alpha_1}_d C, \Gamma$.

($\Delta_0(\Omega_a)$–Coll) Let $a \in Suc$.
There are a formula $\exists z \in M_a(c \in z \wedge \forall x \in c \exists y \in z\, B)$ in Γ with $B \in \Delta_0(\Omega_a)$, a set term c with $|c| < \Omega_a$ and $\alpha_0 < \alpha$ such that $\mathcal{H} \vdash^{\alpha_0}_d \Gamma, \forall x \in c \exists y \in M_a\, B$.

$$\frac{\mathcal{H} \vdash^{\alpha_0}_d \Gamma, \forall x \in c \exists y \in M_a\, B}{\mathcal{H} \vdash^{\alpha}_d \Gamma}\ (\Delta_0(\Omega_a)\text{–Coll})$$

In what follows $\mathcal{H}$ denotes a Skolem hull operator closed under addition and exponentiation to base ω. The following Lemmas 6.23–6.30 are seen as for $\mathsf{ID}^{\mathbb{O}}_1$ in Sect. 6.4.1.

Lemma 6.23 (Weakening) *Assume $\beta \leq \alpha \in \mathcal{H}'$, $d \leq c$ and $\mathsf{k}(\Delta) \subset \mathcal{H}'$ for a Skolem hull operator $\mathcal{H}'$ such that $\forall X \in \mathcal{P}(T(\Omega_\nu))[\mathcal{H}(X) \subset \mathcal{H}'(X)]$. Then*

$$\mathcal{H} \vdash^\beta_d \Gamma \Rightarrow \mathcal{H}' \vdash^\alpha_c \Gamma, \Delta.$$

Lemma 6.24 (Inversion) $\mathcal{H} \vdash^\alpha_d \Gamma, A \Rightarrow \forall i \in J(\mathcal{H}[\{i\}] \vdash^\alpha_d \Gamma, A_i)$ *for* $A \simeq \bigwedge(A_i)_{i \in J}$.

Lemma 6.25 (Boundedness)

$$\mathcal{H} \vdash^\alpha_d \Gamma, \Lambda \,\&\, \alpha \leq \beta < \Omega_{b+1} \,\&\, \beta \in \mathcal{H} \,\&\, \Lambda \subset \Sigma(\Omega_{b+1}) \Rightarrow \mathcal{H} \vdash^\alpha_d \Gamma, \Lambda^{(\beta, \Omega_{b+1})}.$$

Proof By induction on α. When the last inference is a ($\bigvee$) introducing a quantifier $\exists x \in M_{b+1} B(x)$, use the condition (6.18). □

Lemma 6.26 (Embedding) *Let $\Gamma^{(\Omega_\nu)}[\mathbf{x} := \mathbf{a}]$ $(\mathbf{a} \subset RS)$ denote a closed instance of a sequent Γ with restriction of unbounded quantifiers to L_{Ω_ν}. Assume $\mathsf{KP}_\nu \vdash \Gamma$. Then*

$$\exists m, l < \omega \forall \mathbf{a} \subset RS \forall \mathcal{H}[\mathcal{H}[|\mathbf{a}|] \vdash^{\Omega_\nu + l}_{\Omega_\nu + m} \Gamma^{(\Omega_\nu)}[\mathbf{x} := \mathbf{a}]]$$

where $\mathcal{H}$ ranges over Skolem hull operators closed under addition and exponentiation to base ω, and $|\mathbf{a}| = \{|a_1|, \dots, |a_n|\}$ for $\mathbf{a} = (a_1, \dots, a_n)$.

Let us postpone a proof of Embedding Lemma 6.26 in the next Sect. 6.5.2.

Lemma 6.27 (Predicative Cut-elimination) $\mathcal{H} \vdash^{\beta}_{c+\omega^a} \Gamma \Rightarrow \mathcal{H} \vdash^{\varphi\alpha\beta}_{c} \Gamma$ *if* $[c, c + \omega^a[\cap \{\Omega_{a+1} : a < \nu\} = \emptyset$ *and* $\varphi\alpha\beta \in \mathcal{H}$.

Proof By main induction on α with subsidiary induction on β as in the proof of Theorem 5.3. Note that $\varphi\alpha\beta \in \mathcal{H}$ iff $\alpha \in \mathcal{H}$ by (6.17), and $\mathrm{dg}(\exists z \in M_a(c \in z \land \forall x \in c \exists y \in z\, B)) = \Omega_a$ for the main formula $\exists z(z \in M_a \land c \in z \land \forall x \in c \exists y \in z\, B)$ of an inference $(\Delta_0(\Omega_a)\text{-Coll})$ with a successor a.

For example consider the case for a $\beta_0 < \beta$:

$$\frac{\mathcal{H} \vdash^{\beta_0}_{c+\omega^\alpha} \Gamma, \neg C \quad \mathcal{H} \vdash^{\beta_0}_{c+\omega^\alpha} C, \Gamma}{\mathcal{H} \vdash^{\beta}_{c+\omega^\alpha} \Gamma} \; (cut)$$

By SIH we obtain $\mathcal{H} \vdash^{\varphi\alpha\beta_0}_{c} \Gamma, \neg C$ and $\mathcal{H} \vdash^{\varphi\alpha\beta_0}_{c} C, \Gamma$. As in Theorem 5.3 it remains to show by induction on β that

$$\{\Omega_{a+1} : a < \nu\} \not\ni \mathrm{dg}(C) \leq c \;\&\; \mathcal{H} \vdash^{\alpha}_{c} \Gamma, \neg C \;\&\; \mathcal{H} \vdash^{\beta}_{c} C, \Lambda \Rightarrow \mathcal{H} \vdash^{\alpha+\beta}_{c} \Gamma, \Lambda$$

Consider the case $C \simeq \bigvee (C_i)_{i \in J}$

$$\frac{\mathcal{H} \vdash^{\beta_0}_{c} C, C_i, \Lambda}{\mathcal{H} \vdash^{\beta}_{c} C, \Lambda} \; (\bigvee)$$

for some $i \in J$ and $\beta_0 < \beta$. By IH we have $\mathcal{H} \vdash^{\alpha+\beta_0}_{c} C_i, \Gamma, \Lambda$. We can assume $|i| \in \mathsf{k}(C_i)$. On the other hand we have $\mathsf{k}(C_i) \subset \mathcal{H}$ by (6.4). Hence by Inversion Lemma 6.6.1 we have $\mathcal{H} \vdash^{\alpha}_{c} \Gamma, \neg C_i$. We obtain for $\mathrm{dg}(C_i) < \mathrm{dg}(C) \leq c$

$$\frac{\mathcal{H} \vdash^{\alpha}_{c} \Gamma, \neg C_i \quad \mathcal{H} \vdash^{\alpha+\beta_0}_{c} C_i, \Gamma, \Lambda}{\mathcal{H} \vdash^{\alpha+\beta}_{c} \Gamma, \Lambda} \; (cut)$$

□

Theorem 6.7 (Collapsing) *Let $\sigma \in \{\Omega_{a+1} : a < \nu\}$, and $\lambda \in \{\Omega_a : 0 < a \leq \nu\}$. Suppose $\gamma \in \mathcal{H}_\gamma[\Theta]$,*

$$\Theta \subset \mathcal{H}_\gamma(\psi_\sigma(\gamma)) \tag{6.19}$$

for a finite set Θ of ordinals, and $\Gamma \subset \Sigma(\sigma)$. Then for $\hat{\alpha} = \gamma + \omega^{\lambda+\alpha}$

$$\mathcal{H}_\gamma[\Theta] \vdash^{\alpha}_{\lambda+1} \Gamma \Rightarrow \mathcal{H}_{\hat{\alpha}+1}[\Theta] \vdash^{\psi_\sigma(\hat{\alpha})}_{\psi_\sigma(\hat{\alpha})} \Gamma.$$

Proof This is seen by main induction on λ with subsidiary induction on α. From (6.19) and $\forall\rho \geq \sigma(\psi_\rho(\gamma) \geq \psi_\sigma(\gamma))$ we see $\forall\rho \geq \sigma[\Theta \subset \mathcal{H}_\gamma(\psi_\rho(\gamma))]$.

First note that $\psi_\sigma(\hat{\alpha}) \in \mathcal{H}_{\hat{\alpha}+1}[\Theta]$ for (6.17) since $\hat{\alpha} = \gamma + \omega^{\lambda+\alpha} \in \mathcal{H}_\gamma[\Theta]$ by the assumption $\{\gamma, \lambda, \alpha\} \subset \mathcal{H}_\gamma[\Theta]$ with (6.17). Assume $\mathcal{H}_\gamma[\Theta][\Lambda] \vdash^{\alpha_0}_{\lambda+1} \Gamma_0$ with $\alpha_0 < \alpha$ and $\Lambda \subset \mathcal{H}_\gamma(\psi_\sigma(\gamma))$. Then by $\gamma \leq \hat{\alpha}$ and (6.19) we obtain for any $\rho \geq \sigma$ that $\widehat{\alpha_0} \in \mathcal{H}_\gamma[\Theta][\Lambda] \subset \mathcal{H}_\gamma(\psi_\rho(\gamma)) \subset \mathcal{H}_{\hat{\alpha}}(\psi_\rho(\hat{\alpha}))$. This yields, by Proposition 6.3.4, that $\alpha_0 < \alpha \Rightarrow \forall\rho \geq \sigma\left(\psi_\rho(\widehat{\alpha_0}) < \psi_\rho(\hat{\alpha})\right)$.

Second observe that $\mathsf{k}(\Gamma) \subset \mathcal{H}_\gamma[\Theta] \subset \mathcal{H}_{\hat{\alpha}+1}[\Theta]$ by $\gamma < \hat{\alpha} + 1$ and (6.17).

Case 1. The last inference is a $(\bigvee)$.

Let $A \in \Gamma$ be such that $A \simeq \bigvee(A_i)_{i\in J}$, and for an $i \in J$ and an $\alpha(i) < \alpha$

$$\dfrac{\mathcal{H}_\gamma[\Theta] \vdash^{\alpha(i)}_{\lambda+1} \Gamma, A_i}{\mathcal{H}_\gamma[\Theta] \vdash^{\alpha}_{\lambda+1} \Gamma}\ (\bigvee)$$

By SIH it suffices to show $|i| < \psi_\sigma(\hat{\alpha})$ for (6.18). We can assume $|i| \in \mathsf{k}(A_i)$. Then $|i| \in \mathsf{k}(A_i) \subset \mathcal{H}_\gamma[\Theta] \subset \mathcal{H}_\gamma(\psi_\sigma(\gamma))$ by (6.4) and the assumption (6.19). On the other hand we have $|i| < \sigma$ since $A \in \Sigma(\sigma)$. Hence $|i| \in \mathcal{H}_{\hat{\alpha}}(\psi_\sigma(\hat{\alpha})) \cap \sigma = \psi_\sigma(\hat{\alpha})$.

Case 2. The last inference is a $(\bigwedge)$.

Let $A \in \Gamma$ be such that $A \simeq \bigwedge(A_i)_{i\in J}$, and for any $i \in J$, there is an $\alpha(i) < \alpha$ such that

$$\dfrac{\{\mathcal{H}_\gamma[\Theta \cup \mathsf{k}(i)] \vdash^{\alpha(i)}_{\lambda+1} \Gamma, A_i : i \in J\}}{\mathcal{H}_\gamma[\Theta] \vdash^{\alpha}_{\lambda+1} \Gamma}\ (\bigwedge)$$

By SIH it suffices to show that $\forall i \in J(\mathsf{k}(i) \subset \mathcal{H}_\gamma(\psi_\sigma(\gamma)))$. For example consider the case when $A \equiv (\forall x \in a\, B(x))$ for a set term a. Then $J = \{t \in RS : |t| < |a|\}$. Since A is a $\Sigma(\sigma)$-sentence, we have $|a| < \sigma$. On the other hand we have $|a| \in \mathcal{H}_\gamma[\Theta]$ for $\mathsf{k}(a) = \{|a|\}$, and hence $|i| < |a| \in \mathcal{H}_\gamma(\psi_\sigma(\gamma)) \cap \sigma = \psi_\sigma(\gamma)$ for any $i \in J$. Thus we obtain $|i| < \psi_\sigma(\gamma)$ for $\mathsf{k}(i) = \{|i|\}$.

Case 3. The last inference is a $(\Delta_0(\Omega_a)\text{–Coll})$.

There are a sentence $\exists z \in M_a(c \in z \wedge \forall x \in c \exists y \in z\, B)$ in Γ with $B \in \Delta_0(M_a)$, $|c| < \Omega_a$ and $\alpha_0 < \alpha$ such that

$$\dfrac{\mathcal{H}_\gamma[\Theta] \vdash^{\alpha_0}_{\lambda+1} \Gamma, \forall x \in c \exists y(y \in M_a \wedge B)}{\mathcal{H}_\gamma[\Theta] \vdash^{\alpha}_{\lambda+1} \Gamma}\ (\Delta_0(\Omega_a)\text{–Coll})$$

Since $\exists z \in M_a(c \in z \wedge \forall x \in c \exists y \in z\, B) \in \Sigma(\sigma)$, we have $|c| < \sigma$ and $\Omega_a \leq \sigma$. Then $\forall x \in c \exists y(y \in M_a \wedge B)$ is also a $\Sigma(\sigma)$-sentence. SIH yields $\mathcal{H}_{\widehat{\alpha_0}+1}[\Theta] \vdash^{\psi_\sigma(\widehat{\alpha_0})}_{\psi_\sigma(\widehat{\alpha_0})} \Gamma, \forall x \in c \exists y(y \in M_a \wedge B)$.

Case 4. The last inference is a (cut).

For $\mathrm{dg}(C) < \lambda + 1$ and $\alpha_0 < \alpha$, we have

$$\frac{\mathcal{H}_\gamma[\Theta] \vdash^{\alpha_0}_{\lambda+1} \Gamma, \neg C \quad \mathcal{H}_\gamma[\Theta] \vdash^{\alpha_0}_{\lambda+1} C, \Gamma}{\mathcal{H}_\gamma[\Theta] \vdash^{\alpha}_{\lambda+1} \Gamma}\ (cut)$$

Case 4.1. $\mathrm{dg}(C) < \sigma$.

By SIH it suffices to show $\mathrm{dg}(C) < \psi_\sigma(\hat{\alpha})$. We have $\mathsf{k}(C) \subset \mathcal{H}_{\hat{\alpha}}(\psi_\sigma(\hat{\alpha}))$, and $\mathsf{SC}(\mathrm{dg}(C)) \subset \mathsf{SC}(\mathsf{k}(C))$ by Proposition 6.17.1. Hence $\mathrm{dg}(C) \in \mathcal{H}_{\hat{\alpha}}(\psi_\sigma(\hat{\alpha})) \cap \sigma = \psi_\sigma(\hat{\alpha})$.

Case 4.2. $\sigma \leq \mathrm{dg}(C) < \lambda + 1$ and $\mathrm{dg}(C) \notin \{\Omega_{b+1} : b < \nu\}$.

Let $\kappa = \min\{\Omega_{a+1} : \Omega_{a+1} > \mathrm{dg}(C)\} \leq \lambda$. Then $a > 0$ for $\kappa = \Omega_{a+1}$, $\sigma \leq \mathrm{dg}(C) < \kappa < \lambda + 1$, and $\{\neg C, C\} \subset \Sigma(\kappa)$ by Proposition 6.18.1. SIH yields $\mathcal{H}_{\widehat{\alpha_0}+1}[\Theta] \vdash^{\beta}_{\beta} \Gamma, \neg C$ and $\mathcal{H}_{\widehat{\alpha_0}+1}[\Theta] \vdash^{\beta}_{\beta} C, \Gamma$ for $\widehat{\alpha_0} = \gamma + \omega^{\lambda+\alpha_0}$ and $\beta = \psi_\kappa(\widehat{\alpha_0})$. Let $\lambda' = \Omega_a$ for $\kappa = \Omega_{a+1}$. Then $\beta = \lambda' + 1 + \omega^\beta$ and $[\lambda' + 1, \beta] \cap \{\Omega_{b+1} : b < \nu\} = \emptyset$. Since $\mathrm{dg}(C) < \kappa$, we obtain $\max \mathsf{k}(C) < \kappa$ by Proposition 6.18.1, which yields $C \in \Delta(\kappa)$. Moreover we see $\mathrm{dg}(C) < \beta$ as in **Case 4.1**. We obtain

$$\frac{\mathcal{H}_{\widehat{\alpha_0}+1}[\Theta] \vdash^{\beta}_{\lambda'+1+\omega^\beta} \Gamma, \neg C \quad \mathcal{H}_{\widehat{\alpha_0}+1}[\Theta] \vdash^{\beta}_{\lambda'+1+\omega^\beta} C, \Gamma}{\mathcal{H}_{\widehat{\alpha_0}+1}[\Theta] \vdash^{\beta+1}_{\lambda'+1+\omega^\beta} \Gamma}\ (cut)$$

Predicative cut-elimination Lemma 6.27 yields

$$\mathcal{H}_{\widehat{\alpha_0}+1}[\Theta] \vdash^{\varphi\beta(\beta+1)}_{\lambda'+1} \Gamma$$

Now we have $\lambda' < \kappa \leq \lambda$, $\widehat{\alpha_0} + 1 = \gamma + \omega^{\lambda+\alpha_0} + 1 \in \mathcal{H}_\gamma[\Theta] \subset \mathcal{H}_{\widehat{\alpha_0}+1}[\Theta]$ and $\mathcal{H}_\gamma(\psi_\sigma(\gamma)) \subset \mathcal{H}_{\widehat{\alpha_0}+1}(\psi_\sigma(\widehat{\alpha_0} + 1))$ by $\gamma < \widehat{\alpha_0} + 1$. MIH yields

$$\mathcal{H}_{\widehat{\alpha_1}+1}[\Theta] \vdash^{\psi_\sigma(\widehat{\alpha_1})}_{\psi_\sigma(\widehat{\alpha_1})} \Gamma$$

for $\widehat{\alpha_1} = \widehat{\alpha_0} + 1 + \omega^{\lambda'+\varphi\beta(\beta+1)} = \gamma + \omega^{\lambda+\alpha_0} + \omega^{\lambda'+\varphi\beta(\beta+1)} < \gamma + \omega^{\lambda+\alpha} = \hat{\alpha}$ by $\alpha_0 < \alpha$ and $\lambda' + \varphi\beta(\beta + 1) < \kappa \leq \lambda$. Hence $\psi_\sigma(\widehat{\alpha_1}) < \psi_\sigma(\hat{a})$, and we obtain

$$\mathcal{H}_{\hat{\alpha}+1}[\Theta] \vdash^{\psi_\sigma(\hat{\alpha})}_{\psi_\sigma(\hat{\alpha})} \Gamma$$

Case 4.3. $\sigma \leq \kappa = \Omega_{b+1} = \mathrm{dg}(C) < \lambda + 1$ for $b < \nu$.

Then C is a sentence $\exists x \in M_{b+1}\, B(x)$ with $\mathrm{dg}(B(\mathsf{L}_0)) < \kappa$. By $\mathsf{k}(B(\mathsf{L}_0)) \subset \mathcal{H}_\gamma(\psi_\kappa(\gamma)) \cap \kappa$, we obtain $\mathrm{dg}(B(\mathsf{L}_0)) < \psi_\kappa(\gamma)$.

We have $\{C\} \cup \Gamma \subset \Sigma(\kappa)$. From the right upper sequent, SIH yields for $\widehat{\alpha_0} = \gamma + \omega^{\lambda+\alpha_0}$ and $\beta_0 = \psi_\kappa(\widehat{\alpha_0})$

$$\mathcal{H}_{\widehat{\alpha_0}+1}[\Theta] \vdash^{\beta_0}_{\beta_0} C, \Gamma$$

We have $\beta_0 \in \mathcal{H}_{\widehat{\alpha_0}+1}$. Then by Boundedness Lemma 6.25, we obtain

$$\mathcal{H}_{\widehat{\alpha_0}+1}[\Theta] \vdash^{\beta_0}_{\beta_0} C^{(\beta_0, \Omega_{b+1})}, \Gamma$$

On the other hand we have by inversion from the left uppersequent

$$\mathcal{H}_{\widehat{\alpha_0}+1}[\Theta] \vdash^{\alpha_0}_{\lambda+1} \Gamma, \neg C^{(\beta_0, \Omega_{b+1})}$$

SIH with $\Gamma \cup \{\neg C^{(\beta_0, \Omega_{b+1})}\} \subset \Sigma(\kappa)$ yields for $\beta_1 = \psi_\kappa(\widehat{\alpha_1})$ and $\widehat{\alpha_1} = \widehat{\alpha_0} + 1 + \omega^{\lambda+\alpha_0} = \gamma + \omega^{\lambda+\alpha_0} + \omega^{\lambda+\alpha_0} < \gamma + \omega^{\lambda+\alpha} = \hat{\alpha}$

$$\mathcal{H}_{\widehat{\alpha_1}+1}[\Theta] \vdash^{\beta_1}_{\beta_1} \Gamma, \neg C^{(\beta_0, \Omega_{b+1})}$$

On the other hand we have $\widehat{\alpha_i} \in \mathcal{H}_\gamma[\Theta]$ and $\widehat{\alpha_0} < \widehat{\alpha_1}$. We obtain $\beta_0 = \psi_\kappa(\widehat{\alpha_0}) < \psi_\kappa(\widehat{\alpha_1}) = \beta_1$. Also $\mathrm{dg}(C^{(\beta_0, \Omega_{b+1})}) = \max\{\beta_0 + 1, \mathrm{dg}(B(\mathsf{L}_0)) + 1\} < \beta_1$. Consequently

$$\dfrac{\mathcal{H}_{\widehat{\alpha_1}+1}[\Theta] \vdash^{\beta_1}_{\beta_1} \Gamma, \neg C^{(\beta_0, \Omega_{b+1})} \quad \mathcal{H}_{\widehat{\alpha_0}+1}[\Theta] \vdash^{\beta_0}_{\beta_0} C^{(\beta_0, \Omega_{b+1})}, \Gamma}{\mathcal{H}_{\widehat{\alpha_1}+1}[\Theta] \vdash^{\beta_1+1}_{\beta_1} \Gamma}\ (cut)$$

Let $\lambda' = \Omega_b$ for $\kappa = \Omega_{b+1}$. Then $\beta_1 = \lambda' + 1 + \omega^{\beta_1}$ and $[\lambda', \beta_1[\cap\{\Omega_{a+1} : a < \nu\} = \emptyset$. Predicative cut-elimination Lemma 6.27 yields

$$\mathcal{H}_{\widehat{\alpha_1}+1}[\Theta] \vdash^{\varphi\beta_1(\beta_1+1)}_{\lambda'+1} \Gamma$$

Now we have $\lambda' < \kappa \leq \lambda$, $\widehat{\alpha_1} + 1 \in \mathcal{H}_\gamma[\Theta] \subset \mathcal{H}_{\widehat{\alpha_1}+1}[\Theta]$ and $\mathcal{H}_\gamma(\psi_\sigma(\gamma)) \subset \mathcal{H}_{\widehat{\alpha_1}+1}(\psi_\sigma(\widehat{\alpha_1} + 1))$ by $\gamma < \widehat{\alpha_1} + 1$. MIH yields

$$\mathcal{H}_{\widehat{\alpha_2}+1}[\Theta] \vdash^{\psi_\sigma(\widehat{\alpha_2})}_{\psi_\sigma(\widehat{\alpha_2})} \Gamma$$

for $\widehat{\alpha_2} = \widehat{\alpha_1} + 1 + \omega^{\lambda'+\varphi\beta_1(\beta_1+1)} = \gamma + \omega^{\lambda+\alpha_0} \cdot 2 + \omega^{\lambda'+\varphi\beta_1(\beta_1+1)} < \gamma + \omega^{\lambda+\alpha} = \hat{\alpha}$ by $\alpha_0 < \alpha$ and $\lambda' + \varphi\beta_1(\beta_1 + 1) < \kappa \leq \lambda$. Hence $\psi_\sigma(\widehat{\alpha_2}) < \psi_\sigma(\hat{a})$, and we conclude

$$\mathcal{H}_{\hat{\alpha}+1}[\Theta] \vdash^{\psi_\sigma(\hat{\alpha})}_{\psi_\sigma(\hat{\alpha})} \Gamma$$

□

Let $L_{\Omega_\nu+1}(\mathbb{N})$ be a model with the standard model $\mathbb{N}$. The predicate $\mathbb{N}$ is interpreted as natural numbers in the model. Each set term a denotes a set $\mathsf{s}(a) \in L_{\Omega_\nu+1}(\mathbb{N})$ defined as follows. $\mathsf{s}(\mathsf{L}_\alpha) = L_\alpha(\mathbb{N})$, constructible sets from $\mathbb{N}$ in stage α. Namely $L_0(\mathbb{N}) = \mathbb{N}$, the set of urelements, $L_\lambda(\mathbb{N}) = \bigcup_{\alpha<\lambda} L_\alpha(\mathbb{N})$ for limits λ, and $L_{\alpha+1}(\mathbb{N}) = \mathbb{N} \cup \mathrm{Def}(L_\alpha(\mathbb{N}))$, where $\mathrm{Def}(L_\alpha(\mathbb{N}))$ is the set of definable sets over $L_\alpha(\mathbb{N})$. For a compound set term, let $\mathsf{s}([x \in \mathsf{L}_\alpha : \theta^{\mathsf{L}_\alpha}(x, s_1, \ldots, s_n)]) = \{x \in L_\alpha(\mathbb{N}) : L_\alpha(\mathbb{N}) \models \theta(x, \mathsf{s}(s_1), \ldots, \mathsf{s}(s_n))\}$.

Let $T_n = \{\alpha \in T(\Omega_\nu) \cap \omega_n(\Omega_\nu + 1) : G_{\Omega_1}(\alpha) < \omega_n(\Omega_\nu + 1)\}$.

Lemma 6.28 (Truth)

1. $(\mathrm{FiX}^i(\mathsf{PA} + \{\mathrm{TI}(T_n, <) : n \in \omega\}))$
   For each arithmetic *sequent Γ in the language* PA, $\mathcal{H}_\gamma \vdash_0^\alpha \Gamma \Rightarrow \mathbb{N} \models \Gamma$ *if* $\alpha \in T_n$ *for an* $n < \omega$.
2. *If* $\mathcal{H} \vdash_{\Omega_1}^\alpha \Gamma$ *with* $\Gamma \subset \Delta(\Omega_1)$, *then* $L_{\Omega_\nu+1}(\mathbb{N}) \models \Gamma$.

Proof 6.28.2 is seen by induction on α using the fact that $\mathbb{N} \cup \{\mathsf{s}(t) : t \in RS, |t| < \beta\} = L_\beta(\mathbb{N})$ for $\beta \in T(\Omega_\nu) \cap \Omega_1$, i.e., $\beta < \psi_{\Omega_1}(\varepsilon_{\Omega_\nu+1})$. □

Theorem 6.8 *1. For* each arithmetic *sequent Γ, if* $\mathsf{KP}_\nu \vdash \Gamma$, *then*
$\mathrm{FiX}^i(\mathsf{PA} + \{\mathrm{TI}(T(\Omega_\nu) \cap \psi_{\Omega_1}(\omega_n(\Omega_\nu + 1)), <) : n \in \omega\}) \vdash \Gamma$.
2. $\mathsf{KP}_\nu \vdash \Gamma$ and $\Gamma \subset \Sigma(\Omega_1) \Rightarrow \exists m < \omega\left[L_{\Omega_\nu+1}(\mathbb{N}) \models \Gamma^{(\psi_{\Omega_1}(\omega_m(\Omega_\nu+1)))}\right]$.

Proof These are seen as in Theorem 6.5 using Lemmas 6.26, 6.27, 6.28, 6.25, and Theorem 6.7. □

Corollary 6.4 *Both* ID_ν *and* KP_ν *are conservative extensions of* $\mathsf{PA} + \{\mathrm{TI}(T(\Omega_\nu) \cap \psi_{\Omega_1}(\omega_n(\Omega_\nu + 1)), <) : n \in \omega\}$.

Proof By Theorem 6.2 ID_ν is an extension of $\mathsf{PA} + \{\mathrm{TI}(T(\Omega_\nu) \cap \psi_{\Omega_1}(\omega_n(\Omega_\nu + 1)), <) : n \in \omega\}$.

Conversely let $\mathsf{ID}_\nu \vdash A$ for an arithmetic sentence A. Proposition 6.1 yields $\mathsf{KP}_\nu \vdash A$. By Theorem 6.8.1 we obtain $\mathrm{FiX}^i(\mathsf{PA} + \{\mathrm{TI}(T(\Omega_\nu) \cap \psi_{\Omega_1}(\omega_n(\Omega_\nu + 1)), <) : n \in \omega\}) \vdash A$. Theorem 4.15.1 yields $\mathsf{PA} + \{\mathrm{TI}(T(\Omega_\nu) \cap \psi_{\Omega_1}(\omega_n(\Omega_\nu + 1)), <) : n \in \omega\} \vdash A$. □

From Corollary 6.4 with Theorem 4.1 we obtain for example the following.

Theorem 6.9 *1. The 1-consistency* $\mathrm{RFN}_{\Sigma_1^0}(\mathsf{ID}_\nu)$ *of* ID_ν *is equivalent to* $\mathcal{E}^\omega DS_{\psi_{\Omega_1}(\varepsilon_{\Omega_\nu+1})}$.
2. *For computable total function f on $\mathbb{N}$, f is provably recursive in* ID_ν, $f \in Fnc_{\Sigma_1}(\mathsf{ID}_\nu)$ *iff f is α-recursive for an* $\alpha < \psi_{\Omega_1}(\varepsilon_{\Omega_\nu+1})$, $f \in \mathcal{R}^{<\psi_{\Omega_1}(\varepsilon_{\Omega_\nu+1})}$.
3. ID_ν *is Π_1^0-conservative over (one application of a rule)* $(\mathcal{E}^\omega\text{–TI})_{<\psi_{\Omega_1}(\varepsilon_{\Omega_\nu+1})}$ *over* $I\Sigma_1^0$.

6.5.2 Embedding

In this subsection let us prove Embedding Lemma 6.26.

Lemma 6.29 (Tautology) $\mathsf{k}(\{A\} \cup \Gamma) \subset \mathcal{H} \Rightarrow \mathcal{H} \vdash_0^{2d} \Gamma, \neg A, A$ *with* $d = \mathrm{dg}(A)$.

Proof This is seen by induction on $\mathrm{dg}(A)$ using Proposition 6.22. □

Lemma 6.30 (Induction) *For any set term $s \in RS$,*

$$|a| < \Omega_\nu \;\&\; \mathsf{k}(\{F\} \cup \Gamma) \cup \mathsf{k}(a) \subset \mathscr{H} \Rightarrow \mathscr{H} \vdash_0^{f(a)} \Gamma, \Theta, F(a)$$

for $\Theta = \{\neg\forall x \in \mathsf{L}_{\Omega_\nu}[\forall y \in x\, F(y) \to F(x)]\}$ *and* $f(a) = 2(1 + \mathrm{dg}(F(a)) + |a| + 1)$.

Proof By induction on the levels $|a| < \Omega_\nu$.

Suppressing the side sequent Γ, assume $\mathsf{k}(F) \cup \mathsf{k}(a) \subset \mathscr{H}$. Let $d = \mathrm{dg}(F(a))$ and $f(a) - 2 = 2 + 2d + 4|a|$. Tautology Lemma 6.29 yields $\mathscr{H} \vdash_0^{2d} \neg F(a), F(a)$. Let b be such that $|b| < |a|$. We have $\mathscr{H}[\mathsf{k}(b)] \vdash_0^{f(b)} \Theta, F(b)$ by IH, and $\mathrm{dg}(F(b)) \leq d$ by Proposition 6.17.2. Hence $f(b) + 1 < f(a) - 2$. On the other hand we have $\mathscr{H} \vdash_0^0 a \dot\in \mathsf{L}_{\Omega_\nu}$ for $(a\dot\in\mathsf{L}_{\Omega_\nu}) \equiv (0 = 0)$. We obtain for $|a| < f(a)$

$$\dfrac{\mathscr{H} \vdash_0^0 a\dot\in\mathsf{L}_{\Omega_\nu} \qquad \dfrac{\dfrac{\dfrac{\mathscr{H}[\mathsf{k}(b)] \vdash_0^{f(b)} \Theta, F(b)}{\mathscr{H}[\mathsf{k}(b)] \vdash_0^{f(b)+1} \Theta, b\dot\in a \to F(b)\ (|b| < |a|)}}{\mathscr{H} \vdash_0^{f(a)-2} \Theta, \forall x \in a F(x)}\,(\bigwedge) \qquad \mathscr{H} \vdash_0^{2d} \neg F(a), F(a)}{\mathscr{H} \vdash_0^{f(a)-1} \Theta, \forall x \in a F(x) \wedge \neg F(a), F(a)}}{\mathscr{H} \vdash_0^{f(a)} \Theta, F(a)}\,(\bigvee)$$

□

Lemma 6.31 *Let* $\mathsf{k}(a) \cup \mathsf{k}(b) \cup \mathsf{k}(c) \subset \mathscr{H}$, *and* $f(a, b, c) = 7(|a|\#|b|\#|c|)$.

1. $\mathscr{H} \vdash_0^{f(a,b,c)} a \neq b, a \notin c, b \in c$.
2. $\mathscr{H} \vdash_0^{f(a,b,c)} a \neq b, c \neq a, c = b$.
3. $\mathscr{H} \vdash_0^{f(a,b,c)} c \neq b, a \notin c, a \in b$.

Proof By simultaneous induction on the natural sums $|a|\#|b|\#|c|$. We can assume that all of a, b, c are set terms. Let t be a term with $|t| < |c|$, $\mathscr{H}' = \mathscr{H}[\mathsf{k}(t)]$, and $d = \mathrm{dg}(t\dot\in c)$. We have $\mathscr{H}' \vdash_0^{2d} \neg(t\dot\in c), t\dot\in c$ by Tautology Lemma 6.29. By Proposition 6.17.3 we have $2d + 7 < 7|c| \leq f(a, b, c)$. Let $\beta = f(a, b, t)$, and $\gamma = \max\{\beta, 2d\}$. Then $\gamma + 7 \leq f(a, b, c)$. In the following note that $|t| < \gamma + 1$ for (6.18).

Lemma 6.31.1. By IH we have $\mathscr{H} \vdash_0^{\beta} a \neq b, t \neq a, t = b$. In the following $(\vee)^2$ designates that inference rules $(\vee)$ are applied twice.

$$\dfrac{\dfrac{\dfrac{\dfrac{\mathscr{H}' \vdash_0^{2d} \neg(t\dot\in c), t\dot\in c \qquad \mathscr{H}' \vdash_0^{\beta} a \neq b, t \neq a, t = b}{\mathscr{H}' \vdash_0^{\gamma+1} a \neq b, \neg(t\dot\in c), t \neq a, t\dot\in c \wedge t = b}}{\mathscr{H}' \vdash_0^{\gamma+2} a \neq b, \neg(t\dot\in c), t \neq a, b \in c}\,(\in)}{\mathscr{H}' \vdash_0^{\gamma+4} a \neq b, t\dot\in c \to t \neq a, b \in c}\,(\vee)^2}{\mathscr{H} \vdash_0^{\gamma+5} a \neq b, a \notin c, b \in c}\,(\notin)$$

Lemma 6.31.2. By IH we have $\mathcal{H} \vdash_0^\beta a \neq b, t \notin a, t \in b$.

$$\dfrac{\dfrac{\dfrac{\mathcal{H}' \vdash_0^{2d} t\dot{\in}c, \neg(t\dot{\in}c) \quad \mathcal{H}' \vdash_0^\beta a \neq b, t \notin a, t \in b}{\mathcal{H}' \vdash_0^{\gamma+1} a \neq b, t\dot{\in}c \wedge t \notin a, \neg(t\dot{\in}c), t \in b}}{\mathcal{H}' \vdash_0^{\gamma+3} a \neq b, c \neq a, \neg(t\dot{\in}c), t \in b}\,(\exists), (\vee)}{\mathcal{H} \vdash_0^{\gamma+6} a \neq b, c \neq a, \forall x \in c(x \in b)}\,(\vee)^2, (\forall)$$

Similarly we have $\mathcal{H}[\mathsf{k}(s)] \vdash_0^{\delta+3} a \neq b, c \neq a, \neg(s\dot{\in}b), s \in c$ for any s with $|s| < |b|$, where $\delta = \max\{f(a, s, c), 2\mathrm{dg}(s\dot{\in}b)\}$ with $\delta + 7 \leq f(a, b, c)$.

$$\dfrac{\mathcal{H} \vdash_0^{\gamma+6} a \neq b, c \neq a, \forall x \in c(x \in b) \quad \mathcal{H} \vdash_0^{\delta+6} a \neq b, c \neq a, \forall x \in b(x \in c)}{\mathcal{H} \vdash_0^{f(a,b,c)} a \neq b, c \neq a, c = b}$$

Lemma 6.31.3. By IH we have $\mathcal{H}' \vdash_0^\beta t \neq a, t \notin b, a \in b$ for any t with $|t| < |c|$.

$$\dfrac{\dfrac{\dfrac{\mathcal{H}' \vdash_0^{2d} \neg(t\dot{\in}c), t\dot{\in}c \quad \mathcal{H}' \vdash_0^\beta t \neq a, t \notin b, a \in b}{\mathcal{H}' \vdash_0^{\gamma+1} \neg(t\dot{\in}c), t \neq a, t\dot{\in}c \wedge t \notin b, a \in b}}{\mathcal{H}' \vdash_0^{\gamma+3} \neg(t\dot{\in}c), t \neq a, c \neq b, a \in b}\,(\exists), (\vee)}{\mathcal{H} \vdash_0^{\gamma+6} a \notin c, c \neq b, a \in b}\,(\vee)^2, (\forall)$$

□

Lemma 6.32 *1.* $\mathcal{H}[\mathsf{k}(a)] \vdash_0^{6\mathrm{dg}(a)+5} a = a$.
2. $\mathcal{H}[\mathsf{k}(a, b)] \vdash_0^{6dg(b)+1} \neg(a\dot{\in}b), a \in b$ *if* $|a| < |b|$.

Proof By simultaneous induction on $dg(a)$. We can assume that a is a set term.

Proposition 6.32.1. By IH we have $\mathcal{H}[\mathsf{k}(t, a)] \vdash_0^{6\mathrm{dg}(a)+1} \neg(t\dot{\in}a), t \in a$ for any t with $|t| < |a|$.

$$\dfrac{\mathcal{H}[\mathsf{k}(t, a)] \vdash_0^{6\mathrm{dg}(a)+1} \neg(t\dot{\in}a), t \in a}{\mathcal{H}[\mathsf{k}(a)] \vdash_0^{6\mathrm{dg}(a)+5} a = a}\,(\vee)^2, (\forall), (\wedge)$$

Proposition 6.32.2. Let $\mathrm{dg}(a) < \mathrm{dg}(b)$, Then $d = \mathrm{dg}(a\dot{\in}b)\mathrm{dg}(a) < \mathrm{dg}(b)$. Lemma 6.32.1 yields $\mathcal{H} \vdash_0^{6\mathrm{dg}(a)+5} a = a$. Also $2d < 6\mathrm{dg}(b)$ and $\mathrm{dg}(a) < 6\mathrm{dg}(b) + 1$.

$$\dfrac{\dfrac{\mathcal{H}[\mathsf{k}(a, b)] \vdash_0^{2d} \neg(a\dot{\in}b), a\dot{\in}b \quad \mathcal{H}[\mathsf{k}(a)] \vdash_0^{6|\mathrm{dg}(a)|+5} a = a}{\mathcal{H}[\mathsf{k}(a, b)] \vdash_0^{6|\mathrm{dg}(b)|} \neg(a\dot{\in}b), a\dot{\in}b \wedge a = a}}{\mathcal{H}[\mathsf{k}(a, b)] \vdash_0^{6|\mathrm{dg}(b)|+1} \neg(a\dot{\in}b), a \in b}\,(\in)$$

□

Proposition 6.19 $\mathcal{H}[\mathsf{k}(a)] \vdash_0^{6|\mathrm{dg}(a)|+6} a \notin a$.

Proof By induction on $\mathrm{dg}(a)$. We can assume that a is a set term. Let t be a term with $|t| < |a|$. By IH we have $\mathcal{H}[\mathsf{k}(t)] \vdash_0^{6\mathrm{dg}(t)+6} t \notin t$. Hence for $d = \mathrm{dg}(t \dot{\in} a)$, $\mathrm{dg}(t) < \mathrm{dg}(a)$

$$\dfrac{\dfrac{\dfrac{\dfrac{\mathcal{H}[\mathsf{k}(t,a)] \vdash_0^{2d} \neg(t \dot{\in} a), t \dot{\in} a \quad \mathcal{H}[\mathsf{k}(t)] \vdash_0^{6\mathrm{dg}(t)+6} t \notin t}{\mathcal{H}[\mathsf{k}(t,a)] \vdash_0^{6\mathrm{dg}(a)+1} \neg(t \dot{\in} a), t \dot{\in} a \wedge t \notin t}}{\mathcal{H}[\mathsf{k}(t,a)] \vdash_0^{6\mathrm{dg}(a)+2} \neg(t \dot{\in} a), \exists x \in a(x \notin t)}}{\mathcal{H}[\mathsf{k}(t,a)] \vdash_0^{6\mathrm{dg}(a)+3} \neg(t \dot{\in} a), t \neq a}}{\mathcal{H}[\mathsf{k}(a)] \vdash_0^{6\mathrm{dg}(a)+6} a \notin a} \; (\vee)^2, (\notin)$$

□

Lemma 6.33 *1. Let B be one of sentences: $A^{\mathbb{N}}$ for any* PA*-axiom A other than the complete induction, $0 \in \mathbb{N}$, $\forall n \in \mathbb{N}(n+1 \in \mathbb{N})$, $\forall x, y \in M_\nu(x \in y \to y \in \mathbb{S})$, $\forall a \in \mathbb{N}\,(a < \nu \to \exists x \in M_a(x \notin x) \wedge \forall x {\in} M_a \forall y \in x(y {\in} M_a))$, $\forall x {\in} M_\nu(M_x {\in} \mathbb{S})$, $\forall x, y {\in} \mathsf{M}_\nu(x = y \to y = x)$, and $\forall \mathbf{x}, \mathbf{y} \subset M_\nu\,(\mathbf{x} = \mathbf{y} \to f(\mathbf{x}) = f(\mathbf{y}))$ for a function symbol f of an elementary recursive function on $\mathbb{N}$.*
Then $\mathcal{H} \vdash_0^{\omega} B$.

2. *complete induction: for $d = \mathrm{dg}(F)$,*
   $\mathcal{H} \vdash_0^{2d+\omega} \neg F(0), \neg\forall n \in \mathbb{N}(F(n) \to F(n+1)), \forall n \in \mathbb{N}\, F(n)$.
3. *$\mathcal{H}[\mathsf{k}(a,b)] \vdash_0^{\alpha} a \neq b, M_a = M_b$, where*
   $$\alpha = \begin{cases} \Omega_a + 5 & a = b < \nu \text{ is a natural number} \\ 1 & \text{otherwise} \end{cases}.$$
4. *$\mathcal{H} \vdash_0^{\Omega_\nu} \forall a, b \in \mathbb{N}(a, b < \nu \to (a <_\nu b \leftrightarrow M_a \in M_b))$.*
5. *$\mathcal{H} \vdash_0^{\Omega_\nu} \forall b \in \mathbb{N}\left(b < \nu \to (M_c)_{c \leq_\nu b} \in M_{b+1}\right)$.*

Proof Proposition 6.33.3. This is seen from Lemma 6.32.1, and $\mathcal{H} \vdash_0^1 \mathsf{L}_0 = \mathsf{L}_0$ for $\mathsf{L}_0 \equiv M_a$ where a is not a natural number$< \nu$.

Proposition 6.33.4. Let a, b be natural numbers such that $a, b < \nu$. First assume $a <_\nu b$. Then $M_a \equiv \mathsf{L}_{\Omega_a}$ and $M_b \equiv \mathsf{L}_{\Omega_b}$ with $\Omega_a < \Omega_b$. We obtain $\mathcal{H} \vdash_0^0 M_a \in M_b$, and $\mathcal{H} \vdash_0^0 a <_\nu b$.

Next assume $a \not<_\nu b$. We have $\mathcal{H} \vdash_0^0 a \not<_\nu b$, and $b \leq_\nu a$ by the linearity of $<_\nu$. Hence $\Omega_a \geq \Omega_\beta$.

It suffices to show for ordinals α, β, $\mathcal{H}[\mathsf{k}(\alpha, \beta)] \vdash_0^{\omega\beta} \mathsf{L}_\alpha \notin \mathsf{L}_\beta$ if $\alpha \geq \beta$. Let $\alpha \geq \beta$, and $|t| < \beta$. By Proposition 6.19 we have $\mathcal{H}[\mathsf{k}(t)] \vdash_0^{6|\mathrm{dg}(t)+6} t \notin t$. Hence

$$\dfrac{\dfrac{\mathcal{H}[\mathsf{k}(t)] \vdash_0^{6|\mathrm{dg}(t)|+6} t \notin t}{\mathcal{H}[\mathsf{k}(t,\alpha)] \vdash_0^{6|\mathrm{dg}(t)|+9} t \neq \mathsf{L}_\alpha} \; (\wedge), (\exists), (\vee)}{\mathcal{H}[\mathsf{k}(\alpha,\beta)] \vdash_0^{\omega\beta} \mathsf{L}_\alpha \notin \mathsf{L}_\beta} \; (\vee), (\notin)$$

Proposition 6.33.5. Let b be a natural number with $b < \nu$. Let $t \equiv [x \in \mathsf{L}_{\Omega_b+1} : \exists c \in \mathbb{N}(c \leq_\nu b \land x = \langle c, \mathsf{L}_{\Omega_c}\rangle)]$. Then we see $|t| = \Omega_b + 1 < \Omega_{b+1}$, and $\mathscr{H} \vdash_0^{\Omega_b+\omega} \forall x \in t \exists c \in \mathbb{N}\left(c \leq_\nu b \land x = \langle c, \mathsf{L}_{\Omega_c}\rangle \land \forall c \in \mathbb{N}(c \leq_\nu b \to \langle c, \mathsf{L}_{\Omega_c}\rangle \in t)\right)$. □

Lemma 6.34 *Let $\lambda = \omega\lambda \leq \Omega_\nu$ be a limit ordinal, and $\mathscr{H}$ a Skolem hull operator closed under addition and exponentiation with base ω, with $\lambda \in \mathscr{H}$.*

1. (Δ_0-Separation) *Let $B(u, y)$ be a Δ_0-formula.* $\mathscr{H} \vdash_0^\lambda \forall x, y \in \mathsf{L}_\lambda \exists z \in \mathsf{L}_\lambda\, (z = \{u \in x : B(u, y)\})$.
2. (Pair) $\mathscr{H} \vdash_0^\lambda \forall x, y \in \mathsf{L}_\lambda \exists z \in \mathsf{L}_\lambda (x \in z \land y \in z)$.
3. (Union) $\mathscr{H} \vdash_0^\lambda \forall z \in \mathsf{L}_\lambda \exists y \in \mathsf{L}_\lambda \forall x \in z \forall u \in x(u \in y)$.
4. (Δ_0-Collection) *Assume $a \in Suc$, and let $B(u, y, w)$ be a Δ_0-formula. Then* $\mathscr{H} \vdash_0^{\Omega_a+\omega} \forall v, w \in M_a\, [\forall u \in v \exists y \in M_a\, B(u, y, w) \to$ $\exists z \in M_a \forall u \in v \exists y \in z\, B(u, y, w)]$.
5. $\mathscr{H} \vdash_0^{\Omega_\nu} \forall a \in \mathbb{N}(a \leq \nu \land a \in Lim \to (\forall x \in M_a \exists b <_\nu a(x \in M_b)))$, *and* $\mathscr{H} \vdash_0^1 \forall n \in \mathbb{N}(n \in M_0)$.

Proof 6.34.1. Let a, b be RS-terms, $\mathscr{H}' = \mathscr{H}[\mathsf{k}(a, b)]$, and $\max\{|a|, |b|\} + 1 = \alpha < \lambda$. Let $c = [u \in \mathsf{L}_\alpha : u \in a \land B(u, b)]$, and t be such that $|t| < |c| = \alpha < \lambda$. Then $(t \dot{\in} c) \equiv (t \in a \land B(t, b))$, and $\mathscr{H}'[\mathsf{k}(t)] \vdash_0^{\omega\alpha} t \dot{\in} c \to t \in a \land B(t, b)$ by Tautology Lemma 6.29 and Proposition 6.17.3 for $\mathrm{dg}(t \dot{\in} c) < \mathrm{dg}(c) = \omega\alpha$. Hence $\mathscr{H}' \vdash_0^{\omega\alpha+1} \forall u \in c(u \in a \land B(u, b))$. Conversely let t be such that $|t| < |a|$. By Tautology Lemma 6.29, Proposition 6.17.3 and Lemma 6.32.1 we obtain for $d + 1 = \mathrm{dg}(B(t, b)) + 1 < \omega\alpha$

$$\dfrac{\dfrac{\dfrac{\dfrac{\dfrac{\dfrac{\mathscr{H}'[\mathsf{k}(t)] \vdash_0^{6\mathrm{dg}(a)+1} \neg(t \dot{\in} a), t \in a \quad \mathscr{H}'[\mathsf{k}(t)] \vdash_0^{2d} \neg B(t, b), B(t, b)}{\mathscr{H}'[\mathsf{k}(t)] \vdash_0^{\omega\alpha} \neg(t \dot{\in} a), \neg B(t, b), t \in a \land B(t, b)} \quad \mathscr{H}'[\mathsf{k}(t)] \vdash_0^{6\mathrm{dg}(t)+5} t = t}{\mathscr{H}'[\mathsf{k}(t)] \vdash_0^{\omega\alpha+1} \neg(t \dot{\in} a), \neg B(t, b), t \dot{\in} c \land t = t}}{\mathscr{H}'[\mathsf{k}(t)] \vdash_0^{\omega\alpha+2} \neg(t \dot{\in} a), \neg B(t, b), t \in c}}{\mathscr{H}'[\mathsf{k}(t)] \vdash_0^{\omega\alpha+6} t \dot{\in} a \to B(t, b) \to t \in c}}{\mathscr{H}' \vdash_0^{\omega\alpha+7} \forall u \in a(B(u, b) \to u \in c)}$$

Therefore $\mathscr{H}' \vdash_0^{\omega\alpha+8} \forall u \in c(u \in a \land B(u, b)) \land \forall u \in a(B(u, b) \to u \in c)$ for any a, b with $\max\{|a|, |b|\} + 1 = \alpha < \lambda$. $\mathscr{H} \vdash_0^\lambda \forall x, y \in \mathsf{L}_\lambda \exists z \in \mathsf{L}_\lambda\, (z = \{u \in x : B(u, y)\})$ is concluded.

Lemmas 6.34.2 and 6.34.3. For the axiom of pair let $c = [u \in \mathsf{L}_\alpha : u = a \lor u = b]$ with $\max\{|a|, |b|\} + 1 = \alpha < \lambda$. Then we see $\mathscr{H}[\mathsf{k}(a, b)] \vdash_0^{\omega\alpha} a \in c \land b \in c$ from Lemma 6.32.1. For the axiom of union let $c = [u \in \mathsf{L}_\alpha : \exists x \in a(u \in x)]$ with $|a| + 1 = \alpha < \lambda$. Then we see from Lemma 6.32 for any t, s with $|s| < |t| < |a|$

$$\dfrac{\dfrac{\mathscr{H}[\mathsf{k}(a, t, s)] \vdash_0^{2\mathrm{dg}(t \dot{\in} a)} \neg(t \dot{\in} a), t \dot{\in} a \quad \mathscr{H}[\mathsf{k}(t, s)] \vdash_0^{6|t|+1} \neg(s \dot{\in} t), s \in t}{\mathscr{H}[\mathsf{k}(a, t, s)] \vdash_0^{6\mathrm{dg}(a)} \neg(t \dot{\in} a), \neg(s \dot{\in} t), s \dot{\in} c} \quad \mathscr{H}[\mathsf{k}(s)] \vdash_0^{6\mathrm{dg}(s)+5} s = s}{\mathscr{H}[\mathsf{k}(a, t, s)] \vdash_0^{6\mathrm{dg}(a)+1} \neg(t \dot{\in} a), \neg(s \dot{\in} t), s \in c}$$

where $(s \dot{\in} c) \equiv (\exists x \in a(s \in x))$. Hence $\mathscr{H}[\mathsf{k}(a)] \vdash_0^{\omega\alpha} \forall x \in a \forall u \in x(u \in c)$.

Lemma 6.34.4. Let $|c|, |b| < |M_a| = \Omega_a$, and $\mathcal{H}' = \mathcal{H}[\mathsf{k}(c, b)]$. By Tautology Lemma 6.29 we obtain for $d = \mathrm{dg}(\forall u \in c \exists y \in M_a\, B(u, y, b))$

$$\frac{\mathcal{H}' \vdash_0^{2d} \neg(\forall u \in c \exists y \in M_a\, B(u, y, b)), \forall u \in c \exists y \in M_a\, B(u, y, b)}{\mathcal{H}' \vdash_0^{2d+1} \neg(\forall u \in c \exists y \in M_a\, B(u, y, b)), \exists z \in M_a \forall u \in c \exists y \in z\, B(u, y, b)}\ (\Delta_0(\Omega_a)\text{-Coll})$$

where $2d + n < \Omega_a + \omega$ for any $n < \omega$ and any c, b with $|c|, |b| < \Omega_a$.

Lemma 6.34.5. First let $a \leq \nu$ be a limit, and $|t| < \Omega_a$. Pick a natural number $b < \nu$ such that $|t| < \Omega_b$. Then $\mathcal{H}[\mathsf{k}(t)] \vdash_0^{6\mathrm{dg}(t)+7} t \in M_b$ with $M_b \equiv \mathsf{L}_{\Omega_b}$.

Next we see $\mathcal{H} \vdash_0^0 n \in M_0$ from $0 = |n| < \omega = |M_0|$ for any natural number n with $M_0 \equiv \mathsf{L}_{\Omega_0}$ and $\Omega_0 = \omega$. □

Proof Let us show Embedding Lemma 6.26. The lemma is seen as in Lemma 4.4 using Lemmas 6.29, 6.30, 6.31, 6.32, 6.33 and 6.34. □

6.6 Applications of Operator Controlled Derivations

In this section we give two applications of the method of the operator controlled derivations. In Sect. 6.6.1 we deal with a relativized ordinal analysis. Specifically let $x \mapsto \Theta(x)$ be an operation assigning a set $\Theta(x)$ to sets x such that $y \in \Theta(x)$ is given by a Δ_0-formula θ, and the rank of the set $\Theta(x)$ is bounded by a function f_θ of the rank of x with respect to a cumulative and continuous hierarchy $M = \bigcup_\alpha M_\alpha$ of sets. Now ask the problem: How many times can we iterate the operation Θ in the Kripke–Platek set theory $\mathsf{KP}\omega$ with the axiom of Infinity and the axiom $\forall x \exists z[z = \Theta(x)]$? We show that the bound for iterations is a Bachmann–Howard ordinal relative to the function f_θ. An operator here to control derivations is a relativized Skolem hull $\mathcal{H}_\alpha^\theta$.

In Sect. 6.6.2 we show that a set theory $\mathsf{KP}\Pi_{N+1}$ for Π_{N+1}-reflections is proof-theoretically reduced to a set theory of iterations of Π_N-recursively Mahlo operations. A transitive and well-founded model P of $\mathsf{KP}\omega$ controls derivations in such a way that each sets occurring in sequents Γ is in P when $P \vdash_m^\alpha \Gamma$.

6.6.1 A Relativized Ordinal Analysis

Let $\theta(x, y, U)$ be a set-theoretic bounded formula possibly with a unary predicate U in the language $\{\in, U\}$. Except x and y, no free variable occurs in $\theta(x, y, U)$. Let us introduce another kind of bounded quantifiers, *θ-bounded quantifiers*. These are one of forms $\exists y \in \Theta(x)\, A(y)$ and $\forall y \in \Theta(x)\, A(x)$. The intended meanings are $\exists y(\theta(x, y, U) \wedge A(y))$ and $\forall y(\theta(x, y, U) \to A(y))$, resp.

Definition 6.19 1. A formula in the language $\{\in, U\}$ is said to be a *Δ_0^θ-formula* if each quantifier in it is either bounded or θ-bounded.

2. A formula in negation normal form is said to be a Σ^{θ}*-formula* if each quantifier in it is either bounded, θ-bounded or an existential unbounded one.
3. A theory $\mathsf{KP}(\theta)$ is obtained from KP in the language $\{\in, U\}$ by adding the axiom of Infinity $\exists z\,(\exists x \in z(x \in z) \wedge \forall x \in z \exists y \in z(x \in y))$, the axiom

$$(\theta)\ \forall x \exists z \forall y \in \Theta(x)(y \in z)$$

the equality axiom $\forall x, y(x = y \to U(x) \to U(y))$, and extending Δ_0-Separation and Δ_0-Collection to Δ_0^{θ}-Separation and Δ_0^{θ}-Collection, resp.

For a Δ_0^{θ}-formula A, $\exists z[z = \{x \in a : A(x)\}]$ is an instance of the Δ_0^{θ}-Separation. In particular we see that $a \cap U$ is a set.

Remark 6.1 $\mathsf{KP}(\theta)$ is equivalent to an extension of $\mathsf{KP}\omega = \mathsf{KP} +$ (Infinity) with a function symbol Θ and the axiom $\forall x(\Theta(x) = \{y : \theta(x, y, U)\})$.

Fix an interpretation $\mathcal{U}$ of the predicate U. Let $\{M_\alpha\}_{\alpha \in ON}$ be a cumulative and continuous hierarchy of transitive sets M_α such that $M_\alpha \in M_\beta$ if $\alpha < \beta$, $M_\lambda = \bigcup_{\alpha<\lambda} M_\alpha$ for limit λ, and each Δ_0^{θ}-definable subset of M_α is in $M_{\alpha+1}$. The last means that for each Δ_0^{θ}-formula $A(x, y_1, \ldots, y_n, U)$ and $b_1, \ldots, b_n \in M_\alpha$, $\{x \in M_\alpha : A(x, b_1, \ldots, b_n, \mathcal{U})\} \in M_{\alpha+1}$. In particular $M_\alpha \cap \mathcal{U} \in M_{\alpha+1}$. Let $\mathrm{rk}_M(x) = \min\{\alpha \in ON : x \in M_{\alpha+1}\}$ for $x \in M := \bigcup_{\alpha \in ON} M_\alpha$.

We assume that there exists a weakly increasing function f_{θ_M} on ordinals ($\alpha \leq \beta \Rightarrow \alpha \leq f_{\theta_M}(\alpha) \leq f_{\theta_M}(\beta)$) such that for any sets x, y and ordinals α that

$$x \in M_\alpha \,\&\, \theta(x, y, \mathcal{U}) \,\&\, y \in M \Rightarrow y \in M_{f_{\theta_M}(\alpha)} \tag{6.20}$$

From (6.20) we see for $x \in M_\alpha$ that $\Theta_M(x) = \{y \in M : \theta(x, y, \mathcal{U})\} = \{y \in M_{f_{\theta_M}(\alpha)} : \theta(x, y, \mathcal{U})\} \in \mathcal{P}(M_{f_{\theta_M}(\alpha)}) \cap M_{f_{\theta_M}(\alpha)+1}$, $\mathrm{rk}_M(x) < \alpha \,\&\, y \in \Theta_M(x) \Rightarrow \mathrm{rk}_M(y) < f_{\theta_M}(\alpha)$, and $\mathrm{rk}_M(x) < \alpha \Rightarrow \mathrm{rk}_M(\Theta_M(x)) \leq f_{\theta_M}(\alpha)$. Note that each Δ_0^{θ}-sentence is absolute for models M_α such that α is closed under the function f_{θ_M}.

Let $\Sigma(f_{\theta_M})$ be the set of Σ-formulas with a function symbol for the function f_{θ_M}. An ordinal $\lambda > 0$ is said to be f_{θ_M}*-recursively regular* if for any $\Sigma(f_{\theta_M})$-definable function $g : \alpha \to \lambda$ on L_λ with $\alpha < \lambda$, $\sup_{\beta<\alpha} g(\beta) < \lambda$ holds.

Let $\Omega(\theta)$ be an f_{θ_M}-recursively regular ordinal closed under the function f_{θ_M}, $\forall \alpha < \Omega(\theta)(f_{\theta_M}(\alpha) < \Omega(\theta))$. For $X \subset \Omega(\theta)$, $\mathcal{H}_\alpha^{\theta}(X)$ denotes the Skolem hull of $\{0, \Omega(\theta)\} \cup X$ under the addition, the exponential $\alpha \mapsto \omega^\alpha, \alpha > \beta \mapsto \psi_{\Omega(\theta)}^{\theta}(\beta)$ and the function f_{θ_M} as in Definition 6.1.

Definition 6.20 1. $\{0, \Omega(\theta)\} \cup X \subset \mathcal{H}_\alpha^{\theta}(X)$.
2. $\gamma, \delta \in \mathcal{H}_\alpha^{\theta}(X) \Rightarrow \gamma + \delta, \omega^\gamma \in \mathcal{H}_\alpha^{\theta}(X)$.
3. $\gamma \in \mathcal{H}_\alpha^{\theta}(X) \cap \Omega(\theta) \Rightarrow f_{\theta_M}(\gamma) \in \mathcal{H}_\alpha^{\theta}(X)$.
4. $\gamma \in \mathcal{H}_\alpha^{\theta}(X) \cap \alpha \Rightarrow \psi_{\Omega(\theta)}^{\theta}(\gamma) \in \mathcal{H}_\alpha^{\theta}(X)$.

Let $\psi_{\Omega(\theta)}^{\theta}(\alpha) = \min\{\beta < \Omega(\theta) : \mathcal{H}_\alpha^{\theta}(\beta) \cap \Omega(\theta) \subset \beta\}$.

We see that $\psi_{\Omega(\theta)}^{\theta}(\alpha) < \Omega(\theta)$ from the assumption on the ordinal $\Omega(\theta)$ as in Theorem 6.1. We show the following Theorem 6.10.

Theorem 6.10 *For a Σ^θ-formula A, if* $\mathsf{KP}(\theta) \vdash A$*, then* $M_{\psi^\theta_{\Omega(\theta)}(\varepsilon_{\Omega(\theta)+1})} \models A$.

Conversely we see the following as in Theorem 6.1.

Proposition 6.20 *Assume that the function f_{θ_M} is Δ^θ_1-definable in $\mathsf{KP}(\theta)$. Then for each $n < \omega$, Definition 6.20 defines sets $\mathcal{H}^\theta_\alpha(X)$ for any $\alpha < \omega_n(\Omega(\theta)+1)$ and sets $X \subset ON$ of ordinals, and a Θ-recursive, i.e., Σ^θ-map $\psi^\theta : \alpha \mapsto \psi^\theta_{\Omega(\theta)}(\alpha)$ ($\alpha < \omega_n(\Omega(\theta)+1)$) in $\mathsf{KP}(\theta)$.*

Corollary 6.5 *Assume that the function f_{θ_M} is Δ^θ_1-definable in $\mathsf{KP}(\theta)$. Moreover assume that there exists a Δ^θ_1-formula $m(x, y)$ in $\mathsf{KP}(\theta)$ such that $\mathsf{KP}(\theta) \vdash \forall x \exists ! y\, m(x, y)$, and $m(M_\alpha, M_{\alpha+1})$ holds for any ordinals α.*

Then for each $n < \omega$, $\mathsf{KP}(\theta) \vdash \exists x \left(x = M_{\psi^\theta_{\Omega(\theta)}(\omega_n(\Omega(\theta)+1))}\right)$ with $M_0 = \emptyset$.

Examples. Here are two examples for θ, M_α, f_{θ_M} and $\Omega(\theta)$ enjoying (6.20) and definabilities in $\mathsf{KP}(\theta)$.

1. $\theta(x, y, U) \equiv (y \subset x)$ and $M_\alpha = V_\alpha$:
   Then $f_{\theta_M}(\alpha) = \alpha$, and $\Omega(\theta)$ can be any recursively regular ordinal, e.g., $\Omega(\theta) = \Omega_1 = \omega_1^{CK}$. Also we see $\mathcal{H}^\theta = \mathcal{H}$ and $\psi^\theta_{\Omega(\theta)}(\varepsilon_{\Omega(\theta)+1})$ is the Bachmann–Howard ordinal $\psi_{\Omega_1}(\varepsilon_{\Omega_1+1})$. The cumulative hierarchy V_α is Σ^θ-definable since the power set $\mathcal{P}(x) = z$ is defined by the Δ^θ_0-formula $\forall y \in z(y \subset x) \land \forall y \subset x(y \in z)$. $\mathsf{KP}(\theta)$ proves $\forall x \exists z(\mathcal{P}(x) \subset z)$ by the axiom (θ).
2. $\theta(x, y, U) \equiv (y \subset x)$ and $M_\alpha = L_\alpha$:
   By the condensation lemma we have $\mathcal{P}(\kappa) \cap L \subset L_{\kappa^+}$. Hence $f_{\theta_M}(\alpha) = (\alpha^+)^L$ where $(\alpha^+)^L$ is the least cardinal in L larger than $\max\{\alpha, \aleph_0\}$, and $\Omega(\theta)$ is the least weakly inaccessible cardinal.
   We see that the map $\omega \leq \alpha \mapsto \alpha^+$ is Δ^θ_1-definable in $\mathsf{KP}(\theta)$ as follows (Hartogs). Let W be the set of pairs $(X, R) \in \mathcal{P}(\alpha) \times \mathcal{P}(\alpha \times \alpha)$ such that R well-orders X. '$R \subset X \times X$ well-orders X' is defined to be a Δ^θ_0-formula saying that R is a linear ordering, and there is no infinite descending chain with respect to R, in which a θ-universal quantifier $\forall f \subset \omega \times X$ involves. Let $otp(X, R)$ denote the order type of R when R well-orders X, and 0 otherwise. $otp(X, R)$ is Δ_1-definable. Then let $\alpha^+ = \sup\{otp(X, R) + 1 : (X, R) \in W\}$ by Δ_0-Collection.
   $\psi^\theta_{\Omega(\theta)}(\varepsilon_{\Omega(\theta)+1})$ is a fixed point λ of the alephs, $\lambda = (\aleph_\lambda)^L$. For example $\psi^\theta_{\Omega(\theta)}(0)$ is the least fixed point $\sup\{\lambda_n : n < \omega\}$ with $\lambda_0 = \aleph_0$ and $\lambda_{n+1} = (\aleph_{\lambda_n})^L$.

6.6.1.1 Ramified Set Theory

Let us prove Theorem 6.1 as in Sect. 6.5. In what follows by ordinals we mean ordinals in $ON(\theta) := \mathcal{H}^\theta_{\varepsilon_{\Omega(\theta)+1}}(\psi^\theta_{\Omega(\theta)}(\varepsilon_{\Omega(\theta)+1}))$. Let $M := \bigcup_{\alpha < \psi^\theta_{\Omega(\theta)}(\varepsilon_{\Omega(\theta)+1})} M_\alpha$.

Definition 6.21 *RS-terms t*, their *levels* $|t| < \Omega(\theta)$ and *values* $\mathbb{V}(t) \in M_{|t|+1}$ are defined recursively as follows.

1. For each ordinal $\alpha < \psi^{\theta}_{\Omega(\theta)}(\varepsilon_{\Omega(\theta)+1})$, M_α is an RS-term of level $|\mathsf{M}_\alpha| = \alpha$. $\mathbb{V}(\mathsf{M}_\alpha) = M_\alpha$.
2. For each set $a \in M_{\psi^{\theta}_{\Omega(\theta)}(\varepsilon_{\Omega(\theta)+1})}$, a is an RS-term of level $|\mathsf{a}| = \mathrm{rk}_M(a)$. $\mathbb{V}(\mathsf{a}) = a$.
3. Let $A(x, y_1, \ldots, y_n)$ be a Δ^{θ}_0-formula in the language $\{\in, U\}$, and $s_1, \ldots, s_n$ be RS-terms such that $\max\{|s_i| : 1 \leq i \leq n\} < \alpha$.
   Then $[x \in \mathsf{M}_\alpha : A(x, s_1, \ldots, s_n)]$ is an RS-term of level $|[x \in \mathsf{M}_\alpha : A(x, s_1, \ldots, s_n)]| = \alpha$. $\mathbb{V}([x \in \mathsf{M}_\alpha : A(x, s_1, \ldots, s_n)]) = \{x \in M_\alpha : M \models A(x, \mathbb{V}(s_1), \ldots, \mathbb{V}(s_n))\}$.

RS denotes the set of RS-terms.

An *RS-sentence* $A(t_1, \ldots, t_n)$ is obtained from a set-theoretic formula $A(x_1, \ldots, x_n)$ by substituting RS-terms t_i for each x_i. When A is a Δ^{θ}_0-formula, $A(t_1, \ldots, t_n)$ is a Δ^{θ}_0-RS-sentence. Let $\mathsf{k}(A(t_1, \ldots, t_n)) := \{|t_1|, \ldots, |t_n|\}$.

We assign disjunctions or conjunctions to RS-sentences as in Definition 6.15 suppressing the clauses for natural numbers, and changing the clause for Δ^{θ}_0-formulas.

Definition 6.22 1. For Δ^{θ}_0-sentences $A(s_1, \ldots, s_n)$, let

$$A(s_1, \ldots, s_n) :\simeq \begin{cases} \bigwedge(A_i)_{i\in J} & \text{if } M \models A(\mathbb{V}(s_1), \ldots, \mathbb{V}(s_n)) \\ \bigvee(A_i)_{i\in J} & \text{otherwise} \end{cases} \quad \text{with } J := 0.$$

In what follows we consider sentences not in Δ^{θ}_0.

2. $(A_0 \vee A_1) :\simeq \bigvee(A_i)_{i\in J}$ and $(A_0 \wedge A_1) :\simeq \bigwedge(A_i)_{i\in J}$ with $J := 2$.
3. $\exists x \in a\, A(x) :\simeq \bigvee(A(t))_{t\in J}$ and $\forall x \in a\, A(x) :\simeq \bigwedge(A(t))_{t\in J}$ with $J := \{t \in RS : |t| < |a|, M \models t \in a\}$.
4. $\exists x \in \Theta(a)\, A(x) :\simeq \bigvee(A(t))_{t\in J}$ and $\forall x \in \Theta(a)\, A(x) :\simeq \bigwedge(A(t))_{t\in J}$ with $J := \{t \in RS : |t| \leq f_{\theta_M}(|a|), M \models \theta(a, t)\}$.
5. $\exists x\, A(x) :\simeq \bigvee(A(t))_{t\in J}$ and $\forall x\, A(x) :\simeq \bigwedge(A(t))_{t\in J}$ with $J := RS$.

Definition 6.23 The *degree* $\mathrm{dg}(A) < \omega$ of RS-sentences A is defined recursively as follows.

1. $\mathrm{dg}(A) = 0$ for Δ^{θ}_0-sentences A.
   In what follows degrees of sentences not in Δ^{θ}_0 are defined.
2. $\mathrm{dg}(A_0 \vee A_1) = \mathrm{dg}(A_0 \wedge A_1) = \max\{\mathrm{dg}(A_i) : i < 2\} + 1$.
3. $\mathrm{dg}(A) = \mathrm{dg}(B(\mathsf{M}_0)) + 1$ for
   $A \in \{\exists x \in a\, B(x), \forall x \in a\, B(x), \exists x \in \theta(a)\, B(x), \forall x \in \theta(a)\, B(x)\}$.
4. $\mathrm{dg}(\exists x\, B(x)) = \mathrm{dg}(\forall x\, B(x)) = \mathrm{dg}(B(\mathsf{M}_0)) + 1$.

The degrees are defined so that the followings hold for any A.

Proposition 6.21 *Let* $A \simeq \bigvee(A_i)_{i\in J}$. *Then* $\forall i \in J(\mathrm{dg}(A_i) < \mathrm{dg}(A))$.

Let us define a relation $\mathcal{H} \vdash^{\alpha}_{d} \Gamma$ for Skolem hull operators $\mathcal{H}$ on $ON(\theta)$, $\alpha < \varepsilon_{\Omega(\theta)+1}$, $d < \omega$ and RS-sequents, i.e., finite sets of RS-sentences Γ.

By convention let $|0| = |1| = 0$. The relation $\mathcal{H}_\gamma[\Theta] \vdash^{\alpha}_{d} \Gamma$ for finite sets Θ of ordinals is defined as a fixed point of a strictly positive formula in an intuitionistic fixed point theory over a set theory.

Definition 6.24 $\mathcal{H} \vdash^{\alpha}_{d} \Gamma$ holds if

$$\{\alpha\} \cup \mathsf{k}(\Gamma) \subset \mathcal{H} \tag{6.21}$$

and one of the following cases holds:

($\bigvee$) There are $A \in \Gamma$ such that $A \simeq \bigvee(A_i)_{i \in J}$, an $i \in J$ with

$$|i| < \alpha \tag{6.22}$$

and an $\alpha(i) < \alpha$ for which $\mathcal{H} \vdash^{\alpha(i)}_{d} \Gamma, A_i$ holds.

($\bigwedge$) There is an $A \in \Gamma$ such that $A \simeq \bigwedge(A_i)_{i \in J}$, and for any $i \in J$, there is an $\alpha(i)$ such that $\alpha(i) < \alpha$ for which $\mathcal{H}[\{|i|\}] \vdash^{\alpha(i)}_{d} \Gamma, A_i$ holds.

(cut) There are C and α_0, α_1 such that $\mathrm{dg}(C) < d, \alpha_0, \alpha_1 < \alpha, \mathcal{H} \vdash^{\alpha_0}_{d} \Gamma, \neg C$ and $\mathcal{H} \vdash^{\alpha_1}_{d} C, \Gamma$.

(Δ^{θ}_{0}–Coll) There are a formula $\exists z(c \in z \wedge \forall x \in c \exists y \in z\, B)$ in Γ with $B \in \Delta^{\theta}_{0}$, an RS-term c and $\alpha_0 < \alpha$ such that $\mathcal{H} \vdash^{\alpha_0}_{d} \Gamma, \forall x \in c \exists y\, B$.

$$\frac{\mathcal{H} \vdash^{\alpha_0}_{d} \Gamma, \forall x \in c \exists y\, B}{\mathcal{H} \vdash^{\alpha}_{d} \Gamma}\ (\Delta^{\theta}_{0}\text{–Coll})$$

In what follows $\mathcal{H}$ denotes a Skolem hull operator closed under addition, exponentiation to base ω and the function f_{θ_M}. The following Lemmas 6.35–6.40 are seen as for $\mathsf{ID}^{\mathbb{O}}_{1}$ in Sect. 6.4.1.

Lemma 6.35 (Weakening) *Assume $\beta \leq \alpha \in \mathcal{H}'$, $d \leq c$ and $\mathsf{k}(\Delta) \subset \mathcal{H}'$ for a Skolem hull operator $\mathcal{H}'$ such that $\forall X \in \mathcal{P}(ON(\theta))[\mathcal{H}(X) \subset \mathcal{H}'(X)]$. Then*

$$\mathcal{H} \vdash^{\beta}_{d} \Gamma \Rightarrow \mathcal{H}' \vdash^{\alpha}_{c} \Gamma, \Delta.$$

Lemma 6.36 (Inversion) $\mathcal{H} \vdash^{\alpha}_{d} \Gamma, A \Rightarrow \forall i \in J \left(\mathcal{H}[\{|i|\}] \vdash^{\alpha}_{d} \Gamma, A_i\right)$ *for* $A \simeq \bigwedge (A_i)_{i \in J}$.

Lemma 6.37 (Tautology) $\mathsf{k}(\{A\} \cup \Gamma) \subset \mathcal{H} \Rightarrow \mathcal{H} \vdash^{2d}_{0} \Gamma, \neg A, A$ *with* $d = \mathrm{dg}(A)$.

Lemma 6.38 (Truth) *If* $\mathcal{H} \vdash^{\alpha}_{1} \Gamma$ *for* $\Gamma \subset \Delta^{\theta}_{0}$, *then* $M \models \bigvee \Gamma$.

For a Σ^{θ}-sentence B, $B^{(\mathsf{M}_\alpha)}$ denotes the result of restricting every unbounded (existential) quantifier $\exists x$ to $\exists x \in \mathsf{M}_\alpha$. For $\Gamma \subset \Sigma^{\theta}$, $\Gamma^{(\mathsf{M}_\alpha)} := \{B^{(\mathsf{M}_\alpha)} : B \in \Gamma\}$.

Lemma 6.39 (Boundedness)

$$\mathcal{H} \vdash^{\alpha}_{d} \Gamma, \Lambda\ \&\ \alpha \leq \beta < \Omega(\theta)\ \&\ \beta \in \mathcal{H}\ \&\ \Lambda \subset \Sigma^{\theta} \Rightarrow \mathcal{H} \vdash^{\alpha}_{d} \Gamma, \Lambda^{(\mathsf{M}_\beta)}.$$

Lemma 6.40 (Predicative Cut-elimination) $\mathcal{H} \vdash^{\beta}_{2+m} \Gamma \Rightarrow \mathcal{H} \vdash^{\omega_m(\beta)}_{2} \Gamma$.

Let $|\mathbf{a}| = \{|a_1|, \ldots, |a_n|\}$ for $\mathbf{a} = \{a_1, \ldots, a_n\}$.

Lemma 6.41 (Embedding) *Let $\Gamma[\mathbf{x} := \mathbf{a}]$ ($\mathbf{a} \subset RS$) denote a closed instance of a sequent Γ. Assume $\mathsf{KP}(\theta) \vdash \Gamma$. Then*

$$\exists m, l < \omega \forall \mathbf{a} \subset RS \forall \mathcal{H} \left(\mathcal{H}[|\mathbf{a}|] \vdash_m^{\Omega(\theta)+l} \Gamma[\mathbf{x} := \mathbf{a}]\right)$$

where $\mathcal{H}$ ranges over Skolem hull operators closed under addition, exponentiation to base ω and f_{θ_M}.

Proof It suffices to show that $\mathcal{H} \vdash_0^{\Omega(\theta)} A$ for each axiom A in $\mathsf{KP}(\theta)$.

Let $\forall x, y\, A(x, y)$ be the axiom of Extensionality with Δ_0-formula A. Then $M \models A(a, b)$ for any RS-terms a, b. Hence $\mathcal{H}[\{|a|, |b|\}] \vdash_0^0 A(a, b)$, and $\mathcal{H} \vdash_0^2 \forall x, y\, A(x, y)$.

Next for the axiom of Pair, we have $\mathcal{H}[\{|a|, |b|\}] \vdash_0^1 a \in c \land b \in c$ for $c \equiv [x \in M_\alpha : x = a \lor x = b]$ with $\alpha = \max\{|a|, |b|\} + 1$. Hence $\mathcal{H}[\{|a|, |b|\}] \vdash_0^{\alpha+1} \exists z(a \in z \land b \in z)$., and $\mathcal{H} \vdash_0^{\Omega(\theta)} \forall x, y \exists z(x \in z \land y \in z)$. Likewise for the axiom of Union, we see $\mathcal{H} \vdash_0^{\Omega(\theta)} \forall x \exists z \forall u \in x \forall v \in u(v \in z)$ with the RS-term $[v \in M_\alpha : \exists u \in a(v \in u)]$ and $\alpha = |a| + 1$.

For the axiom of Infinity $\exists z\, (\exists x \in z(x \in z) \land \forall x \in z \exists y \in z(x \in y))$, we show that $M \models \forall x \in \mathsf{M}_\omega \exists y \in \mathsf{M}_\omega(x \in y)$. Let $a \in M_n$ with $n < \omega$. Then $a \in M_n \in M_{n+1}$ for $M_\omega = \bigcup_{n<\omega} M_n$. Thus $\mathcal{H} \vdash_0^0 \forall x \in \mathsf{M}_\omega \exists y \in \mathsf{M}_\omega(x \in y)$ with $\omega \in \mathcal{H}$, and $\mathcal{H} \vdash_0^{\omega+1} \exists z\, (\exists x \in z(x \in z) \land \forall x \in z \exists y \in z(x \in y))$.

For the axiom (θ), $\forall x \exists z \forall y \in \Theta(x)(y \in z)$, let $c = [y \in M_{f_{\theta_M}(\alpha)} : \theta(a, y)]$ with $\alpha = |a| + 1$. We claim that $M \models \forall y \in \Theta(a)(y \in c)$. Let $M \models \theta(a, b)$. Then by (6.20) and $a \in M_\alpha$ we obtain $b \in M_{f_{\theta_M}(\alpha)}$, i.e., $|b| < f_{\theta_M}(\alpha)$. Hence $b \in c$. Thus $\mathcal{H}[\{|a|\}] \vdash_0^0 \forall y \in \Theta(a)(y \in c)$, and $\mathcal{H}[\{|a|\}] \vdash_0^{f_{\theta_M}(\alpha)+1} \exists z \forall y \in \Theta(a)(y \in z)$, and $\mathcal{H} \vdash_0^{\Omega(\theta)} \forall x \exists z \forall y \in \Theta(x)(y \in z)$ by $f_{\theta_M}(\alpha) < \Omega(\theta)$ for $\alpha < \Omega(\theta)$.

For Δ_0^θ-Separation, let a, b be RS-terms, and $\max\{|a|, |b|\} + 1 = \alpha$. Let $c = [u \in \mathsf{M}_\alpha : u \in a \land B(u, b)]$ for a Δ_0^θ-formula B. We see that $M \models \forall u \in c(u \in a \land B(u, b)) \land \forall u \in a(B(u, b) \to u \in c)$, and $\mathcal{H} \vdash_0^{\Omega(\theta)} \forall x, y \exists z\, (z = \{u \in x : B(u, y)\})$.

Finally for Δ_0^θ-Collection, let B be a Δ_0^θ-formula. By Tautology Lemma 6.37 we obtain for $d = \mathrm{dg}(\forall u \in c \exists y\, B(u, y, b))$

$$\frac{\mathcal{H}[\{|b|, |c|\}] \vdash_0^{2d} \neg(\forall u \in c \exists y\, B(u, y, b)), \forall u \in c \exists y\, B(u, y, b)}{\mathcal{H}[\{|b|, |c|\}] \vdash_0^{2d+1} \neg(\forall u \in c \exists y\, B(u, y, b)), \exists z \forall u \in c \exists y \in z\, B(u, y, b)}\ (\Delta_0^\theta\text{-Coll})$$

□

Theorem 6.11 (Collapsing) *Suppose $\gamma \in \mathcal{H}_\gamma^\theta[\Lambda]$,*

$$\Lambda \subset \mathcal{H}_\gamma^\theta(\psi_{\Omega(\theta)}^\theta(\gamma)) \tag{6.23}$$

for a finite set Λ of ordinals, and $\Gamma \subset \Sigma^\theta$. Then for $\hat{\alpha} = \gamma + \omega^\alpha$

$$\mathcal{H}_\gamma^\theta[\Lambda] \vdash_2^\alpha \Gamma \Rightarrow \mathcal{H}_{\hat{\alpha}+1}^\theta[\Lambda] \vdash_1^{\psi_{\Omega(\theta)}^\theta(\hat{\alpha})} \Gamma.$$

Proof This is seen by induction on α as in Theorems 6.4 and 6.7.
Case 1. The last inference is a $(\bigvee)$.

Let $A \in \Gamma$ be such that $A \simeq \bigvee(A_i)_{i \in J}$, and for an $i \in J$ and an $\alpha(i) < \alpha$

$$\frac{\mathcal{H}^{\theta}_{\gamma}[\Lambda] \vdash^{\alpha(i)}_{2} \Gamma, A_i}{\mathcal{H}^{\theta}_{\gamma}[\Lambda] \vdash^{\alpha}_{2} \Gamma} \ (\bigvee)$$

We can assume $|i| \in \mathsf{k}(A_i)$. Then we have $|i| \in \mathsf{k}(A_i) \subset \mathcal{H}^{\theta}_{\gamma}[\Lambda] \subset \mathcal{H}^{\theta}_{\gamma}(\psi^{\theta}_{\Omega(\theta)}(\gamma)) \cap \Omega(\theta) = \psi^{\theta}_{\Omega(\theta)}(\gamma)$. Hence $|i| < \psi^{\theta}_{\Omega(\theta)}(\gamma) \leq \psi^{\theta}_{\Omega(\theta)}(\hat{\alpha})$ for (6.22).
Case 2. The last inference is a $(\bigwedge)$.

Let $A \in \Gamma$ be such that $A \simeq \bigwedge(A_i)_{i \in J}$, and for any $i \in J$, there is an $\alpha(i) < \alpha$ such that

$$\frac{\{\mathcal{H}^{\theta}_{\gamma}[\Lambda \cup \{|i|\}] \vdash^{\alpha(i)}_{2} \Gamma, A_i : i \in J\}}{\mathcal{H}^{\theta}_{\gamma}[\Lambda] \vdash^{\alpha}_{2} \Gamma} \ (\bigwedge)$$

By IH it suffices to show that $\forall i \in J(|i| \in \mathcal{H}^{\theta}_{\gamma}(\psi^{\theta}_{\Omega(\theta)}(\gamma)))$. For example consider the case when $A \equiv (\forall x \in \Theta(a)\, B(x))$ for a set term a. Then $J = \{t \in RS : |t| \leq f_{\theta_M}(|a|), M \models \theta(a, t)\}$. We have $|a| \in \mathcal{H}^{\theta}_{\gamma}[\Lambda]$, and hence $|i| \leq f_{\theta_M}(|a|) \in \mathcal{H}^{\theta}_{\gamma}(\psi^{\theta}_{\Omega(\theta)}(\gamma)) \cap \Omega(\theta) = \psi^{\theta}_{\Omega(\theta)}(\gamma)$ for any $i \in J$. Thus we obtain $|i| < \psi^{\theta}_{\Omega(\theta)}(\gamma) \subset \mathcal{H}^{\theta}_{\gamma}(\psi^{\theta}_{\Omega(\theta)}(\gamma))$.
Case 3. The last inference is a $(\Delta^{\theta}_{0}\text{–Coll})$.

There are a sentence $\exists z(c \in z \land \forall x \in c \exists y \in z\, B)$ in Γ with $B \in \Delta^{\theta}_{0}$, and $\alpha_0 < \alpha$ such that

$$\frac{\mathcal{H}^{\theta}_{\gamma}[\Lambda] \vdash^{\alpha_0}_{2} \Gamma, \forall x \in c \exists y\, B}{\mathcal{H}^{\theta}_{\gamma}[\Lambda] \vdash^{\alpha}_{2} \Gamma} \ (\Delta^{\theta}_{0}\text{–Coll})$$

Since $\forall x \in c \exists y\, B$ is also a Σ^{θ}-sentence. IH yields $\mathcal{H}^{\theta}_{\widehat{\alpha_0}+1}[\Lambda] \vdash^{\psi_\sigma(\widehat{\alpha_0})}_{1} \Gamma, \forall x \in c \exists y\, B$.
Case 4. The last inference is a (cut).

For $\mathrm{dg}(C) < 2$ and $\alpha_0 < \alpha$, we have

$$\frac{\mathcal{H}^{\theta}_{\gamma}[\Lambda] \vdash^{\alpha_0}_{2} \Gamma, \neg C \quad \mathcal{H}^{\theta}_{\gamma}[\Lambda] \vdash^{\alpha_0}_{2} C, \Gamma}{\mathcal{H}^{\theta}_{\gamma}[\Lambda] \vdash^{\alpha}_{2} \Gamma} \ (cut)$$

Case 4.1. $\mathrm{dg}(C) = 0$.

IH yields the assertion.
Case 4.2. $\mathrm{dg}(C) = 1$.

Then C is a sentence $\exists x\, B(x)$ with a Δ^{θ}_{0}-formula B. From the right upper sequent, IH yields for $\widehat{\alpha_0} = \gamma + \omega^{\alpha_0}$ and $\beta_0 = \psi^{\theta}_{\Omega(\theta)}(\widehat{\alpha_0})$

$$\mathcal{H}^{\theta}_{\widehat{\alpha_0}+1}[\Lambda] \vdash^{\beta_0}_{1} C, \Gamma$$

We have $\beta_0 \in \mathscr{H}^{\theta}_{\widehat{\alpha_0}+1}$. Then by Boundedness Lemma 6.39, we obtain

$$\mathscr{H}^{\theta}_{\widehat{\alpha_0}+1}[\Lambda] \vdash^{\beta_0}_1 C^{(\mathsf{M}_{\beta_0})}, \Gamma$$

On the other hand we have by inversion from the left uppersequent

$$\mathscr{H}^{\theta}_{\widehat{\alpha_0}+1}[\Lambda] \vdash^{\alpha_0}_2 \Gamma, \neg C^{(\mathsf{M}_{\beta_0})}$$

IH with the Δ^{θ}_0-sentence $\neg C^{(\mathsf{M}_{\beta_0})}$ yields for $\beta_1 = \psi^{\theta}_{\Omega(\theta)}(\widehat{\alpha_1})$ and $\widehat{\alpha_1} = \widehat{\alpha_0} + 1 + \omega^{\alpha_0} = \gamma + \omega^{\alpha_0} + \omega^{\alpha_0} < \gamma + \omega^{\alpha} = \hat{\alpha}$

$$\mathscr{H}^{\theta}_{\widehat{\alpha_1}+1}[\Lambda] \vdash^{\beta_1}_1 \Gamma, \neg C^{(\mathsf{M}_{\beta_0})}$$

On the other hand we have $\widehat{\alpha_i} \in \mathscr{H}^{\theta}_{\gamma}[\Lambda]$ and $\widehat{\alpha_0} < \widehat{\alpha_1}$. We obtain $\beta_0 = \psi^{\theta}_{\Omega(\theta)}(\widehat{\alpha_0}) < \psi^{\theta}_{\Omega(\theta)}(\widehat{\alpha_1}) = \beta_1$. We obtain with $\widehat{\alpha_1} < \hat{\alpha}$ and $\beta_1 < \psi^{\theta}_{\Omega(\theta)}(\hat{\alpha})$

$$\dfrac{\mathscr{H}^{\theta}_{\widehat{\alpha_1}+1}[\Lambda] \vdash^{\beta_1}_1 \Gamma, \neg C^{(\mathsf{M}_{\beta_0})} \quad \mathscr{H}^{\theta}_{\widehat{\alpha_0}+1}[\Lambda] \vdash^{\beta_0}_1 C^{(\mathsf{M}_{\beta_0})}, \Gamma}{\mathscr{H}^{\theta}_{\widehat{\alpha_1}+1}[\Lambda] \vdash^{\beta_1+1}_1 \Gamma} \ (cut)$$

□

Proof Let us show Theorem 6.10. Assume $\mathsf{KP}(\theta) \vdash A$ for a Σ^{θ}-formula A. Embedding Lemma 6.41 yields $\mathscr{H}^{\theta}_0 \vdash^{\Omega(\theta)+l}_{2+m} A$ for some $l, m < \omega$. Predicative cut-elimination Lemma 6.40 yields $\mathscr{H}^{\theta}_0 \vdash^{\alpha}_2 A$ for $\alpha = \omega_m(\Omega(\theta) + l)$, which in turn yields $\mathscr{H}^{\theta}_{\omega^{\alpha}+1} \vdash^{\beta}_1 A$ for $\beta = \psi^{\theta}_{\Omega(\theta)}(\omega^{\alpha})$ by Collapsing Lemma 6.11. We obtain $\mathscr{H}^{\theta}_{\omega^{\alpha}+1} \vdash^{\beta}_1 A^{(\mathsf{M}_{\beta})}$ by Boundedness Lemma 6.39. Thus by Truth Lemma 6.38, we conclude $M \models A^{(\mathsf{M}_{\beta})}$, i.e., $M_{\beta} \models A$ for $\beta = \psi^{\theta}_{\Omega(\theta)}(\omega_{m+1}(\Omega(\theta) + l)) < \psi^{\theta}_{\Omega(\theta)}(\varepsilon_{\Omega(\theta)+1})$. □

6.6.2 *Reducing Π_{n+1}-Reflections to Iterated Π_n-Reflections*

In this subsection a set theory $\mathsf{KP}\Pi_{N+1}$ for Π_{N+1}-reflecting universes is shown to be Π_{N+1}-conservative over iterations of Π_N-recursively Mahlo operations RM_N for each $N \geq 2$. In what follows, let V denote a transitive and well-founded model of the Kripke–Platek set theory with the axiom of infinity, $\mathsf{KP}\omega$, which is a universe in discourse. $P, Q, \ldots$ denote non-empty transitive sets in $V \cup \{V\}$ such that $P \models \mathsf{KP}\omega$. For set-theoretic formulas φ, $P \models \varphi :\Leftrightarrow (P, \in) \models \varphi$.

A Π_i-recursively Mahlo operation RM_i for $2 \leq i < \omega$, is defined through a universal Π_i-formula $\Pi_i(a)$ such that for each Π_i-formula $\varphi(x)$ there exists a natural number n such that $\mathsf{KP} \vdash \forall x[\varphi(x) \leftrightarrow \Pi_i(\langle n, x\rangle)]$. Let $\mathscr{X}$ be a collection of sets.

$$P \in RM_i(\mathscr{X}) :\Leftrightarrow \forall b \in P\,[P \models \Pi_i(b) \rightarrow \exists Q \in \mathscr{X} \cap P(b \in Q \models \Pi_i(b))]$$

(read: P is Π_i-reflecting on $\mathscr{X}$.)

Assume that $P \in \mathscr{X}$ is given by a Δ_0-formula. Then there exists a Π_{i+1}-formula rm_i such that for any non-empty transitive sets $P \in V \cup \{V\}$, $P \in RM_i(\mathscr{X}) \leftrightarrow rm_i^P$, where rm_i^P denotes the result of restricting unbounded quantifiers in rm_i to P.

An iteration of RM_i along a definable relation $\prec$ is defined as follows.

$$P \in RM_i(a; \prec) :\Leftrightarrow a \in P \in \bigcap\{RM_i(RM_i(b; \prec)) : b \in P \models b \prec a\}.$$

Assume that $b \prec a$ is given by a Σ_1-formula. Then there exists a Π_{i+1}-formula $rm_i(\prec)$ such that for any non-empty transitive sets $P \in V \cup \{V\}$ and $a \in P$, $P \in RM_i(a; \prec) \leftrightarrow rm_i^P(\prec)$.

For $2 \leq N < \omega$, $\mathsf{KP}\Pi_N$ denotes a set theory for Π_N-reflecting universes V, which is obtained from $\mathsf{KP}\omega$ by adding an axiom $V \in RM_N$ (the axiom for Π_N-reflection) stating that its universe is Π_N-reflecting. This means that for each Π_N-formula φ, $\varphi(a) \to \exists c[ad_N^c \wedge a \in c \wedge \varphi^c(a)]$ is an axiom, where $ad_2^c :\equiv (\forall x \in c \forall y \in x(y \in c))$, i.e., c is transitive, and for $N > 2$, $ad \equiv ad_N$ denotes a Π_3-sentence such that $P \models ad \Leftrightarrow P \models \mathsf{KP}\omega$ for any transitive and well-founded sets P, cf. Exercise 6.1. $\mathsf{KP}\Pi_2$ is a subtheory of $\mathsf{KP}\omega + (V = L)$, which is interpreted in $\mathsf{KP}\omega$: $\mathsf{KP}\omega + (V = L) \vdash \varphi \Rightarrow \mathsf{KP}\omega \vdash \varphi^L$, cf. Theorem 1.13.

$\mathsf{KP}\Pi_{N+1}$ is much stronger than $\mathsf{KP}\Pi_N$ since Π_N-recursively Mahlo operation RM_N can be iterated in $\mathsf{KP}\Pi_{N+1}$. For example, $\mathsf{KP}\Pi_{N+1}$ proves $\forall \alpha \in ON[V \in RM_N(\alpha; <)]$ by induction on ordinals α. Suppose $\forall \beta < \alpha[V \in RM_N(\beta; <)]$. Let φ be a Π_N-formula such that $V \models \varphi$, and $\beta < \alpha$. We can reflect a Π_{N+1}-formula $V \in RM_N(\beta; <) \wedge \varphi$, and obtain a set P such that $P \in RM_N(\beta; <) \wedge P \models \varphi$. Hence $V \in RM_N(\alpha; <)$. This means that V is in the diagonal intersection $\Delta_\alpha RM_N(\alpha; <)$, i.e., $V \in \bigcap\{RM_N(\alpha; <) : \alpha \in ON \cap V\}$. Since this is a Π_{N+1}-formula, the Π_{N+1}-reflecting universe V reflects it: there exists a set $P \in V$ such that P is in the diagonal intersection, i.e., $P \in \bigcap\{RM_N(\alpha; <) : \alpha \in ON \cap P\}$, and so forth.

6.6.2.1 Conservation

Let $ON \subset V$ denote the class of ordinals, $ON^\varepsilon \subset V$ and $<^\varepsilon$ be Δ-predicates such that for any transitive and well-founded model V of $\mathsf{KP}\omega$, $<^\varepsilon$ is a well order of type $\varepsilon_{\mathbb{K}+1}$ on ON^ε for the order type $\mathbb{K}$ of the class ON in V. $\lceil \omega_n(\mathbb{K}+1) \rceil \in ON^\varepsilon$ denotes the code of the 'ordinal' $\omega_n(\mathbb{K}+1)$, which is assumed to be a closed 'term' built from the code $\lceil \mathbb{K} \rceil$ and n, e.g., $\lceil \alpha \rceil = \langle 0, \alpha \rangle$ for $\alpha \in ON$, $\lceil \mathbb{K} \rceil = \langle 1, 0 \rangle$ and $\lceil \omega_n(\mathbb{K}+1) \rceil = \langle 2, \langle 2, \cdots \langle 2, \langle 3, \lceil \mathbb{K} \rceil, \langle 0, 1 \rangle \rangle \rangle \cdots \rangle \rangle$.

$<^\varepsilon$ is assumed to be a standard epsilon order with base $\mathbb{K}$ as in Definition 4.1 (not on $\mathbb{N}$, but on V) such that $\mathsf{KP}\omega$ proves the fact that $<^\varepsilon$ is a linear ordering, and for any formula φ and each $n < \omega$,

$$\mathsf{KP}\omega \vdash \forall x(\forall y <^\varepsilon x\, \varphi(y) \to \varphi(x)) \to \forall x <^\varepsilon \lceil \omega_n(\mathbb{K}+1) \rceil \varphi(x) \tag{6.24}$$

Theorem 6.12 *For each $N \geq 2$, $\mathsf{KP}\Pi_{N+1}$ is Π_{N+1}-conservative over the theory*

$$\mathsf{KP}\omega + \{V \in RM_N(\lceil \omega_n(\mathbb{K}+1)\rceil; <^{\varepsilon}) : n \in \omega\}.$$

From (6.24) we see that $\mathsf{KP}\Pi_{N+1}$ proves $V \in RM_N(\lceil \omega_n(\mathbb{K}+1)\rceil; <^{\varepsilon})$ for each $n \in \omega$.

Remark 6.2 Since the axiom Power is a Π_3-sentence $\forall a \exists b \forall x \subset a(x \in b)$, and Σ_i-Separation or Π_i-Collection are Π_{i+2}-formulas, we have for each $N \geq 3$, $\mathsf{KP}\Pi_{N+1}$ + (Power) + (Σ_{N-2}-Separation) + (Π_{N-2}-Collection) is Π_{N+1}-conservative over the theory $\mathsf{KP}\omega + \{V \in RM_N(\lceil \omega_n(\mathbb{K}+1)\rceil; <^{\varepsilon}) : n \in \omega\}$ + (Power) + (Σ_{N-2}-Separation) + (Π_{N-2}-Collection).

6.6.2.2 Proof of Theorem 6.12

Let us prove Theorem 6.12. In what follows we work in $\mathsf{KP}\omega$, and let $N \geq 2$ denote a fixed integer. Δ_0 denotes the set of bounded formulas in the language $\{\in\}$ of set theories. Then the classes Σ_{i+1}, Π_{i+1} are defined recursively as usual. Each class Σ_{i+1}, Π_{i+1} is defined to be closed under bounded quantifications $\exists x \in a, \forall x \in a$. Note that except Foundation schema and the axiom of Π_{N+1}-reflection, each axiom in $\mathsf{KP}\Pi_{N+1}$ is a Π_2-formula.

Let us embed $\mathsf{KP}\Pi_{N+1}$ to an infinitary calculus R_N. V denotes a transitive and well-founded model of $\mathsf{KP}\omega$. Consider the language $\mathcal{L}_V = \{\in\} \cup \{c_a : a \in V\}$ where c_a denotes the name of the set $a \in V$. We identify the set a with its name c_a. $\Gamma, \Delta, \ldots$ denote finite sets of sentences in the language $\mathcal{L}_V$. Classes $\Delta_0, \Sigma_{i+1}, \Pi_{i+1}$ of sentences in $\mathcal{L}_V$ are defined as usual.

The assignment of disjunctions and conjunctions to sentences is defined as in Definition 6.15, but each constant c_a is identified with the set $a \in V$.

Definition 6.25 1. For a Δ_0-sentence M with $J := \emptyset$

$$M :\simeq \begin{cases} \bigvee(A_\iota)_{\iota\in J} & \text{if } M \text{ is false in } V \\ \bigwedge(A_\iota)_{\iota\in J} & \text{if } M \text{ is true in } V \end{cases}$$

In what follows consider the unbounded sentences.

2. $(A_0 \vee A_1) :\simeq \bigvee(A_\iota)_{\iota\in J}$ and $(A_0 \wedge A_1) :\simeq \bigwedge(A_\iota)_{\iota\in J}$ for $J := 2$.
3. $\exists x \in a\, A(x) :\simeq \bigvee(A(b))_{b\in J}$ and $\forall x \in a\, A(x) :\simeq \bigwedge(A(b))_{b\in J}$ for $J := \{b : b \in a\}$.
4. $\exists x\, A(x) :\simeq \bigvee(A(b))_{b\in J}$ and $\forall x\, A(x) :\simeq \bigwedge(A(b))_{b\in J}$ for $J := V$.

Definition 6.26 The *degree* $\text{dg}(A) < \omega$ of $\mathcal{L}_V$-sentences A is defined recursively as follows.

1. $\text{dg}(A) = 0$ if $A \in \Delta_0$.
   In what follows consider unbounded sentences A.
2. $\text{dg}(\neg A) = \text{dg}(A)$.
3. $\text{dg}(A) = \max\{\text{dg}(A_i) : i < 2\} + 1$ if $A \equiv (A_0 \vee A_1)$.

4. $\text{dg}(A) = \text{dg}(B(\emptyset)) + 1$ if $A \in \{(\exists x\, B(x)), (\exists x \in a\, B(x)) : a \in V\}$.

Definition 6.27 1. For $\mathcal{L}_V$-sentences A, $\mathsf{k}(A) := \{a \in V : c_a \text{ occurs in } A\}$.
2. For sets Γ of sentences, $\mathsf{k}(\Gamma) := \bigcup\{\mathsf{k}(A) : A \in \Gamma\}$.
3. For sets $X \subset V$, $\mathcal{E}(X)$ denotes the Skolem hull of $\{\text{rk}(a) : a \in X\} \cup \{0\}$ under ordinal addition $(\alpha, \beta) \mapsto \alpha + \beta$ and exponentiation $\alpha \mapsto \omega^\alpha$, where $\text{rk}(a) = \sup\{\text{rk}(b) + 1 : b \in a\}$.
4. For an $\iota \in V$ and transitive set $P \in V \cup \{V\}$, $P(\iota)$ denotes the smallest transitive model $Q \subset V$ of $\mathsf{KP}\omega$ such that $P \cup \{\iota\} \subset Q$.

Note that $\mathsf{k}(A)$ is a finite set of *sets*, not of *ordinals*. Let us define a relation $P \vdash^\alpha_m \Gamma$ for transitive models $P \in V \cup \{V\}$ of $\mathsf{KP}\omega$. The relation $P \vdash^\alpha_m \Gamma$ is defined as a fixed point of a strictly positive formula in the intuitionistic fixed point theory $\text{FiX}^i(\mathsf{KP}\omega)$ over the set theory $\mathsf{KP}\omega$.

Definition 6.28 Let $P \in V \cup \{V\}$ be a transitive model of $\mathsf{KP}\omega$, $\alpha < \varepsilon_{\mathbb{K}+1}$ and $m < \omega$.

$P \vdash^\alpha_m \Gamma$ holds if

$$\mathsf{k}(\Gamma) \subset P \;\&\; \alpha \in \mathcal{E}(\mathsf{k}(\Gamma)) \tag{6.25}$$

and one of the following cases holds:

$(\bigvee)$ $A \simeq \bigvee\{A_\iota : \iota \in J\}$, $A \in \Gamma$, and for an $\iota \in J$ and an $\alpha(\iota) < \alpha$

$$\frac{P \vdash^{\alpha(\iota)}_m \Gamma, A_\iota}{P \vdash^\alpha_m \Gamma}\ (\bigvee)$$

$(\bigwedge)$ $A \simeq \bigwedge\{A_\iota : \iota \in J\}$, $A \in \Gamma$, and $\alpha(\iota) < \alpha$ for any $\iota \in J$

$$\frac{\{P(\iota) \vdash^{\alpha(\iota)}_m \Gamma, A_\iota : \iota \in J\}}{P \vdash^\alpha_m \Gamma}\ (\bigwedge)$$

(cut) $\text{dg}(C) < m$ and $\alpha_0, \alpha_1 < \alpha$

$$\frac{P \vdash^{\alpha_0}_m \Gamma, \neg C \quad P \vdash^{\alpha_1}_m C, \Gamma}{P \vdash^\alpha_m \Gamma}\ (cut)$$

(Ref_{N+1}) $\alpha_0, \alpha_1 < \alpha$ and $A \in \Pi_{N+1}$

$$\frac{P \vdash^{\alpha_0}_m \Gamma, A(c) \quad P \vdash^{\alpha_1}_m \forall z[ad^z \to c \in z \to \neg A^z], \Gamma}{P \vdash^\alpha_m \Gamma}\ (Ref_{N+1})$$

Note that in $(\bigvee)$, the conditions (6.5), (6.18), (6.22) are missing. Also we have $P \vdash^\alpha_m \Gamma \Rightarrow \alpha \in P$ by (6.25) since P is assumed to be a model of $\mathsf{KP}\omega$, which is closed under the function $a \mapsto \mathrm{rk}(a)$, ordinal addition and exponentiation on ordinals$< \mathbb{K}$ and on codes of ordinals$< \varepsilon_{\mathbb{K}+1}$.

The following Lemmas 6.42 and 6.43 are seen easily.

Lemma 6.42 (Embedding) *For each axiom A in $\mathsf{KP}\Pi_{N+1}$, there is an $m < \omega$ such that $P \vdash_m^{\mathbb{K}\cdot m} A$ for any transitive model P of $\mathsf{KP}\omega$.*

Proof Consider the Foundation schema. We see by induction on $\mathrm{rk}(a)$ that for $\mathsf{k}(A) \subset P$, $P(a) \vdash_0^{2\mathrm{dg}(A)+3\mathrm{rk}(a)+2} \neg\forall x(\forall y \in x\, A(y) \to A(x)), A(a)$. □

Lemma 6.43 (Predicative Cut-elimination) $P \vdash_{m+1}^{\alpha} \Gamma \Longrightarrow P \vdash_m^{\omega^\alpha} \Gamma$.

For $\alpha < \varepsilon_{\mathbb{K}+1}$, set $RM_N^\alpha := RM_N(\alpha; <^\varepsilon)$. The following Lemma 6.44 is easily seen, but a crucial fact in reducing Π_{N+1}-reflection.

Lemma 6.44 *Let $\Gamma \subset \Sigma_{N+1}$ and $P \in RM_N^\alpha$. Assume*

$$\exists \xi, x \in P(\xi <^\varepsilon \alpha \wedge \forall Q \in RM_N^\xi \cap P(x \in Q \to \bigvee \Gamma \text{ is true in } Q)).$$

Then $\bigvee \Gamma$ is true in P.

Proof By $P \in RM_N^\alpha$ we have $P \in RM_N(RM_N^\xi)$ for any $\xi \in P$ such that $\xi <^\varepsilon \alpha$.

Suppose that the Π_{N+1}-sentence $\neg \bigvee \Gamma$ holds in P. Then for any $\xi \in P$ with $\xi <^\varepsilon \alpha$ and $x \in P$ there exists a $Q \in RM_N^\xi \cap P$ such that $x \in Q$ and $\neg \bigvee \Gamma$ is true in Q. □

Lemma 6.45 (Elimination of (Ref_{N+1})) *Let $\Gamma \subset \Pi_{N+1}$. Suppose $P_0 \vdash_0^\alpha \Gamma$ and $P_0 \in P \in RM_N^\alpha$. Then Γ is true in P.*

Proof By induction on α. Let $RM_N^\alpha \ni P \ni P_0$ with $P_0 \vdash_0^\alpha \Gamma$.

Case 1. First consider the case when the last inference is a (Ref_{N+1}): we have $\{\alpha_\ell, \alpha_r\} \subset P_0 \subset P$, $\max\{\alpha_\ell, \alpha_r\} <^\varepsilon \alpha$, $A \in \Pi_{N+1}$

$$\cfrac{P_0 \vdash_0^{\alpha_\ell} \Gamma, A(c) \quad P_0 \vdash_0^{\alpha_r} \forall z[ad^z \to c \in z \to \neg A^z(c)], \Gamma}{P_0 \vdash_0^\alpha \Gamma}\ (Ref_{N+1})$$

Note that $c \in P_0$ by (6.25), and $c \in Q$ for any transitive $Q \ni P_0$. Since $<^\varepsilon$ is transitive, we have $P \in RM_N^{\alpha_r}$. From IH we see that

$$\text{either } \forall z \in P[ad^z \to c \in z \to \neg A^z(c)] \text{ or } \bigvee \Gamma^P \text{ is true.} \tag{6.26}$$

On the other hand by IH we have for any $Q \in RM_N^{\alpha_\ell} \cap P$ with $P_0 \in Q$, either $\bigvee \Gamma^Q$ is true or $A(c)^Q$ is true. Hence by (6.26) for any $Q \in RM_N^{\alpha_\ell} \cap P$ with $P_0 \in Q$, $\bigvee \Gamma^Q \vee \bigvee \Gamma^P$ is true. From Lemma 6.44 we see that $\bigvee \Gamma^P$ is true.

Case 2. Second consider the case when the last inference is a $(\bigwedge)$: we have $A \simeq \bigwedge\{A_\iota : \iota \in J\}$, $A \in \Gamma$, and $\alpha(\iota) < \alpha$ for any $\iota \in J$

$$\frac{\{P_0(\iota) \vdash_0^{\alpha(\iota)} \Gamma, A_\iota : \iota \in J\}}{P_0 \vdash_0^{\alpha} \Gamma} \ (\bigwedge)$$

For any $\iota \in P$ we have $P_0(\iota) \in P$. IH yields for any $\iota \in P$ that either $\bigvee \Gamma^P$ is true or A_ι^P is true. If $J = V$, then we are done. If $J = a \in V$, then $a \in P_0 \in P$ and hence $a \subset P$.
Case 3. Third consider the case when the last inference is a $(\bigvee)$: we have $A \simeq \bigvee\{A_\iota : \iota \in J\}$, $A \in \Gamma$, and $\alpha(\iota) < \alpha$ for an $\iota \in J$

$$\frac{P_0 \vdash_0^{\alpha(\iota)} \Gamma, A_\iota}{P_0 \vdash_0^{\alpha} \Gamma} \ (\bigvee)$$

IH yields that either $\bigvee \Gamma^P$ is true or A_ι^P is true. Consider the case when $J = V$. If $\iota \in P$, then we are done. Otherwise the variable x in $\exists x\, B(x) \equiv A$ does not occur in $B(x)$. Hence we can assume $\iota = 0 \in P$. □

Let us prove Theorem 6.12. Let $N \geq 2$, and A be a Π_{N+1}-sentence provable in $\mathsf{KP}\Pi_{N+1}$. For the least transitive and well-founded model $L_{\omega_1^{CK}}$ of $\mathsf{KP}\omega$, by Embedding Lemma 6.42 and Predicative Cut-elimination Lemma 6.43 we obtain for an $m < \omega$, $L_{\omega_1^{CK}} \vdash_0^{\omega_m(\mathbb{K}\cdot m)} A$ with $\emptyset = \mathsf{k}(A)$, and $L_{\omega_1^{CK}} \vdash_0^{\omega_n(\mathbb{K}+1)} A$ for an $n > m$. We obtain by Elimination lemma of (Ref_{N+1}) Lemma 6.45, if $V \in RM_N^{\omega_n(\mathbb{K}+1)}$, then $L_{\omega_1^{CK}} \in V$ and A is true (in V).

The above proof is formalizable in the intuitionistic fixed point theory $\mathrm{FiX}^i(\mathsf{KP}\omega)$ over $\mathsf{KP}\omega$ with (6.24). Theorem 4.15.2 yields what we need:

$$\mathsf{KP}\omega \vdash V \in RM_N(\ulcorner\omega_n(\mathbb{K}+1)\urcorner; <^{\varepsilon}) \to A.$$

Exercises

6.1 Show that there is a Π_3-sentence ad such that ad^d holds iff d is a admissible set.

6.2 In this exercise, let $\Omega := \Omega_1$ and $\psi\alpha := \psi_{\Omega_1}(\alpha)$ for the collapsing function in Definition 6.1 with the binary Veblen function φ.

Show the followings.

1. $\forall\alpha[\psi\Omega \leq \alpha < \Omega \to \psi\alpha = \psi\Omega]$.
2. $\psi(\psi\Omega) = \psi\Omega$ and $\forall\alpha < \Omega[\psi\alpha = \alpha \to \alpha = \psi\Omega]$.
3. $\forall\alpha \leq \psi\Omega[(\psi\alpha = \Gamma_\alpha)\,\&\,(\alpha < \psi\Omega \to \alpha < \psi\alpha)]$.
4. $\psi\Omega = \min\{\alpha : \Gamma_\alpha = \alpha\}$.

6.3 In this exercise, let $\Omega := \Omega_1 = \omega_1$.

Let us define a totally defined collapsing function $\alpha \mapsto \vartheta(\alpha)$, whereas the collapsing function $\alpha \mapsto \psi(\alpha)$ is essentially partial, cf. Exercise 6.2 and Sect. 6.4.2. Let

$E(\alpha)$ denote the set of epsilon numbers $< \Omega$ occurring in the Cantor normal form of α with base ω.

Definition 6.29 1. For $\beta < \varepsilon_{\Omega+1}$ define sets $C(\alpha, \beta) \subset \varepsilon_{\Omega+1}$ and ordinals $\vartheta(\alpha) \leq \Omega$ by simultaneous recursion on ordinals $\alpha < \varepsilon_{\Omega+1}$ as follows.

a. $\{0, \Omega\} \cup \beta \subset C(\alpha, \beta)$.
b. $\gamma, \delta \in C(\alpha, \beta) \Rightarrow \gamma + \delta, \omega^{\gamma} \in C(\alpha, \beta)$.
c. $\gamma \in C(\alpha, \beta) \cap \alpha \Rightarrow \vartheta(\gamma) \in C(\alpha, \beta)$.

$$\vartheta(\alpha) = \min\{\beta \leq \Omega : C(\alpha, \beta) \cap \Omega \subset \beta, E(\alpha) \subset C(\alpha, \beta)\} \tag{6.27}$$

Show the followings for $\alpha, \beta < \varepsilon_{\Omega+1}$.

1. $\vartheta(\alpha) < \Omega$ for any $\alpha < \varepsilon_{\Omega+1}$.
2. Each $\vartheta(\alpha)$ is an ε-number$< \Omega$.
3. $E(\alpha) < \vartheta(\alpha), i.e., \forall \gamma \in E(\alpha)(\gamma < \vartheta(\alpha))$.
4. $\vartheta(\alpha) < \vartheta(\beta)$ iff
either $E(\alpha) < \vartheta(\beta) \,\&\, \alpha < \beta$, or $\vartheta(\alpha) \leq E(\beta) :\Leftrightarrow \exists \delta \in E(\beta)(\vartheta(\alpha) \leq \delta)$.
5. $\vartheta(\alpha) = \vartheta(\beta) \Rightarrow \alpha = \beta$.
6. Let $T_{\vartheta}(\Omega)$ be a set of ordinal terms built from $0, \Omega$ by applying the addition $+$, exponentiation $\alpha \mapsto \omega^{\alpha}$ and the function $\alpha \mapsto \vartheta(\alpha)$. Each ordinal term in $T_{\vartheta}(\Omega)$ is a term over the symbols $\{0, \Omega, +, \omega, \vartheta\}$. Conclude that $(T_{\vartheta}(\Omega), <)$ is elementary recursive.

6.4

Definition 6.30 Let T be a set theory comprising the fragment $\mathsf{KP}\Pi_2$ and $L_{\omega_1^{CK}} \models T$. Define the *$\Pi_2$-ordinal* $|T|_{\Pi_2}$ of T by

$$|T|_{\Pi_2} := \inf\{\alpha \leq \omega_1^{CK} : \forall \Pi_2\text{−sentence} A(T \vdash A \Rightarrow L_{\alpha} \models A)\}.$$

The *Σ_1-ordinal* $|T|_{\Sigma_1}$ is defined similarly.

In this exercise let us show $|T + (V = L)|_{\Pi_2} = |T + (V = L)|_{\Sigma_1}$ for set theories T in Definition 6.30. It suffices to show that $|T + (V = L)|_{\Pi_2} \leq |T + (V = L)|_{\Sigma_1}$.

Suppose $T + (V = L) \vdash \forall x \exists y\, \theta$ for a Δ_0 θ. Let $\lambda = |T + (V = L)|_{\Sigma_1}$ and $\xi < \lambda$. By Δ_0-Collection we obtain

$$T + (V = L) \vdash \forall \alpha \exists z \forall x \in L_{\alpha} \exists y \in z\, \theta \tag{6.28}$$

1. Show the existence of a Σ_1-sentence Ξ such that

$$T + (V = L) \vdash \Xi \tag{6.29}$$

   and $L_\xi \not\models \Xi$.
2. Show that

$$\forall \alpha < \lambda [L_\alpha \models \Xi \Rightarrow \alpha > \xi] \tag{6.30}$$

   for the Σ_1-sentence Ξ in Exercise 6.4.1.
3. Show that $T + (V = L) \vdash \exists z \exists \alpha [\Xi^{(L_\alpha)} \wedge \forall x \in L_\alpha \exists y \in z\, \theta(x, y)]$.
4. Conclude that $L_\lambda \models \forall x \in L_\xi \exists y \theta$.

6.5 Show that $(\Sigma^1_1\text{-AC})_0 + \Pi^{1-}_1-\text{CA}$ is Π^1_2-conservative over $\mathsf{ACA}_0 + \Pi^{1-}_1-\text{CA}$.

6.6

Definition 6.31 Let $<_\nu$ be an elementary recursive well-order of type as in the definitions of theories ID_ν in Sect. 6.1. For simplicity let us write $<$ for $<_\nu$ in this exercise. Let $\text{HJ}_\nu(X, Y) :\Leftrightarrow (Y)_0 = X \wedge \forall \gamma < \nu[\gamma > 0 \rightarrow (Y)_\gamma = W(\sum_{\delta<\gamma}(Y)_\delta)]$, where $W(Y)$ denotes the set of codes e of well-founded and Y-recursive trees $\{e\}^Y$. Then $\Pi^1_1\text{-CA}_\nu$ denotes the axiom $\forall X \exists Y\, \text{HJ}_\nu(X, Y)$. $(\Pi^1_1\text{-CA}_\nu)_0$ denotes an SOA obtained from EA^2 by adding the axiom $\Pi^1_1\text{-CA}_\nu$, and $(\Pi^1_1\text{-CA}_{<\nu})_0 := \bigcup_{\gamma<\nu}(\Pi^1_1\text{-CA}_\gamma)_0$. Cf. Exercise 6.7 for the transfinite induction axiom $\forall X\{Prg[<_\nu, X] \rightarrow \forall n\, X(n)\}$.

Show the followings.

1. $(\Sigma^1_2-\text{AC})_0$ proves $\Delta^1_2-\text{CA}$.
2. $(\Sigma^1_2-\text{DC})_0$ proves $\Sigma^1_2-\text{AC}$
3. $(\Sigma^1_2-\text{DC})_0 \vdash \Pi^1_1-\text{CA}_{<\omega^\omega}$, and $(\Sigma^1_2-\text{DC}) \vdash \Pi^1_1-\text{CA}_{<\varepsilon_0}$.
4. $(\Sigma^1_2\text{-AC})_0$ is Π^1_3-conservative over $(\Pi^1_1\text{-CA})_0$.
5. $(\Sigma^1_2\text{-DC})_0$ is Π^1_3-conservative over $(\Pi^1_1\text{-CA}_{<\omega^\omega})_0$.
6. $(\Sigma^1_2\text{-DC})$ is Π^1_3-conservative over $(\Pi^1_1\text{-CA}_{<\varepsilon})_0$.

6.7 $\mathsf{EA}^2 + \Pi^1_1\text{-CA}_\nu \vdash \text{TI}[<, X]$, where $<$ denotes an elementary recursive well-order of type ν, by which the axiom $\Pi^1_1\text{-CA}_\nu$ is defined.

6.8 The theory $\mathsf{ID}_\nu(W)$ is obtained from ID_ν by restricting the X-positive elementary formula $\mathscr{A}$ to an iteration of (6.15) for generating the class $(P_{\mathscr{W}})_b$ of codes of $P_{\mathscr{W}_{<b}}$-recursive well-founded trees for $b < \nu$. Let $\mathsf{ID}_{<\nu}(W) := \bigcup_{\mu<\nu} \mathsf{ID}_\mu(W)$

1. Show that ID_ν is interpreted in $\mathsf{ACA}_0 + \Pi^{1-}_1\text{-CA}_\nu$.
2. Show that $(\Pi^1_1\text{-CA}_{<\omega^\alpha})_0$ is proof-theoretical reducible to $\mathsf{ID}_{<\omega^\alpha}(W)$.
3. Conclude that $(\Pi^1_1\text{-CA}_{<\omega^\alpha})_0$ is proof-theoretically equivalent to $\mathsf{ID}_{<\omega^\alpha}$.

6.9

Definition 6.32 1. BI denotes the schema stating the fact: 'Let $T \subset {}^{<\omega}\omega$ be a well-founded tree(, which is a set). For a formula $B(s)$ in the language $\mathcal{L}_2$ of SOA, assume $\forall s \notin T\, B(s)$ and $\forall s[\forall x\, B(s * \langle x \rangle) \to B(s)]$. Then $B(\emptyset)$ holds for the empty sequence $\emptyset$'.
2. TI denotes the schema $\mathrm{WO}(<_X) \to \mathrm{TI}[<_X, B]$ for formulas B in the language $\mathcal{L}_2$, where $n <_X m :\Leftrightarrow \langle n, m \rangle \in X$.
3. $\forall^2 E(\Pi^1_0)$ denotes the schema $\forall X\, A(X) \to A(V)$ for first-order formula A and arbitrary abstract $V \equiv \{x\}B(x)$ with formulas B in $\mathcal{L}_2$.

Show the followings.

1. $\mathsf{RCA} + W\text{--CA} + \mathrm{BI}$ is interpreted in ID_1.
2. Show that the schema TI implies BI over ACA_0.
3. Show that the schema BI implies the full complete induction schema Π^2_0-IND over RCA_0.
4. Show that the schema BI implies $\forall^2 E(\Pi^1_0)$ over ACA_0.
5. Conclude that three schemata BI, TI and $\forall^2 E(\Pi^1_0)$ are mutually equivalent over ACA_0.

6.10 For positive operator $\mathcal{A}[X, n, b, Y]$, let $I^{\mathcal{A}}(Y, b) := \bigcap\{X : Cl^{\mathcal{A}}_{Y,b}(X)\}$, and $C^{\mathcal{A}}(Y, b) :\Leftrightarrow (Y)_b \subset I^{\mathcal{A}}(Y, b) \land Cl^{\mathcal{A}}_{Y,b}((Y)_b)$ with
$Cl^{\mathcal{A}}_{Y,b}(X) :\Leftrightarrow \mathcal{A}[X, b, Y] \subset X \Leftrightarrow \forall n\{\mathcal{A}[X, n, b, Y] \to n \in X\}$.
Show the followings are provable in $(\Pi^1_1\text{-CA}_{<\omega^{\alpha+1}}) + \mathrm{BI}$.

1. $\forall b \forall Y\, Cl^{\mathcal{A}}_{Y,b}(I^{\mathcal{A}}(Y, b))$ and $\exists Y\, C^{\mathcal{A}}(Y, 0)$.
2. $\forall n \exists Y \forall b \leq \omega^\alpha \cdot n\, C^{\mathcal{A}}(Y, b)$.
3. $\forall c < \omega^{\alpha+1} \forall Y, Z[\forall b < c(C^{\mathcal{A}}(Y, b) \land C^{\mathcal{A}}(Z, b)) \to Y_{<c} = Z_{<c}]$.
4. $\forall c < \omega^{\alpha+1} Cl^{\mathcal{A}}_{F^{\mathcal{A}}_{<c}, c}(F^{\mathcal{A}}_c)$ for $x \in F^{\mathcal{A}}_c :\Leftrightarrow \exists Y[\forall b \leq c\, C^{\mathcal{A}}(Y, b) \land x \in (Y)_c] \Leftrightarrow \forall Y[\forall b \leq c\, C^{\mathcal{A}}(Y, b) \to x \in (Y)_c]$.
5. $\forall c < \omega^{\alpha+1}[Cl^{\mathcal{A}}_{F^{\mathcal{A}}_{<c}, c}(B) \to F^{\mathcal{A}}_c \subset B]$ for any formula B.

Conclude that $\mathsf{ID}_{\omega^{\alpha+1}}$ is interpretable in $(\Pi^1_1\text{-CA}_{<\omega^{\alpha+1}}) + \mathrm{BI}$.

6.11 Show that $(\Pi^1_1\text{-CA}_\alpha) + \mathrm{BI}$ is proof-theoretically reducible to $\mathsf{ID}_{\alpha\cdot\omega}(W)$.
Conclude that $\mathsf{ID}_{\omega^{\alpha+1}}$ is proof-theoretically equivalent to $(\Pi^1_1\text{-CA}_{<\omega^{\alpha+1}}) + \mathrm{BI}$.

6.7 Notes

An ordinal analysis of impredicative theories is first obtained by Takeuti [33–35]. In [33] a notation system of ordinals is introduced, called ordinal diagrams (of finite order). The simplest system $O(2, 1)$ is essentially equivalent to the notation system $(T_\vartheta(\Omega), <)$ based on ϑ-function in Exercise 6.3, the latter is introduced in Rathjen and Weiermann [30]. Takeuti [34] shows a cut-elimination theorem of a second-order logic calculus obtained from $\boldsymbol{G}_2$ by adding the inference

$$\frac{\Gamma, \exists X\, A(X), A(V)}{\Gamma, \exists X\, A(X)}$$

where V is an arbitrary abstract as long as A is obtained from a first-order formula by replacing second-order variables by Σ^1_1-formulas. Takeuti [35] shows a cut-elimination theorem of a higher-order logic calculus in which a higher-order existential formula $\exists X\, A(X)$ can be inferred from $A(V)$ with arbitrary higher-order abstract V as long as no higher-order free variable occurs in $\exists X\, A(X)$. Note that $A(Y) \to \exists X\, A(X)$ is not provable in the calculus when A contains a higher-order free variable even for variables Y. It is easy to see that each of the cut-elimination theorem yields finitistically the 1-consistency of $\mathsf{ID}_{<\omega}$, or equivalently of $(\Pi^1_1\text{-CA})_0$. Takeuti's proof can be easily modified to a proof based on the well-foundedness of the system $O(\omega, 1)$ of ordinal diagrams, cf. [37]. Buchholz [9] again reveals the secret by showing that Takeuti's proof is closely related to Buchholz' proof with Ω_{n+1}-rule in Sect. 6.4.2, which is introduced in [6, 10]. In each proof the least fixed point is interpreted as a Π^1_1-formula.

In the Stanford report [20], subsystems of second-order arithmetics are set about investigating systematically, and the theories of positive inductive definitions are introduced. Actually I have not seen the report [20], but I heard that a large part of it is reproduced in [13] and Chap. 1 of [10]. For more on the proof-theoretic studies of theories ID_ν, see Buchholz, Feferman, Pohlers and Sieg [10], and Feferman [14]. Feferman [12] shows that $(\Pi^1_1\text{-CA})_0$ and related SOA's are proof-theoretically reducible to theories of iterated positive inductive definitions. For example $(\Pi^1_1\text{-CA})_0$ is reduced to $\mathsf{ID}_{<\omega}$. The reduction is significant in the sense that the impredicativity in defining sets by Π^1_1-formulas is resolved in the hierarchy $I_{\mathscr{A}} = \bigcup_{\alpha<\omega_1^{CK}} I^\alpha_{\mathscr{A}}$, in which each stage $I^\alpha_{\mathscr{A}}$ is defined from the previous stages $I^\beta_{\mathscr{A}}$ $(\beta < \alpha)$ predicatively. As in the cumulative hierarchy $V = \bigcup_\alpha V_\alpha$ of sets by power sets, and the constructible universe $L = \bigcup_\alpha L_\alpha$, the problem lies in the status of the whole class of (constructive) ordinals α.

Pohlers [10, 22, 23] introduces the method of the local predicativity for the hierarchy $I_{\mathscr{A}} = \bigcup_{\alpha<\omega_1^{CK}} I^\alpha_{\mathscr{A}}$, and obtains an ordinal analysis of ID_ν.

Buchholz [8] 'simplifies' the method, and introduces nowadays dominant method, operator controlled derivations in Sect. 6.4. An ordinal analysis of set theory for recursively inaccessible universes is obtained in [8]. Before that Jäger [18] shifts theories to be analyzed in ordinal analysis, from SOA's to set theories. The idea is based on a similarity between the hierarchies $I_{\mathscr{A}} = \bigcup_{\alpha<\omega_1^{CK}} I^\alpha_{\mathscr{A}}$ and $L_{\omega_1^{CK}} = \bigcup_{\alpha<\omega_1^{CK}} L_\alpha$ as seen in Sect. 6.5.

For more on ordinal analysis of theories below Δ^1_2-CA+BI, see (the English translation of the first half of) Rathjen's dissertation [28]. Also see survey articles by Rathjen [26, 27] and [2].

6.7.1 Section 6.2

Notation systems with ψ-functions is introduced in Buchholz [7], and Theorem 6.1 is due to Rathjen [25].

6.7.2 Section 6.3

The proof of Theorem 6.2 is took from Buchholz [5].

6.7.3 Section 6.4

Jäger [19] introduces and investigates the theory $\mathsf{ID}_1^{\mathbb{O}}$ in the name of $\mathsf{PA}\Omega$.

The set theory $\mathsf{KP}\omega$ can be interpreted in $\mathsf{ID}_1^{\mathbb{O}}$ using the structure theory for positive elementary inductive definitions in Moschovakis [21]. Here the Stage Comparison Theorem is a crux, which is easily seen to be provable in $\mathsf{ID}_1^{\mathbb{O}}$. Actually $\mathsf{KP}\omega$ is interpreted in ID_1 by Tapp [38], Sato [31] and Fujimoto [15]. For more on interpretations among $\mathsf{KP}\omega$, ID_1 and BI in Definition 6.32 of Exercise 6.9, see Sato [32].

The interpretation in Proposition 6.15 is took from [4]. Corollary 6.2 is found in [12], and Lemma 6.20 should be a folklore.

6.7.4 Section 6.5

We follow Buchholz [8] in this section.

6.7.5 Subsection 6.6.1

Theorem 6.10 for the case $\theta(x, y, U) \equiv (y \subset x)$ and $M_\alpha = V_\alpha$ is due to Rathjen [29].

6.7.6 Subsection 6.6.2

Theorem 6.12 is took from [3].

6.7.7 *Exercises 6.6.2.2*

Exercise 6.4 is due to Rathjen [24]. Exercise 6.6 is due to Friedman [16], and Cantini [11] by proof theory. Exercise 6.7 is due to Takeuti [1, 36]. Exercises 6.8, 6.9 and 6.10 are due to Feferman [10, 12]. For more on bar induction see Howard and Kreisel [17].

References

1. Arai, T.: A consistency proof of a system including Feferman's ID_ξ by Takeuti's reduction method. Tsukuba J. Math. **11**, 227–239 (1987)
2. Arai, T.: A sneak preview of proof theory of ordinals. Ann. Japan Assoc. Phil. Sci. **20**, 29–47 (2012)
3. Arai, T.: Conservation of first-order reflections. J. Symb. Logic **79**, 814–825 (2014)
4. Arai, T.: Proof-theoretic strengths of weak theories for positive inductive definitions. J. Symb. Logic **83**, 1091–1111 (2018)
5. Buchholz, W.: Normalfunktionen und konstruktive Systeme von Ordinalzahlen. In: Diller, J., Müller, G. H. (eds.) Proof Theory Symposion Keil 1974. Lecture Notes in Mathematics, vol. 500, pp. 4–25. Springer, Berlin (1975)
6. Buchholz, W.: Eine Erweiterung der Schnitteliminationsmethode. Habilitattionsschrift, München (1977)
7. Buchholz, W.: A new system of proof-theoretic ordinal functions. Ann. Pure Appl. Logic **32**, 195–208 (1986)
8. Buchholz, W.: A simplified version of local predicativity. In: Aczel, P.H.G., Simmons, H., Wainer, S.S. (eds.) Proof Theory, pp. 115–147. Cambridge University Press, Cambridge (1992)
9. Buchholz, W.: Explaining the Gentzen-Takeuti reduction steps: a second-order system. Arch. Math. Logic **40**, 255–272 (2001)
10. Buchholz, W., Feferman, S. Sieg, W., Pohlers, W.: Iterated Inductive Definitions and Subsystems of Analysis: Recent Proof-Theoretical Studies. Lecture Notes in Mathematics, vol. 897. Springer, Berlin (1981)
11. Cantini, A.: On the relationship between choice and comprehension principles in second order arithmetic. J. Symb. Logic **52**, 360–373 (1986)
12. Feferman, S.: Formal theories for transfinite iteration of generalized inductive definitions and some subsystems of analysis. In: Kino, A., Myhill, J., Vesley, R.E. (eds.), Intuitionism and Proof Theory, Proceedings of the Summer Conference at Buffalo, N. Y., 1968, pp. 303–325. North-Holland (1970)
13. Feferman, S.: Theories of finite type related to mathematical practice. In: Barwise, J. (ed.), Handbook of Mathematical Logic, pp. 913–971. North-Holland (1977)
14. Feferman, S.: The proof theory of classical and constructive inductive definitions. A forty years saga, 1968–2008. In: Schindler, R. (ed.), Ways of Proof Theory. Ontos Mathematical Logic, vol. 2, pp. 7–30. Ontos Verlag (2010)
15. Fujimoto, K.: Truths, inductive definitions, and Kripke-Platek systems over set theories. J. Symb. Logic **83**, 868–898 (2018)
16. Friedman, H.: Iterated inductive definitions and Σ^1_2-AC. In: Kino, A., Myhill, J., Vesley, R.E., (eds.), Intuitionism and Proof Theory, Proceedings of the Summer Conference at Buffalo, N. Y., 1968, pp. 435–442. North-Holland (1970)
17. Howard, W.A., Kreisel, G.: Transfinite induction and bar induction of type zero and one, and the role of continuity in intuitionistic analysis. J. Symb. Logic **31**, 325–358 (1966)
18. Jäger, G.: Zur Beweistheorie der Kripke-Platek Mengenlehre über den natürlichen Zahlen. Arch. Math. Logik Grundl. **22**, 121–139 (1982)

19. Jäger, G.: Fixed points in Peano arithmetic with ordinals. Ann. Pure Appl. Logic **60**, 119–132 (1993)
20. Kreisel, G., et. al.: Seminar on the Foundations of Analysis. (Mimeographed) Stanford (1963)
21. Moschovakis, Y.N.: Elementary Induction on Abstract Structures. North-Holland, Amsterdam (1974). reprinted from Dover Publications (2008)
22. Pohlers, W.: Cut-elimination for impredicative infinitary systems part I. Ordinal-analysis for ID_1. Arch. Math. Logik Grundl. **21**, 113–129 (1981)
23. Pohlers, W.: A short course in ordinal analysis. In: Aczel, P.H.G., Simmons, H., Wainer, S.S. (eds.), Proof Theory, pp. 27–78. Cambridge University Press, Cambridge (1992)
24. Rathjen, M.: Fragments of Kripke-Platek set theory with Infinity. In: Aczel, P.H.G., Simmons, H., Wainer, S.S., (eds.), Proof Theory, pp. 253–273. Cambridge University Press, Cambridge (1992)
25. Rathjen, M.: How to develop proof-theoretic ordinal functions on the basis of admissible ordinals. Math. Logic Quart. **39**, 47–54 (1993)
26. Rathjen, M.: The realm of ordinal analysis, In: Cooper, S.B., Truss, J.K., (eds.), Sets and Proofs. London Mathematical Society Lecture Notes, vol. 258, pp. 219–279. Cambridge University Press, Cambridge (1999)
27. Rathjen, M.: The art of ordinal analysis, In: International Congress of Mathematicians, vol. II, pp. 45–69. European Mathematical Society, Zürich (2006)
28. Rathjen, M.: Investigations of subsystems of second order arithmetic and set theory in strength between Π^1_1-CA and Δ^1_2-CA+BI: Part I. In: Schindler, R. (ed.), Ways of Proof Theory. Ontos Mathematical Logic, vol. 2, pp. 363–440. Ontos Verlag (2010)
29. Rathjen, M.: Relativized ordinal analysis: the case of power Kripke-Platek set theory. Ann. Pure Appl. Logic **165**, 316–339 (2014)
30. Rathjen, M., Weiermann, A.: Proof-theoretic investigations on Kruskal's theorem. Ann. Pure Appl. Logic **60**, 49–88 (1993)
31. Sato, K.: Full and hat inductive definitions are equivalent in NBG. Arch. Math. Logic **54**, 75–112 (2015)
32. Sato, K.: A new model construction by making a detour via intuitionistic theories IV: a closer connection between KPω and BI. submitted
33. Takeuti, G.: Ordinal diagrams. J. Math. Soc. Jpn. **9**, 386–394 (1957)
34. Takeuti, G.: On the fundamental conjecture of GLC V. J. Math. Soc. Jpn. **10**, 121–134 (1958)
35. Takeuti, G.: On the fundamental conjecture of GLC VI. Proc. Jpn. Acad. **37**, 440–443 (1961)
36. Takeuti, G.: On the inductive definition with quantifiers of second order. J. Math. Soc. Jpn. **13**, 333–341 (1961)
37. Takeuti, G.: Proof Theory, 2nd edn. North-Holland, Amsterdam (1987). reprinted from Dover Publications (2013)
38. Tapp, C.: Eine direkte Einbettung von $\mathsf{KP}\omega$ in ID_1. Diploma thesis, Westfälische Wilhelms-Universität Münster (1999)

Chapter 7
Answers to Exercises

Exercises of Chap. 2

2.2 We have $\boldsymbol{G}_2 \vdash \forall \mathbf{x}[F(\mathbf{x}) \leftrightarrow F(\mathbf{x})]$ for any F. Apply $(\exists^2_{1\text{st}})$.

2.3 Let Λ be a sequent consisting solely of prenex formulas. Define a *sequence* $\Lambda = \Lambda_0, \Lambda_1, \ldots$ by modifying the construction of a searching *tree* in Sect. 2.1.1. Replace 'literals' by 'quantifier-free formulas'. The **Leaf condition** here says that σ is a leaf when $Seq(\sigma) = \bigvee\{B \in \Gamma : B \text{ quantifier-free}\}$ is a propositional tautology. Apply the compactness theorem for the propositional logic when the search results in a fail.

2.4 Let Λ be a sequent which has no proof in Mints normal form. For simplicity assume that Λ contains an $\exists$. Modify the construction of the refutation tree $\mathcal{T}$ in Sect. 2.1.1 as follows.

Analyze a formula B only when the resulting inference is irreducible. For example, in the case $B \equiv \exists x A(x)$, let t be the first term such that $t \notin Term(\sigma; B)$ and $Var(t) \subset Var(Seq(\sigma))$ if such a term exists. Let $Term(\sigma * (0); B) = Term(\sigma; B) \cup \{t\}$. If the resulting inference with the minor formula $A(t)$ is irreducible, i.e., $\boldsymbol{G}_1 \nvdash \neg A(t)$, then analyze the formula B as in Sect. 2.1.1. Otherwise repeat with the last B in the ordering. When there is no term t with $Var(t) \subset Var(Seq(\sigma))$, repeat with the last B in the ordering.

This ends the description of the tree $\mathcal{T}$. We see that $Seq(\sigma) \subset Seq(\tau)$ and $Var(Seq(\sigma)) \subset Var(Seq(\tau))$ if $\sigma \subset \tau \in \mathcal{T}$, and $\dfrac{\{Seq(\sigma * (i)) : \sigma * (i) \in \mathcal{T}\}}{Seq(\sigma)}$ is either an irreducible inference rule in $\boldsymbol{G}_1$ or $Seq(\sigma) = Seq(\sigma * (i))$.

© The Editor(s) (if applicable) and The Author(s), under exclusive license to Springer Nature Singapore Pte Ltd. 2020

T. Arai, *Ordinal Analysis with an Introduction to Proof Theory*, Logic in Asia: Studia Logica Library, https://doi.org/10.1007/978-981-15-6459-8_7

As in Claim 2.1 we see that there exists an infinite path $\mathscr{P}$ through $\mathscr{T}$. [1] Pick such a path $\mathscr{P}$, and let $Seq^+(\mathscr{P}) = \bigcup\{Seq(\sigma) : \sigma \in \mathscr{P}\}$. If $\forall x A(x) \in Seq^+(\mathscr{P})$, then $\exists n \in \omega[A(a_n) \in Seq^+(\mathscr{P}) \vee \boldsymbol{G}_1 \vdash \neg A(a_n)]$, and similarly for $\vee, \wedge$.

Let $Term(\mathscr{P}) := Term(\mathscr{P}; B) := \bigcup\{Term(\sigma; B) : \sigma \in \mathscr{P}\}$, where $Term(\mathscr{P}; B) = Term(\mathscr{P}; C)$ for any existential formulas $B, C \in Seq^+(\mathscr{P})$. If $\exists x A(x) \in Seq^+(\mathscr{P})$, then $\forall t \in Term(\mathscr{P})[A(t) \in Seq^+(\mathscr{P}) \vee \boldsymbol{G}_1 \vdash \neg A(t)]$.

Now let $\mathscr{M}$ be a model such that its universe is $Term(\mathscr{P})$ and $\mathscr{M} \models L :\Leftrightarrow L \notin Seq^+(\mathscr{P})$ for literals L, cf. Remark 2.1. Conclude that $B \in Seq^+(\mathscr{P}) \Rightarrow \mathscr{M} \not\models B$ by *induction on* $\mathrm{dg}(B)$ and the soundness of the calculus $\boldsymbol{G}_1$.

2.5 Assume that $\mathsf{PA} \vdash \exists x B(x)$ for a Π^0_1-formula $B(x)$, but $\exists x B(x)$ is false. Let $\mathscr{A}_0$ consist solely of *purely universal* sentences and proves every true Σ_1-sentence logically, and A_0 denote the conjunction of formulas in $\mathscr{A}_0$. By Theorem 2.16 pick a logical proof of the sequent

$$\neg A_0, \neg\mathscr{A}_1, \exists x[A_0 \wedge B(x)] \tag{7.1}$$

in Mints normal form, where $\mathscr{A}_1$ denotes a (finite) set of universal closures of induction axioms with the assumption A_0 (the block $\forall \mathbf{a}$ binds the parameters in $\forall x A(x)$)

$$\forall x \forall \mathbf{a}[A_0 \wedge A(0) \wedge \forall y(A(y) \to A(y+1)) \to A(x)] \tag{7.2}$$

Consider inferences in such a proof beginning from the very last one deriving the sequent (7.1). Since $\boldsymbol{G}_1 \nvdash \neg A_0$, there must be an inference $(\exists)$ analyzing an existential quantifier $\exists x$ in $\exists x[A_0 \wedge B(x)]$ or in the negation $\neg\forall x$ of (7.2). On the other hand we have for any closed term t, $\boldsymbol{G}_1 \vdash A_0 \to \neg B(t)$ by the assumption and the Σ_1-completeness, and $\boldsymbol{G}_1 \vdash \forall \mathbf{a}[A_0 \wedge A(0) \wedge \forall y(A(y) \to A(y+1)) \to A(t)]$. Therefore the lowermost such inference would be reducible.

2.6 Argue in PA. For a sequent Λ let $\mathrm{dg}(\Lambda) := \max\{\mathrm{dg}(A) : A \in \Lambda\}$. Fix a natural number n, and let Λ be a sequent which has no proof in Mints normal form and $\mathrm{dg}(\Lambda) \leq n$. Let M be the model defined from a path $\mathscr{P}$ through the tree $\mathscr{T}$ constructed in Exercise 2.4. Let $M \models^n B$ denote the satisfaction relation restricted to formulas B with $\mathrm{dg}(B) \leq n$. Then $M \models^n B$ is arithmetical for *each* n. Conclude that $M \not\models^n \bigvee \Lambda$, and $\boldsymbol{G}_1 + (cut) \nvdash \Lambda$.

We have shown that $\mathsf{PA} \vdash Mnf(\bar{n})$ for each n, where $Mnf(x)$ denotes the statement that Mints normal form Theorem 2.16 restricted to sequents of degree $\leq x$.

Formalizing the above proof in $\mathrm{I}\Sigma_1$ we see $\mathrm{I}\Sigma_1 \vdash \forall x \mathrm{Pr}_{\mathsf{PA}}(\ulcorner Mnf(\dot{x})\urcorner)$. Finally observe that Mints normal form Theorem 2.16 is the statement in Π^0_3.

2.9

(1) Apply the Herbrand's Theorem 2.9 to $I\Sigma_0(\mathscr{E}^3) \vdash \exists x \exists z \forall y \forall u[A(x, y, c) \to B(z, u, c)]$.

[1] $\mathscr{T}$ is Δ^0_2 and the left-most path $\mathscr{P}$ is Δ^0_2 in $\mathscr{T}$. Hence $\mathscr{P}$ is Δ^0_3.

(2) Argue in $I\Sigma_0(\mathscr{E}^3)$. Suppose $\lim_{w\to\infty} f(c,w)=\ell$ for an $\ell=0,1$.
Since $\forall x\exists y A(x,y,c)\leftrightarrow \exists z\forall u B(z,u,c)$, we have either $\exists z\forall u B(z,u,c)$ or $\exists x\forall y\neg A(x,y,c)$.
First consider the case when $\exists z\forall u B(z,u,c)$. Then $\forall x\exists y A(x,y,c)$. Hence by (2.21) either $\forall b_0 B(s_0,b_0,c)$ or $\forall b_1 B(s_1(a_0,b_0),b_1,c)$ for some a_0,b_0 with $A(t_0,a_0,c)\wedge\neg B(s_0,b_0,c)$.
If $\forall b_0 B(s_0,b_0,c)$, then $f(c,w)=0$ for any $w\geq\max\{t_0,s_0,y_0\}$, where $y_0=\mu y.A(t_0,y.c)$. Therefore $\ell=0$. Moreover $f(c,w)=1$ for $w<\max\{t_0,s_0,y_0\}$.
Next assume $\forall b_1 B(s_1(a_0,b_0),b_1,c)$ for the minimal $a_0.b_0$ such that $A(t_0,a_0,c)\wedge\neg B(s_0,b_0,c)$. Then let a_1 denote the minimal a_1 such that $A(t_1(a_0,b_0),a_1,c)$. We have $f(c,w)=0$ for any $w\geq\max\{a_0,b_0,a_1\}$, and hence $\ell=0$.
Now consider $w<\max\{a_0,b_0,a_1\}$. Then $f(c,w)=0$ iff $\max\{t_0,s_0,a_0\}\leq w<b_0$. Therefore $\lambda w.f(c,w)$ changes its values at most three times, when $\max\{t_0,s_0,a_0\}<b_0<a_1$.
Next consider the case when $\exists x\forall y\neg A(x,y,c)$. We have $\forall z\exists u\neg B(z,u,c)$. Then $f(c,w)=1$ for any w if $\forall a_0\neg A(t_0,a_0,c)$, and $f(c,w)=1$ for any $w\geq\max\{b_0,b_1\}$ if $\forall a_1\neg A(t_1(a_0,b_0),a_1,c)$ for the minimal a_0,b_0,b_1 such that $A(t_0,a_0,c)$, $\neg B(s_0,b_0,c)$ and $\neg B(s_1(a_0,b_0),b_1,c)$. Therefore $\ell=1$.
Finally assume $\forall a_1\neg A(t_1(a_0,b_0),a_1,c)$, and consider $w<\max\{b_0,b_1\}$. Then $f(c,w)=0$ iff $\max\{t_0,s_0,a_0\}\leq w<b_0$. Therefore $\lambda w.f(c,w)$ changes its values at most two times in this case.
In any cases, (reduction) is shown, and $\lambda w.f(c,w)$ changes its values at most $1+2r(=3$ if $r=1)$ times for any c, i.e.,

$$\forall(w_0<w_1<\cdots<w_{1+2r})\exists i\leq 1+2r[f(c,w_i)=f(c,w_i+1)].$$

Hence (lowering) follows.
(3) Let r be as in (2.20). Define Σ^0_1-formulas $Y_k(c)$, $N_k(c)$ for $k\leq 1+2r$ by

$$\begin{aligned} Y_k(c) :\Leftrightarrow \exists(w_0<w_1<\cdots<w_{k-1})\forall i<k[f(c,w_i)\neq f(c,w_i+1)\\ \wedge f(c,w_{k-1})=0] \\ N_k(c) :\Leftrightarrow \exists(w_0<w_1<\cdots<w_{k-1})\forall i<k[f(c,w_i)\neq f(c,w_i+1)\\ \wedge f(c,w_{k-1})=1]] \end{aligned}$$

for $k>0$, and $Y_0(c):\Leftrightarrow f(c,0)=0$, $N_0(c):\Leftrightarrow f(c,0)=1$. Also put $N_{2r+2}(c):\Leftrightarrow 0=1$.
Then $I\Sigma_0(\mathscr{E}^3)$ proves that $\exists z\forall u B(z,u,c)\leftrightarrow\bigvee\{Y_k(c)\wedge\neg N_{k+1}(c):k\leq 1+2r\}$ for the boolean combination $\bigvee\{Y_k(c)\wedge\neg N_{k+1}(c):k\leq 1+2r\}$ of Σ^0_1-formulas.

2.10 Assume that $T\vdash\exists y\exists x(\neg A_0(y,x)\wedge X(x))\vee\exists z(\overline{X}(z)\wedge\neg B(z)),\Gamma$. Then $\mathbf{G}_1\vdash\exists y\exists x(\neg A_0(y,x)\wedge X(x)),\exists z(\overline{X}(z)\wedge\neg B(z)),\Gamma,\Delta_T(X)$, where $\Delta_T(X)$ consists of the negations of some axioms in T. By using the universal closures

$\forall y[C(y) \to C(\varepsilon x.C(x))]$ of the epsilon axioms (2.15), we obtain $G_{1\varepsilon} \vdash \exists y \exists x(\neg A_0(y, x) \wedge X(x)), \exists z(\overline{X}(z) \wedge \neg B(z)), \Gamma_\varepsilon, \Delta_{T\varepsilon}(X)$, where Γ_ε $[\Delta_{T\varepsilon}(X)]$ is equivalent to Γ $[\Delta_T(X)]$ over the epsilon axioms, resp. Γ_ε nor $\Delta_{T\varepsilon}(X)$ contains no quantifiers $\exists, \forall$.

By Herbrand's Theorem 2.8 there are some terms $t_0, \ldots, t_r$ such that $G_{1\varepsilon} \vdash \bigvee\{\exists x(\neg A_0(t_i, x) \wedge X(x)) : i \leq r\}, \exists z(\overline{X}(z) \wedge \neg B(z)), \Gamma_\varepsilon, \Delta_{T\varepsilon}(X)$. Substitute the quantifier-free formula $A'(x) \equiv \bigwedge\{A_0(t_i, x) : i \leq r\}$ for the variable X. From $T \vdash \Gamma, \forall x(A(x) \vee B(x))$, we obtain $G_{1\varepsilon} \vdash \Gamma, \Gamma_\varepsilon, \Delta_{T\varepsilon}(A')$, and $G_{1\varepsilon} \vdash \Gamma, \Delta_T(A')$ by going back to formulas with quantifiers. From $T \vdash \neg \bigvee \Delta_T(A')$, we obtain $T_\varepsilon \vdash \Gamma$ where T_ε is the union of T and the universal closures of the epsilon axioms. We conclude $T \vdash \Gamma$ from the second epsilon Theorem 2.11.

2.11 For Π_1^0-sentences A, B, $S + \mathrm{RFN}_{\Sigma_1^0}(T)$ proves that $\Pr_T(\ulcorner A \to B \urcorner) \to A \to B$. From this we see that $\mathrm{Con}^{(m)}(T)$ follows from $\mathrm{RFN}_{\Sigma_1^0}(T)$ over S by metainduction on $m < \omega$.

Suppose $S \vdash \forall p, n \exists x\, (\mathrm{Prv}_T(p, \ulcorner \exists x\, A(\dot{n}, x) \urcorner) \to A(n, x)) \to B(y)$ for quantifier-free formulas $A(n, x)$, $B(y)$. By Herbrand's Theorem 2.9 pick terms p_i, n_i and distinct variables $x_i \not\equiv y$ such that $\bigwedge_{i<m} C_i \to B(y)$ is provable in S and $FV(p_i, n_i) \subset \{y\} \cup \{x_j : j < i\} \cup \bigvee_{j<i} FV(p_j, n_j)$, where $C_i :\equiv (\mathrm{Prf}_T(p_i, \ulcorner \exists x\, A(\dot{n}_i, x) \urcorner) \to A(n_i, x_i))$. Argue in S. We have $\neg B(y) \wedge \bigwedge_{i<m-1} C_i \to \mathrm{Prf}_T(p_{m-1}, \ulcorner \exists x\, A(\dot{n}_{m-1}, x) \urcorner) \wedge \neg A(n_{m-1}, x_{m-1})$. We obtain $\neg B(y) \wedge \bigwedge_{i<m-1} C_i \to \neg \exists x\, A(n_{m-1}, x)$ for the variable $x_{m-1} \notin \bigcup_{i<m} FV(p_i, n_i) \cup \{x_j : j < m-1\} \cup \{y\}$. Hence $\neg B(y) \wedge \bigwedge_{i<m-1} C_i \to \Pr_T(\ulcorner \neg \exists x\, A(\dot{n}_{m-1}, x) \urcorner)$ for quantifier-free B, C_i. On the other hand we have $\neg B(y) \wedge \bigwedge_{i<m-1} C_i \to \Pr_T(\ulcorner \exists x\, A(\dot{n}_{m-1}, x) \urcorner)$. Therefore $\neg B(y) \wedge \bigwedge_{i<m-1} C_i \to \neg \mathrm{Con}^{(1)}(T)$, i.e., $S + \mathrm{Con}^{(1)}(T) \vdash \bigwedge_{i<m-1} C_i \to B(y)$. In this way we see inductively that $S + \mathrm{Con}^{(\ell)}(T) \vdash \bigwedge_{i<m-\ell} C_i \to B(y)$ for each $\ell \leq m$. Consequently we obtain $S + \mathrm{Con}^{(m)}(T) \vdash B(y)$.

2.12 First show that $T \vdash \forall x, y \exists z(x, y \prec z)$ and $T \vdash \forall x \exists w \forall y \prec x \forall z \prec y(z \prec w)$. From these we see that $T \vdash \exists y \exists w\, C \leftrightarrow \exists u \exists y \prec u \exists w \prec u\, C$, and that $\Sigma_1^{\prec}$-Col is equivalent to the collection schema $\Delta_0^{\prec}$-Col for $\Delta_0^{\prec}$-formulas B.

Assume that $T + (\Sigma_1^{\prec}\text{–Col}) \vdash \forall x \exists y\, C(x, y)$ with $C \in \Sigma_1^{\prec}$. We can assume that $C \in \Delta_0^{\prec}$. Then $G^{\prec} + (\Delta_0^{\prec}\text{–Col}) \vdash \Gamma_0, \exists y\, C(a, y)$, where Γ_0 is a finite set of negations of axioms in T, and $G^{\prec} + (\Delta_0^{\prec}\text{–Col})$ is obtained from $G^{\prec}$ by adding the following inference rule for the $\Delta_0^{\prec}$-collection schema:

$$\frac{\Gamma, b \not\prec s, \exists y\, B(b, y) \quad \exists x \prec s \forall y \prec d \neg B(x, y), \Gamma}{\Gamma} \; (\Delta_0^{\prec}\text{–Col})$$

for terms s, eigenvariables b, d and $B \in \Delta_0^{\prec}$.

Each sequent in the cut-free proof of $\Gamma_0, \exists y C(a, y)$ is of the form Γ_0, Δ, with $\Delta \subset \Delta_0^{\prec} \cup \Sigma_1^{\prec}$. As in the proof of Theorem 2.12, show by induction on the depth of cut-free proofs that there exists a term t such that $FVar(t) \subset FVar(\Gamma_0 \cup \Delta)$ and $T \vdash \Gamma_0, \Delta^t$.

2.14 Let $B(z) \equiv \forall y \exists x\, C(y, x, z)$ be a Π_2^0-formula. For simplicity let us suppress the parameters. Assume that $I\Delta_0(PR) \vdash B(0)$ and $I\Delta_0(PR) \vdash \forall z(B(z) \to B(z+1))$.

By Herbrand's Theorem 2.8 we can find a primitive recursive function g such that $I\Delta_0(PR) \vdash \forall y\, C(y, g(y), 0)$. Moreover by Herbrand's Theorem 2.9, there are terms $t_i = t_i(y_0, \ldots, y_{i-1}, y, z)$ and $s_i = s_i(y_0, \ldots, y_{i-1}, y, z)$ such that $I\Delta_0(PR)$ proves $\bigvee\{\neg C(t_i(y_0, \ldots, y_{i-1}, y, z), y_i, z), C(y, s_i(y_0, \ldots, y_{i-1}, y, z), z+1) : i \leq r\}$, where $Var(t_i(y_0, \ldots, y_{i-1}, y, z), s_i(y_0, \ldots, y_{i-1}, y, z)) \subset \{y_0, \ldots, y_{i-1}, y, z\}$. Let us define a function $f(y, z)$. First let $f(y, 0) = g(y)$. Next Y_i $(i < r)$ is defined recursively by $Y_i :\equiv f(t_i(Y_0, \ldots, Y_{i-1}, y, z), z)$, and
$C_i :\equiv C(y, s_i(Y_0, \ldots, Y_{i-1}, y, z), z+1) \wedge \bigwedge_{j<i} \neg C(y, s_j(Y_0, \ldots, Y_{j-1}, y, z), z+1)$. Then let

$$f(y, z+1) = \begin{cases} s_0(y, z) & \text{if } C_0 \\ s_1(Y_0, y, z) & \text{if } C_1 \\ \vdots & \vdots \\ s_r(Y_0, \ldots, Y_{r-1}, y, z) & \text{otherwise} \end{cases}$$

Show that $I\Sigma_1(PR) \vdash \forall z \forall y\, C(y, f(y, z), z)$ by induction on z, and conclude that $I\Delta_0(PR) \vdash \forall z \forall y\, C(y, f(y, z), z)$ from Theorem 2.14.

2.16 This is seen as in Theorem 2.12.

2.17 Consider the theory $I\Sigma_1(\mathsf{g})$ in a language of arithmetic with the function symbol g. Suppose $f \in Fnc_{\Sigma_1}(I\Sigma_1 + A^+)$, and let C be a Σ^0_1-formula which defines f in $I\Sigma_1 + A^+$. Then $I\Sigma_1 + A^+ \vdash \forall x \exists! y\, C$, and hence $I\Sigma_1(\mathsf{g}) \vdash \forall x[\exists y\, C \vee \exists u \neg A(u, \mathsf{g}(u))]$. Then from Theorem 2.14 we see that there exists a function F primitive recursive in g such that either $C(x, F(x))$ or $\neg A(F(x), g(F(x)))$ for any x. Since $A(u, g(u))$ is true for any u, we obtain $C(x, F(x))$. This means that $f = F$ is primitive recursive in g.

Exercises of Chap. 3

3.1

1 No formula $t \notin N$ is a major formula of an inference, cf. Remark 3.1.
3 By induction on k. Consider the case when Δ is a lowersequent of an inference other than (cut). Its uppersequents are N-positive. By IH we can assume that the inference is an (S) for an $m < k$:

$$\frac{(N) \vdash^m_0 \Gamma, t \in N, S(t) \in N}{(N) \vdash^k_0 \Gamma, S(t) \in N}\ (S)$$

Under an assignment of free variables, we have, by IH, that one of Γ, $t \in N$ and $S(t) \in N$ holds in $\mathbb{N}_{1+m}$. We can assume that $t \in N$ holds in $\mathbb{N}_{1+m}$ by Exercise 3.1.2. Therefore $S(t) \in N$ holds in $\mathbb{N}_{1+k}$ by $k > m$.
5 By induction on n.
6 Cf. *Proof* of Theorem 4.17.

7 Assume the hypothesis Hyp$^+$ and let $k = n + m$. We show $A_n(f^{(m)}(0))$ by induction on $m \le k$.
Exercise 3.1.6 yields the case $m = 0$. Assume $m > 0$. Then $f^{(m)}(0) \equiv f(0, f^{(m-1)}(0))$. Therefore $A_n(f^{(m)}(0))$ follows from (3.7), $A_n(0)$, and IH, $A_{n+1}(f^{(m-1)}(0))$.

3.3

2 This is seen as in Lemma 3.21 using Exercise 3.3.1.
3 Let $\boldsymbol{G}_{2\varepsilon} \vdash \Gamma_0$. Deleting inferences $(\forall)$ from the given $\boldsymbol{G}_{2\varepsilon}$-proof of Γ_0, we obtain a $\boldsymbol{G}_{2\varepsilon}(\forall)^-$-proof of Φ, Γ_0, where $\Phi = \{\exists x\, A_i(x) \land \neg A_i(a_i) : i < k\}$ such that the free variable a_i does not occur in $\exists x\, A_j(x) \land \neg A_j(a_j)$ for any $j < i$. Exercise 3.3.2 yields a $\boldsymbol{G}_{2\varepsilon}$-proof of a $\lor$-expansion Φ', Γ'_0 of Φ, Γ_0, in which neither $(\forall)$ nor (2ε) occurs. Substitute a relation constant for every second-order ε-predicate to get a proof of $\widehat{\Phi}, \widehat{\Gamma_0}$. $\widehat{\Phi}, \widehat{\Gamma_0}$ is a $\lor$-expansion of Φ, Γ_0, and $\widehat{\Gamma_0}$ is ε-free.
This means that each formula in $\widehat{\Phi}$ is of the form $\exists x\, A_{in}(x) \land \neg A_{in}(a_{in})$, which is ε-free and obtained from $\exists x\, A_i(x) \land \neg A_i(a_i)$ in Φ by renaming the free variable a_i by a fresh one a_{in}, and substituting relation constants and variables for second-order ε-predicates. In particular the free variable a_{in} does not occur in $\exists x\, A_{jm}(x) \land \neg A_{jm}(a_{jm})$ for any $j < i$ and any n, m.
First bind existentially the free variables a_{jm} occurring in $\widehat{\Gamma_0}$ to get a $\lor$-expansion $\tilde{\Gamma_0}$ of Γ_0, and then bind universally the free variables $a_{(k-1)n}$, and then binding $a_{(k-2)m}$, and so on, we obtain $\boldsymbol{G}_1 \vdash A_0, \ldots, A_{k-1}, \tilde{\Gamma_0}$ for $A_i \equiv \{\forall y_{in}(\exists x\, A_{in}(x) \land \neg A_{in}(y_{in}))\}_n$. On the other hand we have $\boldsymbol{G}_1 \vdash \exists y_{in}(\exists x\, A_{in}(x) \to A_{in}(y_{in}))$ for each i and n. Namely $\boldsymbol{G}_1 \vdash \neg\forall y_{in}(\exists x\, A_{in}(x) \land \neg A_{in}(y_{in}))$. Finally a series of (cut)'s yields $\boldsymbol{G}_1 + (cut) \vdash \tilde{\Gamma_0}$.

3.4 Let $\boldsymbol{G}_{2\varepsilon A}$ be the second-order ε-calculus obtained from $\boldsymbol{G}_{2\varepsilon}$ by expanding 'predicates' to second-order terms. The inference (AC) is a derived rule in $\boldsymbol{G}_{2\varepsilon A}$ since if both of $\Gamma, \exists Y\, C(x, Y)$ and $\exists x \neg C(x, (Z)_x), \Gamma$ is provable in $\boldsymbol{G}_{2\varepsilon A}$, then by substituting $V :\equiv \{(y_1, \ldots, y_n, x)\}(\varepsilon Y.C(x, Y))(y_1, \ldots, y_n)$ for the eigenvariable Z, we obtain a proof of $\exists x \neg C(x, (V)_x), \Gamma$, where $\exists x \neg C(x, (V)_x) \equiv \exists x \neg C(x, \varepsilon Y.C(x, Y))$.

Suppose $F_A + \boldsymbol{G}'_{2at}(\mathrm{AC})$ proves $\exists Y\, B(Y)$. Then $\boldsymbol{G}_{2\varepsilon A}$ proves $\Gamma, B(\varepsilon Y.B)$, where Γ is a set of negations of universal closures of formulas $A(t, V, F_A(V))$, which is ε-free. Theorem 3.12 in the previous exercise yields a $\boldsymbol{G}_1$-proof of an ε-free $\lor$-expansion $\Gamma \cup \{\exists B(W_i) : i < p\}$.

Exercises of Chap. 4

4.1 First consider Theorem 4.16.1. Show by *metainduction* on k that for $\Pi_0(U)$-formulas A, $I\Sigma_0(U) \vdash Prg[<, A] \to \forall\alpha < \omega \cdot k\, A(\alpha)$, where $\omega \cdot 0 := 0$, and $\omega(k + 1) := \omega \cdot k + \omega$.

Suppose that $I\Sigma_0(U)$ proves $Prg[<, A] \to \forall\alpha < \omega \cdot k\, A(\alpha)$ for any $\Pi_0(U)$-formula A as IH. For a $\Pi_0(U)$-formula A, assume $Prg[<, A]$. For the $\Pi_0(U)$-formula $B(n) :\Leftrightarrow A(\omega \cdot k + \omega^0 \cdot n)$, we see $B(0)$ and $\forall n(B(n) \to B(n+1))$ from $Prg[<, A]$ and $\forall\alpha \leq \omega \cdot k\, A(\alpha)$. Hence $I\Sigma_0(U)$ proves $\forall n\, B(n)$, i.e., $\forall n\, A(\omega \cdot k + \omega^0 \cdot n)$, and $\forall\alpha < \omega \cdot (k+1)\, A(\alpha)$.

Theorem 4.16.2 is seen by inspection of the proof of Theorem 4.1.1. Show by metainduction on $n - m \in \omega$ that for $n > 0$, $m \leq n$ and $\Pi_{m+1}(U)$-formulas A $I\Sigma_n(U) \vdash Prg[<, A] \to \forall\alpha < \omega_{n-m}(k)A(\alpha)$ for *each* k.

Claim 4.1 holds for $\Pi_n(U)$-formulas A and $I\Sigma_n(U)$ since $B(n) \equiv (\forall\gamma < \beta + \omega^\delta \cdot n\, A(\gamma))$ is $\Pi_n(U)$-formula and $I\Pi_n(U) = I\Sigma_n(U)$.

4.2 By Theorem 4.16.2 in Exercise 4.1 we have $I\Sigma_n \vdash \mathrm{TI}[<_\alpha, \Pi_1]$ for each $\alpha < \omega_{n+1}$.

4.3 Argue in $I\Sigma_n(U)$.

1 Let A be a $\Pi_n(U)$-formula. Assume that $Prg[<^1, A]$ and $\forall\delta <^1 \alpha\, \mathrm{i}[A](\delta)$. Assuming $A(\beta)$, show $A(\beta + \omega^\alpha)$ using the facts $\gamma <^1 \beta + \omega^0 = \beta + 1 \Leftrightarrow \gamma = \beta$, $\gamma <^1 \beta + \omega^{\delta+1} \Leftrightarrow \exists n \in \omega(\gamma = \beta + \omega^\delta \cdot n)$ and $\gamma <^1 \beta + \omega^\lambda \Leftrightarrow \exists\delta <^1 \lambda \exists n \in \omega(\gamma = \beta + \omega^\delta \cdot n)$ for limit λ. Note that $B(n) :\Leftrightarrow A(\beta + \omega^\delta \cdot n)$ is a Π_n-formula.

2 Suppose $Prg[<^1, A]$ for a $\Pi_m(U)$-formula A. We see inductively that $Prg[<^1, A^{(1)}], \ldots, Prg[<^1, A^{(n+1-m)}]$ by Exercise 4.3.1, where $A^{(0)} = A$, and $A^{(k+1)} = \mathrm{i}[A^{(k)}]$. Note that $A^{(k)}$ is a $\Pi_{m+k}(U)$-formula. We obtain $A^{(n+1-m)}(0), \ldots, A^{(0)}(0)$.

Fix a positive integer k arbitrarily. Show that $\forall\alpha < \omega_{n_0}(\omega^0 \cdot k)\, A^{(n+1-m-n_0)}(\alpha)$ by metainduction on $n_0 \leq n + 1 - m$. Theorem 4.17 then follows from the case $n_0 = n + 1 - m$. The case $n_0 = 0$ is seen from $Prg[<^1, A^{(n+1-m)}]$ and $A^{(n+1-m)}(0)$.

Suppose $\forall\beta < \omega_{n_0}(\omega^0 \cdot k)\, A^{(n+1-m-n_0)}(\beta)$ for $n_0 < n + 1 - m$. Each $\alpha < \omega_{n_0+1}(\omega^0 \cdot k) = \omega^{\omega_{n_0}(\omega^0 \cdot k)}$ is written $\alpha = \omega^{\beta_0} p_0 + \cdots + \omega^{\beta_l} p_l$ for some positive integers $p_0, \ldots, p_l$ and $\beta_l < \cdots < \beta_0 < \omega_{n_0}(\omega^0 \cdot k)$. By IH we have $A^{(n+1-m-n_0)}(\beta_i)$, i.e., $\mathrm{i}[A^{(n-m-n_0)}](\beta_i)$ for $i \leq l$. For $0 \leq h \leq l+1$, let $\alpha_h = \omega^{\beta_0} p_0 + \cdots + \omega^{\beta_{h-1}} p_{h-1}$. For $h \leq l$, we see $A^{(n-m-n_0)}(\alpha_h) \to \forall p\, A^{(n-m-n_0)}(\alpha_h + \omega^{\beta_h} p)$ by induction on p applied to a $\Pi_{n-m-n_0}(U)$-formula $B(p) :\Leftrightarrow A^{(n-m-n_0)}(\alpha_h + \omega^{\beta_h} p)$. Hence by induction on h applied to another $\Pi_{n-m-n_0}(U)$-formula, we obtain $\forall h \leq l+1\, A^{(n-m-n_0)}(\alpha_h)$ from $A^{(n-m-n_0)}(0)$. Therefore $\forall\alpha < \omega_{n_0+1}(\omega^0 \cdot k)\, A^{(n-m-n_0)}(\alpha)$.

4.4 First show the following Embedding lemma for fragments, cf. Lemma 4.4.

1. Assume $I\Sigma_0(U) \vdash \Gamma(\mathbf{a})$. Then there exist $k, m, c < \omega$ such that for any $\mathbf{n}$, $\vdash^{\omega k+m}_{c} \Gamma(\mathbf{n})$ holds.
2. Assume $I\Sigma_n(U) \vdash \Gamma(\mathbf{a})$ for $n > 0$. Then there exist $k, m < \omega$ such that for any $\mathbf{n}$, $\vdash^{\omega k+m}_{\omega+n} \Gamma(\mathbf{n})$ holds.

Then show the following for fragments, cf. Lemma 4.5 using the facts $\alpha < \omega^2\ \&\ c < \omega \Rightarrow c\alpha < \omega^2$, and $\alpha < \omega^2 \Rightarrow \omega \cdot 2_n(\alpha) < 2_n(\omega^2) = \omega_{n+1} = \omega_{n+1}(1)$ for $n > 0$:

Let $\Gamma(\mathbf{a})$ be a sequent in which no free variable other than the variables $\mathbf{a}$ occurs. Assume $I\Sigma_n(U) \vdash \Gamma(\mathbf{a})$ for an $n \geq 0$. Then there exists an $\alpha < 2_n(\omega^2)$ such that $\forall \mathbf{m}\{\vdash_1^\alpha \Gamma(\mathbf{m})\}$.

4.5 This follows from Exercise 4.4 Note that (4.11) is provable in $I\Sigma_0(U)$, and $I\Sigma_n(U) \vdash \mathrm{TI}[\prec, U] \Rightarrow I\Sigma_{n+1}(U) \vdash \mathrm{TI}[\prec, U^*]$, cf. *Proof* of Theorem 4.2. The latter is seen as follows. Since $I\Sigma_1(U)$ proves the Σ_1-collection schema, each $\Sigma_n(U^*)$-formula is equivalent to a $\Sigma_{n+1}(U)$-formula over $I\Sigma_1(U)$. Hence $I\Sigma_n(U^*) \subset I\Sigma_{n+1}(U)$ for $n > 0$. Moreover we have $I\Sigma_0(U^*) \subset I\Sigma_1(U)$, cf. Lemma 2.14 in p.65 of [1].

4.8 The easy half is seen from Proposition 4.1. For the other direction suppose that $\mathsf{PA} + \mathrm{TI}(< \Lambda)$ proves the formula $\neg A^-(c) \to A^+(c)$, where $A^-(c) \equiv \exists x \forall y \neg A(x, y, c)$ and $A^+(c) \equiv \exists z \forall u\, B(z, u, c)$ with quantifier-free A, B. Then $\mathsf{PA} + \mathrm{TI}(< \Lambda)$ proves the Σ_2^0-formula $\exists x \forall y\, C(x, y, c) \leftrightarrow \exists x \forall y[\neg A((x)_0, (y)_0, c) \lor B((x)_1, (y)_1, c)]$ with an elementary recursive predicate C. As in Sect. 4.2.3, define a tracing function $\{\sigma(c, w)\}_w$. In upper sequents of a $(\forall\omega)$, go through the upper sequents as long as $C(x_a, y_a, \bar{c})$ is true. Now let us define a primitive recursive function f as follows. $f(c, 0) = 1$. Alternate values $f(c, w+1) = 1 - f(c, w)$ if $Seq_c(\sigma(c, w+1))$ is an upper sequent of an inference other than $(\forall\omega)$. Suppose $Seq_c(\sigma(c, w+1))$ is the n-th upper sequent of a $(\forall\omega)$, and $\sigma(c, w+1) = b * \langle n\rangle$. $f(c, w+1) = 0$ iff $A(x_b, (n)_0, \bar{c}) \to B(z_b, (n)_1, \bar{c})$ is true and $\exists k \leq n\, A(x_b, (\bar{k})_0, \bar{c})$ holds. Namely $f(c, w+1) = 0 \Leftrightarrow [A(x_b, (n)_0, \bar{c}) \to B(z_b, (n)_1, \bar{c})] \,\&\, \exists k \leq n\, A(x_b, (\bar{k})_0, \bar{c})$.

Suppose $\sigma(c, w)$ is on a $(\forall\omega)$. Until a witness k such that $A(x_b, (\bar{k})_0, \bar{c})$ is found, $f(c, w) = 1\, (w < k)$. After a witness k has been found, $f(c, w) = 0\, (w \geq k)$ as long as $A(x_b, (\bar{n})_0, \bar{c}) \to B(z_b, (\bar{n})_1, \bar{c})$ is true.

Therefore if the tracing function $\sigma(c, w)$ goes through the upper sequents of the $(\forall\omega)$, then either $\lim_{w\to\infty} f(c, w) = 1$ and $\forall y \neg A(x_b, y, \bar{c})$, or $\lim_{w\to\infty} f(c, w) = 0$ and $\forall u B(z_b, u, \bar{c})$. The function f is seen to enjoy the conditions (reduction), and $f(c, u)$ changes the values at most twice in the upper sequents of a $(\forall\omega)$.

Now define h as follows. $h(c, 0) = 3 \cdot ord_c(\emptyset)$. In what follows put $a = \sigma(c, w+1)$ and let $Seq_c(a)$ be an upper sequent of an inference $Rule_c(b)$ with $a = b * \langle n\rangle$.

1. The case when $Rule_c(b)$ is an inference rule other than $(\forall\omega)$: $h(c, w+1) := 3 \cdot ord_c(\sigma(c, w+1))$.
2. The case when $n = 0$ and $Rule_c(b) = (\forall\omega)$: $h(c, w+1) := 3 \cdot ord_c(\sigma(c, w+1)) + 2$.
3. The case when $n > 0$, $Rule_c(b) = (\forall\omega)$: If $f(c, w+1) = f(c, w)$, then let $h(c, w+1) := h(c, w)$, where $\sigma(c, w+1) = \sigma(c, w) \oplus 1$.
   If $f(c, w) = 1 \,\&\, f(c, w+1) = 0$, then $\sigma(c, w+1) = \sigma(c, w) \oplus 1$ and $n = \min\{k : A(x_b, (\bar{k})_0, \bar{c})\}$. Let $h(c, w+1) := 3 \cdot ord_c(\sigma(c, w+1)) + 1$.
   If $f(c, w) = 0 \,\&\, f(c, w+1) = 1$, then $A(x_b, (\bar{n})_0, \bar{c}) \to B(z_b, (\bar{n})_1, \bar{c})$ is false and $\sigma(c, w+2) = \sigma(c, w+1) * \langle 0\rangle$. Let $h(c, w+1) := 3 \cdot ord_c(\sigma(c, w+1))$.

Then f and h is seen to enjoy (weakly descending) and (lowering).

4.9 These are seen as in Theorem 4.1. In proving the consistency of the fragment $I\Sigma_n(\mathcal{E}^3_*)$, restrict proofs to ones in which every formula is in $\Sigma_n(\mathcal{E}^3_*) \cup \Pi_n(\mathcal{E}^3_*)$.

4.12 This is seen as in Theorem 4.11. Specifically let $C_0(\alpha)$ be defined for $\alpha < \omega^\omega$ by $C_0(0) = 0$ and $C_0(\omega^{x_1} i_1 + \omega^{x_2} i_2 + \cdots + \omega^{x_\ell} i_\ell) = \max\{i_p : 1 \leq p \leq \ell\}$. For $k \geq 2$, let $C_{0k} := \{\alpha < \omega^\omega : C_0(\alpha) < k\}$. It is clear that $\forall \alpha, \beta \in C_{0k}[\alpha < \beta \leftrightarrow G_k(\alpha) < G_k(\beta)]$. Let $P_{0k}\alpha = \max\{\beta < \alpha : \beta \in C_{0k}\}$ for $\alpha < \omega^\omega$. Then for the flat Goodstein sequence $\{y_k\}_k$ of y, we obtain $y_k = G_{2+k} P_{2+k} \cdots P_3 \alpha$ for $G_2 \alpha = y$, i.e., $\alpha = \omega^{x_1} + \cdots + \omega^{x_n}$ when $y = 2^{x_1} + \cdots + 2^{x_n}$ with $x_1 > \cdots > x_n \geq 0$. Thus it suffices to show that the statement $\forall \alpha \in C_{02} \exists k \geq 2[P_{2+k} P_{2+k-1} \cdots P_3 \alpha = 0]$ is independent from $I\Sigma_1$. We see as in Theorem 4.12 that the statement implies the fact that there is no primitive recursive and infinite descending chain $\{\delta_i\}_i$ of ordinals $\delta_i < \omega^\omega$ such that $C_0(\delta_i) \leq 1 + i$. The latter fact yields $\mathcal{E}^\omega DS_{\omega^\omega}$ as follows, cf. Theorem 4.10. Let $\omega^\omega > \alpha_0 > \alpha_1 > \cdots$ be a primitive recursive descending chain of ordinal terms α_k. Consider the primitive recursive function $f_{C_0}(k) = C_0(\alpha_{k+1})$. We have $C_0(g_n(k_1, x)) \leq \max\{k_1 + 1, x\}$ for the function $g_n : \mathbb{N}^2 \to \omega^{n+1}$ in (4.21). Let $j : \mathbb{N}^2 \to \omega^n$ be primitive recursive function such that $x < C_0(\alpha_{k+1}) \Rightarrow j(k, x+1) < j(k, x), C_0(j(k, x)) \leq \max\{k+1, x\}$. For $i \geq \ell_0 = C_0(\alpha_0)$, let k, x be numbers such that $i = C_0(\alpha_0) + \cdots + C_0(\alpha_k) + x$ and $x < C_0(\alpha_{k+1})$. Then set $\delta_i = \omega^n \alpha_k + j(k, x)$. Note here that $C_0(\alpha_k) > 0$ for $\alpha_k > 0$. Let N be a number such that $\omega^{N - \ell_0 + 1} > \omega^n \alpha_0$. For $i < \ell_0$ let $\delta_i = \omega^{N-i}$. Then the primitive recursive sequence $\{\delta_i\}_i$ is descending, and $C_0(\delta_i) \leq i + 1$. Finally $\mathcal{E}^\omega DS_{\omega^\omega}$ yields the 1-consistency $\mathrm{RFN}_{\Sigma_1}(I\Sigma_1)$ of $I\Sigma_1$ by Exercise 4.9.2.

4.13

1 (Inversion) is seen by induction on α. For the case when $k \vdash^\alpha_m \Gamma, \exists x A(x)$ is the conclusion of an $(\exists)$, use **(W1)**. For the case when $k \vdash^\alpha_m \Gamma, \forall x A(x)$ is the conclusion of an $(\forall)$, use **(W4)**.

2 Assume that A is either a literal or an existential formula. We show the assertion by induction on β.
By **(W0)**, **(W1)** and Exercise 4.13.1 we can assume that A is not a literal and Δ, A is the conclusion of an $(\exists)$ with the main formula $A \equiv \exists x B(x)$. We have $k \vdash^{\beta_0}_m B(n), \Delta, A$ with $\beta_0 <_k \beta$ and $n <_k \beta$. IH yields $k \vdash^{\alpha\#\beta_0}_m B(n), \Gamma, \Delta$.
Case 1 $\mathrm{dg}_1(A) \neq 0$: Then $\mathrm{dg}_1(B(n)) < \mathrm{dg}_1(A) \leq m$. (Inversion) in Exercise 4.13.1 yields $k \vdash^{\alpha\#n}_m \Gamma, \neg B(n)$. We obtain $\alpha\#\beta_0, \alpha\#n <_k \alpha\#\beta$ by **(W0)**. By a cut we obtain the assertion.
Case 2 $\mathrm{dg}_1(A) = 0$: Then B is a literal. When $B(n)$ is true, (Inversion) in Exercise 4.13.1 yields $k \vdash^{\alpha\#n}_m \Gamma, \neg B(n)$. We obtain $k \vdash^{\alpha\#n}_m \Gamma, \Delta$ by Exercise 4.13.1 with $\alpha\#n <_k \alpha\#\beta$. Otherwise we obtain $k \vdash^{\alpha\#\beta_0}_m \Gamma, \Delta$ from $k \vdash^{\alpha\#\beta_0}_m B(n), \Gamma, \Delta$ and Exercise 4.13.1 with $\alpha\#\beta_0 <_k \alpha\#\beta$.

3 By induction on α using (Reduction) in Exercise 4.13.2, **(W1)** and **(W2)**.

4 By induction on α. Assume that $\alpha_0 <_k \alpha$, $m <_k \alpha$ and $k \vdash^{\alpha_0}_0 \exists x A, A(m)$.
Case 1 $A(m)$ is false: By Exercise 4.13.1, $k \vdash^{\alpha_0}_0 \exists x A$ holds. By IH we obtain the assertion, since $\alpha_0 <_k \alpha \Rightarrow \psi_k(\alpha_0) < \psi_k(\alpha)$.
Case 2 $A(m)$ is true: We see $m = \psi_k(m) < \psi_k(\alpha)$ by induction on $m < \omega$ using the fact $n <_k n + 1$.

5 When Γ follows from a $(\forall)$, use **(W3)** $n <_n \omega$. When Γ follows from a complete induction, use the fact $2n+1 <_k \omega+n$, which follows from **(W3)** and **(W4)**.
6 Assume $\mathsf{PA} \vdash \exists y A(x,y)$ for a $\exists y A(x,y) \in \Sigma_1$. By (Embedding) in Exercise 4.13.5, $\forall k, n \in \mathbb{N}\{k \vdash_m^{\beta_0+n} \exists y A(n,y)\}$ with an ordinal $\beta_0 = \omega \cdot l + c$. Putting $k := n$, we obtain $\forall n \in \mathbb{N}\{n \vdash_m^{\beta_0+n} \exists y A(n,y)\}$ and by $(<_n)$, $\forall n \in \mathbb{N}$ $\{n \vdash_m^{\beta} \exists y A(n,y)\}$ for $\beta = \beta_0 \# \omega = \omega \cdot (l+1) + c$. By (Elimination) in Exercise 4.13.3, we obtain $\forall n \in \mathbb{N}\{n \vdash_0^{\alpha} \exists y A(n,y)\}$ for $\alpha = \omega_m(\beta)$. From (Collapsing) in Exercise 4.13.4, we see that there exists an $i < \psi_n(\alpha)$ for which $A(n,i)$ is true.

4.15

2 By induction on the rank $\alpha = \mathrm{rk}(c)$.
3 This is seen as in Lemma 4.4 using Exercises 4.15.1 and 4.15.2.
4 As in Lemma 4.10, by induction on α using (4.28). Note that the partial truth definition for Π_{k+l}-formulas is available in T, where the increase l of the formula complexity is due to the definable class $I_{\prec}^{\alpha}$.
5 Suppose $T(U) \vdash \mathrm{TI}[\prec, U]$. Then $\forall c \in V\{(prg)_V \vdash_0^{\omega_n(\Omega+1)} U(\bar{c})\}$ for an $n < \omega$, where we can assume that the witnessing derivation enjoys the condition in Exercise 4.15.4 for a $k < \omega$. We obtain $\forall c \in V\{c \in I_{\prec}^{\omega_n(\Omega+1)}\}$. The whole proof is formalizable in $\mathrm{FiX}^i(T)$, i.e., $\mathrm{FiX}^i(T) \vdash \forall a(a \in I_{\prec}^{\omega_n(\Omega+1)})$. We conclude $T \vdash \forall a(a \in I_{\prec}^{\omega_n(\Omega+1)})$ by Theorem 4.15.2.

Exercises of Chap. 5

5.1

1 Since $C(\prec)$ is a Σ_1^1-formula, we obtain $\neg\forall X(C(X) \leftrightarrow \mathrm{WO}(X))$ by Π_1^1-completeness of $\mathrm{WO}(X)$. Let $\prec$ be a set such that $\neg(C(\prec) \leftrightarrow \mathrm{WO}(\prec))$. Since ATR_0 proves $\mathrm{WO}(\prec) \to C(\prec)$, we obtain $C(\prec)$ and $\neg\mathrm{WO}(\prec)$. This means that $\prec$ is an ill-founded linear ordering.
2 First assume $x \in Z_l$. Let $b \in E$ be such that $x \in (Y)_b$, and $c \in D$. Then $b \prec c$ yields $x \in (Y)_b \subset (Y)_c$. Hence $x \in Z_u$. Conversely assume $x \in Z_u$. Then $x \in (Y)_{b_0}$ for $b_0 \in D$. Let c be such that $x \in (Y)_c$ and $x \notin \bigcup_{d \prec c}(Y)_d$. It suffices to show $c \in E$. Let $b \in D$, and $d \in D$ be such that $d \prec b$. Then $x \in (Y)_b$, and hence $b \not\prec c$. We see $b \neq c$ from $x \in (Y)_d$ and $x \notin \bigcup_{d \prec c}(Y)_d$. Hence $c \prec b$. Thus $c \in E$.
3 First we show $x \in Z_l \to A(Z_l, x)$. Assume $x \in Z_l$. Let $b \in E$ be such that $x \in (Y)_b$. Since E is closed downward, i.e., $c \prec b \in E \to c \in E$, we can assume $x \notin \bigcup_{c \prec b}(Y)_c$. Then $A(\bigcup_{c \prec b}(Y)_c, x)$ and $A(Z_l, x)$ by the positivity. Second let us show $A(Z_u, x) \to x \in Z_u$. Assume $A(Z_u, x)$ and let $b \in D$. We have $Z_u \subset \bigcup_{c \prec b}(Y)_c$ since $\exists c \in D(c \prec b)$. The positivity yields $A(\bigcup_{c \prec b}(Y)_c, x)$, and hence $x \in (Y)_b$. Thus $x \in Z_u$.
4 Both Z_u and Z_l are sets by ACA.

5.2 $(\Sigma_1^1\text{-AC})_0 = (\Sigma_0^1\text{-AC})_0$ is seen from Δ_0^0-CA, $\exists X \exists Y\, A(X,Y) \leftrightarrow \exists Z\, A((Z)_0, (Z)_1)$. $(\Sigma_0^1\text{-DC})_0 = (\Sigma_1^1\text{-DC})_0$ is seen similarly.

5.3 Let A, B be Σ^1_1-formulas. Assume $\forall y(\neg A(y) \leftrightarrow B(y))$. Then $\forall y(A(y) \lor B(y))$, and $\forall y \exists X[(0 \in X \land A(y)) \lor (0 \notin X \land B(y))]$. Σ^1_1-AC yields the existence of a set Z such that $\forall y[(0 \in (Z)_y) \land A(y)) \lor (0 \notin (Z)_y \land B(y))]$. On the other hand we have $\forall y \neg[A(y) \land B(y)]$. Hence $\forall y[0 \in (Z)_y \leftrightarrow A(y)]$, and $\forall y[y \in X \leftrightarrow A(y)]$ for $X = \{y : 0 \in (Z)_y\}$.

5.4 Argue in $(\Sigma^1_1\text{-DC})_0$. Let $A(n, Y)$ be a Σ^1_1-formula, and assume $\forall n \exists Y A(n, Y)$. We have $\forall n \forall X \exists Y B(n, X, Y)$ for $B(n, X, Y) :\Leftrightarrow A(n, Y)$. Pick a set Z such that $\forall n B(n, (Z)_{<n}, (Z)_n)$, i.e., $\forall n A(n, (Z)_n)$.

Next consider Σ^1_1-IND. We have Σ^1_1-AC, and Δ^1_1-CA by Exercise 5.3. In particular we have Π^1_0-IND. Let $B(n, X, Y)$ be the formula $(n = 0 \land A(0, Y)) \lor (n \neq 0 \land (A(n \dot{-} 1, (X)_{n \dot{-} 1}) \to A(n, Y))$ for a formula $A(n, Y) \in \Pi^1_0$. Assuming $\exists X A(0, X)$ and $\forall n(\exists X A(n, X) \to \exists X A(n + 1, X))$, we have $\forall n \forall X \exists Y B(n, X, Y)$. Pick a set Z such that $\forall n B(n, (Z)_{<n}, (Z)_n)$. This means that $A(0, (Z)_0)$ and $\forall n(A(n, (Z)_n)) \to A(n + 1, (Z)_{n+1}))$ by $((Z)_{<n+1})_n = (Z)_n$. By Π^1_0-IND we conclude $\forall n A(n, (Z)_n)$.

Finally assume $\forall n, X \exists Y A(n, X, Y)$ for a Σ^1_1-formula A. Let $B(n, X, Y) :\Leftrightarrow [(n = 0 \land Y = U) \lor (n \neq 0 \land A(n \dot{-} 1, (X)_{n \dot{-} 1}, Y))]$. Then $\forall n, X \exists Y B(n, X, Y)$. By Σ^1_1-DC pick a set Z such that $\forall n B(n, (W)_{<n}, (W)_n)$. Then we obtain $(W)_0 = U$ and $A(n, (W)_n, (W)_{n+1})$ for any n.

5.5

1 Arguing in $(\Sigma^1_1\text{−DC}_\xi)_0$, assume $\forall \beta, X \exists Y A(\beta, X, Y)$. $B(0)$ is seen from the assumption.
Let λ be a limit ordinal, and assume $\forall \delta < \lambda\, B(\delta)$.
Let $\{\lambda_n\}_n$ be a fundamental sequence such that $\forall n(\lambda_n < \lambda_{n+1} < \lambda)$ and $\lambda = \sup_n \lambda_n$. Let an ordinal γ and a set X_0 with $\mathscr{A}(X_0, \gamma)$ be given. Put $\eta_0 = \gamma$ and $\eta_{n+1} = \gamma + \xi^{\lambda_n}$. Then $\sup_n \eta_n = \gamma + \xi^\lambda$. From $\forall n\, B(\lambda_n)$ we obtain the following for $\xi^{\lambda_n} + \xi^{\lambda_{n+1}} = \xi^{\lambda_{n+1}}$

$$\forall n \forall X \exists Y[\mathscr{A}(X, \eta_n) \to (X)_{<\eta_n} = (Y)_{<\eta_n} \land \mathscr{A}(Y, \eta_{n+1})].$$

By $\Sigma^1_1\text{−DC}_\omega$, pick a set Z such that $(Z)_0 = X_0$ and

$$\forall n[\mathscr{A}((Z)_n, \eta_n) \to ((Z)_n)_{<\eta_n} = ((Z)_{n+1})_{<\eta_n} \land \mathscr{A}((Z)_{n+1}, \eta_{n+1})].$$

By Π^1_0-IND with Exercise 5.4 we obtain $\forall n\, \mathscr{A}((Z)_n, \eta_n)$ and $\forall n[((Z)_n)_{<\eta_n} = ((Z)_{n+1})_{<\eta_n}]$. Let $W = \{(x, \beta) : \exists n(\beta < \eta_n \land (x, \beta) \in (Z)_n)\}$. By the arithmetical comprehension axiom W is a set. From $\forall n[((Z)_n)_{<\eta_n} = ((Z)_{n+1})_{<\eta_n}]$ we see that $(W)_{<\eta_n} = (Z)_n$. Hence $(W)_{<\gamma} = (X_0)_{<\gamma}$ and $\forall n \mathscr{A}((W)_{<\eta_n}, \eta_n)$. We conclude $\mathscr{A}(W, \xi^\lambda)$.
Finally assume $B(\alpha)$. Let an ordinal γ and a set X_0 with $\mathscr{A}(X_0, \gamma)$ be given. Put $\lambda(\zeta) = \gamma + \xi^\alpha \zeta$. Let $\lambda \in Lim$ denote the formula saying that 'λ is a limit ordinal', and $C(\zeta, X, Y)$ denote the following formula:

$$C(\zeta, X, Y) :\Leftrightarrow [\zeta = 0 \land Y = X_0] \lor$$
$$\exists\zeta_0[\zeta = \zeta_0 + 1 \land (\mathscr{A}((X)_{\zeta_0}, \lambda(\zeta_0)) \to ((X)_{\zeta_0})_{<\lambda(\zeta_0)} = (Y)_{<\lambda(\zeta_0)} \land \mathscr{A}(Y, \lambda(\zeta))]$$
$$\lor[\zeta \in Lim \land \forall\eta < \zeta\mathscr{A}((X)_\eta, \lambda(\eta)) \to Y = \bigcup_{\eta<\zeta}((X)_\eta)_{<\lambda(\eta)}]$$

We have $\forall\zeta < \xi\forall X\exists Y\, C(\zeta, X, Y)$ by $B(\alpha)$ and the arithmetical comprehension axiom. By Σ^1_1−DC$_\xi$, pick a set Z such that $\forall\zeta < \xi\, C(\zeta, (Z)_{<\zeta}, (Z)_\zeta)$. Then $(Z)_0 = X_0$, and for the successor $\zeta = \zeta_0 + 1$, $\mathscr{A}((Z)_{\zeta_0}, \lambda(\zeta_0)) \to ((Z)_{\zeta_0})_{<\lambda(\zeta_0)} = ((Z)_\zeta)_{<\lambda(\zeta_0)} \land \mathscr{A}((Z)_\zeta, \lambda(\zeta))$. Moreover when $\zeta \in Lim$, $\forall\eta < \zeta\mathscr{A}((Z)_\eta, \lambda(\eta)) \to (Z)_\zeta = \bigcup_{\eta<\zeta}((Z)_\eta)_{<\lambda(\eta)}$. By TI$[<_\xi, \Pi^1_0]$ we obtain $\forall\zeta < \xi\mathscr{A}((Z)_\zeta, \lambda(\zeta))$ and $((Z)_\zeta)_{<\lambda(\eta)} = ((Z)_\eta)_{<\lambda(\eta)}$ for any $\eta < \zeta < \xi$.
Let $W = \{(x, \beta) : \exists\zeta < \xi(\beta < \lambda(\zeta) \land (x, \beta) \in (Z)_\zeta)\}$. By the arithmetical comprehension axiom, W is a set. We see that $(W)_{<\lambda(\zeta)} = (Z)_\zeta$ for any $\zeta < \xi$. Hence $(W)_{<\gamma} = (X_0)_{<\gamma}$ and $\forall\zeta < \xi\mathscr{A}((W)_{<\lambda(\zeta)}, \lambda(\zeta))$. We conclude $\mathscr{A}(W, \lambda(\xi))$ with $\lambda(\xi) = \gamma + \xi^{\alpha+1}$.

2, 3 Exercises 5.5.2, 5.5.3 follow from Exercise 5.5.1 and Theorem 4.1.1.

5.6 For the iterated Π^1_0−CA, note that $\forall X\exists Y(Y = \{n : A(n, X)\})$ is a Π^1_2-formula for $A \in \Pi^1_0$, and $(\Sigma^1_1\text{−DC})_0 \vdash \Pi^1_0$−CA. The assertions follow from Exercises 5.5.2 and 5.5.3.

5.7 Arguing in (Δ^1_1−CA), assume $\forall\beta, X\exists!Y\, A(\beta, X, Y)$ and $\forall\gamma < \alpha\, H(\gamma)$ for a Π^1_0-formula A and $\alpha < \varepsilon_0$. Note that we have the transfinite induction schema TI$[<_\alpha, B]$ for any formula B and for each $\alpha < \varepsilon_0$ by Theorem 4.1.1. We need to show $H(\alpha)$. The uniqueness $\forall Z, W[\mathscr{A}(Z, \alpha) \land \mathscr{A}(W, \alpha) \to (Z)_{<\alpha} = (W)_{<\alpha}]$ follows from the assumption and the transfinite induction up to α. Then $W = \{(x, \beta) : \beta < \alpha \land \exists Z\exists\gamma < \alpha[\beta < \gamma \land \mathscr{A}(Z, \gamma) \land (x, \beta) \in Z]\} = \{(x, \beta) : \beta < \alpha \land \forall Z\forall\gamma < \alpha[\beta < \gamma \land \mathscr{A}(Z, \gamma) \to (x, \beta) \in Z]\}$, and W is a set by Δ^1_1-comprehension axiom. We obtain $\mathscr{A}(W, \alpha)$. Thus $H(\alpha)$ is shown, and this yields $\exists Z\mathscr{A}(Z, \alpha)$.

5.8 This follows from Exercise 5.7. Note that a Π^1_0−CA is of the form $\forall X\exists!Y(Y = \{n : A(n, X)\})$, and $(\Delta^1_1\text{−CA})_0 \vdash \Pi^1_0$−CA.

5.9 The axioms $\{\forall X\exists Y A(X, Y) : A \in \Phi\}$ over EA^2 yields a set enjoying the axioms $D[A]_n$ $(A \in \Phi)$ of the predicate symbol D^U_A for each $n < \omega$. From Exercise 5.5.2 [5.5.3] we see that $\{\forall X\exists Y A(X, Y) : A \in \Phi\} + (\Sigma^1_1\text{−DC})_0$ $[\{\forall X\exists Y A(X, Y) : A \in \Phi\} + (\Sigma^1_1\text{−DC})]$ models $(D[\Phi]_{<\omega^\omega})_0$ $[(D[\Phi]_{<\varepsilon_0})_0]$, resp.

5.10 Although this follows from Theorem 3.13 in Exercise 3.4, let us give a proof by means of an asymmetric interpretation.

Let us introduce a sequent calculus $D[\Phi] + \boldsymbol{G}_2(\text{AC})$ for $\{\forall X\exists Y A(X, Y) : A \in \Phi\} + (\Sigma^1_1\text{−AC})_0$. $D[\Phi] + \boldsymbol{G}_2(\text{AC})$ is obtained from the second-order sequent calculus $\boldsymbol{G}_2$ by adding initial sequents for set variables X and $A \in \Phi$

$$\Gamma, \exists Y A(X, Y)$$

and the inference rule (AC)

$$\frac{\Gamma, \exists Y\, C(x, Y)}{\Gamma, \exists Z \forall x\, C(x, (Z)_x)}\ (\mathrm{AC})$$

where C is a Π^1_0-formula[2] in $\mathcal{L}_2$, x is an eigenvariable.

Assume $\{\forall X \exists Y A(X, Y) : A \in \Phi\} + (\Sigma^1_1\text{–AC})_0 \vdash \exists Z\, C(U, Z)$. Then there exists a proof P_0 of a sequent $\Gamma_0, \exists Z\, C(U, Z)$ in $D[\Phi] + \boldsymbol{G}_2(\mathrm{AC})$ for a set Γ_0 of negations of Π^1_1-axioms (complete induction axiom and arithmetic axioms) in EA^2.

Let $\Phi_0 = \{A_i\}_{i<k}$ be a finite set of formulas such that $B' \in \Phi_0$ if $\exists Y B(X, Y)$ is a major formula of an initial sequent in P_0, where the formula B' is defined from B in (5.19).

Let $A(a, X, Y) :\Leftrightarrow \bigvee_{i<k}[a = i \wedge A_i(X, Y)] \vee [a = k \wedge J(X, Y)]$. By the assumption $A \in \Phi$.

Let $\Gamma, \exists Y\, B(X, Y)$ be an initial sequent in P_0 for $B \in \Phi_0$. For $A_i \equiv B' \in \Phi_0$, supposing $X \in \mathcal{D}_A(n)$, we have $B(X, Y) \leftrightarrow A_i((D^U_A)_{<n}, Y)$, and $A(i, (D^U_A)_{<n}, ((D^U_A)_n)_i)$. Thus $X \in \mathcal{D}_A(n) \to \exists Y \in \mathcal{D}_A(n+1) B(X, Y)$.

Next note that the Turing jump $U_0 = ((D^U_A)_{<n})'$ is in $Set((D^U_A)_{<n+1})$ since $J((D^U_A)_{<n}, U_0)$ and $U_0 = ((D^U_A)_{<n+1})_k$.

Eliminate cut inferences partially from P_0 to get a proof P of the same Σ^1_1-sequent such that every formula occurring in the proof is either a Σ^1_1-formula or a Π^1_1-formula, cf. Remark 3.1.

Let Γ be a sequent occurring in the proof P. We show by induction on the depth of proofs that there exists an $m < \omega$ such that for any n, $(D[\Phi]_{<\omega})_0 \vdash \Gamma[n; m]$. In particular we obtain $(D[\Phi]_{<\omega})_0 \vdash \Gamma_0[0; m], \exists Z \in \mathcal{D}_A(m) C(U, Z)$ for $U \in \mathcal{D}_A(0)$. For each $\neg\forall X B \in \Gamma_0$, $(\neg\forall X B)[0; m] \equiv (\exists X \in \mathcal{D}_A(m) \neg B)$ is the negation of an axiom in $(D[\Phi]_{<\omega})_0$. Hence we obtain $(D[\Phi]_{<\omega})_0 \vdash \exists Z \in \mathcal{D}_A(m) C(U, Z)$.

Argue in $(D[\Phi]_{<\omega})_0$. First consider the case when the last inference is an (AC):

$$\frac{\Gamma, \exists Y\, C(x, Y)}{\Gamma, \exists Z \forall x\, C(x, (Z)_x)}\ (\mathrm{AC})$$

By IH we have an m such that for any n,

$$\Gamma[n; m], \exists Y \in \mathcal{D}_A(n+m)\, C(x, Y)$$

$\exists Y \in \mathcal{D}_A(n+m)\, C(x, Y)$ is equivalent to $\exists y \in \Delta^{U_1}_1\, C(x, y)$ for $U_1 := (D^U_A)_{<n+m}$. Let

$$\begin{aligned} u \in (Z)_x &:\Leftrightarrow \exists y(y = \mu y_0(y_0 \in \Delta^{U_1}_1 \wedge C(x, y_0)) \wedge \{y\}^{U_1}(u) \simeq 0) \\ &\leftrightarrow \forall y(y = \mu y_0(y_0 \in \Delta^{U_1}_1 \wedge C(x, y_0)) \to \{y\}^{U_1}(u) \simeq 0) \end{aligned}$$

Z is Δ^0_{1+k} in U_1 for a $k > 0$, and hence $Z \in Set((D^U_A)_{<n+m+k}))$. Thus we obtain by (5.18)

---

[2] We can restrict C to Π^0_2-formulas.

$$\Gamma[n; m+k], \exists Z \in \mathcal{D}_A(n+m+k)\forall x\, C(x, Y)$$

Second consider the case when the last inference is a (cut) with a Π^1_1-cut formula $\forall Y\, B$.

$$\frac{\Gamma, \exists Y \neg B \quad \forall Y\, B, \Gamma}{\Gamma}\ (cut)$$

By IH we have an m such that for any n, n_0

$$\Gamma[n; m], \exists Y \in \mathcal{D}_A(n+m)\neg B \text{ and } \forall Y \in \mathcal{D}_A(n_0)B, \Gamma[n_0; m]$$

Hence $\forall Y \in \mathcal{D}_A(n+m)B, \Gamma[n+m; m]$. By a (cut) we obtain $\Gamma[n; m], \Gamma[n+m; m]$. Equation (5.18) yields $\Gamma[n; m \cdot 2]$.

5.11 As in the proof of Exercise 5.10 introduce a sequent calculus $D[\Phi] + \boldsymbol{G}_2(\text{DC})$ for $\{\forall X \exists Y A(X, Y) : A \in \Phi\} + (\Sigma^1_1\text{−DC})_0$. $D[\Phi] + \boldsymbol{G}_2(\text{DC})$ is obtained from the sequent calculus $D[\Phi] + \boldsymbol{G}_2(\text{AC})$ by replacing the inference rule (AC) by the inference rule (DC):

$$\frac{\Gamma, \exists Y\, C(n, X, Y)}{\Gamma, \exists Z \forall n < \omega\, C(n, (Z)_{<n}, (Z)_n)}\ (\text{DC})$$

where C is a Π^1_0-formula in $\mathcal{L}_2$, x is an eigenvariable.

Assume $\{\forall X \exists Y A(X, Y) : A \in \Phi\} + (\Sigma^1_1\text{−DC})_0 \vdash \exists Z\, C(U, Z)$. Then there exists a proof P_0 of a sequent $\Gamma_0, \exists Z\, C(U, Z)$ in $D[\Phi] + \boldsymbol{G}_2(\text{DC})$ for a set Γ_0 of negations of Π^1_1-axioms. Let $\Phi_0 = \{A_i\}_{i<k}$ be a finite set of formulas such that $A' \in \Phi_0$ if $\exists Y\, B(X, Y)$ is a major formula of an initial sequent in P_0, and let $A(a, X, Y) :\Leftrightarrow \bigvee_{i<m}[a = i \wedge A_i(X, Y)] \vee [a = m \wedge J(X, Y)]$.

Eliminating cut inferences partially, we obtain $\vdash^k_1 \Gamma_0, \exists Z\, C(U, Z)$ for a $k < \omega$, which means that there exists a proof of $\Gamma_0, \exists Z\, C(U, Z)$ in $D[\Phi] + \boldsymbol{G}_2(\text{DC})$ such that every formula occurring in the proof is either a Σ^1_1-formula or a Π^1_1-formula.

Let Γ be a sequent occurring in the proof P. We show by induction on the depth k of proofs

$$(D[\Phi]_{<\omega^\omega})_0 \vdash \Gamma[\alpha; \omega^{1+k}]$$

for any α. Then we obtain $(D[\Phi]_{<\omega^\omega})_0 \vdash \Gamma_0[0; \omega^k], \exists Z \in \mathcal{D}_A(\omega^k)C(U, Z)$. For each $\neg\forall X B \in \Gamma_0$, $(\neg\forall X B)[0; \omega^k] \equiv (\exists X \in \mathcal{D}_A(\omega^k)\neg B)$ is the negation of an axiom in $(D[\Phi]_{<\omega^\omega})_0$. Hence we obtain $(D[\Phi]_{<\omega^\omega})_0 \vdash \exists Z \in \mathcal{D}_A(\omega^k)C(U, Z)$.

Argue in $(D[\Phi]_{<\omega^\omega})_0$. Consider the case when the last inference is a (DC) for a $k > 0$:

$$\frac{\vdash^{k-1}_1 \Gamma, \exists Y\, C(n, X, Y)}{\vdash^k_1 \Gamma, \exists W \forall n < \omega\, C(n, (W)_{<n}, (W)_n)}\ (\text{DC})$$

By IH we have for any α,

$$\Gamma[\alpha; \omega^k], \forall n < \omega \forall X \in \mathcal{D}_A(\alpha)\exists Y \in \mathcal{D}_A(\alpha + \omega^k)\, C(n, X, Y)$$

$\forall n < \omega \forall X \in \mathcal{D}_A(\alpha)\exists Y \in \mathcal{D}_A(\alpha + \omega^k)\, C(n, X, Y)$ is equivalent to $\forall n < \omega \forall x \in \Delta_1^{U_\alpha} \exists y \in \Delta_1^{U_{\alpha+\omega^k}}\, C(n, x, y)$ for $U_\alpha := (D_A^U)_{<\alpha}$.

Fix a code x_0 for the empty set, i.e., $Set(x_0) = \emptyset$. Let $B(w, n)$ denote a formula expressing that w is a sequence in length $(n + 1)$, $(w)_0 = x_0$, and $\forall m < n[(w)_m \in \Delta_1^{\tilde{U}_m} \wedge (w)_{m+1} = \mu y(y \in \Delta_1^{\tilde{U}_{m+1}} \wedge C(m, (w)_{<m}, y))$, where $\tilde{U}_m = U_{\alpha+\omega^k m}$ and $(w)_{<m} \in \Delta_1^{\tilde{U}_m}$ such that

$$\{(w)_{<m}\}^{\tilde{U}_m}(p, u) \simeq \begin{cases} \{(w)_p\}^{\tilde{U}_p}(u) & \text{if } p < m \\ 0 & \text{otherwise} \end{cases}$$

This means $Set((w)_{<m}) = \sum_{p<m} Set((w)_p)$. By induction on n we see that $\forall n \exists! w\, B(w, n)$.

Let

$$\begin{aligned} u \in (W)_n &:\Leftrightarrow \exists w(w = \mu w_0(B(w_0, n)) \wedge \{(w)_n\}^{\tilde{U}_n}(u) \simeq 0) \\ &\leftrightarrow \forall w(w = \mu w_0(B(w_0, n)) \rightarrow \{(w)_n\}^{\tilde{U}_n}(u) \simeq 0) \end{aligned}$$

We see that $W \in Set((D_A^U)_{<\alpha+\omega^{k+1}})$. Thus we obtain by (5.18)

$$\Gamma[\alpha; \omega^{k+1}], \exists W \in \mathcal{D}_A(\alpha + \omega^{k+1})\forall n < \omega C(n, (W)_{<n}, (W)_n)$$

5.12 An infinitary calculus $D[\Phi] + \boldsymbol{G}_\omega(\mathrm{DC})$ is obtained from $D[\Phi] + \boldsymbol{G}_2(\mathrm{DC})$ by replacing the inference rule $(\forall)$ by the ω-rule $(\forall\omega)$.

Assume $\{\forall X \exists Y A(X, Y) : A \in \Phi\} + (\Sigma_1^1\text{−DC}) \vdash \exists Z\, C(U, Z)$. Then there exists a proof P_0 of a sequent $\Gamma_0, \exists Z\, C(U, Z)$ in $D[\Phi] + \boldsymbol{G}_\omega(\mathrm{DC})$ for a set Γ_0 of negations of arithmetic axioms. Here the complete induction schema is replaced by $(\forall\omega)$. The depth of P_0 is bounded by ω^2, and its cut degree is finite, where the degree of Π_1^1-formulas and Σ_1^1-formulas is defined to be 0. Write the fact by $\vdash_{<\omega}^{<\omega^2} \exists Z\, C(U, Z)$.

Eliminating cut inferences partially we obtain $\vdash_1^{<\varepsilon_0} \Gamma_0, \exists Z\, C(U, Z)$, which means that there exists a proof of $\Gamma_0, \exists Z\, C(U, Z)$ in $D[\Phi] + \boldsymbol{G}_\omega(\mathrm{DC})$ such that every formula occurring in the proof is either a Σ_1^1-formula or a Π_1^1-formula.

Let Γ be a sequent such that $\vdash_1^a \Gamma$. As in the proof of Exercise 5.11 we see by induction on the depth a of proofs that $\bigvee \Gamma[\alpha; \omega^{1+a}]$ is true for any α. Formalizing it in $(D[\Phi]_{<\varepsilon_0})_0$ through a partial truth definition, we obtain $(D[\Phi]_{<\varepsilon_0})_0 \exists Z \in \mathcal{D}_A(\alpha), C(U, Z)$ for an $\alpha < \varepsilon_0$.

5.13 The assertions on proof-theoretic ordinals follow from the conservations and Theorem 5.4.

Corollary 5.4.1 follows from Exercises 5.9, and 5.10 since $(\Sigma_1^1\text{−AC})_0$ proves the arithmetic comprehension axioms by Exercise 5.3. Corollary 5.4.2 follows from Exercises 5.9 and 5.11, and Corollary 5.4.3 follows from Exercises 5.9 and 5.12.

5.14 Let Z be the ω-th jump of a given set X. Let $M = \{Y : \exists n(Y \leq_T (Z)_n)\}$, where $Y \leq_T X$ denotes that Y is Turing reducible to X. M is seen to be a countable coded ω-model of ACA_0 with $X \in_\omega M$.

5.15

1 This is seen as in Theorem 5.9.
2 This is seen as in Theorem 5.10.
3 In $\mathsf{ACA} + \mathrm{WOP}(\mathsf{g})$ we see that the transfinite induction up to $\mathsf{g}'(a)$ for each $a < \varepsilon_0$ since $\mathrm{TI}(\mathsf{g}'(a))$ is progressive in a. Hence $|\mathsf{ACA} + \mathrm{WOP}(\mathsf{g})| \geq \mathsf{g}'(\varepsilon_0)$. Conversely let $\mathsf{ACA} + \mathrm{WOP}(\mathsf{g}) \vdash \mathrm{TI}[\prec]$ for an arithmetic relation $\prec$. Then we obtain a $(prg)^\infty + (WP)^\infty + (cut)$-derivation of $E_\prec(n)$ such that its depth is at most ω^2, the 2-degree $\mathrm{dg}_2(C) < \omega$ of its cut formulas C, cf. Definition 2.2. Using Theorem 3.3, eliminate cut inferences to get $(prg)^\infty + (WP)^\infty \vdash^\alpha_\alpha E_\prec(n)$ for an $\alpha < \varepsilon_0$. From the fact $(prg)^\infty + (WP)^\infty \vdash^\alpha_\alpha E_\prec(n)$, Lemma 5.17 and Theorem 5.12 we obtain $\vdash_0^{F(\alpha,\alpha)+\alpha} E_\prec(n)$ for any n in the calculus $\mathbf{G}_{0\omega}(\emptyset) + (prg)^\emptyset$. Then as in Theorem 5.10, we see that $|\prec| \leq \omega^{F(\alpha,\alpha)+\alpha+1} < \mathsf{g}'(\varepsilon_0)$.

Exercises of Chap. 6

6.1 This is seen from the fact that there exists a Π_2-universal formula $\Pi_2(a)$.
6.2

1 We show $\psi\alpha = \psi\Omega$ for any α with $\psi\Omega \leq \alpha < \Omega$. By Proposition 6.3.7 we have $\psi\Omega = \mathcal{H}_\Omega(0) \cap \Omega$. We see $\mathcal{H}^n_\Omega(0) \subset \mathcal{H}_\alpha(0)$ by induction on $n < \omega$. For example, $\beta \in \mathcal{H}_\Omega(0) \cap \Omega = \psi\Omega \Rightarrow \beta \in \mathcal{H}_\alpha(0) \cap \alpha$ by $\alpha \geq \psi\Omega$, and hence $\psi\beta \in \mathcal{H}_\Omega(0) \cap \mathcal{H}_\alpha(0)$. Therefore $\psi\Omega = \mathcal{H}_\Omega(0) \cap \Omega \subset \mathcal{H}_\alpha(0) \cap \Omega = \psi\alpha$. Thus we have shown $\forall\alpha[\psi\Omega \leq \alpha < \Omega \to \psi\alpha = \psi\Omega]$.
2 $\psi(\psi\Omega) = \psi\Omega$ is shown in Exercise 1. Assume $\psi\alpha = \alpha < \Omega$. Then $\mathcal{H}_\Omega(0) \subset \mathcal{H}_\alpha(0)$. For example, $\beta \in \mathcal{H}_\Omega(0) \cap \Omega \Rightarrow \beta \in \mathcal{H}_\alpha(0) \cap \Omega = \psi\alpha = \alpha$. This means $\alpha = \psi\alpha = \psi\Omega$. Namely $\psi\Omega$ is the unique fixed point of the ψ-function.
3, 4 Let us show $\forall\alpha \leq \psi\Omega[(\psi\alpha = \Gamma_\alpha) \,\&\, (\alpha < \psi\Omega \to \alpha < \psi\alpha)]$ by induction on α. Consider the case when $\lambda \leq \psi\Omega$ is a limit ordinal. By IH we have, for any $\alpha < \lambda$, $\psi\lambda \geq \psi\alpha > \alpha$, i.e., $\alpha \in \mathcal{H}_\lambda(\psi\lambda) \cap \lambda$. Hence $\psi\alpha < \psi\lambda$. IH yields $\psi\lambda \geq \sup\{\psi\alpha : \alpha < \lambda\} = \Gamma_\lambda$. On the other hand we have $\psi\lambda = \mathcal{H}_\lambda(0) \cap \Omega \subset \Gamma_\lambda$ by IH. Therefore $\psi\lambda = \Gamma_\lambda \geq \lambda$. If $\lambda < \psi\Omega$, then $\lambda < \psi\lambda$.

6.3

1 Define recursively countable ordinals $\{\beta_n\}_n$ by $\beta_0 = \max(\{0\} \cup E(\alpha)) + 1$, and $\beta_{n+1} = \min\{\beta < \Omega : C(\alpha, \beta_n) \cap \Omega \subset \beta\}$. Since $C(\alpha, \beta)$ is countable for countable ordinals β, we see $\beta_{n+1} < \Omega$ from $\beta_n < \Omega$. Then the countable ordinal $\beta = \sup_n \beta_n$ enjoys $E(\alpha) \subset C(\alpha, \beta)$ and $C(\alpha, \beta) \cap \Omega \subset \beta$.
2 Since the set $C(\alpha, \beta)$ is closed under addition and exponentiation with base ω, $\vartheta(\alpha)$ is an ε-number.
3 This is seen from the definition (6.27), i.e., from $E(\alpha) \subset C(\alpha, \vartheta(\alpha)) \cap \Omega \subset \vartheta(\alpha)$.
4 If $\vartheta(\alpha) \leq E(\beta)$, then $\vartheta(\alpha) < \vartheta(\beta)$ follows from Exercise 3. Assume $E(\alpha) < \vartheta(\beta) \,\&\, \alpha < \beta$. Then $E(\alpha) \subset C(\beta, \vartheta(\beta))$, and $\alpha \in C(\beta, \vartheta(\beta))$ since $\{0, \Omega\} \subset$

$C(\beta, \vartheta(\beta))$, and the set is closed under addition and exponentiation. Hence we obtain $\alpha \in C(\beta, \vartheta(\beta)) \cap \beta$. This yields $\vartheta(\alpha) \in C(\beta, \vartheta(\beta)) \cap \Omega \subset \vartheta(\beta)$. Thus we have shown that

$$\vartheta(\alpha) \leq E(\beta) \vee (E(\alpha) < \vartheta(\beta) \,\&\, \alpha < \beta) \Rightarrow \vartheta(\alpha) < \vartheta(\beta) \tag{7.3}$$

Conversely assume that $E(\beta) < \vartheta(\alpha)$ and (either $\vartheta(\beta) \leq E(\alpha)$ or) $\beta \leq \alpha$. If $\beta < \alpha$, then we see $\vartheta(\beta) < \vartheta(\alpha)$ by (7.3). Otherwise we have $\vartheta(\alpha) = \vartheta(\beta)$. Therefore $\vartheta(\beta) \leq \vartheta(\alpha)$, i.e., $\vartheta(\alpha) \not< \vartheta(\beta)$.

5 This is seen from Exercise 6.3.4.

6.4

1 By the minimality of λ and $\xi < \lambda$ there exists a Σ_1-sentence Ξ such that $T + (V = L) \vdash \Xi$ and $L_\xi \not\models \Xi$.

4 From Exercise 6.4.3 we see $L_\lambda \models \exists z \exists \alpha[\Xi^{(L_\alpha)} \wedge \forall x \in L_\alpha \exists y \in z\theta(x, y)]$. Pick an $\alpha < \lambda$ so that $L_\alpha \models \Xi$ and $L_\lambda \models \forall x \in L_\alpha \exists y \theta(x, y)$. By (6.30) we obtain $\alpha > \xi$.

6.5 Since the axiom Π^{1-}_1-CA is essentially a Σ^1_2-sentence, this follows from the fact that $(\Sigma^1_1$-AC$)_0$ is Π^1_2-conservative over ACA_0, Corollary 5.4.1 in Exercise 5.13.

6.6

1 This is seen as in Exercise 5.3.

2 This is seen as in Exercise 5.4.

3 These are seen as in Exercise 5.6.

4, 5,6 These are seen as in Exercises 5.10, 5.11 and 5.12 by considering the hyper-jumps $W(Y)$ instead of the jumps Y', and using the Π^1_1-completeness of W, i.e., $\forall X\, A(X, Y) \leftrightarrow \forall e \in W(X)\, A(X, Set(e))$.

6.7 Let $\mathscr{B}[X, n, b, Y] :\Leftrightarrow \left(n \in \bigcup_{x<b}(Y)_x \to Prg[<, X] \to X(b)\right)$. Let $Q = (Q_b)_{b<\nu}$ be the family of sets Q_b defined recursively by $\forall b < \nu \forall n\, (n \in Q_b \leftrightarrow \forall X\, \mathscr{B}[X, n, b, \sum_{c<b} Q_c])$. This means that for any $b < \nu$ and any n, $n \in Q_b \leftrightarrow \left(n \in \bigcup_{c<b} Q_c \to \forall X(Prg[<, X] \to X(b))\right)$. Let $A(b) :\Leftrightarrow (0 \in Q_b)$. Then we obtain $A(c) \leftrightarrow (\exists x < c\, A(x) \to \forall X(Prg[<, X] \to X(c)))$. Since $Prg[<, X] \to \forall c < b\, X(c) \to X(b)$, we obtain $\forall b < \nu[\forall x < b\, A(x) \to Prg[<, X] \to X(b)]$. In other words, $\forall b < \nu\, A(b)$. Therefore $\forall b < \nu \forall X(Prg[<, X] \to X(b))$.

6.8

1 This is seen as in Proposition 6.15.

2 This is seen as in Lemma 6.20.

6.9

1 As in Corollary 6.2 we see that $\mathsf{RCA} + W-\mathrm{CA} + \mathrm{BI} \vdash A \Rightarrow \mathsf{ID}_1 \vdash A^r$ for the same interpretation A^r.

2 Given a well-founded tree $T \subset {}^{<\omega}\omega$, let $<_{KB}$ be the Kleene-Brouwer ordering on T. Then $<_{KB}$ is a well-ordering by ACA_0, cf. Proposition 1.10, and TI yields the transfinite induction schema on $<_{KB}$. Now assume $\forall s \notin T\, B(s)$

and $\forall s[\forall x\, B(s * \langle x\rangle) \to B(s)]$. Then we obtain $Prg[<_{KB}, B]$, and hence $\forall s \in T\, B(s)$. In particular $B(\emptyset)$.

3 Assuming $C(0) \land \forall x(C(x) \to C(S(x)))$, we need to show $C(a)$. For the well-founded tree $T = \{s \in {}^{<\omega}\omega : a > lh(s)\}$, we have $s \notin T \to C(a \dot{-} lh(s))$ and $\forall x\, C(a \dot{-} lh(s * \langle x\rangle)) \to C(a \dot{-} lh(s))$. BI yields $C(a \dot{-} lh(\emptyset))$, i.e., $C(a)$.

4 Argue in ACA_0 + BI. Let $A(X)$ be a first-order formula. For example let $A(X) \equiv (\exists x \forall y\, R(x, y, X))$ with a quantifier-free formula R.
Let $\forall f_X \forall f \exists x S_A(\overline{j(f_X, f)}(x)) \leftrightarrow \forall X \exists x \forall y\, R(x, y, X)$ be its Π^1_1-normal form such that the set $\{s \in {}^{<\omega}\omega : \neg S_A(s)\}$ is a tree with an elementary recursive predicate S_A, cf. Theorem 1.2, where f_X denotes the characteristic function of the set X, $j(g, f)(x) = j(g(x), f(x))$, i.e., $j(g, f)$ denotes the join of the functions g, f. Assume $\forall f_X \forall f \exists x S_A(\overline{j(f_X, f)}(x))$, and $\forall x \exists y \neg R(x, y, V)$ for an abstract V. Let $F(x, y) :\Leftrightarrow (y \simeq \mu y.\neg R(x, y, V))$. Then $\forall x \exists! y\, F(x, y)$ and $\forall x \exists s(s = \bar{F}(x))$ by the previous Exercise 6.8.3. We obtain $\forall x \neg S_A(\overline{j(f_V, F)}(x))$, cf. Remark 1.1.
Let $B(s) :\Leftrightarrow (s = \overline{j(f_V, F)}(lh(s)) \to \exists x\, S_A\left(\overline{j(f_V, F)}(lh(s) + x)\right))$. Then we obtain $S_A(s) \to B(s)$ and $\forall s[\forall x B(s * \langle x\rangle) \to B(s)]$. BI yields $B(\emptyset)$, i.e., $\exists x\, S_A(\overline{j(f_V, F)}(x))$. This is a contradiction.

6.10

1 Let $(Y)_0 = I^{\mathscr{A}}(\emptyset, 0)$. Then $C^{\mathscr{A}}(Y, 0)$.

2 It suffices to show $\exists Y \forall b \le \omega^\alpha \cdot n\, C^{\mathscr{A}}(Y, b) \to \exists Y \forall b \le \omega^\alpha \cdot (n+1)\, C^{\mathscr{A}}(Y, b)$. Assume $\forall b \le \omega^\alpha \cdot n\, C^{\mathscr{A}}(Y, b)$. Let $(Z)_b = (Y)_b$ for $b \le \omega^\alpha$, and $(Z)_{\omega^\alpha \cdot n+1+\gamma} = I^{\mathscr{A}}(Z_{<\omega^\alpha \cdot n+1+\gamma}, \omega^\alpha \cdot n + 1 + \gamma)$. Such a set Z exists by Π^1_1-$\mathrm{CA}_{<\omega^{\alpha+1}}$. Then $\forall b \le \omega^\alpha \cdot (n+1)\, C^{\mathscr{A}}(Z, b)$.

3 This follows from transfinite induction on c.

4 This is seen from Exercises 6.10.2 and 6.10.3.

5 By Exercise 6.10.2 let Y be a set such that $\forall b \le c\, C^{\mathscr{A}}(Y, b)$. In particular $(Y)_c \subset F^{\mathscr{A}}_{Y_{<c}, c}$. By Exercise 6.8 with $\forall^2 E(\Pi^1_0)$ we obtain $Cl^{\mathscr{A}}_{Y_{<c}, c}(B) \to (Y)_c \subset B$. Exercise 6.10.3 yields $Y_{<c+1} = F^{\mathscr{A}}_{<c+1}$.

6.11 As in Corollary 6.2 we see that $(\Pi^1_1\text{-}\mathrm{CA}_\alpha) + \mathrm{BI} \vdash A \Rightarrow \mathsf{ID}_{\alpha \cdot \omega}(W) \vdash A^r$, where A^r is obtained from A by restricting QX ($Q \in \{\exists, \forall\}$) to sets in $\bigcup_{n<\omega} \Delta_1^{W_{\alpha \cdot n}}$.

Reference

1. Hájek, P., Pudlák, P.: Metamathematics of first-order arithmetic. Perspectives in Mathematical Logic. Springer, Berlin (1993)

Index

© The Editor(s) (if applicable) and The Author(s), under exclusive license to Springer Nature Singapore Pte Ltd. 2020

T. Arai, *Ordinal Analysis with an Introduction to Proof Theory*, Logic in Asia: Studia Logica Library, https://doi.org/10.1007/978-981-15-6459-8

V

W

The manufacturer's authorised representative in the EU is Springer Nature Customer Service Centre GmbH, Europaplatz 3, 69115 Heidelberg, Germany. If you have any concerns regarding our products, please contact ProductSafety@springernature.com

Printed and bound by CPI Group (UK) Ltd, Croydon, CR0 4YY
30/09/2026
02225558-0012